JAPAN SOLO

EIJI KANNO
AND
CONSTANCE O'KEEFE

WARNER BOOKS

A Warner Communications Company

JAPAN SOLO

Originally published by Nitchi Map-Publishing Co., Ltd.
2-2-15, Nishi-Kanda, Chiyoda-ku, Tokyo 101, Japan

Warner Books Edition

Warner Books, Inc., 666 Fifth Avenue, New York, NY 10103

 A Warner Communications Company

Maps by Eiji Kanno
Photos and illustrations
  courtesy of the Japan National Tourist Organization;
  Tourist Associations of Aichi, Aomori, Ehime, Fukushima, Gifu, Hiroshima, Ishikawa,
  Iwate, Kagawa, Kanagawa, Kochi, Kyoto, Mie, Miyagi, Nagano, Nagasaki, Nara,
  Osaka, Shimane, Shizuoka, Tokyo, Wakayama, and Yamaguchi Prefectures
Book design by Takayuki Okada
Cover design by Jackie Merri Meyer

Printed in Japan for Warner Books by Shalom Printing Co., Ltd.

First Warner Books Trade Paperback/Printing: April 1988
10 9 8 7 6 5 4 3 2 1

Library of Congress Cataloging in Publication Data

Kanno, Eiji.
  Japan solo.

  Includes index.
  1. Japan—Description and travel—1945-
Guide-books. I. O'Keefe, Constance. II. Title.
DS805.2.K36 1988   915.2'0448   87-28002
ISBN 0-446-38821-1 (pbk.) (U.S.A.)
      0-446-38822-x (pbk.) (Canada)

A Message to the Readers of
This Greatly Expanded Edition of JAPAN SOLO

Mr. Eiji Kanno and Miss Constance O'Keefe, two of our brilliant former colleagues of the Japan National Tourist Organization have done a splendid job of updating and adding to JAPAN SOLO, a guide book labeled by the New York Times as the indispensable book for independent travelers.

JAPAN SOLO reflects the authors' extensive knowledge not only of Japan but also of what international travelers want to know about Japan. Mr. Kanno and Miss O'Keefe visited all the destinations contained in the book and walked all the Walking Tour Courses recommended in the book.

Three strengthened features add to the book – 193 maps, an advanced set of 'Conversation Cards' and expanded timetables.

Japan has always been a country for tourists – hospitable people, well-organized safety features, good public transportation. The Japan National Tourist Organization has as its priority objective to have the visitor come back again – none of this one-time stress.

JNTO has organized over 20,000 Good-will Guides to help your stay in Japan to be of pleasure and of understanding, and there is a toll-free Travel-phone service 365 days of the year.

We believe that tourism is a passport to peace – people to people contacts are one of the surest ways to bring us closer to each other in the global village.

JAPAN SOLO, the best answer to a guide book that we have seen, will offer you a golden key to meet people – the biggest attraction Japan has to offer international travelers.

Shunichi Sumita

Shunichi Sumita
President
Japan National Tourist Organization

January 1988

4

CONTENTS

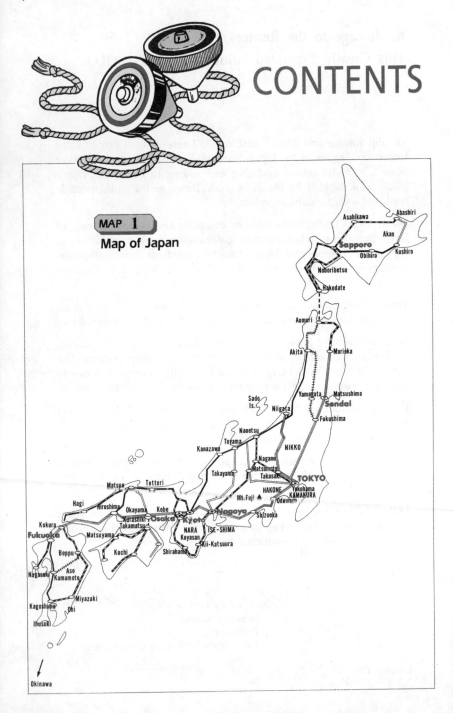

MAP **1**

Map of Japan

Abashiri
Asahikawa
Akan
Sapporo
Kushiro
Obihiro
Noboribetsu
Hakodate

Aomori
Akita
Morioka
Yamagata
Matsushima
Sado Is.
Niigata
Sendai
Fukushima
Naoetsu
Toyama
NIKKO
Kanazawa
Nagano
Takayama
Matsumoto
Takasaki
TOKYO
Matsue
Tottori
HAKONE
Yokohama
KAMAKURA
Mt. Fuji ▲
Odawara
Hagi
Hiroshima
Okayama
Kobe
Nagoya
Shizuoka
Kokura
Kurashiki
Osaka
Kyoto
Takamatsu
NARA
ISE-SHIMA
Fukuoka
Matsuyama
Koyasan
Beppu
Kochi
Kii-Katsuura
Shirahama
Nagasaki
Aso
Kumamoto
Kagoshima
Miyazaki
Obi
Ibusuki

Okinawa

6

● CITY/RESORT GUIDE

● LIST OF MAPS

PREFACE
TO THE SECOND EDITION

When the first edition of **Japan Solo** appeared in 1985, we told our readers that our goal was to provide the detailed practical information one needs to travel in Japan independently. Our aim is the same with this second edition.

We have retained, and worked to improve, the three features we believe set **Japan Solo** apart from other guides. The maps, Conversation Cards and timetables are designed to help you surmount the language barrier that hinders most foreign visitors to Japan and take full advantage of Japan's efficient and economical public transportation. Using them, and spending time planning in advance should enable you to enjoy a trip to Japan as much as possible.

This second edition contains a total of 193 maps. At the beginning of each chapter, there is a map outlining the area. The locations of major places of interest, major accommodations, and inter- and intra-city transportation networks are indicated. More detailed maps, picturing downtown sections of each destination as well as its tourist attractions, follow. They also pinpoint the exact locations of train stations, bus stops, major hotels, restaurants, shops, landmarks, etc.

The second innovation of the first edition, the "Conversation Cards," are placed at the end of this text, on special perforated pages. You can use the Conversation Cards to figure out train/subway fares, to locate the right track for the particular train/subway you want, or to make sure that you'll get off the train/subway at the right place. Fill in the particular information you need, show the card to a Japanese passerby, and help is on the way! It's much more efficient than trying to ask for help, because most Japanese have trouble understanding spoken English, despite the fact that they are usually able to read it quite well.

Photo by B. Jackson

This second edition still includes detailed timetables for all of the public transportation we recommend. The timetables are collected in a special section in the back of the book. Easy reference numbers on the maps coordinate with the timetables. Using this system, you have access to the same information Japanese travelers use to plan their own sightseeing excursions.

We have expanded the scope of the book, and it now includes information on all parts of Japan. The information on the "Golden Route" areas of Japan remains the most detailed. Information on the more remote destinations is less detailed because smaller cities are easier to navigate and because we suspect that intrepid off-the-beaten-track explorers like more of a challenge!

We are extremely grateful for the support of our families and friends, in both Japan and the U.S., as well as for the many suggestions, comments and constructive criticisms we received from readers of the first edition. We hope that both will continue.

Eiji Kanno

Constance O'Keefe

January, 1988
New York City

Remarks, Details and Survival Tips

How to Use This Book and Its Maps

The destinations introduced in this guide are arranged in rough geographical order starting at Tokyo and moving west to Kyoto, and then southwest to Kyushu. Areas north of Tokyo (Hokkaido Island and Tohoku or the northern part of the main island) are placed at the end of the book. We've walked every one of the suggested itineraries in this book. There is an area map at the beginning of each section on a city or resort, followed by a suggested itinerary for the particular city or resort and an explanation of intra-city transportation. Details on places of interest are then presented – in the order in which we think they should be visited. Regional, city and district maps are placed to coordinate with the text. Regional maps follow the introductory matter and precede the detailed information on destinations. We suggest that you use these regional maps to locate major destinations and plan intra-city transportation. The city maps outline intra-city transportation networks, the location of downtown areas, places of interest, etc. Once you understand how an area is laid out in general terms, proceed to the more detailed walking tour maps on the pages that follow. You can use them much more easily than the big city maps.

The maps in the book generally adhere to the following principles:
★ Places of interest for tourists;
● Hotels and other accommodations;
▲ Restaurants and other eating and drinking establishments;
▲ Department stores and souvenir shops;
⊙ Public buildings, such as city halls, post offices and bus terminals;
● Signs and landmarks. This information is included merely to help you get your bearings;

Solid lines always indicate railways. Japan Railways (JR) trains (i.e., all of the trains on which you can use your Rail Pass) are always indicated with black lines, except on some detailed city maps;

Private railways are always indicated in red, except on some detailed city maps;

When several different lines appear on the same map, each line is given its own distinctive presentation; and

Seas, lakes, rivers, creeks and other bodies of water are indicated by diagonal black lines.

All regional, city and walking tour maps are drawn to scale.

Safety and Security

Japan is one of the safest countries in the world. Robberies are very rare and impersonal violent crime is virtually unknown. Even pickpockets tend to avoid foreigners! It is because Japan is so safe that we are able to wholeheartedly encourage you to travel there on your own.

Geography and Population

The Japanese archipelago stretches 1,860 miles (3,000 km.) from northeast to southwest along the eastern coast of the Asian Continent. The country has four major islands (from north to south – Hokkaido, Honshu, Shikoku and Kyushu), and about 4,000 small islands. The total area of Japan is about 146,000 square miles (378,000 square kilometers). Although it is one and a half times the size of the U.K., it is only one-twenty-fifth the size of the U.S., and the whole country is only about the size of the state of California. Three-fourths of

Japan is mountainous and covered with forests. The highest peak is Mt. Fuji (12,388 feet or 3,776 m.). Japan's other high mountains are grouped in the middle of the main island of Honshu and form the "Japan Alps." Several volcanic ranges that run through the islands of Japan have created a unique topography and account for the large number of hotsprings located throughout the country. Only 15% of the land is arable, and residential areas account for only 3% of the total land of the country.

Some 121 million people (about half the size of the population of the U.S.) are crowded onto these mountainous islands. Post-war industrialization and housing shortages have resulted in incredibly high population density in all of the major cities. Eleven cities have populations of more than one million. The nation's capital, Tokyo, has about 8.4 million people within its city limits, and an additional 3.2 million in its suburbs. Yokohama, the second largest city, with a population of 3 million, is located only 18 miles (29 km.) from Tokyo. Between these two giant cities is Kawasaki, the nation's ninth largest city, with a population of 1.1 million. These three cities form the world's largest megalopolis.

Climate

The map of Japan below is overlaid on a map of the East Coast of the United States, at the same latitude, to facilitate comparisons. The climate of Japan is similar to that of the East Coast of the United

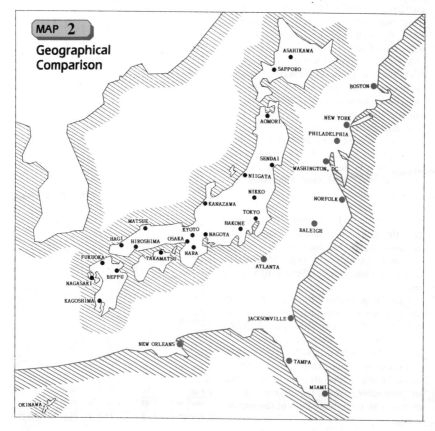

MAP 2

Geographical Comparison

States. Japan has four distinctively different seasons. Spring begins in March (April in northern Honshu and Hokkaido) and lasts until the middle of June. Plum and peach blossoms appear in March, heralding the blooming of the cherry trees in early April and Japan's annual spring time love affair with these beautiful blossoms. The first cherry blossoms appear in the southern part of Kyushu around March 20. The "Cherry Blossom Frontier" then moves gradually toward the northeast. Full bloom in the Kyoto/Osaka and Tokyo areas is usually around April 5. The northern part of Japan is in full bloom by the middle of April. The cherry trees are easily affected by slight changes in temperatures, and the period of full bloom varies slightly from year to year. With warm temperatures and stable weather, April and May are very comfortable months for traveling in Japan. This comfortable weather usually continues until the second week of June, when the rainy season sets in.

Summer begins with the rainy season. With the exception of Hokkaido Island, high humidity and temperatures, along with occasional showers, prevail over the entire country. This is not an ideal season for traveling, but many landscaped gardens are said to look most attractive during a shower or just after a rainfall. The rainy season usually ends in the middle of July. Hot yet stable weather lasts until late August or early September. Areas of high altitude, such as Hakone, Nikko, Koyasan, the Japan Alps and Mt. Asozan, are pleasantly cool throughout the summer. September is typhoon season, but most of these storms remain at sea with only about three or four a year coming ashore. Severe damage is rare.

Autumn is marked by occasional quiet showers in late September and early October. After this short rainy period, Japan has a two-month-long period of stable, comfortable weather, with brilliant blue skies and pleasant temperatures. Japan's scenic beauty reaches its peak in the middle of November, when the country is bedecked with the intense hues of the autumn leaves.

Winter begins with cold western winds blown in by Siberian high pressure systems. The areas along the Japan Sea Coast and the mountainous areas of the interior receive heavy snowfalls throughout the win-

Average Temperatures in Major Cities

	Tokyo		Kyoto		Fukuoka		Sapporo	
Jan.	°F	°C	°F	°C	°F	°C	°F	°C
High	49	10	48	9	49	10	30	−1
Low	33	1	32	0	36	2	16	−9
Average	41	5	39	4	42	6	23	−5
Feb.								
High	50	10	49	10	51	10	32	0
Low	34	1	33	1	37	3	17	−9
Average	42	5	40	5	44	6	24	−4
Mar.								
High	55	13	56	13	57	14	38	4
Low	40	4	37	3	41	5	24	−4
Average	47	8	46	8	49	10	31	0
Apr.								
High	65	18	67	20	66	19	52	11
Low	50	10	47	9	50	10	35	2
Average	57	14	57	14	58	14	43	6
May								
High	73	23	76	24	74	23	64	18
Low	58	15	56	13	57	14	45	7
Average	65	18	65	18	65	18	54	12
June								
High	78	25	81	27	79	26	70	21
Low	65	18	64	18	65	18	53	12
Average	71	22	72	22	72	22	61	16
July								
High	84	29	88	31	87	31	77	25
Low	72	22	73	23	74	24	62	16
Average	77	25	79	26	80	27	68	20
Aug.								
High	87	31	91	33	89	32	79	26
Low	75	24	74	23	75	24	63	18
Average	80	27	82	28	81	27	70	21
Sep.								
High	80	27	83	28	82	28	71	22
Low	68	20	67	19	68	20	54	12
Average	73	23	74	23	74	23	62	17
Oct.								
High	70	21	73	23	73	23	61	16
Low	57	14	55	13	56	13	42	6
Average	63	17	63	17	64	18	51	11
Nov.								
High	62	17	63	17	64	18	47	8
Low	47	8	44	7	47	8	32	0
Average	54	12	53	11	55	13	39	4
Dec.								
High	58	12	53	12	54	12	35	2
Low	38	3	36	2	40	4	23	−5
Average	45	7	44	6	47	8	29	−2

ter, and become winter sports paradises. Even though walking tours are often difficult in these areas in winter, the rugged, snow-covered mountains are scenes of magnificent natural beauty. Most areas on the Pacific coast, especially those southwest of Tokyo, have clear skies and low humidity. Temperatures are mild and seldom fall below freezing. In these areas of the Pacific coast, winter is really not at all a bad time for sightseeing.

Language

Pronunciation. Hepburn romanization is used throughout this book because we believe it is the easiest system for foreigners who want to pronounce Japanese words correctly. There are only five vowels in Japanese – **a** (pronounced like "ah"), **i** ("i" of itch), **u** ("oo" of food), **e** ("e" of bet), and **o** (pronounced like "oh"). All consonants are pronounced the same as in English (if in doubt, you should use a hard rather than a soft sound). Japanese is a language of syllables, not individual letters. The five vowels are separate syllables. All other syllables combine the vowels with a consonant or a consonant blend, e.g. **Na, ri, ta, ryo,** and **shi**. Except for occasional doubling of consonants between syllables (e.g., Jakkoin), virtually the only exception is **n**, which can be a syllable all by itself. The name of the Japanese city Sendai has four syllables: **Se-n-da-i**. To pronounce it correctly be sure to pronounce each separate syllable. Even long words like Amanohashidate become manageable when you separate them thusly: **A-ma-no-ha-shi-da-te**. Remember that each Japanese vowel counts as a separate syllable and that long vowels in Japanese count as two syllables. For example, Tokyo and Osaka are each four syllable words: **To-o-kyo-o** and **O-o-sa-ka**.

Japanese makes no distinction between singular and plural nouns or pronouns, or between present and future tenses. Many English sounds – such as "c", "f", "v", and especially the difference between "r" and "l", are very difficult for Japanese to say; it

is also difficult for them to distinguish these sounds when they hear them. Bear this in mind when conducting conversations. Speak slowly and distinctly, and be patient.

Japanese Suffixes. Typically, there is confusion on how to handle Japanese suffixes when translating into English. For example, "Kiyomizudera" is usually translated as Kiyomizu Temple ("Kiyomizu" is the name of the temple, and "dera" means temple), while "Nanzenji" is usually translated as Nanzenji Temple ("Nanzen" is the name of the temple, and "ji" is another suffix that means temple). To avoid this kind of confusion, this text leaves all Japanese suffixes attached, and adds explanatory English nouns. Therefore, Kiyomizudera is translated as Kiyomizudera Temple, and Nanzenji as Nanzenji Temple. Nagoyajo (the castle in the city of Nagoya) is Nagoyajo Castle, and Asozan (an active volcano in Kyushu) is Mt. Asozan. The only exception is Fujisan because the mountain is already world famous as "Mt. Fuji." To impress the Japanese you meet, delete the explanatory English word and use the full Japanese name.

Conversation Cards

After World War II, English became a mandatory subject for all junior and senior high school students, and most university students. Most Japanese have therefore studied English for at least several years, and know enough to understand written English pretty well. But the schools place all their emphasis on grammar and translation, and the average Japanese has few opportunities to practice speaking English. It is therefore difficult to find Japanese who understand spoken English well. To make the situation worse, most of them are embarrassed that they're not good at English, and believe that they don't understand anything at all. As a result, they often fail to understand even easy questions that they would be able to answer if they were not paralyzed by embarrassment and self-consciousness. To help you ask Japanese passersby simple questions when you need help during your travels in Japan, this book includes nine different kinds of Conversation Cards. Several copies of each card are attached at the back of this book so that you can tear them out and use them while traveling. Remember to **print** your questions clearly on the cards. Handwriting is not easy for Japanese to read. A list of the types of Conversation Cards and instructions on how to use them follow:

Train Rides

Looking for train and subway stations.

Card 1 – Where is the following train/ subway station?

Circle either train or subway and fill in the name of the station and the name of the line you are looking for.

* You shouldn't have much difficulty finding train stations. However, in some huge complexes that house several different lines – including JR, city subways, and private railways – you'll need to use this card to locate the station for the particular line you want.

			下の電車の発車ホーム番号を教えてください	
STATION			Where is the following train/subway station? (Circle either train or subway and fill in the name of the station and the name of the line.)	
	Circle either one		路線名 Line Name	駅名 Destination
1	Train 電車	Subway 地下鉄		
2	電車	地下鉄		
3	電車	地下鉄		
4	電車	地下鉄		
5	電車	地下鉄		

Purchasing tickets for subways and short-distance commuter trains.

Card 2 – How much is the fare to the following station?

Fill in the name of your destination and the name of the line you want to take.

* Tickets for subways and short-distance commuter trains are usually sold in vending machines. Because Japanese train and subway fares vary with the distance traveled, and because the fare tables are often written only in Japanese, you will probably use

this Card frequently to make sure that the ticket you're purchasing is for the proper amount.

		下の電車の発車ホーム番号を教えてください	
TICKET		How much is the fare to the following station? (Fill in the name of your destination and the name of the line you want to take.)	
	路線名 Line Name		目的駅 Destination
1			
2			
3			
4			
5			

Looking for train platforms.

Card 3 – What is the number of the platform for the following train to the destination listed below?

Fill in the name of the line, the name of the train you plan to take, and the name of your destination. If the train is a local and does not have a name, write "Donko." The best person to show this card to is the railway employee at the entrance gate. Show your ticket as well.

		下の電車の発車ホーム番号を教えてください		
PLATFORM		What is the platform number for the following train to the destination listed below? (If the train is a local and does not have a name, write "Donko" in the train name column.)		
	路線名 Line Name	電車名 Train Name		目的駅 Destination
1				
2				
3				
4				
5				

Purchasing a reserved ticket.

Card 4 is designed so that you can easily fill in all the information necessary to purchase a reserved seat ticket. Present the completed card to the clerk at the ticket window.

	座席指定申込書					If you have a Rail Pass you can register reservations for JR trains free of charge. Show the Pass with this form.				
RESERVATION	Application for reserved seats					Your Rail Pass cannot be used for private railways.				
乗車日 (Date of Trip)	月 (month)		日 (date)	人数 No. of Psns	大人 Adults	枚	子供 Children	枚		
出発駅 Departure				目的駅 Destination					Station	
			Station							
座席の種類 (Check either one) Class of Seat	□グリーン車 First Class		□普通車 Coach Class		□禁煙席 Nonsmoking section, if available					
第一希望 First Choice	電車名 Train Name				出発時間 Dep. Time		時 (hour)		分 (minute)	
第二希望 Second Choice	電車名 Train Name				出発時間 Dep. Time		時 (hour)		分 (minute)	
第三希望 Third Choice	電車名 Train Name				出発時間 Dep. Time		時 (hour)		分 (minute)	

Streetcars and Buses

Looking for a stop.

Card 5 – Where is the stop for the streetcar (or bus) going to the following stop?

Circle either streetcar or bus and fill in the name of your destination.

		下の行先の市電またはバス乗場を教えてください	
BUS STREETCAR		Where is the stop for the streetcar (or bus) going to the following destination? (Circle either streetcar or bus and fill in the name of your destination.)	
	Circle either one		目的駅 Destination
1	Streetcar 市電	Bus バス	
2	市電	バス	
3	市電	バス	
4	市電	バス	
5	市電	バス	

Asking about the arrival of your train, streetcar or bus at your destination (for use while on the train, streetcar or bus).

Card 6 – I am going to the following place. Please let me know when we near the destination.

Fill in the name of your destination and show the card to a fellow passenger.

	私は下の目的地まで行きます 目的地が近づいたら教えてください		
DESTINATION	I am going to the following place. Please let me know when we near the destination. (On the train, streetcar or bus) (Fill in the name of your destination and show the card to a fellow passenger.)		
1		6	
2		7	
3		8	
4		9	
5		10	

Taxis

Card 7 – Please take me to the following place.

Fill in the name of your destination.

	下の目的地まで行ってください		
TAXI	Please take me to the following place. (For a taxi driver) (Fill in the name of your destination.)		
1		7	
2		8	
3		9	
4		10	
5		11	
6		12	

Checking Baggage

Card 8 – Where are the coin lockers or a short-term baggage check room?

Train stations have either coin lockers (usually 200 yen per day) or a short-term baggage check room with an attendant. The former can accommodate only carry-on size bags, and you'll need to find the latter for large bags. The check rooms are more convenient for tourists, but many of them are being replaced by coin lockers.

手荷物一時預り所
または
コインロッカーを
教えてください
Where are the coin lockers or
a short-term baggage check room?

One More Important Question

Card 9 -Where is a rest room?

All train stations, department stores and most tourist destinations have rest rooms.

お手洗の場所を
教えてください
Where is a rest room?

Travel Phone

The most convenient information service for you while traveling in Japan is the toll-free Travel Phone. This is the toll-free telephone service operated by Japan National Tourist Organization (JNTO) to provide travel information free of charge, from 9:00 AM to 5:00 PM daily. Outside Tokyo and Kyoto you can call either 0120-222-800. (for information on Eastern Japan) or 0120-444-800 (for information on Western

Japan). In Tokyo you can reach the Tourist Information Center at 502-1461 (a 10 yen call), and in Kyoto you can reach the Information Center by calling 371-5649. To use the toll free number, pick up the receiver of a blue or yellow phone (there is no dial tone until you insert your money), insert a 10 yen coin, and then dial the appropriate number. You will be connected to an Information Center and your 10 yen coin will be returned at the end of your call.

Good-will Guide

This volunteer program was launched by JNTO to help visitors overcome any language difficulty. So far, more than 24,000 Japanese have registered with JNTO or with local governments to serve as volunteer good-will guides. They wear distinctive blue badges and are happy to give directions and answer questions in English.

What to Pack

Clothes. Japan is located in the North Temperate Zone and has four distinct seasons. Jackets or sweaters should be enough in the spring and autumn. Summer is hot and humid and only very light clothes are needed. In the winter a light overcoat or a raincoat with a liner will be enough. Casual clothes are fine for sightseeing, but Japanese usually get dressed up when they're going out to shop or to eat, so you'll probably want to be a little more formal yourself on these occasions.

Supplies at Japanese hotels and ryokans. A fresh *nemaki* (sleeping robe) is provided for your use every night. They are **not** giveaways. If you want to keep one as a souvenir, ask the hotel or ryokan clerk if it's possible to buy one. Towels, soap, washcloths, toothbrushes and toothpaste are standard supplies at all regular accommodations. If you are staying at inexpensive accommodations (i.e., where the charge is less than 12,000 yen for a twin room at a western style hotel, or less than

10,000 yen per person for a Japanese style room plus two meals), these items will not necessarily be supplied (but you'll always be able to purchase them at such places).

Shoes. Bring a pair of comfortable shoes for your walking tours. Don't expect to be able to purchase shoes in Japan. It'll probably be impossible to find any big enough. Because you have to take your shoes off when you enter most temples and shrines, socks are indispensable, especially in the winter, when the wooden corridors of these old, unheated buildings are very chilly.

Medicines. Japan's medical services and facilities meet the highest international standards. If you have prescription medicines you should be sure to pack them. Hotels can help with emergencies.

Electrical products. Electric current in Japan is 100 volts. Fifty cycles is the standard in Tokyo and to the northeast, and 60 cycles in Nagoya, Kyoto, Osaka and areas to the southwest. Most electrical products used by North American travelers, such as electric shavers and hair dryers, will just run a little slower than they do at home. More sensitive devices won't work properly unless they are adjusted.

Others. Japanese always carry tissue paper and handkerchiefs because public toilets often don't have toilet paper or hand towels. These items are always available at the newsstands in train stations.

Shopping and Money

Tax Free Shopping. Foreign visitors to Japan can avoid taxes by patronizing the authorized stores that display "Tax-Free" signs. Be sure to carry your passport with you because the store clerks have to complete special forms and attach them to the passport. These forms will be collected by the customs officials when you leave Japan. Tax free shopping is available in major department stores, hotel arcades and other tourist locations. The tax exemptions vary from 5 to 40 percent, and the items available include precious and semi-precious gems, pearls, electronic goods, watches and cameras.

Currency. The Japanese currency is the yen. There are three kinds of bills – 1,000 yen, 5,000 yen, and 10,000 yen – and several denominations of coins – 1 yen, 5 yen, 10 yen, 50 yen, 100 yen, and 500 yen.

Banks at Narita (New Tokyo International) Airport and Osaka International Airport are open for all arriving flights. You can also convert foreign currency into Japanese yen at banks, hotels and other established tourist facilities that display an "Authorized Money Exchanger" sign. There is no currency black market in Japan. The conversion rate is always a bit more advantageous at banks than at other locations. There are no restrictions on reconversion of unused yen to other currencies. You can also take up to 5 million yen out of Japan. The Japanese yen constantly fluctuates against foreign currencies. fluctuates against other foreign currencies. Our best guess, as of December 1987, is that its future value will be somewhere around US$1.00 = 120 yen.

Credit Cards. Major credit cards, such as American Express, Master Card, Visa and Diners Club, are accepted at major tourist facilities, including hotels, restaurants and souvenir shops. Inexpensive facilities usually do not accept credit cards.

Traveler's Checks. Traveler's checks are accepted at established tourist facilities. However, inexpensive places which cater mainly to Japanese usually do not accept traveler's checks. You should exchange your traveler's checks for Japanese yen at banks.

Cash. Japan is still pretty much a cash society. Because it is safe to do so, people usually carry large amounts of cash, and most Japanese still prefer cash to credit cards.

Service Charges and Tax

Personal tipping is not customary in Japan. Instead of tipping, a 10 – 15% service charge is automatically added to your bill at most major restaurants and accommodations. However, many inexpensive restaurants do not add a service charge. The few porters who do work at airports

¥10,000

¥5,000

¥1,000

¥500   ¥100

¥50   ¥10

¥5   ¥1

and train stations charge a standard per piece fee of 200 – 300 yen.

If the charge at an accommodation is less than 5,000 yen per person per night, no tax is levied. If the charge is 5,000 yen or more, a 10% tax will be added to your bill. At restaurants, if your bill is 2,500 yen or more per person, a 10% tax is added. If you want to save money, don't charge your breakfast to your hotel bill. If you pay for your breakfast separately no tax will be levied (provided, of course, that the bill is less than 2,500 yen per person), but if you charge your meal to your hotel bill and pay the entire amount when you check out, the total charge will be subject to a 10% tax (except at Tokyo and Osaka hotels).

Water, Food and Drinks

Water. Tap water is safe everywhere in Japan.

Food. Food (even what's sold by street vendors) is also safe.

Drinks. A variety of soft drinks, including international and Japanese brands, are available, but diet soft drinks with saccharin are not allowed to be sold in Japan. Most Japanese are not familiar with 100% fruit juice; when they talk about "juice" they usually mean soda pop.

Major hotels have refrigerators in every room so that guests always have easy access to cold beer and soft drinks, but anything you take from one of these refrigerators will be very expensive. Inexpensive hotels usually have vending machines for soft drinks and beer in the lobby. Prices are tolerable, but still higher than the prices in the stores. You might want to consider taking beverages out and bringing them to your room (see below). Alcoholic beverages are not unusually expensive, but this does not mean that they are cheap. If you drink alcohol regularly you should purchase some at an airport duty-free shop before you leave your own country. You can bring in up to three regular-sized bottles of any kind of alcoholic beverage duty free.

Take Out. A variety of take out foods and canned soft drinks and alcoholic beverages are sold in the basements of department stores. If you feel like relaxing in your hotel room but don't want to spend the money for room service, you should buy food and beverages at these places. Many housewives shop for dinner for their families at these establishments, which have wide selection at inexpensive prices.

Morning Service. If you don't want a big breakfast at your hotel, find a coffee shop nearby. Most of them serve a "morning service" special for 350 – 500 yen. The special consists of coffee or tea, toast, a boiled egg, and a small salad or a piece of fruit.

Table Manners

At Japanese restaurants, except for the most prestigious and expensive ones, you are expected to find an empty table and seat yourself.

As soon as you are seated at a restaurant or coffee shop you'll be presented with an *oshibori* – a hot towel (a cold one in summer). You can use the towel to clean your hands and wipe your face (Women should stop with the hands!). At most restaurants, except those which specialize in Western food, disposable chopsticks (which are very clean because they are used just once) are provided; pull them apart at the top. If you ask for a knife, fork or spoon, don't be surprised if the restaurant doesn't have any. Don't eat your soup with a spoon. In Japan it's proper to "drink" your soup. Pick up the bowl and drink the broth; use your chopsticks for the contents. Don't be surprised if you hear Japanese slurping their soup or noodles (It's often quite loud!). Slurping is **good** manners in Japan, and demonstrates one's appreciation.

Useful Hints

Rest Rooms

In real emergencies you can always stop in a coffee shop. You'll probably find it well worth the 300   400 yen it will cost you for a cup of coffee or a soft drink. If you are in a city, department stores and hotels are good places to take refuge. All train stations have rest rooms but they are almost always dirty and are sometimes inside the ticket barriers (another advantage for holders of Japan Rail Passes, who have unlimited access to all JR trains and platforms – for whatever the reason). Rest rooms in office buildings are not locked. Public rest rooms are not clean, but will do in emergencies.

Hotels, department stores and fancy restaurants and coffee shops have Western-style toilets. But if you are traveling as the

Japanese travel, you should expect to encounter a lot of Japanese-style toilets. Japanese style requires squatting rather than sitting. Actually, it's supposed to be better for you, and it's certainly cleaner. Once you get used to it you might find that you prefer it.

Baggage Handling

Trains in Japan are not equipped to accommodate the big bags of international travelers. Train stations in Japan are generally very large and have many staircases and underground passages connecting the various platforms and entrances/exits, but it's almost impossible to find a porter. It's torture trying to lug big bags through these huge, confusing and often very crowded stations. Plan a separate baggage transfer between major cities such as Tokyo and Kyoto. Even if you plan to travel extensively, consider arranging several side trips using Tokyo and Kyoto as your bases. There are more details in the Transportation Chapter below.

Traffic on the Left

As in the U.K., traffic on the left is the rule in Japan. Not only automobiles, but also trains and subways run on the left. Be careful when you're waiting for a train at a local station or for a bus on an empty street. If you don't think about it, you're likely to wait on the right hand side facing your destination!

Japan has the largest number of cars per square foot in the world. Because traffic is so heavy, pedestrian bridges and underground passages are quite commonplace. Use these facilities and cross only at intersections. Don't jaywalk. Japanese obey traffic signals, and drivers aren't prepared for pedestrians who don't.

Why You Shouldn't Drive in Japan

There are several reasons why we recommend that foreigners travel on the trains rather than by car. First of all, except on a few expressways, road signs are only in Japanese. If you can't read Japanese, it is extremely difficult to drive around in Japan. Secondly, many Japanese cities were laid out during the feudal era, with the streets arranged in complicated patterns for strategic, defensive purposes. Even for Japanese it is not easy to get around in these cities by car. Thirdly, renting a car costs far more than taking trains. Even though car rentals themselves are not too expensive, gas costs about three times what it does in the U.S., and tolls are extremely expensive. For example, the one-way toll from Tokyo to Kyoto is 11,900 yen, which is almost the same amount as the Shinkansen fare for the same distance. The fourth reason is that trains are much faster than cars. For example, the Shinkansen takes a little less than three hours to make the trip from Tokyo to Kyoto, but driving the same distance usually takes eight hours, even on the expressway. Even if you have experience driving on the left and are able to manage manual shifts (which are standard on rental cars), it does not mean that you can drive in Japan enjoyably. Experiencing the efficiency and punctuality of public transportation should be part of your discovery of the country.

National Holidays

Jan. 1 – New Year's Day (Only January 1 is a legal holiday, but government offices and corporations are closed from December 29 through January 3.)

Jan. 15 – Adults' Day

Feb. 11 – Founding of the Nation Day

Mar. 21 – Vernal Equinox Day

Apr. 29 – Emperor's Birthday

May 3 – Constitution Day

May 5 – Children's Day (Most Japanese take a long break at this time, bridging these three holidays with the weekends before or after them. As a result, the period from April 28 through May 6, called "Golden Week," is the period of the largest movement of people throughout the country.)

Sep. 15 – Respect for the Aged Day

Sep. 23 – Autumn Equinox Day

Oct. 10 – Health-Sports Day

Nov. 3 – Culture Day

Nov. 23 – Labor Thanksgiving Day

Business Hours

Department Stores are open from 10:00 AM to 6:00 PM (till 6:30 PM on Saturdays and Sundays). They are closed once a week on a weekday. Closing days differ from store to store, so in major cities at least one store is open on any given weekday.

Other Stores. Smaller stores are usually open from 10:00 AM to 8:00 PM. (Some are open till 10:00 PM). They usually close once a week or once every two weeks, on a weekday.

Banks. Banks are open from 9:00 AM to 3:00 PM on weekdays and from 9:00 AM to 12:00 noon on Saturdays. They are closed on Sundays and on the second and third Saturdays of each month. Banks at Narita (New Tokyo International) Airport and Osaka Airport are open for all arrival flights year round.

Time Difference

All of Japan is in a single time zone. Japanese standard time is nine hours ahead of G.M.T., 14 hours ahead of New York, 15 hours ahead of Chicago and 17 hours ahead of Los Angeles. If it is 7:00 AM in New York it is 9:00 PM in Japan (plus 14 hours). If it is 4:00 PM in Los Angeles it is 9:00 AM the next day in Japan (plus 17 hours).

When you travel to Japan from the U.S. you lose one day (arriving in Japan the following day). When you return from Japan to the U.S. you gain one day (arriving in the U.S. on the same day – usually even before you left Japan!).

Postal Services

Mail boxes in Japan are red. You can buy stamps in your hotel or at local post offices.

Telephone Service within Japan

Public phones in Japan usually have two slots, one for 10 yen coins and another for 100 yen coins. A local call costs 10 yen for the first three minutes. The cost of a long distance call varies depending on the city you call. If you have no idea about the cost of a long distance call you want to make, insert several 100 yen coins. Unused coins will be returned after your call.

International Telephone Service

In major Japanese cities, international telephone calls can be arranged at your hotel. Further information is available from KDD (International Telegram and Telephone Co.) at (03) 270-5111. When you call from Tokyo you don't have to use the (03) area code.

Churches

Large Japanese cities have a selection of churches and synagogues. Check with the concierge of your hotel.

English Newspapers

Four English language newspapers are published daily – three in the morning and one in the evening. They are sold at newsstands in train stations and at major hotels. International news magazines (usually Asian editions) are also sold at major hotels and bookstores.

Massage Service at Accommodations

Japanese masseuses are renowned (justifiably) for their skill. Massages can be arranged at most accommodations – Western style hotels as well as Japanese inns. The charge is 2,000 – 3,000 yen for 30 minutes.

Guides and Hired Cars

If you plan to sightsee using a car and a guide, you'll have to hire a chauffeur-driven car and a guide separately, because these two services are completely separate in Japan. The standard charge for a tourist guide is 20,000 – 30,000 yen per day. You'll also have to pay for the guide's transportation. If you take a guide on an overnight trip, you'll also have to pay for the guide's accommodations and meals. The cost of a chauffeur-driven car varies from city to city. A typical rate is about 5,000 – 6,000 yen per hour. A guide and a hired car can be arranged for at your accommodations. You can also make arrangements through the Japan Guide Association. About 1,000 active licensed guides belong to the association (Phone: (03) 213-2706).

About the Japanese

Japan's Roots

Archeological discoveries have confirmed that the Japanese archipelago was inhabited as long as 10,000 years ago. Contrary to the belief popular in Japan that the "Yamato race" is monotribal, recent studies indicate that the Japanese are a mixture of various Asian races, including Mongolians, Chinese, Koreans and Southeast Asians, who inhabited Japan before the archipelago split away from the continent. Even after the Japanese islands floated away from the continent, many Asian peoples, especially Koreans and Chinese, emigrated to Japan, adding new strains to Japanese native stock and creating the "Japanese" as they are today. Despite all the evidence to contrary, the myth that the Japanese are a monotribal people who conquered the uncivilized inhabitants of their islands still persists and is an important part of the view most Japanese have of themselves and of their nation. It was used to fan the flames of the nationalism that consumed Japan in the period between the Meiji Restoration and the end of World War II.

Japan is located only 110 miles (176 km.) from the Korean peninsula. Throughout its history, this proximity to the continent has enabled Japan to import advanced culture and technologies from various Asian countries, especially China. At the same time, the roughness of the Japan Sea and the primitive equipment and rudimentary navigational techniques of ancient times kept Japan relatively free from military and political interference by other countries. Japan created its own unique culture, based on the imports from the continent, adopting and "Japanizing" them, much as it has done in the modern era with its adoptions and modifications of Western cultures and technologies.

Religion

Japan's native religion is Shinto. Because it originated in the daily life of the people during the primitive era, all sorts of natural objects and phenomena were considered gods or the work of gods. A naturalistic religion, it does not involve belief in any specific creator and has no scriptures. After the Meiji Restoration (in 1868), Shinto was established as the national religion. The new government, organized in the name of the emperor, portrayed the Shinto gods as progenitors of the imperial family as a means of legitimating its authority. After World War II Shinto lost its official status.

Buddhism was introduced into Japan in the 6th century. It deeply influenced the philosophical life of the Japanese, introducing for the first time the belief in eternal life. Buddhism first spread among the aristocrats, and was used as the spiritual base of the unified nation. Zen is one of Buddhism's sects and was especially popular with the military classes. It emphasized serenity of mind and freedom from worldly desires, to be achieved not through the study of scripture, but rather through the practice of meditation. A number of Buddhist groups are active today, and most of them have, either formally or informally, a substantial influence on political affairs.

But neither Buddhism nor Shintoism has much real influence on the everyday life of today's Japanese. In Japan religion is usually regarded as merely the provider of social ceremonies. Ceremonies related to birth, coming of age, and marriage are usually performed according to Shinto rites, while those related to death utilize Buddhist rites: most Japanese do not think it at all strange to be involved with more than one religion at a time.

Christianity, introduced in the middle of the 16th century, but then banned during the period of Japan's isolation, was reintroduced after the Meiji Restoration. Despite great missionary efforts and the establishment by Christians of many useful social institutions, such as hospitals and schools, neither Catholicism nor Protestantism has attracted many followers. The total number of Christians is estimated to be 700,000 – 900,000.

Airport Transportation

Narita Airport
(New Tokyo International Airport)

There are several means of public transportation between Narita Airport and the city of Tokyo:

I. Airport Limousine Bus

This is the most popular and the easiest way to get to Tokyo. The Airport Limousine Bus information and ticketing counter is located in the arrivals lobby right outside of the Customs Hall. There is a huge orange English sign. This company operates several bus routes as explained below.

(1) Between Narita Airport and Tokyo City Air Terminal (TCAT)

This is the main Airport Limousine Bus route. Buses operate about every 15 minutes. The ride takes 60 – 70 minutes, and the fare is 2,500 yen. From TCAT, most hotels are within a 1,500 – 3,000 yen taxi ride (10 – 20 minutes). At TCAT, the buses arrive on the third floor. Escalators take you down to the baggage claim area on the ground floor. Plenty of taxis are always waiting at the TCAT exit.

(2) Between Narita Airport and Tokyo Station

A direct bus from the airport to Tokyo Station operates twice an hour. This service is especially convenient for those who are headed for other cities, such as Kyoto, by the Shinkansen. The ride takes 60 – 70 minnutes, and the fare is 2,600 yen. Service from Tokyo Station to Narita Airport is available two or three times an hour from dawn to dusk. The bus stop at Tokyo Station is on the Yaesu side of the Station.

(3) Between Narita Airport and Shinjuku District

There are direct buses twice an hour on this route. The buses stop at Shinjuku Station, the Keio Plaza Hotel, the Century Hyatt Hotel, and the Tokyo Hilton. The ride takes about 2 hours and the fare is 2,700 yen. Buses from the Shinjuku district (making the same stops) to Narita Airport run from early in the morning till late in the afternoon, about twice an hour.

(4) Direct Buses Between Narita Airport and Major Hotels in Tokyo

In addition to the special service to the Shinjuku area hotels, there is also direct Airport Limousine Bus service to other ma-

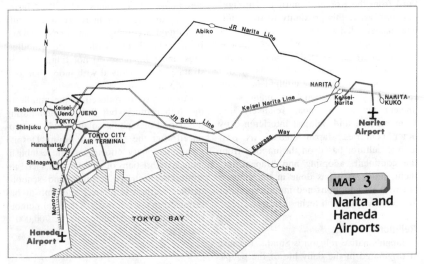

MAP **3**

Narita and Haneda Airports

jor hotels in Tokyo. Most buses from the airport to the hotels operate in the afternoon and the early evening (from 2:00 PM to 9:00 PM). Several buses make the reverse trip from the major hotels to the airport, directly. Check with the hotel staff for times. The rides take 80 – 120 minutes, and the fare is 2,700 yen.

Hotels served by the Airport Limousine Bus: Akasaka Prince, Akasaka Tokyu, ANA Tokyo, Ginza Tokyu, Grand Palace, Imperial, Metropolitan, New Otani, New Takanawa Prince, Okura, Pacific Meridien, Palace, Shimbashi Daiichi, Sunshine City Prince, Takanawa Prince and Tokyo Prince.

(5) Between Narita Airport and Haneda Airport

Most domestic flights operate from Haneda Airport ("Old" Tokyo International Airport). The two airports (Narita and Haneda) are connected by Airport Limousine Bus service every 20 – 30 minutes, from morning till night. The ride takes 80 minutes and the fare is 2,700 yen.

II. Airport Express Bus

This second company (with a name frustratingly similar to the first) operates direct buses about once an hour to major hotels in Tokyo. It too has an information and ticketing counter in the arrivals lobby at Narita Airport (not far from the Airport Limousine Bus counter). If you cannot find a convenient bus to your hotel with the Airport Limousine Bus service, check with this company for a direct bus to your hotel.

In addition to those hotels listed at (3) and (4) above, the following hotels are served by the Airport Express Bus: Miyako Tokyo, Tokyo Marunouchi and Shiba Park.

III. Keisei Line Skyliner Train

Keisei Electric Railway (private) operates limited express trains between Narita-Kuko (Narita Airport) Station and Keisei-Ueno Station in Tokyo. The train is called Skyliner, and runs every 40 minutes. The ride takes exactly 61 minutes, and the fare is 1,500 yen, which includes a limited express reserved seat surcharge. The station is located on the airport grounds. Shuttle buses take you the short distance from the arrivals building to the station. Stop at the Keisei Information Counter in the arrivals lobby if you decide to use this way of getting to Tokyo.

IV. Japan Railways

JR train service is less convenient than the other methods of transportation between the airport and Tokyo, and is recommended only for those who want to make maximum use of a Japan Rail Pass. JR Narita Station is a 25-minute bus ride from Narita Airport. Connecting buses stop right outside the arrivals building. The shuttle bus fare of 350 yen is covered by the Rail Pass (the bus is a JR bus). The Sobu Line runs between Narita Station and Tokyo Station, via Chiba. The Narita Line connects Narita with Ueno Station (via Abiko). Both trains operate about once an hour and both trips take about 80 minutes.

V. Taxis

Taxis are plentiful at Narita Airport, and the drivers are quite willing to take you the long distance to your hotel in Tokyo, but the ride costs about 24,000 yen.

Haneda Airport
("Old" Tokyo International Airport)

Airport Limousine Bus between Narita and Haneda Airports: Explained above.

Airport Limousine Bus between Haneda Airport and Hotels in Tokyo: The following hotels are served by the Airport Limousine Bus. The buses run about once every hour and the ride takes 50 – 60 minutes (The fare is 1,000 yen): Akasaka Prince, Akasaka Tokyu, Century Hyatt, Keio Plaza, New Otani and Tokyo Hilton.

Monorail between Haneda Airport and Hamamatsucho Station: There is frequent monorail service between Haneda Airport and Hamamatsucho Station in Tokyo (a 15 minute ride).

Taxis: A taxi trip from Haneda Airport to any major Tokyo hotel will cost about 5,000 yen.

Osaka Airport

Osaka Airport functions as a gateway to three major cities in the Kansai district – Osaka, Kyoto and Kobe. There is no train service between Osaka Airport and these three cities, but airport buses are available. Taxis are plentiful at the airport, but you had better stay away from them, especially when you go to Kyoto.

I. To and From Kyoto

Airport Limousine Bus: There is service between Osaka Airport (from Domestic Arrivals Building – 200 meters from International Arrivals Building) and Kyoto Station (Hachijo-guchi or the southern side of the station) three times an hour each way from early in the morning till at night. In addition, hourly buses operate between Osaka Airport and major hotels in Kyoto. The ride takes 60 – 100 minutes, and the fare is 700 – 800 yen depending on your destination.

Hotels in Kyoto served by the Airport Limousine Bus: ANA Kyoto, International Kyoto, Kyoto, Kyoto Grand, Kyoto Tokyu, New Miyako, New Hankyu.

Taxi: A taxi trip from Osaka Airport to major hotels in Kyoto takes about 60 minutes, and the ride costs about 20,000 yen.

II. To and From Osaka

Taxi: Because a taxi ride to major hotels in Osaka costs about only 4,000 yen, this is the most convenient and easiest method of transportation to Osaka. Because there are no convenient buses serving major hotels in Osaka, you had better take a taxi to your hotel if you have large suitcases. If you are traveling light, you can take the Airport Bus (below) to Osaka or Shin-Osaka Station, and catch a taxi from there.

Airport Bus: There is also frequent bus service to various points in the city of Osaka, including Osaka Station (a 30 minute ride; 380 yen) and Shin-Osaka Station (the Shinkansen station) (a 25 minute ride; 290 yen).

III. To and From Kobe

Airport Limousine Bus: There is service three times an hour from dawn to dusk. The bus stop near Sannomiya Station (the main train station in Kobe) is pictured on Map 99 (upper right). The ride takes 40 minutes and the fare is 620 yen.

Taxi: A taxi trip between Osaka Airport and major hotels in Kobe costs about 10,000 yen.

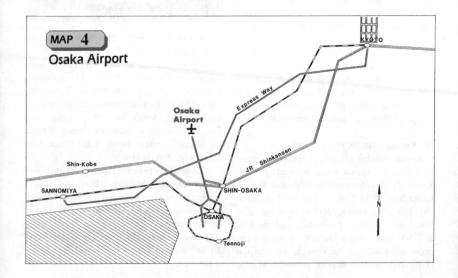

Other Major Airports in Japan

With the expansion of the national air network, air travel has become popular, especially from Tokyo and Osaka to Kyushu and Hokkaido.

Haneda (Tokyo), Osaka, Nagoya, Fukuoka and Sapporo are five key airports in Japan. Several daily flights are operated to most local airports from these key cities, especially from Haneda and Osaka.

In addition, one to three daily flights each way operate between Tokyo (Narita Airport) and such major cities as Osaka, Nagoya, Fukuoka and Sapporo to provide easy connections to international flights to and from Narita.

Bus or train services between the airports and downtown areas are explained in each city section.

MAP 5

Major Airports in Japan

Entrance Requirements

Visas

Citizens of the U.S. and Australia must obtain tourist visas to enter Japan (There is no charge for these visas). Canadians and British subjects do not need visas. Citizens of other countries should check with the nearest Japanese Embassy or Consulate.

In the United States you can apply for your Japanese visa at the Embassy of Japan or at one of the following Consulates General of Japan:

Embassy of Japan, Washington, D.C.
Tel: (202) 939-6800.

Consulates General of Japan
1. Atlanta, GA
   Tel: (404) 892-2700.
2. Boston, MA
   Tel: (617) 973-9772.
3. Chicago, IL
   Tel: (312) 280-0400.
4. Honolulu, HI
   Tel: (808) 536-2226.
5. Houston, TX
   Tel: (713) 652-2977.
6. Kansas City, MO
   Tel: (816) 471-0111.
7. Los Angeles, CA
   Tel: (213) 624-8305.
8. New Orleans, LA
   Tel: (504) 529-2101.
9. New York, NY
   Tel: (212) 371-8222.
10. Portland, OR
    Tel: (503) 221-1811.
11. San Francisco, CA
    Tel: (415) 921-8000.
12. Seattle, WA
    Tel: (206) 682-9107.

Customs

The following can be brought into Japan duty free:
- Up to three regular sized bottles of alcoholic beverages.
- 20 packs of cigarettes (400 cigarettes), or 100 cigars, or 500 grams of pipe, powdered or chewing tobacco.
- Two ounces of perfume.
- Two timepieces in addition to the one the traveler is using (Maximum value of 30,000 yen each).
- In addition to the items listed above, souvenirs whose combined market value is less than 200,000 yen.

The following cannot be brought into Japan under any circumstances:
- Illegal drugs, including marihuana (Don't try it; you'll be in big trouble!). Properly labeled prescription drugs are fine.
- Pornographic books, pictures, films and other items.

Other Requirements

Vaccinations are not required unless you are visiting Japan after traveling in an affected area.

Security checks at Japanese airports are rather strict. You're likely to be frisked at the entrance gates to the departure wings.

There is no departure tax per se at Japanese airports. However, if you leave Japan from Narita (New Tokyo International) Airport, a 2,000 yen "airport utility charge" will be imposed.

Airlines

In addition to Japan Air Lines and All Nippon Airways, the flag carriers of most nations serve Japan. From the United States, United, Northwest, American and Delta provide service between virtually all major American cities and Tokyo (Narita Airport) and Osaka.

Transportation within Japan

Some Advice
How to Use Japanese Common Sense

Trains are the most convenient and efficient method of travel in Japan. Most Japanese cities are conveniently linked by the Japan Railways (JR) network. In the larger cities and major resort areas, private railways provide parallel and supplementary service.

All long distance trains (whether JR or private) have reserved seats. To make your trip as comfortable as possible you should make reservations for the long distance trains as soon as you arrive in Japan. If you are not able to make reservations, don't worry because all long distance trains also have nonreserved cars, and you will usually be able to get a seat. The "Hikari" Shinkansen (bullet train) between Tokyo and Kyoto, for example, has 16 cars, five of which are nonreserved. On the slower "Kodama" Shinkansen on the same line, 11 of the 16 cars are nonreserved.

At least one nonreserved car and one reserved car on all long distance trains are nonsmoking cars. The number of nonsmoking cars has been gradually increasing. Smoking is prohibited on all short-distance and commuter trains.

Japanese trains are not designed to accommodate the large suitcases and bags that many international travelers use. Except in the green car (first class) of the Shinkansen, there is no space for luggage other than on the overhead rack (though there is sometimes some space behind the last seat in a car). You can leave your big bags outside the door of the car. They will be safe (Japan really is as safe as all the promotional materials claim). If you feel uneasy, go to the door whenever the train stops at a station. This won't be too much of a bother because long distance trains only stop at major stations. Small and medium sized bags can be stowed on the overhead racks.

* If you want to travel light in Japan, you should arrange separate baggage delivery between hotels. Same day delivery is available between such major cities as Tokyo, Kyoto and Osaka. In order to use this service it is important to have advance hotel reservations at your next destination. Separate delivery costs about 1,500 yen per bag, depending on the size of the bag and the distance involved.

When planning your itinerary, consider the most effective use of baggage delivery between major cities. For example, if you plan a Tokyo – Kyoto – Inland Sea – Central Japan – Tokyo route, you should:

– Travel on the Shinkansen to Kyoto with your big bags (or arrange separate delivery).

– Then make a two-night three-day excursion to the Inland Sea area from Kyoto. You can check your large bags at your hotel in Kyoto, and just carry a smaller bag on the Inland Sea trip.

– Returning to Kyoto, arrange for separate baggage delivery to Tokyo, and then travel to Central Japan with only a smaller bag. When you return to Tokyo from your visit to Central Japan, your baggage will be waiting for you at your hotel.

By arranging your trip this way, you carry your large bags only once (or not at all), between Tokyo and Kyoto.

During the following periods, trains are very crowded. Avoid them. When we say **avoid**, we mean it. These are major holiday periods, and most Japanese take a family vacation or travel back to their original home towns for big family get-togethers. The inter-city trains at these times look something like the famous rush hour subways of Tokyo – the ones where professional pushers cram everyone into the car! Pick another time or stay in a major tourist destination such as Tokyo or Kyoto. Stay off the trains.

– New Year's Holidays: Dec. 28 – Jan. 4
– Golden Week: April 28 – May 6
– Obon Period: August 12 – 18

Japan Railways (JR)

As with most of the passenger railways in the world, the Japanese National Railways (JNR) has been suffering from massive deficits. In an attempt to rationalize the industry, the Japanese Diet passed a law to privatize the JNR and split it into six regional passenger railway companies: (1) JR (Japan Railways) Hokkaido; (2) JR Eastern Japan (Tokyo and northern mainland); (3) JR Tokai (central mainland); (4) JR

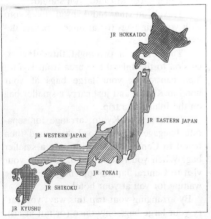

MAP **6**   Six JR Companies

JR HOKKAIDO

JR EASTERN JAPAN

JR WESTERN JAPAN

JR TOKAI

JR SHIKOKU

JR KYUSHU

Western Japan (Kyoto/Osaka and western mainland); (5) JR Shikoku; and (6) JR Kyushu. The law went into effect on April 1, 1987.

Even though privatization may eventually have an influence on fares and schedules, there will be no drastic changes in the near future. Long-distance trains now run inter-regionally operated jointly by the new companies, and schedules and fares in effect at the time of the changeover continue without major changes. As far as passengers are concerned, there might as well still be a nationwide JNR network. Best of all, the Japan Rail Pass is also administered jointly, and can be used on trains of each of the six new companies.

TYPES OF JR TRAINS

1. Shinkansen

Popularly known as the bullet trains. Because all the English signs in the JR stations refer to these as "Shinkansen" rather than "bullet train," "Shinkansen" is used throughout this book when referring to this super express train. Only major cities have stations on the Shinkansen lines, in some cases separate from the stations for other lines, because the Shinkansen runs on its own special tracks.

There are now three Shinkansen lines operating in Japan:

(1) West-bound from Tokyo
(Tokaido-Sanyo Shinkansen)

This Shinkansen runs between Tokyo and Hakata (Fukuoka) via such major cities as Nagoya, Kyoto, Osaka, Kobe and Hiroshima. Most foreigners have this line in mind when they refer to the Shinkansen. When "the" Shinkansen is referred to in this book, this is the line we mean. There are more details on the Shinkansen below.

(2) North-bound from Ueno, Tokyo
(Tohoku Shinkansen)

This line connects Tokyo's Ueno Station with Morioka via Utsunomiya, Sendai, Ichinoseki, etc. Thanks to this new bullet train, Tohoku has become an easily accessible destination from Tokyo. You will use this line to visit all of the four major destinations in Tohoku introduced in this book. We will refer to this bullet train as the Tohoku Shinkansen.

(3) Japan Sea-bound from Ueno, Tokyo
(Joetsu Shinkansen)

This train runs from Tokyo's Ueno Station to Niigata on the Japan Sea Coast. Destinations introduced here along this line are Mt. Tanigawadake, Niigata and Sado Island, and we refer to it as the Joetsu Shinkansen.

2. Limited Express Trains
3. Express Trains

These are long distance trains that operate on regular tracks. A limited express uses fancier and more spacious cars and makes fewer stops than an express. The extra charges are higher for a limited express than for an express, but the surcharge for a limited express is cheaper than that for a Shinkansen.

4. Local Trains

Local trains operate over comparatively short distances and serve the everyday needs of the people. These trains are convenient for traveling around in the larger cities, or for making side trips from these larger cities. Only a basic fare is required on this type of train.

In the timetables attached at the end of this book, we have selected the most convenient trains for the destinations we introduce, taking into consideration comfort, ease and speed as well as economy.

CLASSES OF SERVICE

There are two classes of service, first class and coach class, on Shinkansen trains, limited express trains, most express trains, and some local trains. There's an extra charge for the Green Car (the name JR gives its first class cars).

Sleeping berth service is available on some long distance night trains. However, sleeping berth charges (quite expensive) are not covered by a Japan Rail Pass and the berths are not big enough for most foreigners.

FARE SYSTEMS

Because there are four types of trains and two classes of service, total train fares vary depending on their combination. For example, if you take a local train, you will pay only the basic fare. If you take a Green Car on a limited express train, you have to pay (1) the basic fare, (2) a limited express surcharge, and (3) a Green Car surcharge.

The distinctive Greencar (First Class) symbol, here on the Shinkansen.

Reserved tickets office at a JR station.

Don't worry. We have calculated total fares for all the long distance train rides we have suggested in this guidebook and included them in the timetable section at the end of the book.

HOW TO PURCHASE AND USE TICKETS

* If you are using a Japan Rail Pass, skip this section and proceed to the next section, **JAPAN RAIL PASS.**

Reserved Seats

You can make reservations and purchase tickets at JR stations. Because there are no English-speaking clerks at the ticket windows except in a few of the largest stations, Conversation Card 4 will help you purchase tickets. In large JR stations there are spe-

cial "Reserved Ticket" offices that are distinguishable by their green signs. If the station does not have a green ticket office, you can purchase both reserved seat tickets and nonreserved seat tickets at the regular ticket windows.

Nonreserved Seats for Longer Distance Trains

Purchase tickets at regular ticket windows.

Commuter Train Tickets

Because the fares are low, these tickets are usually sold in vending machines. Fares, which vary with the distance traveled, are usually listed only in Japanese (there are only a few English fare tables in all of Japan). If you can't figure out the fare, write the name of your destination on Conversation Card 2 and show it to a Japanese passerby.

Ticket Check

When you go through the entrance gate, your ticket will be punched. Keep the ticket with you. On long distance trains a conductor usually checks tickets, but they are usually not checked on commuter trains. All tickets have to be returned at the exit gate when you reach your destination.

JR Ticket vending machines.

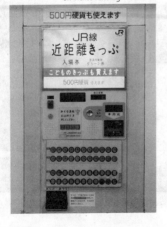

JAPAN RAIL PASS

For foreign visitors to Japan, the six Japan Railway companies, working as a single entity, make available the specially discounted Japan Rail Pass. The Pass entitles the bearer to unlimited travel on the entire JR rail, bus and boat system.

Eligibility

A Japan Rail Pass voucher can be purchased by any foreign tourist visiting Japan on a tourist visa or a transit visa (Sorry, holders of diplomatic, student or business visas **cannot** use Japan Rail Passes). A Japan Rail Pass cannot be purchased in Japan. The Pass (actually a voucher that you exchange for a pass once you arrive in Japan) must be obtained **before** you leave for Japan.

Types of Japan Rail Passes and Prices

There are two types of Japan Rail Passes – ordinary car (coach class) and Green Car (first class). One week, two week and three week passes are available at the following prices (in yen):

Type	7 days	14 days	21 days
Coach	27,000	43,000	55,000
First-class	37,000	60,000	78,000

How to Purchase a Japan Rail Pass

A voucher for a Japan Rail Pass can be purchased from your travel agent.

Exchange of a Voucher for a Pass

Upon arrival in Japan, you can exchange your voucher for your Pass at any of the following JR stations from 10:00 AM to 6:00 PM: Tokyo, Ueno, Shinjuku, Yokohama, Nagoya, Kyoto, Osaka, Hiroshima, Hakata, Kumamoto, Niigata, Nishi-Kagoshima, Sendai and Sapporo.

If you land in Japan at Narita Airport, however, we definitely recommend that you change your voucher for your pass at the JR counter right in the airport arrivals lobby. The JR counter, which is open from 7:00 AM to 11:00 PM daily, is located on the concourse just outside the Customs Hall. When you exchange your voucher specify the date on which you'd like your one, two or three week pass to start running.

Seat Reservations

The Japan Rail Pass entitles its holder to make seat reservations for ordinary cars or green cars depending on the type of Pass. Plan your long distance train rides in advance and request reservations at the time you exchange your voucher (There's no additional charge for reservations). If you change your schedule while you are traveling, you can change your reservations at any of the major JR stations, or just abandon your reserved seat and take a non-reserved seat on another train. Sleeping berths (all reserved) are not covered by the Japan Rail Pass. An additional surcharge will be collected if you request a sleeping berth reservation.

DINING CARS AND CATERING SERVICES

Most long-distance trains have either a dining car or a buffet car. In addition, there are vendors on every long-distance train who walk up and down the aisles with baskets or wagons (keep your legs out of the aisle!). You can buy sandwiches, box lunches, coffee, soft drinks, Japanese tea, beer, whiskey, and even local souvenirs from these vendors.

• **REST ROOMS**

On long-distance trains almost every other car has a rest room.

Private Railways

Private railways usually operate commuter trains in large cities and deluxe tourist trains from large cities to nearby resorts. In this guide we have introduced them when we believe they are more convenient than the JR (Even in these situations we have also introduced parallel JR service, if it exists, for the information of Japan Rail Pass holders). As with JR, reserved-seat tickets are sold at the ticket windows and commuter train tickets are sold in vending machines.

Subways

There are subways in Tokyo, Nagoya, Kyoto, Osaka, Kobe, Hakata, Yokohama, Sapporo and Sendai. Tickets are sold in vending machines (All subway stations in Nagoya, which is not known as Japan's most cosmopolitan city, have at least one fare board in English). Subway stations (except for most Tokyo stations) are equipped with automatic entrance and exit gates like those in San Francisco and Washington, D.C. At the entrance, you have to insert your magnetized ticket in the slot at the front of the gate. The ticket is checked magnetically and the bar across the entrance retracts if the ticket is valid. Pick up your ticket from the slot on the other side of the barrier. At your destination, you again insert your ticket into the machine. You can then exit, but the ticket does not come out this time. You have to buy a new ticket for each trip. If the ticket you bought was for less that the required amount, an alarm bell sounds and a puzzled station clerk will arrive on the scene to settle the difference with you. Most Tokyo subways work like the trains. Have your ticket punched when you enter, make sure that you hold on to it, and turn it in when you exit. During rush hours Tokyo subways really are as horribly crowded as everyone says. It's probably best to avoid them then.

Buses and Streetcars

Buses are especially important means of public transportation in Kyoto, Nara and most smaller cities. Streetcars provide tourists with convenient and inexpensive transportation in Hakodate, Hiroshima, Matsuyama, Kochi, Kagoshima, Kumamoto and Nagasaki. This book provides detailed information in the city sections on the bus networks and streetcar systems. Both streetcars and buses are usually operated by a driver only, and you are required to deposit the exact fare into the box near the driver when you get off. Many local bus systems charge only one flat fare, but others operate on a zone fare system. When you get on a bus, make sure to check to see if there's a machine that issues *seiri-ken*, or fare zone tickets. If there is, be sure to take one. When you're ready to get off the bus, match the number on your *seiri-ken* ticket with the number on the fare board posted at the front of the bus (usually above the driver's seat) to determine your fare, and deposit the *seiri-ken* along with your fare as you exit the bus. If you don't have a *seiri-ken* ticket to surrender, you may be charged the maximum fare possible for the route. Make sure you have a good supply of 100, 50 and 10 yen coins in these cities (On some long distance buses you might encounter 1,000 yen bill changers, but don't count on them being

there).

Don't hail taxis as a matter of course. Follow our suggestions and you will not only save money but also have many additional experiences available only when you travel as the Japanese do.

Taxis

Taxis are plentiful all over Japan. If you follow the suggestions in this book, you'll probably only need to use them when transferring your big suitcases from train stations to hotels. (In some local destinations, where public transportation is not as convenient, you may have to rely on taxis more often). Empty taxis can be recognized by the red light in front of their windshields. Fares vary slightly from city to city. The average basic fare is 470 yen for the first 1.25 miles (2 km.), and 80 yen for each additional quarter mile (about 0.4 km.). From 11:00 PM to 5:00 AM a 20% surcharge is added. The maximum number of passengers is four. Taxi trunks can only accommodate two large suitcases. The left-hand side rear doors on all taxis are operated by the driver. When a taxi stops for you, wait for the door to open, and once you're inside wait for it to be closed. Keep your hands to yourself or you'll find your fingers closed inside the door! When you arrive at your destination, pay the exact amount shown on the meter (no tipping) and wait again for the door to open. When you get out you should just walk away (Don't worry about the door). Neither the right-hand side front nor rear doors are automatic.

Bicycles

In many destinations, rental bicycles offer the most convenient and inexpensive means of transportation to explore the area. When this is the case, we suggest bicycles and include information on where to rent them.

How to Use the Maps and Timetables in This Book

The seven district maps on the following pages show details of intercity transportation networks throughout Japan, starting at Kyushu Island, and then moving northeast to Hokkaido. Tourist destinations introduced in this book are shown on these maps in red.

To give you a clear idea of city connections, the maps stick to the following principles:

(1) Railways are indicated with solid lines. A variety of lines are used to show different train lines clearly. Black lines indicate JR lines (those on which you can use a Japan Rail Pass), and red lines indicate private lines.

(2) Broken lines indicate buses (on land) and boats (at sea). Again, black lines stand for JR services (on which you can use your Rail Pass), and red lines private companies.

(3) Each train line, bus and boat suggested in this book has been assigned its own number. To reinforce the distinction between JR and private transportation companies, the numbers 1 to 199 are used for JR lines and numbers 200 and above for private lines.

Timetables for each transportation service, numbered in this way, are included at the back of the book, in numerical order, in a special timetable section.

The timetables at the end of this book, like official timetables in Japan, use military time, e.g., 6:00 AM is expressed as 06:00, while 6:00 PM is 18:00; 10:00 AM is 10:00, while 10:00 PM is 22:00.

The maps also indicate a number of train lines that are not specifically referred to in this book. These lines do not have numbers and their timetables are not included. These lines were added to the maps for more adventurous travelers, who may wish to travel to off-off-the-beaten-track destinations, using these local trains.

When planning your itinerary, first find the train line, bus or boat you want to use. Determine its number, and then use the number to find its timetable.

Enjoy planning your itineraries. Once you start, you'll begin to gain an appreciation of the extent and the efficiency of Japan's public transportation system.

There are more detailed explanations on timetables at the beginning of the timetable section below.

Kyushu

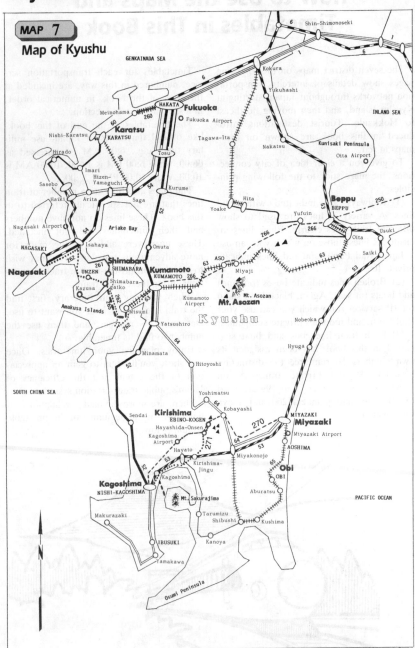

MAP 7

Map of Kyushu

Chugoku and Shikoku

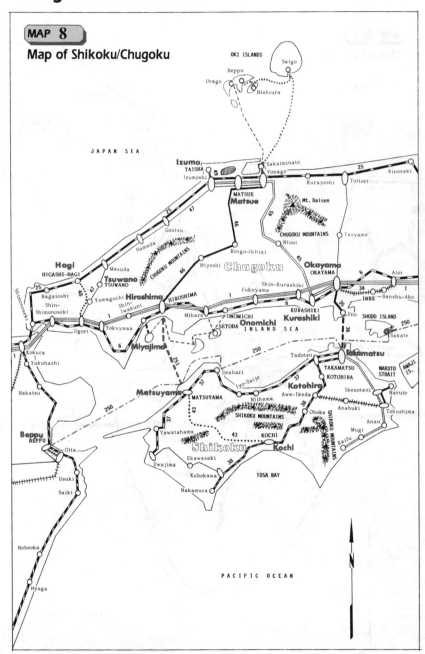

MAP 8

Map of Shikoku/Chugoku

Kansai

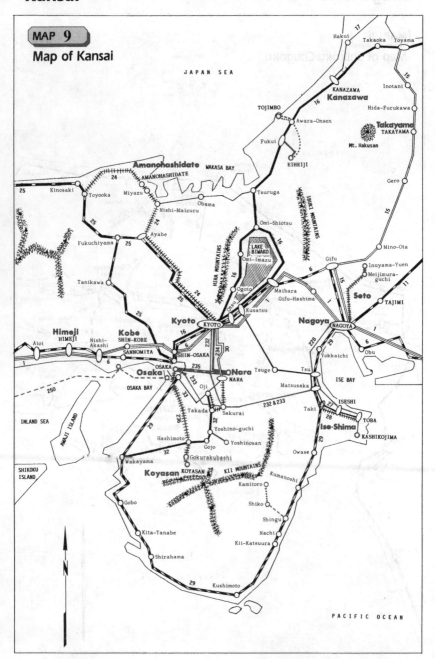

MAP **9**

Map of Kansai

Tokai, Hokuriku and Kanto

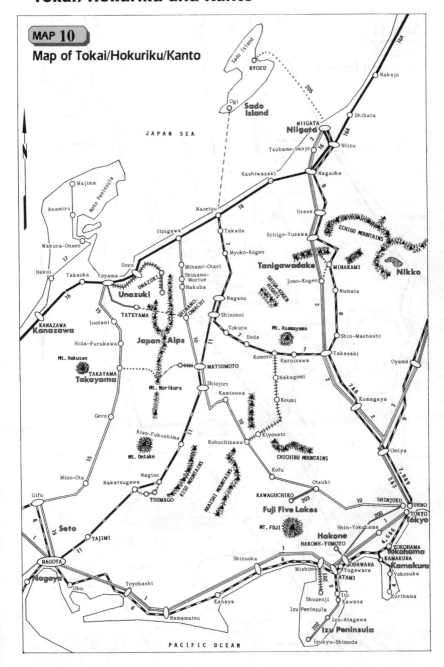

MAP 10

Map of Tokai/Hokuriku/Kanto

Southern Tohoku

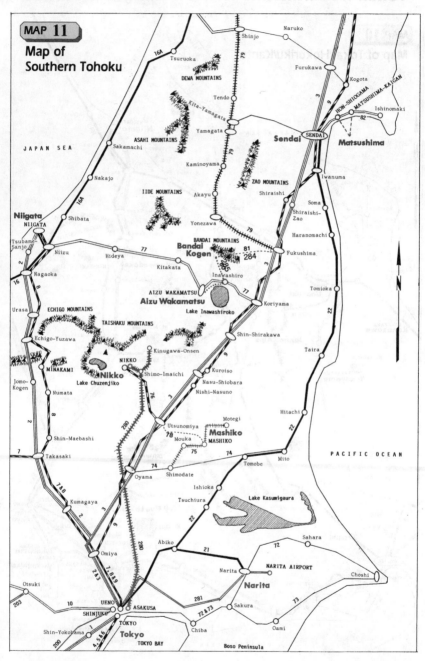

MAP 11

Map of Southern Tohoku

Northern Tohoku

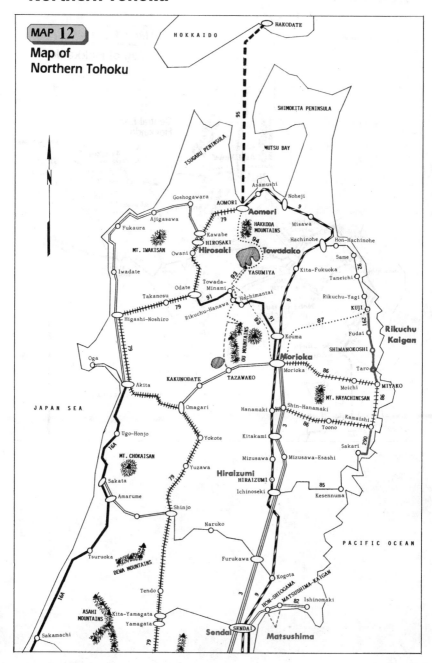

MAP 12

Map of
Northern Tohoku

Hokkaido

Accommodations

Introduction

In 1949 the Japanese Diet passed a special law to encourage construction of high quality accommodations suitable for foreign guests. The law provided low cost government loans for construction of hotels or ryokans (Japanese inns) that met official standards. Since then many facilities have benefited from this law. The number of government-registered hotels has increased from 30 to more than 450, and registered ryokans increased from 2 to over 1,600. Today the Japan Hotel Association and the Japan Ryokan Association represent operators of Japan's top hotels and ryokans. Most member hotels have 300 – 1,000 rooms, and member ryokans generally have 15 – 100 rooms.

But that's not the entire story. Most of these new accommodations, eager for the prestige and the profits connected with an international clientele, tried to extend their best courtesy to foreign guests. Many had good experiences and are still working to develop their international reputations. But others were discouraged by the inevitable problems – language barriers, differences in customs, no-shows, etc. – and gradually grew reluctant to accept foreign guests. Some just decided that it is less trouble and more profitable to cater to Japanese guests. All of the facilities listed in this book, however, accept foreign guests. Each listing includes price information, and the figure quoted includes service charges and tax. (Most listings of hotel and ryokan rates do not include these charges, but all accommodations add them to your bill automatically. Hotels add a 10% service charge and ryokans add 10 – 15% and the Japanese government, like most, is quite conscientious about collecting its additional 10% in tax.) You should therefore be able to get a much more realistic idea of what accommodations will really cost you.

Reservations

There are about 90,000 accommodation facilities of various types throughout Japan, ranging from five-room minshuku (small family-run inns) to giant first class hotels with more than 2,000 rooms. Almost all of them are crowded during the spring (from the middle of March to the end of May), summer (from the middle of July to the end of August), autumn (October and November) tourist seasons, and the New Year's holidays (from December 29 through January 3). Most hotels in the large cities have occupancy rates above 80%. Occupancy rates at accommodations in smaller cities and resorts fluctuate from 60 – 100%. If you are traveling during the busy seasons, you should absolutely make reservations well in advance. Under any circumstances, making reservations in advance will make your life far easier.

It is possible, nevertheless, to travel in Japan without reservations. Hotel and ryokan reservation offices are located in major train stations. Though the clerks probably won't speak English, they should be able to help you find an accommodation for the night. Needless to say, conveniently located, reasonable accommodations sell first. If you try to make reservations at the last minute, especially during the busy seasons, you may end up staying at a rather expensive accommodation or one that is inconveniently located.

For many foreign tourists in Japan the most important task of each day is visiting the reservations office in the train stations to find a place to stay for the night. "Keep your itinerary flexible" sounds like good advice, but doing so is not necessarily enjoyable. Careful advance planning is especially important when you are traveling extensively in a limited time period. Otherwise you'll waste valuable sightseeing and leisure time trying to find places to stay.

Selecting Accommodations

When selecting accommodations, you should pay attention not only to the rates but also to the locations. Even if you can find inexpensive accommodations, you'll end up spending your savings on taxis if they can't be reached easily by public transportation or on foot.

Alternate Western style hotels and Japanese style ryokans in your itinerary. Even if you think that you are not interested in trying a ryokan, you should try one for at least one or two nights. As you will find in the detailed explanation of ryokans that follows, they are small properties where you can expect much more personalized service. You can experience Japanese life style and have closer contact with Japanese people when staying at a ryokan. If you are very interested in ryokans, allocate more nights for them. However, we do recommend that you stay at a Western style hotel once in a while to refresh yourself in familiar surroundings. It is important to remember that ryokan rates usually include two meals (dinner and breakfast the next morning). Eating in ryokans does deprive you of opportunities to eat out and to explore on your own. In the larger cities, where there are a variety of restaurants, Western style accommodations are recommended.

Hotels

Deluxe and First-class Hotels
(18,000 yen and up for a twin room)

Hotels in this category are designed to serve foreign visitors and Japanese VIPs. In polls of the world's best hotels, many of them have ranked near the top. They are usually quite big and have fancy lobbies, large meeting and banquet rooms, and a variety of boutiques and shops. Most of the hotels in this category have more than 500, and some of them have as many as 1,500 to 2,000 rooms. Travel agencies have offices in these hotels to assist guests in making travel arrangements. Pick-up service for guided tours is usually available. These hotels often maintain special "business service salons" to provide foreign business people with information, assistance and secretarial services. A variety of restaurants, bars and lounges are located in the hotels. Most of the hotels in this category have representative agencies and/or their own sales offices in the United States and other countries to accept overseas reservations.

Standard Hotels
(14,000 – 18,000 yen for a twin room)

Hotels in this category are usually smaller (100 – 500 rooms) and do not have luxurious lobbies designed to impress. They don't have "business service salons" for foreign business people, and don't necessarily tailor their services to foreign visitors. However, each of these hotels has English-speaking employees and foreign guests shouldn't have any real communications problems. Standard features of these hotels include several restaurants, a coffee shop and a bar. Most of these hotels use representative agencies to accept reservations overseas.

Business Hotels
(14,000 yen and less for a twin room)

Business hotels were developed to provide Japanese businessmen with convenient, inexpensive accommodations. They usually have 100 – 200 rooms, most of them singles. All the fancy elements of most hotels, such as spacious lobbies, room service, and even bellboys, are non-existent. Rooms are smallish, but each has its own pre-fab bath unit (the tubs aren't big enough for most foreigners, but taking a shower should be no problem). Though some business hotels have several restaurants, most of them have only one or two restaurants that do double or triple duty – as coffee shops in the morning, as bars at night. The staff usually does not speak English, but standard check-in and check-out procedures shouldn't cause any problems. In the past few years, many of these hotels have been organized in a flat-rate "Japan Hotel Pass" system, and overseas reservations have become possible through several wholesale travel companies.

Ryokans

Eighty-three thousand of Japan's 90,000 accommodation facilities can be classified as ryokans. The name "ryokan" covers a wide variety of Japanese-style facilities, from the very expensive to the very economical.

Common features of ryokans are:
- the number of rooms at each property is very small, usually 20 – 40 rooms;
- guest rooms have *tatami* mat floors – you have to remove your shoes;
- instead of beds, *futon* mattresses are spread on the floor (and folded away in closets during the day);
- meals (dinner and breakfast the next day) are included in the rate, and the menu, which is selected by the chef rather than the guest, varies with the season.
- the entrance is locked up at night (usually after 11 PM).

Facilities and services vary greatly depending on price.

Traditional Deluxe Ryokans

(36,000 yen and up for two persons with breakfast and dinner)

These distinguished ryokans represent traditional, refined Japanese values, and their service is geared to individual clients. Staying at a ryokan in this category can be an extremely intimate and memorable way to experience Japanese hospitality. Meals are genuine Japanese cuisine. Private bathrooms and air-conditioning are standard.

Modern Deluxe Ryokans

(30,000 – 40,000 yen for two persons with breakfast and dinner)

These ryokans combine Japanese tradition with western convenience. The buildings are usually modern concrete structures, and public space is similar to a regular hotel. However, the guest rooms are authentic Japanese style, and meals are authentic Japanese cuisine. Private bathrooms and air-conditioning are standard. A number of ryokans in this category are located in famous hotspring resorts and are often the best available in the area.

First-class Ryokans

(24,000 – 34,000 yen for two persons with breakfast and dinner)

These ryokans have similar facilities and services to the above Modern Deluxe Ryokans, but are more modest in facilities and cuisine. These ryokans offer a good chance to experience Japanese life-style at a reasonable price. Private bathrooms and air-conditioning are standard.

Standard Ryokans

(18,000 – 26,000 yen for two persons with breakfast and dinner).

These ryokans are popular among young Japanese and are often used for school excursions and small group tours. They are modest concrete buildings or wooden houses. Meals are simple and similar to those eaten by Japanese in daily life. A private bathroom is rather exceptional and communal bathrooms may be shared with other guests.

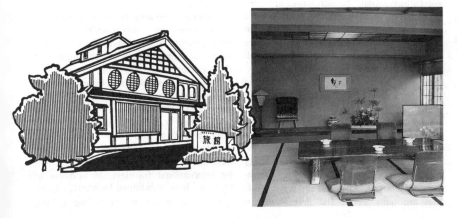

Economy Ryokans and Minshukus
(10,000 – 18,000 yen for two persons with breakfast and dinner).

Ryokans in this category are similar to regular houses. Meals are simpler and common baths are shared by all the guests. They are probably most comparable to bed-and-breakfast type cheap accommodations, and are not the places where you'll experience traditional Japan. **Minshuku** are small family-operated accommodations and can be classified in this category. Minshuku were originally developed to provide extra accommodations in resort areas during busy seasons. Most minshukus are remodeled private homes, and the rooms are usually smaller than those of regular ryokans.

Shukubo

Shukubo are temple lodgings. Their facilities are very similar to those of standard ryokans. But there are two distinct differences:
– the lodgings are attached to temples, and located in the temple precincts; and
– the meals served are vegetarian.

The best place to experience shukubo is Koyasan. There are about 50 accommodations available in Koyasan, and they are all temple lodgings.

* The price benchmarks quoted here are based on Tokyo and Kyoto standards. Prices are often lower in local cities.

Restaurants and Pubs

A number of restaurants and pubs, as well as several discos, are introduced in this guidebook. All of them are clearly pictured on the detailed maps. In the interest of saving space, detailed information on restaurants in smaller cities is omitted. You can always find inexpensive and reasonable restaurants in the downtown areas of such cities and prestigious and expensive restaurants in the good hotels. Sample menus and prices, especially for the inexpensive and reasonable restaurants, are also included below. Most Japanese restaurants offer set-menu specials. These are usually good buys, but substitutions are not allowed. In addition to the main dish, a set-menu meal will typically include an appetizer, pickles, soup, green tea and rice – or soup, rice and one cup of coffee with dinner if the main dish is Western.

In this book restaurants are classified into the following categories: Inexpensive Restaurants; Reasonable Restaurants; Moderate Restaurants; and Expensive Restaurants.

Inexpensive Restaurants. These are restaurants where most items on the dinner menu are less than 1,500 yen. They are inexpensive but not cheap. They serve meals that are quite good, and give value for money spent. They are used by budget **and** quality conscious Japanese. You will agree that Japan is not always expensive if you dine at these restaurants.

Reasonable Restaurants. These are restaurants that serve dinners at somewhere between 1,500 yen and 3,000 yen. You can enjoy a variety of cuisines, including Japanese, Western, Chinese, etc. If you want a good dinner in a pleasant atmosphere, these restaurants are ideal. If they are located near office buildings, they also often serve special lunch menus for the white collar workers at 1,000 – 1,500 yen. These lunches are always good buys.

Moderate Restaurants. These restaurants serve dinners for 3,000 – 6,000 yen. They have pleasant atmospheres, the menus are varied and imaginative and the quality of the food served is quite good.

Expensive Restaurants. This category includes restaurants that serve dinners at more than 5,000 yen (usually around 10,000 yen). Their excellent reputations reflect both their food and their service. These establishments are usually patronized by business people on expense accounts and by international travelers. In addition to those we have mentioned by name, all restaurants in major hotels belong to this category. Most Japanese use these places only on special occasions, such as wedding anniversaries, alumni reunions or very classy dates. They serve specialties, and, if your budget allows, you should sample a few of them while you are in Japan. But, unless you are the kind of person who always stays at the Helmsley Palace in New York, and who always eats your meals in the hotel, don't make a habit of patronizing these restaurants. "Expensive" means "expensive," with an exclamation point, especially in these days of the strong yen!

At several places in the text we've also mentioned coffee shops. Japanese love these establishments because customers are never hurried along. You might come to appreciate them too because they are good places to sit down, relax and rest your feet when you're tired. Coffee is still considered a bit of an exotic luxury in Japan. It's expensive, and you don't get automatic refills. If you order tea you have to ask for milk or it will come with lemon. Many coffee shops are pretty utilitarian affairs, with rather standardized decor, but some have decors worthy of the exotic beverage they serve. You might, for example, find a "Viennese" coffee shop, a rock and roll coffee shop, or a space ship coffee shop. The whimsy adds to the charm. Coffee shops always have tea, coffee, "cake-sets" – tea or coffee plus a piece of fancy cake –, ice creams, sandwiches, and, sometimes, a few other light snacks. Most coffee shops (and many restaurants as well) have display cases out front with plastic models of the dishes they serve. If you have trouble making yourself understood you can always walk the waiter or waitress out front with you and just point to what you want.

Another way to get a quick lunch or snack is to buy a box lunch ("bento"). These are always Japanese style; the contents vary from town to town, and often include local specialties. The divided containers usually have a few portions of fish or meat along with vegetables, rice and Japanese pickles. You can buy *bento* in most large train stations and, in the case of the Shinkansen and other long distance trains, on the train itself. They usually cost 600 – 1,200 yen (slightly higher on the Shinkansen).

There is a remarkable difference in the clientele of Japanese-style and Western-style pubs (and wine houses). The former are usually used by groups of business colleagues, while the latter are often used by couples on dates. Beer halls occupy a middle ground. The atmosphere of Western style pubs is not too different from those you're used to at home. But if you go to a Japanese pub, you'll see lots of differences. First, you will find that the majority of the customers are male (the number of women patrons has increased in recent years). Secondly, you will find that Japanese drink a lot – you'll sometimes be convinced that Japan is a nation of alcoholics. Thirdly, you will find that many of the drinkers are engaged in conversations that seem quite intense. In the Japanese business world (which is also the most important community for the majority of people), it is considered rather uncouth to express one's opinion too clearly or to object to another's proposal openly. So after work Japanese businessmen often go drinking with their office colleagues. Over drinks, they discuss differences of opinion, seek compromises, and sound each other out before presenting proposals formally. Thus, pubs are places where a great deal of business is conducted, and a great many decisions made, before even the preliminary memos begin to make the rounds in the office. Pubs are also important places for younger employees, because it is only in such establishment that they are free to ease their frustrations in the workplace by criticizing their "untalented" bosses. Such behavior, "under the influence," is viewed as a necessary safety valve, and involves no adverse consequences for those whose tongues are loosened by alcohol.

It is rather difficult to clearly separate Japanese pubs from Japanese restaurants. Even in restaurants much more alcohol is consumed than in regular Western restaurants. Those facilities which emphasize drinking have been classified here as pubs, and those which serve substantial meals have been labeled restaurants.

The following are typical popular dinner menus:

Tempura. 天婦羅 Tempura is deep-fried seafood and vegetables. It usually includes shrimp, white fish, squid, eggplant, green pepper and onion. A special dipping sauce is also served. A set menu tempura lunch or dinner usually costs 800 – 1,500 yen. At tempura specialty restaurants, if you eat a la carte, costs can be quite astronomical.

Sukiyaki. すき焼 Sukiyaki is probably the Japanese dish most popular with foreigners. Thinly sliced beef, and vegetables, tofu and Japanese vermicelli are cooked in an iron pan in a special broth. Raw egg is used as a dip. A sukiyaki lunch or dinner costs around 3,000 – 5,000 yen. You may wish to order extra slices of beef (1,000 – 2,000 yen more).

Shabu-shabu. しゃぶしゃぶ Shabu-shabu is a cousin of sukiyaki. A brass pot with a chimney in its center is placed on the table. Thinly sliced beef and ingredients similar to those used for sukiyaki are prepared on a large tray. Guests dip these ingredients into the boiling water in the pot for a few seconds to cook them, and then eat them after dipping them again in a special sauce that is served separately. The price of shabu-shabu is similar to that of sukiyaki.

Sushi. 寿司 Sushi is a Japanese invention. Various types of thinly sliced raw fish are served atop small rice patties. Fish and vegetables are also rolled up with rice in seaweed wrappers. A set menu sushi dinner usually includes about 10 different types of sushi and costs 800 – 1,500 yen. A la carte orders at sushi counters are usually substantially more than the set menu meals. Be ready to pay a minimum of 5,000 yen.

Kaiseki. 懐石 Kaiseki is an authentic Japanese full course dinner. The meal usually consists of about 10 different courses, and features the delicacies of the season. The best way for foreign tourists to try a kaiseki meal in a relaxed atmosphere is to stay at a deluxe or first class ryokan in a traditional city like Kyoto. Inexpensive ryokans seldom serve this type of full course Japanese dinner. If you try a kaiseki dinner at an authentic Japanese restaurant, you should budget a minimum of 8,000 – 10,000 yen. A simplified kaiseki lunch at 3,000 – 5,000 yen is a good compromise.

The following are typical side dishes served at Japanese pubs as accompaniments to the drinks:

Robatayaki. 炉端焼 In any given area, the robatayaki pubs are usually the most popular. A variety of seafood, meats and vegetables are arranged in front of the counter where guests are seated. You can

Yakitori

order whatever you want to have broiled on the hearth. Because you can just point, the language barrier is no problem.

Yakitori. 焼鳥 Yakitori is barbecued chicken shish kebab. This is one of the most popular snacks with alcoholic beverages.

Sashimi. さしみ Sashimi is thinly sliced raw fish. Unlike sushi, where the raw fish is served on top of small rice patties, sashimi is just the slices of fish. Another popular side dish with drinkers.

Nabemono. 鍋物 Nabemono means "things cooked in an earthen bowl." Various ingredients and broth bases are used in the different versions of this popular dish, and its name varies with the ingredients used. *Chankonabe*, for example, was concocted by sumo wrestlers. It uses fish, chicken and vegetables. Another nabemono dish – *Ishikarinabe* – uses salmon and vegetables. Nabemono dishes are a special treat on cold winter nights.

For many Japanese, eating and drinking at pubs is a substitute for dinner. After drinking a lot people will order **onigiri** おにぎり (rice balls that contain small pieces of broiled salmon, cod roe or pickled plums), or **ochazuke** お茶漬 (green tea poured over a bowl of rice and topped with broiled salmon, cod roe or pickled plums).

Sashimi and Nabemono

The following are typical lunch or inexpensive dinner dishes:

Noodles. 麺類 Ramen, soba and udon are all varieties of Japanese noodles. They are usually served in large bowls, with soup broth and a choice of toppings such as scraps of meat or seafood, vegetables, seaweed and Japanese condiments. They range in price from 400 to 800 yen.

Donburi 丼物 **or Rice Bowl Dishes.** These popular dishes are served atop a large bowl of rice. They are cheap, substantial food. *Katsudon*, the most typical, is a deep-fried pork cutlet atop rice; *Oyakodon* is chicken and egg atop rice; *Gyudon* is beef and onion atop rice; and *Unadon* is broiled eel atop rice. The first three range in price from 500 to 800 yen, and unadon is usually 1,200 to 1,800 yen. At rather expensive restaurants, the *-don* suffix becomes *-ju*, and your meal is served in an attractive lacquer box.

Curry Rice. カレーライス This is a unique Japanese concoction. It's cheap, and it fills you up for 500 to 800 yen, but don't expect to be reminded in way of Bombay, unless you go to restaurants specializing in Indian cuisine.

Introduction to Kanto 関東

Except for the approximately 100 years of the Kamakura Era, the Kanto Region was Japan's less developed area, and the Kansai (Kyoto/Nara/Osaka) Region prospered as the nation's political, economic and cultural center. The Kanto became the nation's focal point when Ieyasu Tokugawa established his shogunate in Edo (Tokyo) in 1603. After the Meiji Restoration in 1868, the capital officially moved to Tokyo, and since then the area has developed into one of the world's biggest and most advanced urban areas.

Tokyo is Japan's New York, Washington, Chicago, Los Angeles and San Francisco all rolled into one. It is the seat of Government, the nation's business capital, and the center for international finance, education, communications, transportation, and fashion. It is a giant magnet for the Japanese people, and one of every four of them now live in the Kanto Region, which, as the city spreads ever further, is rapidly becoming synonymous with Tokyo Metropolitan Area. Its fast pace, its population density, its drastic space limitations and its spiraling real estate prices make New York seem relatively slow, empty, spacious and reasonably priced. Be prepared for an encounter with fast-moving 21st century urban life.

Narita Airport, the gateway to Japan, is northeast of Tokyo. In addition to Tokyo itself, the region includes such major destinations as Nikko, Mashiko, Kamakura, Hakone, Fuji Five Lakes and the Izu Peninsula. There is convenient train service from Tokyo to all of these destinations.

Nikko

Nikko, a National Park, is also famous as a site of the magnificent Toshogu Shrine.

If you have a Japan Rail Pass, you should use the Tohoku Shinkansen (No. 3 between Ueno and Utsunomiya) and the JR Nikko Line (No. 76 between Utsunomiya and Nikko). If you don't have a Rail Pass, use the private Tobu Railways (No. 280), which provides less expensive direct train service between Asakusa and Nikko.

Mashiko

Mashiko is the Kanto district's busiest and most famous pottery center.

You can take the Tohoku Shinkansen (No. 3) to Oyama, and then the JR local trains (No. 74 between Oyama and Shimodate, and No. 75 between Shimodate and Mashiko). There are several through trains daily from Oyama to Mashiko. If you combine your visit to Mashiko with one to Nikko, remember that there is bus service from Mashiko to Utsunomiya (about once an hour; not listed in this book). You can visit Mashiko first, and then proceed to Nikko for an overnight stay.

Kamakura

During the 12th – 13th centuries, Kamakura was the center of the nation, when the first shogunate established, for the first time, a capital removed from the emperor's city of Kyoto. Modern Kamakura jealously guards the many historical legacies of its medieval prosperity.

The JR Yokosuka Line (No. 4) operates frequent commuter trains between Tokyo and Kurihama via Kamakura.

Hakone

Hakone is a National Park famous for its magnificent view of Mt. Fuji. Hakone is also a renowned hotspring resort.

As with Nikko, you can take either JR or a private railway. The Shinkansen (No. 1) runs from Tokyo to Odawara, the gateway station to Hakone. A private Odakyu Railways train (No. 200) runs between

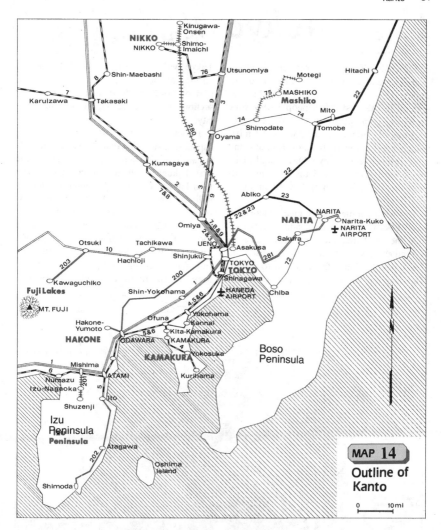

MAP **14**

**Outline of
Kanto**

0   10mi

Shinjuku and Hakone-Yumoto via Odawara. If you don't have a Japan Rail Pass,
the Odakyu is much cheaper.

Fuji Five Lakes

The center of Fuji Five Lakes is Kawaguchiko. You can take the JR Chuo Line
(No. 10) from Shinjuku to Otsuki, and
then the private Fujikyu Railways (No.
203) to Kawaguchiko, the terminal station.
You can use your Rail Pass for the portion
of the trip between Shinjuku and Otsuki

only.

Izu Peninsula

There are several famous hotspring resorts in Izu Peninsula, such as Ito, Shimoda
and Shuzenji. You'll have to use both JR
trains and private railways to visit these resorts: JR trains to the gateway cities of Ito
and Mishima, and then the private railways. Several daily trains operate over both
lines directly between Tokyo and Shimoda
(No. 202) or Shuzenji (No. 201).

Tokyo 東京

Officially, Tokyo consists of 23 urban wards spread over an area of 230 square miles (590 square km.) and suburbs that extend to the west. Most people who work in Tokyo commute from the adjacent prefectures of Saitama, Kanagawa and Chiba, which are located to the north, south and east respectively. Tokyo Disneyland, Disney's third property and the first one outside the U.S., is actually located in Chiba Prefecture.

But what people usually mean when they say "Tokyo" is the area inside or just outside the JR Yamanote Loop Line, an area 4.5 miles (7 km.) from east to west, and 7.6 miles (12 km.) from north to south. The map on the next page that compares Tokyo with New York is good for getting an idea of the size of the city. The central part of Tokyo is divided into several subsections that are really cities within the city.

Tokyo is much newer than most Japanese cities. Its real development only began in 1603 when Ieyasu Tokugawa, the first Tokugawa Shogun, selected the town then known as Edo as headquarters for his military government. During the 265-year reign of the Tokugawas, Edo functioned as the nation's administrative center even though Kyoto, the home of the emperors, remained the nominal capital. After the Imperial forces regained power in 1868 (the Meiji Restoration), Edo officially became

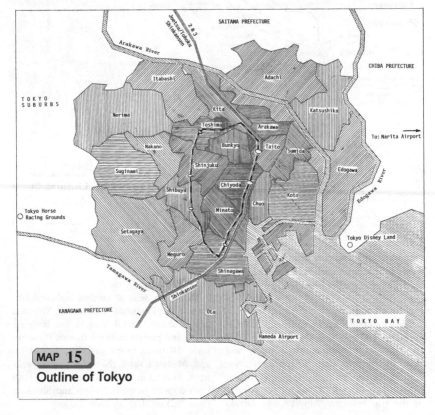

MAP 15

Outline of Tokyo

the capital and was renamed Tokyo (eastern Kyoto or eastern capital). Emperor Meiji moved to Tokyo and established his court in what had been the Shogun's Edojo Castle. Unlike the Tokugawa Shogunate, which had kept the nation isolated from the rest of the world, the new government aggressively imported advanced Western technology and scientific knowledge and worked to develop modern industries. Tokyo was devastated in World War II, but was rebuilt quickly (and, some say, haphazardly). Today it is an ultra-modern city rushing toward the 21st century. The Tokyo area has a population of 11,588,000. It is the nation's political, economic, commercial, educational, communications and entertainment capital.

Tokyo District by District

We have divided Tokyo into seven districts (listed here in the order in which they are introduced in the text):

1. Eastern Tokyo

This area includes: Ginza, Tokyo's Fifth Avenue, with its huge department stores and elegant shops; Tsukiji, which is famous for its Central Fish Market; Harumi, a man-made island and the site of the Tokyo International Trade Show Grounds; Marunouchi and Otemachi, the areas near Tokyo Station, the nation's business center and home of the headquarters of many major Japanese corporations; and the Imperial Palace to the west of Marunouchi. The Palace moats and Nijubashi Bridge with a turret of the old Edojo Castle in the background is one of the most picturesque and typical of Japanese scenes, recorded by thousands on film every year. The Palace's East Garden is a spacious park, incredibly quiet for Tokyo. A few of the old rock walls of Edojo Castle, including the base of the donjon, are still standing. The northern part of the Imperial Palace is now Kitanomaru-Koen Park and home to the National Museum of Modern Art and other public institutions.

2. Central Tokyo

Kasumigaseki is the political and administrative center of Japan. The Diet Building and most government offices are located in this area. Toranomon is home to modern office buildings. ARK Hill (Akasaka **R**oppongi **K**not) is a new urban development to the south of Toranomon. The area's skyscrapers are home to a number of offices of foreign corporations, and also feature very expensive apartments specially designed for foreign executives. ARK Hill is expected to grow into Tokyo's investment center and an "International Village." Akasaka is a world famous night spot with an astonishing concentration of high-class restaurants and other entertainment facilities.

3. Western Tokyo

Shinjuku is the new downtown of Tokyo. Western Shinjuku is home of most of the city's new skyscrapers. Eastern Shinjuku has two faces – one as a fashionable shopping center with department stores, specialty shops and restaurants; and the other a bustling young people's playground where

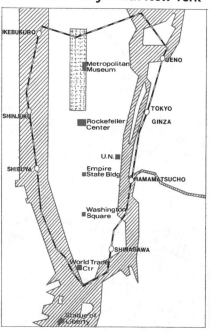

MAP 16   Comparative Map of Tokyo with New York

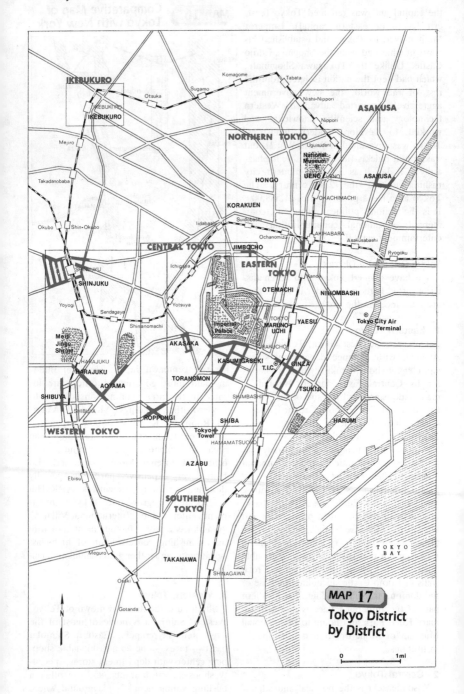

MAP **17**
Tokyo District by District

0   1mi

MAP 18   Tokyo's Transportation Network

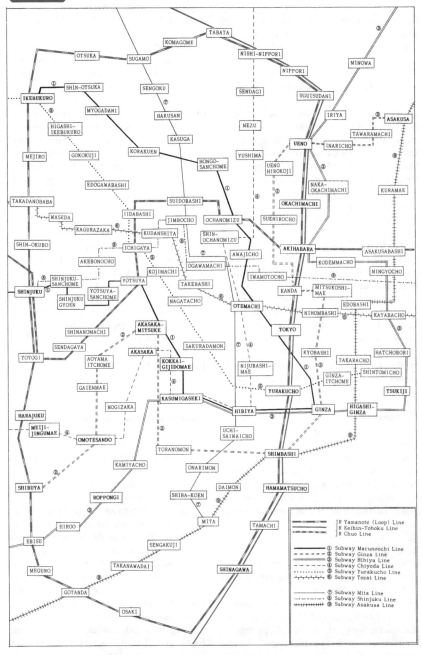

night never visits and where pornographic enterprises flourish. Shibuya, once known for its inexpensive shops, restaurants and pubs for white-collar workers, has developed into a fashion center. Harajuku is now the fashion center for teenagers. On Sundays, when the streets are closed to traffic, Tokyo's "takenoko" (bamboo shoots) gather here in their outlandish outfits to dance in the street to the music of big radios and cassette players. Aoyama is an adult fashion center that boasts of famous name shops and boutiques such as Hanae Mori, Issey Miyake, Paul Stuart and Brooks Brothers. Omotesando Boulevard, which connects Aoyama with Harajuku, is a lovely tree lined promenade, and an ideal place for a leisurely stroll.

4. Northern Tokyo

Ueno is the cultural center of Tokyo. The National Museum, Metropolitan Festival Hall, the Zoological Garden and other cultural facilities are located in spacious Ueno-Koen Park. Hongo is home to Tokyo University, one of the most prestigious in Japan. Akihabara is the world famous discount paradise for electric and electronic products. Jimbocho is famous for its innumerable bookstores. Korakuen boasts a sports and entertainment complex.

5. Asakusa

Asakusa, famous for its Kannon Temple, is one of the few areas that preserves the nostalgic atmosphere of Tokyo's old "shitamachi" downtown. Wholesalers of restaurant utensils are concentrated on nearby Kappabashi Street and doll wholesalers in Asakusabashi. You can find unusual souvenir items here.

6. Southern Tokyo

Southern Tokyo is still, for the most part, a residential area. Several international hotels are located in Takanawa and Shinagawa. Azabu is home to many embassies. Tokyo Tower and Zojoji Temple are the attractions of Shiba. Roppongi is another typical Tokyo night spot. Unlike Akasaka, which is patronized by members of the political establishment and business people on expense accounts, Roppongi is popular with the relatively young and with many of the foreign residents of Tokyo.

7. Ikebukuro

This is one of Tokyo's largest shopping and night life areas. But, because its habitues are typically commuters from Saitama Prefecture (who are roughly the equivalent of the "bridge and tunnel" crowd in New York City), Ikebukuro has been considered a bit of a second-class downtown. Sunshine City features Tokyo's tallest building and the city's best observatory. Tokyo Antique Hall, which moved here from Jimbocho in 1987, offers unique souvenirs at bargain prices.

Tokyo's Transportation Network

To transport millions of commuters from suburban areas to the city, Tokyo has developed extensive railway and subway networks. For tourists, however, many of them have little value. To avoid confusion and to give you a clear idea of which of Tokyo's public transportation facilities will be useful to you, only three essential JR lines and nine essential subway lines are pictured on the map.

JR (Japan Railways)

All the stations you need to know in order to get around Tokyo easily are clearly pictured on the seven district maps and eight sub-district maps that appear on the following pages. Because the JR stations are so important to the everyday life of Tokyo, you shouldn't have trouble recognizing the stations.

The JR Yamanote Loop Line (Green Line): This line surrounds the central part of Tokyo. It takes about one hour to make the trip around the loop. All major stations, such as Tokyo, Ueno, Shinjuku, Shibuya and Ikebukuro, are on this loop line.

In most JR stations the name of the line, e.g., "Yamanote Line" or "Keihin-Tohoku Line," and the direction of the train, e.g., "for Shibuya and Shinjuku" or "for Shimbashi and Tokyo," are written in both Japanese and English on many signboards. At smaller stations you shouldn't have any

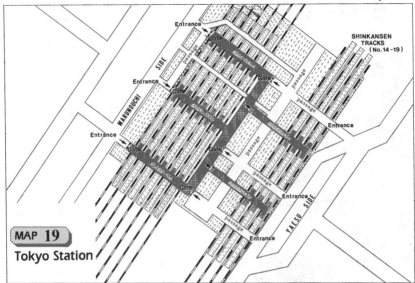

MAP 19
Tokyo Station

problem finding the track number of the train you want.

Subways

All the stations essential for tourist travel in Tokyo are clearly pictured on the following maps. Entrances are clearly marked "subway" in both Japanese and English. At large stations, such as Shinjuku, Ginza and Otemachi, long underground passages connect the platforms of the various lines. There are also signs in English on every subway platform. Tokyo subway maps and fare boards show each line with a different color, and the trains themselves are painted to coordinate with this color scheme. If you ever have difficulty finding the subway you want, you should go back to the surface and walk to the approximate location of the station as pictured on the map. You will find the entrance to the line you want around the area.

To help you get familiar with the subway system, the same symbols used on the Tokyo Transportation Map are also used on the district maps. For example:

The Marunouchi Line is always represented by a bold solid line; the Ginza Line is always represented by double dotted lines; the Hibiya Line is always represented

by double solid lines; etc.

Refer back to the Tokyo Transportation Map when you want to check subway or train connections as you move from one district to another.

Eastern Tokyo

Establishment Tokyo

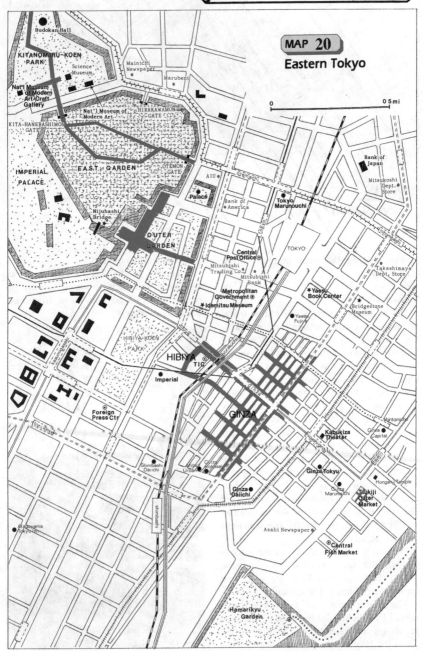

MAP 20
Eastern Tokyo

0 _____ 0.5 mi

Budokan Hall

KITANOMARU-KOEN PARK

Science Museum

Mainichi Newspaper

Marubeni

Nat'l Museum of Modern Art Craft Gallery

Nat'l Museum of Modern Art

HIRAKAWAMON GATE

KITA-HANEBASHIMON GATE

E.A.S.T. GARDEN

OTEMON GATE

IMPERIAL PALACE

Palace

Nijubashi Bridge

OUTER GARDEN

AIU

Otemachi

Bank of America

Tokyo Marunouchi

Bank of Japan

Mitsukoshi Dept. Store

TOKYO

Takashimaya Dept. Store

Central Post Office

Mitsubishi Trading Co.

Mitsubishi Bank

Metropolitan Government

Idemitsu Meseum

Yaesu Book Center

Bridgestone Museum

Yaesu Fujiya

HIBIYA-KOEN PARK

HIBIYA

TIC

Imperial

Foreign Press Ctr

GINZA

Shimbashi Daiichi

Mitsui Urban

Ginza Kokusai

Ginza Daiichi

Ginza Marunouchi

Kabukiza Theater

Ginza Capital

Shintomicho

Ginza Tokyu

Honganji Temple

Tsukiji Outer Market

Atagoyama Tokyo Inn

shimbashi

Asahi Newspaper

Central Fish Market

Hamarikyu Garden

Home of the Ginza and the Imperial Palace, Eastern Tokyo is the city's most popular district for foreign visitors. Tokyo Station, where the Shinkansen originates for Kyoto and Osaka, is also located here. The Ginza is explained in detail at the end of this section.

Imperial Palace　皇居

The Imperial Palace grounds are divided into four parts: (1) the actual palace, (2) Outer Garden, (3) East Garden, and (4) Kitanomaru-Koen Park. The actual palace is the Emperor's residence and is closed to the public.

Imperial Palace Outer Garden　皇居外苑

The Outer Garden is a spacious park with numerous pine trees and pebble-covered pedestrian paths. The area is popular with tourists, both Japanese and foreign, during the daytime, and with amorous couples in the evening. If you are a camera fan, the shot of Nijubashi Bridge with the Palace's turret and moats behind it is not to be missed.

Imperial Palace East Garden　皇居東御苑

What is now the Imperial Palace East Garden used to be the main grounds of Edojo Castle. Otemon Gate was the main entrance to the castle grounds, and even today most visitors use this gate to visit the East Garden after their stroll through the Outer Garden. Though most of the castle buildings were lost to repeated fires, the garden grounds still contain the Hundred-Guard Office, huge old stone walls, and neatly maintained ponds, flowerbeds and pine trees. The stone base of the donjon is at the northeastern end of the grounds. The grounds are open to the public from 9:00 AM to 4:00 PM, but visitors are not admitted after 3:00 PM. Closed on Mondays and Fridays, but the Garden is open if those days happen to be a holiday. At the entrance visitors receive numbered cards that have to be turned in when exiting. There are three gates – Otemon, Kita-Hanebashimon and Hirakawamon. Visitors can enter and exit at any of the three. Admission free.

Kitanomaru-Koen Park　北の丸公園

The Park is now home to several museums and public facilities. **The National Museum of Modern Art – Craft Gallery** 国立近代美術館工芸館　is housed in a brown brick building. It displays the highest quality crafts of contemporary masters, including textiles, ceramics, glass ware, lacquer ware, wooden ware, bamboo ware, metal works, etc. (10:00 AM to 5:00 PM. Closed on Mondays. Admission 300 yen). **The National Museum of Modern Art** 国立近代美術館 holds special exhibitions of the works of modern and contemporary painters and sculptors. **The Science Museum** 科学技術館　is always crowded with school children. The exhibits are not particularly interesting for adults, but this is a good place to get an idea of how the scientific education of Japanese children is organized and conducted (9:30 AM to 4:50 PM. Closed only during New Year's Holidays). The National Archives and Budokan Hall (Japan's largest public hall – used for concerts, conventions, etc.) are also located in the Park.

After your visit to Kitanomaru-Koen Park you can continue your walking tour to Yasukuni Jinja Shrine (see Central Tokyo) or Jimbocho (see Northern Tokyo).

Marunouchi　丸の内

Marunouchi is the area sandwiched between the Imperial Palace moats and the JR lines. Before it was developed, the area was known as Mitsubishi Meadow, and it is now home to many corporate headquarters, especially those of the Mitsubishi conglomerate. Many American financial corporations also have Japanese subsidiaries here. For tourists, Marunouchi is really nothing more than rows of modern concrete and glass office buildings. However, it is here that you can see what the members of Japan's business elite look like.

Yaesu   八重洲

Yaesu is the area to the east of Tokyo Station. As with Marunouchi, modern office buildings line both sides of wide streets. **Kokusai Kanko Kaikan Building** 国際観光会館 , right next to Tokyo Station, houses information offices of local prefectural governments. Free travel brochures (mostly written in Japanese only) are available here. Local specialty products and souvenir items are also sold at these offices. **Yaesu Underground Shopping Center** 八重洲地下街 is connected with Tokyo Station and stretches to the east. Rather characterless stores and reasonable restaurants are located in this huge, confusing underground town. **Bridgestone Museum** ブリヂストン美術館 is owned by Japan's largest tire company (9:00 AM to 5:00 PM. Closed on Mondays. Admission 300 yen). **Yaesu Book Center** 八重洲ブックセンター , one of the largest bookstores in Japan, contains as many as one million books. If you tire of looking at the books, you can take a coffee break on the mezzanine.

Tsukiji   築地

(Lower right, map 20)

Tsukiji Central Fish Market 築地中央卸売市場：This wholesale market handles all the fish and meat consumed in the Tokyo area. Because of the overwhelming volume of trade in fish and fish products, it is popularly called the Central Fish Market. The business between the fishermen and the wholesalers is conducted early in the morning, between 5:20 AM and 6:00 AM. From 6:00 AM to 9:00 AM the market is crowded with purchasers from retail stores and restaurants. The many small restaurants in the market serve sushi, tempura, noodles, etc. The restaurants are busy, noisy, no-frills affairs, but the food is excellent and they are very inexpensive. The Market is closed on Sundays and holidays, on August 15 and 16, and for the New Year's Holidays. If you want to see the early morning trading, take a taxi from your hotel. If you visit the market a little later, you can take the No. 1 bus from the western side of Shimbashi Station.

Tsukiji Outer Market 築地場外市場：Small shops that sell fish, other foodstuffs and various consumer products crowd the lanes near the Central Fish Market. The Outer Market is for members of the general public who want small quantities of the freshest food and other inexpensive items. This is one of the two best places to learn about what goes home in shopping baskets to the kitchen of typical Tokyoites, with Ameya-Yokocho near Ueno being the other one (see Northern Tokyo).

Honganji Temple 築地本願寺 , near the Outer Market, is an Indian-style temple, the only one of its kind in Japan. This massive stone structure, built in 1935 after the 1680 original was destroyed by the Kanto Earthquake, is the main hall of Tsukiji Honganji Temple. ¯ is temple has church-like pews, which are quite a novelty in Japan. There are Japanese-style rooms at both sides of the altar. The temple combines traditional atmosphere and modern practicality, and provides busy Tokyoites with a place of worship.

One Restaurant in Tsukiji – Edogin: If you want to enjoy excellent sushi at a reasonable price, this is the place. The restaurant is busy and not fancy at all. At lunch time Deluxe Sushi is your best bet (2,000 yen). Even the bargain 1,200 yen lunch gives you a good sampling of marvelously fresh sushi. In the evening, 5,000 yen is usually enough to cover a good a la carte sampling. The restaurant does not have an English sign, but the paper lanterns at its entrance are a good landmark.

Hamarikyu Garden

浜離宮庭園

(Lower center, map 20)

This garden was built about 330 years ago at the order of Tsunashige Matsudaira, a feudal lord. Later, it was ceded to the sixth Tokugawa Shogun, Ienobu, who used it for duck hunting. After the Meiji Restoration the garden became the property of the Imperial Household Agency and was used for outdoor parties for the nobles and for receptions for foreign guests of honor. General Ulysses S. Grant, the 18th President of the United States, was entertained here when he visited Japan. Later, the garden was given to the Tokyo Metropolitan Government and opened to the public (9:00 AM to 4:30 PM. Closed on Mondays. Admission 200 yen). Shimbashi is the station closest to Hamarikyu Garden (0.5 miles or 0.8 km.).

Boats to Asakusa operate from the pier in Hamarikyu Garden about once every hour (480 yen for a 40 minute ride). The Sumidagawa River provided the main means of transportation in the Edo Era (17th – 19th centuries), and the areas along the river were, at that time, the most prosperous in the city. The center of Tokyo moved west only with the development of the railroad and other surface transportation. The view from the boat is not particularly noteworthy, but the ride is an interesting way to see the face this huge city never shows to the casual tourist.

Ginza   銀座

Ginza literally means silver mint. The area was so named when the Tokugawa Shogunate built its mint here in 1612. The Ginza is now Tokyo's established shopping district. Instead of minting silver coins, the area now collects millions and millions of yen every day from the customers who patronize its many stores, restaurants and bars.

Outline of the District

The Ginza is a rectangular area sandwiched between Sotobori-dori Street on the northwest and Showa-dori on the southeast. The area is divided into eight long rectangular zones by narrower streets that run perpendicular to these boundaries; these narrow blocks are numbered 1-chome through 8-chome. The center of the Ginza is the large intersection made by Chuo-dori Street and Harumi-dori Street. The famous round building (San-ai) and clock tower are located at this intersection. Many department stores and specialty shops line Chuo-dori Street; it is always crowded with window shoppers. The area is closed to traffic on Saturdays (3:00 PM to 6:00 PM) and on Sundays (12:00 noon to 6:00 PM). To the northwest of the Ginza is **Yurakucho** 有楽町 (around the JR Yurakucho Station), with many modern office buildings. **Hibiya** 日比谷 is a theater and restaurant district. Many foreign airlines have offices in this area. **Hibiya-Koen Park** is an oasis for the *Ginzakko* (Ginza natives and Ginza patrons). Spacious gardens are arranged around a large pond, and the Park contains an open-air concert hall, a public hall and a library. A French restaurant named **Matsumotoro** is Tokyo's version of "Tavern on the Green" in New York's Central Park. The suggested walking tour course is marked in red on the Ginza Map.

Tourist Information Center (T.I.C.)

The Japanese government's free Tourist Information Center is located on Harumi-dori Street near the elevated JR tracks. This is one of the three T.I.C.'s operated by the Japan National Tourist Organization (the other two are located at Narita Airport and in Kyoto). JNTO's toll-free travelphone is answered at the Tokyo and Kyoto T.I.C.'s.

Kabukiza Theater 歌舞伎座 (Lower right, map 21)

The Kabuki drama has a four hundred year history. Of the many traditional Japanese theater arts (Kabuki, Noh, Kyogen, Bunraku and Gagaku), Kabuki is probably the most accessible for foreigners. It is famous for its colorful stage settings and stylized acting style. There are no actresses in Kabuki plays, but it is often said that the female impersonators who take these roles are more feminine than the real thing. Matinees start at 11:00 AM, and evening performances at 4:30 PM. Admission tickets range in price from 1,500 yen to 10,000 yen. An English "Earphoneguide" can be rented for 600 yen. A recorded tape provides information on the story, actors' props, etc., as the drama progresses. Reservations can be made through your hotel, or you can call the Kabukiza Theater at 541-8597.

Museums in the Area

Idemitsu Museum 出光美術館 (upper left, map 21) is located on the ninth floor of its building. The museum specializes in Japanese and Oriental (mostly Chinese) antiquities, and is especially renowned for its collection of pottery and ceramics (10:00 AM to 5:00 PM. Admission 500 yen). **Riccar Museum** リッカー美術館 (middle left, map 21) is famous for its collection of *ukiyoe*, Japanese wood-block prints (10:00 AM to 5:00 PM. Admission 500 yen).

Shopping

Department stores are open from 10:00 AM to 6:00 PM. They are closed once a week on weekdays. Because the closing days vary from store to store, you can find at least a few stores open on any given day of the week. There are three major stores along Chuo-dori Street – from north to south, **Matsuya**, **Mitsukoshi** and **Matsuzakaya**. On Harumi-dori Street are the two **Hankyus**, **Seibu** and **Nishi-Ginza** Department Stores. To the north of the JR Yurakucho Station is **Sogo** Department Store. **American Pharmacy** (upper left, map 21) sells American drugs; **Mikimoto** (upper center) is world famous for its cultured pearls; **Ginza Hakuhinkan** (lower center) specializes in toys; and **International Arcade** (middle left) is located under the elevated JR tracks and houses 24 specialty shops that handle everything from traditional handicrafts to the most advanced electronic products (very touristy but convenient for busy travelers).

Restaurants
Inexpensive Restaurants

A number of small restaurants are located on the second floor of Yuraku Food Center near JR Yurakucho Station (narrow buildings constructed under the elevated expressway). You can find a variety of cuisines here, from Japanese and Chinese, to Italian and Continental, at very reasonable prices (600 – 2,000 yen for lunch and dinner).

Japanese Restaurants

Tenkuni is a tempura restaurant. The original is at Ginza 8-chome (lower center, map 21), and a branch is in the Kintetsu Building (middle center). Both reasonably priced. **Ten-ichi** (middle center) is a more famous and accordingly more expensive tempura restaurant. **Unkai** (lower left) is a shabu-shabu restaurant (moderate) and **Rangetsu** (middle center) is famous for sukiyaki (moderate). **Tsukiji-Uemura** (5th floor of Hakuhinkan Building, lower center) serves a variety of Japanese food (moderate).

Western & Steak Restaurants

Italian (middle center) and **Capri** (upper

French restaurant owned by a famous chansonnier (moderate). **Lion** (lower center) is a Sapporo beer hall restaurant that serves a wide variety of foods. **Mikasa Kaikan** (middle center) contains several famous restaurants. **Haruna** is an excellent French restaurant and **Yamato** is a steak and seafood restaurant (both expensive).

Other Restaurants

Totenko in Twin Tower Building (upper left) is a moderate Chinese restaurant. **Maharao** in Mitsui Building (upper left) and **Nair's** (middle right) are inexpensive yet excellent Indian restaurants. **Ashoka** (lower center) is another Indian restaurant with higher prices.

right) serve spaghetti, pizza and other Italian foods at reasonable prices. **Jardin** (middle center) serves French home-style cuisine (moderate). **Suehiro** (middle center) and **Volks** (lower center) are famous for their reasonable steaks. **Maison de France** in Twin Tower Building (upper left) is a

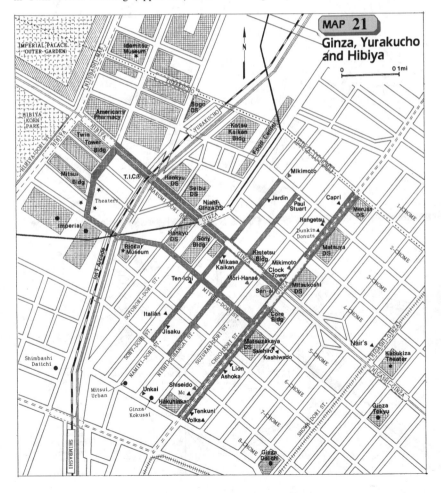

Central Tokyo

Governmental Tokyo

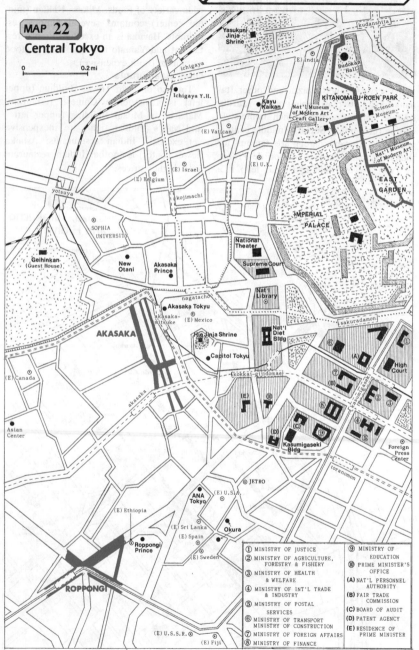

MAP 22
Central Tokyo

0   0.2 mi

Yasukuni Jinja Shrine

kudanshita

(E) India

Budokan Hall

ichigaya

Ichigaya Y.H.

Kayu Kaikan

KITANOMARU KOEN PARK

Nat'l Museum of Modern Art Craft Gallery

Science Museum

(E) Vatican

Nat'l Museum of Modern Art

(E) Israel

(E) U.K.

(E) Belgium

EAST GARDEN

yotsuya

kojimachi

SOPHIA UNIVERSITY

IMPERIAL PALACE

Geihinkan (Guest House)

National Theater

New Otani

Akasaka Prince

Supreme Court

nagatacho

Nat'l Library

Akasaka Tokyu

akasaka-mitsuke

(E) Mexico

sakuradamon

AKASAKA

Hie Jinja Shrine

Nat'l Diet Bldg

⑥

(A)

①

High Court

Capitol Tokyu

(kokkai-gijidomae)

⑦

(B)

(E) Canada

akasaka

(E)

⑩

⑧

②

③

Asian Center

(D)

(C)

⑨

④

Kasumigaseki Bldg

Foreign Press Center

toranomon

JETRO

ANA Tokyo

(E) U.S.A.

(E) Ethiopia

(E) Sri Lanka

(E) Spain

Okura

Roppongi Prince

(E) Sweden

ROPPONGI

(E) U.S.S.R.

(E) Fiji

① MINISTRY OF JUSTICE
② MINISTRY OF AGRICULTURE, FORESTRY & FISHERY
③ MINISTRY OF HEALTH & WELFARE
④ MINISTRY OF INT'L TRADE & INDUSTRY
⑤ MINISTRY OF POSTAL SERVICES
⑥ MINISTRY OF TRANSPORT MINISTRY OF CONSTRUCTION
⑦ MINISTRY OF FOREIGN AFFAIRS
⑧ MINISTRY OF FINANCE

⑨ MINISTRY OF EDUCATION
⑩ PRIME MINISTER'S OFFICE
(A) NAT'L PERSONNEL AUTHORITY
(B) FAIR TRADE COMMISSION
(C) BOARD OF AUDIT
(D) PATENT AGENCY
(E) RESIDENCE OF PRIME MINISTER

Most governmental institutions are concentrated in Kasumigaseki and Nagatacho, including the National Diet, most Ministries and the Supreme Court. The area can be reached easily by many subways.

The wide street in front of Ministry of Foreign Affairs is lined with a number of cherry trees. Japan's National Flower blooms in early April to announce the beginning of a new fiscal year to the area's elite bureaucrats.

Akasaka, Tokyo's most prestigious night spot, is explained in detail at the end of this section.

Government of Japan

Japan's modern government, established after World War II, is based on the new Constitution, which was promulgated on November 3, 1946 and came into effect six months later. Under the new Constitution, the Emperor, who had held sovereign power, became a symbol of the State, and sovereign power is declared to rest with the people. Three independent governmental branches, the legislative, the executive and the judiciary, operate on checks-and-balances principles.

Legislature

The Diet consists of two Houses, the House of Representatives (513 seats) and the House of Councillors (252 seats). The House of Representatives has much more real power than the House of Councillors. More than seven parties have seats in the Diet. The Liberal Democratic Party ("LDP") has held the majority in both Houses since 1955. The Socialists, Komeito (Clean Government), Communists and Democratic Socialists are the other major political parties. An apportionment controversy has raged for many years in Japan. In some rural districts, it takes as few as 50,000 votes to elect a Representative, while in the big city districts, a candidate typically needs 150,000 votes to win a seat in the Diet. This gerrymandering in favor of the rural areas (which happen to be LDP strongholds) is often cited as the reason for Japan's persistent protectionism of agricultural products.

Executive

Executive power rests with the Cabinet. The Prime Minister is elected by the Diet. Typically, the chairman of the majority party is elected Prime Minister. The other ministers who form the Cabinet are selected by the Prime Minister, usually from the Diet members. The following are the major ministries: Ministry of Justice; Ministry of Foreign Affairs; Ministry of Finance; Ministry of International Trade & Industry (the famous, or, in the eyes of some, the notorious MITI); Ministry of Education; Ministry of Health & Welfare; Ministry of Agriculture, Forestry & Fisheries; Ministry of Transport; Ministry of Postal Services; Ministry of Labor; Ministry of Construction; Ministry of Home Affairs; and Prime Minister's Office. Under the supervision of the Prime Minister's Office are: Defense Agency; Science & Technology Agency; National Police Agency; Environment Agency; Imperial Household Agency, etc.

Judiciary

The court system consists of the Supreme Court, regional high courts, district courts and a number of summary courts.

Take A Break

If you are in the Kasumigaseki area during lunch time, a variety of restaurants are available in the basement of Kasumigaseki Building 霞が関ビル, the first skyscraper in Japan (147 m. or 450 feet) (lower right of map 22). There is an observatory on the 36th floor of the building.

National Theater 国立劇場

National Theater (middle center, map 22) stages traditional Japanese theatricals, such as Kabuki, Bunraku and Noh, from time to time. An English "Earphone-Guide" is available at the theater.

Yasukuni Jinja Shrine 靖国神社

Yasukuni Jinja Shrine (upper center, map 22) enshrines the spirits of 2.5 million soldiers who died in the wars since the Meiji Restoration. The shrine has been controversial for a long time. Left-wing political groups have accused the conservative parties of disregarding the tragedy these wars brought to the nation and of trying to revitalize Japanese militarism by putting too much emphasis on this shrine and the chauvinism they say it encourages. In spite of all this, the shrine grounds are famous as one of the best places in Tokyo to enjoy cherry blossoms in early April.

Akasaka   赤坂

Akasaka is Tokyo's most sophisticated night spot. Because the area is patronized primarily by politicians and bureaucrats busy plotting strategy, by businessmen on company expense accounts, by high society people, and by foreign VIP's visiting Tokyo, prices are generally quite high. The Marunouchi and Ginza subway lines serve Akasakamitsuke Station and the Chiyoda subway line stops at Akasaka Station.

A Few Places of Interest before Dusk

Suntory Museum サントリー美術館 (upper center, map 23) houses about 2,000 traditional Japanese art objects, including paintings, lacquer ware, glass ware and women's ornaments. A tea-house is attached to the museum, and, if it's not occupied by a group, you can enjoy real tea-ceremony powdered green tea there (300 yen). (10:00 AM to 5:00 PM. Until 7:00 PM on Friday. Closed on Mondays. Admission 500 yen).

Hie Jinja Shrine 日枝神社 (middle right): The entrance is marked by a big torii gate. At the end of the street are steep stone steps lined with numerous small red torii gates. Watch your head when passing under them. This authentic shrine is quite impressive, and the precincts are unexpectedly quiet despite the shrine's location right next to the bustling play town.

Restaurants and Night Spots

Tamachi-dori and **Hitotsugi-dori** Streets are crowded with all sorts of restaurants, pubs, discos and pachinko pinball parlors (both streets are shaded in red on the map). Misuji-dori Street, located between them, is a rather quiet street that is home to many extremely expensive Japanese-style restaurants. These restaurants have private rooms that are used for business negotiations and VIP entertaining. *Geisha* are often called to these establishments to enhance the party atmosphere. Stay away from these places unless you are invited by Japanese business associates. They are much too expensive for anyone not on a very generous expense account.

Japanese Restaurants

Tsunahachi (8F) and **Fukusuke** (7F) are in Belle Vie Akasaka (upper center). The former serves tempura and the latter sushi (moderate). **Ten-ichi** (middle center) is a famous expensive tempura restaurant. **Zakuro** in TBS Kaikan (lower left) serves superb sukiyaki and shabu-shabu (expensive). **Akasakatei, Chachatei, Suisha** and **Inakaya** (all middle center) are Japanese pub restaurants (moderate).

Western and Steak Restaurants

Stew Kettle (middle center) has a full line of stew dishes (reasonable). **Al Dente** in Belle Vie Akasaka is an Italian spaghetti restaurant (reasonable). **Manos** (lower center) serves authentic Russian dishes (reasonable). **Suehiro** (middle left) and **Volks** (upper center) are reasonable steak houses, while **Misono** (lower left) is a renowned steak restaurant (expensive). **Fisherman's Wharf** (middle left) is an American-style seafood restaurant (expensive). **Granata** and **Shido** are in TBS Kaikan. Granata serves authentic Italian cuisine and Shido French (both expensive).

Other Restaurants and Pubs

Seoul (middle center) is a Korean barbecue restaurant, probably the best place to eat your fill of beef at a reasonable price. **Nangokushuka** in Belle Vie Akasaka is great if you're hungry for Chinese food (reasonable). **The Taj** (middle center) is known for its authentic Indian curry (reasonable). **Hai Whan** (middle center) is famous for its Chinese-style seafood dishes (expensive).

Discos

Mugen and **Byblos** (middle center) are well known discos often frequented by foreign visitors.

Detour

If you have a chance to walk on Hitotsu-gi-dori Street, visit **Akasaka Fudo Hall** 赤坂不動尊 (middle left). Although the Hall itself is only a small structure housing an image of the god Fudo, the narrow path leading to the hall is illuminated by small lanterns, and is especially exotic and romantic in the evening.

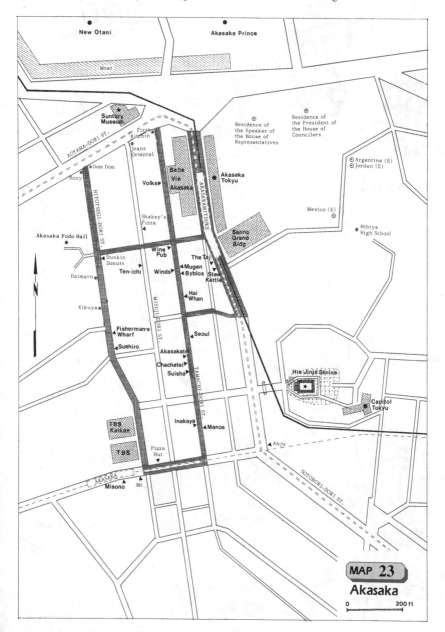

MAP **23**
Akasaka

0   200 ft

Western Tokyo

◈ **Fashionable Tokyo**

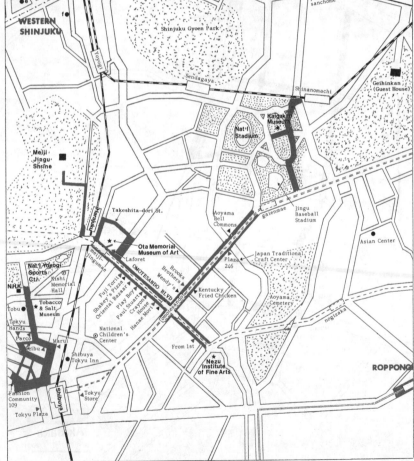

a — Shinjuku Prince
b — Tokyo Hilton
c — Century Hyatt
d — Keio Plaza
e — Shinjuku Washington
f — Sunroute Tokyo

MAP 24
Western Tokyo

EASTERN SHINJUKU

WESTERN SHINJUKU

SHINJUKU

shinjuku-gyoenmae

yotsuya sanchome

Shinjuku Gyoen Park

Yoyogi

Sendagaya

Shinanomachi

Geihinkan (Guest House)

Kaigakan Museum

Nat'l Stadium

Meiji Jingu Shrine

Jingu Baseball Stadium

galenmae

Asian Center

Takeshita-dori St.

Aoyama Bell Commons

Japan Traditional Craft Center

Harajuku

Ota Memorial Museum of Art

Plaza 246

Aoyama Cemetery

Laforet

Brooks Brothers

Wendy's

Kentucky Fried Chicken

nogizaka

meiji

jingumae

OMOTESANDO BLVD

Nat'l Yoyogi Sports Ctr.

N.H.K.

Kishi Memorial Hall

Tobacco & Salt Museum

Fuji Torii

Shakey's Pizza

Oriental Bazaar

Play Boy

Paul Stuart

Crayon House

Hanae Mori

Tobu

Tokyu Hands

Parco

Seibu

Marui

National Children's Center

From 1st

Nezu Institute of Fine Arts

ROPPONGI

Shibuya Tokyu Inn

Fashion Community 109

Tokyu Plaza

Shibuya

Tokyu Store

0   0 5 mi

Shibuya   渋谷

Shibuya is reached by either the JR Yamanote Loop Line or the Ginza subway line. As a large terminal where suburban commuters transfer from commuter trains to city transportation, Shibuya has a great many shopping, eating and drinking establishments. However, until recently Shibuya was just a typical white-collar workers' area. **Parco**, a new concept fashion building full of boutiques and accessory stores, has changed the character of the area. Parco attracted the young ladies, and other fashionable new enterprises sprang up to cater to the new traffic. Koen-dori Street has become a promenade for young couples, connecting Shibuya, National Yoyogi Sports Center, Meiji Jingu Shrine and Harajuku.

Shopping In Shibuya

Tokyu Plaza 東急プラザ (lower left, map 24), **Fashion Community 109, Seibu, Marui Fashion, Parco, Parco Part II,** and **Parco Part III** are the major shopping buildings in the area. **Tokyu Hands** 東急ハンズ is a new department store that specializes in various do-it-yourself products for Sunday carpenters and hobbyists.

Shibuya to Harajuku

Tobacco & Salt Museum たばこと塩の 博物館 (lower left) is probably the only museum of its kind in the world. Especially interesting are the numerous packages collected from all over the world. The fourth floor displays wood-block prints featuring smoking. (10:00 AM to 5:30 PM. Closed on Mondays. Admission 100 yen).

NHK 日本放送協会 (Japan Broadcasting Corporation) (lower left): There is a 0.4 mile (0.6 km.) long tour path through the main building that leads visitors past several studios and panel displays featuring popular programs of the past. Sound effects and film techniques are demonstrated. Because the displays are explained only in Japanese, foreigners may have difficulty understanding them, but it is still interesting to see the workings of a popular con-

temporary industry (10:00 AM to 5:00 PM. Closed the fourth Monday of each month. Admission free).

National Yoyogi Sports Center 国立 代々木競技場: The two indoor arenas here were constructed for the 1964 Olympic Games. The unique designs of these arenas still fascinate visitors. You can see the inside of the large arena if it is not being used for a competition (10:00 AM to 4:00 PM).

Harajuku   原宿

Meiji Jingu Shrine 明治神宮 is dedicated to Emperor Meiji, who was responsible for Japan's modernization. The present buildings were reconstructed in 1958. The shrine grounds provide the people of Tokyo with a refuge from the concrete welter (9:00 AM to 5:00 PM). Admission to the Treasure House in the precincts costs 200 yen.

Teenager Fashion Streets: On Takeshita-dori Street and the northern part of Meiji-dori Street (both are shaded red) there are countless small boutiques and fashion shops. Vendors at the flea market near Harajuku Station sell ornaments and accessories that appeal to young girls. Open-air discos are held on Sundays on Omotesando Boulevard (western side of Harajuku Station or northern side of Yoyogi Sports Center).

Ota Memorial Museum of Art 太田記念 美術館 houses 12,000 wood-block prints of famous artists such as Sharaku and Hiroshige. The exhibits are changed periodically. (10:30 AM to 5:30 PM. Closed on Mondays, and from the 25th through the end of each month. Admission is 500 yen).

Aoyama   青山

Omotesando Boulevard 表参道 is lined with lovely gingko trees and is probably the most beautiful street in Tokyo. After crossing Meiji-dori Street, there are two antique stores – **Fuji Torii** and **Oriental Bazaar.** Once you pass these two shops you've entered Aoyama.

Aoyama 青山 is a residential area especially popular with artists, professionals and foreign residents. Many designer boutiques and fashionable shops have sprung up in the area to serve this elite clientele. Fashions here are sophisticated and cosmopolitan - very different from Shibuya's appeal to trendy young adults and from Harajuku's bizarre allure for teens. **Hanae Mori's** sleek glass showcase for her exquisite designs is on Omotesando Boulevard, along with American stores such as **Play Boy** and **Paul Stuart.** Across Aoyama-dori Street, on the way to the Nezu Institute of Fine Arts, are **Lamia** and **From 1st** (Issey Miyake has his boutique here). Major fashion buildings on Aoyama-dori Street are **Aoyama Bell Commons, Teijin Men's Shop,** and **Brooks Brothers** of New York.

Japan Traditional Craft Center 全国 伝統的工芸センター is located on the second floor of Plaza 246. Handicraft products from all parts of Japan, including lacquer ware, pottery, silk clothing and accessories, are displayed and sold here. **Crayon House** クレヨン・ハウス on Omotesando Boulevard has a small book store on the second floor that stocks children's picture books from around the world.

The Nezu Institute of Fine Arts 根津 美術館 : This jewel-box museum houses about 8,000 works of art from Japan and other parts of the Orient. The collection includes several National Treasures (9:30 AM to 4:30 PM. Closed on Mondays and for the entire month of August. Admission 500 yen).

Jingu-gaien Park 神宮外苑 : Literally, the Outer Garden of Meiji Jingu Shrine. Omotesando Boulevard above was originally designed as the main approach connecting the Shrine and this Outer Garden. Kaigakan Museum in the Park, a unique rock building, exhibits paintings featuring Emperor Meiji (9:00 AM to 4:30 PM). The Park also contains the National Stadium, the main site for the 1964 Tokyo Olympic Games and still the nation's most prestigious sports center, Jingu Baseball Stadium, the home of the professional Yakult Swallows, and other sports facilities. The area, with its countless gingko trees, provides refreshing promenades and is especially beautiful in autumn when the leaves turn yellow.

Western Shinjuku
西新宿

In the last fifteen years Western Shinjuku has undergone the most drastic changes of any area of Tokyo. The area used to be nothing more than a sleepy small town whose only claim to fame was that it was the location of the reservoirs that provided millions of Tokyoites with their water. But starting with the completion of the Keio Plaza Hotel, more than 10 skyscrapers have been constructed in the area, and development is planned to continue into the 21st century. The skyscrapers include Shinjuku Mitsui Building (225 m. or 686 feet), Shinjuku Center Building (223 m. or 680 feet), Shinjuku Sumitomo Building, Shinjuku Nomura Building (both are 210 m. or 641 feet), and Yasuda Kasai Kaijo Building (200 m. or 610 feet). The Tokyo Metropolitan Government is scheduled to move here in several years.

The JR Yamanote Loop Line, and the Marunouchi and Shinjuku subway lines serve Shinjuku Station (The private Odakyu Railways also uses Shinjuku as its terminal, operating, as explained below in the Hakone Chapter, a special train from here to Hakone). Shinjuku is Tokyo's biggest train terminal and has extensive, confusing underground passages and shopping malls. Many derelicts live in the air-conditioned underground area. They are usually drunk and dirty, but not at all violent.

Free Observatories: The 53rd floor of Shinjuku Center Building (No. 3), the 50th floor of Shinjuku Nomura Building (No. 1) and the 51st floor of Shinjuku Sumitomo Building (No. 5) have free observatories.

Togo Seiji Museum 東郷青児美術館 ： About 100 works of Seiji Togo, a great master of paintings of girls, are displayed on the 42nd floor of Yasuda Kasai Kaijo Building (No. 2). The Museum has recently added the notoriously expensive (5,300 million yen!) Van Gogh Sunflowers. The museum also has an observatory gallery overlooking the Shinjuku area (9:30 AM to 4:30 PM. Closed on Saturdays, Sundays and national holidays. Admission 300 yen).

Shinjuku NS Building 新宿ＮＳビル (No. 7): At only 440 feet (134 m.) this building is dwarfed by many of its neighbors, but its unique interior – with an empty core up to a glass roof – opened a new chapter in Japanese architecture. A 24-foot (7 m.) tall antique clock stands in the lobby of the first floor. The basement exhibition hall is one of Tokyo's largest. Nineteen computer companies have showrooms on the fifth floor.

Discount Camera Shops: Tokyo's two leading discount camera shops, Yodobashi and Doi are located near the station.

Shinjuku Chuo Koen 新宿中央公園 or Shinjuku Central Park is a popular jogging route for those staying at the area's hotels. The Park is also an oasis for Shinjuku's amorous couples in the evening.

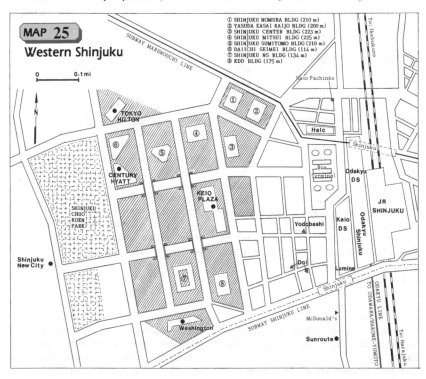

Restaurants

As a general rule, the higher up the floor on which restaurants are located, the more expensive their prices. However, all of the following restaurants serve good food at reasonable prices, and have magnificent views of Tokyo as well.

Shinjuku NS Building: Orizuru-tei (30F) is a good choice if you want to sample Japanese dishes. **Suehiro** (29F) serves steak (800 yen for lunch and 2,500 yen for dinner). **Ise** (29F) specializes in tonkatsu (pork cutlet). **The Old Kitchen** has a varied continental menu. **Hakkaku** is a robatayaki pub. This is a good place to sample Japanese seafood and sake.

Shinjuku Nomura Building: Tempura Tsunahachi (49F) serves set menu tempura meals. **Miyoshitei** (49F) serves a combination of Japanese and Chinese food. **Swiss Chalet** (50F) serves dinners that start at 2,200 yen.

Disco: The Samba Club, with an atmosphere of studied sophistication, is located on the ground floor of the Century Hyatt Hotel.

Eastern Shinjuku
東新宿

Everything new under the rising sun, especially everything new with young people, makes its first appearance in Eastern Shinjuku. If the behavior of young people is a barometer of future social trends, Eastern Shinjuku is certainly the place to get an idea of where Japanese society is headed, for better or worse.

There are two distinct areas in Eastern Shinjuku. The southern part, from Shinjuku-dori Street south, is a traditional shopping and restaurant area. The northern part, to the north of Yasukuni-dori Street, called Kabukicho, is Tokyo's biggest amusement center. It is estimated that Kabukicho's population during the daytime is only 3,000, but that its nighttime population swells to an astonishing 400,000. Kabukicho is drinking places, discos, snack shops, trysting places for young couples, and pornographic salons. It crackles with

the energy of the young people who throng its streets. It is alluring, seductive, enticing, gaudy, tawdry, vulgar, exhilarating and exciting all at once. The destination of desires, it is a place where the veils that usually mask human emotions are torn aside. A lot of scams and bunco schemes are operated here, but violent crimes are seldom heard of. Kabukicho is especially safe for foreign tourists because the denizens of the streets are afraid to even talk to foreigners. Don't be afraid to visit Kabukicho, but if you are a woman, don't stay in the area alone after 8:00 PM. After then most of the men will be drunk and, inspired by alcohol, quite likely to make propositions that you probably won't find welcome. Kabukicho is quite an experience and will teach you a lot about Tokyo.

As explained in the Western Shinjuku district section, Shinjuku is the biggest train terminal in Tokyo, served by the JR Yamanote and Chuo Lines, the Marunouchi and Shinjuku subway lines, etc. If you visit Shinjuku by either subway line, the Shinjuku-Sanchome Station is also convenient for Eastern-Shinjuku. The area's undergrounds have been also developed into shopping centers with complicated passages. When leaving Shinjuku, it's best to stay on the surface and walk to the approximate location of the station to find an entrance with an English sign. Though becoming very popular with foreign visitors, the Shinjuku Station area still lacks adequate English signs.

Stores

Isetan (middle center, map 26) is a huge department store especially popular with young people. **Mitsukoshi** and **Marui** are other major shopping buildings. **Kinokuniya Bookstore** (middle center) has an inventory of 400,000 books. Believe it or not, 40,000 of them are foreign books, most of them in English. **Sakuraya** and **Yodobashi** (near Shinjuku Station) are two more discount camera stores. **JC Tax-Free** (lower center) handles electric and electronic products, and other souvenir items, and caters to foreign tourists. An **antique flea market** is held on the first Saturday and on the

third Sunday of each month in the precincts of Hanazono Jinja Shrine (middle
center) from dawn till dusk.

Shinjuku Gyoen Garden 新宿御苑

With huge Japanese and Western gardens, Shinjuku Gyoen Garden is an oasis
for busy city people. With 1,900 cherry
trees, the Garden is crowded with
thousands of cherry blossom lovers in early
April (9:00 AM to 4:00 PM. Closed on
Mondays. Admission 120 yen).

Restaurant

Japanese Restaurants: Hinodezushi
(sushi) and **Tempura Tsunahachi** (tempura)
are located in Studio Alta (middle left,
map 26). Both reasonably priced. **Funa-
bashiya** (middle center) is an authentic
tempura restaurant (moderate). **Amimoto**
(upper center) is a Japanese pub restaurant

famous for its fresh seafood (moderate).

Western Restaurants: Takayama Land
Kaikan (middle center) accommodates
several reasonable restaurants. **Essen** (5F)
is a popular German restaurant, and
Suehiro (6F) serves steaks, sukiyaki and
shabu-shabu. **Stew Ukraine** (middle center)
serves a variety of Russian stews (reasonable).

**Other Restaurants: Korean Barbecue
Tokaien** (middle center) serves Korean bar-
becue at very reasonable prices. **Baien** is a
Chinese restaurant (reasonable).

Pubs: Jazz Club Pit Inn (middle center)
features live jazz performances. **Pub Sher-
lock Holmes** (6F of American House, middle left) is an English-style pub. **Shinjuku
Wine House** (5F of Saison Plaza, middle
center) is a good place to sample Japanese
wines at reasonable prices. Imported wines
are also served.

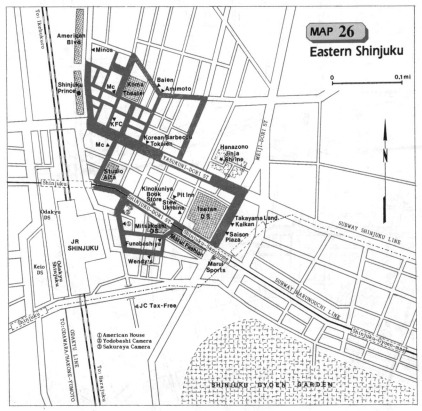

MAP 26
Eastern Shinjuku

Northern Tokyo

◉ Cultural Tokyo

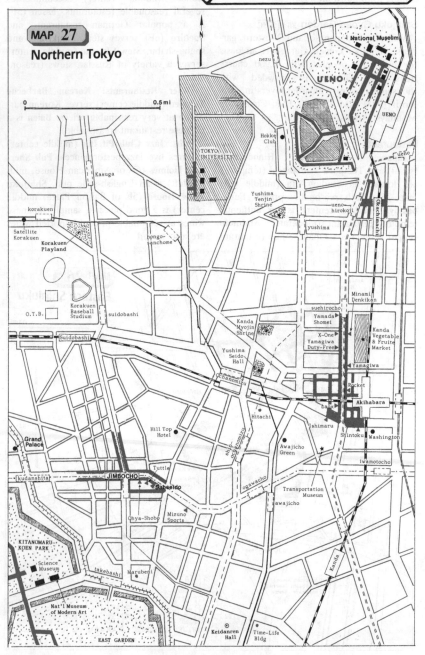

MAP 27

Northern Tokyo

0 — 0.5 mi

- National Museum
- nezu
- UENO
- UENO
- Hokke Club
- TOKYO UNIVERSITY
- Kasuga
- Yushima Tenjin Shrine
- korakuen
- Satellite Korakuen
- Korakuen Playland
- hongo-sanchome
- ueno-hirokoji
- yushima
- O.T.B.
- Korakuen Baseball Stadium
- suidobashi
- Suidobashi
- Minami Denkikan
- suehirocho
- Yamada Shomei
- X-One Yamagiwa Duty-Free
- Kanda Vegetable & Fruite Market
- Kanda Myojin Shrine
- Yamagiwa
- Yushima Seido Hall
- Ochanomizu
- Rocket
- Laox
- Akihabara
- Hitachi
- Ishimaru
- Hill Top Hotel
- Shintoku
- Washington
- Grand Palace
- Awajicho Green
- iwamotocho
- kudanshita
- Tuttle
- JIMBOCHO
- Sanseido
- ogawacho
- Transportation Museum
- awajicho
- Ohya-Shobo
- Mizuno Sports
- KITANOMARU-KOEN PARK
- Science Museum
- takebashi
- Marubeni
- Kanda
- Nat'l Museum of Modern Art
- EAST GARDEN
- Keidanren Hall
- Time-Life Bldg

Northern Tokyo is home to many educational and cultural institutions.

Ueno, with many museums and other cultural facilities, is the center of the area, and is explained in detail at the end of this section.

Jimbocho   神保町

Jimbocho (lower left, map 27) is a scholars' and students' area, especially famous as a mecca for bookstores, particularly second-hand books. More than 50 bookstores line the southern side of Yasukuni-dori Street, on both sides of Jimbocho Station. Traditionally, Japan has absorbed advanced cultures, science and technology by way of written documents, from China and other Asian countries in olden times, and from European countries and the U.S. in modern times. The Japanese love of books developed as a result of these experiences, and still endures even though TV and other audio-visual media have, in recent years, diminished what used to be the overwhelming popularity and power of the written word.

Some Bookstores of Interest

Sanseido has the greatest floor space of any Japanese bookstore. If you want to take a look at just one Japanese bookstore, this is the place. **Ohya-Shobo** handles an extensive inventory of old Japanese books, hand-written documents (calligraphy) and wood-block prints. **Charles E. Tuttle** deals in new Western (mostly English language) books. Tuttle also has published a number

of English books introducing Japanese culture as well as English translations of Japanese novels.

Akihabara   秋葉原

Akihabara (middle right, map 27) is world famous as Japan's bargain basement for electrical and electronic products. When you arrive in Akihabara you'll be confronted with a confusing jumble of colorful signs inviting you to sample the various wares of this electronic bazaar. The area is always bustling with bargain hunters, and the busy streets always have a bit of the air of a festival.

Transportation Museum 交通博物館 (lower right, map 27) illustrates the development of air, land and ocean transportation, with special emphasis on trains, and is very popular with the young (9:30 AM to 5:00 PM. Closed on Mondays).

Kanda Myojin Shrine 神田明神 (middle center, map 27) is famous for its Kanda-Matsuri Festival (May 14 – 16). In addition to the procession of miniature shrines, formally dressed geisha girls participate in the parade.

Korakuen & Hongo   後楽園, 本郷

Korakuen (middle left, map 27) is a huge sports and entertainment complex. Korakuen Baseball Stadium, the only covered stadium in Japan, is home to the Tokyo Giants, the most popular ball team in Japan. Korakuen Playland is a paradise for Tokyo kids. Bowling alleys, an ice skating rink, an off-track-betting parlor and a boxing gymnasium are also located in the complex.

Tokyo University (upper center, map 27), famous for its symbolic red gate, is located in Hongo, and is one of the most prestigious educational institutions in Japan.

Korakuen Playland

Ueno　上野

Ueno is one of Tokyo's largest terminals, where the Tohoku Shinkansen, Joetsu Shinkansen and other north-bound long-distance JR trains originate. The private Keisei Railways operates special trains from Ueno to Narita Airport. You can reach Ueno by the JR Yamanote Loop Line, and the Ginza and Hibiya subway lines.

Ueno-Koen Park　上野公園

Ueno-Koen Park is a spacious wooded area to the west of Ueno Station. Several museums, concert halls, Ueno Zoo and other cultural institutions are located there.

Tokyo National Museum 東京国立美術館 (upper right, map 28) consists of the following halls: **The Main Hall,** which houses Japanese fine and applied arts; **The Gallery of Oriental Antiquities,** which features historical and artistic objects of China, India and other Asian countries; **The Hyokeikan Gallery,** which specializes in Japanese archeological relics; and **The Gallery of Horyuji Treasures,** which contains the priceless Buddhist treasures of Nara's Horyuji Temple. The Museum is open from 9:00 AM to 4:30 PM. Closed on Mondays. The Gallery of Horyuji Treasures is open only on Thursday. Even on Thursday, if it is rainy or very humid, the Gallery may be closed in order to protect the fragile relics. A 250 yen admission charge covers all four halls.

Ueno Zoo 上野動物園 (upper center, map 28) is home to about 8,300 animals from all over the world. The most popular animals here are the pandas presented by the Chinese government. A monorail connects the Aquarium with the main grounds (9:30 AM to 4:30 PM. Closed on Mondays).

The National Science Museum 国立科学博物館 (upper right, map 28) is the Japanese version of New York's Natural History Museum (9:00 AM to 4:30 PM. Closed on Mondays). **The National Museum of Western Art** 国立西洋美術館 (upper right, map 28) contains carvings and statues, many of them by Rodin, as well as

a number of paintings of the French Impressionist school (9:30 AM to 5:00 PM. Closed on Mondays). **Metropolitan Festival Hall** 東京文化会館 (middle right, map 28) is the mecca for classical music concerts, operas and ballet performances. **The Metropolitan Art Museum** 東京都美術館 (upper center, map 28) is mainly used for exhibitions of the works of younger Japanese artists.

Toshogu Shrine 東照宮 (middle center) was built in 1627 to honor the spirit of Ieyasu Tokugawa, the first Tokugawa Shogun. The structure is painted vermilion and decorated with gold foil and numerous carvings. Both sides of the approach are lined with many stone lanterns (9:30 AM to 5:00 PM. Admission 100 yen).

Shinobazu-no-ike Pond 不忍池： On your way down the hill to Shinobazu-no-ike Pond, you will pass through numerous small red torii gates that lead to the precincts of Hanazono Jinja Shrine. On an island in the center of the pond stands a small hall called Bentendo. This hall contains the image of Benzaiten, the goddess of wealth. Don't forget to pay your respects to Her!

Shitamachi Museum 下町美術館 (lower center, map 28): This small two-story museum was founded in 1980 thanks to the efforts of the people of the Ueno area. It features various objects used in the daily life of the people in the late 19th and early 20th centuries. Reconstructed buildings, including a modest residence, a merchant's showroom and a candy shop, are on display, along with related utensils. Visitors can get an idea of the lost life of the *Edokko* children of Tokyo who lived in the traditional *shitamachi* (9:30 AM to 4:30 PM. Closed on Mondays. Admission 200 yen).

Ameya-Yokocho Shopping Street
アメヤ横丁

Ameya-Yokocho Street is a narrow lane along the west side of the elevated JR tracks between Ueno and Okachimachi Stations (lower right, map 28). The area was originally developed as a wholesale market for candies and snacks. "Ameya" means candy store, and "Yokocho" means narrow

lane. Nowadays, the shopping street is lined with about 400 retail discount stores that sell food, clothing, jewelry, sporting goods, etc. The area always has a festive atmosphere, especially in the late afternoon, when housewives crowd the shops to purchase what they need for the family dinner. Walk down the crowded alley to experience something of the casual, everyday life of the people of Tokyo.

Restaurants

Ueno Seiyoken (middle center) opened right after the Meiji Restoration in 1868 and introduced Western cuisine to Japan. The grill is located in a quiet corner of Ueno-Koen Park and overlooks Shinobazu-no-ike Pond. Rather expensive, but quality is excellent. **Totenko** (lower left): This eight-story Chinese restaurant is proud of its fantastic view of Shinobazu-no-ike Pond and the thickly wooded Ueno-Koen Park. The 7th floor grill serves a fine lunch. **Ueno Fugetsudo** (lower center) is famous for its sponge cake (which is also retailed all over Japan). You can enjoy this famous delicacy in the first-floor cafe. The second floor serves Western food, such as beef stew and salmon steak.

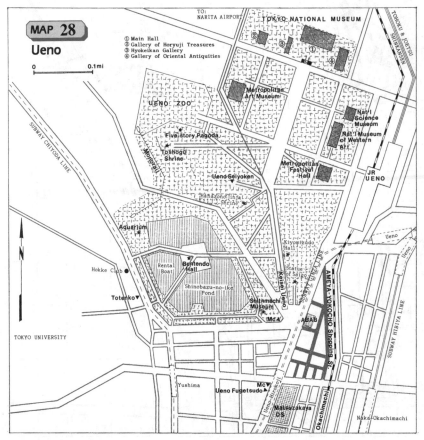

MAP 28
Ueno

0   0.1mi

① Main Hall
② Gallery of Horyuji Treasures
③ Hyokeikan Gallery
④ Gallery of Oriental Antiquities

Asakusa

Nostalgic Tokyo

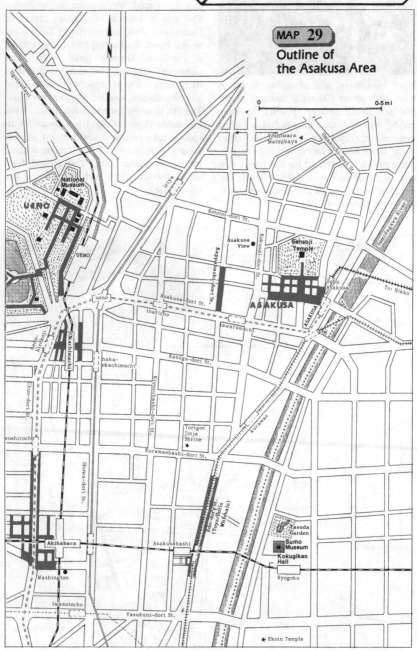

MAP 29

**Outline of
the Asakusa Area**

Asakusa has prospered as a temple town throughout Japanese history. Sensoji Temple (popularly known as Asakusa Kannon Temple) is the oldest temple in Tokyo. Until recently Asakusa was also the entertainment center of Tokyo, and was especially famous for its comedies and girls' revue. Though the entertainment centers have shifted to other areas, Asakusa has stubbornly preserved the nostalgic atmosphere of the traditional *shitamachi* downtown of the common people. For transportation to Asakusa, you can take either the Ginza or the Asakusa subway line. The boat ride from Hamarikyu Garden (see Eastern Tokyo section) is also recommended.

The private Tobu Railways operates special trains from Tobu-Asakusa (middle right, map 30) to Tobu-Nikko. See the Nikko chapter below.

Sensoji Temple 浅草寺

Kaminarimon Gate is the entrance to the main approach to the Temple. Gods of Wind and Thunder stand in the niches on both sides of the Gate, and an 11-foot (3.3

m.) tall red lantern hangs from it. Both sides of the main approach, called Nakamise Street, are lined with souvenir shops decorated with colorful small lanterns. Shin-Nakamise is an arcade lined with modern stores, restaurants and traditional souvenir shops. At the end of the arcade are many movie houses and other theaters reminiscent of the old Asakusa.

Kappabashi Street 合羽橋商店街

Both sides of this street are lined with shops which handle various restaurant products, such as lacquer ware, pottery, small decorative objects like lanterns and umbrellas, the menu stands found in authentic Japanese restaurants, and the plastic displays of foods used in the windows of many restaurants and coffee shops. Though the primary clients of these stores are restaurant owners, retail sales to the general public are also made. The southern part of Kappabashi Street is especially interesting. Many items much more interesting than what you can find in regular souvenir shops are available here.

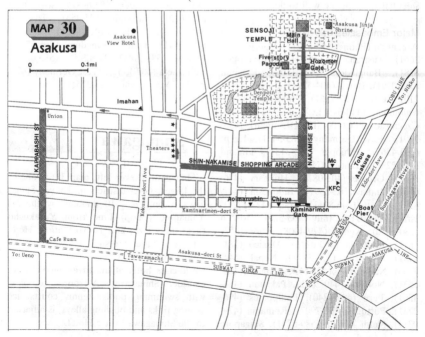

Restaurants in Asakusa

Try authentic Japanese cuisine in this nostalgic old downtown. **Chinya** (middle center, map 30) is famous for sukiyaki and shabu-shabu (moderate). **Aoimarushin** (middle center, map 30): The name Aoimarushin is famous throughout Japan as *the* restaurant for tempura. The higher up you go in this seven-story restaurant, the better the facilities become, and the higher the prices go (reasonable). **Imahan** (upper left, map 30) is another big-name sukiyaki restaurant (moderate).

Other Places of Interest

Kokugikan Hall 国技館 , in front of Ryogoku Station on the JR Sobu Line (lower right of map 29), is the home of sumo wrestling. Fifteen-day tournaments are held here three times a year in January, May and September. The Hall also houses the **Sumo Museum** 相撲博物館 , which exhibits photographs of grand champions and historic sumo-related items (9:30 AM to 4:30 PM. Closed on Saturdays, Sundays and national holidays).

Yasuda Garden 安田庭園 is a Japanese-style landscaped garden near Kokugikan Hall (9:00 AM to 4:30 PM).

Asakusabashi 浅草橋 (lower center, map 29) is a famous toy and doll wholesale district. Many such stores line Edo-dori Street and most of them also will sell directly to consumers.

Southern Tokyo

◈ Diplomatic Tokyo

A number of embassies are located in Southern Tokyo, which is basically a residential zone for the well-to-do.

Major Embassies in Tokyo

Argentina (Phone: 592-0321), Algeria (711-2661), Australia (453-0251), Austria (451-8281), Bangladesh (442-1501), Belgium (262-0191), Brazil (404-5211), Canada (408-2101), Chile (452-7561), China (403-3380), Colombia (440-6451), Cuba (449-7511), Czechoslovakia (400-8122), Denmark (496-3001), East Germany (585-5401), Egypt (463-4565), Ethiopia (585-3151), Finland (442-2231), France (473-0171), Ghana (409-3861), Greece (403-0871), Hungary (476-6061), India (262-2391), Indonesia (441-4201), Iran (446-8011), Iraq (423-1727), Israel (264-0911), Italy (453-5291), Jordan (580-5856), Kenya (479-4008), Korea (452-7611), Malaysia (463-0241), Mexico (581-1131), Morocco (478-3271), Nepal (444-7303), Netherlands (431-5126), Nigeria (468-5531), Norway (440-2611), Pakistan (454-4861), Peru (406-4240), Philippines (496-2731), Portugal (400-7907), Romania (479-0311), Saudi Arabia (589-5241), Singapore (586-9111), South Africa (265-3366), Spain (583-8531), Sri Lanka (585-7431), Sudan (406-0811), Sweden (582-6981), Switzerland (473-0121), Tanzania (425-4531), Thailand (441-0352), Turkey (470-5131), Uganda (469-3641), United Kingdom (265-5511), U.S.A. (583-7141), U.S.S.R. (583-4224), Venezuela (409-1501), West Germany (473-0151), Yugoslavia (447-3751), and Zaire (423-3981).

Shinagawa   品川

Shinagawa (lower left, map 31) is one of the largest hotel districts in Tokyo. Shinagawa is only 8 – 10 minutes by the JR Yamanote (Loop) Line from Yurakucho (near the Ginza) and Tokyo Station. Hotel rates in the area are slightly lower than the Tokyo norm. If you want to stay at a world-class hotel at an advantageous rate, consider Shinagawa. A sports complex, with swimming pools, tennis courts, ice skating rinks and bowling alleys, is adjacent to the Shinagawa Prince Hotel.

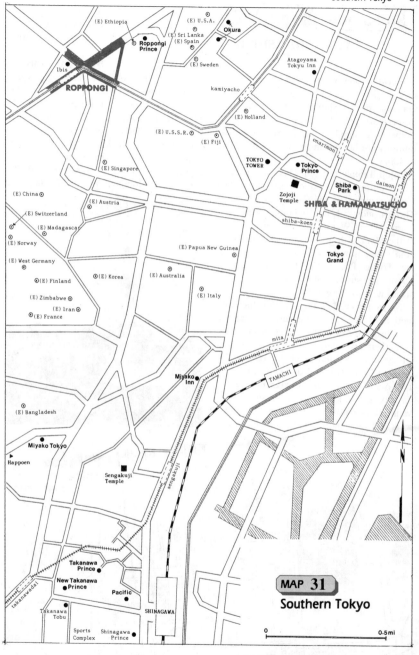

MAP **31**
Southern Tokyo

0   0.5mi

Shiba and Hamamatsucho 芝，浜松町

World Trade Center 世界貿易センター (152 meters or 498 feet high) rises next to Hamamatsucho Station. The 40th floor observatory provides a panoramic view of Tokyo. A number of inexpensive restaurants are housed in the basement of the building.

Zojoji Temple 増上寺 : This temple prospered during the Edo era as one of the family temples of the Tokugawa shoguns. Though most of the buildings were lost during World War II, the artistic structures of the Main Gate to the temple and Nitenmon Gate, now located in the grounds of the Tokyo Prince Hotel, remain intact. There are statues of fierce guardians in niches next to the gates.

Tokyo Tower 東京タワー : With the completion of Tokyo's many new skyscrapers, the observatories of this radio tower have lost their popularity. But the Special Observatory, located at an altitude of 250 meters (820 feet) is still the highest point in Tokyo and commands an extensive view of the city and Tokyo Bay. Admission to the Main Observatory (150 m. or 492 feet) costs 600 yen, and an additional 400 yen is charged for entrance to the Special Observatory. Though it is expensive, it is a must-see for those who enjoy high altitude views.

Shibarikyu Garden 芝離宮庭園 : This garden was built about 300 years ago as part of the private residence of Tadaatsu Okubo, a top shogunate official. After the Meiji Restoration, the garden belonged to the imperial family for a time, and then was given to the Tokyo Metropolitan Government. Its oddly shaped pine trees are especially delightful (9:00 AM to 4:30 PM. Closed on Monday. When Monday is a

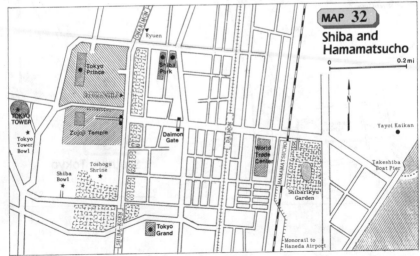

MAP 32
Shiba and Hamamatsucho

holiday, open on Monday and closed on Tuesday).

Roppongi   六本木

Roppongi is popular among Tokyo's young sophisticates and "artists." It also appeals to many foreign residents because it is easily accessible from the embassies located in the area, and because a liberal atmosphere pervades the neighborhood. This has helped to give Roppongi an international flavor. Roppongi in recent years has become so caught up in its night life, especially its discos, that it's no longer much of a residential area, but it is a very enjoyable place for urban night owls. The Hibiya subway line (Roppongi Station) is the only method of public transportation to Roppongi.

Please note that, as with Tokyo's other night life areas, it is very difficult to catch a cab for a short distance ride late in the evening (after 11:30 PM). Cab drivers try to pick up passengers headed for suburban residential areas, and are reluctant to provide their services to those staying at downtown hotels.

Restaurants in Roppongi
Japanese Restaurants

Inagiku in the basement of Sunroser Building (middle left, map 33) is the Roppongi branch of the world famous Inagiku tempura restaurant (moderate). **Osho** (middle center) is a Japanese-style pub-restaurant (moderate). **Seryna** (middle center) is an elegant shabu-shabu restaurant (expensive).

Western Restaurants

Berni Inn (middle center) serves reasonable steaks. **Stew Kettle** is a stew specialist (reasonable). **Double Ax** (middle center) is a Greek restaurant and **Tokyo Swiss Inn** (upper center) a renowned Swiss establishment (both moderate).

Other Restaurants

Bungawan Solo (lower left) serves **Indonesian** and **Raja** (lower left) Indian cuisine (both reasonable). **Rozan** (lower left) is an authentic Chinese restaurant (moderate), while Hai-Kung (middle center) is a Chinese-style seafood restaurant (expensive). **Mr. James** is a pub with live Dixie and Country and Western music. There are also a variety of restaurants in **Roa Building** (lower center).

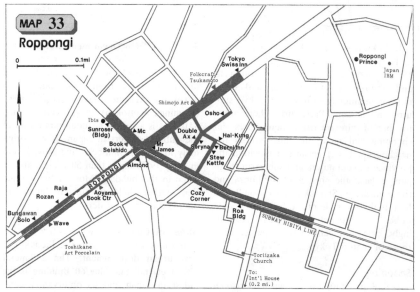

Ikebukuro

◈ **Panoramic Tokyo**

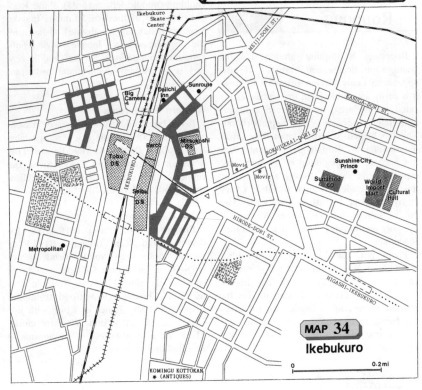

MAP **34**

Ikebukuro

0   0.2mi

Ikebukuro is one of the largest terminals in Tokyo. It is served by, in addition to the JR Yamanote Loop Line, the Marunouchi and Yurakucho subway lines and three more commuter lines from the Tokyo suburbs and Saitama Prefecture. There are a number of different department stores and shopping and night life zones within the neighborhood, but because it is within the province of commuters and suburban shoppers, it lacks the prestige of the Ginza and the panache of Shinjuku. What you'll find here is the life style of the common people rather than the rich and famous. Accordingly, prices in general are cheaper than those of central Tokyo.

Shopping

Ikebukuro Station is sandwiched between **Seibu** and **Parco** Department Stores on the east, and the **Tobu** Department Store on the west. **Mitsukoshi** Department Store is just a few minutes from the station.

Tokyo Antique Hall 古民具骨董館 (Komingu Kottokan) (lower center, map 34): This is a sort of headquarters for all of the antique dealers in Japan. It was originally located in Jimbocho and moved here in early 1987. More than 50 dealers are located in this building. Most of the antique flea markets held throughout Japan are operated by these dealers.

Sunshine City サンシャイン・シティー

Sunshine City is the name of Ikebukuro's new urban development. The 240-meter (787 feet) tall **Sunshine 60 Building** is the tallest in Japan and its observatory commands the best view of Tokyo (10:00 AM to 8:00 PM). **World Import Mart Building** contains a permanent exhibition of international products imported into Japan, as well as a planetarium, an aquarium, and a branch of Mitsukoshi Department Store. Many foreign national tourist boards also have offices in this building. **The Cultural Hall** next to World Import Mart Building houses the Orient Museum (Egyptian antiquities) and Sunshine Theater.

Some Extra Information

Small restaurants, drinking places, movie theaters and other entertainment properties are located on both sides of Ikebukuro Station (shown in shaded red).

Ikebukuro is only 15 minutes by subway from the Ginza and Tokyo Station. Hotel rates in this neighborhood are below the Tokyo norm. If you want to stay at a nice hotel without spending too much money, consider Ikebukuro.

Major Festivals in Tokyo

January 6: Dezomeshiki New Year Parade by firemen at Harumi near Ginza. Firemen in traditional uniforms perform acrobatic stunts atop tall bamboo ladders.

February 3: Setsubun Festival at Sensoji Temple in Asakusa. Bean-throwing ceremonies are held to ensure good fortune throughout the year.

April 8: Hanamatsuri Festival at Sensoji Temple in Asakusa celebrates the birthday of Shakya.

April 21 – 23: Spring Festival at Yasukuni Jinja Shrine.

Middle of May: Kanda Matsuri Festival in the Kanda area and Sanja Matsuri Festival in the Asakusa area both feature processions of miniature shrines.

Middle of June: Torigoe Jinja Festival near Asakusa and Sanno Matsuri Festival in Akasaka (Hie Jinja Shrine) feature processions of miniature shrines.

July 13 – 16: Mitama Matsuri Festival at Yasukuni Jinja Shrine.

Middle of July: Shoro Nagashi Festival: a number of paper lanterns with lighted candles are floated on the Imperial Palace moat near Kitanomaru-Koen Park.

Last Saturday of July: Fireworks Festival on the Sumidagawa River near Asakusa.

Beginning of August: Takigi Noh (open-air Noh performance) at Hie Jinja Shrine in Akasaka.

Middle of October to Middle of November: Kiku Matsuri Chrysanthemum Show at Sensoji Temple in Asakusa.

October 27 – November 3: Flea market of second-hand books in Kanda (Jimbocho).

Beginning of November: Meiji Jingu Shrine Festival features performance of traditional arts and demonstrations of martial arts.

Middle of December: Gasaichi flea market features New Year decorations (at Sensoji Temple in Asakusa).

Sanja Matsuri Festival

Accommodations in Tokyo

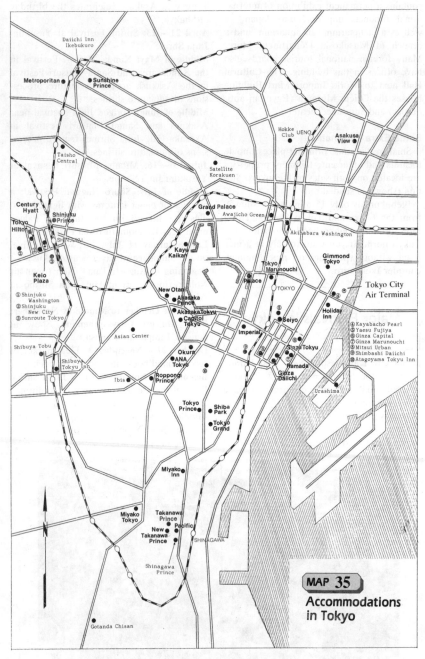

Daiichi Inn
Ikebukuro

Metropolitan   ● Sunshine
                  Prince

Taisho
Central

Hokke
Club   UENO   Asakusa
                      View

Satellite
Korakuen

Century
Hyatt   ● Grand Palace
Tokyo   Shinjuku   ● Awajicho Green
Hilton   Prince
         SHINJUKU   ● Akihabara Washington

         Kayu   Tokyo   Gimmond
         Kaikan   Marunouchi   Tokyo
Keio   ● Palace
Plaza   Palace
① Shinjuku   ○ TOKYO   Tokyo City
  Washington   New Otani   Air Terminal
② Shinjuku   ● Akasaka
  New City   Prince
③ Sunroute Tokyo ● Akasaka Tokyu   ● Seiyo   Holiday
                 ● Capitol   Inn
Asian Center   Tokyu   Imperial   Ginza Tokyu ④ Kayabacho Pearl
                                                      ⑤ Yaesu Fujiya
Shibuya Tobu   Okura   ● Ramada   ⑥ Ginza Capital
                           ● ANA   ⑦ Ginza Marunouchi
Shibuya   Ibis   Tokyo   Ginza   ⑧ Mitsui Urban
Tokyu Inn   ● Roppongi   Daiichi   ⑨ Shimbashi Daiichi
                 Prince   ⑩ Atagoyama Tokyu Inn
                                          ● Urashima
                Tokyo   Shiba
                Prince ● ● Park
                         ● Tokyo
                           Grand

                Miyako
                Inn ●

    Miyako   Takanawa
    Tokyo ●   Prince
                New ● Pacific
                Takanawa
                Prince   SHINAGAWA

                Shinagawa
                Prince

                                    MAP 35

                                    **Accommodations
                                    in Tokyo**

● Gotanda Chisan

1. Hotels

(1) Deluxe Hotels

Imperial Hotel 帝国ホテル
   (Middle center, map 35. 1,135 rooms)
   Add: 1-1-1, Uchisaiwaicho, Chiyoda-ku.
   Tel: (03) 504-1111.

Hotel Okura ホテルオークラ
   (Middle center, map 35. 980 rooms)
   Add: 2-10-4, Toranomon, Minato-ku.
   Tel: (03) 582-0111.

Palace Hotel パレスホテル
   (Middle center, map 35. 404 rooms)
   Add: 1-1-1, Marunouchi, Chiyoda-ku.
   Tel: (03) 211-5211.

Akasaka Prince Hotel 赤坂プリンスホテル
   (Middle center, map 35. 760 rooms)
   Add: 1-2, Kioicho, Chiyoda-ku.
   Tel: (03) 234-1111.

Hotel New Otani & Tower
   ホテルニューオータニ
   (Middle center, map 35. 2,057 rooms)
   Add: 4-1, Kioicho, Chiyoda-ku.
   Tel: (03) 265-1111.

Capitol Tokyu Hotel
   キャピトル東急ホテル
   (Middle center, map 35. 468 rooms)
   Add: 2-10-3, Nagatacho, Chiyoda-ku.
   Tel: (03) 581-4511.

Keio Plaza Inter-Continental Hotel
   京王プラザホテル
   (Middle left, map 35. 1,500 rooms)
   Add: 2-2-1, Nishi-Shinjuku, Shinjuku-ku.
   Tel: (03) 344-0111.

ANA Hotel Tokyo 東京全日空ホテル
   (Middle center, map 35. 900 rooms)
   Add: 1-12-33, Akasaka, Minato-ku.
   Tel: (03) 505-1111.

Century Hyatt Hotel
   センチュリーハイヤットホテル
   (Middle left, map 35. 800 rooms)
   Add: 2-7-2, Nishi-Shinjuku, Shinjuku-ku.
   Tel: (03) 349-0111.

Tokyo Hilton Hotel 東京ヒルトンホテル
   (Middle left, map 35. 858 rooms)
   Add: 6-6-2, Nishi-Shinjuku Shinjuku-ku.
   Tel: (03) 344-5111.

Hotel Pacific ホテルパシフィック
   (Lower center, map 35. 854 rooms)
   Add: 3-13-3, Takanawa, Minato-ku.
   Tel: (03) 445-6711.

New Takanawa Prince Hotel
   新高輪プリンスホテル
   (Lower center, map 35. 1,010 rooms)
   Add: 3-13-1, Takanawa, Minato-ku.
   Tel: (03) 442-1111.

Miyako Hotel Tokyo 都ホテル東京
   (Lower center, map 35. 483 rooms)
   Add: 1-1-50, Shiroganedai, Minato-ku.
   Tel: (03) 447-3111.

Hotel Seiyo ホテル西洋
   (Middle right, map 35. 80 rooms)
   Add: 1-11-2, Ginza, Chuo-ku.
   Tel: (03) 535-1111.

(2) First-class Hotels

Tokyo Prince Hotel 東京プリンスホテル
   (Middle center, map 35. 484 rooms)
   Add: 3-3-1, Shiba-Koen, Minato-ku.
   Tel: (03) 432-1111.

Takanawa Prince Hotel
   高輪プリンスホテル
   (Lower center, map 35. 386 rooms)
   Add: 3-13-1, Takanawa, Minato-ku.
   Tel: (03) 447-1111.

Ginza Tokyu Hotel 銀座東急ホテル
   (Middle right, map 35. 445 rooms)
   Add: 5-15-9, Ginza, Chuo-ku.
   Tel: (03) 541-2411.

Hotel Grand Palace ホテルグランドパレス
   (Middle center, map 35. 480 rooms)
   Add: 1-1-1, Iidabashi, Chiyoda-ku.
   Tel: (03) 264-1111.

Sunshine City Prince Hotel
   サンシャイン・シティプリンスホテル
   (Upper left, map 35. 1,166 rooms)
   Add: 3-1-5, Higashi-Ikebukuro,
   Toshima-ku.
   Tel:(03) 988-1111.

Roppongi Prince Hotel
   六本木プリンスホテル
   (Middle center, map 35. 221 rooms)
   Add: 3-2-7, Roppongi, Minato-ku.
   Tel: (03) 587-1111

Akasaka Tokyu Hotel 赤坂東急ホテル
   (Middle center, map 35. 566 rooms)
   Add: 2-14-3, Nagatacho, Chiyoda-ku.
   Tel: (03) 580-2311.

Hotel Metropolitan ホテルメトロポリタン
   (Upper left, map 35. 818 rooms)
   Add: 1-6-1, Nishi-Ikebukuro,
   Toshima-ku.
   Tel:(03) 980-1111.

Shinjuku Prince Hotel 新宿プリンスホテル
 (Middle left, map 35. 571 rooms)
 Add: 1-30-1, Kabukicho, Shinjuku-ku.
 Tel: (03) 440-1111.

Asakusa View Hotel 浅草ビューホテル
 (Upper right, map 35. 342 rooms)
 Add: 3-17, Nishi-Asakusa, Taito-ku.
 Tel: (03) 842-2111.

(3)   Standard Hotels

Tokyo Marunouchi Hotel
 東京丸の内ホテル
 (Middle right, map 35. 210 rooms)
 Add: 1-6-3, Marunouchi, Chiyoda-ku.
 Tel: (03) 215-2151.

Shiba Park Hotel 芝パークホテル
 (Middle center, map 35. 370 rooms)
 Add: 1-5-10, Shiba-Koen, Minato-ku.
 Tel: (03) 433-3131.

Ginza Daiichi Hotel 銀座第一ホテル
 (Middle right, map 35. 812 rooms)
 Add: 8-13-1, Ginza, Chuo-ku.
 Tel: (03) 542-5311.

Hotel Kayu Kaikan ホテル霞友会館
 (Middle center, map 35. 127 rooms)
 Add: 8-1, Sanbancho, Chiyoda-ku.
 Tel: (03) 230-1111.

Tokyo Grand Hotel 東京グランドホテル
 (Middle center, map 35. 170 rooms)
 Add: 2-5-3, Shiba, Minato-ku.
 Tel: (03) 454-0311.

Miyako Inn Tokyo 都イン東京
 (Lower center, map 35. 405 rooms)
 Add: 3-7-8, Mita, Minato-ku.
 Tel: (03) 454-3111.

Holiday Inn Tokyo ホリデーイン東京
 (Middle right, map 35. 119 rooms)
 Add: 1-13-7, Hatchobori, Chuo-ku.
 Tel: (03) 553-6161.

Hotel Gimmond Tokyo
 ホテルギンモンド東京
 (Middle right, map 35. 221 rooms)
 Add: 1-6, Nihombashi, Chuo-ku.
 Tel: (03) 666-4111.

(4)   Business Hotels

Shimbashi Daiichi Hotel 新橋第一ホテル
 (Middle center, map 35. 1,106 rooms)
 Add: 1-2-6, Shimbashi, Minato-ku.
 Tel: (03) 501-4411.

Ginza Marunouchi Hotel 銀座丸の内ホテル
 (Middle right, map 35. 114 rooms)
 Add: 4-1-12, Tsukiji, Chuo-ku.
 Tel: (03) 543-5431.

Shinagawa Prince Hotel
 品川プリンスホテル
 (Lower center, map 35. 1,016 rooms)
 Add: 4-10-30, Takanawa, Minato-ku.
 Tel: (03) 440-1111.

Shinjuku Washington Hotel
 新宿ワシントンホテル
 (Middle left, map 35. 1,300 rooms)
 Add: 3-2-9, Nishi-Shinjuku, Shinjuku-ku.
 Tel: (03) 343-3111.

Hotel Ibis ホテルアイビス
 (Middle center, map 35. 200 rooms)
 Add: 7-14-4, Roppongi, Minato-ku.
 Tel: (03) 403-4411.

Yaesu Fujiya Hotel 八重洲富士屋ホテル
 (Middle right, map 35. 377 rooms)
 Add: 22-9-1, Yaesu, Chuo-ku.
 Tel: (03) 273-2111.

Mitsui Urban Hotel 三井アーバンホテル
 (Middle right, map 35. 263 rooms)
 Add: 8-6-15, Ginza, Chuo-ku.
 Tel: (03) 572-4131.

Hotel Sunroute Tokyo
 ホテルサンルート東京
 (Middle left, map 35. 544 rooms)
 Add: 2-3-1, Yoyogi, Shinjuku-ku.
 Tel: (03) 375-3211.

Shinjuku New City Hotel
 新宿ニューシティホテル
 (Middle left, map 35. 406 rooms)
 Add: 4-31-1, Nishi-Shinjuku,
 Shinjuku-ku.
 Tel: (03) 375-6511.

Ginza Capital Hotel 銀座キャピタルホテル
 (Middle right, map 35. 255 rooms)
 Add: 2-1, Tsukiji, Chuo-ku.
 Tel: (03) 543-8211.

Atagoyama Tokyu Inn 愛宕山東急イン
 (Middle center, map 35. 269 rooms)
 Add: 1-6-6, Atago, Minato-ku.
 Tel: (03) 431-0109.

Tokyo Hotel Urashima 東京ホテル浦島
 (Middle right, map 35. 1,001 rooms)
 Add: 2-5-23, Harumi, Chuo-ku.
 Tel: (03) 533-3111.

Gotanda Chisan Hotel 五反田チサンホテル
(Lower left, map 35. 353 rooms)
Add: 6-1-1, Nishi-Oi, Shinagawa-ku.
Tel: (03) 785-3211.
Daiichi Inn Ikebukuro 第一イン池袋
(Upper left, map 35. 140 rooms)
Add: 1-42-8, Higashi-Ikebukuro,
Toshima-ku.
Tel: (03) 982-4126.
Kayabacho Pearl Hotel
茅場町パールホテル
(Middle right, map 35. 270 rooms)
Add: 1-2-5, Shinkawa, Chuo-ku.
Tel: (03) 553-8080.
Taisho Central Hotel
大正セントラルホテル
(Upper left, map 35. 200 rooms)
Add: 1-27-7, Takadanobaba,
Shinjuku-ku.
Tel: (03) 232-0101.
Tokyo Green Hotel Awajicho
東京グリーンホテル淡路町
(Middle right, map 35. 226 rooms)
Add: 2-6, Kanda-Awajicho, Chiyoda-ku.
Tel: (03) 255-4161.
Akihabara Washington Hotel
秋葉原ワシントンホテル
(Middle right, map 35. 314 rooms)
Add: 1-8-3, Kanda-Sakumacho,
Chiyoda-ku.
Tel: (03) 255-3311.
Satellite Hotel Korakuen
サテライトホテル後楽園
(Upper center, map 35. 251 rooms)
Add: 1-3-3, Kasuga, Bunkyo-ku.
Tel: (03) 814-0202.
Shibuya Tobu Hotel 渋谷東武ホテル
(Middle left, map 35. 200 rooms)
Add: 3-1, Udagawacho, Shibuya-ku.
Tel: (03) 476-0111.
Shibuya Tokyu Inn 渋谷東急イン
(Middle left, map 35. 224 rooms)
Add: 1-24-10, Shibuya, Shibuya-ku.
Tel: (03) 498-0109.
Asian Center アジア会館
(Middle center, map 35. 180 rooms)
Add: 8-10-32, Akasaka, Minato-ku.
Tel: (03) 402-6111.

Hokke Club (Ueno Ikenohata)
法華クラブ上野池ノ端店
(Upper right, map 35. 330 rooms)
Add: 2-1-48, Ikenohata, Taito-ku.
Tel: (03) 882-3111.

2. Ryokans

There used to be a few traditional, authentic ryokans in Tokyo. However, all of them have been converted to very expensive restaurants in the past years. Therefore we could not find any ryokan which represents the serenity and relaxation of a Japanese inn.

The following four ryokans (all inexpensive), however, have some atmosphere of a Japanese inn.

Mikawaya Bekkan 三河屋別館
Add: 1-31-11, Asakusa, Taito-ku.
Tel: (03) 843 2345.
A 5 minute walk from Asakusa Station on the Ginza subway line.
Sawanoya Ryokan 沢の屋旅館
Add: 2-3-11, Yanaka, Taito-ku.
Tel: (03) 822-2251.
A 7 minute walk from Nezu Station on the Chiyoda subway line.
Ryokan Sansuiso 旅館山水荘
Add: 2-9-5, Higashi-Gotanda,
Shinagawa-ku.
Tel: (03) 441-7454.
A 5 minute walk from Gotanda Station on the JR Yamanote (Loop) Line.
Suigetsu Hotel 水月ホテル
Add: 3-3-21, Ikenohata, Taito-ku.
Tel: (03) 822-4611.
A 3 minute walk from Nezu Station on the Chiyoda subway line.

Nikko 日光

Nikko is located about 80 miles (128 km.) north of Tokyo. Its excellent reputation as a tourist attraction is well deserved; in just a one-day excursion from Tokyo, visitors can enjoy both the great natural beauty of Lake Chuzenjiko and Kegon-no-Taki Falls, and the impressive cultural artifacts of the magnificent Toshogu Shrine.

Nikko's history as a sacred region began in 782 when the priest Shodo erected Shihonryuji Temple (the original of today's Rinnoji Temple). Shihonryuji prospered as a training center for priests of the Tendai sect, and at its peak the precincts were filled with more than 300 minor temples and other buildings. But the temple went into serious decline when Hideyoshi Toyotomi completed the unification of Japan at the end of the 16th century. Because its congregation had supported his opponent during the civil wars, the great Hideyoshi seized the manors that had been held by the temple. Nikko began to regain the prominence of its glorious past when, at the suggestion of the priest Tenkai, an adviser to the Tokugawas, it was selected in 1617 as the site of the mausoleum of Ieyasu Tokugawa, the first Tokugawa Shogun. Toshogu Shrine was completed in 1636 at the order of the third Shogun, Iemitsu. No expense was spared. It is estimated that the Tokugawas expended the equivalent of 200 million of today's dollars in erecting this memorial. Master artisans, including architects, sculptors and painters all worked together to achieve the splendor of Toshogu Shrine, which is a living memorial to the high artistic standards and achievements of 17th century Japan.

Transportation to Nikko

There are two ways to get to Nikko, either directly by the private Tobu Nikko Line, or on JR (which involves two trains – the Tohoku Shinkansen and the JR Nikko Line). The Tobu Line is more convenient and less costly, and should be your choice unless you have a Japan Rail Pass. Nikko can also be incorporated at the end of a trip to Tohoku.

1. Tobu Nikko Line

The Tobu Nikko Line operates convenient service between Asakusa Station 東武浅草駅 and Tobu-Nikko Station 東武日光駅. Asakusa is easily accessible from most places in Tokyo via the Ginza subway line. The exact location of Asakusa Station is pictured on map 30. The ticket office is located on the first floor of the building and the platforms are on the second floor.

Two types of trains run to Tobu-Nikko: Limited Expresses and Rapid Service Trains. The Limited Express is a specially

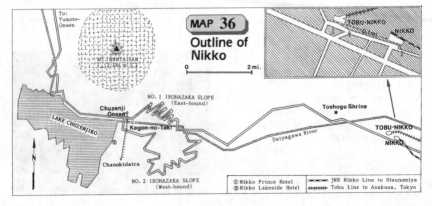

MAP 36
Outline of Nikko
0   2 mi.

To: Yumoto-Onsen
MT. NANTAISAN (2,484 m.)
NO. 1 IROHAZAKA SLOPE (East-bound)
Chuzenji Onsen
Kegon-no-Taki
LAKE CHUZENJIKO
Chanokidaira
NO. 2 IROHAZAKA SLOPE (West-bound)
Toshogu Shrine ★
Daiyagawa River
TOBU-NIKKO
NIKKO

① Nikko Prince Hotel
② Nikko Lakeside Hotel
▬▬▬ JNR Nikko Line to Utsunomiya
╫╫╫╫ Tobu Line to Asakusa, Tokyo

designed deluxe train, and if you want to guarantee yourself a seat you should make advance reservations, especially if you're traveling on a holiday. The Rapid Service Train is a regular commuter train and has only nonreserved seats. The rapid service train is about half of the cost for the Limited Express. See No. 280 for the schedule.

2. Japan Railways

There is no JR direct train to Nikko from Tokyo. The fastest way to reach Nikko by JR is the combination of the Tohoku Shinkansen (No. 3, from Ueno to Utsunomiya 宇都宮駅), and the JR Nikko Line (No. 76, from Utsunomiya to Nikko 日光駅). The JR Nikko Line is a commuter line. All seats are unreserved.

Outline of Nikko

As pictured on map 36, Nikko's major cultural and historical attractions are located about 1.3 miles (2 km.) from the train stations. The area's natural wonders are on the eastern side of the Lake Chuzenjiko. The train stations are at an altitude of about 2,000 feet (600 m.), the surface of the Lake at 4,163 feet (1,269 m.), and Mt. Nantaisan at 8,150 feet (2,484 m.). "Nikko" thus encompasses not only a wide area but also an area with great differences in altitude. To facilitate the flow of traffic on the mountainous roads of the area, special one-way toll roads have been constructed to and from the Lake. The southern road, No. 2 Iroha-zaka Slope, is used for the west-bound traffic up to the lake, while the northern road, No. 1 Irohazaka Slope, is used for the east-bound traffic back down from the lake. "Iroha" is the name of the 48 character Japanese syllabic alphabet. The roads were so named because of the many (but not exactly 48) hairpin curves on the slopes.

Suggested Itinerary
Nikko Station to Chuzenji-Onsen by Bus

Nikko buses have both Japanese and English signs. In order to get to Chuzenji-Onsen 中禅寺温泉 you can take a bus headed for either Chuzenji-Onsen or

Yumoto-Onsen 湯元温泉. At the JR Nikko Station the bus for Chuzenji-Onsen uses stop No. 2, and the bus for Yumoto-Onsen uses stop No. 3. Departure times of the buses are coordinated with the arrival times of the JR Nikko Line trains.

* If you plan to visit only the Toshogu Shrine area, you can also take the bus headed for Nishi-Sando, from stop No. 5. Nishi-Sando stop is pictured at the lower left of map 38.

At Tobu-Nikko Station the bus for Chuzenji-Onsen uses stop No. 2, and the bus for Yumoto-Onsen uses stop No. 1.

* The bus for Nishi-Sando uses stop No. 9.

Because the Tobu Nikko Line trains arrive more frequently than the JR trains, there are more buses out of Tobu-Nikko Station.

Chuzenji-Onsen Area (Map 37)

Chanokidaira 茶ノ木平 (5,308 feet, or 1,618 m.) commands a great view of Lake Chuzenjiko and the 8,200-foot (2,500 m.) high mountains surrounding the Lake. To reach the observatory you take a ropeway from Chuzenji-Onsen (a short 6 minute ride).

A sightseeing boat operates on the Lake every hour from the Boat Pier pictured on map 40. The cruise takes 55 minutes.

The Observatory of Kegon-no-Taki Water Falls 華厳ノ滝展望台 is reached by an elevator, which is only a five-minute walk from Chuzenji-Onsen bus stop. The dynamic 325-foot (99 m.) high water falls are known as the best in Japan. The falls are especially impressive in the spring when the snow melts and the run off from the lake swells the falls far beyond their normal size.

Chuzenji-Onsen to Nishi-Sando

Catch a bus headed for Nikko Station at either Chuzenji-Onsen or Kegon-no-Taki bus stop. These buses run about once every 30 minutes, and the ride to Nishi-Sando 西参道 takes about 30 minutes.

Toshogu Area (Map 38)

Toshogu Shrine, Futarasan Jinja Shrine and Rinnoji Temple (and its Daiyuinbyo) are the attractions in this area. When you purchase an admission ticket, ask for "Nisha-Ichiji-Kyotsuken, (二社一寺共通券)" the combination ticket for all three. With this ticket, you'll have access to most areas of the shrines and the temple, but you'll have to pay additional admission to see some of the special treasures, as explained below.

Daiyuinbyo 大猷院廟 (Upper left)

Daiyuinbyo is the mausoleum of Iemitsu Tokugawa, the third Shogun, who established the strong, isolated-by-choice government that ruled Japan for 250 years. The mausoleum was built in 1653. Compared to the lavish, colorful Toshogu

Shrine, this complex is small and modestly decorated, but it harmonizes beautifully with its natural setting and reflects the careful attention the architects obviously paid to the complex. Most of the buildings are National Treasures or Important Cultural Properties (8:00 AM to 5:00 PM. Till 4:00 PM in winter. The basic ticket gives you access to all the buildings on the grounds of Daiyuinbyo).

Futarasan Jinja Shrine 二荒山神社 (Upper left)

Futarasan Jinja Shrine is only a short walk northeast from Daiyuinbyo. Until Toshogu Shrine was constructed, Futarasan Jinja Shrine, dedicated to the god of Mt. Futarasan (or Mt. Nantaisan), was the center of Shintoism in Nikko for about 800 years. The present main buildings were donated in 1619 by the second Tokugawa Shogun. The old cedar trees that surround the pre-

MAP 37
Lake
Chuzenjiko

0   0.1mi.

To: Yumoto-Onsen

LAKE CHUZENJIKO

Sightseeing Boat

To: Chanokidaira

KEGON-NO-TAKI

CHUZENJI ONSEN

Kegon-no-Taki Water Falls

Ropeway

Elevator

OBSERVATORY

To: Nikko

From: Nikko

cincts contribute to the sacred and solemn atmosphere of the Shrine (8:00 AM to 5:00 PM. Till 4:00 PM in winter. The basic ticket gives you access to all the buildings in the precincts).

Toshogu Shrine Treasure House 東照宮宝物館 (Middle center)

The Treasure House contains about 250 artistic and historical objects, of which approximately 60 – 70 are displayed in turn. The treasures include samurai armor, swords, paintings, portraits of Tokugawa shoguns, etc. (9:00 AM to 4:30 PM. Till 4:00 PM in winter. Admission 300 yen).

Toshogu Shrine 東照宮 (Upper center)

Passing under a huge torii gate on the Omote-Sando Path, you will see Five-Story Pagoda on your left. The original was destroyed by fire and the present pagoda was built in 1818. Omotemon Gate is the main and the only entrance to the Shrine. Two Deva Kings stand in the niches at the sides of the vermilion gate. The 66 carvings on the Gate presage what is waiting inside the precincts.

Three buildings on the right hand side of the path are warehouses for the costumes and equipment used each spring and fall for the Festival of the Procession of the Warriors (May 18 and October 17). On the walls of Kami-Jinko are two rather strange carvings of elephants. When Tanyu Kano, a master painter of the Kano School, drew the original design, there were no elephants in Japan; he had only read about them. Walls of the Shinkyusha (Stable for Sacred Horses) feature eight carvings that depict the life of monkeys (as an allegory of human existence). The second scene is the famous "hear-no-evil, see-no-evil, speak-no-evil" monkeys. Passing through the torii gate, you will see Yomeimon Gate (National Treasure) at the top of the stone steps. The 36-foot (11 m.) tall gate is entirely covered with innumerable (actually more than 400) carvings painted brilliant shades of gold, vermilion, blue, and green. Corridors (National Treasures) stretch in both directions from Yomeimon Gate and surround the main buildings (National Treasures). On the western side of the Yomeimon Gate is Honchido Hall, which is famous for the dragon painting on its ceiling. The original building was lost to fire in

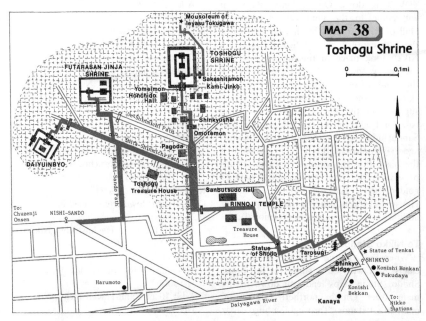

1961 and the present one was completed in 1963. The dragon was painted from the original design by Nampu Katayama, a modern master. If you clap your hands under the head of the dragon, the resulting echo is said to sound like the sound of the dragon roaring (An additional 200 yen admission is required). Each of the main buildings boasts of its own carvings; especially famous is the Sleeping Cat (very small) in the East Corridor. You can see it on the upper left hand side as you cross the East Corridor toward Sakashitamon Gate. The mausoleum of Ieyasu Tokugawa is located to the north of Toshogu Shrine at the end of the long stone stairway (An additional 300 yen is collected at Sakashitamon Gate).

Rinnoji Temple 輪王寺 (Lower center)

Walking down Omote-Sando Path you will come to the impressive Sanbutsudo Hall of Rinnoji Temple on your left. Until the 17th century, most religious activity in Nikko took place in this temple. Though the glory days of the temple, when thousands of priests were housed in its precincts, vanished with Hideyoshi Toyotomi's suppression, the temple still plays a leading role for Buddhism in the Nikko area. The Sanbutsudo Hall contains three Buddha images (Entrance to this Hall is included in the basic ticket). Sorinto Tower is an impressive golden structure decorated with 24 golden bells. Entrance to the Treasure House and the attached garden requires an additional 300 yen admission (optional).

To Nikko Station

When you emerge from the temple precincts, you will see a statue of the priest Shodo. Stone steps lead you down to the main street. On the northern side of the main street stands "Tarosugi," a huge cedar

tree. Several years ago the Ministry of Construction insisted that Tarosugi be cut down in order to facilitate the flow of traffic, and this venerable giant was spared only after a long court battle between the Temple and the Ministry. As you cross Daiyagawa River, look to your right to see the "Shinkyo" (Sacred Bridge). On the other side of the Daiyagawa River stands a statue of the priest Tenkai. The stop for buses to Nikko Station is in front of Konishi Hotel Honkan. Most buses go to Tobu-Nikko Station first, and then to the JR Station. Some of them terminate at Tobu-Nikko Station, but the JR Station is only a few minutes walk from Tobu Station.

Accommodations in Nikko
1. Hotels

Nikko Kanaya Hotel 日光金谷ホテル
   (First-class: lower right, map 38.
   85 rooms)
   Add: 1300, Kami-Hachiishicho, Nikko.
   Tel: (0288) 54-0001.
Nikko Prince Hotel 日光プリンスホテル
   (First-class: 78 rooms. On the northern
   shore of Lake Chuzenjiko).
   Add: 2485, Chugushi, Nikko.
   Tel: (0288) 55-0661.
Nikko Lakeside Hotel
   日光レークサイドホテル
   (First-class: 100 rooms. On the northern
   shore of Lake Chuzenjiko).
   Add: 2482, Chugushi, Nikko.
   Tel: (0288) 55-0321.

2. Ryokans

Harumoto 春茂登
   (Standard: lower left, map 38. 22 rooms)
   Add: 5-13, Yasukawacho, Nikko.
   Tel: (0288) 54-1133.
Konishi Bekkan 小西別館
   (Standard: lower right, map 38.
   24 rooms)
   Add: 1115, Kami-Hachiishicho, Nikko.
   Tel: (0288) 54-1105.
Fukudaya 福田屋
   (Standard: lower right, map 38,
   31 rooms)
   Add: 1036, Kami-Hachiishicho, Nikko.
   Tel: (0288) 54-0389.

Mashiko 益子

Mashiko-yaki pottery dates back to the Nara Era (the 8th century). The modern success of *Mashiko-yaki* began in 1853 when Keizaburo Otsuka started production of everyday potteryware in this small town. *Mashiko-yaki* was elevated to the level of art by Shoji Hamada, and was introduced worldwide by Bernard Leach, an English potter. More than 150 kilns are located in the peaceful farm town of Mashiko (Many of them are indicated by stars on the map.)

Transportation to Mashiko

You can take the Tohoku Shinkansen (No. 3), or the JR Tohoku Line's commuter train (frequent operation) from Tokyo's Ueno Station to Oyama. Then the JR Mito Line (No. 74) from Oyama to Shimodate, and the JR Mooka Line (No. 75) from Shimodate to Mashiko. There are several direct trains from Oyama to Mashiko daily. There is also bus service between Mashiko Station and Utsunomiya Station. If you plan to travel to Nikko after your visit to Mashiko, this bus line provides very convenient connections.

Kyohan Center 共販センター

(Middle right, map 39)

This large complex is operated jointly by the Mashiko potters. It functions not only as a shop but also as a museum, displaying both old and contemporary products of Mashiko.

Mashiko Sankokan Museum 益子参考館

(Upper right, map 39)

This is the workshop where Shoji Hamada devoted his life to developing *Mashiko-yaki* into one of the most popular artistic potteries. This warehouse converted into a museum displays his art works as well as photographs introducing his life. Mr. Hamada was designated a Living National Treasure. All the displays have English explanations.

Ryokan in Mashiko

Mashiko Nanmaso 益子南間荘

(Standard: outside of the map; 10 minutes by taxi from Mashiko Station)
Add: 4264, Mashiko, Tochigi Pref.
Tel: (02857) 2-5155.

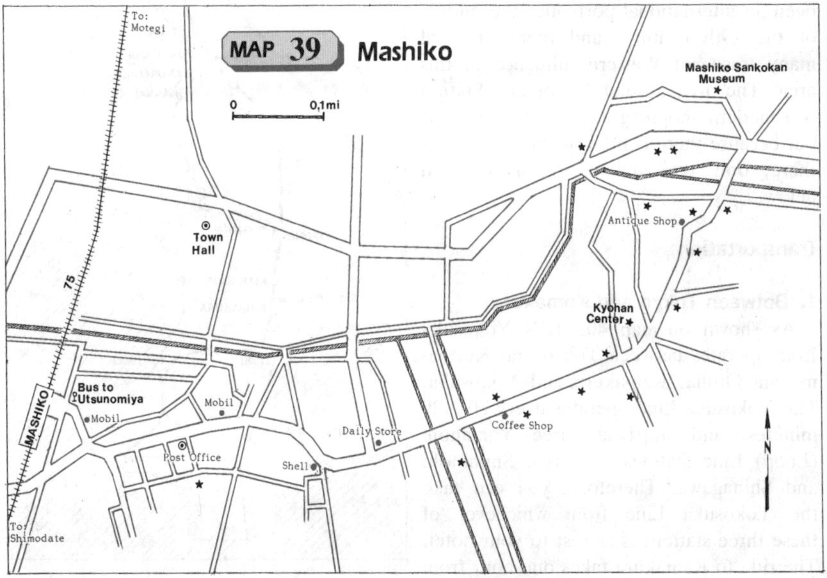

Kamakura & Yokohama 鎌倉，横浜

Outline of the Area

As pictured on map 40, Kamakura (lower left) is located about 30 miles (48 km.) southwest of Tokyo. Foreign tour groups usually skip this city or visit only the Great Buddha. But Kamakura is definitely worth exploring, and has much more to offer visitors. This once prosperous feudal city is on a direct train line from Tokyo and is an ideal day excursion from the capital.

Yokohama is included here as an additional destination for those who stay in Tokyo for a longer period. Located between Tokyo and Kamakura, Yokohama stretches northeast to southwest, with Tsurumi Station (middle center) at the northeastern end of the city, and Hongodai (lower center) at its southwestern border. The center of the city, both geographically and functionally, is the area around Yokohama, Sakuragicho and Kannai stations. With a population of 3,001,000, Yokohama is Japan's second largest city – larger than Osaka, Nagoya and Kyoto. Kannai has been an international port since the middle of the 19th century, and there are still many traces of Western influence in this area. The area around Yokohama Station is a modern shopping and business district, but because there is little of special interest there, only the Kannai area is detailed below.

Transportation

1. Between Tokyo and Kamakura

As shown on map 40, JR's Yokosuka Line operates between Tokyo and Kurihama via Ofuna, Kamakura and Yokosuka. The Yokosuka Line operates every 10 – 20 minutes, and stops at three Yamanote (Loop) Line stations – Tokyo, Shimbashi and Shinagawa. Therefore, you can take the Yokosuka Line from whichever of these three stations is closest to your hotel. The ride to Kamakura takes one hour from Tokyo, 57 minutes from Shimbashi, and 50 minutes from Shinagawa.

There are two important stations in Kamakura, Kamakura 鎌倉駅 and Kita-Kamakura 北鎌倉駅. Before you get on the train decide what your first destination will be so you'll know which of these stations you want. You can use your Rail Pass if you have one.

MAP 40
Outline of Kamakura/ Yokohama

—— JR YOKOSUKA LINE
—— JR KEIHIN–TOHOKU LINE
———— JR YAMANOTE (LOOP) LINE
—— JR SHINKANSEN

0   5mi

Tabata
Ueno
Tokyo
TOKYO
SHIMBASHI
SHINAGAWA
SHIN-YOKOHAMA
Tsurumi
Yokohama
YOKOHAMA
SAKURAGICHO
KANNAI
TOKYO BAY
OFUNA
Hongodai
KITA-KAMAKURA
Kamakura
KAMAKURA
Zushi
Yokosuka
SAGAMI BAY
Kurihama

On the way to Kamakura, you can see an 82-foot (25 m.) tall Kannon (Goddess of Mercy) statue from the right-hand side of the train on a hill near Ofuna Station. As the train leaves the station, look back to get a good look at her merciful face.

2. In Kamakura

Kamakura's major temples and shrines are located between Kita-Kamakura and Kamakura. A walking tour is the ideal way to visit these places.

The Great Buddha and Hasedera Temple are located near Hase Station 長谷駅 (lower left, map 41) on the Enoden (the *Eno*shima *Den*tetsu) Line. This line originates at Kamakura Station; Hase is the third stop, and the ride from Kamakura takes only five minutes. You cannot use a Rail Pass on this line.

3. Between Tokyo and Kannai

JR's blue colored commuter line between Omiya (to the north of Tokyo, outside of map 40), and Yokohama is called the Keihin-Tohoku Line, and the Negishi commuter line runs from Yokohama further south to Ofuna. Though the names of the lines are different, most of the trains from the Tokyo area run through Ofuna via Yokohama and Kannai 関内駅. In Tokyo, the Keihin-Tohoku Line runs parallel to the Yamanote (Loop) Line at the 14 major stations located between Tabata and Shinagawa. The Keihin-Tohoku Line operates every 2 – 10 minutes. The ride from Tokyo takes 50 minutes to Kannai. You can use your Japan Rail Pass. Some trains terminate at stations along the way. If this happens, just wait for a few minutes for the next train going in the same direction.

4. Between Kamakura and Kannai

If your time is limited, it is a good idea to visit Kannai on your way back to Tokyo from Kamakura and enjoy authentic Western or Chinese cuisine in this international port area. The ride on the Yokosuka Line from Kamakura to Ofuna takes only 7 minutes. The Keihin-Tohoku (Negishi) Line will take you from Ofuna to Kannai in another 27 minutes.

Kamakura
鎌倉

The first military government in Japanese history was established in Kamakura by Shogun Yoritomo Minamoto in 1192. Before the Minamoto family seized control of the country, the Taira family, another powerful military clan (which the Minamoto destroyed) had already played an influential role in the imperial government in Kyoto. The Minamotos made history by establishing a government independent, both geographically and structurally, from Kyoto. The second and the third Minamoto shoguns were assassinated, and political power shifted to the family of Yoritomo's wife, the Hojos. Succeeding generations of the Hojo family installed puppet shoguns, reserving for themselves the powerful office of regent. The military government of Kamakura lasted until 1333. During these 141 years, Kamakura prospered as Japan's political, economic, cultural and religious center. Zen Buddhism was especially popular among the samurai class, and flourished here in the stronghold of the Shoguns.

Japan was attacked by the forces of the Yuan Dynasty of China twice, in 1274, and again in 1281. The Kamakura government, led by Regent Tokimune Hojo, successfully defeated the Mongolian invaders, thanks in part to fortuitous typhoons (Kamikaze, or Divine Wind), but these wars caused the Kamakura Shogunate great financial difficulties. The local lords whose military support had made the victories possible expected recognition, gratitude and hard cash in return for their contributions, and felt that the Shogunate was not supplying any of them. Emperor Godaigo capitalized on this situation, rallying these dissatisfied lords to his cause. With their support the imperial forces defeated the Kamakura forces and the Emperor was restored to political power in 1333. The Emperor's ascendancy was, however, very short lived, and in 1336, the Ashikaga family seized power and established a new Shogunate.

After the fall of the Hojos, Kamakura

never reappeared on the historical scene. It remained a sleepy temple town with agriculture and fishing its only industries. Since World War II it has become a high-class residential district. Its many carefully preserved cultural relics testify to the glory the

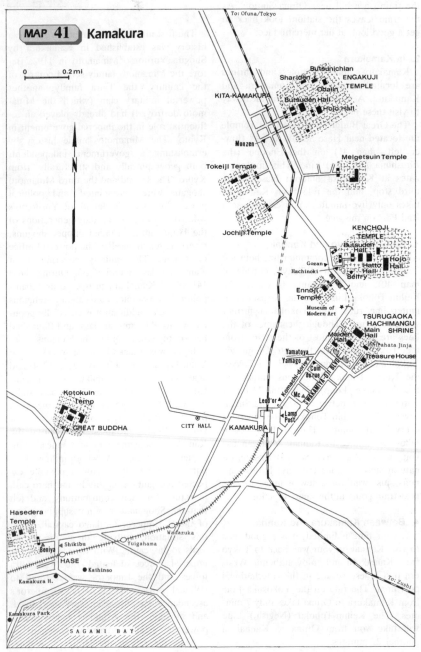

MAP 41   Kamakura

0   0.2 mi

To: Ofuna/Tokyo

Shariden   Butsunichian
KITA-KAMAKURA   Obaiin   ENGAKUJI TEMPLE
Butsuden Hall
Hojo Hall

Monzen

Meigetsuin Temple

Tokeiji Temple

Jochiji Temple

KENCHOJI TEMPLE
Butsuden Hall
Gozan   Hatto Hall   Hojo Hall
Hachinoki   Belfry

Ennoji Temple

Museum of Modern Art

TSURUGAOKA HACHIMANGU SHRINE
Main Hall
Maiden Hall   Shirahata Jinja
Treasure House

Yamatoya
Yamago   Komachi-dori
Coin de rue

Kotokuin Temp   Leud'or   Mc

GREAT BUDDHA   CITY HALL   Lamp Post   KAMAKURA

Hasedera Temple

Beniya   Shikibu   Yuigahama   Wadazuka
HASE

Kaihinso

Kamakura H.

To: Zushi

Kamakura Park

SAGAMI BAY

area enjoyed in the medieval era.

Suggested Itinerary

The full day walking tour starts from Kita-Kamakura Station as explained below. If you want to see just the highlights of Kamakura, take a train to Kamakura Station and visit Tsurugaoka Hachimangu Shrine, Hasedera Temple, and finally the Great Buddha.

Engakuji Temple 円覚寺 (Upper right, map 41)

Engakuji Temple was built in 1282 to honor the victims of the wars against the Mongolian invaders. In the Kamakura of the time, Engakuji was second in importance only to Kenchoji Temple, and, at the peak of its prosperity, its precincts contained more than 50 minor temples and other buildings. Even though most of the original buildings were lost in fires, the reconstructions preserve the atmosphere of a powerful Zen temple. What might be the original Shariden Hall (National Treasure) still stands, and is Engakuji's most important historical relic. You can't go through the gate in front of Shariden, but you can get a glimpse of part of this famous building. The garden of Butsunichian and Obaiin are open to the public. Obaiin is the mausoleum of Tokimune Hojo and has a well maintained garden located at the foot of a steep cliff. Japanese powdered tea is served in the garden of Butsunichian (350 yen, including a 100-yen admission). If you are interested in tasting real Japanese tea ceremony tea (it's green and bitter!), Butsunichian is a good place to enjoy it in a casual atmosphere. The entrance to Butsunichian is a small wooden door (Don't hit your head!). The precincts of Engakuji Temple are open to the public from 8:00 AM to 5:00 PM. Admission is 100 yen.

Tokeiji Temple 東慶寺 (Middle center)

Tokeiji Temple was a nunnery until the Meiji Restoration, and was popularly known as the "Divorce Temple." In the feudal era, women were not allowed to initiate divorces, no matter how cruel their husbands. A special law promulgated by the wife of Tokimune Hojo designated Tokeiji Temple as the place where unhappily married women could seek refuge as a last resort. Once a woman escaped into the precincts, no one was allowed to remove her. The temple still has a bit of the delicate atmosphere of a nunnery, and the precincts are filled with the flowers of the season (8:30 AM to 5:00 PM. Admission 50 yen). The Treasure House in the temple's precincts is open from 10:00 AM to 3:00 PM (Closed on Mondays). The admission is 300 yen.

Jochiji Temple 浄知寺 (Upper center, optional)

Kamakura-kaido Street is the main road connecting Kita-Kamakura and Kamakura. The traffic is always heavy and there's only a narrow sidewalk – be careful!

The entrance to Jochiji Temple is at the top of a long moss-covered stone stairway. The unique gate houses a temple bell on its second floor. All the temple's magnificent original buildings were destroyed by fires over the course of history, and the present buildings were constructed about 50 years ago. There is a neatly trimmed garden behind the Main Hall. Statues of the Seven Gods of Fortune stand at the northern end of the precincts (9:00 AM to 4:30 PM. Admission 100 yen).

Meigetsuin Temple 明月院 (Upper right, optional)

Meigetsuin Temple is known as the Temple of Hydrangeas because of the thousands of these bushes in its grounds. It is especially beautiful in June when they are all in bloom. Japanese find them particularly appealing in the rain, which is fortunate since the rainy season begins in mid-June. Thousands visit Kamakura just to see the hydrangeas in bloom. Even though Meigetsuin Temple is bit off the walking tour route, we recommend that you visit here if you are in Japan in June (8:30 AM to 5:00 PM. Admission 100 yen).

Kenchoji Temple 建長寺 (Middle right)

Kenchoji, erected in 1253 as a training center for Zen priests, is the most important Zen temple in Kamakura. At the peak of its prosperity, the grounds contained more than 50 buildings, but all the original buildings were lost in successive fires. The present reconstructions were based on the original models. The bronze bell in the belfry near Sanmon Gate is a National Treasure. The precincts are in complete harmony with nature and are filled with the solemn atmosphere of Zen Buddhism. The huge buildings, arranged in a straight line and surrounded by a thick pine forest, are on a grand scale that helps one imagine how magnificent Kamakura must have been when the Shoguns ruled from here (8:30 AM to 4:30 PM. Admission 200 yen).

Ennoji Temple 円応寺 (Middle right, optional)

Steep narrow stone steps set between stone walls lead to the gate of Ennoji Temple, which is also known as "Temple of the Ten Kings of Heaven." In the Kamakura era people believed that Ten Kings of Heaven sat in judgment on all souls after death, admitting them to heaven or damning them to hell. Wooden statues of these Kings are housed in this small temple. Unless you are especially interested in sculpture, you should skip this temple (9:00 AM to 5:00 PM. Admission 100 yen).

Tsurugaoka Hachimangu Shrine 鶴が岡 八幡宮 (Middle right)

Passing under the covered portion of the road, the street turns right, and you will see the modern Kanagawa Prefecture Museum of Modern Art. The slow downward slope leads to the back gate of Tsurugaoka Hachimangu Shrine. The long flight of stone steps that begins at the torii gate leads you to the highest point of the precincts and the Main Hall. The Shrine was built in 1180 at the order of Yoritomo Minamoto, the first Kamakura Shogun. It is especially popular among Japanese because it is associated with the tragic story of two brothers of the Minamoto family, Yoritomo and his younger brother, Yoshitsune, who are both credited with establishing the Kamakura Shogunate. As a matter of fact, Yoritomo did not participate in

even one of the clashes with the Tairas, and Yoshitsune fought all the battles. However, once the Minamoto forces had triumphed, it was Yoritomo, as the elder brother, who would, in the normal course of events, have assumed all the power won through the military clashes. To keep Yoritomo from exercising what would have been, in effect, absolute power over the entire nation, supporters of the imperial court in Kyoto moved to destabilize the situation by maneuvering to have Yoshitsune appointed to high office. Learning of this plot, Yoritomo sent retainers to Kyoto to assassinate his younger brother. Yoshitsune managed to escape from Kyoto and took refuge in Hiraizumi, which was governed by the Fujiwara family. But Yoshitsune's lover, Shizu, was arrested by Yoritomo's force and taken to Kamakura. Because she had been a famous dancing girl when she met Yoshitsune, Yoritomo ordered Shizu to entertain him and his wife. Enduring the humiliation involved, Shizu made the forced performance an emotional expression of her love for Yoshitsune and her anxiety about his fate in his remote exile. Maiden Hall, located at the foot of the stone steps to the Main Hall, is where Shizu danced 800 years ago. Incidentally, Yoshitsune and the Fujiwaras were destroyed by forces dispatched from Kamakura in 1189; with this there remained no challengers to Yoritomo, who established the Kamakura Shogunate. Shirahata Jinja Shrine, also located here, was built to honor Yoritomo and Sanetomo, the first and the third Kamakura Shoguns. The Treasure House displays artistic and historical objects related to Zen Buddhism (9:00 AM to 4:00 PM. Closed on Mondays. Admission 150 yen).

Kamakura Station and Vicinity

Wakamiya-oji Boulevard 若宮大路 leads to Tsurugaoka Hachimangu Shrine from Kamakura Station. In the stretch that runs between the two huge torii gates, one at the southern end of the Shrine precincts and the other near McDonald's, a pedestrian path runs in the central part of the boulevard. Cherry trees on both sides of the path make this approach to the Shrine especially beautiful in early April when the pale pink flowers are in bloom. During the New Year's Holidays the boulevard is thronged with visitors because millions of Japanese visit this Shrine to make their New Year's Resolutions. There are many souvenir shops and restaurants along the boulevard. Komachi-dori Street 小町通り runs to the west of Wakamiya-oji Boulevard. This street represents the modern face of Kamakura with many (perhaps too many) Western restaurants, souvenir shops, coffee shops and boutiques.

To Hase

The Enoden Line's Kamakura station is at the western side of the JR station. It is easier to find the ticket vending machines and the entrance if you go around the JR station.

Hasedera Temple 長谷寺 (Lower right)

The first thing you see upon entering the precincts of Hasedera Temple is a lovely garden. Stone steps lead to the main grounds of the temple. On the way, you will see hundreds of small stone images of Jizobosatsu (God of Travelers and Children). The colorful pinwheels attached to each image were placed there by grieving parents of stillborn babies and children who died young. Unlike most temples in Kamakura, which open their precincts but not their interior halls to the public, Hasedera Temple allows visitors inside both its Amida Hall and Kannon Hall. After looking at just the exteriors of temple buildings, the encounters you will have here with the images of many Buddhas and other Gods is very impressive. Especially important is the 30-foot (9 m.) tall Eleven-Faced Kannon housed in Kannon Hall. This golden image was carved in 721 and is the tallest wooden statue in Japan. Another group of stone Jizobosatsu images stands at the western end of the grounds. One more attraction of this temple is the marvelous view of Sagami Bay from the southern part of the grounds (7:00 AM to 5:40 PM. Admission 100 yen).

Great Buddha 鎌倉大仏 (Middle left)

The Great Buddha, the main object of worship at Kotokuin Temple 高徳院 , is popular world-wide, and attracts visitors all year round. The 37-foot (11.3 m.) tall bronze image was cast in 1252. It is Japan's second largest statue (The largest is the Great Buddha of Todaiji Temple in Nara). This Buddha was originally housed in a wooden hall, which was swept away by a tidal wave in 1495. Since then the Buddha has sat in the open air. There's an entrance to the interior of the statue at the right side of its base (as you face the Buddha). Steep ladders go up to a small window at the top of the back of the statue (Additional 20 yen) (7:00 AM to 5:45 PM. Admission 100 yen).

To Kamakura Station

A bus to Kamakura Station stops right in front of the grounds of the Great Buddha. Be sure to take a *seiri-ken* ticket when you get on the bus. You can also walk back to Hase Station and take an Enoden train to Kamakura.

Restaurants

Monzen, near Tokeiji Temple (middle center), and **Hachinoki,** near Kenchoji Temple (middle right), serve authentic Japanese lunches (moderate). **Coin de rue** on Komachi-dori Street (middle center) is a famous French restaurant (moderate). **Gozan**, near Kenchoji Temple, is a coffee shop.

Souvenir Shops

Yamago on Komachi-dori Street (middle center) deals in bamboo handicrafts. A number of souvenir shops on Wakamiya-oji Boulevard have good inventories of *Kamakura-bori*, a special Kamakura craft. (Carved wooden items lacquered and relacquered many times in either black or vermilion). **Yamatoya** on Komachi-dori Street sells various handicraft items. **Shikibu** near Hase Station (lower left) is known for its Japanese dolls and antiques. **Objects of Art Beniya** near Hasedera Temple (lower left) is an authentic antique store.

Yokohama (Kannai)

横浜(関内)

In the feudal era Yokohama was a small farming and fishing village. In the middle of the 19th century, when the Tokugawa Shogunate reluctantly abandoned its policy of isolation and opened several Japanese ports to Western traders, Yokohama was selected as one of them. At that time nearby Kanagawa (middle center, map 42) was the main port in the area, but it was too busy a place for the authorities to be able to adequately protect the Western traders against assassins, so the Shogunate had a new port constructed at Yokohama, which was a rather isolated place. Yokohama was the only place the western traders were allowed to live and work. Moats were constructed to make the area unassailable, and check-points were set up on all the bridges to prevent the fanatics who wanted no foreigners in the country from entering the compound. The area inside the moats was Kannai (Inside the Checkpoints), while the rest of the area was called Kangai (Outside the Checkpoints). After the Meiji Restoration, the new imperial government emphasized international trade. Yokohama grew rapidly and became Japan's largest port. Kannai became the center of the new city. Once Yokohama was opened to the traders, many Chinese also took up residence in the city and today part of Kannai is a bustling Chinatown. Kannai is a living display of Japanese, Western and Chinese cultures, and has an exotic and rather cosmopolitan air quite different from that of other Japanese cities.

Walking Tour in Kannai

The sidewalks along Bashamichi Street 馬車道 are paved with bricks, which is very unusual in Japan, and the buildings still have the atmosphere of the late 19th and early 20th centuries, when Japan first embraced Westernization. Kanagawa Prefectural Museum 神奈川県立博物館 , a Western style building with a domed top, is on the left side of Bashamichi Street (upper left, map 43). The first floor of the Museum features nature displays, the second floor archaeology, and the third sculptures and paintings of medieval and modern times.

In 1854, Japan ended its more than 200 year long period of isolation by signing its first treaty of friendship with the United States. A monument commemorating the signing of this important document is near the Silk Center (upper center). The Silk Museum, シルク博物館 located on the second and third floors of the Silk Center Building, has displays that explain the silk production process. Fine silk products are also displayed here (9:00 AM to 4:30 PM).

Yamashita-Koen Park 山下公園 is a green oasis for urbanites. In the center of the park are water fountains and a Statue of the Goddess of Water presented to Yokohama by San Diego, its sister city. The Marine Tower マリンタワー (348 feet,

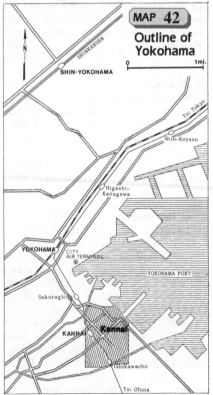

MAP 42

Outline of Yokohama

0 _____ 1mi.

SHINKANSEN

N

SHIN-YOKOHAMA

To: Tokyo

Shin-Koyasu

Higashi-Kanagawa

YOKOHAMA

CITY AIR TERMINAL

YOKOHAMA PORT

Sakuragicho

KANNAI · Kannai

Ishikawacho

To: Ofuna

or 106 m. tall) was built to commemorate the 100th anniversary of the opening of Yokohama Port. Its Observatory is at an altitude of 328 feet (100 m.). If the weather permits, visitors can enjoy panoramic view in all directions, even as far as Mt. Fuji (10:00 AM to 7:30 PM. Till 8:00 PM in summer and till 6:00 PM in winter).

Chinatown 中華街

Chinatown starts at East Gate and stretches to North Gate via Hairomon Gate. About 100 Chinese restaurants are located along the main street and the alleys and lanes that branch off from it.

Restaurants in Kannai

The following are restaurants with good reputations for authentic international cuisines. You can have a good dinner at around 3,000 yen.

Western Food

Scandia is a Scandinavian restaurant; **Hofbrau** is a German beer hall restaurant (both of them are pictured in the upper center). **Rome Station** (middle right) specializes in Italian food. **Bashamichi Jubankan** (upper left) is a red brick building. The first floor is a coffee shop, the second an English-style bar, and the third a grill. The grill is a little more expensive than the other three restaurants listed above.

Chinese Food

You can pick any one of the hundreds of restaurants in Chinatown. The following have good reputations: **Kaihokaku, Minyan, Tung Fat, Chungking,** and **Tonkoh** (all of them are pictured on map 43).

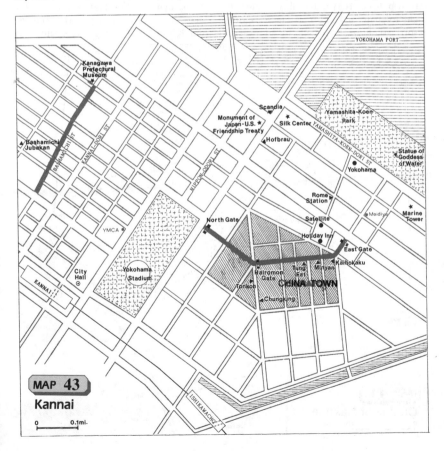

MAP **43**

Kannai

0   0.1mi.

Hakone 箱根

Hakone is a National Park and mountain resort about 50 miles (80 km.) southwest of Tokyo. Volcanic activity is responsible for the area's beautiful, complex topography. The many "hells" emitting steam and sulphur fumes found amid the 4,300-foot (1,300 m.) tall mountains testify to the great geological forces still at work underfoot. The calm surface of Lake Ashinoko reflects the symmetrical figure of Mt. Fuji as it rises to 12,399 feet (3,776 m.) northwest of the Lake. Japanese think this is one of the world's most beautiful natural sights; we're sure you'll agree. Hakone is easily a day trip from Tokyo, but if you have a night to spare and linger in this hotspring resort, you'll treat yourself to an experience you won't soon forget.

Transportation

The usual gateway to Hakone is Odawara (middle right, map 44). Odawara is easily accessible from Tokyo by the JR Shinkansen (Tokyo Station) or the Odakyu Line (Shinjuku Station).

1. Shinkansen

The "Kodama" Shinkansen stops at Odawara Station 小田原駅 (The "Hikari" does not). Odawara is the second stop from Tokyo. The ride from Tokyo Station takes only 42 minutes. You also have to use the "Kodama" Shinkansen if you visit Hakone from Kyoto, or if you go to Kyoto after

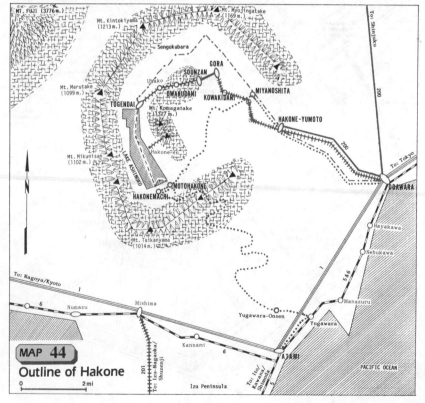

MAP 44
Outline of Hakone

0   2 mi

your visit to Hakone. The ride from Odawara to Kyoto takes about 3 hours. See No. 1 for the Shinkansen schedules.

2. Odakyu Line

This private railway operates frequent service between Shinjuku Station (in Tokyo) and Odawara Station, including a special limited express train called the "Romance Car," which features attendants and luxurious seating. Most Romance Cars go beyond Odawara, to Hakone-Yumoto Station 箱根湯本駅 (upper right, map 44), but some terminate at Odawara. Because Hakone-Yumoto is on the (private) Hakone Tozan Tetsudo Line, which originates at Odawara Station, and which you will use for transportation within the Hakone area, you can get off at either Odawara or Hakone-Yumoto. See No. 200 for the schedule of major "Romance Cars."

Tickets for the Romance Cars are only for reserved seats. If there are no seats available on the Romance Cars (though it's very rare), you can take one of Odakyu's regular express trains. These are designed to serve commuters and operate about once every 30 minutes. The ride to Odawara Station takes about 1 hour and 50 minutes. All the express trains terminate at Odawara Station. If you intend to return to Tokyo on the Romance Car, you should purchase your return ticket before you leave Shinjuku.

3. Transportation in Hakone

The most exciting way to reach Lake Ashinoko is to use the Hakone Tozan Tetsudo Line from Odawara to Gora, a cable car from Gora to Sounzan and a ropeway from Sounzan to Togendai. If you go this way, you can visit the Open-Air Museum and Owakudani "Hell" on the way to the Lake. Unless you are really afraid of heights and ropeways, we definitely recommend that you follow this route.

If you don't want to take the 2.5 mile (4 km.) ropeway trip between Sounzan and Togendai, your alternative is to take a bus from Odawara to Togendai via Sengokubara (the bus route is indicated on map 44). The bus terminal at Odawara Station is in front of the south (main) exit. Use the underground passage to reach the bus terminal. The bus to Togendai operates from stop No. 4 every 15 – 20 minutes. Stop No. 3 is for the bus to Hakone-machi, at the southern side of Lake Ashinoko; it operates every 10 – 15 minutes. As pictured on map 44, these two buses run on the same route until they get to Miyanoshita, then branch off, one to the north and one to the south. From Togendai you can take a boat to Hakone-machi, and then take a bus back to Odawara via Hakone-Yumoto.

Suggested Itinerary

Odawara to the Open-Air Museum by Train

The Hakone Tozan Tetsudo Line operates about once every 20 minutes. After leaving Hakone-Yumoto Station, the mountain train climbs up hills switch backing three times on the way. The famous accommodations, Fujiya Hotel and Naraya Ryokan, are near Miyanoshita Station. Your first stop is Chokokunomori Station 彫刻の森駅 (upper right, map 45). The Hakone Open-Air Museum is only a few minutes walk from the station. If you are not interested in the museum, you can take the train directly to Gora Station, the next stop after Chokokunomori and the last stop on the line. The ride to Chokokunomori takes about 50 minutes from Odawara and about 35 minutes from Hakone-Yumoto.

The Hakone Open-Air Museum 彫刻の森美術館 displays many fine works of contemporary Japanese and Western sculpture

in a spacious open-air setting. An indoor exhibition hall features paintings and sculptures of Picasso, Takamura, etc. Harmoniously matched to its natural surroundings, the Museum attracts hundreds of thousands of visitors every year (Open year round. 9:00 AM to 5:00 PM. Till 4:00 PM in winter. Admission 1,000 yen).

Gora 強羅 (Upper right, map 45)

Gora is located at an altitude of 2,000 feet (600 m.), on the eastern slope of Mt. Sounzan (3,730 feet or 1,137 m. above sea level). If you are staying the night in Hakone, the following are optional sightseeing destinations in the Gora area:

Gora-Koen Park 強羅公園 is a French-style rock garden. The Park also contains the Hakone Natural Museum, the Alpine Botanical Garden and the Tropical Bird House (Open year round. 9:00 AM to 5:00 PM. Till 9:00 PM in summer).

Hakone Museum 箱根美術館 displays many priceless Japanese, Chinese and Korean ceramic and porcelain masterpieces. The museum's garden is also famous for its refined design (9:00 AM to 4:00 PM. Closed on Thursdays).

Gora to Sounzan 早雲山 by Cable Car

The cable car station is in the same building as the train station. The cable car operates every 15 minutes, and the ride to Sounzan takes 9 minutes. There are four intermediate stations – Koen-shimo, Koen-kami, Naka-Gora and Kami-Gora. With a through ticket from Gora to Sounzan you can stop over at any one of them. For example, Hakone Museum, mentioned above, is only a one-minute walk from Koen-kami Station.

Sounzan to Owakudani 大湧谷 by Ropeway

Small cabins, each with a capacity of only 12 persons, operate at one minute intervals from 9:30 AM to 4:00 PM between Sounzan and Togendai, a distance of 2.5 miles (4 km.). There are two intermediate stations – Owakudani and Ubako. If you have a through ticket, you're allowed to stop over at an intermediate station. The ride takes 10 minutes from Sounzan to Owakudani, and an additional 25 minutes from Owakudani to Togendai. If you want to get off the ropeway at Owakudani Station (and we recommend that you do), sig-

nal to the station employee, who will open the cabin door from the outside. The highlight of the ropeway ride is when it passes over Owakudani Valley just before it arrives at the Owakudani Station. Far below you can see steam escaping from the rug-

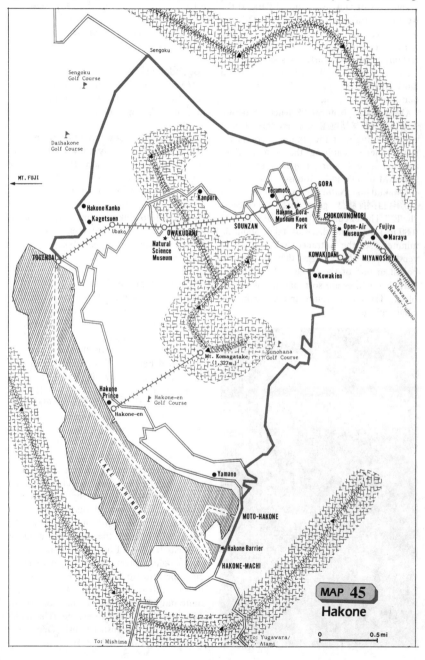

MAP 45
Hakone

0   0.5mi

ged mountains.

The second floor of the Owakudani Station houses a restaurant which commands a grand view of Hakone National Park. If the weather permits, you can see Mt. Fuji rising above the lower mountains to the northwest. Unfortunately, the menu of the restaurant is not nearly as special as the view. But because the 1,000 – 1,500 yen lunch includes the view, it has to be classified as a real bargain.

Owakudani Natural Science Museum 大湧谷自然科学博物館 , a modern three-story building near the station, displays various objects featuring the history, flora and fauna of Hakone (Open year round. 9:00 AM to 5:00 PM. Admission 300 yen).

Owakudani Natural Exploration Path 大湧谷自然探勝路 goes through volcanic "hells." The circular path is about 0.4 miles (680 m.) long, and the walk takes about 30 minutes. At the entrance to the Path, a vendor sells black eggs that have been boiled in one of the "hells": the yolks are hard, the whites are soft, and the shells are black. Try one if you're interested in volcanic cuisine.

Owakudani to Togendai by Ropeway

Continue your ride to Togendai via the ropeway. Because Owakudani is the highest point on the route, the cabin descends slowly toward Lake Ashinoko. The view of the Lake beneath your feet is breathtaking.

Togendai 桃源台

If you skip the ropeway ride and take a bus from Odawara to Togendai, your itinerary will begin here.

Togendai to Hakone-machi by Boat

Togendai Pier is only a few minutes walk from the ropeway station. Boats leave every 30 – 40 minutes, and all boats that originate at Togendai go to Hakone-machi. Usually they go to Hakone-machi first and then to Moto-Hakone, but a few stop at Moto-Hakone first, and then continue to Hakone-machi. The cruise takes 30 to 40 minutes.

Hakone-machi 箱根町

If you still have time before you have to go back to Odawara (or Hakone-Yumoto) to catch your train, you should visit **Hakone Barrier** 箱根関所跡 , a five-minute walk from the boat pier. In the Edo era, the main road between Tokyo and Kyoto (the "Tokaido" so vividly illustrated in Hiroshige's wood-block prints) ran through Hakone. To keep the minor feudal lords from rebeling, the Tokugawa shoguns forced the lords' wives to live in Edo, and the lords themselves had to make formal, compulsory visits to the city every other year. These trips to Edo cost the lords a great deal because they traveled in grand processions accompanied by hundreds of retainers. The financial burden was even heavier for those lords unfriendly to the Tokugawas because they had been assigned to areas far from Edo. At Hakone Barrier the shoguns checked on the number of guns the lords took into the Edo area. The Barrier also served as a checkpoint on the route out of Edo, ensuring that none of the wives would be able to escape. The buildings here are reconstructions. (Open year round. 9:00 AM to 4:30 PM).

Hakone-machi to Odawara by Bus

There is frequent bus service between Hakone-machi and Odawara Station via Hakone-Yumoto Station, operated by different companies. The ride to Hakone-Yumoto takes about 40 minutes and the ride to Odawara Station takes exactly one hour.

Hakone-en 箱根園 and Mt. Komagatake 駒ヶ岳

Though not included in our suggested itinerary, Hakone-en is another major attraction in Hakone. Located on Lake Ashinoko near Hakone Prince Hotel, Hakone-en is a recreation complex that includes an aquarium, a barbecue garden, an archery field, swimming pools, a golf course, and tennis courts.

A ropeway operates between Hakone-en and the summit of Mt. Komagatake (1,327 m. or 4,354 feet). The mountain top observatory commands a graceful view of Mt. Fuji over Lake Ashinoko. There is an ice skating rink near the observatory.

If you stay at the Prince Hotel, we recommend that you visit Hakone-en and Mt. Komagatake.

Accommodations in Hakone

1. Hotels

Hakone Prince Hotel 箱根プリンスホテル
   (Deluxe: middle left, map 45. 96 rooms)
   Add: 144, Moto-Hakone, Hakonemachi.
   Tel: (0460) 3-7111.
Fujiya Hotel 富士屋ホテル
   (First-class: upper right, map 45. 149 rooms)
   Add: 359, Miyanoshita, Hakonemachi.
   Tel: (0460) 2-2211.
Hotel Kowakien ホテル小湧園
   (First-class: upper right, map 45. 257 rooms)
   Add: 1297, Ninotaira, Hakonemachi.
   Tel: (0460) 2-4111.
Hakone Kanko Hotel 箱根観光ホテル
   (First-class: upper left, map 45. 100 rooms)
   Add: 1245, Sengokubara, Hakonemachi.
   Tel: (0460) 4-8501.

Yamano Hotel 山のホテル
   (First-class: lower center, map 45. 93 rooms)
   Add: 80, Moto-Hakone, Hakonemachi.
   Tel: (0460) 3-6321.
Hotel Kagetsuen ホテル花月園
   (Standard: upper left, map 45. 44 rooms)
   Add: Sengokubara, Hakonemachi.
   Tel: (0460) 4-8621.

2. Ryokans

Naraya 奈良屋
   (Deluxe: upper right, map 45. 15 rooms)
   Add: 162, Miyanoshita, Hakonemachi.
   Tel: (0460) 2-2411.
Kanporo 冠峰楼
   (Deluxe: upper center, map 45. 17 rooms)
   Add: 1251, Sengokubara, Hakonemachi.
   Tel: (0460) 4-8551.
Terumoto 照本
   (First-class: upper center, map 45. 50 rooms)
   Add: 1320, Gora, Hakonemachi.
   Tel: (0460) 2-3177.
Hakone Kowakien 箱根小湧園
   (First-class: Same location as Hotel Kowakien. 352 rooms)
   Add: 1297, Ninotaira, Hakonemachi.
   Tel: (0460) 2-4111.

Izu Peninsula 伊豆半島

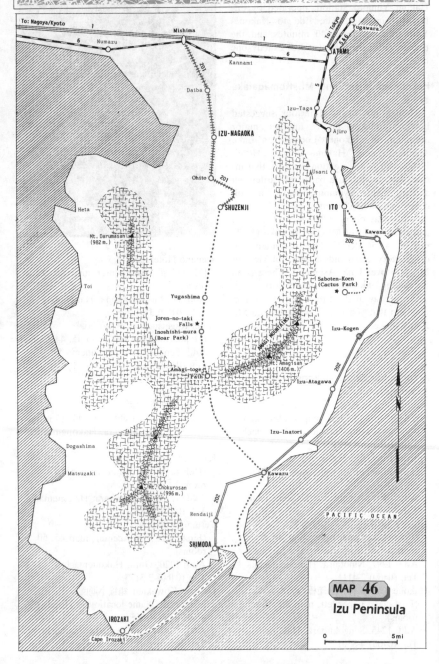

MAP 46
Izu Peninsula

0   5mi

Izu Peninsula is a wide area stretching 60 km. (37 miles) from north to south and 33 km (20 miles) from east to west. A number of hotspring resorts are scattered across the peninsula, along the sea coast and in quiet valleys. Many people visit Izu to stay at a hotspring, to relax away from busy city life, and to enjoy the excellent fresh seafood served there.

If you want to combine a stay in a hotspring with sightseeing, the following is a typical two-day itinerary from Tokyo:

Day 1. Tokyo/Shimoda

Several direct trains run between Tokyo Station and Izukyu-Shimoda Station (about a 3 hour ride). The train runs on the JR Line between Tokyo and Ito, and then on the private Izukyu Line between Ito and Izukyu-Shimoda. (You can use your Rail Pass for the JR portion only.) Afternoon sightseeing in Shimoda and Cape Irozaki. Overnight in Shimoda.

Day 2. Shimoda/Shuzenji/Tokyo

Take a pleasant bus ride from Shimoda to Shuzenji across the picturesque Amagi mountains (a 2 hour ride). On the way, if you wish, you can visit Inoshishimura (Boar Park) and Joren-no-taki Falls. At Inoshishimura, trained boars and badgers perform a show. The Park and the Falls are just a 15 minute walk from each other. From Shuzenji you can take a direct train back to Tokyo Station (2 hours and 20 minutes). The train runs on the Izu-Hakone Tetsudo Line between Shuzenji and Mishima, and on the JR Line between Mishima and Tokyo. (Your Rail Pass is good for the JR portion only.)

* If you plan to continue your trip to the west, e.g., to Kyoto, you can take a local train from Shuzenji to Mishima, and then catch the Shinkansen.

Atami

Major Hotsprings and Accommodations

Atami   熱海

(Upper right, map 46)

Only a 55 minute ride on the Shinkansen from Tokyo, Atami is the largest resort in Izu. There are several famous and authentic ryokans here, as well as many large hotels/ryokans catering to groups. **MOA Museum** (8 minutes by taxi from Atami Station) is a large complex owned by a religious organization. The museum exhibits priceless paintings, pottery and other art objects, some of which are National Treasures. (Closed on Thursdays.)

1. Hotels in Atami

New Fujiya Hotel ニューフジヤホテル
(First-class: 316 rooms. 5 min. by taxi from Atami Station)
Add: 1-16, Ginzacho, Atami.
Tel: (0557) 81-0111.

Chateautel Akanezaki シャトーテル赤根崎
(First-class: 300 rooms. 15 min. by taxi from Atami Station)
Add: Akane, Kamitaga, Atami.
Tel: (0557) 67-1111.

2. Ryokans in Atami

Atami Sekitei 熱海石亭
(Deluxe: 40 rooms. 5 min. by taxi from Atami Station)
Add: 6-17, Wadacho, Atami.
Tel: (0557) 81-7191.

Taikanso 大観荘
(Deluxe: 45 rooms. 10 min. walk from Atami Station)
Add: 7-1, Hayashigaokacho, Atami.
Tel: (0557) 81-8137.

Horai 蓬莱
(Deluxe: 17 rooms. 5 min. by car from Atami Station)
Add: 750-6, Izusan, Atami.
Tel: (0557) 81-5151.

Seikanso 静観荘
(First-class. 122 rooms. 8 min. walk from Atami Station)
Add: 3-8, Sakimicho, Atami.
Tel: (0557) 81-5101.

Atami Grand Hotel 熱海グランドホテル
(First-class. 96 rooms. 15 min. walk from
Atami Station)
Add: 6-38, Higashi-Kaigancho, Atami.
Tel: (0557) 81-0311.

Ito 伊東

(Upper right, map 46)

Ito is another large hotspring resort
along the picturesque sea coast.
Saboten Koen サボテン公園 (Cactus Park),
located on pleasant Mt. Omuroyama, has
several huge pyramidal greenhouses and
features 5,000 cactuses transplanted from
around the world. Buses operate between
Ito Station and Saboten-Koen frequently.
The ride takes 35 minutes.

1. Hotel in Ito
Kawana Hotel 川奈ホテル
(Deluxe: 113 rooms. 15 min. by taxi
from Ito Station)
Add: 1459, Kawana, Ito.
Tel: (0557) 45-1111.
2. Ryokans in Ito
Nagoya 那古野
(Deluxe: 13 rooms. 10 min. by taxi from
Ito Station)
Add: 1-1-18, Sakuragaoka, Ito.
Tel: (0557) 37-4316.
Yonewakaso よねわか荘
(Deluxe: 18 rooms. 5 min. by taxi from
Ito Station)
Add: 2-4-1, Hirono, Ito.
Tel: (0557) 37-5111.
Hotel Kawaryo ホテル川良
(Deluxe: 85 rooms. 10 min. walk from
Ito Station)
Add: 1-1-3, Takenouchi, Ito.
Tel: (0557) 37-8181.
Ito Hotel Juraku 伊東ホテル聚楽
(First-class: 104 rooms. 15 min. walk
from Ito Station)
Add: 281, Oka, Ito.
Tel: (0557) 37-3161.
Ito Suimeiso 伊東水明荘
(First-class: 100 rooms. 5 min. by taxi
from Ito Station)
Add: 8-18, Yudacho, Ito.
Tel: (0557)37-5171.

Atagawa 熱川

(Middle right, map 46)

There are several large ryokans in Atagawa. Many retreats owned by companies
and associations are also located here. All
of the accommodations introduced below
have hotspring swimming pools (available
year round). **Atagawa Banana-Wani-en**
熱川バナナ・ワニ園 (Banana and Croco-
dile Park) is in front of Izu-Atagawa
Station, and features more than 400 croco-
diles gathered from all over the world.
Several huge greenhouses in the Park
contain tropical plants.

Ryokans in Atagawa
Atagawa Yamatokan 熱川大和館
(First-class: 60 rooms. 10 min. walk from
Izu-Atagawa Station)
Add: 986-2, Naramoto, Izucho.
Tel: (0557) 23-1126.
Hotel Daitokan ホテル大東館
(First-class: 113 rooms. 10 min. walk
from Izu-Atagawa Station)
Add: 980, Naramoto, Izucho.
Tel: (0557) 23-1111.
Atagawa View Hotel 熱川ビューホテル
(First-class: 55 rooms. 10 min. walk from
Izu-Atagawa Station)
Add: 1271, Naramoto, Izucho.
Tel: (0557) 23-1211.
Atagawa Daiichi Hotel 熱川第一ホテル
(Standard: 58 rooms. 8 min. walk from
Izu-Atagawa Station)
Add: 1267-2, Naramoto, Izucho.
Tel: (0557) 23-2200.

Shimoda 下田

(Lower center, map 46)

Shimoda is the most popular destination
in Izu. Shimoda prospered as early as the
Edo Era as an intermediate port for trade
ships between Tokyo and Osaka. In 1854
the Japan-US Friendship Treaty was signed
here, and Townsend Harris, the first U.S.
Consul General to Japan, arrived in Shimoda two years later. A ropeway near Izukyu-
Shimoda Station climbs to **Mt. Nesugata-**

yama 寝姿山. The observatory commands a panoramic view of Shimoda Port and the Pacific Ocean. **Cape Irozaki** 石廊崎 is at the southern tip of Izu Peninsula. We suggest that you take a bus from Izukyu-Shimoda Station to Irozaki Todai (Lighthouse), the last stop (a 50 minute ride). A promenade to the lighthouse passes a huge "Jungle Park" greenhouse. The lighthouse stands on a steep cliff overlooking the Pacific Ocean. Take a boat from Irozaki for the return trip to Shimoda (a 40 minute ride).

1. Hotels in Shimoda

Shimoda Prince Hotel 下田プリンスホテル
(Deluxe: 134 rooms. 5 min. by taxi from Izukyu-Shimoda Station)
Add: 1547-1, Shirahama, Shimoda.
Tel: (05582) 2-7575.

Shimoda Tokyu Hotel 下田東急ホテル
(First-class: 117 rooms. 5 min. by taxi from Izukyu-Shimoda Station)
Add: 5-12-1, Shimoda.
Tel: (05582) 2-2411.

2. Ryokans in Shimoda

Seiryuso 清流荘
(Deluxe: 33 rooms. 5 min. by taxi from Izukyu-Shimoda Station)
Add: 2-2, Kawauchi, Shimoda.
Tel: (05582) 2-1361.

Hotel Izukyu ホテル伊豆急
(First-class: 164 rooms. 10 min. by taxi from Izukyu-Shimoda Station)
Add: 2732-7, Shirahama, Shimoda.
Tel: (05582) 2-8111.

Shuzenji 修善寺

(Upper center, map 46)

Shuzenji is a prestigious traditional hotspring resort. Most accommodations are located about 2 km. (1.2 miles) to the west of Shuzenji Station, in a long narrow valley along the Katsuragawa River. Shuzenji was famous as long ago as the 9th century. The second Kamakura Shogun, Yoriie, was assassinated here in 1204. The Treasure House of Shuzenji Temple displays historic objects related to the Kamakura Shogunate.

Ryokans in Shuzenji

Yagyu-no-sho 柳生の庄
(Deluxe: 14 rooms. 10 min. by taxi from Shuzenji Station)
Add: 1116-6, Shuzenji.
Tel: (0558) 72-4126.

Arai Ryokan 新井旅館
(Deluxe: 41 rooms. 10 min. by taxi from Shuzenji Station)
Add: 970, Shuzenji.
Tel: (0558) 72-2007.

Shuzenji Sekitei 修善寺石庭
(Deluxe: 12 rooms. 10 min. by taxi from Shuzenji Station)
Add: 1163, Shuzenji.
Tel: (0558) 72-2841.

Katsuragawa 桂川
(Deluxe: 72 rooms. 5 min. by taxi from Shuzenji Station)
Add: 860, Shuzenji.
Tel: (0558) 72-0810.

Hotel Miyuki ホテルみゆき
(First-class: 111 rooms. 5 min. by taxi from Shuzenji Station)
Add: 870-1, Shuzenji.
Tel: (0558) 72-2112.

Izu-Nagaoka 伊豆長岡

(Upper center, map 46)

Izu-Nagaoka is another famous hotspring town. The Hojo family, which captured the political power of the Kamakura Shogunate after the assassination of the third Minamoto Shogun, was originally from this town. The observatory on Mt. Katsuragiyama, which can be reached by ropeway, has a panoramic view of the Amagi mountains, Mt. Fuji, and the Pacific Ocean.

Ryokans in Izu-Nagaoka

Sanyoso 三養荘
(Deluxe: 20 rooms. 5 min. by taxi from Izu-Nagaoka Station)
Add: 270, Domanoue, Izu-Nagaoka.
Tel: (05594) 8-0123.

Nagaoka Sekitei 長岡石亭
(Deluxe: 19 rooms. 10 min. by taxi from Izu-Nagaoka Station)
Add: 55, Minami-Onoue, Izu-Nagaoka.
Tel: (05594) 8-2841.

Fuji Five Lakes 富士五湖

Fuji Five Lakes are located to the north of Mt. Fuji, scattered in wild forests. Kawaguchiko is the center of the area, and most of the accommodations in the area are located on the southeastern shore of Lake Kawaguchiko (Funazu district). A bus runs from Kawaguchiko Station to the fifth grade of Mt. Fuji. Many retreats owned by companies and colleges are located in the Lake Yamanakako area. The other three lakes – Saiko, Shojiko and Motosuko – are less developed. Unless you drive, visiting all the five lakes is very difficult. We suggest that you relax in the beautiful natural setting, enjoying a magnificent view of Mt. Fuji. The area is an ideal overnight destination from Tokyo. Even a full day excursion from Tokyo is possible if you visit only the Lake Kawaguchiko area.

Transportation to Kawaguchiko

To get to Kawaguchiko from Tokyo, you have to use two trains: first a limited express train on the JR Chuo Line (No. 10) from Tokyo's Shinjuku Station to Otsuki (1 hour), and then the private Fujikyu train (No. 203) from Otsuki to Kawaguchiko (50 minutes).

In July and August, special through trains from Shinjuku to Kawaguchiko run a few times daily.

Tenjozan Observatory 天上山展望台

The ropeway station is a 15 minute walk from Kawaguchiko Station. The gondola brings you up to the top of Mt. Tenjozan

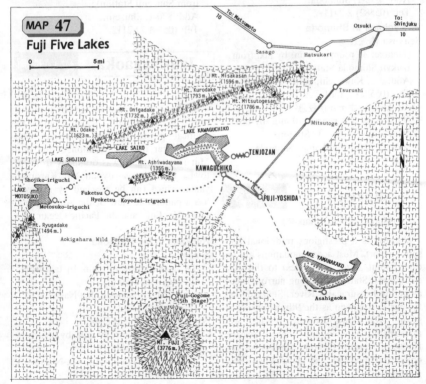

MAP 47
Fuji Five Lakes

0   5mi

(1,104 meters or 3,622 feet) in just three minutes. The observatory commands a great view of Mt. Fuji to the south and Lake Kawaguchiko below.

Sightseeing Boat

A 30 minute sightseeing boat around Lake Kawaguchiko leaves from near the ropeway station and operates frequently. Mt. Fuji viewed beyond the blue water of the lake appears in a new and quite impressive guise.

Other Lakes

You can visit the other four lakes by bus from Kawaguchiko Station. If you must choose only one of them, we suggest that you visit Lake Motosuko. **Lake Motosuko** 本栖湖 is located at the westernmost end of the five lakes. The bus ride from Kawaguchiko Station takes about one hour. The bus runs through Aokigahara Wild Forest, with a view of Mt. Fuji from time to time. Lake Motosuko is the deepest of the five lakes (138 meters) and has the clearest water.

Lake Yamanakako 山中湖 is the largest of the five. The bus ride from Kawaguchiko Station takes about 35 minutes (Asahigaoka is the bus stop for Lake Yamanakako). A 30 minute sightseeing boat operates from the pier near the bus stop. You can enjoy a grand view of Mt. Fuji from yet another angle.

Fuji-Gogome 富士五合目

If you want to see Mt. Fuji from closer up, you should take a bus from Kawaguchiko to Fuji-Gogome (the 5th grade of Mt. Fuji). The hour drive through the wild forests (called the "Fuji Subaru Line") is refreshing and thrilling. There are restaurants and souvenir shops at the Fuji-Gogome Terminal. The bus operates from April 5 through November 8.
* Please note that there is bus service from Fuji-Gogome to Tokyo's Shinjuku Station via the Chuo Expressway (about a 3 hour ride).

Fujikyu Highland 富士急ハイランド

Fujikyu Highland is an amusement and sports complex, located in front of Fujikyu-Highland Station. The playland contains all sorts of amusement facilities, from a merry-go-round to double-loop jet coasters. If you are traveling with children, this is an ideal place to enjoy family activities, while still enjoying a great view of Mt. Fuji. The playland is also popular in winter, when its five ice skating rinks are open. The area has very stable weather, and Mt. Fuji appears with its snow-covered graceful shape in a clear blue sky.

Ryokans near Lake Kawaguchiko
Hotel Kogetsukan ホテル湖月館
   (First-class: 48 rooms. 15 min. walk from
   Kawaguchiko Station)
   Add: 4014, Funazu, Kawaguchiko-machi.
   Tel: (05557) 2-1180.
Hotel Konanso ホテル湖南荘
   (First-class: 41 rooms. 12 min. walk from
   Kawaguchiko Station)
   Add: 4020, Funazu, Kawaguchiko-machi.
   Tel: (05557) 2-2166.
Maruei Hotel 丸栄ホテル
   (First-class: 51 rooms. 5 min. by taxi
   from Kawaguchiko Station)
   Add: 498, Kodachi, Kawaguchiko-machi.
   Tel: (05557) 2-1371.
Kawaguchiko Daiichi Hotel
   河口湖第一ホテル
   (First-class: 45 rooms. 15 min. walk from
   Kawaguchiko Station)
   Add: 61, Asakawa, Kawaguchiko-machi.
   Tel: (05557) 2-1162.
Hotel Yamakitaso ホテル山北荘
   (Standard: 32 rooms. 15 min. walk from
   Kawaguchiko Station)
   Add: 1132, Asakawa, Kawaguchi-
   ko-machi.
   Tel: (05557) 2-1245.

Hotel near Lake Kawaguchiko
Fuji View Hotel 富士ビューホテル
   (First-class: 62 rooms. 10 min. by taxi
   from Kawaguchiko Station)
   Add: 511, Katsuyama-mura, Minami-
   Tsuru-gun.
   Tel: (05558) 3-2211.

Narita 成田

Narita (population of 76,000) is the home of the New Tokyo International Airport (Narita Airport). For most tourists Narita is nothing more than the city they pass through to get to Tokyo. However, the area contains two important and interesting tourist attractions – Shinshoji Temple and the National Museum of Japanese History, which is in nearby Sakura City.

These two places are worth visiting from Tokyo if you have an extra day. They are especially recommended for those who must spend a night in Narita while waiting for a connecting flight to other countries. Starting from Narita Airport, you need three hours to visit Shinshoji Temple. You need six hours to visit both the Temple and the Museum.

Shinshoji Temple 成田山新勝寺

Shinshoji Temple is located about a 15 minute walk from both the JR Narita Station and the Keisei-Narita Station 京成成田駅, which are only about 150 meters (0.1 miles) away from each other. Bus service is available between Narita Airport and JR Narita Station ＪＲ成田駅 (the bus

stop is marked on map 49). If you visit Narita from Tokyo, you can take a private Keisei Line commuter train from Keisei-Ueno Station to Keisei-Narita Station (about a 60 minute ride), or either the JR Sobu Line commuter train (from Tokyo to Narita) or the JR Narita Line commuter train (from Ueno to Narita). The ride takes about 80 minutes via either route.

In 939, when the social status of samurai or soldiers was still low despite their service to the aristocracy, a Kanto samurai, Masakado Taira, organized a rebellion against the reign of the imperial court in Kyoto. Though the rebellion was suppressed and Masakado was killed in 940, the uprising presaged the rise of samurai power in Japanese history. The original Shinshoji Temple was built at the order of Emperor Sujaku during the rebellion. He hoped that this act of piety would result in his ultimate triumph. The gods were evidently pleased with his offering. The Temple was moved to the present location in 1705.

The entrance to the main approach (shaded red) to Shinshoji Temple is marked by an arch. The main approach is

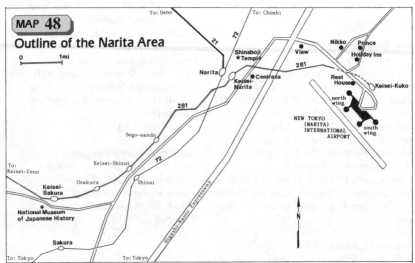

MAP 48
Outline of the Narita Area
0   1mi

lined on the both sides with souvenir shops, restaurants and stores. There are several ryokans near the Niomon Gate that put up the many pilgrims who come to the temple from all over Japan. The huge precincts include a number of impressive buildings, including the Main Hall, a three-story pagoda, and Daito Pagoda. Naritasan-Koen Park, adjacent to the temple, has beautiful gardens designed around three ponds. Shin-

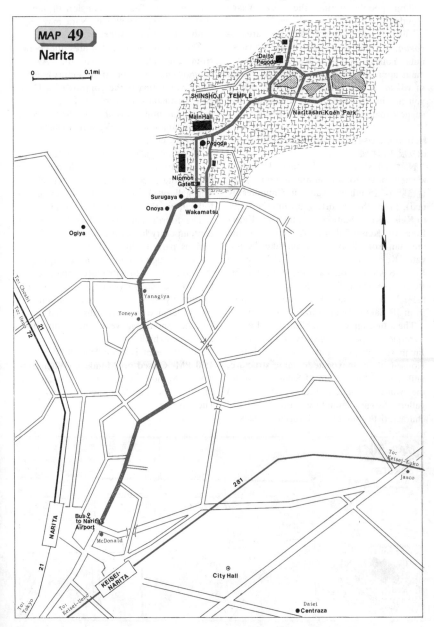

shoji Temple is one of the most popular temples in the Tokyo area. Several million people visit the temple year round to pray for the safety and prosperity of the households. The temple attracts more than three million people during the New Year's Holiday.

The special souvenir of the area is *yokan*, a sweet paste cake made of chestnuts. Yoneya and Yanagiya, located on the main approach, are two famous producers of *yokan*. Narita is also famous for eels. If you are in the area during lunch time, we suggest that you try *unadon* or *unaju*.

National Museum of Japanese History
国立歴史博物館

National Museum of Japanese History is located near Keisei-Sakura Station 京成佐倉駅 (a 15 minute walk, or 5 minutes by taxi). From the airport, you can take a bus to Keisei-Kuko Station, and then the Keisei Line to Keisei-Sakura. If you visit the museum from Tokyo, you can take the private Keisei Line from Keisei-Ueno to Keisei-Sakura. You can also take the JR Boso Line from Tokyo Station to Sakura 佐倉駅. It takes about 15 minutes by taxi from JR Sakura Station to the museum.

The Museum was established in 1981 to introduce Japanese history to both the Japanese people and foreign visitors. Housed in an unexpectedly large structure, built on the former site of Sakurajo Castle, the Museum contains four galleries. Each gallery displays miniature reproductions of characteristic buildings of various stages of Japanese history. Authentic cultural artifacts are displayed.

The first gallery features the period from pre-history (7,500 BC) through the establishment of the central power in Nara (the 8th century). The reproduction of Japan's first permanent capital in Nara may especially interest the visitor.

The second gallery features the period from the Heian Era to the Azuchi-Momoyama Era (the 16th century). Especially interesting is the contrast of a Heian Era aristocrat's mansion and a civil war period samurai mansion. The first encounter by Japanese with Western civilization is also featured here.

The third gallery features the Edo Era. A reproduction of a typical Edo downtown depicts the people's life in the feudal era. The gallery also offers information on the folk culture that flourished in this era.

The fourth and last gallery features the contemporary life of the Japanese people in various parts of the archipelago.

Even though one of the main purposes of the Museum is to introduce Japanese history to the foreign visitor, the displays unfortunately lack English explanations. A pretty detailed pamphlet distributed at the entrance should, however, help you understand the exhibits.

The Museum is open from 9:30 AM to 4:30 PM. Closed on Mondays (When Sunday or Monday is a national holiday, the Museum opens on Monday and is closed on Tuesday).

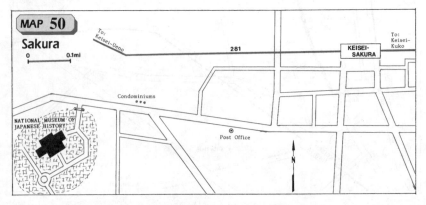

MAP 50
Sakura
0   0.1mi

To: Keisei-Ueno

281

KEISEI-SAKURA

To: Keisei-Kuko

Condominiums

NATIONAL MUSEUM OF JAPANESE HISTORY

Post Office

N

Hotels in Narita

Narita Prince Hotel 成田プリンスホテル
  (First-class: 329 rooms)
  Add: 560, Tokko, Narita.
  Tel: (0476)33-1111.

Hotel Nikko Narita ホテル・日航成田
  (First-class: 523 rooms)
  Add: 500, Tokko, Narita.
  Tel: (0476) 32-0032.

Holiday Inn Narita ホリデーイン・成田
  (First-class: 244 rooms)
  Add: 320-1, Tokko, Narita.
  Tel: (0476) 32-1234.

Narita View Hotel 成田ビューホテル
  (First-class: 493 rooms)
  Add: 700, Kosuge, Narita.
  Tel: (0476) 32-1111.

Airport Rest House
  エアポート・レストハウス
  (First-class: 210 rooms)
  Add: Narita Airport, Narita.
  Tel: (0476) 32-1212.

Hotel Centraza Narita
  ホテル・セントラーザ
  (Standard: 268 rooms)
  Add: 1-1-5, Hiyoshidai, Tomisato-cho,
  Inba-gun.
  Tel:(0476) 93-8811.

Except for Hotel Centraza Narita, which is located in downtown Narita, all the other hotels are located in or near the airport. Complimentary bus service is provided from time to time between the airport terminal building and each hotel.

Boso Peninsula
房総半島

The Boso peninsula arches around the eastern side of Tokyo Bay. A number of resorts have been developed here, especially along the Pacific ocean coast, for Tokyoites. The area is still seldom visited by foreign tourists. We have selected two representative destinations.

Awa-Kamogawa

With rugged coastal line, Awa-Kamogawa is famous for its picturesque marine scenery, and is often called "the Matsushima of Boso." Awa-Kamogawa is also famous for Kamogawa Sea World (five minutes by bus from Awa-Kamogawa Station). This large complex contains several pavilions and outdoor pools, featuring a number of sea animals from around the world. Open year round. 9:00 AM to 5:00 PM.

Admission 1,600 yen. Limited express trains on the JR Sotobo Line run between Tokyo and Awa-Kamogawa Stations in two hours.

Ryokans in Awa-Kamogawa

Kamogawa Grand Hotel
    鴨川グランドホテル
    (First-class: 136 rooms. 0.5 miles from
    Awa-Kamogawa Station)
    Add: 820, Hiroba, Kamogawa.
    Tel: (04709) 2-2111.

Kamogawa Sea World Hotel
    鴨川シーワールドホテル
    (First-class: 76 rooms. 0.8 miles from
    Awa-Kamogawa Station)
    Add: 1137-48, Nishimachi, Kamogawa.
    Tel: (04709) 2-2121.

Cape Inubosaki

Cape Inubosaki has steep cliffs that climb out of the Pacific Ocean. The contrast of the white of Inubosaki Lighthouse and the blue of the Pacific has always been a popular theme for camera fans and painters. The inside of the Lighthouse is open to the public, and the observatory commands a dynamic view of the ocean. Inubosaki Marine Park is an aquarium near the Lighthouse. The gateway to the Cape is Choshi. Limited express trains on the JR Sobu Line connect Tokyo Station with Choshi in two hours. From Choshi Station you can take the private Choshi Denki Tetsudo Line to Inubo (a 19 minute ride).

Ryokans in Cape Inubosaki

Grand Hotel Isoya グランドホテル磯屋
    (First-class: 121 rooms. 0.2 miles from
    Inubo Station)
    Add: 10292, Inubosaki, Choshi.
    Tel: (0479) 24-1111.

Inubosaki Keisei Hotel 犬吠崎京成ホテル
    (Standard: 40 rooms. 0.2 miles from
    Inubo Station)
    Add: 9575, Inubosaki, Choshi.
    Tel: (0479) 22-8111.

Along the Joetsu Shinkansen

上越新幹線方面

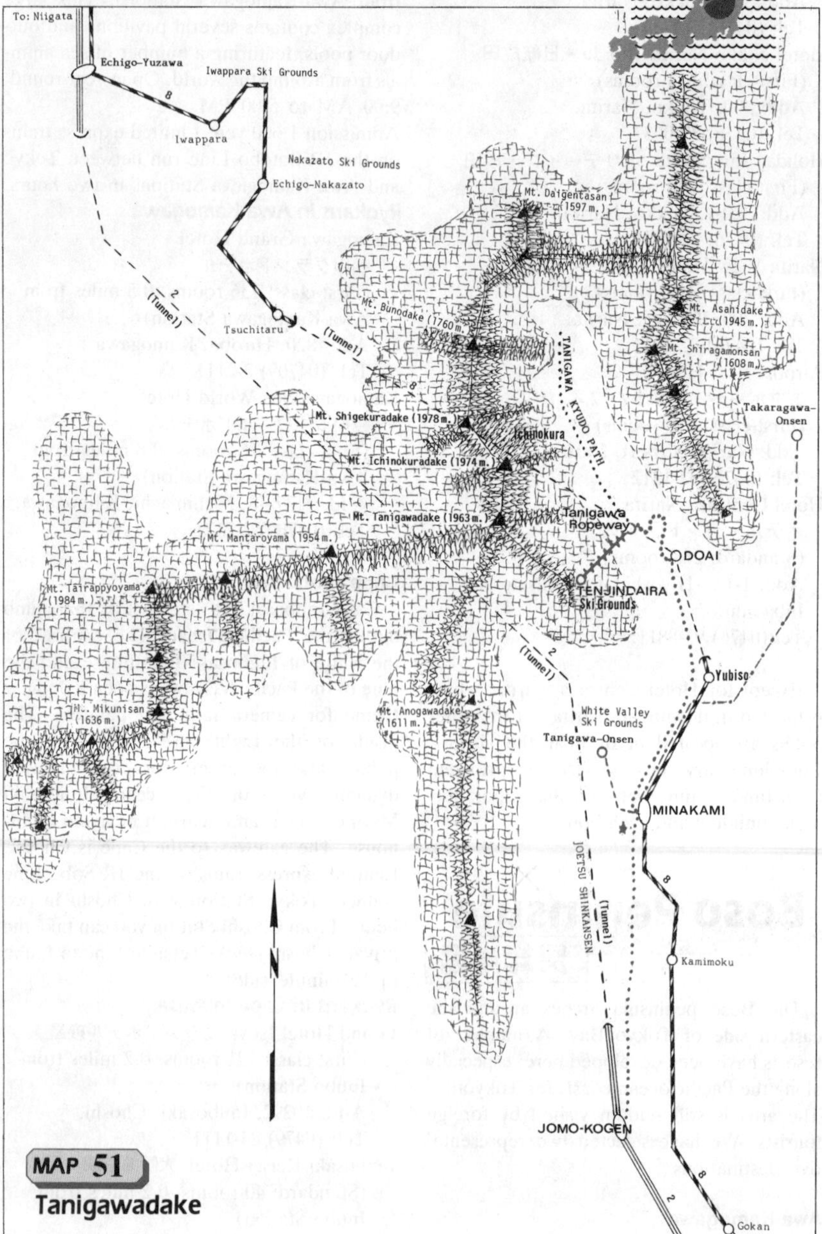

To: Niigata

Echigo-Yuzawa

Iwappara Ski Grounds

Iwappara

Nakazato Ski Grounds

Echigo-Nakazato

Mt. Daigentasan (1597 m.)

Mt. Bunodake (1760 m.)

Mt. Asahidake (ca) 1945 m.

(Tunnel)

Tsuchitaru

(Tunnel)

TANIGAWA KYUDO PATH

Mt. Shiragamonsan (1608 m.)

Mt. Shigekuradake (1978 m.)

Ichinokura

Takaragawa-Onsen

Mt. Ichinokuradake (1974 m.)

Mt. Tanigawadake (1963 m.)

Tanigawa Ropeway

Mt. Mantaroyama (1954 m.)

DOAI

Mt. Tairappoyama (1984 m.)

TENJINDAIRA Ski Grounds

(Tunnel)

Yubiso

Mt. Mikunisan (1636 m.)

Mt. Anogawadake (1611 m.)

White Valley Ski Grounds

Tanigawa-Onsen

MINAKAMI

JOETSU SHINKANSEN

(Tunnel)

Kamimoku

N

JOMO-KOGEN

MAP 51
Tanigawadake

0   2 mi

Gokan

To: Ueno, Tokyo

The Joetsu Shinkansen runs between Tokyo's Ueno Station and Niigata on the Japan Sea coast, across the Tanigawadake mountains via the Dai-Shimizu Tunnel.

Northwestern winds from Siberia blow across the Japan Sea in the winter, absorbing moisture. As they rise along the Tanigawa mountains, they are cooled and cause heavy snowfalls on the northern side of the mountains (Niigata Prefecture), while the southern side has dry, cold winds. The Shinkansen enters a tunnel on the southern side, and emerges on the north. "The train came out of the long tunnel into the snow country," the striking first sentence of Yasunari Kawabata's novel vividly describes this phenomenon. It is also a precise and accurate description of the experience of winter time travelers to this area. A number of ski resorts have been developed in Niigata Prefecture. There are also many hotspring resorts along the Joetsu Line, such as Minakami and Echigo-Yuzawa.

In this chapter we introduce three destinations:

(1) Mt. Tanigawadake, a mecca for Tokyo mountain climbing enthusiasts;
(2) Niigata, an undistinguished provincial urban center; and
(3) Sado Island.

Mt. Tanigawadake can be visited in a full day excursion from Tokyo. If you're able to stay overnight, you can enjoy one of the area's hotspring resorts.

Niigata and Sado can be visited in a 4-day excursion from Tokyo as follows:

Day 1.   Ueno/Niigata
The Joetsu Shinkansen from Tokyo to Niigata (2 hours). Afternoon sightseeing and overnight in Niigata.

Day 2.   Niigata/Sado
Boat from Niigata to Ryotsu on Sado (1 hour by jetfoil or 2 hours 30 minutes by ferry). Visit Senkakuwan and Aikawa in the afternoon. Overnight in Ryotsu or Aikawa.

Day 3.   Sado
Visit Ogi and Shukunegi. Overnight in Ryotsu.

Day 4.   Sado/Niigata/Tokyo
Boat from Ryotsu to Niigata, and then return to Tokyo, or proceed to other destinations, such as Unazuki or Kanazawa, on the Japan Sea coast.

Tanigawadake 谷川岳

Transportation to Mt. Tanigawadake

You can take the Joetsu Shinkansen from Ueno to Jomo-Kogen 上毛高原駅 (lower right, map 51). The ride takes 70 minutes on the slower "Toki" train. Or, you can take a limited express train on the JR Joetsu Line from Ueno to Minakami 水上駅 (middle right, map 51). The ride takes 2 hours 15 minutes. The bus to the Tanigawa-Ropeway terminus 谷川岳ロープ ウェー駅 takes 25 minutes from Minakami Station and 55 minutes from Jomo-Kogen Station. When you take a bus from Jomo-Kogen, you may have to change buses at Minakami Station (there are only a few direct buses from Jomo-Kogen to Tanigawa-Ropeway).

Tanigawa Kyudo Path 谷川旧道

Because of heavy snow in the area in the winter, the Tanigawa mountains have precipitous cliffs and snowy ravines for their comparatively low heights (less than 2,000 m. above sea level), and the mountains are very popular among rockclimbers. Tanigawa Kyudo Path, starting at Tanigawa-Ropeway bus terminus, is an extension of the bus road from Minakami. It is wide enough for cars, but they are restricted beyond the Tanigawa-Ropeway terminus. The road is closed from November till the end of May because of the danger of snow avalanches. The path curves skirting along the mountain side. Forty minutes from the bus terminus you will see Machiga, the first ravine. Machiga Ravine マチガ沢 is broad and rises gradually towards Mt. Tanigawadake. Forty minutes from Machiga you will reach Ichinokura Ravine 一ノ倉沢 . This ravine is quite precipitous. Looking up the cliffs rising sharply into the sky, you can understand why Ichinokura is a mecca for rockclimbers, and also why this threatening ravine has taken more than 500 young lives.

Ropeway to Tenjindaira 天神平

Returning to the bus terminus, take a ropeway to Tenjindaira. Small cabins operate frequently to halfway up Mt. Tanigawa-dake. Tenjindaira is a challenging ski grounds proud of its long season from the end of November till the middle of May. You can have a panoramic view of the nearby mountains. A leisurely stroll will give you a chance to enjoy the mountain flowers. You can return via the same route to Minakami or Jomo-Kogen.

Ryokans in the Area

1. Minakami Onsen Spa 水上温泉
(Near Minakami Station. Largest of the area's hotsprings.)
Hotel Juraku ホテル聚楽
(Deluxe: 246 rooms)
Add: 665, Yuhara, Minakami-machi.
Tel: (02787) 2-2521.
Fujiya Hotel 藤屋ホテル
(First-class: 82 rooms)
Add: 719, Yuhara, Minakami-machi.
Tel: (02787) 2-3270.
Kikufuji Hotel 菊富士ホテル
(First-class: 38 rooms)
Add: 750, Yuhara, Minakami-machi.
Tel: (02787) 2-3020.

2. Tanigawa Onsen Spa 谷川温泉
(Ten minutes by bus from Minakami Station. A quiet resort in woods.)
Kinseikan 金盛館
(Standard: 17 rooms)
Add: 544, Tanigawa, Minakami-machi.
Tel: (02787)2-3260.

3. Takaragawa Onsen Spa 宝川温泉
(Forty minutes by bus from Minakami Station. An isolated hotspring spa famous for its large open-air baths.)
Osenkaku 旺泉閣
(First-class: 52 rooms)
Add: 1899, Fujiwara, Minakami-machi.
Tel: (02787) 5-2121.

4. Echigo-Yuzawa Onsen Spa
(Near Echigo-Yuzawa Station.)
Yuzawa New Otani Hotel 湯沢ニューオタニホテル (First-class: 97 rooms)

Add: 337-1, Yuzawa, Yuzawa-machi.
Tel: (02578) 4-2191.

Niigata 新潟

On the 'opposite' side of the country, on the Japan Sea coast, lies Japan's *Yukiguni,* Snow Country. Transformed by the mounds of snow that bury it in winter, and blessed with uniformly pleasant weather in summer, this remote area is famous for a tranquility conducive to contemplation, and its hearty people are direct and open in a way you won't often encounter in the rarified atmosphere of Japan's cities. It was this area that Yasunari Kawabata celebrated in his famous 1947 novel *Yukiguni.* Niigata, with a population of 400,000, is the largest city in this area, and the capital of the prefecture as well as of the Snow Country.

Most of Niigata's attractions for visitors are located across the Shinanogawa River from the station, on the island that lies between the River and the Japan Sea.

Niigata's downtown area, through which virtually every bus line passes, is called Furumachi. The biggest intersection is where Furumachidori Street crosses Nishiboridori Street. Mitsukoshi Department Store is on the southwest corner and Daiwa Department Store on the northeast corner.

The Nishibori Rosa Underground Shopping Area runs under Furumachi's Nishiboridori Street. There are entrances at both the Mitsukoshi and Daiwa Department Stores. The underground area has two wings: "6th Avenue" is all smart, stylish shops and boutiques. "7th Avenue" is also mostly shops, with a few restaurants and snack bars at the far end.

Transportation to Niigata

Niigata is the terminus of Japan's newest bullet train, the Joetsu Shinkansen (No. 2). Many believe that this Shinkansen line was built primarily at the insistence of former Prime Minister Kakuei Tanaka, a native son of Niigata, as the ultimate Japanese pork barrel project. Niigata is connected by the JR Hokuriku Line (No. 16) with Kanazawa, Kyoto and Osaka.

Air service is also available from such major cities as Osaka, Nagoya, Sapporo, Sendai, and Fukuoka. An airport bus runs between Niigata Airport and Niigata Station (a 30 minute ride).

Transportation in Niigata

The best way to get around Niigata is on the city's buses. There's a bus terminal in front of the train station, to your left as you emerge from the station. Because so many buses originate at the Station, it's probably a good idea to use Conversation Card 5 to make sure you get on the right bus.

Places of Interest

Hakusan-Koen Park 白山公園 . Catch the bus bound for Hakusankoen-mae stop at the station. The Park, located in the city's cultural zone, contains Hakusan Jinja Shrine, which was established in the 10th or 11th century, and a spectacular garden. Take some time to walk around the garden: it has two ponds, one with a curved bridge, and the second with an arbor overhead. In the spring, the garden's beautiful lotus, wisteria and azalea blooms make it especially attractive.

Nihonkai Tower 日本海タワー (optional). This observatory is 1.5 miles (2.4 km.) from Niigata Station – 10 minutes by bus. Catch the bus bound for Nihonkai Tower-mae stop from the station. When you get

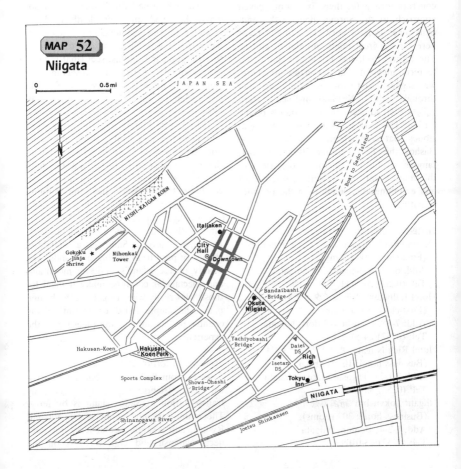

off the bus walk back the way the bus came until you see the entrance. Hours: 9:00 AM to 5:00 PM; 10:00 AM to 4:00 PM in winter. Take the elevator up, and follow the red arrows up the stairs when you get off. On one of the landings you'll see displays from Niigata's three sister cities – Galveston (U.S.A.), Khabarovsk (U.S.S.R.) and Harbin (China). The tower is 191 feet (62.6 meters) tall, and boasts a 360 degree view. The Japan Sea lies to the North and the West, and the city itself to the East and the South. You can sit still and see it all in the 20 minutes it takes the Tower to make one full revolution.

Gokoku Jinja 護国神社 (optional). You can walk the short distance from Nihonkai Tower to the Shrine. Through the large concrete torii gate, there is a long, paved approach to the Shrine, lined with wind-bent pines (you're very close to the coast here) and a great many monument stones. The Shrine itself has nothing in particular to recommend it, but if you do stop here, we suggest that you wander into and through the **Nishikaigan-Koen Park** 西海岸公園 adjacent to the grounds of the Shrine. The park is dotted with monument stones that commemorate, among others, Basho, the 17th century Buddhist poet, famous for his travels to remote areas of the country and for his verses, often short and epigrammatic, celebrating the beauties of nature.

Hotels in Niigata

Okura Hotel Niigata オークラホテル新潟
  (First-class: 300 rooms).
  Add: 6-53, Kawabatacho, Niigata.
  Tel: (0252) 24-6111.
Hotel Italiaken ホテルイタリア軒
  (First-class: 101 rooms).
  Add: 7-1574, Nishibori-dori, Niigata.
  Tel: (0252) 24-5111.
Hotel Rich Niigata ホテルリッチ新潟
  (Business hotel: 103 rooms.)
  Add: 2-1-21, Higashi-Odori, Niigata.
  Tel: (0252) 43-1881.
Niigata Tokyu Inn 新潟東急イン
  (Business hotel: 309 rooms).
  Add: 1-2-4, Benten, Niigata.
  Tel: (0252) 43-0109.

Sado Island 佐渡

Isolated from the main island by a trip that takes more than two hours by modern ferry from Niigata, it is easy to imagine why Sado Island was a place of exile in the middle ages and a prison colony during the Edo era. With an area of 857 sq. mi., Sado Island is the fifth largest of Japan's islands.

One of the most famous of the early residents of Sado Island was Emperor Juntoku, who lost out in a 1221 attempt to wrest control from the Kamakura Shogunate, which was in fact controlled by hereditary regents of the Hojo family. Regent Yoshitoki Hojo banished the emperor to Sado, where he lived until his death in 1242. Another famous medieval-era resident of Sado Island was Nichiren, the founder of the still popular Buddhist sect (that reduces the essentials of religious observance to chanting *Namu-Myo-Ho-Renge-Kyo*), who was exiled on the island from 1271 until 1274.

Sado Island is at its best between April and October, and winter visits are really not recommended. The weather is harsh, the crossings from Honshu can be quite rough, bus services on the island are severely reduced, and once the autumn equinox has passed, the sun sets quite early (it's usually completely dark by 5:00 PM), limiting the time available for sightseeing. In other seasons, Sado is a delightful change of pace from the bigger islands. The beauty of the island's majestic mountains and spectacular coastline make it ideal for those who really want to get off the beaten path. The simple and direct warmth of the country people adds to the pleasure of the experience.

Transportation to Sado Island

Aside from flights from Niigata to Ryotsu, Sado Island's capital city, the only transportation to Sado Island is by ferry. The main ferry line connects Niigata and Ryotsu, and a supplemental ferry line connects Naoetsu and Ogi, a town on the southern coast of Sado Island. As the ferry pulls into Ryotsu port on Sado Island, you can see the island's mountains, green and wrinkled, that seem to march all the way down to the edge of the water.

Transportation on Sado Island

The only means of public transportation are taxis and buses. An extensive bus network covers the island. Fares vary with the distance traveled. Frequency of service varies from route to route, and with the season. Once you've figured out what you want to visit on the island, we recommend that you ask for a bus schedule at the Ryotsu port building or at any of the other

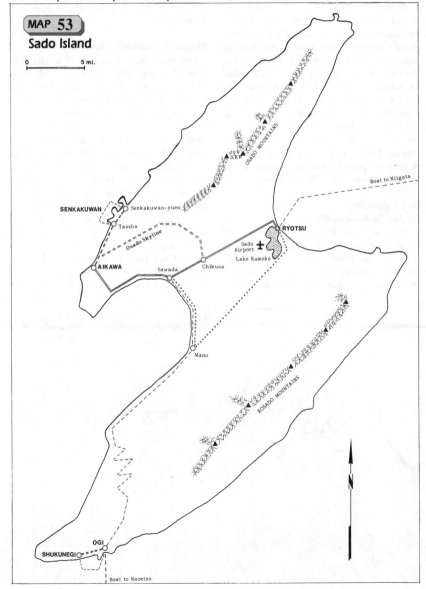

MAP 53
Sado Island

0 ___ 5 mi.

SENKAKUWAN
Senkakuwan-yuen
Tassha
Osado Skyline
OSADO MOUNTAINS
Boat to Niigata
RYOTSU
Sado Airport
Lake Kamoko
AIKAWA
Sawada
Chikusa
Mano
KOSADO MOUNTAINS
OGI
SHUKUNEGI
Boat to Naoetsu

N

bus terminals. Ask for a *teiki* bus 定期バス schedule (or you'll get the schedule for the regularly scheduled (Japanese language only) tour buses), and tell the attendant the name of your starting point and your destination, e.g., "Ogi – Shukunegi."

Ryotsu 両津

Ryotsu is Sado Island's capital and largest city. It also has the most accommodations, and its status as the hub of the island's transportation system makes it the most convenient jumping off place for day tours of the island. The city is dominated by Kamoko Lake, which is 10.6 mi. (17 km.) wide and which is connected to the Japan Sea by a narrow inlet. Many of the city's ryokans boast lake-view rooms. Ryotsu is also the home of Sado Island's famous Okesa Odori Folkdance. Performances are presented every evening during tourist season at Okesa Kaikan Hall.

Day 1 Itinerary
Ryotsu to Aikawa 相川

The bus from Ryotsu to Aikawa runs about once every half hour. As the bus traverses the island you begin to realize that you're really out in the country. Sado Island has two parallel mountain chains,

one in the northwest and the other in the southeast, with a fertile farmland plain between the two. The bus crosses the island on the plain, and the mountains are visible in the distance. The bus makes a terminal-type stop at Sawada Bus Station after it rumbles through the town of Sawada. Stay put: it'll continue to Aikawa shortly. The Ryotsu-Aikawa trip takes about 1 hour and 15 minutes.

Places of Interest in Aikawa

Old Gold Mine 佐渡金山. The taxi ride from the bus terminal to the Old Gold Mine costs about 800 yen. The Aikawa taxi company is right next to the bus terminal. Because the route to the Gold Mine from the town of Aikawa is uphill, we recommend that you take a taxi to the mine, and walk back. Gold was first discovered on Sado Island in 1601. During the Edo era, this mine, Japan's most famous, reached the height of its prosperity. Aikawa at the time had a population of approximately 100,000 (Today, the population of the entire island is 80,000, and declining). The mine's tunnels covered 250 mi. (400 km.) – the distance between Aikawa and Tokyo – and some of them extended as far as 1,969 ft. (600 m.) below sea level. The mine was

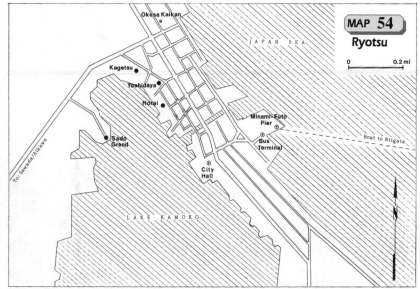

MAP 54
Ryotsu

worked by prison slave labor, and served as a major source of revenue for the Tokugawa Shogunate. Some mining is still done here on a small scale. Today the mine is primarily a living museum. Dioramas and mechanical models demonstrate the privations of the lives of the miners, who dug many of the old tunnels with only hammers and chisels. The path through the display area winds down through the tunnels of the mine, and if you look closely you can still see a few traces of gold and silver in the walls. Hours 8:00 AM to 6:00 PM.

If you walk back to Aikawa from the Old Gold Mine, you might want to stop at the following, all of which are optional: **Aikawa Museum** 相川郷土美術館. Displays of Edo period maps, pictures, scrolls and everyday items, including implements used for mining. The second floor has woven goods, and the third, pottery (8:30 AM to 5:00 PM. Closed on Sundays in January and February). **Sado Hangamura Museum** 佐渡版画村 (Woodblock Print Museum).

This museum is located in a beautiful old wooden building, and has a lovely garden with twisted pines in front of it. It displays the works of members of local woodblock print clubs. Recommended only for devotees of woodblock prints (9:00 AM to 5:30 PM. Closed December through February and on Mondays in November). Near the Aikawa Bus Terminal there are a few *Mumyoyaki* Pottery Shops. *Mumyoyaki* is a distinctive (and expensive!) red-hued pottery made with clay from the Gold Mine.

Aikawa to Senkakuwan 尖閣湾

Buses from Aikawa to Tassha 達者 operate about once an hour (a 15 minute ride). When the weather is good, you can take a 40 minute boat trip from Tassha that circles Senkakuwan Bay for a close-up view of the spectacular coast and its exotic rock formations. This trip is, in our opinion, the biggest attraction in the Aikawa area.

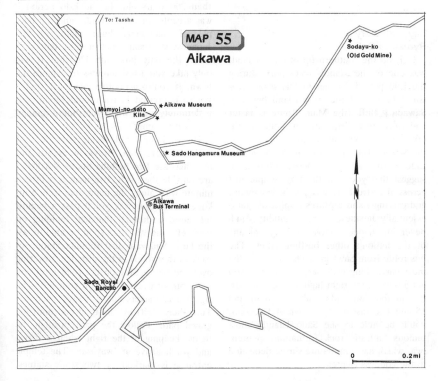

MAP 55
Aikawa

To: Tassha

Sodayu-ko
(Old Gold Mine)

Mumyoi-no-sato
Kiln

Aikawa Museum

Sado Hangamura Museum

Aikawa
Bus Terminal

Sado Royal
Rancho

N

0   0.2 mi

Sado Skyline Drive (optional) 佐渡スカイ
ライン

The only public transportation available
on the Sado Island Skyline, which runs
through the mountains between Aikawa
and Chikusa, is on Japanese tour buses.
The Skyline Tour Route starts from Ryotsu
and stops at Aikawa, Senkakuwan and the
Old Gold Mine before returning to Ryotsu.
Japanese tours are notorious for their su-
perficiality and rushed atmospheres, and
you won't be able to understand the explanations of the tour guide, but these
tours are the easiest way to get around the
Aikawa area and might be worth it for the
scenic skyline route. A taxi trip on the Skyline from Aikawa to Chikusa 千種 will cost
you about 3,000 – 3,500 yen. You can catch
a bus back to Ryotsu in Chikusa. The April
1 – November 30 Japanese sightseeing bus
schedule is as follows: Morning tour (7:50
AM to 11:50 AM), and Afternoon tour
(12:20 PM to 5:10 PM). The tour costs
3,600 yen.

Day 2 Itinerary
Ryotsu to Ogi

Ogi, on the southern tip of Sado Island,
was one of the island's main ports during
the Edo period. To get to Ogi from Ryotsu, take one of the cross island buses to
Sawada 佐和田 (the Main Route is faster
and runs more frequently than the Southern Route; a 50 minute ride). Transfer at
the Sawada Bus Station terminal to the Ogi
Line. If you have a wait between buses, we
suggest that you visit the tiny temple just
across the street. It has lovely woodwork
and carvings, and captures a spirit of quint-
essentially Japanese rustic tranquility you'll
never just happen across in Tokyo or any
of the nation's other bustling cities. The
bus route from Sawada to Ogi runs, for the
most part, along the coast, so be sure you
get a seat on the right hand side of the bus.
It's another long ride – about 1 hour and
15 minutes. Just past the town of Takazaki,
you'll be able to see Sado Island's most
famous fantastic rock formation, Benten-
iwa, which has a miniature shrine dedicated
to the goddess Benten.

Ogi 小木

Ogi is most famous for a unique form of
transportation – its tubs. These tubs, or
taraibune, can easily accommodate three or
more people. Rent your tub at the
taraibune port, to your right and on the
coast as you exit from the Ogi Bus Terminal. If you have time to spare in Ogi, we
suggest that you explore Shiroyama-Koen
Park. A quiet shrine, Kisaki Jinja, stands
at its foot, and the path behind it leads you
up the hill. The paths in the park itself are
punctuated with pavilions for picnicking, and
observatories with great views of the Japan
Sea.

Ogi to Shukunegi 宿根木

The Shukunegi Line bus connects Ogi
and Shukunegi (a 15 minute ride). Boat
service is also available between them (a 20
minute ride).

You can also rent *taraibune* at Shukunegi, a tiny traditional town. All of its
houses are wooden, and many are more
than 200 years old. In the Edo period it
was a center of export trade, and the people of Shukunegi built many of the
Japanese style ships that in those days provided the only link with Honshu. It will
only take you a few minutes to explore the
town. If you're a photography buff, and if
you're interested in traditional Japan, this
is definitely a day when you should remember your camera.

The traditional sightseeing attractions of
the Shukunegi area, **Iwayasan** 岩谷山 and
the **Shiawase Jizo Buddha Statue** 幸福地蔵,
are outside the town. **Iwayasan** is a fifteen
minute walk along the main road from Shukunegi. On your way you'll pass a beautiful, large traditional thatched building on
your left, and will then soon be able to see
the large Shiawase Jizo Buddha Statue set
back in the woods in the distance, towering
over the fields. Stay on the road until you
see a brown wooden post on your left. The
sign has characters but also says "400 m."
Turn there (left) off the road and onto the
gravel path. Follow the path through the
fields, keeping to the right when it forks,
and you'll arrive at Iwayasan. The temple
entrance is marked by two stone statues,

and by another sign that says "200 m." and points in the direction of the Shiawase Jizo Buddha Statue. Visit Iwayasan first. Go through the lantern entrance and up the steps. At the top there is a circular area ringed with tiny Buddha statues. The clearing also has huge trees, the biggest of which is in front of the cave that houses the temple. Numerous tiny statues of Buddhas line the cave, and seven very old images of Buddha are also carved right into its walls.

When you leave Iwayasan, continue on the path, following the "200 m." sign to the **Shiawase Jizo Buddha Statue**. The Shiawase Jizo stands 58 ft. (17.5 m.) tall. His temple, appropriately enough for the 'Happiness Buddha', is a thoroughly cheerful place. There's a smaller, seated laughing Buddha to the right of the big statue, and huge tubs (*taraibune*-type) are scattered around the temple area. One of the tubs has even been given a roof and turned into a mini-temple! Walk straight away from the statue back to the road. There's a bus stop nearby where you can catch a bus back to Ogi (a 10 minute ride), or you can return on the boat.

Ryokans in Sado
1. Ryotsu
Sado Grand Hotel 佐渡グランドホテル
(First-class: middle left, map 54.
107 rooms)

Add: 4918-1, Kamoshiro, Ryotsu.
Tel: (02592) 7-3281.
Yoshidaya Hotel 吉田家ホテル
(First-class: upper center, map 54.
50 rooms)
Add: 261-1, Ebisu, Ryotsu.
Tel: (02592) 7-2151.
Kagetsu Hotel 花月ホテル
(Standard: upper center, map 54.
29 rooms.)
Add: 262, Ebisu, Ryotsu.
Tel: (02592) 7-3131.
Hotel Horai ホテル蓬莱
(Standard: upper center, map 54.
28 rooms).
Add: 261, Ebisu, Ryotsu.
Tel: (02592) 7-2141.

2. Aikawa
Sado Royal Hotel Bancho
佐渡ロイヤルホテル万長
(First-class: lower left, map 55.
87 rooms)
Add: 58, Shimoto, Aikawa-machi.
Tel: (02597) 4-3221.

3. Ogi
Hotel New Kihachiya ホテルニュー喜八屋
(Standard: upper right, map 56.
38 rooms)
Add: Ogicho, Ogi-machi.
Tel: (02598) 9-3131.

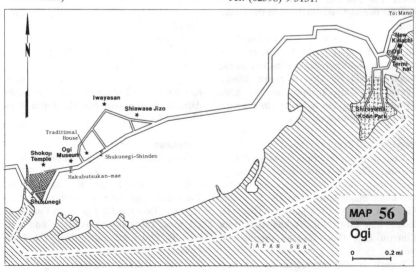

MAP 56
Ogi

0   0.2 mi

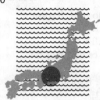

Introduction to Central Japan 中部日本

Central Japan is a vast area between Tokyo and Kyoto, the modern and the traditional capitals of Japan, and the two most popular destinations in Japan. You can incorporate some of the destinations in the Central Japan Chapter of this book to add interest to a standard Tokyo/Kyoto tour.

Nagoya, the Tokugawas' castle town and the third most important business city in Japan (following Tokyo and Osaka) is at the center of the Pacific Ocean side of Central Japan. To the south of Nagoya is Ise-Shima National Park. Ise is the site of Ise Jingu Shrine, Japan's most important Shinto shrine. There are many scenic ocean resorts in Ise-Shima National Park, such as Toba and Kashikojima.

In the middle of Central Japan rise the Japan Alps, the roof of Japan. Matsumoto and Takayama, both historic cities, are located at eastern and western ends of the Japan Alps respectively. There are several scenic routes across the Japan Alps. Kamikochi and Unazuki are two of the most popular overnight destinations in the mountains.

Kanazawa, a historic city governed by the second largest feudal lord of the Edo Era, is the most popular destination on the Japan Sea side of Central Japan. Eiheiji Temple and Cape Tojimbo are two extra destinations that can be visited in conjunction with a trip to Kanazawa.

Nagoya

Nagoya is the transportation center of the area. The Shinkansen connects Nagoya conveniently with Tokyo, Kyoto, Osaka, and other major cities. The JR Takayama Line (No. 15), the JR Chuo Line (No. 11), the JR Kise Line (No. 29), and the private Kintetsu Line (No. 228) all originate at Nagoya.

Nagoya is also connected by air with Tokyo (both Narita and Haneda Airports), Sapporo, Hakodate, Sendai, Niigata, Kochi, Matsuyama, Fukuoka, Nagasaki, Oita, Miyazaki, Kagoshima, and Naha (Okinawa). Airport buses run frequently between the Meitetsu Bus Center (near Nagoya Station) and Nagoya Airport (a 40 minute ride).

Ise-Shima

From Nagoya, there are two ways to visit the Ise-Shima area (Iseshi and Toba Stations). The private Kintetsu Railways (No. 228) operates direct trains between Nagoya and Kashikojima via Iseshi and Toba. If you have a Japan Rail Pass, you can combine two JR trains to visit Ise-Shima – the JR Kise Line (No. 29) from Nagoya to Taki, and the JR Sangu Line (No. 28) from Taki to Iseshi or Toba.

From Kyoto and Osaka, the private Kintetsu Railways also operates direct trains to Iseshi, Toba and Kashikojima (No. 232 and No. 233).

Takayama

The most popular route to Takayama is on the JR Takayama Line (No. 15), which connects Nagoya and Toyama via Takayama. Starting from Tokyo, there is also a route to Takayama across the Japan Alps via Matsumoto. See the Japan Alps Chapter for details.

Kanazawa

From Kyoto/Osaka, you can take a direct train on the JR Hokuriku Line (No. 16).

If you travel to Kanazawa from Takayama, you have to change trains at Toyama. Take the JR Takayama Line (No. 15) from Takayama to Toyama, and then the JR Hokuriku Line (No. 16) from Toyama to Kanazawa.

If you visit Kanazawa after a trip to Sado

Island, you can take the JR Hokuriku Line (No. 16) from Niigata to Kanazawa.

Japan Alps

Kamikochi, Mt. Norikuradake, the Tate- yama-Kurobe Alpine Route (which connects Shinano-Omachi and Toyama), and Unazuki are explained in the Japan Alps Chapter.

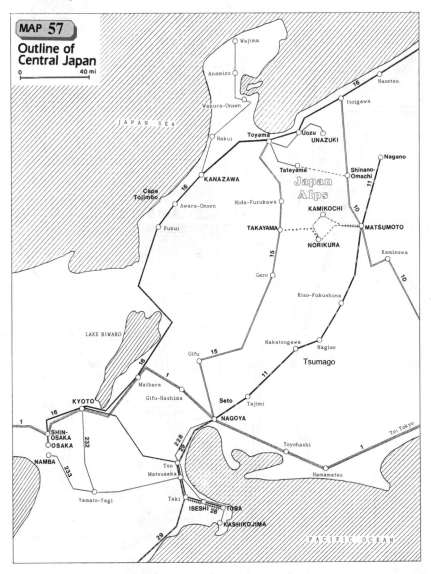

MAP 57
Outline of Central Japan
0   40 mi

Nagoya 名古屋

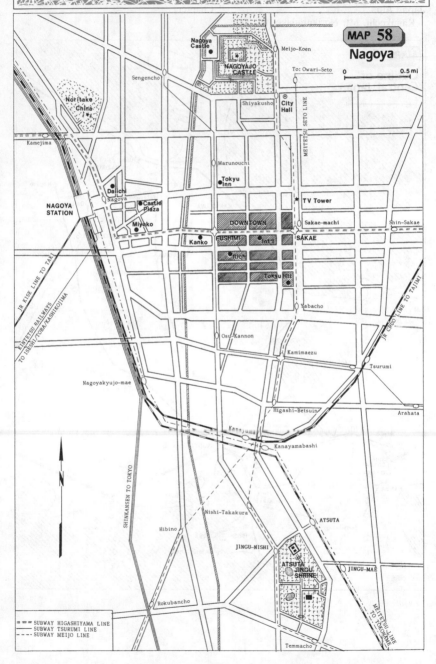

MAP 58
Nagoya

Nagoya Castle
NAGOYAJO CASTLE
Meijo-Koen
To: Owari-Seto
0   0.5 mi

Sengencho
Shiyakusho
City Hall

Noritake China

Kamejima

Marunouchi

Tokyu Inn

TV Tower

NAGOYA STATION
Daiichi
Nagoya
Castle Plaza
Miyako

DOWNTOWN
Sakae-machi
Shin-Sakae

Kanko
FUSHIMI   Int'l   SAKAE
Rich
Tokyu Htl

Yabacho

Osu-Kannon

Kamimaezu

Tsurumi

Nagoyakyujo-mae

Higashi-Betsuin
Arahata

Kanayama
Kanayamabashi

N

Nishi-Takakura

ATSUTA

Hibino

JINGU-NISHI

ATSUTA JINGU SHRINE
JINGU-MAE

Rokubancho

Temmacho

MEITETSU SETO LINE
JR KISE LINE TO TAKI
KINTETSU RAILWAYS TO ISESHI/TOBA/KASHIKOJIMA
SHINKANSEN TO TOKYO
JR CHUO LINE TO TAJIMI
MEITETSU LINE TO TOKONAME

=== SUBWAY HIGASHIYAMA LINE
—— SUBWAY TSURUMI LINE
--- SUBWAY MEIJO LINE

Major attractions in the Nagoya area include the city itself, three pottery villages (Seto, Tajimi and Tokoname), and Tsumago.

In the civil war period (the 15th – 16th centuries), the Nagoya vicinity was the scene of major battles of feudal lords such as Nobunaga Oda and Ieyasu Tokugawa. At the beginning of the 17th century, when the Tokugawa Shogunate gained control over the entire country and incorporated Nagoya into the area under its direct administration, the real development of the area began. Nagoyajo Castle, a massive symbol of the power of the Tokugawa family, was completed in 1612. Most of the city, including the Castle, was destroyed during World War II. Ironically, this destruction hastened the development of Nagoya as a modern city. Wide streets were laid out in the center of the city to accommodate heavy modern traffic. To keep a bit of green within the city, each of these streets was designed with a grassy median strip with trees. Nagoyajo Castle was reconstructed in 1959 as the spiritual symbol of the city. Nagoya is often called Chukyo (Central Capital) because it is located between the modern capital, Tokyo (Eastern Capital), and the ancient capital, Kyoto (Western Capital). Though the city has never been the official capital of Japan, it has always been the focal point for the Central Japan district.

Outline of the City

Nagoya's downtown area, Sakae, is about 1.5 miles (2.5 km.) from Nagoya Station, but the station district, and especially its underground shopping and restaurant malls, has itself become another city center. Many office buildings are located around the station. Governmental offices of both Nagoya City and Aichi Prefecture are southeast of Nagoyajo Castle. There are two major places of interest in Nagoya – Nagoyajo Castle (upper center, map 58) and Atsuta Jingu Shrine (lower center). If you have extra time, you can also visit the Noritake China Factory (upper left), the TV Tower (middle center) and the Tokugawa Museum (northeastern part of the city; outside the map).

Transportation in Nagoya

There are four subway lines in the city. They provide tourists with an easy means of public transportation to all major places of interest. The **Higashiyama** subway line (No. 1) runs east to west, and connects Nagoya Station with Fushimi and Sakae, the major downtown area of Nagoya. The Meijo subway line (No. 2) and a second **Meijo** subway line (No. 4) run north to south on the same tracks between Ozone and Kanayama (lower center) via Shiyakusho (the closest stop to Nagoyajo Castle) and Sakae. At Kanayama Station the No. 2 subway branches off to the south for Nagoya Port, and the No. 4 heads toward the suburbs in the southeast toward Atsuta Jingu Shrine. Between Ozone and Kanayama the No. 2 and No. 4 trains alternate – i.e., if a No. 2 train is the first to come along a No. 4 will be next. The **Tsurumi** subway line runs from the northwest to the southeast. It is probably not of much use to tourists.

All signs at the subway stations are written in both Japanese and English. If you refer to map 58, you shouldn't have any difficulty at all getting around the city. At virtually all subway stations, at least one fare table is written in English.

Places of Interest
Nagoyajo Castle 名古屋城

The Castle is a five minute walk from Shiyakusho Station on the Meijo subway line. The original castle was famous for the twin gold dolphins on the top of the donjon as well as for the grandeur of its structure. The present donjon was reconstructed in 1959, and two new golden dolphins were placed atop its roof. These replacements are the symbol of the Castle. The donjon's modern conveniences include elevators that take you to the top of the building. The observatory affords an extensive view of City of Nagoya and the Nobi Plain. The lower floors of the donjon house a museum that displays various artistic and historic objects rescued from the fire that destroyed the original castle. Ninomaru Garden to the east of the donjon is typical of the refined castle gardens for which Japan is so famous (9:30 AM to 4:30 PM. Admission 250 yen).

Atsuta Jingu Shrine 熱田神宮

You can take the Meijo Line subway (No. 4), the JR Tokaido Line or the Meitetsu Tokoname Line to the Shrine.

Atsuta Jingu, set in densely wooded grounds, is one of the most important shrines in all of Japan. It was erected in the third century. The Shrine is especially famous as the repository of one of the emperor's three sacred symbols, the *Kusanagi-no-Tsurugi* (Grass Mowing Sword). The other two, the Mirror and the Jewel, are preserved at Ise Jingu Shrine and at the Imperial Palace respectively. Atsuta Jingu Shrine is still an object of deep respect among the people, and millions of worshippers visit here during the New Year's Holiday. Amateur groups often stage weekend performances in Noh Hall.

Noritake China Factory のりたけチャイナ

The factory is a ten minute walk from Nagoya Station and a five minute walk from Kamejima subway station. Noritake is Japan's largest ceramics company, and its refined products are popular all over the world. The company welcomes foreign tourists to the factory to observe the manufacturing process. An English-speaking guide escorts you and explains details. You are requested to make reservations at the Welcome Center (561-7111 ext. 251). The factory is closed on weekends.

Tokugawa Museum 徳川美術館

Tokugawa Museum is a 10 minute walk from Ozone Station on the Meijo subway line, the JR Chuo Line, or the Meitetsu Seto Line. It was built on the grounds of the former mansion of a high-ranking retainer of the Tokugawa family. Although the Museum houses 10,000 treasures, such as swords, suits of armor, paintings, pottery, lacquerware and other works of art, only a limited number of them can be displayed in the three small chambers at once. The world famous scroll of the story of Prince Genji (*Genji Monogatari*) is displayed only once a year, and unless you happen to be in Nagoya during the time of this special exhibition, it is probably not worth allocating precious time to this Museum.

Nagoya Station Vicinity

To the east of Nagoya Station there is a huge underground shopping center, the total length of which is 3.75 miles (6 km.). It's so extensive that natives of the city as well as foreign visitors can easily get lost. The surface of the area is a business area. Although the district is bustling during the day, it is rather quiet in the evening.

Sakae Downtown 栄

Sakae is Nagoya's version of Tokyo's Ginza. Shopping, eating and drinking establishments are clustered on the streets here. There's another extensive underground shopping area under the Sakae subway stations and the Meitetsu Seto Line's Sakae-machi Station (which is itself underground). In the center of 328-foot (100 m.) wide Hisaya-dori Street is a park and the city's 590-foot (180 m.) tall TV Tower. The tower has an observatory at an altitude of 295 feet (90 m.).

Restaurants in Sakae

Akbar (lower center, map 59) is located in the basement of a modern building, and serves a variety of Indian curry dishes (inexpensive). **Riviere** (upper right) is a seafood restaurant and **Kaen** (middle center) is a Korean barbecue restaurant (both reason-

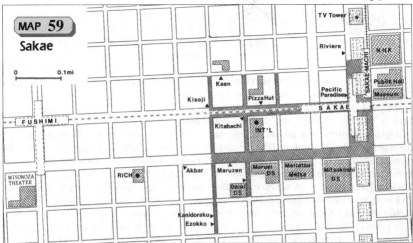

able). **Chinese Yamucha Miramar** (not pictured on map 59, but at the same location as **Akbar** above) serves Chinese set menu dinners at 2,500 – 4,000 yen. **Kitahachi** (middle center) is a typical sushi bar restaurant. An a la carte dinner may cost 3,000 – 5,000 yen. **Kisoji** (middle center) is an authentic Japanese restaurant. In addition to the Japanese set menu, the restaurant also serves Shabu-shabu (moderate). **Kanidoraku** (lower center) is a crab specialist, and has a huge mechanical crab for a sign (moderate). **Ezokko** (lower center) is a robatayaki pub. Typical dishes are 300 – 600 yen. **Pacific Paradise** (middle right) is a wine house (reasonable).

Accommodations in Nagoya
First-class Hotels
Hotel Nagoya Castle
   ホテルナゴヤキャッスル
   (Upper left, map 58, 250 rooms)
   Add: 3-19, Hinokuchicho, Nishi-ku.
   Tel: (052) 521-2121.
Nagoya Kanko Hotel 名古屋観光ホテル
   (Middle center, map 58, 505 rooms)
   Add: 1-19-30 Nishiki, Naka-ku.
   Tel: (052) 231-7711.
Nagoya Tokyu Hotel 名古屋東急ホテル
   (In Sakae downtown, outside of map 58, 380 rooms)
   Add: 4-chome, Sakae, Naka-ku.
   Tel: (052) 251-2411.

International Hotel Nagoya
   名古屋国際ホテル
   (Middle center, map 58, 254 rooms)
   Add: 3-23-3, Nishiki, Naka-ku.
   Tel: (052) 962-3111.
Nagoya Miyako Hotel 名古屋都ホテル
   (Middle left, map 58, 390 rooms)
   Add: 4-9-10, Meieki, Nakamura-ku.
   Tel: (052) 571-3211.
Standard Hotels
Hotel Castle Plaza
   ホテルキャッスルプラザ
   (Middle left, map 58, 258 rooms)
   Add: 4-3-25, Meieki, Nakamura-ku.
   Tel: (052) 582-2121.
Meitetsu Grand Hotel 名鉄グランドホテル
   (Middle left, map 58, 242 rooms)
   Add: 1-2-4, Naeki, Nakamura-ku.
   Tel: (052) 582-2211.
Business Hotels
Nagoya Daiichi Hotel 名古屋第一ホテル
   (Middle left, map 58)
   Add: 3-27-5, Meieki, Nakamura-ku.
   Tel: (052) 581-4411.
Nagoya Tokyu Inn
   名古屋東急イン（丸の内）
   (Middle center, map 58, 187 rooms)
   Add: 2-17-18, Marunouchi, Naka-ku.
   Tel: (052) 202-0109.
Hotel Rich Nagoya ホテルリッチ名古屋
   (Middle center, map 58, 101 rooms)
   Add: 2-3-9, Sakae, Naka-ku.
   Tel: (052) 231-5611.

Seto

瀬戸

In Japan, ceramics are popularly called "Seto-mono" (objects of Seto). It is believed that pottery production started in Seto in the 8th century, and that Japan's first glazed pottery was produced here in the middle of the 9th century. The development of artistic pottery was advanced when new Chinese technology was introduced by Toshiro Kato in the 13th century, but the civil wars scattered the skilled potters to remote areas, and Seto suffered a long stagnant period. The city was revitalized by the efforts of Tamikichi Kato, who introduced advanced ceramic technology in the early 19th century. Today Seto prospers as Japan's largest producer of everyday ceramic products. Seto is the most typical of all Japanese pottery centers and has a long history as such.

Seto is described below in detail. There are two more famous pottery villages near Nagoya:

Tajimi 多治見 is the home of Mino Pottery, which originated with craftsmen from Seto who took refuge in the Tajimi area during the civil wars. The simple yet refined designs and color schemes used by this school of pottery have long been favored for the tea ceremony.

Tokoname 常滑 pottery originated in the 12th century, and is noted for its natural finish. The Tokoname School uses only simple, natural glazes or leaves its products unglazed. Tokoname vases are especially prized. The city now prospers as Japan's chief producer of industrial earthenware pipes.

Seto

Of the many pottery villages located all over Japan, Seto is proud that it has the longest history. The river running in the middle of the city is dark white from all the pottery clay, and the major streets are crowded with shops that display the products of the workrooms. Seto's Pottery Festival, which is held on the third Saturday and Sunday of September, is the largest open air market of this kind and attracts hundreds of thousands of visitors to the city. On map 60, the major pottery stores are indicated with red stars.

Ceramic Center 陶磁器センター (middle center, map 60) is a Seto pottery museum. About 250 fine works, both old and new, are displayed on the second floor. The first floor is a souvenir shop and sells a variety of products at prices that range from about 250 yen to more than 1 million yen.

Hosenji Temple 宝泉寺 (lower right) has an impressive two-story pagoda.

Seto-Koen Park 瀬戸公園 (middle right) is located in an elevated place. The hexagonal hall, made itself of pottery, contains a monument to Toshiro Kato, originator of

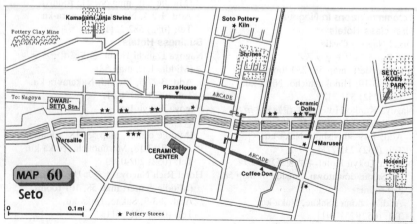

MAP 60

Seto

0   0.1 mi

★ Pottery Stores

Seto pottery. The 11-foot (3.3 m.) tall hall, built in 1866, is the largest pottery product in Japan, and a very impressive structure.

Toningyo Juhachibankan 陶人形十八番館 (middle right), a pottery shop specializing in pottery dolls, has an English sign "Ceramic Dolls." This store is always up on new trends in pottery making and is a good place to look for small souvenir items.

Soto Pottery Kiln 創陶 (upper center) teaches pottery making to amateurs. All visitors are invited to join in the work on Sundays and holidays (10:00 AM to 3:00 PM). There is nominal charge (1,000 – 2,000 yen) to cover materials. On weekdays the kiln is open only to registered members (1:00 PM to 3:00 PM), but visitors can still observe the potters at work.

Kamagami Jinja Shrine 窯神神社 (upper left) is located on a small hill atop a long flight of stone steps. The Shrine has several ceramic lion dogs (Guardians of the Shrine). A statue of Tamikichi Kato, who revitalized the city in the early 19th century, is located in the Shrine's precincts. There is a good view of the city from the shrine.

Pottery Clay Mine (upper left): This source of the clay used by the city's potters is to the west of Kamagami Jinja Shrine.

Seto's Pottery Festival

Tsumago
妻籠

During the Edo era, when the Tokaido Post Road was the principal link between Tokyo and Kyoto along the coast, Nakasendo Path, which branches off the Tokaido at Nagoya and runs through the mountainous inland, was another important trunk route connecting the Shogun's city of Edo (Tokyo) and the Emperor's city of Kyoto. A number of post towns that catered to travelers on foot or on horseback prospered along Nakasendo Path. Tsumago was one of them.

With the development of the Pacific coast cities after the Meiji Restoration, traffic between Tokyo and Kyoto (or Osaka) shifted to the Tokaido route, and Nakasendo became only a supplemental route. In the early 20th century, the completion of the JR Chuo Line (No. 11) connecting Nagoya and Nagano sounded the death knell for the post towns of the Nakasendo. Most accommodations and rest facilities disappeared, including those in Tsumago.

To recreate the historic setting of a typical Edo era town, and to attract nostalgic tourists, the ruins in Tsumago were reconstructed in the 1960's. A half-mile stretch of the old Nakasendo Path in Tsumago is flanked by wooden houses reconstructed in the style of the 18th century. This area is a camera buff's delight. Many of these reconstructed buildings house restaurants, souvenir shops and small museums, of the 'tourist-trap' type.

Transportation to Tsumago

The closest train station to Tsumago is Nagiso, which is connected with Nagoya by the JR Chuo Line (No. 11). The ride from Nagoya to Nagiso takes only 70 minutes.

Buses run frequently between Nagiso Station and Tsumago Bus Terminal (a 10 minute ride). The historic district is only a few minutes walk from the terminal.

Tsumago can be easily visited in a one day excursion from Nagoya.

Ise-Shima 伊勢，志摩

Ise-Shima National Park offers two major attractions – beautiful marine scenery created by the rugged coast, and solemn Ise Jingu Shrine. The private Kintetsu Railways operates direct trains from Nagoya (No. 228), Kyoto (No. 232) and Osaka (No. 233), and the area attracts several million travelers year round, tourists as well as pilgrims to Ise Jingu Shrine.

Toba

鳥羽

Toba is the center of Ise-Shima National Park, and most tourists to Ise-Shima spend

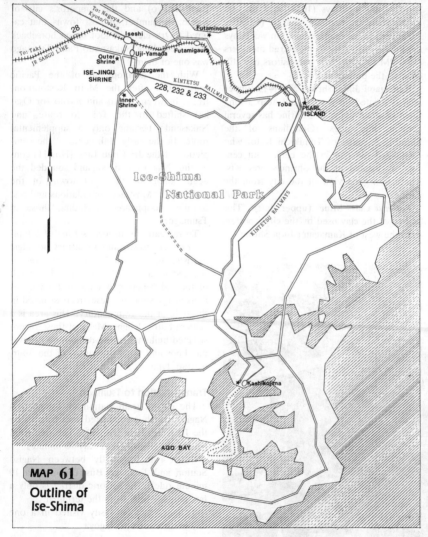

MAP 61
Outline of Ise-Shima

a night or two in Toba. Many hotels and ryokans are also located along scenic Toba Bay.

Mikimoto Pearl Island 御木本真珠島

Only a five minute walk from Toba Station, this small island is connected to the mainland by a covered bridge. Kokichi Mikimoto started his experiments with cultured pearls here in the late 19th century. He succeeded in culturing pearl hemispheres in 1893 and round pearls in 1905. A variety of pearl products are on display in the museums and the women pearl divers give demonstrations every 40 – 60 minutes (8:30 AM to 5:00 PM. In the winter 9:00 AM to 4:30 PM. Admission 800 yen).

Toba Aquarium 鳥羽水族館

Toba Aquarium is just a few minutes walk from Mikimoto Pearl Island. This large complex consists of several halls. In addition to the fish of the area, rare marine animals, such as Alaskan sea otters and Baikal seals, are also on display here. The adjacent museum has an extensive collection of sea shells (8:00 AM to 5:00 PM. Admission 1,200 yen).

Sightseeing Boat in Toba Bay

A 50-minute sightseeing boat trip around Toba Bay operates frequently from the pier near Toba Station. The view of the rugged coast of Toba Bay is absolutely magnificent. You can also get off the boat at Mikimoto Pearl Island (1,200 yen).

Hotel in Toba

Toba Hotel Int'l 鳥羽国際ホテル
(First-class: upper center, map 62, 102 rooms)
Add: 1-23-1, Toba, Mie Prefecture.
Tel: (0599) 25-3121.
* 45 Japanese rooms are available in the annex.

Ryokans in Toba

Todaya Bekkan 戸田家別館
(First-class: upper center, map 62, 123 rooms)
Add: 1-24-26, Toba, Mie Prefecture.
Tel: (0599) 25-4126.
Toba Grand Hotel 鳥羽グランドホテル
(Standard: upper left, map 62, 42 rooms)
Add: 239-9, Obamacho, Toba, Mie Prefecture.
Tel: (0599) 25-4141.

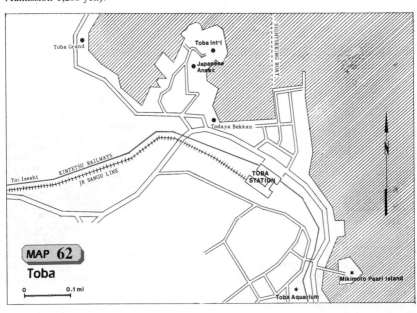

MAP 62
Toba

0   0.1 mi

Toba Grand
Toba Int'l
Japanese Annex
Todaya Bekkan
SIGHTSEEING BOAT
To: Iseshi
KINTETSU RAILWAYS
JR SANGU LINE
TOBA STATION
N
Mikimoto Pearl Island
Toba Aquarium

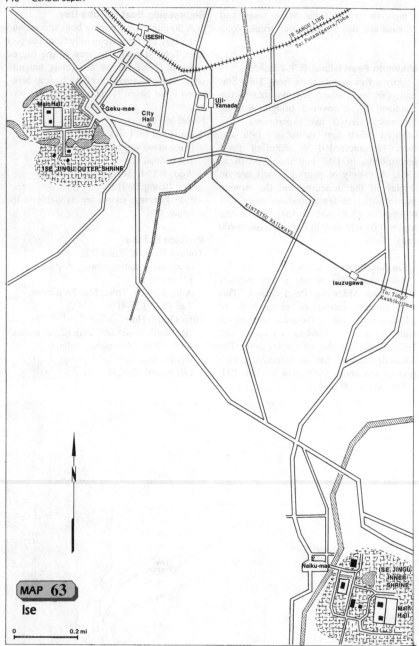

MAP 63
Ise

0   0.2 mi

Ise Jingu Shrine
伊勢神宮

Ise Jingu Shrine consists of two major shrines (Outer Shrine and Inner Shrine) and many minor buildings.

The Outer Shrine 外宮 (upper left, map 63), a seven minute walk from Iseshi Station 伊勢市駅, honors the Goddess of the Harvest. The wide main approach is lined with tall cedar trees, through which you can see Magatama-ike Pond. The main shrine is a complex of several buildings. The main hall, made of white Japanese cypress, uses a unique *Yuiitsu-Shinmeizukuri* design.

The Inner Shrine 内宮 (lower right, map 63) is located 3.9 miles (6.2 km.) to the southeast of the Outer Shrine. The Shrines are connected by a bus that runs every 15 minutes. The Inner Shrine is dedicated to the Goddess of the Sun, mythological ancestress of the imperial family. Crossing the clear Isuzugawa River by bridge, the wide main approach leads to the main hall of the inner shrine. Huge cedar trees line both sides of the approach and enhance the sacred atmosphere of the grounds. The main shrine also employs the *Yuiitsu-Shinmeizukuri* style and is located on a hillside.

Because the main worship halls of both Shrines are reconstructed every 20 years in accordance with Shinto practice and tradition, the structures are new. They are, however, considered good examples of simple design and make the best possible use of the natural beauty of the wood.

Buses from the Inner Shrine to Iseshi Station run every 15 minutes.

Kashikojima
賢島

(Lower center, map 61)

Kashikojima, a terminus of the Kintetsu Railways, is on the southern side of Shima Peninsula. Ago Bay, with a number of small islands and pearl beds, features the most beautiful marine scenery of the area.

A one-hour boat tour around peaceful and picturesque Ago Bay operates frequently from a pier near Kashikojima Station. Shima Marineland is an aquarium that is home to more than 2,500 fish of the area (9:00 AM to 5:00 PM).

Hotel in Kashikojima
Shima Kanko Hotel 志摩観光ホテル
  (First-class)
  Add: Kashikojima, Agocho,
  Mie Prefecture.
  Tel: (05994) 3-1211.

Ryokan in Kashikojima
Shin-Kashikojimaso 新賢島荘
  (First-class, 57 rooms)
  Add: 738, Kashikojima, Agocho,
  Mie Prefecture.
  Tel: (05994) 3-1221.

Futaminoura
二見ヶ浦

(Upper center, map 61)

Futaminoura is famous for two rocks the sea has eroded in a distinctive way. They are called the Husband-Wife rocks, and are joined by a thick straw rope. In the summer the beach is crowded with sea bathers.

Ryokans in Futaminoura
Futamikan 二見館
  (The Old Wing is a very traditional ryokan. The New Wing is first-class, 42 rooms)
  Add: 569-2, Ko, Futami-machi,
  Mie Prefecture.
  Tel: (05964) 3-2003.
Hamachiyokan
  浜千代館
  (Standard ryokan, 33 rooms)
  Add: 537-26, Ko, Futami-machi,
  Mie Prefecture.
  Tel: (05964) 3-2050.

Takayama 高山

Takayama Valley is located at the western foot of the Japan Alps. The Alps in this area consist of a number of 10,000-foot (3,000 m.) tall mountains, and are called the roof of Japan. When Hideyoshi Toyotomi unified Japan after almost 250 years of civil war, the feudal lord Nagachika Kanamori was assigned to govern the Takayama area in 1586. During the next 100 years, the Kanamori family successfully encouraged the development of agriculture and handicrafts and made Takayama one of the most prosperous local cities in Japan. In 1692, defeated in a political struggle with the Tokugawa Shogunate, the Kanamori family was exiled to a northern area of Japan, and Takayama fell under the direct control of the Tokugawa Shogunate. Because the Shogunate's principal interest in this prosperous area was in collecting taxes, economic activities were even further encouraged. Protected by the power of the Shogunate, Takayama merchants and craftsmen expanded their activities into the territories of other feudal lords, and underwrote cultural activities at home with the profits they made elsewhere. The elaborate floats still used in Takayama Festivals testify to the economic prosperity and high cultural standards achieved by the people of Takayama.

Takayama Matsuri Festival

As you approach Takayama from the direction of either the Pacific Ocean or the Japan Sea, the train goes along a narrow, beautiful river basin surrounded by mountains. The train ride is enjoyable in all seasons, but especially wonderful in winter, when the mountains are covered with snow. Though your activities will be restricted by the snow and the severe winter cold, the winter train ride is recommended as a detour on your way to Kyoto from Tokyo or on your way back to Tokyo from Kyoto. It is amazing that a city as lovely as Takayama was built in such an isolated mountain valley.

Transportation in Takayama

Buses are the only means of public transportation in Takayama City. Taxis are also plentiful. Since major places of interest are located in a comparatively narrow area, you won't even have to use the buses except to visit Hida-no-sato Village in Western Takayama.

If you are a cycling fan, a rental cycle can be arranged at your accommodations.

Outline of Takayama

The main part of the city is to the east of the JR Takayama Line tracks. In addition to business and governmental offices, there are a number of places of historical interest in this part of the city. The area to the west of the railroad tracks is mountainous and less developed. Hida-no-sato Village (an open-air museum) and Hida Minzokukan (Hida Folklore Museum) are here. They are perched on the mountain sides surrounded by thick forests.

Suggested Itinerary

One and a half days are ideal for a visit to Takayama: a half day for Western Takayama, and a full day for Eastern Takayama, and this is how the itineraries are organized. If you can allocate only one day for Takayama, skip the places marked optional.

Western Takayama

Takayama Station to Hida-no-sato by Bus

There is counter-clockwise circle line bus service from Takayama Station to Hida-no-sato and Minzokukan-mae. The bus leaves from bus stop No. 4 at Takayama Station three times an hour (Take a *seiri-ken* fare zone ticket upon boarding, and pay when you get off).

On your way to Hida-no-sato, you will see a huge golden temple building (probably the biggest structure in Takayama). It is the recently constructed headquarters of the Mahikari religious group. This glaringly modern building is quite incongruous in the quiet surroundings of a mountain village.

Hida-no-sato Village 飛驒の里

Hida-no-sato Village is Takayama's

equivalent of Williamsburg, Virginia. Old farm houses, which were destined to be destroyed for the construction of dams or because their owners planned to move to larger cities, have been moved here and preserved as living museums. They illustrate the life style of farmers and craftsmen of the Takayama area. More than 30 buildings are situated on a hillside around a small pond. Many of them are also used for demonstrating the production processes of handicrafts such as lacquerware, carving, dyeing, woodenware, and handmade paper. The village is located in an elevated area and provides visitors with a good view of the city, with the Japan Alps rising in the background. The Village is open from 8:30 AM to 5:00 PM. The 300 yen admission ticket also entitles you to entrance to Hida Minzokukan (Hold on to your ticket until you get there!).

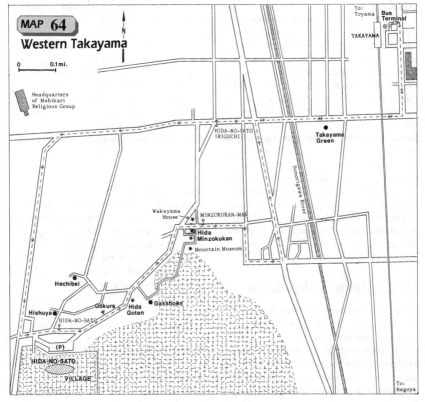

Hida-no-sato Village to Hida Minzokukan

The walk from Hida-no-sato Village to Hida Minzokukan is itself a trip through the living museum of the traditional Takayama area. The descending road is dotted with old houses, most of which are now souvenir shops or restaurants. Especially noteworthy are Gokura and Hida Goten. Neither of them have English signs, but you will have no difficulty recognizing them. Gokura is an antique shop, in a big old converted warehouse. Because it handles comparatively large-sized antiques, most of them won't be suitable for souvenirs, but the shop itself is like a museum. Hida Goten is the biggest wooden structure in Takayama. It was originally constructed as a rich farmer's house and was moved here for preservation. Its complicated roof and beautiful wall designs are very impressive.

Hida Minzokukan (Folklore Museum) 飛騨民族館

Hida Minzokukan consists of four buildings. Wakayama House was built in 1751 and transferred to this site in 1959. It is a good example of the *Gasshozukuri* architectural style – with a steep roof shaped like hands joined in prayer. You can step inside to see the interior and its antique furniture and handicraft items. A grain storehouse and an old one-story house are other examples of the everyday environment of the people of the Edo era. The Mountain Museum exhibits materials collected in the Japan Alps by the Hida Mountaineering Club, but the arrangement of the displays unfortunately lacks a focus.

You can take the circle bus back to Takayama Station. It won't take more than 20 minutes even if you walk back to Takayama Station.

Eastern Takayama

There is another circle bus line in Eastern Takayama. If you follow the suggested itinerary, you won't use it.

* If your time in Takayama is limited, you should take the bus from the station to Kusakabe Mingeikan-mae (upper right, map 65). The bus leaves from stop No. 2 at

Takayama Station every 10 – 15 minutes.

Kokubunji Temple (optional) 国分寺

Kokubunji Temple was originally erected at the order of Emperor Shomu in 746 (Kokubunji Temples were built all over Japan at that time as subordinate branch temples of Nara's Todaiji Temple, or Temple of the Great Buddha). The original buildings were burnt down during the civil wars. The present Main Hall was built in 1615 by the Kanamori family. The three-story pagoda, built in 1807, is the only one of this type in the Takayama area. A huge gingko tree in the precincts is 1,200 years old, and has been designated a Natural Monument. Entrance to the temple grounds is free of charge.

Shunkei Kaikan 春慶会館 (optional)

Shunkei Kaikan, a white warehouse-like building, exhibits exquisite lacquerware of the Shunkei School. The Shunkei School, established in Takayama at the beginning of the 17th century, is famous for its technique of making use of the natural beauty of the grains of the woods. (8:30 AM to 5:00 PM).

Open-Air Market 朝市

An open-air market is held in the morning along the eastern bank of the Miyagawa River. The market was originally organized by farmers in the Takayama vicinity to sell fresh vegetables to the people of the city. The tradition still continues. Souvenir and snack vendors have joined in as well, to squeeze a few yen from tourists. The market is a treasure trove of local color and local flavors (6:00 AM to 12:00 noon).

Kusakabe House 日下部民芸館

The Kusakabes, a merchant family, prospered under the Tokugawa Shogunate. Although their house was destroyed by fire

MAP 65
Eastern Takayama

0   0.1mi.

in 1875, it was reconstructed in 1879, with careful attention paid to all details. The high ceiling supported by complicated beams and pillars is a good example of the unique architectural designs of the area (9:00 AM to 4:30 PM. Admission 200 yen). **Yoshijima House** 吉島家, another merchant's house adjacent to the Kusakabe House, is open to the public from 9:00 AM to 5:00 PM (optional).

Kusakabe House to Yatai Kaikan

On your way from Kusakabe House to Yatai Kaikan, you will pass **Hida Koshokan** 飛騨工匠館 (Hida Craftsmen's Shop). This is basically a souvenir shop. Demonstrations of wood carvings are held in the shop

and representative works of contemporary masters are displayed in its warehouse annex. Unless you are a real handicrafts buff, it is better to skip Hida Koshokan. Passing two torii gates, you will see the brilliant main hall of **Sakurayama Hachiman Jinja Shrine** 桜山八幡宮神社. The present structure is a 1976 reconstruction.

Yatai Kaikan 屋台会館

Yatai Kaikan in the shrine precincts is a modern concrete building. Festival floats, which are still used for Takayama Festivals every spring (April 14 – 15) and fall (October 9 – 10), are stored here. The elaborate decorations and delicate carvings of the floats testify to the high artistic skill of the craftsmen of Takayama. Four of the existing 11 floats are always exhibited in turn. A number of dolls in traditional costume are displayed along with the floats and recorded festival music is played to help visitors imagine the atmosphere of the festival (8:30 AM to 5:00 PM. Admission 380 yen).

Shishi Kaikan 獅子会館 (optional)

Shishi Kaikan is another small museum adjacent to Yatai Kaikan. The shishi is a legendary creature believed to be a protector of peaceful daily life. A variety of shishi dances are performed all over Japan, especially in the Takayama area. The faces of shishi masks used in the dances differ slightly from area to area. About 300 of these masks have been collected from all over Japan and are on display on the first floor of Shishi Kaikan. The second floor displays artistic works such as hanging scrolls and folding screens. A short demonstration of the traditional puppet show, performed on the floats during Takayama Festivals, is given here every 10 minutes. Because the stage is in the dining room, the atmosphere is a bit strange, but the complicated movements of the puppets are fascinating. (9:00 AM to 4:30 PM).

Takayama Betsuin Temple 高山別院 (optional)

Takayama Betsuin Temple is the regional headquarters of the Jodo-Shinshu sect of Buddhism. The temple was originally built in 1509 and was destroyed by fire many times. The present structure is a recent reconstruction. Karamon Gate at the southern edge of the precincts is impressive. Entrance to the grounds is free of charge.

Kami-Sannomachi Street 上三之町通り

Kami-Sannomachi Street preserves the atmosphere of the Edo era town. The old buildings on both sides of the street are used as stores, restaurants, snack shops and galleries, but still maintain an 18th century ambience. Enjoy a coffee break or shopping in this unique setting. Several museums, such as **Fuji Art Gallery** and **The Local Museum Hida** are located in the area. Most of them capitalize a bit on the popularity of Takayama.

Takayama Jinya 高山陣屋

Takayama Jinya is a palace that was used as an administrator's office and residence from 1692 until the Tokugawa Shogunate was overthrown in 1868. It is the only building of its kind that is still standing. The palace's Kitashirasu (civil court), Oshirasu (criminal court), Hiroma (chambers), rice warehouses and other facilities give visitors an idea of how the Shogunate conducted official business (8:45 AM to 5:00 PM. Closed on Wednesdays. Admission 200 yen). **An open-air market** is held in the square in front of the palace entrance every morning (6:00 AM to 12:00 noon).

Shopping

Many souvenir shops are located around the tourist attractions. If you want to combine an evening stroll and shopping, Kokubunji-dori Street (middle center, map 65) has many shops handling handicraft items (These shops close around 8:00 PM).

Restaurants

Jizake-en (middle center, map 65) is a Japanese style pub. Thirteen different brands of sake brewed in the Takayama area are available here. The sake barrels piled at the entrance are a good landmark and make this pub easy to find. **Mikado** (middle center, map 65) is a small Japanese restaurant. In addition to pork cutlet and tempura, it has a special set menu dinner ("Sansai Teishoku," or assorted mountain vegetables). Inexpensive, **Shotenko** (middle center, map 65) is a Chinese restaurant (inexpensive). **Steak House** (lower center, map 65) serves a reasonable steak dinner.

Accommodations in Takayama
1. Hotels

Hida Hotel Plaza ひだホテルプラザ
  (First-class: upper left, map 65, 150 rooms)
  Add: 2-60, Hanaokacho, Takayama.
  Tel: (0577) 33-4600.
Takayama Green Hotel 高山グリーンホテル
  (First-class: middle right, map 64,

184 rooms)
Add: 2-180, Nishino-Isshikicho,
Takayama.
Tel: (0577) 33-5500.

2. Ryokans

Kinkikan 金亀館
(Deluxe: middle center, map 65,
9 rooms)
Add: 48, Asahicho, Takayama.
Tel: (0577) 32-3131.

Hishuya 飛州屋
(Deluxe: lower left, map 64. 16 rooms)
Add: 2581, Kami-Okamotocho,
Takayama.
Tel: (0577) 33-4001.

Sogo Palace Takayama ソーゴパレス高山
(Standard: middle center, map 65,
33 rooms)
Add: 54, Suehirocho, Takayama.
Tel: (0577) 33-5000.

Daimaru Ryokan 大丸旅館
(Standard: middle left, map 65,
26 rooms)
Add: 6-6, Hanasatocho, Takayama.
Tel: (0577) 32-0630.

Hachibei 八兵衛
(Minshuku: lower left, map 64,
12 rooms)
Add: 2561, Kami-Okamotocho,
Takayama.
Tel: (0577) 33-0573.

Gero　下呂

Gero is a hotspring town, with a number
of modern buildings nestled in a narrow
valley along the Masudagawa River. There
are more than 30 ryokans in Gero. Only
two hours by the JR Takayama Line (No.
15) from Nagoya, this hotspring is one of
the most popular weekend destinations for
residents of that metropolitan area. Its proximity to Takayama, which is only one
hour away by train, has helped Gero also
attract tourists from around the country
who want to combine a visit to historic
Takayama with a relaxing overnight stay at
a hotspring.

Takayama Jinya

As is the case with many hotspring resorts near huge cities (such as Atami Spa
and Tokyo, and Arima Spa and Osaka),
the town of Gero has a rather racy night
life, and features quite a few strip joints,
bars and cabarets. But the town is proud of
its vigorous hotsprings, and its reputation
as one of Japan's three best hotspring resorts. Vacationers from large Japanese
cities find this a pleasant, relaxing atmosphere. If you like hotsprings, you should
consider staying overnight in Gero, as most
Japanese do, before or after your trip to
Takayama.

Ryokans in Gero

Hotel Suimeikan ホテル水明館
(Deluxe, 178 rooms)
Add: 1268, Koda, Gerocho.
Tel: (05762) 5-2800.

Ogawaya 小川屋
(First-class, 86 rooms)
Add: 570, Yunoshima, Gerocho.
Tel: (05762) 5-3121.

Gero Yamagataya 下呂山形屋
(First-class, 60 rooms)
Add: 260-1, Yunoshima, Gerocho.
Tel: (05762) 5-2601.

Hotel Yoshino ホテルよし乃
(Standard, 129 rooms)
Add: 1138-1, Mori, Gerocho.
Tel: (05762) 5-3200.

Hotel Gerokan ホテル下呂館
(Standard, 55 rooms)
Add: 1075, Mori, Gerocho.
Tel: (05762) 5-2028.

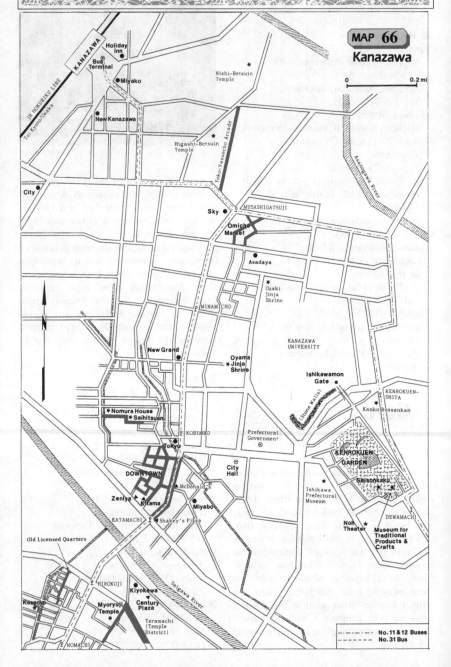

Kanazawa 金沢

MAP **66**

Kanazawa

0   0.2 mi

JR HOKURIKU LINE

To: Kyoto/Osaka

KANAZAWA

Holiday Inn

Bus Terminal

● Miyako

● New Kanazawa

● City

Nishi-Betsuin Temple

Higashi-Betsuin Temple

Toko-Yasuecho Arcade

Asanogawa River

● Sky

MUSASHIGATSUJI

Omicho Market

● Asadaya

Ozaki Jinja Shrine

MINAMICHO

New Grand ●

Oyama Jinja Shrine

KANAZAWA UNIVERSITY

Ishikawamon Gate

(Stone Walls)

KENROKUEN-SHITA

Kanko Bussankan

Nomura House
Saihitsuan

KORIMBO

Prefectural Government

KENROKUEN GARDEN

Seisonkaku

ToKyu

DOWNTOWN

City Hall

McDonald's

Ishikawa Prefectural Museum

DEWAMACHI

Zeniya ● Kitama

● Miyabo

KATAMACHI   Shakey's Pizza

Noh Theater

Museum for Traditional Products & Crafts

Old Licensed Quarters

HIROKOJI

Kiyokawa ●

Century Plaza

Saigawa River

Kosenyo

Myoryuji Temple

Teramachi (Temple District)

NOMACHI

- - - - - No. 11 & 12 Buses

- - - - - No. 31 Bus

During the period of Japan's civil wars (15th to 16th centuries), the Jodo-Shinshu sect of Buddhism established an autonomous government in Kanazawa. It was the only one of many such experiments to survive the onslaughts of neighboring feudal lords. The independent government stayed in power from 1488 to 1580, when the area was attacked by the forces of Nobunaga Oda, who by then had almost realized his great ambition of terminating the civil wars and uniting the nation.

During the Edo period, Kanazawa was the home of Japan's second most powerful feudal family, the Maedas (The most powerful was, of course, the Tokugawas). To avoid confrontations with the Tokugawas, the Maedas stressed cultural activities rather than military affairs. Kutani pottery, Kaga Yuzen dyeing and other crafts were developed to high standards here and they still flourish today. Kanazawa is a modern city, but its many historical and cultural sites still testify to the area's unique historical background.

Transportation to Kanazawa

Kanazawa Station is served by the JR Hokuriku Line. The JR Hokuriku Line (No. 16) originates at Osaka and runs northeast via Kyoto, Fukui, Awara-Onsen, Kanazawa, etc. Some trains terminate at Kanazawa, but many operate further northeast along the Japan Sea coast to Toyama and Niigata. When you travel from Takayama to Kanazawa, you have to take the Takayama Line to Toyama, and then transfer to the Hokuriku Line.

Outline of the City

The most important tourist attraction of Kanazawa, Kenrokuen Garden (lower right, map 66), is located about 1.5 miles (2.4 km.) southeast of JR Kanazawa Station (upper left, map 66). Major places of interest, such as Ishikawamon Gate, Seisonkaku Mansion, and the Museum for Traditional Products & Crafts, are also located in the vicinity of Kenrokuen Garden.

Samurai houses are preserved in the area to the west of Kanazawa's main street (middle left, map 66). Saihitsuan, located in the same area, is a small Kaga Yuzen dyeing factory. Oyama Jinja Shrine (middle center, map 66) is also within walking distance.

Kanazawa's downtown stretches north to south along the main street (between Musashigatsuji bus stop and Katamachi bus stop). Most shops are between Musashigatsuji and Minamicho, while business offices are between Minamicho and Korimbo, and eating and drinking places between Korimbo and Katamachi. Government offices are to the east of Korimbo.

Kosenyo (lower left, map 66), the only Kutani pottery kiln in the city, is located to the south of the Saigawa River. Myoryuji Temple, which is famous for its complicated interior structure, and which is nicknamed "Ninja Temple," as well as the surviving buildings of the former licensed quarters are within walking distance of the pottery kiln.

Transportation in Kanazawa

Using just three of the city's bus lines you can easily cover Kanazawa's major places of interest. As pictured on map 66, the No. 31 bus runs south from Kanazawa Station along the main street. The No. 11 and No. 12 buses operate from Kanazawa Station to the southeast. You can use these buses to reach Kenrokuen Garden and other major tourist destinations.

Suggested Itinerary

It is rather difficult to cover all the places introduced below. If you have only one full day in Kanazawa, skip the places marked as optional.

Seisonkaku 成巽閣 (optional)

Take No. 11 or No. 12 bus to Dewamachi stop. Seisonkaku is a one-minute walk from this stop (lower right, map 66). Seisonkaku was constructed in 1863 by the 13th lord of the Maeda family as a residence for his mother. This two-story building is a monument of elegantly tasteful design. Seikoken Tea House and Hikakutei (Flying Crane Garden) are attached to the mansion (8:30 AM to 4:30 PM. Closed on Wednesdays).

Museum for Traditional Products & Crafts 伝統産業工芸館

With the completion of the new Prefectural Museum this institution has focused its attention on traditional arts and crafts. All sorts of handicraft items, including pottery, Yuzen dyeing, lacquerware, gold, metal and wood items, handmade toys and papers, are displayed here. The displays illustrate the glories of the high artistic standards the area developed during the feudal era (9:00 AM to 4:30 PM. Closed on Thursdays and National Holidays. Admission 100 yen).

Ishikawa Prefectural Museum 石川県立美術館 (optional)

This newly constructed museum is famous for its display of Kutani ware. A large pheasant-shaped incense burner (National Treasure) made by Ninsei Nonomura, master of the Kutani School of pottery, is the pride of the collection. Most of the halls of the Museum are used for special exhibitions (9:00 AM to 4:30 PM. Closed irregularly).

Kenrokuen Garden 兼六園

Kenrokuen literally means "a refined garden incorporating six different features." The famous features of the Garden are

vastness, solemnity, precise arrangements, antiquity, elaborate use of water and scenic charm. Kenrokuen Garden was originally built in the 1670's by the fifth lord of the Maeda family. Succeeding generations expanded the garden and each added something of its own taste to it. The Garden as it stands today was completed by the 12th lord in 1837. This Garden is popularly known as one of Japan's three best gardens, with the other two being Kairakuen in Mito and Korakuen in Okayama. From the top parts of the Garden, visitors can command a good view of the city, and can even see the Japan Sea in the distance (6:30 AM to 6:00 PM; 8:00 AM to 4:30 PM in winter. Admission 100 yen).

Ishikawamon Gate 石川門

Ishikawamon Gate was the southern entrance to Kanazawajo Castle. The entire compound was burned down in 1881 and only a few structures, including the Gate, survived the fire. The magnificence of the Gate gives modern visitors some idea of the power of the Maeda family, and the beautifully arranged stone walls around the Gate testify to the craftsmanship of the era. The castle grounds are now used by Kanazawa University, the Kanazawa local courts and other public offices. Though visitors can enter the Ishikawamon Gate area, the grounds themselves are not open to the public.

Kanko Bussankan 観光物産館 (optional)

Kanko Bussankan is a commercial building near Kenrokuen-shita bus stop. Demonstrations of handicraft production, including Yuzen dyeing, gold foil, pottery, toys and lacquerware are held on the third floor (9:00 AM to 5:00 PM. Closed on Thursdays only in winter). The first floor of the building is a souvenir shop and the second a restaurant.

Kenrokuen to Samurai Houses

Enjoy a leisurely walk from Kenrokuen to the governmental district. There are a number of Kutani pottery shops along the street. Crossing downtown, you will soon be in the Nagamachi district.

Samurai Houses and Saihitsuan

The Nagamachi district was inhabited by high ranking samurai during the Edo era. Several samurai houses and tile-roofed mud walls along the narrow street have been preserved. **Saihitsuan** 彩筆庵 (optional), one of these houses, has been converted to a small Kaga Yuzen dye works. Kanazawa is proud of the high artistic standards of Kaga Yuzen dyeing, which is comparable to the fine work done in Kyoto. The delicate hand-painting process is demonstrated here (9:00 AM to 4:00 PM). **Nomura House** 野村家 (optional), which was actually moved here from another part of the city, provides visitors a chance to see the interior of the house of a high-ranking samurai. A small but authentic Japanese-style garden is attached to the house, and armor and other samurai utensils are displayed in its various rooms (9:00 AM to 5:00 PM).

Oyama Jinja Shrine (optional) 尾山神社

Oyama Jinja Shrine was erected in 1873 in memory of Toshiie Maeda, the first lord of the Maeda family. The Shrine's three-story Shimmon Gate is famous for its colorful stained glass windows on the third level; this is a very unusual structure for Japan. The Shrine's garden skillfully combines a pond, rocks, islets and bridges. Entrance to the temple grounds is free of charge.

Omicho Market 近江町市場

Omicho Market will probably be the last visit of your full-day sightseeing in Kanazawa. The Market is the kitchen of Kanazawa. About 200 small shops, most of which handle foodstuffs, cluster under narrow covered alleys. Visitors are amazed at the variety of seafood and the reasonable prices.

Other Places of Interest

Kosenyo Pottery Kiln 光仙窯 (lower left, map 66) is the only kiln located in Kanazawa City. This small factory, which looks like a regular house from the outside, carries out all the processes of pottery making, from designing and firing to painting. Demonstrations of the skillful craftsmanship involved are sure to fascinate visitors. There is no admission charge, but it is courteous to purchase at least a small item at the souvenir shop (8:30 AM to 5:00 PM. Closed on Sundays).

Former Licensed Quarters 西郭 (lower left, map 66). Nishi-Kuruwa used to be one of Kanazawa's three licensed quarters. The establishments have been converted to drinking places. Several buildings have preserved their original appearance, and are good subjects for photographers. A gatehouse used as a checkpoint to keep the girls from escaping from the district has also been preserved.

Myoryuji Temple 妙立寺 (lower left, map 66). A number of temples are located on the southern side of the Saigawa River. Among them is Myoryuji Temple. Because of its complicated structure, with 29 staircases and 21 secret chambers, the Temple is popularly known as *Ninja-dera*, or Temple for Secret Agents. Guided tours are organized from time to time so that visitors don't get lost in this tricky temple. Travelers who only have limited time should skip Myoryuji because advance reservations are required. In addition, you have to listen to a taped lecture (in Japanese) before the tour. If you have time to make a visit here, ask your hotel to make a reservation for you at (0762) 41-2877.

Ozaki Jinja Shrine 尾崎神社 (middle center, map 66) is often described as Kanazawa's version of the famous Toshogu Shrine in Nikko. Actually, to demonstrate their loyalty to the Tokugawa Shogunate, local lords all over Japan had Toshogu-type shrines built and dedicated to Ieyasu Tokugawa. Ozaki Jinja Shrine is one of them. The Shrine has deteriorated and does not retain its original magnificence.

Yoko- Yasuecho Arcade 横安江町アーケ
ード (upper center, map 66) is lined with
many modern stores. Several shops dealing
in Buddhist altars are scattered among
them. The arcade can be an alternative
destination, especially if you happen to get
caught in a rain storm.

Edo-mura Village 江戸村 (41 minutes by
bus from Kanazawa Station). If you are
staying in Kanazawa for an extended
period, you should consider a visit to Edo-
mura Village, an open-air museum that features about 20 buildings of the Edo era.
Each building represents the typical dwelling of a different social class of the era.
You can see the homes of farmers, merchants, craftsmen, priests and warriors.
Dampuen 檀風苑 ,   another   open-air
museum that displays the tools and products of various craftsmen, is connected to
Edo-mura by frequent mini-bus service.
Both facilities are open from 8:00 AM to
6:00 PM. To reach Edo-mura Village, take
the No. 12 bus from Kanazawa Station or
Kenrokuen-shita. The bus operates about
once every 30 minutes. Edo-mura Village is
a few minutes walk from Yuwaku Spa,
湯湧温泉, the last stop on the line.

Restaurants in Kanazawa

Because Kanazawa is famous for fresh
seafood caught in the Japan Sea, we recommend that you try an authentic Japanese
restaurant for dinner.

Kitama (lower left, map 66). This 122-
year old establishment serves a variety of
set menu dinners (moderate). **Zeniya** (near
Kitama above) is an authentic counter-style
Japanese restaurant (moderate). **Century
Plaza** (lower left, map 66). This modern
restaurant overlooks the Saigawa River.
Jimbei, located on the first floor, serves
traditional Japanese dinners (moderate).

Accommodations in Kanazawa
1. Hotels
Kanazawa Tokyu Hotel 金沢東急ホテル
  (First-class: middle center, map 66,
  250 rooms)
  Add: 2-1-1, Korimbo, Kanazawa.
  Tel: (0762) 31-2411.

Kanazawa New Grand Hotel
  金沢ニューグランドホテル
  (First-class: middle center, map 66,
  190 rooms)
  Add: 1-50, Takaokamachi, Kanazawa.
  Tel: (0762) 33-1311.
Kanazawa Miyako Hotel 金沢都ホテル
  (First-class: upper left, map 66,
  92 rooms)
  Add: 6-10, Konohanacho, Kanazawa.
  Tel: (0762) 31-2202.
Holiday Inn Kanazawa ホリデーイン金沢
  (First-class: upper left, map 66,
  181 rooms)
  Add:L 1-10, Horikawacho, Kanazawa.
  Tel: (0762) 23-1111.
Kanazawa Sky Hotel 金沢スカイホテル
  (Standard: upper center, map 66,
  133 rooms)
  Add: 15-1, Musashimachi, Kanazawa.
  Tel: (0762) 33-2233.
Hotel New Kanazawa ホテルニュー金沢
  (Business hotel: upper left, map 66,
  117 rooms)
  Add: 2-14-10, Honcho, Kanazawa.
  Tel: (0762) 23-2255.
Kanazawa City Hotel 金沢シティーホテル
  (Business hotel: upper left, map 66,
  209 rooms)
  Add: 6-8, Showamachi, Kanazawa.
  Tel: (0762) 33-2233.

2. Ryokans
Asadaya 浅田屋
  (Deluxe: middle center, map 66,
  5 rooms)
  Add: 23, Jukkenmachi, Kanazawa.
  Tel: (0762) 31-2228.
Miyabo みやぼ
  (Deluxe: lower center, map 66,
  38 rooms)
  Add: 3, Shimo-Kakinokibata, Kanazawa.
  Tel: (0762) 31-4228.
Kiyokawa きよ川
  (Deluxe: lower left, map 66, 26 rooms)
  Add: 7-1, Kiyokawamachi, Kanazawa.
  Tel: (0762) 41-6123.
Hakuunro Hotel 白雲楼ホテル
  (Yuwaku Spa, near Edo-mura Village,
  100 rooms)
  Add: Yuwakucho, Kanazawa.
  Tel: (0762) 35-1111.

Eiheiji Temple & Cape Tojimbo

永平寺, 東尋坊

Two important places of interest are located between Kanazawa and Kyoto. Cape Tojimbo is on the beautiful, rugged Japan Sea coast, and Eiheiji Temple is still a prosperous training center for Zen priests.

If you want to visit the Temple and the Cape on your way to Kanazawa from Kyoto/Osaka, take the Keifuku Echizen Line from Fukui to Eiheiji (The train runs about once every hour). When you finish your visit to Eiheiji Temple, take a direct bus to Cape Tojimbo (Check the schedule of this bus service as soon as you arrive at Eiheiji Station because there are only two buses daily – one in the morning and the other around noon). After enjoying the view of the Japan Sea, take a bus (frequent operation) to Awara-Onsen Station to catch a train to Kanazawa. If you travel this route in reverse, from Kanazawa to Kyoto/Osaka, visit Cape Tojimbo first. Then take a bus to Eiheiji Temple. After the visit to the temple take the Keifuku Echizen Line to Fukui Station and catch the train to Kyoto/Osaka.

Eiheiji Temple 永平寺

Eiheiji Temple, a 10 minute walk from the train station, was founded in 1244 as a Zen monastery. Two hundred monks live there, devoting themselves to Zen training. Visitors, including foreigners, are first guided to a reception hall for a 15 minute long (and rather tedious) explanation, in Japanese, of the temple's history and facilities. An English brochure is given to foreigners. Visiting this temple is the best way to understand how Zen training is conducted. The temple is open to the public from 5:00 AM to 5:00 PM. (Admission tickets are sold in vending machines!).

Cape Tojimbo 東尋坊

The Cape is famous for its pillars of dark greyish andesite. Fifty-meter (164 feet) tall cliffs supported by these pillars extend along the Japan Sea coast, creating a beautiful, rugged coastline. A 30-minute sightseeing boat operates frequently from the tip of the Cape. The view of the cliffs from the water is much more impressive than what you'll see staying on land. If your time is limited, take the elevator to the top of Tojimbo Tower. The observatory is located 328 feet (100 m.) above sea level, and commands a wide view of the Cape area. The area is filled with souvenir shops, vendors and restaurants, and is a little noisy.

MAP 67

Eiheiji Temple & Cape Tojimbo

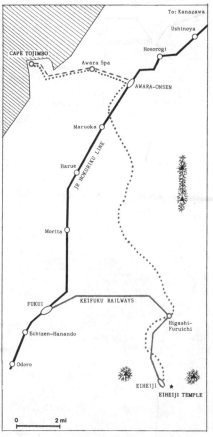

The Japan Alps 日本アルプス

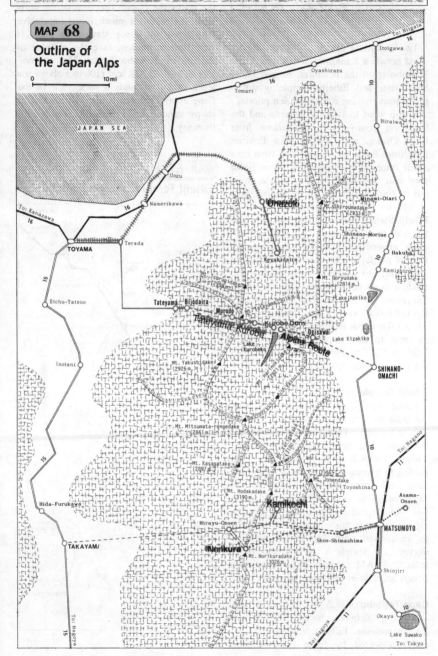

MAP **68**

Outline of
the Japan Alps

0   10mi

The Japan Alps are often referred to as the roof of Japan. There are three major mountain ranges in the Japan Alps – from north to south, the Hida mountains or the Northern Alps, the Kiso mountains or the Central Alps, and the Akaishi mountains or the Southern Alps. The Northern Alps have the most precipitous and scenic mountains, and the phrase "Japan Alps" usually refers to this area. The highest peak of the Northern Alps is Mt. Hodakadake (3,190 m. or 10,466 ft.), and there are several other mountains that top 3,000 meters, such as Mt. Yarigatake, Mt. Norikuradake and Mt. Tateyama.

Two JR lines run from north to south parallel to the Northern Alps – the JR Oito Line (No. 10) on the east, and the JR Takayama Line (No. 15) on the west. There are two scenic routes that connect these two JR lines across the Northern Alps.

The southern trans-Alps route runs between Matsumoto and Takayama via Mt. Norikuradake, a typical alternative for a trip between Tokyo and Takayama. Leaving Tokyo in the morning, you can arrive in Takayama in the afternoon, after enjoying a magnificent view of the Japan Alps (The route is closed from the middle of October through the middle of May). If you can stay overnight in the area, we suggest that you visit the beautiful Kamikochi valley (The bus road to Kamikochi is closed from the middle of November through the end of April).

The route on the northern side of the Alps, called the Tateyama-Kurobe Alpine Route, runs between Shinano-Omachi and Toyama. The route was made possible thanks to the construction of tunnels under the precipitous mountains in the heart of the Japan Alps, which were used originally for the construction of Kurobe Dam, Japan's largest. Traveling on buses, a trolley, a cable cars, a ropeway, and a train, you can cross one of the highest and most scenic parts of the Japan Alps (The route is closed from the middle of November through the end of April). Starting from Tokyo, you'll be a little rushed to complete this route in one day, but it's not impossible. We suggest that you stay at one of accommodations in Shinano-Omachi. If you travel east-bound, e.g., returning from Kanazawa to Tokyo, you can catch a late afternoon train to Tokyo at Shinano-Omachi. Be forewarned that you may wish to spend more time here, especially in Murodo.

Unazuki is a hotspring resort at the northern end of the Japan Alps. A small train runs between Unazuki and Keyakidaira along the scenic Kurobe gorge. If you plan to travel to Kanazawa after a visit to Niigata and Sado Island (See the "Along the Joetsu Shinkansen" chapter), or if you have one extra day between your trip from Takayama to Kanazawa (or reverse), you should consider a visit to Unazuki.

Norikuradake
乗鞍岳

After the spring thaw, as an alternate route to the Shinkansen from Tokyo to Nagoya, and the JR train from Nagoya to Takayama, you can take the JR Chuo Line from Tokyo (Shinjuku Station) to Matsumoto (3 hours by limited express), and then cross the Japan Alps using a private railway and two bus lines.

Matsumoto 松本

Matsumoto (population of 194,000) is famous for its castle (a 20 minute walk from JR Matsumoto Station). The castle has Japan's oldest donjon, built in the 16th century (National Treasure).

Three Business Hotels in Matsumoto

Matsumoto Tokyu Inn 松本東急イン
   (In front of Matsumoto Station, 99 rooms).
   Add: 1-2-37, Fukashi, Matsumoto.
   Tel: (0263) 36-0109.
Matsumoto Daini Tokyu Inn
   松本第2東急イン
   (In front of Matsumoto Station, 158 rooms).
   Add: 1-3-21, Fukashi, Matsumoto.
   Tel: (0263) 36-0109.
Hotel Sunroute Matsumoto
   ホテルサンルート松本
   (10 minute walk from Matsumoto Station, 90 rooms).
   Add: 1-1, Agata, Matsumoto.
   Tel: (0263) 33-3131.

Matsumoto to Takayama

You take the private Matsumoto Dentetsu Line from Matsumoto to Shin-Shimashima 新島々, the last stop. The train operates about once every hour, and the ride takes 30 minutes.

The bus between Shin-Shimashima and Norikura 乗鞍 operates three times a day from the middle of May through the middle of October (Extra buses are added in the peak season of July and August). The ride takes about 2 hours. Norikura bus terminal

is located at an altitude of 2,730 m. (8,957 ft.), and you will command an extensive view of the Japan Alps. You can also take a walk to some of the nearby peaks as you wait for a connecting bus to Takayama.

The bus from Norikura to Takayama 高山 also operates three times a day from the middle of May through the middle of October (extra buses in July and August). The ride takes 1 hour 30 minutes.

Kamikochi
上高地

If you can stay overnight in the Japan Alps before visiting Takayama, we suggest that you visit Kamikochi, instead of crossing the Japan Alps via Norikura. In this case, you follow the same route from Tokyo to Shin-Shimashima (the JR Chuo Line and the private Matsumoto Dentetsu Line). Then, you take a bus to Kamikochi from Shin-Shimashima Station. The bus operates from the end of April through the middle of November about once every hour (a 75 minute ride). After a memorable night in the scenic valley, you take a bus from Kamikochi to Norikura. This bus operates three times a day from the middle of May through the middle of October (Extra buses are added in July and August), and the ride takes 2 hours. After your visit to Norikura, you can take a bus from Norikura to Takayama (details above in the Norikura section). If you decide to skip Norikura, you can change buses at Hirayu-Onsen.

Needless to say, you can just visit Kamikochi, or make a circle trip to Kamikochi and Norikura from Tokyo, without crossing the Japan Alps to Takayama.

Kamikochi, one of Japan's most famous valleys, is at an altitude of 1,500 m. (4,921 ft.). It is bisected by the Azusagawa River, and surrounded by the Japan Alps. It has some of the most picturesque mountain scenery in Japan. Kamikochi is a popular starting point for mountaineers who are headed for Mt. Hodakadake and Mt. Yarigatake. The hikers who also love this area dress just as casually as the mountaineers. This is a good chance for you to use your knapsack and blue jeans and casual shirts and sweaters.

In Kamikochi you can enjoy a stroll along the crystal-clear Azusagawa River and relish the beautiful view of the rugged mountains, which are covered by snow most of the time. Kappabashi Bridge with Mt. Hodakadake in the background is snapped by hundreds of thousands of camera fans every year. The view of Taishoike Pond with the Alps towering in the distance has long been popular with painters.

Accommodations In Kamikochi
1. Hotel
Imperial Hotel 上高地帝国ホテル
(Deluxe: 75 rooms)
Add: Kamikochi, Azumimura.
Tel: (0263) 95-2001.

2. Ryokans
Shirakabaso 白樺荘
(Standard: 58 rooms)
Add: 4468, Kamikochi, Azumimura.
Tel: (0263) 95-2131.
Kamikochi Onsen Hotel 上高地温泉ホテル
(Standard: 69 rooms)
Add: 4469, Kamikochi, Azumimura.
Tel: (0263) 95-2311.
Gosenjaku Ryokan 五千尺ホテル
(Standard: 31 rooms)
Add: 4468, Kamikochi, Azumimura.
Tel: (0263) 95-2111.
Nishiitoya 西糸屋
(Standard: 30 rooms)
Add: 4469-1, Kamikochi, Azumimura.
Tel: (0263) 95-2206.
Shimizuya Ryokan 清水屋
(Standard: 35 rooms)
Add: 4469, Kamikochi, Azumimura.
Tel: (0263) 95-2121.

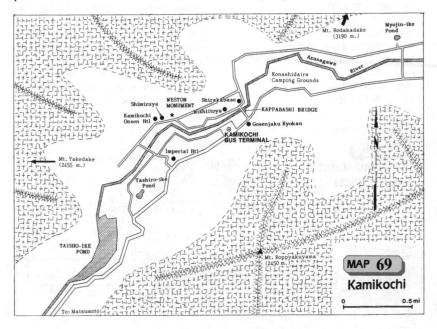

Tateyama-Kurobe Alpine Route

立山―黒部アルペンルート

The Tateyama-Kurobe Alpine Route traverses the northern part of the Japan Alps, utilizing various means of transportation.

From Tokyo (Shinjuku Station) you can take the JR Chuo Line. Many limited express trains on the Chuo Line (No. 10) run beyond Matsumoto onto the JR Oito Line. Use one of these direct trains to Shinano-Omachi (about 4 hours). Take a bus from Shinano-Omachi Station to Ogisawa (a 35 minute ride). If you stay overnight in Shinano-Omachi, Omachi-Onsen spa is on this bus route (a 15 minute ride from Shinano-Omachi).

Accommodations in Omachi-Onsen

Omachi New Otani Hotel
  大町ニューオータニホテル
  Add: 2883-7, Taira, Omachi.
  Tel: (0261) 22-4400.
Tateyama Prince Hotel
  立山プリンスホテル
  Add: 2884-10, Taira, Omachi.
  Tel: (0261) 22-5131.
Keisuien 景水苑
  Add: 2884-13, Taira, Omachi.
  Tel: (0261) 22-5501.

Kurobe Kanko Hotel 黒部観光ホテル
  Add: 2822, Taira, Omachi.
  Tel: (0261) 22-1520.

A trolley bus runs in the tunnel under the Ushiro-Tateyama mountains, from Ogisawa to Kurobe Dam 黒部ダム. There's a 1 km. long pedestrian path atop the Dam. The 186 m. (610 ft.) tall dam falls precipitously into Kurobe ravine on your right.

Next take an underground cable car from Kurobeko 黒部湖 to Kurobe-daira 黒部平, and then transfer to the steep ropeway to Daikanbo 大観峰. The ropeway ascends 500 meters in just 7 minutes. Take another bus, which runs in a tunnel under the Tateyama mountains, to Murodo 室堂, the highest point along the route. The huge Murodo bus terminal seems a bit incongruous with the alpine scenery of the area. In this area you can usually see lingering snow till the end of July. Well maintained pedestrian paths extend from the bus terminal to nearby scenic ponds and "Jigoku-dani" volcanic hells (a 20 minute walk).

The bus route descends from Murodo to Bijodaira 美女平, traveling through the spacious Midagahara plateau. In May and June the plateau is still covered with thick snow. A cable car brings you from Bijodaira down to Tateyama Station 立山駅. You take the private Toyama Chiho Tetsudo Line from Tateyama to Toyama Station 富山駅, which is also served by the JR Takayama and Hokuriku Lines.

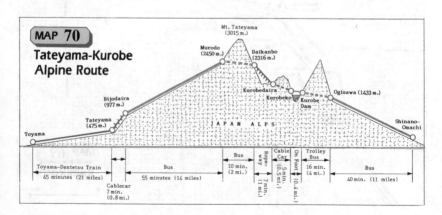

MAP 70
Tateyama-Kurobe Alpine Route

Unazuki and Kurobe Gorge

宇奈月，黒部峡谷

We recommend arriving in Unazuki late in the day, relaxing at one of the town's many hotspring hotels, and starting for Kurobe Gorge and Keyakidaira early the next morning.

Unazuki 宇奈月 is the terminal of the private Toyama Chiho Tetsudo Railroad. You can catch the Line at Toyama or Uozu, on the JR Hokuriku Line. When headed for Unazuki from Toyama or Uozu, don't be concerned when the train changes direction at Kamiichi: strange as it might seem, you're still going in the right direction. The ride takes 1 hour from Toyama, and 30 minutes from Uozu. At Unazuki Station, vans from the ryokans of the town line up to meet the incoming trains.

Accommodations in Unazuki

Unazuki Grand Hotel 宇奈月グランドホテル
(Deluxe: 96 rooms)
Add: 267, Togen, Unazuki-machi.
Tel: (07656)2-1111.
Unazuki New Otani 宇奈月ニューオータニ
ホテル (Deluxe: 115 rooms)
Add: 352-7, Unazuki-machi.
Tel: (07656) 2-1041.

Enraku 延楽 (Deluxe: 77 rooms)
Add: 347-1, Unazuki-machi.
Tel: (07656) 2-1221.
Entaijiso 延対寺荘 (Deluxe: 58 rooms)
Add: 53-1, Unazuki-machi.
Tel: (07656) 2-1231.
Hotel Togen ホテル桃源
(First-class: 64 rooms)
Add: 22-1, Unazuki-machi.
Tel: (07656) 2-1131.

The Kurobe Kyokoku Tetsudo Railroad Station is in a separate building from the Toyama Chiho Tetsudo Station, about 200 meters away. Both stations have coin lockers where you can leave your bags for the day. The Kurobe Kyokoku Tetsudo Railroad is a narrow-gauge line, more like a trolley than a train. When you buy your ticket, you'll have the option of an open or enclosed car. The trip along the Gorge to Keyakidaira takes approximately an hour and a half. The route winds along the edge of both sides of the Gorge, slipping in and out of tunnels, over bridges and past huge dams. When you get off the train at Keyakidaira, walk through the station and go down two flights of steps for the hiking path to the Sarutobi Observation Platform, which will be to your left. The walk to Sarutobi will take about 15 minutes. If you're lazy, there's an observatory right on the roof of the station. No matter which way you choose to go, the views are breathtaking.

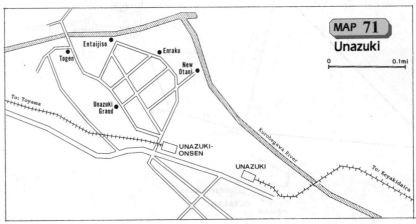

MAP 71
Unazuki

0   0.1mi

Introduction to Kansai 関西

Until the 1868 Meiji Restoration, the Kansai region was the political, economic, and cultural center of Japan. A number of places of interest and importance are located in the region. The following five districts will be introduced in this guidebook:

Kyoto. The world famous historic city.

Kyoto was the nation's capital for about 1,100 years from 794 to 1868, and still is the cultural center of Japan.

Nara. The oldest capital of Japan prospered in the 6th to 8th centuries. Many tourists visit Nara in just one day excursions from Kyoto, but the city has a lot

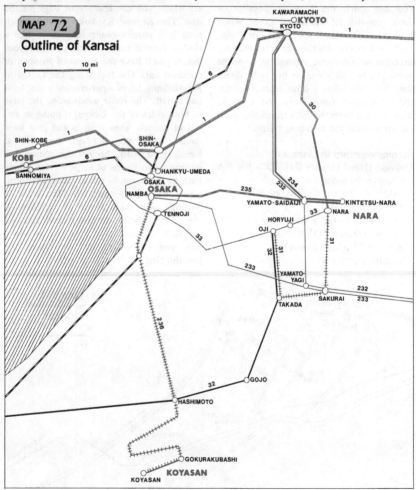

MAP 72

Outline of Kansai

0   10 mi

more to offer.

Osaka. The industrial and commercial center of Western Japan. Foreign visitors, with the exception of business travelers, usually omit Osaka from their sightseeing itineraries. Compared to the shogun's city of Tokyo (Edo) and the emperor's city of Kyoto, Osaka is known as the people's city. Osaka shows visitors another face of Japan, and is a good indication of what the Japan of the 21st century will be like.

Kobe. This exotic international port city is a gourmet's paradise, especially noted for its Kobe beef.

Koyasan. Located in an isolated mountain region, Koyasan is a training center for Buddhist priests. Koyasan is also renowned for its many shukubo (temple lodgings) and vegetarian meals.

To facilitate your understanding of the inter-city transportation network, Kansai train connections are outlined here.

Between Kyoto and Nara

The JR Nara Line (No. 30) runs commuter trains between Kyoto and Nara (the ride takes 68 minutes). The private Kintetsu Kyoto Line (No. 234) operates deluxe cars for tourists between these cities.

Between Kyoto and Osaka

The JR Tokaido-Sanyo Line operates commuter trains between Kyoto and Nishi-Akashi that stop at Osaka and Sannomiya (the main station in Kobe). The ride between Kyoto and Osaka takes 50 minutes. If you have a Japan Rail Pass, you can take the Shinkansen (No. 1). The ride between Kyoto and Shin-Osaka takes only 17 minutes. If you don't have a Pass, the ride is too costly. From Shin-Osaka Station, you can take the JR Tokaido-Sanyo commuter train to Osaka Station. If you are going to Osaka's Namba area, the Midosuji subway line is available from Shin-Osaka Station.

The private Hankyu Kyoto Line connects downtown Kyoto (Kawaramachi) and Umeda (The private railways and the city subways use the name Umeda for their stations near JR's Osaka Station). The ride on the limited express takes 38 minutes.

Between Kyoto and Kobe

The JR Tokaido-Sanyo Line is available for this connection. The ride between Kyoto and Sannomiya takes about one and a half hours. If you have a Japan Rail Pass, you can also take the Shinkansen between Kyoto and Shin-Kobe. The ride takes only 35 minutes.

Between Kyoto and Koyasan

You have two choices for a visit to Koyasan from Kyoto. The first, and more popular route is via Osaka. The private Nankai Koya Line provides convenient transportation between Osaka (Namba Station) and Koyasan (Gokurakubashi Station). The limited express, which uses deluxe "tourist" cars, takes one and a half hours, and the express, which uses commuter cars, takes one hour and 45 minutes. Namba Station in Osaka can be reached easily by the Midosuji subway line from Shin-Osaka and Osaka (Umeda) Stations.

The second route is via Nara. You have to take five trains on this route: (1) Kyoto to Nara on the JR Nara Line; (2) Nara to Oji on the JR Kansai Line; (3) Oji to Gojo on the JR Wakayama Line; (4) Gojo to Hashimoto on another JR Wakayama Line; and (5) Hashimoto to Gokurakubashi on the private Nankai Koya Line. All trains are local, and the trip takes about 4 hours altogether.

Between Osaka and Nara

The JR Kansai Line operates between Nara Station and Minatomachi Station in Osaka in the morning and in the evening. The same commuter trains run between Nara Station and Osaka Station during the day. If in doubt, take the train from Tennoji Station on the Osaka Kanjo (Loop) Line (the ride takes about 30 minutes). The trains stop at Horyuji Station (a 15 minute walk to Horyuji Temple). The private Kintetsu Nara Line operates deluxe cars specially designed for tourists. The ride between Namba Station and Nara Station takes about 30 minutes.

Between Osaka and Kobe

The JR Tokaido-Sanyo Line connects these two cities (Osaka Station and Sannomiya Station) in 35 minutes.

The private Hankyu Kobe Line operates between Umeda Station and Sannomiya Station. The ride takes 27 minutes by express and 42 minutes by local.

Kyoto 京都

The fertile land between the Kamogawa and Katsuragawa Rivers has been inhabited since the pre-historic era, and Emperor Kammu chose the area as his capital in 794. Kyoto, the "Seat of the Emperor," was laid out in a Chinese-style grid, with broad streets running east to west, and avenues north to south. During the civil wars of the 15th and 16th centuries, Kyoto was the scene of almost constant violence, and many of the city's cultural treasures were destroyed. When Hideyoshi Toyotomi finally succeeded in unifying the nation at the end of the 16th century, Kyoto was rebuilt. Modern Kyoto retains many of the structures and much of the charm of that era, and is today the home of more than 200 Shinto shrines, 1,500 Buddhist temples, and many other buildings of historical significance such as Nijojo Castle, Kiyomizu-dera Temple, Sanjusangendo Hall, Ryoanji Temple and the old Imperial Palace. It is also the home of several major museums, including the Kyoto National Museum.

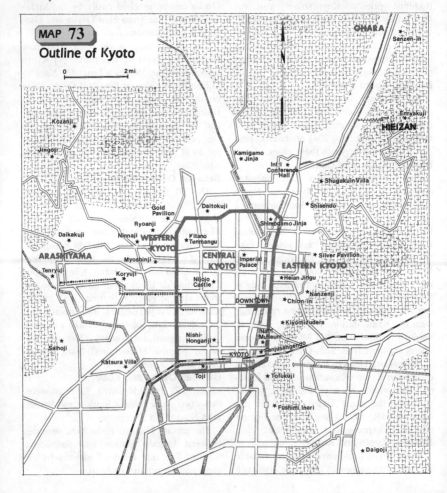

MAP 73
Outline of Kyoto

0   2mi

Outline of The Area

Higashi-oji-dori Street on the east, Nishi-oji-dori Street on the west, Kujo-dori Street on the south and Kita-oji-dori Street on the north are the boundaries of central Kyoto (shaded red on map 73). Despite the fact that this area is only about half the size of central Tokyo, many of Kyoto's most interesting and important sites are located far beyond this core area. Careful advance planning is therefore indispensable if you want to make the best use of your valuable time and money.

Suggested Itineraries

The itineraries that follow allocate one day for Central Kyoto, two days for Eastern Kyoto (we have also included suggestions for a one day itinerary in Eastern Kyoto), one day each for Western Kyoto, Arashiyama and Northern Kyoto (for a total of 5 days). Southern Kyoto also has several interesting destinations, and we have explained several places of interest at the end of this chapter as supplemental destinations for an extra day.

Katsura Detached Villa has a reputation as something special, but we believe its popularity is partly a result of the fact that you have to obtain special permission to visit it. You must apply for permission in advance by telephone at (075) 211-1211, and then visit the office of the Imperial Household Agency, at least one day before the day of your visit, to fill out an application form. You must also present your passport. You waste valuable time making these preparations and, because the time of your visit is determined by the Agency, advance planning becomes rather difficult (applications from overseas are not accepted). Although the Villa's refined buildings and lovely garden make it worth visiting, it is still only one of the many places in Kyoto with impressive buildings and excellent gardens. When your time is limited, it should not be taken up making such arrangements. The Villa is closed on Saturday afternoon, all day Sunday, and during the New Year's holidays. Applicants must be over 20 years of age, and the maximum size of groups admitted is four persons. The location of the Imperial Household Agency's Kyoto Office is pictured on map 77.

Another temple in the southwestern portion of the city, Saihoji, has the same kind of reputation as Katsura Detached Villa – and the same sort of requirements. Popularly called Kokedera, or Moss Temple, Saihoji Temple does have a lovely garden, but permission to visit can only be obtained by means of advance application to the temple by mail (Saihoji Temple, Matsuo-Kamigaya-cho, Ukyo-ku, Kyoto). A maximum of five applications are accepted at once. Once permission is obtained, you must make your visit at the time set by the temple. All visitors to the temple are required to listen to a one hour lecture – in Japanese only — before they are allowed to see the garden, and are expected to make a donation of 3,000 yen before they leave.

Central Kyoto is outlined first, followed by Eastern Kyoto, Western Kyoto, Arashiyama and Northern Kyoto. This order is designed to promote easy understanding of the layout of the city for those who read this guide, and does not reflect destination priorities. We suggest that you spend your time in Kyoto as follows:

– If you have only one day:
  Visit Eastern Kyoto (combining the two one-day itineraries as suggested in the text that follows).
– If you have two days:
  Add Western Kyoto.
– If you have three days:
  Add Central Kyoto.
– If you have four days:
  Add Arashiyama.
– If you have five days:
  Add Northern Kyoto.
– If you have six days:
  Congratulations! Follow all the itineraries as written.
– If you have more than six days:
  Add "Other Places of Interest."

Connections with Other Cities

Kyoto can be reached from all major Japanese cities by Shinkansen. The Shinkansen platforms, as pictured on map 74, are located at the southernmost side of Kyoto Station, on the second floor. When you arrive at Kyoto by Shinkansen, you have to go through two exits. The first exit, where your Shinkansen surcharge ticket is collected, is before the connecting passages – the bridge on the western side or the underground passage on the eastern side. Keep your basic fare ticket; it is collected at the second, general exit (if you have one ticket for both the Shinkansen charge and the basic fare, just show it at the first exit). Most major places of interest and most major hotels are located to the north of Kyoto Station, so you should walk through the connecting passage to the general exits on

the north side of the station. However, if you are staying at the New Miyako Hotel, or have big bags and do not want to carry them through the station, you can go out through the southern exit (Hachijo-guchi), which is adjacent to the Shinkansen platforms, and catch a taxi right in front of the exit. Your fare will be a little higher, but sparing yourself a long trek with your luggage is probably worth it.

Platform No. 5 is for the JR rapid service commuter train for Osaka, and No. 8 for the JR train to Nara. The Kintetsu private railway operates trains to Nara and to Ise/Shima from the southwestern corner of the station.

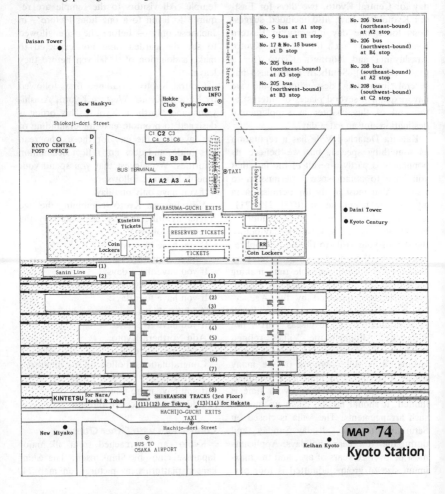

MAP 74
Kyoto Station

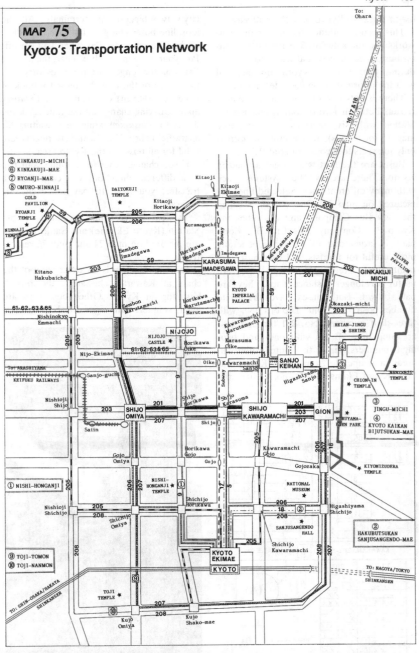

MAP 75

Kyoto's Transportation Network

Major Buses in Kyoto and the Subway

This section outlines the major bus networks and the subway. Specific instructions on buses, the subway and trains to be used during your visit to Kyoto are included with the information on each destination.

There is only one subway line in the city. It runs between Kyoto Station and Kitaoji Station with six intermediate stops (see map 75 for details). It is useful for tourists only for visits to Kyoto Imperial Palace.

Buses are the best way to get around in Kyoto. There are two bus systems, each with many different lines. Selected lines are pictured on map 75. One system is called the City Bus Company and the other the Kyoto Bus Company. The City Bus Company is larger and its lines are generally more useful for tourists. All City buses are painted pale green. The Kyoto buses are useful for longer distance trips; they are pale brown. Both buses have the route number posted on front. The bus lines with three-digit numbers (No. 201 through 208) are loop lines. Buses with one- and two-digit numbers serve the outer suburban areas, and operate from either Kyoto Station (Kyoto Ekimae) or Sanjo Keihan, the

city's two biggest bus terminals. All the loop line buses charge a flat fare regardless of distance you ride. Pay when you get off. Put your fare in the box near the driver. Fares on the longer distance lines vary with the length of the ride. If you get a book of tickets (1,000 yen) you won't have to worry about carrying change all the time. Ask the driver for *kaisu-ken* while he is waiting for a traffic light. The *kaisu-ken* tickets are valid for all buses in the Kyoto area.

If you change buses to continue your trip in a different direction, you cannot get a transfer; you have to pay for each ride separately.

The two biggest bus terminals, Kyoto Station (Kyoto Ekimae) and Sanjo Keihan, are pictured on map 74 and map 76 respectively.

The Chart below is an exact copy of the chart at Kawaramachi-Sanjo, the busiest bus stop in Kyoto. Other bus stops are much simpler. The signs for Kyoto buses

have round tops – ⚲ – while those for City buses have flag-shaped tops –⚑ . As shown on the Chart, the name of the stop is written in both Japanese and English. The upper part of each bus stop chart ("A" on the Chart) shows your present location and the location of the other bus stops with the same name (there are 10 stops named Kawaramachi-Sanjo). Imagine that you are at Kawaramachi-Sanjo stop No. 2, on the northeastern corner of the intersection. The No. 2 stop is served by the No. 17 and No. 205 buses. If you want to take a south-bound No. 205 bus, you are in the right place (Remember that traffic is on the left in Japan!). The schedule for the south-bound 205 bus is written on the lower part

("B" on the Chart) of the bus chart. If you are looking for the stop for the north-bound No. 5 bus, look at the upper part of the chart and find No. 5 on the left-hand side of the street. Stop No. 6 is where you should wait for the bus. Go to stop No. 6 and check the schedule for the north-bound No. 5 bus on the lower portion of the chart. It's easy once you understand how it's organized.

Tourist Information

The Japanese Government's free Tourist Information Center (TIC) is located on the ground floor of the Kyoto Tower building (upper center, map 74). Closed on Saturday afternoon and all day Sunday.

Downtown Kyoto
◆ Shopping and Nightlife

Kyoto's main shopping area and night life establishments lie on both sides of the Kamogawa River along Shijo-dori Street. Gion is on the eastern and Pontocho and Shinkyogoku on the western side of the river. Although the Kyoto Station area has become a new downtown, "Downtown Kyoto" still means Gion, Pontocho and Shinkyogoku.

| Gion | 祇園 |

For Japanese the name "Gion" still conjures up images of traditional, almost magical establishments where guests (usually men) enjoy drinks and sophisticated Japanese dishes while being entertained by *maiko* (apprentice geisha) dancers, but few have actually had this experience. And Gion itself, like the traditional entertainment areas in most Japanese cities, has changed a great deal in modern times: many traditional drinking places have been replaced by contemporary, convenient, but rather characterless cabarets and bars. Nevertheless, some sections of Gion still

stubbornly preserve the atmosphere of the ancient capital, and the area still features many good restaurants, which are slightly more expensive than those on the other side of the Kamogawa River. Gion is a great place for a leisurely evening stroll and a good dinner.

Strolling in Gion

The southern part of Hanami-koji Street between Shijo-dori Street and Gion Corner is lined with traditional buildings with wooden lattice windows and lanterns at their entrances. Walking here will give you a taste of what the old entertainment quarters were like. **Shinmonzen-dori Street** 新門前通り, between Yamato-oji Street and Hanami-koji Street (middle center, map 76, shaded in red), is a street of crowded wooden houses, most of which house art and antique shops. They are open till 6:00 PM. This street is a must-see for anyone interested in good antiques or authentic backstreet atmosphere. **Kasagen** (lower right, map 76, on Shijo-dori Street), another good place to look for souvenirs, specializes in traditional paper umbrellas.

Theaters

Minamiza 南座 Theater (lower center, map 76) is the oldest theater in Japan. During the feudal era, entertainers, whose social status was very low, performed in public on the dry bed of the Kamogawa River. When kabuki was created, in the early part of the Edo era, it was first performed there as well. The new drama became so popular with the general public in Kyoto that Japan's first permanent theater was established where Minamiza Theater stands today. There are three or four kabuki programs performed at Minamiza Theater each year (each run lasts 20 – 25 days).

Gion Kaburenjo 祇園歌舞練場 Theater (lower right) is a training center for the *maiko* of the Gion area. Once a year, in April, a public dance performance is given. 1987 marked the 115th occasion of this annual event.

Gion Corner ギオンコーナー is a small theater (250 seats) attached to Gion Kaburenjo Theater. It was specially designed to introduce foreign tourists to a variety of traditional Japanese arts. Gion Corner is not the place to go if you expect high artistic standards, but it does allow you to sample a bit of everything, including Japanese dance, bunraku puppet theater, gagaku court dance and music, tea ceremony, etc. in just one hour. The theater is open from March 1 through Nov. 29. Two performances are held daily, at 8:00 PM and 9:10 PM. Admission is 2,000 yen.

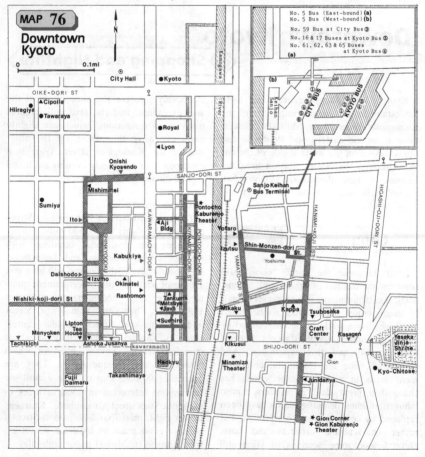

Restaurants

Kikusui (lower center) is a Western restaurant in a four-story building. The restaurant on the first floor serves a "Service Steak Dinner" at 1,700 yen. The excellent grill on the second floor charges more than 5,000 yen for dinner. **Yotaro** (middle center, on Yamato-oji Street) is a tempura restaurant. The set menu tempura dinner is 3,000 yen. **Junidanya** (lower right) is located in the midst of the traditional quarter. A tempura dinner is 2,300 yen, and steak is 4,500 yen. **Kappa** (middle center) has plastic food displays outside the entrance. This Japanese restaurant serves shabu-shabu at 3,000 yen. "Kappa Gozen," a Japanese-style set menu dinner is a treat for both the eyes and the taste buds (3,000 yen). **Restaurant Izutsu** (middle center) and **Mikaku** (middle center) are both steak restaurants. The former is rather Westernized while the latter is Japanese style (both expensive). Sukiyaki and shabu-shabu are also served at Mikaku.

Kawaramachi 河原町

Strolling in Kawaramachi

The intersection of Kawaramachi-dori and Shijo-dori streets (lower left) is Kyoto's version of the Ginza. Three large department stores, **Hankyu, Takashimaya**, and **Fujii Daimaru**, and modern as well as traditional specialty shops line Shijo-dori Street. **Jusanya** (lower left, near the entrance to Shinkyogoku) deals in all sorts of exotic combs and hair ornaments. **Tachikichi** (lower left) is the main store of a famous Kiyomizu-yaki pottery chain. **Matsuya** (middle center, on Kawaramachi-dori Street) sells Kyoto pottery dolls.

Northeast of the main intersection are Pontocho-dori and Kiyamachi-dori Streets, two more of Kyoto's typical night life areas. **Pontocho-dori Street** 先斗町通り has more old buildings, while **Kiyamachi-dori Street** 木屋町通り, which runs along the narrow Takasegawa River, features modern buildings with colorful neon signs. **Pontocho**

Kaburenjo Theater 先斗町歌舞練場 (middle center, near the Kamogawa River), like the Gion Kaburenjo, is a training center for the *maiko* of the area. This theater stages two performances of *maiko* dances a year, from May 1 – 24 and from October 15 to November 7, and as with the Gion dances, these have been a tradition for more than 115 years.

Shinkyogoku 新京極 is the name given to the two shopping arcades that run north from Shijo-dori Street. The arcades display innumerable souvenir items in reasonable price ranges. Most of the stores close around 8:00 PM. The area also has many movie theaters.

Nishiki-koji-dori Street 錦小路通り runs west from Shinkyogoku. A torii gate is a good landmark to help you find the entrance. This narrow covered street is Kyoto's food market. There are more than 150 stores, all of which handle food or food-related items; you will find a lot of products you have never seen before.

Restaurants

Japanese: Okinatei (middle left) features sukiyaki and shabu-shabu. Yakitori is also served as an appetizer to accompany Japanese sake or beer (moderate). **Izumo** (middle left) is an excellent, very reasonable sushi bar. The restaurant has a number of plastic sushi displays outside its entrance. **Tankuma** (middle center) is one of the most famous authentic Japanese restaurants in Kyoto (expensive).

Western & Steak: Lipton Tea House (lower left) serves Western food, cakes and good tea at reasonable prices. **Manyoken** (lower left) is an authentic French restaurant (moderate). **Lyon** (upper center) is another well known French restaurant located on the 9th floor of the modern Asahi Kaikan Building (moderate). **Suehiro** (middle center) is a steak house (moderate). **Cipolla** (upper left, on Oike-dori Street) is a deluxe Italian restaurant (expensive).

Others: Ashoka (lower left) is an Indian restaurant. A variety of curries and shish kebab are priced reasonably. **Java** (middle center) serves curry and Western food (both reasonable).

Central Kyoto

Glorious Kyoto

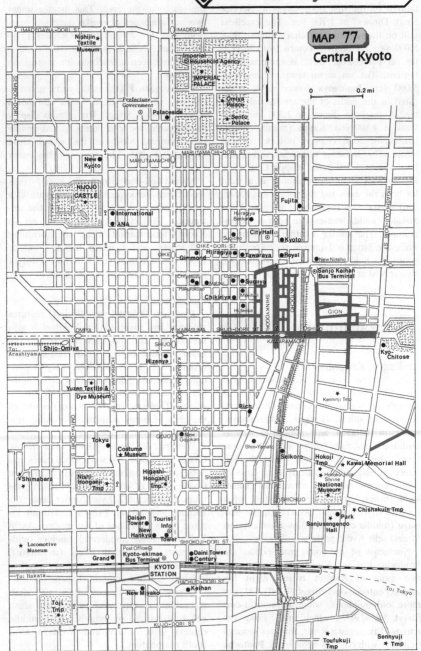

MAP 77

Central Kyoto

0   0.2 mi

Despite the fact that the 20th century has put its mark on Central Kyoto, several important historical jewels, including Kyoto Imperial Palace, Nijojo Castle, Nishi-Honganji Temple and Toji Temple still stand amid the concrete welter. There are also several interesting museums scattered throughout the area. Avoid Sundays and Mondays for this itinerary because the Imperial Palace is closed on Sundays and Nijojo Castle is closed on Mondays.

Kyoto Imperial Palace 京都御所 (Upper center, map 77)

Even though Japanese must apply in advance for permission to visit the Imperial Palace, foreign visitors are accorded special privileges, but you will only be admitted if you arrive at the office of the Imperial Household Agency in the Palace grounds by 9:40 AM (bring your passport). To get to the Palace you can take a subway to Imadegawa Station or take a bus to Karasuma-Imadegawa stop. The 30-minute English guided tour starts at 10:00 AM at Seishomon Gate. An afternoon English guided tour starts at 2:00 PM. To join the afternoon tour you have to arrive at the Household Agency's Office by 1:40 PM. There is no afternoon tour on Saturday and no tours at all on Sunday. Admission is free.

Kyoto Imperial Palace has been destroyed by fire many times, and the present buildings date from 1855. The original palace, built in 794 when the capital was moved to Kyoto, was located to the west of the present building, and was twice its size. The covered corridor that surrounds the spacious, white-gravel courtyard has three gates. The guided tour will take you to the courtyard, and give you a chance to take a close look at Shishinden Hall, the symbolic palace building at the northern end of the courtyard. The most important ceremonies of the imperial family, such as the installation of a new emperor, are still held here. Visitors are then led to the Oikeniwa (Pond Garden), a lovely Japanese-style garden. On the left-hand side of the garden are Kogosho (Minor Palace for Small Receptions) and Gogakumonjo (Study Hall). Turning to the left, the guide leads you back to Seishomon Gate where you entered the Palace.

Nishijin Textile Museum 西陣織会館 (optional) (Upper left, map 77)

Nishijin Textile Museum is about 0.4 miles (0.7 km.) from the Palace. If you skip this Museum, walk to Nijojo castle from the Imperial Palace.

The history of Nishijin textiles began in 794 when the newly organized imperial court established a special new agency for textiles. It produced refined and elegant textiles for the imperial family and the aristocracy for centuries. During the "Onin-no-Ran" civil war of the 15th century, the central part of Kyoto was reduced to ashes. The textile craftsmen scattered to various parts of Japan, where they learned new patterns and skills. After the war, when the craftsmen returned to Kyoto, they gravitated to the area called Nishijin and established a guild. Since then, the name Nishijin has been synonymous with fine textile products.

The Nishijin Textile Museum was constructed in 1976 to display contemporary products and to demonstrate weaving techniques. Its dark, seven-story building is quite distinctive. A special feature of the museum is its live *kimono* fashion show, with lovely models wearing extremely expensive and elaborate *kimono* in a variety of patterns and colors. The show is presented at regular intervals between 10:00 AM and 4:00 PM. (quite touristy).

Nijojo Castle 二条城 (Upper left, map 77)

Nijojo Castle was built in 1603 as a residence for Ieyasu Tokugawa, the first Tokugawa Shogun. This castle served as the shogun's temporary residence whenever the Edo-based Tokugawas visited Kyoto. In 1868, when the 15th Tokugawa Shogun, Yoshinobu, relinquished power to the imperial court (the Meiji Restoration), the castle became the temporary seat of the emperor's new government. Despite the stern appearance of the moats and stone walls that surround the castle grounds, the buildings inside are clearly those of a gracious noblemen's estate. The castle has two

major complexes – the Honmaru Palace located inside the inner moats, and the Ninomaru Palace in the eastern grounds. The major attractions of the castle are in the Ninomaru Palace section because the original Honmaru Palace and its donjon were destroyed by fire in the 18th century. The present Honmaru Palace was built as the residence of Prince Katsura and was moved from Kyoto Imperial Palace to its present site in 1893. Several Western elements are incorporated in its design, but the interior is closed to the public except for short periods in spring and fall.

The original architectural beauty and lavish interior decorations of the Ninomaru Palace (National Treasure) are still intact. Entrance to Ninomaru Palace is through the brilliantly designed Karamon Gate. The six buildings of the palace are each divided into many chambers, all of which are decorated with exceptional paintings, carvings and metal works. The corridor of the first building is designed to squeak like a nightingale whenever people walk on it. It is said that this is an alarm device designed to prevent assassins from penetrating to the inner halls. Especially noteworthy are the paintings on the sliding screens in Ohiroma Hall. The hall was used for the meetings of shoguns and feudal lords. It's easy to recognize this hall because a number of dolls in formal costumes are arranged here to represent the scene when the 15th Tokugawa Shogun announced his decision to return the power of government to the Emperor. Ninomaru Garden, designed by Enshu, is, in its own right, as famous as the castle. Nijojo is open from 8:45 AM to

4:00 PM (Closed on Mondays. When Monday is a holiday, it's open on Monday and closed on Tuesday. Admission, covering both Ninomaru Palace and the Garden, is 450 yen).

Nishi-Honganji Temple 西本願寺 (Lower left, map 77)

Take a south-bound No. 9 bus from the stop on the eastern side of Horikawa-dori Street, in front of Nijojo Castle. This is the only bus that goes directly to Nishi-Honganji stop.

As pictured on map 77, there are two Honganji Temples, Nishi (West) and Higashi (East), side by side. Honganji Temple was the headquarters of the Jodoshinshu or Ikkoshu sect of Buddhism, the only feudal era sect that reached the farmers and the poor. The sect's religious teachings also had definite political and economic overtones, and for that reason, Jodo-shinshu was constantly oppressed by the rulers and its headquarters moved from place to place. Nevertheless, it remained tremendously influential. In the 15th century, in the central Japan Sea Coast area of Kanazawa, adherents of the sect managed to defeat the local feudal lord and establish an autonomous government that ruled for as long as 100 years. In Osaka, the sect accumulated enough military might to wage an 11-year battle against Nobunaga Oda. When Hideyoshi Toyotomi finally succeeded in unifying the nation, he realized that it would be necessary to make concessions to this powerful group: he sponsored construction of the headquarters for the sect in Kyoto in 1591. But when Ieyasu

Tokugawa came to power, he plotted against Jodo-shinshu. He threw his support behind Kyojo, a priest who had failed in his own political maneuvering within the sect, and had another temple constructed for Kyojo to the east of the original headquarters. He then split the subordinate temples of the sect all over Japan into two groups. Since then, the original temple has been called Nishi-Honganji, and the new one Higashi-Honganji. The main building of the east (Higashi) temple is much larger (as a matter of fact this 1895 structure is the largest wooden structure in Kyoto), but many objects of historical and artistic significance are found in the west (Nishi) temple.

Entrance to the Nishi-Honganji Temple precincts is free of charge. Upon entering at either Goeidomon Gate (northern side) or Hondomon Gate, visitors encounter huge, impressive 300-year old wooden structures. Among the temple's many buildings, the most important are Daishoin Hall, which runs from east to west, and Karamon Gate, which is located along the southern walls. Karamon Gate was originally located at Fushimijo Castle, which was constructed by Hideyoshi Toyotomi and is said to have been magnificently lavish. Unfortunately, Ieyasu Tokugawa had Fushimijo Castle destroyed when he defeated the dictatorial Toyotomi family and founded the Tokugawa Shogunate. The elaborate carvings and decorations on Karamon Gate give us some idea of the lost splendors of the castle. Daishoin Hall was also moved to Nishi-Honganji from Fushimijo Castle. A guided tour (in Japanese) is conducted at Daishoin Hall four times a day, at 10:00 AM, 11:00 AM, 1:30 PM and 2:30 PM (Morning tours only on Saturday). Permission to enter the Hall must be obtained at the temple office in the grounds. Each of the many sections of Daishoin Hall has elegant paintings, carvings and other 16th century decorations. Two Noh stages and a small garden are attached to the Hall. If you follow our suggested itinerary, you probably won't arrive in time for the last tour, but it's still worthwhile visiting the temple to see the grandeur of one of the most influential Buddhist sects.

The Costume Museum 風俗美術館 (lower left, near Nishi-Honganji Temple) is a small establishment on the fifth floor of an office building. An English sign is posted at the entrance of the building. The museum displays Japanese costumes from prehistoric times to the Meiji era. Unexpectedly beautiful (9:00 AM to 5:00 PM. Closed on Sundays. Admission 300 yen).

* If you call it a day at Nishi-Honganji Temple, find your way back to your hotel by referring to map 75. Kyoto Station will probably provide the best connection for other buses or for the subway.

Toji Temple 東寺 (Lower left, map 77)

If you are continuing on to Toji Temple, leave Nishi-Honganji Temple through the southern gate and go to Omiya-dori Street. You can walk all the way to Toji Temple in 15 minutes.

Toji Temple, officially called Kyo-o-gokokuji Temple, was originally erected in 796 by imperial edict. In 818, Emperor Saga gave the temple to Kukai, the founder of Shingon Buddhism, as headquarters for his sect. The original buildings were burnt down during the civil wars, but the major structures were rebuilt between the 15th and 17th centuries. A number of important religious objects from the 8th and 9th centuries have survived and are preserved in the temple. The ticket office is located inside the temple grounds, at the entrance to the main part of the temple. The temple also has a spacious garden with three ponds. At the southern end of the garden stands Japan's tallest five-story pagoda (184 feet or 56 m. tall, National Treasure), which was built in 1644. The Kondo (Main Hall), built in 1606, is another National Treasure. The Kodo (Lecture Hall), constructed in 1491, contains 21 statues of Buddha, gods and guardians; fifteen of these date from the 8th and 9th centuries and have been designated National Treasures. On the 21st of each month a flea market is held in the temple precincts (The temple is open from 9:00 AM to 4:00 PM Admission 300 yen).

Eastern Kyoto

◈ Contemplative Kyoto

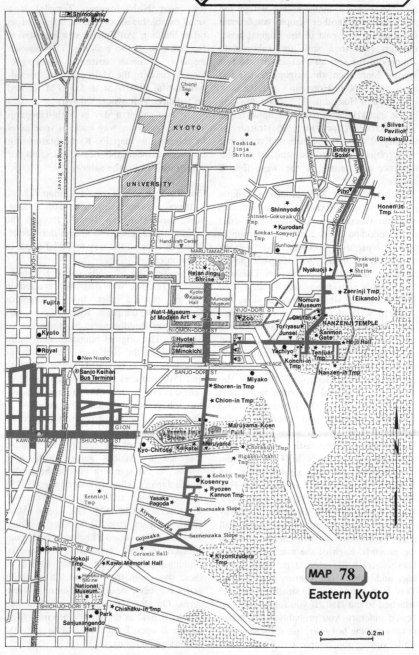

MAP **78**

Eastern Kyoto

0   0.2 mi

Eastern Kyoto nestles against Higashi-yama (Eastern Mountain). The area contains innumerable temples and shrines in quiet settings, and provides visitors with an ideal opportunity to appreciate the natural beauty and cultural splendors of this ancient capital city. The famous Silver Pavilion, Nanzenji Temple, Heian Jingu Shrine and Kiyomizudera Temple are just a few examples of the delights of this area. This is the area we give top priority, and Eastern Kyoto is introduced in two one-day itineraries.

* If your time is limited and you want to see just the highlights of the area, take the following modified itinerary: Start your tour at Silver Pavilion. After the visit, take a south-bound No. 5 bus to Kyoto Kaikan Bijutsukan-mae stop. Visit Heian Jingu Shrine, and then make a walking tour to Chion-in Temple, Maruyama-Koen Park and Kiyomizudera Temple.

Day 1 – Northern Part of Eastern Kyoto
Heian Jingu Shrine 平安神宮 (Middle center, map 78)

Heian Jingu Shrine can be reached by either the No. 5 bus (Kyoto Kaikan Bijutsukan-mae on the southern main approach), or the No. 203 bus (Okazaki-michi stop on the northeastern corner of the shrine on Marutamachi-dori Street).

Heian Jingu Shrine was built in 1895 to commemorate the 1,100th anniversary of the city of Kyoto, and dedicated to two famous emperors – Kammu, the founder of Kyoto, and Komei, the last emperor to live in the city. The Shrine consists of the East and West Honden (Main Halls), the Daigokuden (Great Hall of State), two pagodas, the Otemon Gate (Main Gate), a spacious white-gravel front yard, and a garden. A huge torii gate stands to the south of the Shrine at the entrance to the broad main approach. The brightly colored vermilion-red buildings are reduced scale replicas of the first Imperial Palace. The garden at the rear of the Shrine is famous for its weeping cherries, maples, azaleas, irises and water lilies. The garden is a living relic of the brilliant days of the imperial and aristocratic families at the dawn of Japanese history

(The precincts are open throughout the day. The garden is open from 8:30 AM to 5:00 PM. Until 4:30 PM in winter. Admission to the garden is 300 yen).

Silver Pavilion 銀閣寺 (Upper right, map 78)

Take the No. 5 bus from Kyoto Kaikan Bijutsukan-mae to Ginkakuji-michi stop.

Silver Pavilion, popularly called Ginkakuji Temple in Japanese and formally known as Jishoji Temple, was built in 1482 by Shogun Yoshimasa Ashikaga. The power of the Ashikaga Shogunate was eclipsed as a result of the civil war of the 15th century, and Yoshimasa retired from the world of politics to spend his days in this exquisite country retreat indulging himself in wine, women and cultural activities. He intended that his villa be a counterpart to the famous Gold Pavilion that his grandfather, Yoshimitsu, had built, and planned to have the entire structure covered with silver foil. But he died before this was accomplished, and his grand residence was converted into a temple. Even without the glimmer of silver foil, it is a magnificent structure. The garden, with a pond, pine trees and carefully arranged "mountains" of sand, supposedly the work of Soami, is one of Kyoto's most attractive. The trees along the neatly maintained curved entrance path form a beautiful green screen (8:30 AM to 5:00 PM. In winter 9:00 AM to 4:30 PM. Admission 200 yen).

Path of Philosophy 哲学の道

The 0.75-mile (1.2 km.) walkway along the small creek from Ginkakuji Temple to Nyakuoji Jinja Shrine is called the Path of Philosophy. It is lined with cherry, willow and maple trees and is completely traffic free. All through Japanese history, famous priests and philosophers have wandered along this quiet path, lost in contemplation. Today, the path still lives up to its name: it is a favorite haunt of teachers and students, and is especially conducive to quiet contemplation.

Honen-in Temple 法然院 (optional) (Upper right, map 78)

Honen-in Temple is a short walk east from the Path of Philosophy. Coffee & Tea Lounge **Pino** is a good landmark for finding the street that leads to the temple. This small thatched temple was built in 1680 in honor of the priest Honen, one of the greatest figures in the history of Japanese Buddhism. Honen liberated the new religion from the narrow circle of the ruling class and propagated it to the general public, emphasizing the equality of all human beings in the eyes of Buddha. The highlight of the temple is the approach to the main buildings. The narrow path, with its thick canopy of venerable trees, is incredibly quiet. The piles of sand on both sides of the path are arranged to reflect and complement the beauties of the seasons (Free admission to the grounds).

Zenrinji Temple 禅林寺 (optional) (Middle right, map 78)

Zenrinji Temple was erected in 856 by the priest Shinsho. The temple is popularly known as Eikando to honor the memory of the 11th century priest Eikan, who tended to the physical as well as the spiritual needs of the people. The original buildings were destroyed in the civil wars of the 15th century, but many were reconstructed. The halls are connected by covered corridors. If all the sliding paper doors are closed, you can open them and enter the inside of the hall, to worship or just to look at the paintings on the walls. Be sure to close the doors behind you. (A Japanese sign asks visitors to "keep the doors closed so pigeons can't get in!")

The temple is famous for its unique image of Buddha looking back over his shoulder, which is in Amidado Hall at the southern end of the complex. You can only reach Amidado by climbing one of the staircases at the southern end of the complex. At the top of the opposite staircase is a pagoda where visitors can command a grand view of the city of Kyoto. The temple is especially famous for its maple trees. The brilliance of their autumnal tints has always been a popular theme with Japanese poets (9:00 AM to 4:00 PM. Admission 350 yen).

Nomura Museum 野村美術館 (optional) (Middle right, map 78)

This museum was established recently to display the collection of Tokushichi Nomura, founder of one of Japan's biggest conglomerates (Nomura Securities, Daiwa Bank, etc.). The collection includes hanging scrolls, paintings, pottery and tea ceremony utensils (10:00 AM to 4:30 PM. Closed on Mondays. Admission 500 yen).

Nanzenji Temple 南禅寺 (Middle right, map 78)

Nanzenji Temple is Kyoto's most important Zen temple. It was constructed as a villa for Emperor Kameyama in 1264. The original buildings were burnt down during the civil wars, and those standing today were constructed in the late 16th century. Entrance to the precincts is free of charge. **Sanmon Gate** 山門, built in 1628, is famous for the splendid view of Kyoto from its top floor, which is reached by a steep, narrow stairway. Unless you really enjoy climbing, it's better to spend your time and money on other facilities in the precincts (Admission to Sanmon Gate is 150 yen. Open from 9:00 AM to 5:00 PM). **Hojo Hall** 方丈 (National Treasure) was moved here from Kyoto Imperial Palace in the early 17th century. Its chambers are divided by sliding doors covered with brilliant paintings of the Kano school. The garden attached to the hall is in typical Zen style, with stones, elaborately-shaped trees and sand. The stones and trees clustered in one area of the spacious garden are said to represent tigers crossing a stream (300 yen).

There are three more minor temples here with beautiful gardens (optional). **Nanzen-in Temple** 南禅院 is located at the southern end of the precincts. A small creek (actually runoff from Lake Biwako) flows on an elevated brick waterway, which was a very unusual structure in the feudal era. The path to Nanzen-ji Temple goes under this Roman-like structure. The garden is designed around a pond surrounded by wild trees from Higashiyama Mountain. Reflecting its beginnings as an imperial villa, the garden features many elegant maple trees and beautiful mosses. **Konchiin Temple** 金地院 is famous for its elaborate garden. The *bonsai* trees, rocks and sand of the garden represent deep mountains and an ocean with two islands. This typically Japanese use of limited space is considered one of the best works of Enshu. **Tenjuan Temple** 天寿庵 also has an attractive garden.

Restaurants in the Area

Okutan is a famous restaurant in the Nanzenji Temple grounds that specializes in *yudofu* (bean curd dipped in boiling water). The Nanzenji area is famous for imaginative *yudofu* cuisine and Okutan is the oldest restaurant of its kind (moderate). **Junsei**, located to the west of the temple, is another famous *yudofu* restaurant. **Yachiyo**, one of the most famous ryokans in Kyoto, has a restaurant in the grounds. The restaurant serves a Japanese-style set menu lunch in lacquer boxes. **Hyotei** (No. 1 in the middle of map 78) is one of the most famous and most expensive authentic Japanese restaurants. Though it has no English sign, this restaurant is housed in a traditional building and displays a distinctive sign shaped like a gourd. A full course dinner here costs more than 20,000 yen, but a special set menu lunch called "Shokado Bento" is only about 3,500 yen. There are two more famous restaurants in the neighborhood, **Minokichi** (No. 2), famous for tempura, and another **Junsei** (No. 3).

Shoren-in Temple 青蓮院 (optional) (Middle center, map 78)

Shoren-in, popularly called Awata Palace, is famous as the residence of the head about of the Tendai sect of Buddhism. In the past, this position was so highly regarded that it was always reserved for a member of the imperial family. The present buildings were erected in 1895. Especially notable are the sliding screens of the Main Hall, survivors of an earlier time, graced with paintings by Mitsunobu Kano, Motonobu Kano, and other leading artists of the late 16th and early 17th centuries. The garden, which is considered one of the best in Kyoto, was designed in part by Soami, and in part by Enshu, two of Japan's greatest landscape artists (9:00 AM to 5:00 PM. Admission 300 yen).

Chion-in Temple 知恩院 (Middle center, map 78)

Chion-in Temple, erected in 1234, is the grand headquarters of the Jodo sect of Buddhism, and is one of the largest and most famous temples in all of Japan. The oldest of the buildings that have survived the repeated fires that ravaged the temple are the Main Hall and the Abbot's Quarters, which date from 1633 and 1639. Chion-in's two-story Sanmon Gate, at a height of 79 feet (24 m.), is considered the most imposing of all the temple gates in Japan. The corridor connecting the Main Hall with the Daihojo Hall is so constructed that at every step the floor emits a sound resembling the song of the nightingale. This wonderful quirk of construction is thought to be the work of Jingoro Hidari, the master sculptor famous for the Sleeping Cat at Toshogu Shrine in Nikko. The sliding screens of the Daihojo Hall are decorated with beautiful paintings of the Kano school. The garden attached to the abbot's apartments is the work of Enshu. The belfry houses the largest temple bell in Japan, which was cast in 1633. Seventeen people are needed to ring it! Entrance to the precincts is free of charge. The entrance to the inside of the buildings is located at the northern side of the Main Hall (9:00 AM to 5:00 PM. Admission 300 yen).

Maruyama-Koen Park 円山公園 (Middle center, map 78)

Maruyama-Koen Park, Kyoto's main public park, is a beautiful landscaped garden laid out at the foot of Higashiyama Mountain at the eastern end of Shijo-dori Street. The Park is really a series of gardens designed around ponds. There are many vendors, restaurants and souvenir shops, and the Park always has a festival atmosphere. This is the last stop on the first-day of the walking tour of Eastern Kyoto. Take your time and relax. You are very close to Gion, and can easily spend your evening there. **Yasaka Jinja Shrine** 八坂神社 , a vermilion shrine on the way to Gion, is famous as the host of Gion Matsuri Festival, Kyoto's biggest festival (held in July every year).

Day 2 – Southern Part of Eastern Kyoto

The second day itinerary starts at Maruyama-Koen Park. Gion bus stop provides the best public transportation access to Maruyama-Koen Park.

Maruyama-Koen Park

The Park itself was explained at the end of the Day 1 itinerary. If you are a good walker, we recommend that you start the day with a visit to **Chorakuji Temple** 長楽寺 (middle center, map 78), which is on a mountain slope at the top of a long stone stairway. The entrance to the approach is lined with elegant, dark-purple lanterns. Chorakuji Temple is famous because it was here that Kenreimon-in, daughter of Kiyomori Taira and mother of Emperor Antoku, renounced the world when the Taira clan was defeated by Yoritomo Minamoto at the end of the 12th century. Kenreimon-in became a nun and spent the rest of her days at Jakkoin Temple in Ohara (see Northern Kyoto section).

Ryozen Kannon Temple 霊山観音 (optional) (Lower center, map 78)

Ryozen Kannon Temple, which is located at the top of a flight of stone steps not quite as long as those of Chorakuji, has no real historical value, but features an outdoor Kannon statue. According to its inscription, this 79 foot (24 m.) tall statue was erected in 1955 as a "Memorial to the World's Unknown Soldiers Who Perished in World War II." In exchange for your 100 yen admission you are handed a burning joss stick that should be inserted in the box in front of the Kannon's image.

Kiyomizudera Temple 清水寺 (Lower center, map 78)

The path to Kiyomizudera Temple is lined with old wooden buildings and is a good example of a typical backstreet of the ancient capital. Most of buildings house souvenir shops that are stocked to their eaves with inexpensive traditional items such as *Kiyomizu-yaki* pottery, Kyoto dolls, bamboo crafts, etc. There are also many traditional snack shops and tea shops here. On your way to Kiyomizudera Temple, be sure to try one of the free samples of Yatsuhashi cookies. These are the souvenir that Japanese visitors to Kyoto most often purchase for the folks back home. They come in two varieties – soft, sweet dumplings stuffed with sweet bean paste, or hard, curved cookies that taste a bit like ginger snaps. Only the latter travel well. The five-story Yasaka Pagoda can be seen from the approach to Kiyomizudera Temple.

Kiyomizudera Temple, erected in 798, is dedicated to the Eleven-headed Kannon. The present structures were rebuilt in 1633 at the order of the third Tokugawa Shogun. The two-story West Gate serves as the main entrance. Statues of the guardian Kongo-Rikishi stand in niches at both sides of the gate. The Main Hall, which extends out over a cliff and which is supported by 139 giant pillars, is quite a unique structure, and probably the only National Treasure you can walk on in shoes. There is a

wide, wooden veranda across the front of the Main Hall where visitors can enjoy a panoramic view of Kyoto and its surroundings. It is quite thrilling to look down at the deep valley that lies below the veranda. The precincts are open from dawn till dusk, and admission to the veranda is 100 yen.

Chishakuin Temple 智積院 (optional)
(Lower left, map 78)

Chishakuin Temple is famous for its brilliant paintings of the Hasegawa School (a rival of the Kano School), and its garden. The colorful paintings, which feature the beauties of the four seasons, are displayed in a special exhibition hall. Because they are arranged at the height they would normally be in a Japanese style room, you have to sit down to really appreciate them. The garden, laid out about 400 years ago, centers around a large pond that extends under a veranda. Because most people hurry directly to Sanjusangendo Hall from Kiyomizudera Temple, you can spend a quiet, relaxed time at this garden. (9:00 AM to 4:30 PM. Admission 300 yen).

Sanjusangendo Hall 三十三間堂 (Lower left, map 78)

Sanjusangendo Hall is the popular name given to Rengeoin Temple. It was so named because of the 33 ("sanjusan") spaces between the pillars in the long, narrow hall. Although the hall is only 33 feet (10 m.) wide, it is 394 feet (120 m.) long. The original temple, erected in 1164 at the order of the retired but still powerful Emperor Goshirakawa, was destroyed by fire in 1249 and rebuilt in 1266. Its chief image is a wooden, thousand-handed Kannon in a seated position. This National Treasure was carved in 1254 by Tankei, a master sculptor of the Kamakura era. The Kannon is surrounded by statues of 28 faithful followers (National Treasures), and an additional one thousand and one smaller statues of the Kannon fill the remainder of the gallery. It is said that everyone can find at least one face like that of a friend (or sweetheart?) among these 1,001 images (8:00 AM to 4:40 PM. Till 3:40 PM in winter. Admission 300 yen).

Kyoto National Museum 京都国立美術館
(Lower left, map 78)

Kyoto National Museum was built in 1879 by the Imperial Household Agency as a repository for precious art objects and other treasures. It is divided into three sections – history, fine arts, and handicrafts. Its 17 exhibit rooms house some 2,000 pieces of rare and valuable art, and historical and religious objects. Set aside as much time as possible for this museum (9:00 AM to 4:00 PM. Closed on Mondays. Admission 250 yen).

Other Places of Interest

Kawai Memorial Hall 河井寛次郎記念館 (lower left, map 78) displays representative art works of Kanjiro Kawai, the most distinguished potter of the *Kiyomizu-yaki* school.

Hokoji Temple 方広寺 (lower left, map 78; to the north of the National Museum) was built at the order of Hideyoshi to house Japan's biggest image of Buddha. Larger even than that of Nara's Todaiji Temple (which is today Japan's biggest statue), the huge Buddha was recast three times before finally falling victim to fires and earthquakes. Only the old stone walls along the western side of the precincts remain to give us an idea of Hideyoshi's grand scheme for the temple complex. A large temple bell, cast at the order of Hideyori Toyotomi, Hideyoshi's successor, also stands in the temple grounds. The inscriptions on the bell say, "Peace for the Nation, and Prosperity for the People." Two of the Chinese characters used in the inscription are characters used in Ieyasu Tokugawa's name as well. On the inscription these two characters were split – unluckily – and another character interspersed. Ieyasu took this as an insult and claimed that the unlucky inscription illustrated Hideyori's desire to destroy his influence. For Ieyasu this constituted an excuse to commence hostilities, and the resulting battle at Osakajo Castle led to the ascendancy of the Tokugawas and the collapse of the Toyotomi family. **Hokoku Jinja Shrine** 豊国神社, in the Hokoji Temple precincts, was built to honor Hideyoshi Toyotomi.

Western Kyoto

◈ **Traditional Kyoto**

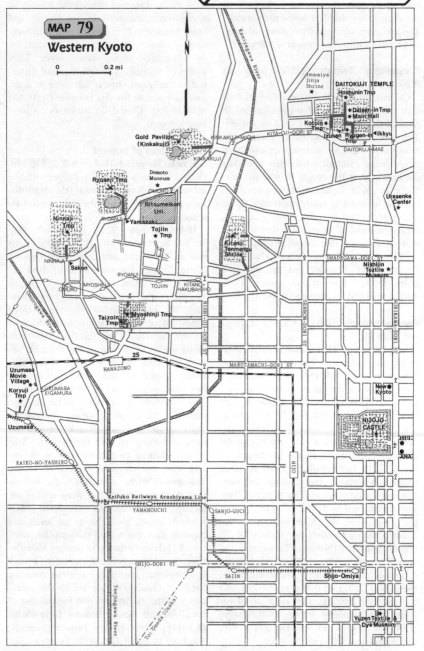

MAP **79**

Western Kyoto

0   0.2 mi

Kamiyagawa River

Amamiya
Jinja
Shrine
★

DAITOKUJI TEMPLE

Hoshunin Tmp
★   ★Daisen-in Tmp
★Main Hall

Kotoin
Tmp ★   ★ ★Ryugen-in ★Ikkyu
Izusen   Tmp

KITA-OJI-DORI ST

DAITOKUJI-MAE

Gold Pavilion
(Kinkakuji)

KINKAKUJI-MICHI

KINKAKUJI

Urasenke
Center
★

Ryoanji Tmp
★

Domoto
Museum

OMURO

Ritsumeikan
Uni

RYOANJI   Yamazaki

Ninnaji
Tmp

Tojiin
★ Tmp

Kitano
Tenmangu
Shrine

IMADEGAWA-DORI ST

Nishijin
Textile ★
Museum

NINNAJI

★ Sakon

RYOANJI

OMURO   MYOSHINJI

TOJIIN

KITANO-
HAKUBAICHO

SENBON-DORI ST

HORIKAWA-DORI ST

Omurogawa River

Taizoin
Tmp

Myoshinji Tmp

25

HANAZONO

MARUTAMACHI-DORI ST

Uzumasa
Movie
Village
★
UZUMASA
EIGAMURA

Koryuji
Tmp
★

New ●
Kyoto

**NIJOJO
CASTLE**

JR●
ANA●

Uzumasa

OIIN

KAIKO-NO-YASHIRO

Keifuku Railways Arashiyama Line

YAMANOUCHI

Sanjo-Guchi

SHIJO-DORI ST

SAIIN

Shijo-Omiya

Toji Oneta (Osaka)

Tenjingawa River

Yuzen Textile &
Dye Museum ★

Western Kyoto, adjacent to the central part of the city, is home to famous temples such as the Gold Pavilion and Ryoanji, with its austerely beautiful rock garden. Western Kyoto is also the home of Uzumasa Movie Village, Japan's Hollywood.

The itinerary of Western Kyoto starts at Daitokuji Temple. After your visit, take a bus to Gold Pavilion, and then to Ryoanji Temple. After enjoying the Rock Garden, continue your bus ride to Ninnaji Temple. Then you walk (or take a short bus ride) to Myoshinji Temple. Walking through the broad expanse of Myoshinji Temple from the north gate to the south gate, take a bus to the Movie Village, and then walk to Koryuji Temple, the last stop of the day.

Daitokuji Temple 大徳寺 (Upper right, map 79)

Daitokuji is a large temple located in the northwestern corner of Kyoto city. The entrance to the temple precincts is near Daitokuji-mae bus stop on the No. 205 and No. 206 loop lines.

The original temple was founded in 1319, but was lost to fire during the 1467 civil war. The temple was revitalized by Hideyoshi Toyotomi in the 16th century, and many smaller buildings in the precincts were constructed by local feudal lords, to express their loyalty to Hideyoshi. Sanmon Gate, Buddha Hall, Lecture Hall and the Main Hall are located in a straight line from south to north, surrounded by about 20 subordinate temples. Several of them are open to the public. The most famous among them is **Daisen-in Temple** 大仙院 (National Treasure). The temple has one of Japan's most famous Zen gardens: with rocks and sand, it represents a grand view of mountains, ravines and the ocean. Sliding screens feature brilliant paintings of the Kano School. (9:00 AM to 5:00 PM. Admission 300 yen). **Hoshun-in Temple** 芳春院 features a lovely pavilion and a garden designed around a pond (8:30 AM to 4:30 PM. Admission 200 yen).

Gold Pavilion 金閣寺 (Upper center, map 79)

Gold Pavilion (whose popular Japanese

name is Kinkakuji) can be reached by the No. 205 or No. 206 bus from Daitokuji-mae (to Kinkakuji-michi stop). Kinkakuji-michi stop is a 3 minute walk to the temple.

Gold Pavilion, formally Rokuonji Temple, was constructed in 1397 by the third Ashikaga Shogun, Yoshimitsu, who spent the latter part of his life here in retirement. His son, Yoshimochi, in accordance with the dictates of his father's will, had the villa converted to a Buddhist temple. The garden still reflects the beauty of the refined contemplative life of the Ashikagas, but most of the original buildings have been destroyed by repeated fires, including the tragic loss, by arson, in July 1950, of the precious Gold Pavilion itself. A new Gold Pavilion – an exact reproduction of the original – was erected on the same spot in October 1955. After walking through Chumon Gate, you will see two shimmering gold pavilions. One is the three-story golden building with a bronze phoenix on its roof. The other is its reflection in the calm, beautiful pond that lies in front of the Pavilion. The walls of the Pavilion are completely covered with gold foil. (9:00 AM to 5:00 PM. Until 5:30 PM in summer. Admission 300 yen).

Domoto Museum 堂本美術館 (optional) (Upper center, map 79)

If you enjoy contemporary art, you should visit Domoto Museum, which is located at Kinugasa bus stop. Take the No. 59 bus from Kinkakuji-mae stop right in front of the temple. The modern three-story museum displays paintings, sculptures and other works of Insho Domoto (10:00 AM to 5:00 PM. Admission 500 yen. Closed on Mondays).

Ryoanji Temple 竜安寺 (Upper left, map 79)

If you don't visit Domoto Museum, you should still take the No. 59 bus, but should stay on it to Ryoanji-mae stop. Ryoanji Temple belongs to the Rinzai sect of Zen Buddhism, and was founded in 1473 by Katsumoto Hosokawa, a powerful Kyoto feudal lord, whose grave is in the temple grounds. It is famous for its rock garden. Consisting of only rocks and pebbles, it is regarded as the quintessential Zen garden. Some say that the 15 rocks arranged on the surface of white pebbles look like islands on a huge ocean, while others think that they look like tigers crossing a big river. The rocks are so arranged that visitors can only see 14 of them at once, no matter what the angle from which they view the garden (except perhaps from the air!) (8:00 AM to 5:00 PM. Admission 300 yen).

After visiting Ryoanji Temple you may, due to the lack of time, have to choose only two destinations from the following five attractions. The selection depends on your interest. Our suggestion is the combination of the Movie Village and Koryuji Temple. For that option, you need to take a short taxi ride from Ryoanji Temple to the Movie Village.

Ninnaji Temple 仁和寺 (optional) (Middle left, map 79)

Take the No. 59 bus three stops, from Ryoanji-mae stop to Omuro Ninnaji stop (or you can walk the distance in 10 minutes). Ninnaji Temple was formerly known as Omuro Palace. Emperor Koko, the Temple's first patron, ordered work on it begun in 886, but passed away before it was completed. His successor, Emperor Uda had the work completed two years later, and when he retired became the temple's first abbot. Originally, there were more than 60 buildings scattered around the temple precincts, but frequent fires have reduced their number. The oldest buildings still standing date from the first half of the 17th century. The five-story pagoda, about 108 feet (33 m.) tall, was built in 1637. The Main Hall (National Treasure) at the northernmost end of the precincts was formerly the Main Ceremonial Hall of the Imperial Palace and was moved here in the early 17th century. The Main Hall contains a wooden image of Amitabha (National Treasure) as its chief object of worship. Admission to the temple grounds is 100 yen. It costs an additional 300 yen to see the interior of Goten Hall, the palace the abbots used as their residence. The Treasure House is open to the public only for two weeks in the fall (9:00 AM to 4:00 PM).

Myoshinji Temple 妙心寺 (optional) (Middle left, map 79)

You can easily walk the 0.5 mile (0.8 km.) distance from Ninnaji to Myoshinji, and frequent bus service is also available. Take the No. 8, No. 10 or No. 26 bus from the stop right in front of the South Gate of Ninnaji Temple (make sure to take one going east, from the northern side of the road).

Upon entering the precincts of Myoshinji Temple at the North Gate, you'll feel that you're walking along a stone path running between temple after temple. Myoshinji, like Daitokuji Temple, is one of the few temples that has enough of its original buildings intact to give you some idea of the magnificent scale of Japan's traditional temple architecture. It was founded in 1337 on the site of Emperor Hanazono's imperial villa. There are more than 40 minor buildings, and each has its own refined garden. Japan's oldest bell (National Treasure), cast in 698, hangs in a belfry near South Gate. Four of Myoshinji's buildings are open to the public:

Main Hall: You will see the entrance on your left just after passing under the elevated corridor between the main buildings. The main attraction of the Main Hall is the picture of a dragon painted on the ceiling of Hatto (Ceremonial) Hall. The painting is often described as "A Dragon Glaring in Eight Directions" because his eyes seem to stare at you no matter where you stop to look up at him (9:00 AM to 4:00 PM. Admission 300 yen). **Taizoin Temple** 退蔵院 , erected in 1404, is renowned for its landscaped garden, which represents a

Uzumasa Movie Village

stream coursing down a mountain and forming a river. The grounds are quiet and quite beautiful (9:00 AM to 5:00 PM. Admission 300 yen).

Uzumasa Movie Village 太秦映画村
(optional) (Lower left, map 79)

Take the No. 61, No. 62 or No. 63 bus (west-bound) at Myoshinji-mae stop (southern side of the temple) to Uzumasa Eigamura (Eigamura is "Movie Village" in Japanese). The official name of the bus stop is "Hachigaokacho," but "Uzumasa Eigamura" is used much more frequently.

Uzumasa Movie Village, owned by the Toei Movie Company, has large open-air sets that recreate the buildings, bridges and streets of feudal and modern Japan. There are also indoor studios and museums. You can watch as the cameras roll on famous movie stars dressed in period costumes. It takes one hour just to tour the facilities, and a thorough visit to this world through the looking glass will probably take two or three hours. The village is closed on the 4th Tuesday, Wednesday and Thursday of July, and from December 21 to January 1. Admission is 1,100 yen.

Koryuji Temple 広隆寺 (optional) (Middle left, map 79)

Koryuji Temple is just a 10 minute walk from the Uzumasa Movie Village. If you skip the Movie Village, continue your bus ride from Myoshinji to Uzumasa.

A huge wooden gate marks the entrance to the precincts of Koryuji Temple, which was founded in 622 by Kawakatsu Hata, one of Kyoto's most powerful aristocrats. It was designed as a memorial for Regent Shotoku, who promulgated Japan's first "Seventeen-Article" Constitution. The newly constructed Reihoden Treasure House is home to more that 50 masterpieces of Asu-

ka, Nara and Heian sculpture. The exquisite statues, all of which were originally objects of worship, reflect the artistic splendor of those ancient eras, and many of them are National Treasures. Perhaps the most famous of all is the Miroku-Bosatsu, which was selected as Japan's first National Treasure and well deserves this honor. Strong yet gentle, serene and compassionate, the enigmatic beauty of the face of this Buddha casts its spell over every visitor to the Treasure House. The Treasure House is open from 9:00 AM to 5:00 PM. Admission is 300 yen. The Keiguin Hall (National Treasure) is an elegant octagonal structure located in the northwestern part of the temple precincts.

* You can take the private Keifuku Arashiyama Line train from Uzumasa to Shijo Omiya, and then a bus to your hotel.

Places for Lunch

Yamazaki, located near Ryoanji Temple, is a handy place for a light, inexpensive lunch. **Sakon** is in front of Ninnaji Temple. This restaurant serves a wide variety of set menu Japanese lunches (reasonable). The Movie Village has a huge restaurant that serves everything from noodles to fancy Japanese, Chinese and Western dishes.

Yuzen Textile & Dye Museum 友禅美術館
(Middle left, map 77)

If you arrive at Shijo Omiya Station in mid afternoon, and if you are interested in traditional Japanese textiles, we recommend that you visit the Yuzen Textile and Dye Museum, which is only an 8-minute walk from Shijo Omiya. Like Nishijin Textiles, Yuzen Dyeing, which dates from 794, got its start with imperial patronage. The first floor of the museum is used for displays of Yuzen masterpieces, and the second and third floors are devoted to demonstrations of the traditional technique. Yuzen *kimono* are extremely expensive, but smaller items such as ties, folding fans and scarves are affordable, and make excellent presents for friends and relatives back home. The many bamboo trees at its entrance make the museum easy to find (9:00 AM to 5:00 PM. Admission 300 yen).

Arashiyama

Poetic Kyoto

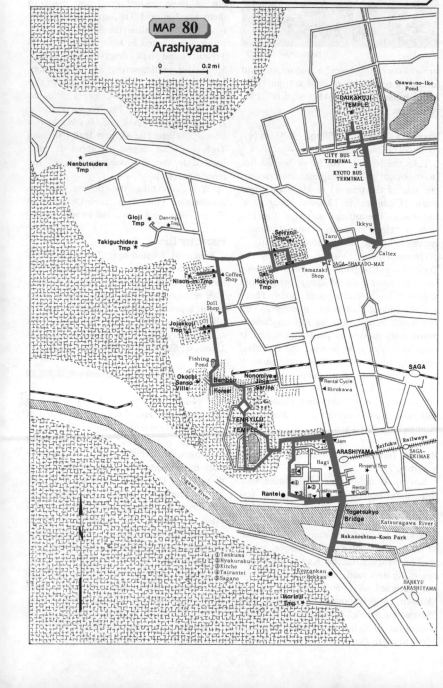

MAP **80**
Arashiyama

0   0.2 mi

The peaceful surroundings, gentle mountains and the clear waters of the Katsuragawa River made the Arashiyama district a favorite of emperors and nobles throughout Japanese history. Arashiyama preserves peaceful natural settings as they were in the feudal era. Because of its historical importance, we give top priority to Eastern Kyoto, but we personally love this westernmost part of Kyoto most. Walking along the narrow paths here and visiting the area's many historic sites, are, in our opinion, the best way to experience the beauty that is Kyoto.

Arashiyama Station is 4.5 miles (7.2 km.) from Shijo Omiya. The Keifuku Arashiyama trains that connect the two operate every 10 – 15 minutes. The ride takes 20 minutes.

There are several bicycle rental shops near Arashiyama Station and Togetsukyo Bridge for cycling fans, but we recommend that you enjoy walking through the area.

Togetsukyo Bridge 渡月橋 (Lower right, map 80)

Arashiyama stretches along the Katsuragawa River (the river is also called Oigawa). The view from the northern bank of the river of Togetsukyo Bridge with the beautiful Arashiyama foothills in the background is especially lovely. It is no wonder that throughout Japanese history, emperors, aristocrats and shoguns loved the area. Modern Japanese, too, are particularly fond of this area.

Tenryuji Temple 天竜寺 (Middle center, map 80)

Tenryuji Temple was founded in 1339 by Takauji, the first Ashikaga Shogun, in memory of Emperor Godaigo. The noted priest and landscape artist, Muso-Kokushi, was its first abbot. The temple was repeatedly ravaged by fire. and the present buildings date only from 1900, but the famous garden preserves the style of the 14th century original. Complementing its natural surroundings, the Tenryuji garden testifies to the great creative abilities of the Ashikaga era artists who planned it (8:30 AM to 5:00 PM. Admission 350 yen. An additional 100 yen for the interior).

Okochi Sanso Villa 大河内山荘 (optional) (Middle center, map 80)

When you leave Tenryuji Temple from the north exit (if you see a small pond with an image of Buddha and a statue of a frog, you'll know you're going in the right direction for the north exit), you'll pass through a narrow street with thousands of beautiful bamboos. The westernmost part of Kyoto is famous for its bamboo forests, and this one is considered the best. Enjoy the green serenity of the bamboos – and be thankful that you're on foot – this is something you'd never see from a tour bus.

Okochi Sanso Villa, the lavish home of Denjiro Okochi, a famous star of samurai films is of no interest itself, but the garden is beautiful, and the view of Arashiyama and the city of Kyoto from the upper part of its grounds is splendid (9:00 AM to 5:00 PM. The 700 yen admission – which includes powdered tea and a cake – is a bit too expensive).

Jojakkoji Temple 常寂光寺 (Middle center, map 80)

The approach to the main buildings of Jojakkoji Temple passes through two gates and up old stone steps. The view of the thatched roofs of the gates from the top of the steps is especially lovely, so don't forget to look back. A two-story pagoda stands at the highest point of the grounds, and is surrounded by many trees. The temple is also famous for its colorful maple leaves in November (9:00 AM to 5:00 PM. Admission 200 yen).

Nison-in Temple 二尊院 (Middle center, map 80)

Nison-in Temple was erected in 841 at the order of Emperor Saga. The approach to the main grounds is up a wide, stone-paved slope lined on both sides with cherry, maple and other trees whose beauty varies with the seasons. The main hall houses two images of Buddha. Visitors can ring the temple's "Bell of Happiness." Its sound is not particularly distinctive, but ringing it is an interesting experience. (9:00

AM to 5:00 PM. Admission 200 yen).

Detour

After your visit to Nison-in Temple, our suggested itinerary is that you head east to Hokyoin and Seiryoji Temples. If you are a good walker and have enough time to make a detour, we suggest that you visit three temples to the north.

Gioji Temple 祇王寺 and **Takiguchidera Temple** 滝口寺 were the scenes of sentimental love stories of olden times. Although they have little historic value, these two small temples standing in beautiful bamboo forests are quite impressive.

Nenbutsudera Temple 念仏寺 is in an area called Adashino. Adashino was the extreme end of Kyoto, and the dead bodies of the poor and the unknown were discarded here. After the Meiji Restoration, the scattered bones were collected and buried in the grounds of Nenbutsudera Temple. Thousands of stone images of Buddha, dedicated to the dead, sit in the precincts – a very unusual scene.

Hokyoin Temple 宝筐院 (optional) (Middle center, map 80)

Even few Japanese know about this temple. The tombs of two men, Yoshiakira

Ashikaga and Masatsura Kusunoki, who were fierce rivals during Japan's medieval era, are located side by side in the precincts of Hokyoin Temple. Masatsura helped Emperor Godaigo regain power from the Kamakura Shogunate. Even though the Emperor triumphed in 1333, he was again soon supplanted, this time by the Ashikagas. Yoshiakira had great respect for his enemy Masatsura, and when he died in battle, Yoshiakira had this temple built to honor Masatsura's memory, and left instructions that he himself was to be buried next to his old enemy. The wooded precincts are extremely quiet and very peaceful (9:00 AM to 5:00 PM. Admission 300 yen).

Seiryoji Temple 清涼寺 (optional) (Middle center, map 80)

This temple, popularly known as Saga-Shakado (Saga Buddha Hall), was originally the villa of an imperial prince. It was converted to a temple to provide a home for a sandalwood image of Sakyamuni that had been imported from China. There are several buildings in the temple's spacious grounds, including Sutra Hall at the eastern end of the grounds, repository of thousands and thousands of sutras arranged on revolving shelves. Supposedly, if you spin the shelves once, it has the same effect as reading the innumerable volumes of sutras contained on them! Admission to the precincts is free of charge, but it costs 200 yen to enter the main hall and the garden attached to it (9:30 AM to 4:30 PM).

Daikakuji Temple 大覚寺 (Upper right, map 80)

Daikakuji Temple was originally built as a villa for Emperor Saga in the early 9th century. After its conversion to a temple, the abbots were selected from the imperial family and the temple maintained its high social status and reputation as one of Kyoto's most important establishments. The original structures were destroyed by fires and the present buildings date from the 16th century. Many of these buildings are connected by corridors (watch your head because they are only about 6 feet tall). Brilliant paintings of the Kano School are displayed in the chambers along the corridors. The temple's Osawa-no-Ike Pond was designed so that Emperor Saga could enjoy the pleasures of boating at his country retreat. It is surrounded by a promenade lined with cherry, maple and pine trees (9:00 AM to 4:30 PM. Admission 300 yen).

* As pictured on map 80, the Kyoto Bus and City Bus terminals are a bit of a distance from each other. Because Kyoto Bus has more frequent service back to the city, you should check that schedule first. The No. 61 goes to Sanjo Keihan bus terminal while the No. 71 and the No. 81 go to Kyoto Station. Only the No. 28 operates from the City Bus terminal, and it goes back to Kyoto Station. The ride to either Kyoto Station or Sanjo Keihan terminal takes about 50 minutes.

Restaurants in Arashiyama

There are a number of famous restaurants along the northern bank of Oigawa River, such as **Tankuma, Hyakuraku, Kitcho, Tairantei** and **Sagano**. Drop in at one of them for an authentic Japanese lunch (2,000 – 4,000 yen). If you're in the mood for a Western lunch, **Coffee & Hamburger Hagi**, near Arashiyama train station, serves quick inexpensive lunches.

Northern Kyoto
◈ Panoramic Kyoto

Check map 81 first. Enryakuji Temple is located on top of Mt. Hieizan, which separates the city of Kyoto and Lake Biwako. Ohara is located further to the north in a rural district. The suggested itinerary for Northern Kyoto involves visits to Ohara in the morning and Enryakuji Temple in the afternoon. Because the visit to Enryakuji Temple requires at least a 0.6 mile (1 km.) walk on a mountain path (one that is *not* steep), those who don't want to walk too much should spend more time in Ohara and return to the city directly.

Transportation to Ohara from the City

As pictured on map 75, you can take either the No. 17 or No. 18 bus from Kyoto Station to Ohara. If it is easier for you to start from Sanjo Keihan bus terminal, take either the No. 16 or No. 17 bus. At Kyoto Station, the buses leave from stop D (pictured on map 74, upper left). From Sanjo Keihan terminal, catch your bus at the Kyoto Bus (5) stop (pictured on map 76, upper right). The trip from Kyoto Station takes about one hour, and the trip from Sanjo Keihan to Ohara takes about 40 minutes.

MAP 81
Outline of Northern Kyoto

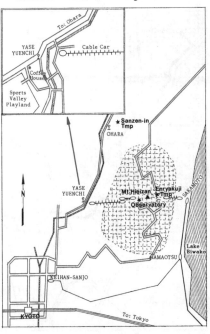

Ohara 大原

Ohara, located in the quiet northern suburbs of Kyoto, is surrounded by mountains. Though the area is slowly modernizing, it still preserves much of the atmosphere of the ancient capital. Several destinations in this area are real gems. If you plan to visit Enryakuji Temple (and we recommend that you do), visit the temples on the eastern side of Ohara, skipping Jakkoin Temple, which is located on the western side. If you decide to skip Enryakuji Temple, you should be sure to include a visit to Jakkoin.

Sanzen-in Temple 三千院 (Lower right, map 82)

The approach to Sanzen-in Temple is a gentle paved slope that runs alongside a small creek. Many souvenir shops and restaurants are, unfortunately, located here as well, cluttering up and commercializing this lovely natural setting. Sanzen-in Temple was originally located in Mt. Hieizan and was a branch of Enryakuji Temple. The temple was moved to its present site in the

15th century. There are three buildings and beautiful gardens in the spacious precincts. The main hall houses an Amitabha trinity: the two disciples that flank Buddha are seated, which is quite unusual – it makes these goddesses seem very relaxed and merciful. The temple grounds and the approach have a reputation as one of Kyoto's best maple viewing locations in November (8:30 AM to 5:00 PM. Until 4:30 PM in winter. Admission 400 yen).

Jikkoin Temple 実光院 (optional) (Middle right, map 82)

Jikkoin Temple is only 0.1 miles north of Sanzen-in temple, but because group tours only visit Sanzen-in and then rush off to Jakkoin Temple on the other side of Ohara, Jikkoin Temple and the other temples located north of Sanzen-in are never very crowded. Unlike most temples, Jikkoin does not have a ticket office at its entrance. Upon entering the gate, you should ring the gong. The admission of 400 yen should be paid to the young lady who will lead you to a chamber overlooking a small garden. Powdered tea and a cake are

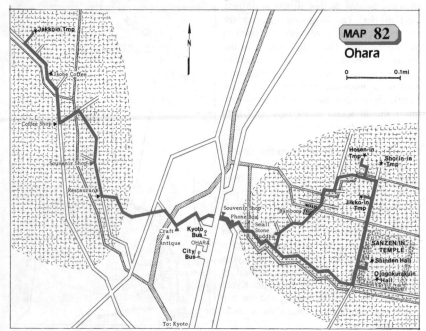

MAP 82
Ohara

served. Because the tea is served in a very casual manner, you can just relax and enjoy the delicate flavor of the tea and the view of the beautifully manicured garden, even if you don't know anything about the etiquette of tea ceremony. This temple also has a collection of tiny bells in one corner of the visitors' chamber, each of which has a distinctive but delicate tone. When the temple was a training center for new monks, the bells were used to help the novices learn their prayers (9:00 AM to 5:00 PM).

Shorin-in Temple 勝林院 (optional) (Middle right, map 82)

The grounds of this temple are quite extensive. Even from the outside visitors can see a building that dates from 1013. Shorin-in Temple is famous as the place where the priest Honen (remember Honen-in Temple in Eastern Kyoto?) debated and refuted the high ranking priests of other sects (9:30 AM to 5:00 PM. Admission 100 yen).

Hosen-in Temple 宝泉院 (optional) (Middle right, map 82)

Hosen-in Temple is famous for its 500-year old pine tree shaped like Mt. Fuji; this marvelous example of the gardener's art is just inside the entrance. As with Jikkoin Temple, there is no ticket window. This time you have to hit a wooden gong to inform the staff of your arrival. Again, you pay a 400 yen admission and are led to a chamber where tea and a cake are served in a casual manner. The room faces a beautiful bamboo forest and the pillars on that side of the room are arranged like an oversize frame so that the garden looks like a huge picture – and a very beautiful one at that (9:00 AM to 5:00 PM).

To Go or Not to Go to Enryakuji

If you have decided to visit Enryakuji Temple, take a Kyoto Bus back to Yase-Yuenchi (Yase Playland), which you passed on your way to Ohara in the morning. You can take any of the following Kyoto Buses: No. 11, No. 13, No. 14, No. 15, No. 16, No. 17 or No. 18.

If you are not going to visit Enryakuji Temple, visit Jakkoin Temple in Ohara, and then take a bus back to the city. Again, the No. 16 and No. 17 Kyoto Buses go to Sanjo Keihan terminal, and the No. 17 and No. 18 Kyoto Buses go to Kyoto Station.

Jakkoin Temple 寂光院 (Upper left, map 82)

Jakkoin Temple, erected in 594, is famous as the scene of a Taira clan tragedy. After ascending the ladder of power at the imperial court, the Taira clan was destroyed by the Minamotos. Empress Kenreimonin, a daughter of Kiyomori Taira and mother of Emperor Antoku, renounced the world at Chorakuji Temple, and lived the rest of her life at Jakkoin praying for the repose of the souls of her son and other members of the Taira family. The temple is located at the top of a long stone stairway, and is surrounded by thick woods. If you are lucky enough to be at Jakkoin at a quiet time, its solemn atmosphere will remind you of this heroine's tragic life 800 years ago (9:00 AM to 5:00 PM. Until 4:30 AM in winter. Admission 350 yen).

Mt. Hieizan 比叡山

To Mt. Shimeidake 四明岳

Yase cable car station is a few minutes walk from Yase-Yuenchi bus stop (upper left, map 81). The cable car operates every 30 minutes. Transfer to the ropeway at Hiei for the trip to Sancho stop. The ropeway operates every 30 minutes.

A revolving observatory is located on the top of Mt. Shimeidake (admission 300 yen). If the weather permits, you have a panoramic view of Lake Biwako to the east, Osaka Bay to the west and the surrounding mountains.

Enryakuji Temple 延暦寺

Walking away from the observatory, find the small hut pictured on map 83. This hut (very dirty rest rooms) marks the beginning of the path to Enryakuji Temple. The narrow mountain path zigzags down amid huge cedar trees. You can see a ski area below the path. As pictured on map 83, several sign posts (with signs written in Japanese) lead you to the temple. Once you come to a large stone monument with a carving of the Amitabha trinity, the temple precincts are not far at all. The path crosses over a road just before the temple.

If you are a good walker, we recommend that you visit the West Precincts first. They are to the north, and further down the slope. The return walk is pretty tough even though the approach is paved. If you decide to visit the West Precincts, use the bridge to cross the road. The major structures in the West Precincts are Jodoin Temple, Ninaido Hall and Shakado Hall, the main hall at the northern end of the grounds. All the buildings are surrounded by huge cedar trees, and since the number of visitors is relatively small, the precincts are filled with an atmosphere of esoteric Buddhism.

The East Precincts are what most visitors see at Enryakuji Temple. Enryakuji was founded by the priest Saicho in 788. Enryakuji and Koyasan are the two giants of Japanese Buddhism and have played leading roles throughout their 1,200-year long histories. Many new religious sects were established by priests who studied at Enryakuji Temple. At the peak of its prosperity, Enryakuji Temple contained 3,000 buildings in three major precincts and in the surrounding valleys. The temple even organized a private military force as big as that of a feudal lord. Because of this force, and because of the temple's influence in political matters, Nobunaga Oda attacked Enryakuji in 1571. Most of the buildings were burned to the ground and thousands of soldiers, priests and other residents of the temple grounds were killed in the battle. Most of the present structures were constructed in the middle of the 17th century. Konponchudo Hall is the main hall of the temple. Toto Pagoda is a recently completed gigantic two-story brilliant red structure.

How to Return to the City

Take a bus back to the city. The No. 6 (going to Sanjo Keihan terminal), the No. 7 (to Kyoto Station via Sanjo Keihan) and

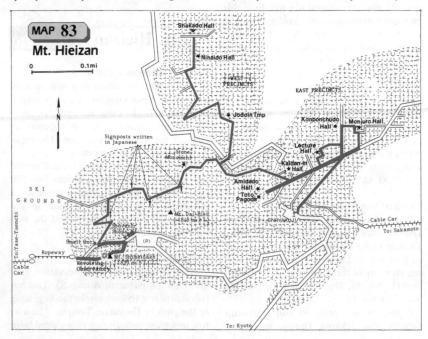

MAP 83
Mt. Hieizan
0   0.1mi

the No. 51 (to Kyoto Station) buses all stop at the Enryakuji stop. Because each bus operates only every 2 – 3 hours, take whichever one comes first (there is at least one bus every hour). The ride to Kyoto Station takes about one hour. Enryakuji is not the first stop for these buses, so make sure that the bus you get on is headed for Kyoto.

As indicated on map 81, there is another way to go back to Kyoto via Lake Biwako: a cable car to Sakamoto, and then a 15 minute walk to Sakamoto train station. The Keihan Ishiyama Sakamoto Line to Hamaotsu, and then the Keihan Kyozu Line to Keihan Sanjo in Kyoto. Though the view of Lake Biwako from the cable car is fantastic, the rest of the connections are time consuming and the train rides boring, and we do not recommend this route for tourists unless you allocate one full day for Hieizan and Lake Biwako, and plan to stop at Hamaotsu to enjoy a boat ride on Lake Biwako.

Other Places of Interest in Kyoto

Byodoin Temple 平等院

Byodoin Temple, popularly known as Phoenix Temple, was originally built as a villa for Michinaga Fujiwara, the most powerful aristocrat of the Heian Era. His son, Yorimichi, converted the villa to a temple, and intended to create a Heaven on earth by adding many more magnificent structures and gardens. Even though most of the buildings were lost in the war at the middle of the 14th century, Phoenix Hall still stands in a garden designed around a large pond.

Byodoin Temple is located in Uji to the south of Kyoto (actually half way to Nara). The temple is a 15 minute walk from Uji Station 宇治駅 on the JR Nara Line (a 20 minute ride from Kyoto Station).

Fushimi Inari Shrine 伏見稲荷 (Lower center, map 73)

Fushimi Inari Shrine is the headquarters

Jidai Matsuri Festival

of about 40,000 Inari shrines all over Japan. The origin of the shrine is not clear. The shrine was moved to the present site in 1438. Through a huge Torii Gate, a number of vermilion structures stand in the spacious grounds. Beyond the main precincts, a number of small shrines are scattered along the mountainous paths on Mt. Inariyama. Most parts of the path are beneath hundreds of thousands of vermilion torii gates contributed by people from all around Japan.

Fushimi Inari Shrine is a few minutes walk from Inari Station 伏見稲荷駅 on the JR Nara Line. Inari is the second stop from Kyoto Station, and the ride takes only 5 minutes.

Tofukuji Temple 東福寺 (Lower right, map 73)

Erected in 1255, Tofukuji Temple is one of the five most important Zen temples in Kyoto. The huge Sanmon Gate and the Main Hall were constructed in this century. However, there are about 25 subordinate temples in the wide precincts, and each one has its own garden. Especially noteworthy is **Hojo**方丈 , which has a rock garden and a moss garden (9:00 AM to 4:20 PM).

Tofukuji Temple is a 15 minute walk from Tofukuji Station on the JR Nara Line. Tofukuji is the first stop from Kyoto Station.

Daigoji Temple 醍醐寺 (Lower right, map 73)

Mt. Daigosan rises in the southwestern corner of Kyoto City. The whole mountain is part of the precincts of Daigoji Temple, and more than 70 buildings are scattered over the mountain. The temple precincts are divided into two parts: Shimo-Daigo (lower Daigo) and Kami-Daigo (upper Daigo).

The main approach to Shimo-Daigo is lined on both sides with cherry trees. **Sanpoin Temple** 三宝院, a subordinate temple on the grounds, is famous for its paintings of the Kano School and its landscaped garden (9:00 AM to 5:00 PM). **Hojuin** 宝聚院 (Treasure House) exhibits Buddha images, paintings, and other temple treasures. The Treasure House is open to the public only twice a year (early April to early May, and mid October to mid November). An elegant five-story pagoda is the only structure that survives from the time of the founding of the temple in 951.

Kami-Daigo was a training center for Buddhist priests. A 3.5 km. (2 mile) long steep path runs in the woods from Shimo-Daigo to Kami-Daigo. In the grounds of Kami-Daigo are several historic structures built in the 12th through the 15th centuries. If you like hiking, you should visit Kami-Daigo (a roundtrip hike from Shimo-Daigo takes about 3 hours).

To visit Daigoji Temple, you can take the "Higashi-9" City Bus from Keihan-Sanjo Bus Terminal to Sanpoin-mae 三宝院前 bus stop (about 40 minutes).

Katsura Detached Villa 桂離宮 (Lower left, map 73)

Katsura Detached Villa is located in a bamboo forest on the western side of the Katsuragawa River. To visit the Villa, you must apply for permission to the Imperial Household Agency Kyoto office located in the Kyoto Imperial Palace (See the Suggested Itineraries section above for more details). The date and time for your visit will be set by the Agency. The visit takes about 40 minutes, and only Japanese language tours are available.

The Villa was constructed over a period of 50 years starting 1620. The garden was built around a large pond with five small islets. The main villa and several small tea houses line the pond.

The Villa is a 5 minute walk from Katsura-rikyu-mae 桂離宮前 bus stop. You can take the No. 33 or No. 60 bus from Kyoto Station.

Shugakuin Detached Villa 修学院離宮 (Middle right, map 73)

As with Katsura Detached Villa, the property is administered by the Imperial Household Agency. You have to apply for permission in advance.

This detached villa was constructed by the Tokugawa Shogunate in 1655 to entertain the emperor of the time. Three large gardens are located in a broad hilly area and pedestrian paths connect the gardens. The upper garden, designed around a large pond, is most impressive. The upper garden also commands a good view of the area.

You can take the No. 5 City Bus from Kyoto Station to Shugakuin-rikyu-michi 修学院離宮道. The bus passes Sanjo Keihan Bus Terminal and Ginkakuji-michi. The entrance of the Detached Villa is about a 10 minute walk from the bus stop.

Shisendo 詩仙堂 (Middle right, map 73)

Shisendo was built in 1641 by Jozan Ishikawa, a famous poet of the Edo Era. He lived here in isolation from the worldly life. The garden is considered one of the best in Kyoto. You should not forget Shisendo if you are in the area for a visit to Shugakuin Detached Villa.

Shisendo is a 5 minute walk from Ichijoji-Sagarimatsu bus stop, which is also served by the No. 5 City Bus.

Major Festivals in Kyoto

April 8: Hanamatsuri Festival to celebrate the birthday of Shaka. Held at many temples, such as Chion-in (Eastern Kyoto), Nishi-Honganji (Central Kyoto) and Seiryoji Temple (Arashiyama).

May 3: Kankosai Festival of Fushimi Inari Shrine. Miniature shrines are carried on main streets, such as Gojo-dori and Kawaramachi-dori Streets.

May 15: Aoi Matsuri Festival features a colorful imperial procession on main streets in the city from the Imperial Palace to Kamigamo Jinja Shrine.

Third Sunday of May: Mifune Matsuri Festival reproduces the scene of boating by nobles (near Togetsukyo Bridge in Arashiyama).

June 1 – 2: Takigi Noh (open-air Noh performance) at Heian Jingu Shrine.

July 17: Gion Matsuri Festival. A 1,000 year old festival featuring a gorgeous procession of festival floats on main streets in the city.

August 16: Gozan Okuribi Festival or Bonfires on Five Mountains. Spectacular bonfires are lighted on the city's five mountains. The fires can be seen from downtown.

August 16: Manto Nagashi Festival. A number of paper lanterns with candles are floated on the river to send the spirits of ancestors back to Heaven (during the middle of August, they are supposed to visit). The festival is held in the Arashiyama area.

Second Sunday of October: Jinkosai Festival features a procession of miniature shrines and festival floats on Nishi-oji-dori Street.

October 22: Jidai Matsuri Festival is a living reproduction of Japanese history. A huge procession featuring various costumes from olden times to the Meiji Restoration is held on main streets in the city.

Second Sunday of November: Momiji Matsuri or Maple Viewing Festival. Traditional music and many dances and dramas are performed on boats in the Arashiyama area.

Gion Matsuri Festival

Accommodations in Kyoto

1. Hotels

(1) Deluxe Hotels

Miyako Hotel 都ホテル
(Middle center, map 78.
480 rooms)
Add: Sanjo-Keage, Higashiyama-ku,
Kyoto.
Tel: (075) 771-7111.

Takaragaike Prince Hotel
宝が池プリンスホテル
(Near Int'l Conference Hall, upper right
of map 73. 322 rooms).
Add: Takaragaike, Sakyo-ku, Kyoto.
Tel: (075) 712-1111.

ANA Hotel Kyoto 京都全日空ホテル
(Upper left, map 77. 302 rooms).
Add: Nijojo-mae, Horikawa-dori,
Nakagyo-ku, Kyoto.
Tel: (075) 231-1155.

(2) First-class Hotels

Hotel Fujita ホテルフジタ
(Upper right, map 77. 195 rooms).
Add: Nishizume, Nijo-Ohashi, Naka-
gyo-ku, Kyoto.
Tel: (075) 222-1511.

Kyoto Grand Hotel 京都グランドホテル
(Lower left, map 77. 578 rooms).
Add: Horikawa-Shichijo,
Shimogyo-ku, Kyoto.
Tel: (075) 341-2311.

Kyoto Tokyu Hotel 京都東急ホテル
(Lower left, map 77. 437 rooms).
Add: Gojo-sagaru, Horikawa-dori,
Shimogyo-ku, Kyoto.
Tel: (075) 341-2511.

New Miyako Hotel 新都ホテル
(Lower center, map 77. 714 rooms).
Add: Nishi-Kujoincho, Minami-ku,
Kyoto.
Tel: (075) 661-7111.

Int'l Hotel Kyoto 京都国際ホテル
(Upper left, map 77. 332 rooms).
Add: Nijo-sagaru, Aburakoji,
Nakagyo-ku, Kyoto.
Tel:(075) 222-1111.

Kyoto Royal Hotel 京都ロイヤルホテル
(Middle right, map 77. 395 rooms).
Add: Kawaramachi, Sanjo,
Nakagyo-ku, Kyoto.
Tel: (075) 223-1234

Kyoto Hotel 京都ホテル
(Middle right, map 77. 507 rooms).
Add: Kawaramachi-Oike,
Nakagyo-ku, Kyoto.
Tel: (075) 211-5111.

(3) Standard Hotels

Hotel New Hankyu Kyoto
ホテル新阪急京都
(Lower center, map 77. 320 rooms).
Add: Shiokoji-Shinmachi, Shimogyo-ku,
Kyoto.
Tel: (075) 343-5300.

Kyoto Century Hotel
京都センチュリーホテル
(Lower center, map 77. 243 rooms).
Add: Shiokoji-sagaru, Higashino-Toin-
dori, Shimogyo-ku, Kyoto.
Tel: (075) 351-0111.

Kyoto Park Hotel 京都パークホテル
(Lower right, map 77. 307 rooms).
Add: 644-2, Sanjusangendo-Mawari-
machi, Higashiyamaku, Kyoto.
Tel: (075) 523-3111.

Hotel Gimmond Kyoto
ホテルギンモンド京都
(Middle center, map 77. 142 rooms).
Add: Takakura-kado, Oike-dori, Naka-
gyo-ku, Kyoto.
Tel: (075) 221-4111.

Hotel New Kyoto ホテルニュー京都
(Upper left, map 77. 242 rooms).
Add: Horikawa-Marutamachi,
Kamigyo-ku, Kyoto.
Tel: (075) 801-2111.

Kyoto Palaceside Hotel
京都パレスサイドホテル
(Upper center, map 77. 120 rooms).
Add: Shimodachi-uri, Karasumadori,
Kamigyo-ku, Kyoto.
Tel: (075) 431-8171.

Holiday Inn Kyoto ホリデーイン京都
(Near Shimogamo Jinja Shrine, middle
center of map 73. 270 rooms).
Add: 36, Nishi-Hirakicho, Takano,
Sakyo-ku, Kyoto.
Tel: (075) 721-3131.

Kyoto Tower Hotel 京都タワーホテル
(Lower center, map 77. 148 rooms.)
Add: Karasuma-Shichijo-sagaru,
Shimogyo-ku, Kyoto.
Tel: (075) 361-3211.

(4) Business Hotels

Hotel Rich Kyoto ホテルリッチ京都
(Middle center, map 77. 109 rooms).
Add: Gojo-agaru, Kawaramachi-dori,
Shimogyo-ku, Kyoto.
Tel: (075) 342-1131.

Kyoto Tokyu Inn 京都東急イン
(10 minutes by taxi from Kyoto Station.
437 rooms).
Add: 35-1, Hananookacho, Kami-Kazan,
Yamashina-ku, Kyoto.
Tel: (075) 593-0109.

Kyoto Dai-ni Tower Hotel
京都第二タワーホテル
(Lower center, map 77. 306 rooms).
Add: Higashino-Toindori-Shichijo-
sagaru, Shimogyo-ku, Kyoto.
Tel: (075) 361-3261.

Kyoto Dai-san Tower Hotel
京都第三タワーホテル
(Lower center, map 77. 122 rooms).
Add: Shinmachidori-Shichijo-sagaru, Shi-
mogyo-ku, Kyoto.
Tel: (075) 343-3111.

Hotel Keihan Kyoto ホテル京阪
(Lower center, map 77. 308 rooms).
Add: Higashi-Kujo, Minami-ku, Kyoto.
Tel: (075) 661-0321.

2. Ryokans
(1) Deluxe Ryokans

Tawaraya Ryokan 俵屋
(Middle center, map 77. 19 rooms).
Add: Fuyacho-Anegakoji-agaru,
Nakagyo-ku, Kyoto.
Tel: (075) 211-5566.

Hiiragiya Ryokan 柊家
(Middle center, map 77. 33 rooms).
Add: Fuyacho-Anegakoji-agaru,
Nakagyo-ku, Kyoto.
Tel: (075) 211-5566.

Sumiya Ryokan 炭屋
(Middle center, map 77. 26 rooms).
Add: Fuyachodori-Sanjo-sagaru,
Nakagyo-ku, Kyoto.
Tel: (075) 221-2188.

Seikoro 晴鴨楼
(Lower right, map 77. 24 rooms)
Add: Tonyachodori-Gojo-sagaru,
Higashiyama-ku, Kyoto.
Tel: (075) 561-0771.

Yachiyo 八千代
(Middle right, map 78. 26 rooms).
Add: 34, Nanzenji-Fukuchicho,
Sakyo-ku, Kyoto.
Tel: (075) 771-4148.

(2) First-class Ryokans

Chikiriya 千切家
(Middle center, map 77. 49 rooms).
Add: Tominokoji-nishiiru, Takoyakushi-
dori, Nakagyo-ku, Kyoto.
Tel: (075) 221-1281.

Kosenryu 弘扇龍
(Lower center, map 78. 17 rooms).
Add: 363-22, Masuyamachi, Higashi-
yama-ku, Kyoto.
Tel: (075) 561-0605.

Kyo-Chitose 京千歳
(Middle right, map 77. 13 rooms).
Add: 545, Gionmachi-Minamigawa,
Higashiyama-ku, Kyoto.
Tel: (075) 531-0157.

Hizenya 肥前屋
(Middle center, map 77. 38 rooms).
Add: Karasuma-nishiiru, Ayanokoji-dori,
Shimogyo-ku, Kyoto.
Tel: (075) 361-8421.

Yoshiima Ryokan 吉今旅館
(Middle center, map 76. 19 rooms).
Add: Yamotooji-Higashiiru, Shinmon-

zen, Higashiyama-ku, Kyoto.
Tel: (075) 561-2620.

Mikihan Ryokan 三木半旅館
(Middle center, map 77. 39 rooms).
Add: Fuyacho-kado, Rokkaku-dori,
Nakagyo-ku, Kyoto.
Tel: (075) 221-0428.

Hotel New Nissho ホテルニュー日昇
(Middle right, map 77. 87 rooms).
Add: 2-57, Sanjo-Ohashi-Higashi,
Higashiyama-ku, Kyoto.
Tel: (075) 761-8111.

Hotel Chiyosuzu ホテル千代鈴
(Middle center, map 77. 33 rooms).
Add: Sanjo-sagaru, Higashino-Toindori,
Nakagyo-ku, Kyoto.
Tel: (075) 241-4136.

Hotel Sugicho ホテル杉長
(Upper center, map 77. 49 rooms).
Add: Oike-agaru, Tominokoji,
Nakagyo-ku, Kyoto.
Tel: (075) 241-0106.

Hiiragiya Bekkan 柊家別館
(Upper center, map 77. 14 rooms).
Add: Gokocho-Nijo-sagaru, Nakagyo-ku,
Kyoto.
Tel: (075) 231-0157.

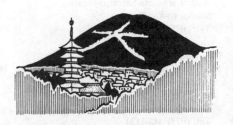

(3) Standard Ryokans

Hotel Matsui ホテル松井
(Middle center, map 77. 42 rooms).
Add: Takakura-Higashiiru, Rokkaku-
dori, Nakagyo-ku, Kyoto.
Tel: (075) 221-3535.

Ryokan Hakurokuso 旅館白鹿荘
(Middle center, map 77, 53 rooms).
Add: Higashino-Toin-Higashiiru,
Rokkaku-dori, Nakagyo-ku, Kyoto.
Tel: (075) 221-7846.

Hotel Uojien ホテルウオジ苑
(Middle center, map 77. 30 rooms).
Add: Sanjo-sagaru, Tominokoji-dori,
Nakagyo-ku, Kyoto.
Tel: (075) 221-2411.

Ryokan Hideoka 旅館秀岡
(Middle center, map 77. 19 rooms).
Add: Tominokoji-Higashiiru,
Takoyakushi-dori, Nakagyo-ku, Kyoto.
Tel: (075) 221-2667.

Shin-Yamato 新大和
(Lower right, map 77. 31 rooms).
Add: Gojo-Minamiiru, Teramachi-dori,
Shimogyo-ku, Kyoto.
Tel: (075) 361-5331.

New Gojokan ニュー五條館
(Lower middle, map 77. 34 rooms).
Add: Gojo-sagaru, Fumeimon-dori,
Shimogyo-ku, Kyoto.
Tel: (075) 351-0952.

Three Sisters' Inn (Rakutoso) 洛東荘
(Near Heian Jingu Shrine)
Add: 81, Higashi-Furukawa, Okazaki,
Sakyo-ku, Kyoto.
Tel: (075) 761-6336.

(4) Inexpensive Ryokans

Hiraiwa Ryokan 平岩旅館
Add: 314, Hayaocho, Kaminoguchi-
agaru, Ninomiyadori, Shimogyo-ku,
Kyoto.
Tel: (075) 351-6748. 16 rooms.

Ryokan Kyoka 旅館京花
Add: Higashino-Toin-Higashi-iru, Shimo-
Juzuyamachi-dori, Shimogyo-ku, Kyoto.
Tel: (075) 371-2709. 10 rooms.

Matsubaya Ryokan 松葉家旅館
Add: Higashino-Toin-Higashiiru, Kami-
Juzuyamachi-dori, Shimogyo-ku, Kyoto.
Tel: (075) 351-3727. 11 rooms.

Shichijoso 七条荘
Add: Higashi-Futasujime-Minamiiru,
Shichijo-Ohashi, Higashiyama-ku, Kyoto.
Tel: (075) 541-7803. 10 rooms.

Ryokan Hinomoto 旅館ひのもと
Add: 375, Kotakecho, Kawara-
machi-Matsubara-agaru, Shimogyo-ku,
Kyoto.
Tel: (075) 351-4563. 6 rooms.

Gion Umemura 祇園梅村
Add: 102, Hakata, Shijo-Yamato-oji-
sagaru, Higashiyama-ku, Kyoto.
Tel: (075) 525-0156. 11 rooms.

Amanohashidate 天の橋立

Amanohashidate, the "Bridge of Heaven," is the name of the place where, as the story goes, two figures of Japanese mythology, the god *Izanagi-no-Mikoto* and the goddess *Izanami-no-Mikoto*, stood while they conceived the islands of Japan, to which Izanami later gave birth. The "Bridge of Heaven" is actually a 2.2 mile (3.6 km.) long pine-clad sandbar that separates Miyazu Bay from Asoumi Lagoon. Geography and mythology aside, Amanohashidate is indisputably a beautiful place, as evidenced by its popularity as a summer resort for the upper classes of the Osaka – Kyoto – Kobe Kansai area and its official designation as a place of scenic beauty (It's part of the traditional "Scenic Trio" that all Japanese try to visit at one point in their lives – the other two places being Matsushima near Sendai and Miyajima in the Inland Sea near Hiroshima). Because of its popularity, it's best to visit Amanohashidate before or after the summer season.

Transportation to Amanohashidate

See No. 24 for the JR trains to Amanohashidate. The trip from Kyoto is an especially lovely one. The train runs along the Hozugawa River for much of the trip, and once it passes Saga, goes through a beautiful forested area. About 1 hour and 25 minutes after the train leaves Kyoto, it changes direction, at a town called Ayabe, and then again after it stops at Nishi-Maizuru Station, but is still headed for Amanohashidate!

Viewing Amanohashidate

When you get off the train from Kyoto in Amanohashidate, cross over the track and exit. Coin lockers are to your left as you leave the station, and a ticket stand for the sightseeing boat that will take you across Asoumi Lagoon to Ichinomiya (Kasamatsu-Koen Park) and the best traditional view of Amanohashidate is on the right. The best bargain is a combination sightseeing ticket for 1,300 yen.

Turn right from the station onto the town's main street, turn left at the first street you come to, and then right through the parking lot. Follow the path through the grounds of Chionji Temple. You'll be able to see the boat pier straight ahead. Your ticket will be punched when you get on the boat. The fifteen minute trip across the lagoon to the town of Ichinomiya gives you a view of the Amanohashidate sand bar on your right.

When you get off the boat at Ichinomiya, walk through the large yellow torii gates that you'll see straight ahead. When you reach the main Shrine building, turn left and follow the path that curves around to the right after you pass under another yellow torii. Turn left at the next corner, and in one block you come to a street crammed full of souvenir shops; the entrance to the cog railway-type cable car and the chair lift is on your right. The cable car and lift run about once every 15 minutes. Part of your ticket will be collected at the entrance. The four minute cable car ride takes you to Kasamatsu Park, which provides the most celebrated view of Amanohashidate.

When you get off the cable car, go up the steps to the observatory (There's another observatory to your left as you get off the cable car, but it is completely ruined by tacky restaurants and souvenir shops and loudspeakers blaring sentimental music). The observatory up the steps is *the* one. Japanese believe that one's view of Amanohashidate is enhanced if you stand with your back to it, lean down and look at it upside down, through your legs. From this perspective, the Bridge of Heaven is supposed to look like it's suspended in mid-air! Give it a try! Even straight on, the view is quite nice.

If you're in the mood for a hike, you can follow the path out of the observatory and up the mountain. After a pretty hard 15-minute climb, which itself provides great glimpses of Asoumi Lagoon and the mountains, you'll come to Nariaiji Temple. If you don't want to hike, you can take a bus from the Bus Station next to the cable car terminus – 300 yen one way). The temple dating back to the beginning of the 8th century, belongs to the Koyasan-Shingon sect of Buddhism, and is the 28th stop on the pilgrimage tour of 33 Western Japan Kannon temples. The red entrance gate to the temple has many colorful carvings of animals. The Main Hall also features lavishly detailed carvings. There's a snack shop and garden adjacent to the temple grounds.

Exploring Amanohashidate

When you arrive back on the Amanohashidate side of the lagoon (Monju) after your observation of the Bridge of Heaven, you can explore it for yourself. Cars are forbidden on the sandbar. It's a lovely place to stroll or cycle. You can rent a bike at a shop just the other side of the second of the two bridges that lead you to Amanohashidate.

Amanohashidate View Land 天の橋立ビューランド (optional)

The entrance to this recreation center atop a steep peak is only a short walk from the train station. Turn right off the main street, cross the railroad tracks, and turn left when you come to the arch over the street. The ticket window is on your right. A round trip ticket for the chair lift ride to the top of the mountain is 700 yen. If you have long legs, be careful on the way up. The view from the top is quite different from the Kasamatsu Park view across the lagoon, and also breathtakingly beautiful. From this perspective, you see out toward the Japan Sea. It's impossible to say which view is better. Amanohashidate View Land also features a garden, lawn croquet, go-carts, an archery range, a monkey house, an aviary, various other amusement-park-type rides and a restaurant.

Evening Strolls

Several of Amanohashidate's ryokans feature, along with the usual luxurious amenities of Japanese inns, fantastic views of the lagoon. If you're not lucky enough to get a view along with your room, you

should join the evening strollers. The Monju area around Chionji Temple and the boat pier includes one street with restaurants and souvenir shops. If you want to escape the commercial area, you can do so within a few quick steps. The island between the Monju area and the sandbar and the sandbar itself are literally at your feet. It's hard to imagine lovelier places to enjoy a sunset.

Ryokans in Amanohashidate
Genmyoan 玄妙庵
   (Deluxe: middle center, map 85.
   32 rooms).
   Add: 32, Monju, Miyatsu.
   Tel: (07722) 2-2171.
Monjuso 文珠荘
   (Deluxe: upper center, map 85.
   14 rooms).
   Add: 466, Monju, Miyatsu.
   Tel: (07722) 2-2151.
Monjuso Shinkan 文珠荘新館
   (Deluxe: middle center, map 85.
   38 rooms).
   Add: 510, Monju, Miyatsu.
   Tel: (07722) 2-4101.
Amanohashidate Hotel 天の橋立ホテル
   (First-class: upper left, map 85.
   55 rooms).
   Add: 310, Monju, Miyatsu.
   Tel: (07722) 2-4111.
Shoeiro 松影楼
   (Standard: upper center, map 85.
   22 rooms).
   Add: 468-1, Monju, Miyatsu.
   Tel: (07722) 2-3317.

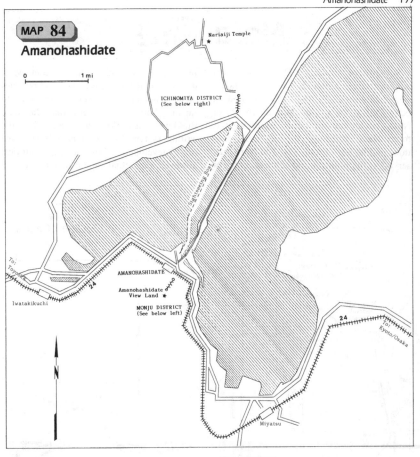

MAP **84**
Amanohashidate

0   1 mi

Nariaiji Temple ★

ICHINOMIYA DISTRICT
(See below right)

Sightseeing Boat

To:
Toyooka

Iwatakikuchi

24

AMANOHASHIDATE

Amanohashidate
View Land ★

MONJU DISTRICT
(See below left)

24

To:
Kyoto/Osaka

N

Miyatsu

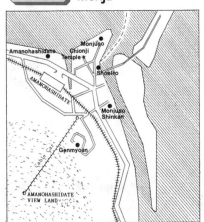

MAP **85**   **Monju**

Monjuso

Amanohashidate
Chionji
Temple ★

Shoeito

AMANOHASHIDATE

Monjuso
Shinkan

Cable Car

Genmyoan

AMANOHASHIDATE
VIEW LAND

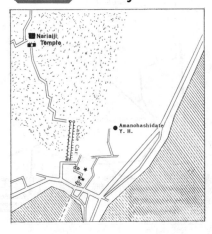

MAP **86**   **Ichinomiya**

Nariaiji
Temple

Cable Car

Amanohashidate
Y. H.

Nara 奈良

Somewhere around A.D. 350, the first administrative center for a united Japan was established, in the area of modern Nara (not at the site of the modern city of Nara, but in the southern part of what is today Nara Prefecture: around Asuka Station, middle left of map 87). The Nara area served as the political and cultural center of

Japan until the end of the 8th century. It was here that the cultures and technologies of continental Asia were introduced to Japan. And it was here that Japanese Buddhism first flourished, and that the writing system for the Japanese language first developed. For many centuries, however, the actual capital was moved to a

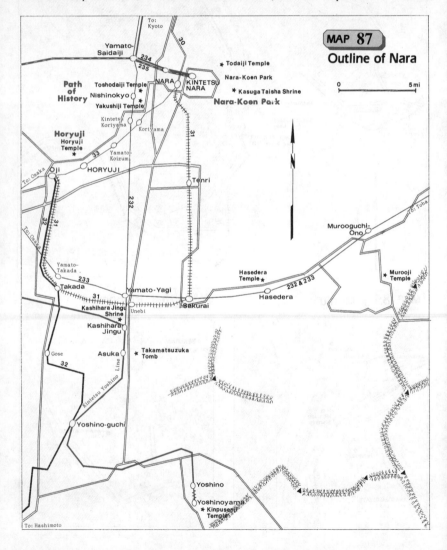

MAP **87**

Outline of Nara

0 _____ 5 mi

new place each time a new emperor ascended the throne. Japan's first permanent capital was founded in Nara in 710 by Emperor Kammu. Today's visitors to the city will find many portions of this ancient capital dating from the 6th – 8th centuries still intact. As of 794, when the capital was moved to Kyoto, Nara lost its political significance, and was thus spared the damage other areas suffered during the civil wars. Modern industrialization has also passed Nara by. With great foresight, modern Nara's inhabitants decided to construct the spacious garden park that now surrounds the area containing Nara's venerable structures.

We have allocated two days for Nara although most tours only visit it as a one-day excursion from Kyoto. The reason these visits are so short is that there are virtually no accommodations in Nara large enough for tour groups. Two days are not enough to even begin to appreciate Nara: we have selected and described what we believe are the most precious of this ancient capital's many jewels. Individual travelers who stay overnight in Nara have the extra treat of being able to stroll in Nara-Koen Park in the early morning or in the evening. This beautiful garden park, home to Nara's famous tame deer, is completely peaceful during these hours, and the only other visitors are likely to be the ghosts of the lords and ladies of Japan's ancient aristocracy.

If, unfortunately, you have only one day for Nara, you will have to follow your own instincts in choosing between the Nara-Koen Park area and the southwestern area (Path of History and Horyuji Temple).

Transportation to Nara
1. From Kyoto
The JR Nara Line (No. 30) connects Nara with Kyoto. Trains operate about once every 30 minutes. All the trains are locals that originate at Kyoto Station and terminate at JR's Nara Station. The ride takes 68 minutes.

The private Kintetsu Kyoto Line (No. 234) also operates between Kyoto and Nara (Kintetsu-Nara Station). There are three types of trains on this line – locals, expresses and limited expresses. The locals and expresses serve commuters, but the limited express trains, which use deluxe cars with reserved seats, cater to tourists. Local and express trains operate every 10 – 30 minutes, but a transfer is required at Yamato-Saidaiji Station, two stops before Kintetsu-Nara Station, your destination. The limited express trains, which operate every 30 minutes, whisk passengers directly to Kintetsu-Nara Station in only 33 minutes.

2. From Osaka
Commuter trains between Osaka and Nara operate on the JR's Kansai Line (No. 33) almost every 20 minutes. All the trains are locals. They stop at Horyuji Station on their way to Nara, thus making it easy for those staying in Osaka to visit the southwestern part of Nara. From 7:30 AM to around 9:00 AM, the trains originate at Minatomachi Station. Between 9:00 AM and 4:30 PM they originate at Osaka Station. From 5:00 PM till 10:00 PM they again originate at Minatomachi Station. All the trains stop at Tennoji Station on the JR Osaka Kanjo (Loop) Line. Return trains operate the same way.

The private Kintetsu Railways also operates a Kintetsu Nara Line (No. 235) between Kintetsu-Namba Station in Osaka and Kintetsu-Nara Station. As is the case with the Kintetsu trains from Kyoto, there are three types of trains: locals, expresses, and limited expresses. The limited express has deluxe cars with all reserved seating, and operates once every hour. The ride takes 31 minutes. The express and local trains operate frequently, and take 10 – 20 minutes longer than the limited express.

Day 1 – The Nara-Koen Park Area
As shown on map 88, famous sites such as Todaiji Temple and Kasuga Taisha Shrine are located to the east of the city center. Circle bus lines – running both clockwise and counter-clockwise – operate frequently and are quite convenient for tourists. Recorded English announcements herald the next stop. The buses operate on a 120-yen flat fare system (pay upon board-

ing). The clockwise loop bus is No. 2, while the counter-clockwise loop is No. 1. The loop these buses make is indicated on map 88 with a red dotted line, and the names of major bus stops are also shown.

Todaiji Temple 東大寺 (Upper right, map 88)

Todaiji Temple was originally constructed at the order of Emperor Shomu in 752. Though most tourists see only the statue of the Great Buddha in the main building (Daibutsuden), the wide temple precincts contain a number of buildings and sculptures of great historical and cultural significance. **Nandaimon Gate** 南大門 (National Treasure) is the main entrance to the temple. The Gate, reconstructed in 1199, is supported by 19 pillars, and is a good example of the Chinese architectural technology the Japanese imported in the 12th century. There are two 26-foot tall statues of guardians in niches on both sides of the gate. These two National Treasures,

carved in 1203 by Unkei and Kaikei, are representative of the high artistic achievements of the Kamakura era.

Kaidan-in Hall 戒檀院 (optional) located to the west of the main building. In the medieval era, Kaidan-in was the most important ceremonial Buddhist hall in all of Japan, and was the site of ordinations of new priests. The small hall is particularly famous for the exquisite clay images of the Four Heavenly Guardians (National Treasures) that were produced in the 7th century. (8:00 AM to 4:30 PM. Admission 200 yen).

The present huge **Daibutsuden Hall** 大仏殿 (Hall of the Great Buddha, National Treasure) was constructed in 1708 after repeated fires. The hall, 187 feet (57 m.) wide, 164 feet (50 m.) deep, and 157 feet (48 m.) tall, is the largest wooden structure in the world. However, the original, built in 752, was 1.5 times larger than the present hall. In front of the hall stands a 15-foot (4.5 m.) tall octagonal bronze lantern

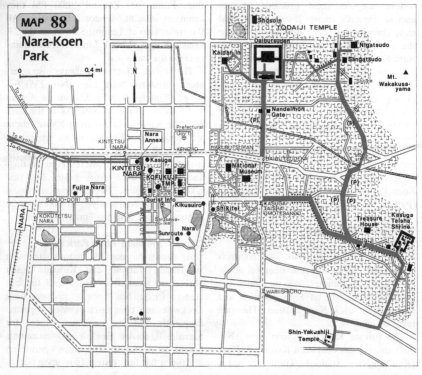

(National Treasure) which is noteworthy for its fine carvings of Heavenly Maidens. **The Image of the Great Buddha** in the Daibutsuden Hall is the holiest object of Todaiji Temple. Completed in 752, the original was damaged several times by fire and earthquake. The present 53-foot (16 m.) tall statue was repaired quite extensively in 1692 (7:30 AM to 5:30 PM. Admission 200 yen).

To the east of the main buildings, atop a flight of stone steps, there are several structures including the old Bath House and Belfry (National Treasure). Further to the east, in an elevated location, are **Nigatsudo Hall** 二月堂 (February Hall), **Sangatsudo Hall** 三月堂 (March Hall), and **Shigatsudo Hall** (April Hall). The view of the city of Nara from the corridor of Nigatsudo Hall is not to be missed. Nigatsudo is also famous as the home of an elaborate fire festival held in early March. Sangatsudo Hall, built in the middle of the 8th century, is the oldest building in the Todaiji complex. It contains more than 10 statues produced in the 8th century (8:00 AM to 5:30 PM. Admission 200 yen).

Kasuga Taisha Shrine 春日大社 (Middle right, map 88)

Passing Tamukeyama Shrine, walk to the south skirting the western foot of Mt. Wakakusayama (1,115 feet, or 342 m.). The right side of the street is lined with souvenir shops and restaurants. As the paved street curves toward the left, you will see a flight of stone steps on your right. Take this short cut down to the small stream at the bottom, and walk across Kasuga Taisha Shrine's wide parking lot. **The Treasure House** 春日大社宝物館 (optional) of the Shrine, located at the southern end of the parking lot, is housed in a modern two-story concrete building. It displays the Shrine's treasures, which include Noh masks and equipment for Shinto ceremonies (8:30 AM to 4:30 PM).

To the south of the Treasure House stands a torii gate, the formal entrance to Kasuga Taisha Shrine (As a matter of fact, this is the second of the Shrine's torii gates. The first is located far to the west, near the National Museum). Both sides of the approach to the Shrine are lined with stone lanterns of various sizes and shapes. Altogether there are about 3,000 lanterns along the approach. Twice a year, in early February and in the middle of August, all of them are lighted, creating a solemn, dream-like atmosphere. Through the torii gate, you come first to Tochakuden (Arrival Hall), then to Minamimon Gate (South Gate), entrance to the main buildings of Kasuga Taisha Shrine. Covered red and green corridors extend in two different directions from the gate, and surround the major buildings of the Shrine. The Shrine was originally erected in 710, and its buildings were reconstructed periodically according to Shinto tradition, which requires that places of worship be pulled down and then completely rebuilt at regular intervals (usually every 20 years). The spacious grounds of the Shrine are inside Minamimon Gate. Several of the natural wood buildings, including Haiden Hall (Offering Hall) and Naoraiden (Entertainment Hall), are used for various Shinto ceremonies. Behind Chumon Gate (Middle Gate) are four Honden Halls (Main Shrines), each in the same architectural style and each a National Treasure. They were last rebuilt in 1893, supposedly for the 56th time (8:30 AM to 4:00 PM. Admission 50 yen).

Shin-Yakushiji Temple 新薬師寺 (optional) (Lower right, map 88)

After you pass Wakamiya Jinja Shrine, the narrow path enters a thick, refreshing and romantic forest. Crossing a wider street, you'll come to a T-shaped intersection, where you should turn right. The traffic mirror and the small store are good landmarks to help you find the street that leads to Shin-Yakushiji Temple.

Shin-Yakushiji Temple was originally erected in the middle of the 8th century at the order of Empress Komyo, in thanksgiving for the recovery of Emperor Shomu from a serious illness. Only the original Dining Hall (the present Main Hall, National Treasure) has been preserved; the other buildings were destroyed by fire and typhoon and were reconstructed after the 13th century. At the center of the dark Main Hall sits the image of Yakushi-Nyorai (God of Medicine, National Treasure), which is surrounded by clay images of Twelve Divine Generals. Eleven of the 12 originals remain, and are National Treasures. They are especially famous for their powerful, dynamic expressions (8:30 AM to 5:30 PM. Admission 300 yen).

Nara National Museum 奈良国立美術館
(Optional) (Middle center, map 88)

If you are lucky enough to be in Nara between the end of October and beginning of November, you should definitely visit the Museum because that is the one time of the year that the treasures of Todaiji Temple (kept in Shosoin House) are displayed.

The Museum consists of two buildings. The Main Hall, patterned on a traditional Japanese architectural style, has a display of Buddhist images that illustrates how ideas of divine beings changed over the centuries. The Western-style annex displays archeological relics, most of which were found in old tombs (9:00 AM to 4:30 PM. Admission 250 yen. Closed on Mondays).

Kofukuji Temple 興福寺 (Middle center, map 88)

Kofukuji Temple was constructed in the early 700's by Fuhito Fujiwara, a leading aristocrat of the time. Patronized by emperors, the temple has enjoyed incomparable prosperity throughout its history. The precincts were once filled with 175 buildings, all of which were destroyed by fire. The present buildings, much smaller in scale than the originals, were built after the 13th century. **The five-story pagoda** 五重塔 (National Treasure) is the second highest pagoda (164 feet or 50 m.) in Japan (the

tallest is the Toji Temple's pagoda in Kyoto). The present pagoda was built in 1426 as an exact replica of the 730 original. **The Tokondo Hall** 東金堂 (National Treasure) was rebuilt in 1415 from the plans of the 726 original. **The Treasure House** 宝物堂 is a concrete building that houses more than 20 National Treasure statues along with many other fine objets d'art (9:00 AM to 5:00 PM. Admission 400 yen). **Hokuendo** 北円堂 and **Nan-endo** 南円堂 Halls are octagonal buildings constructed in the 13th and 18th centuries respectively. The three-story pagoda (National Treasure) was erected in 1143.

Sarusawa-no-Ike Pond 猿沢池
(Middle center, map 88)

Before walking back to either the JR Nara or Kintetsu Nara Station, visit this pond south of Kofukuji Temple. With the five-story pagoda in the background, the pond is an especially lovely not-to-be-missed camera shot.

Tourist Information

Nara Municipal Tourist Information Center is located on Sanjo-dori Street near Sarusawa-no-Ike Pond (middle center, map 88).

Day 2 – The Southwestern Part of Nara

As shown on map 87, three major temples, Toshodaiji Temple, Yakushiji Temple, and Horyuji Temple, are located in this area. The No. 52 bus conveniently connects these three historical sites, originating at Daibutsuden, and stopping at Kintetsu-Nara, JR Nara, Toshodaiji Temple, Yakushiji Temple and Horyuji Temple (last stop). The No. 63 bus also provides service to Toshodaiji Temple. The ride to Toshodaiji Temple, your first stop of the day, takes about 20 minutes from Kintetsu-Nara Station (The buses have recorded English announcements). Make sure you take a *seiri-ken* fare zone ticket upon boarding.

Toshodaiji Temple 唐招提寺

(Upper center, map 89)

The No. 52 bus stop is on the main street, only 0.2 miles (0.3 km.) from the South Gate of Toshodaiji Temple. The No. 63 bus stops right in front of the Gate.

Toshodaiji Temple was erected in 759 by the Chinese priest Ganjin, who visited Japan at the invitation of Emperor Shomu. Ganjin was 66 when he finally arrived in Japan, twelve years after the invitation was issued. His attempts to reach Japan from the continent were thwarted by political interference by Chinese officials, five shipwrecks, and various diseases, one of which left him blind. Despite these difficulties, Ganjin fulfilled the imperial commission and supervised the construction of this magnificent temple.

Toshodaiji Temple, unlike most other temples, has suffered no fires or other accidents; its original buildings still stand. Kondo Hall (Main Hall, National Treasure) contains a 10-foot tall image of Sakya as its main object of worship. The eight pillars at the front of Kondo Hall are entastic (i.e., they balloon almost imperceptibly). This borrowing from Greek architecture testifies to the fact that cultural exchange via the "Silk Road" had an impact even in Nara as early as the 8th century. Behind Kondo Hall is Kodo Hall (Lecture Hall, National Treasure), which was moved from Nara Imperial Palace in celebration of Ganjin's completion of the temple. Nara Imperial

Palace was completely destroyed in a later era, and this Kodo Hall is the only relic we have today of palace architecture of the Nara era. A graceful atmosphere pervades the precincts. (8:30 AM to 4:00 PM. Admission 300 yen). The Treasure House is open to the public from March 20 to May 19 in the spring, and from September 15 to November 5 in the fall.

Yakushiji Temple 薬師寺

(Lower center, map 89)

The street connecting Toshodaiji and Yakushiji Temples is popularly called the "Path of History" because emperors and nobles used this path when they visited these two important temples.

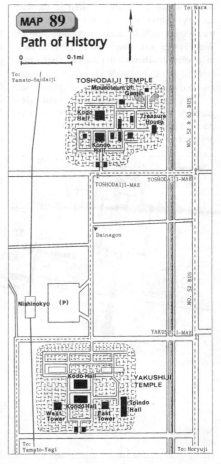

Yakushiji Temple was originally erected in the Asuka district (further to the south) by Emperor Temmu in 680, and was moved to its present location in 718. The gorgeous buildings of Yakushiji were called "Heavenly Palace," and the temple enjoyed the patronage of successive emperors. Unfortunately, all of the buildings except East Tower, a three-story pagoda constructed in 730, were destroyed by fires and earthquakes. The 112-foot (34 m.) tall East Tower Pagoda looks like it has six stories because of the three decorative roofs placed between the real ones. The balanced beauty of East Tower has been described as "frozen music." Toindo Hall was built in the Kamakura Era (the 13th century) and houses a Kannon statue crafted in the 7th century (National Treasure). Kondo Hall was rebuilt in 1976, and a reconstruction of West Tower was completed in 1981, as part of a very controversial project. These two replicas of the originals are painted vermilion and seem glaringly out of place, set as they are against the subdued elegance of the other buildings, but those who planned these new buildings took the long perspective – because they knew it would eventually settle, they had the new West Tower built to stand slightly taller than East Tower. Thus, the original balance of the two towers will be restored in the future, albeit the distant future.

Horyuji Temple 法隆寺

Because of its isolated location, foreign tourists often skip Horyuji. This is a mistake. In light of its historical importance and the number of treasures exhibited there, Horyuji Temple should be given great, if not top, priority in the Nara area.

Pine trees flank the main approach to the temple, which was originally erected in 607 by Prince Shotoku, the promulgator of the first Japanese constitution. The original structures were destroyed by fire in 670, but the present buildings of the Western Precincts were reconstructed immediately, at the end of the 7th century. They are possibly the oldest wooden structures in the world. The buildings in the Eastern Precincts were built sometime later, around 739. All the buildings of Horyuji are National Treasures. On both sides of Chumon Gate are images of Deva Kings that were sculpted in 711. Inside the Gate is the

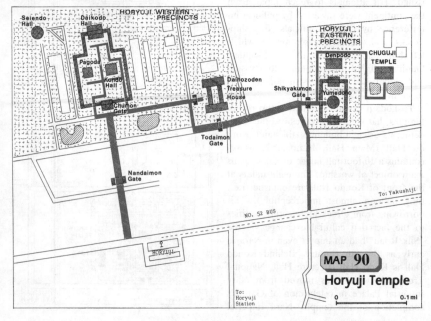

MAP 90
Horyuji Temple

main part of Horyuji Temple. At your right is Kondo Hall (Main Hall). At your left is a five-story pagoda (112 feet, or 34 m. tall), with roofs that decrease in size toward the top; the pagoda projects an ethereal yet stable image. Inside the pagoda are 95 images clustered in four groups. The varied faces of these images reflect the artistic realism of the era. There are several other old buildings to the east of the corridors. At the eastern end of the Western Precincts is **Daihozoden** 大宝蔵殿 (Great Treasure House). This concrete building preserves hundreds of temple treasures, including images, statues, carvings and metalwork from the 7th and 8th centuries. Leave the Western Precincts through Todaimon Gate and walk east to the end of the wide lane, where Shikyakumon Gate (a typical four-legged gate), the entrance to the Eastern Precincts of Horyuji Temple, is located. The main hall of this part of Horyuji is Yumedono Hall, an octagonal building constructed in 739. Yumedono Hall is surrounded by covered corridors. Dempodo Mansion, located to the north of the corridors, is representative of mansion architecture for the nobles of the 8th century. Horyuji Temple is open to the public from 8:00 AM to 5:00 PM (till 4:30 PM in winter). Admission is 400 yen.

Chuguji Temple 中宮寺

Chuguji Temple is adjacent to the northeastern corner of the Eastern Precincts of Horyuji Temple. It has the quiet neatness of a nunnery, and is especially famous for its wooden statue of Miroku-Bosatsu (National Treasure), whose soft and tender features have been pronounced the consummate expression of mercy. It is said that her face changes delicately with changes in temperature or humidity (9:00 AM to 4:15 PM. Until 3:45 PM in winter. Admission 300 yen).

Back to Nara City

Take the north-bound No. 52 bus from Horyuji stop to either JR Nara or Kintetsu-Nara Station. The ride takes 51 minutes to the former and 54 minutes to the latter.

You can also take the JR Kansai Line train from Horyuji Station to Nara. You can walk south from Horyuji bus stop for about 10 minutes, to JR Horyuji Station. Trains run every 30 minutes, and the ride takes only 12 minutes.

Places of Interest in Southern Nara

Kashihara Jingu Shrine 橿原神宮 (Middle left, map 87)

Japan's first history book, *Nihonshoki*, reports that the court of the nation's first emperor, Jimmu, was at the site of what is now Kashihara Jingu Shrine. As a general matter, however, the veracity of the *Nihonshoki* must be doubted because it was compiled with the aim of glorifying the imperial court rather than accurately recording the events that led to the establishment of Japan's first central government. It should be viewed as a collection of myths rather than facts. It is, nevertheless, true that the first imperial court was established in this area.

Kashihara Jingu Shrine was constructed in 1889 and dedicated to Emperor Jimmu. On the occasion of the mythological 2,600th anniversary of the foundation of Japan in 1940, 1.5 million trees were planted here by volunteers from all over the country. Today, the grand shrine buildings stand in spacious grounds surrounded by thick woods.

Kashihara Archeological Museum 橿原考古博物館 is located in the shrine grounds. The museum displays archeological objects unearthed in the area. Clay images and other items found in the old tombs are also exhibited in the museum. (9:00 AM to 4:30 PM. Closed on Mondays and national holidays.)

Kashihara Jingu Shrine is a five minute walk from Kashihara Jingu Station 橿原神宮駅. The station is served by the private Kintetsu Line from Kyoto (a 60 minute ride) and Osaka. From Kintetsu-Nara you can take a Kintetsu train to Yamato-Saidaiji, and then another Kintetsu train from Yamato-Saidaiji to Kashihara Jingu.

Takamatsuzuka Tomb 高松塚古墳 (Middle left, map 87)

To the south of Kashihara Jingu Shrine (the second stop from Kashihara Jingu on the Kintetsu Line) is Asuka 飛鳥. This area is thought to have been the center of the Yamato imperial courts until the first permanent capital was constructed in Nara in 710. A number of tombs of emperors and aristocrats have been found in and around Asuka. Takamatsuzuka Tomb, only 5 meters tall and 54 meters in circumference, is one of the smaller ones in the area. It became famous in 1962, when the members of the Kashihara Archeological Institute found a colorful fresco in one of the stone chambers in the tomb. The fresco, drawn around the turn of the 7th century, has been almost perfectly preserved, and is one of the most important archeological findings in Japan. The tomb is not open to the public. Instead, **Takamatsuzuka Hekigakan** 高松塚壁画館 (Fresco Hall) was built next to the tomb and displays a reproduction of the fresco of the same size as the original. (9:00 AM to 4:30 PM).

Yoshino 吉野 (Lower center, map 87)

Kinpusenji Temple was originally erected in Mt. Yoshinoyama as a training center for Buddhist priests. The temple grounds cover a hillside, which is dotted by a number of buildings. The current main hall, Zaodo 蔵王堂, was built in 1591 under the sponsorship of Hideyoshi Toyotomi, and is Japan's second largest wooden structure (after Nara's Todaiji Temple). Yoshinoyama is especially famous for its cherry blossoms in April. The cherry trees start blooming at the foot of the mountain in early April, and then gradually ascend the mountain, with the trees on the summit blooming at the end of April.

Yoshino Station 吉野駅 is about 40 minutes from Kashihara Jingu Station on the private Kintetsu Yoshino Line. A cable car operates from near Yoshino Station to Yoshinoyama 吉野山 (a 5 minute ride).

Hasedera Temple 長谷寺 (Middle center, map 87)

Hasedera Temple is often called "the Temple of Flowers," because a variety of flowers bloom in the grounds from spring through fall. Hasedera is especially famous for its peonies, which bloom from the end of April to the middle of May. A number of buildings stand in densely wooded precincts on the mountain side. Major buildings, including the grand Main Hall and a five-story pagoda, are connected by covered stone steps. (8:30 AM to 5:00 PM).

Hasedera Temple is a 20 minute walk from Hasedera Station 長谷寺駅 on the Kintetsu Line. You can take this Kintetsu Line from either Yamato-Yagi or Sakurai Station.

Murooji Temple 室生寺 (Middle right, map 87)

Murooji Temple is located in a quiet valley of the Muroogawa River. Established

by Kobo-daishi, who also founded Koya-san, Murooji is popularly called "Women's Koya" because the temple allowed women to visit throughout its history, while Koya-san did not accept women visitors until modern times.

Magnificent buildings are scattered on the hillside, and stone steps connecting these historic structures run through beautiful forests. The most impressive building among them is a 16 m. (53 ft.) tall, five-story National Treasure pagoda. The pagoda, viewed from the bottom of the stone steps at its front, has been featured in many posters and pictorial books, and is a not-to-be-missed shot for camera fans.

A bus between Murooguchi-Ono 室生口大野 and Murooji Temple runs about once every hour (a 15 minute ride).

Major Festivals in Nara

January 15: Grass Burning Festival at Mt. Wakakusayama in Nara-Koen Park. Fires are set at 6:00 PM. Todaiji and Kofukuji Temples, silhouetted against the fire, create a spectacular image.

February 2 or 3 (on the day of Bean Scattering Festival): Mantoro Festival at Kasuga Taisha Shrine. About 3,000 lanterns are lit and create a magical, solemn atmosphere.

March 1 – 14: Omizutori Festival at Nigatsudo Hall of Todaiji Temple. A fire festival every night, with the biggest one on the 12th.

May 2: Shomu-Tenno-sai at Todaiji Temple. The festival is designed to honor the founder of the Temple of the Great Buddha. A colorful parade in traditional costumes is held.

May 11 – 12: Takigi Noh at Kofukuji Temple. Firelight Noh performances by masters of the four major Noh schools in Japan (from 4:00 PM).

August 14 – 15: Mantoro Festival at Kasuga Taisha Shrine (See above).

August 15: Daimonji-Okuribi Festival. A

spectacular bonfire in the shape of the character for "big" is lighted at 8:00 PM on Mt. Koenzan, not far from the city.

September 15: Shiba-Noh. A firelight Noh performance on the grass meadow of Nara-Koen Park (from 5:30 PM).

December 17: Kasuga-Wakamiya-On-matsuri. A large procession with all participants dressed in traditional costumes.

Accommodations in Nara

1. Hotels

Nara Hotel 奈良ホテル
(First-class: middle center, map 88. 67 rooms).
Add: Nara-Koen-nai, Nara.
Tel: (0742) 26-3300.

Hotel Fujita Nara ホテルフジタ奈良
(First-class: middle left, map 88. 120 rooms).
Add: 47-1, Sanjomachi, Nara.
Tel: (0742) 23-8111.

Hotel Sunroute Nara
ホテルサンルート奈良
(Business hotel: middle center, map 88. 95 rooms).
Add: 1110, Takahatake-machi, Nara.
Tel: (0742) 22-5151.

2. Ryokans

Shikitei 四季亭
(Deluxe: middle center, map 88. 18 rooms).
Add: 1163, Takabatake-machi, Nara.
Tel: (0742) 22-5531.

Kikusuiro 菊水楼
(Deluxe: middle center, map 88. 18 rooms).
Add: 1130, Takabatake-Bodaimachi, Nara.
Tel: (0742) 23-2001.

Kasuga Hotel 春日ホテル
(First-class: middle center, map 88. 43 rooms).
Add: 40, Noborioji-machi, Nara.
Tel: (0742) 22-4031.

Seikanso 静観荘
(Inexpensive: lower center, map 88. 12 rooms).
Add: 29, Higashi-Kitsujicho, Nara.
Tel: (0742) 22-2670.

Osaka 大阪

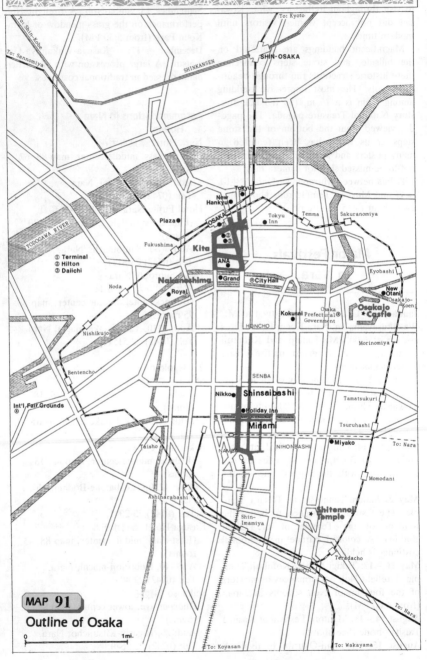

To: Shin-Kobe
To: Kyoto
To: Sannomiya
SHIN-OSAKA
SHINKANSEN
To: Shin-Kobe

YODOGAWA RIVER

Tokyu
New
Hankyu
Plaza ●
● OSAKA
Tokyu Inn
Temma
Sakuranomiya

Fukushima
Kita
① ②③
ANA
Kyobashi

① Terminal
② Hilton
③ Daiichi

Noda
Nakanoshima
● Grand
● City Hall
New Otani
Osakajo-Koen

● Royal
Kokusai ●
Osaka Prefectural Government
Osakajo Castle

Nishikujo

Morinomiya

Bentencho
HONCHO

SENBA

Int'l Fair Grounds
Nikko ●
Shinsaibashi
Tamatsukuri

● Holiday Inn
Tsuruhashi

Minami

Taisho
NAMBA
NIHONBASHI
● Miyako
To: Nara

Ashiharabashi
Momodani

Shin-Imamiya
Shitennoji Temple

Teradacho

TENNOJI

To: Koyasan
To: Wakayama
To: Nara

MAP 91
Outline of Osaka

0 ——— 1mi.

At the dawn of Japanese history, when Japan was divided into many small "nations," powerful clans were based in the Osaka area. These fiefdoms later formed the core of the unified nation. Osaka was once the capital of Japan for a short period in the 7th century, but when a permanent capital was established first in Nara, and then in Kyoto, Osaka disappeared from the political scene. Osaka's modern prosperity as a merchant city began at the end of the 16th century, when Hideyoshi Toyotomi built Japan's largest castle here. During the Edo period (1603 – 1868), Osaka prospered as a distribution center. The local feudal lords sent the products of their territories, mainly rice, to Osaka, where the merchants arranged distribution to Edo and other large cities. The city was administered directly by the Tokugawa Shogunate, and was called the "Kitchen of Japan." Although its population of 2,635,000 makes it the country's third largest city (trailing Yokohama), Osaka, a confident, bustling industrial and commercial center, is clearly Japan's "Second City."

Many Japanese corporations have headquarters in Osaka, and the city plays host to a number of foreign business visitors every year. However, Osaka is often omitted from the itineraries of foreign tourists to Japan. There is no denying that Osaka lacks the historical and cultural significance that appeals to foreign tourists. But, as the transportation center of the Kansai region, Osaka is an ideal base for exploration of several Kansai destinations. Osaka also has many more hotels than Kyoto, and rooms are usually available when Kyoto hotels are full during the peak tourist seasons of spring and fall.

Outline of the City

The city of Osaka has 26 wards and is spread over a wide area, but all the main municipal and business areas are clustered inside and immediately outside the JR Osaka Kanjo (Loop) Line. As pictured in the upper left of map 92, the area of Central Osaka is about half the size of the central area of Tokyo. There are two major shopping and eating districts in Osaka. One is

called "Kita" (North); it is an area of newly constructed modern buildings and extensive underground shopping centers. The other is called "Minami" (South) and "Shinsaibashi," and is located right in the center of the JR loop. Shinsaibashi is a fashionable shopping quarter, while Minami is famous for its eating and drinking facilities and theaters. Public institutions such as Osaka City Hall and Osaka Festival Hall are located on Nakanoshima island. Major business offices are located in the Osaka Station area, on Nakanoshima Island, and along the Midosuji main boulevard (running to the south from Osaka Station). Osaka's two major historical sites are Osakajo Castle and Shitennoji Temple. Osaka International Fair Grounds (middle left, map 91), where most large trade shows are held, are located just outside the JR loop.

Transportation to Osaka

Osaka is connected with other major cities, such as Tokyo, Nagoya, Kyoto, Hiroshima and Fukuoka, by the Shinkansen (No. 1). The Shinkansen Station in Osaka is called Shin-Osaka (New Osaka) and is located about 3 km. (2 miles) to the north of Osaka Station.

As explained in the Introduction to Kansai section, JR commuter trains and private railways conveniently connect Osaka with Kyoto, Kobe, Nara and Koyasan, major places of interest in the Kansai region.

Those with Japan Rail Passes can use the Shinkansen even for the short distance between Kyoto and Osaka. Regular travelers shouldn't take the Shinkansen because the short trip is too costly.

Transportation in Osaka
1. Subways

We have selected five of Osaka's lines, and indicated them with red lines on map 92. You will probably use only the Midosuji subway line (indicated with double dotted lines), which connects Shin-Osaka Station, Umeda Station (near JR's Osaka Station), Shinsaibashi, Namba and Tennoji, Osaka's most important stations.

2. JR Osaka Kanjo Line

This loop line surrounds the central part of Osaka. Orange-colored trains run every 3 – 10 minutes and a trip around the whole loop takes 37 minutes.

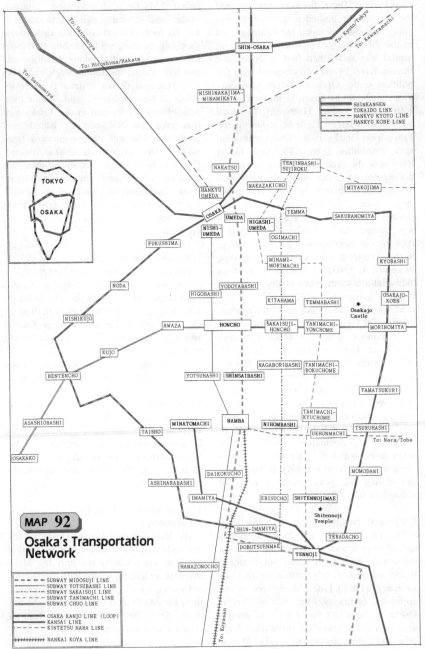

MAP 92

Osaka's Transportation Network

- SUBWAY MIDOSUJI LINE
- SUBWAY YOTSUBASHI LINE
- SUBWAY SAKAISUJI LINE
- SUBWAY TANIMACHI LINE
- SUBWAY CHUO LINE

- OSAKA KANJO LINE (LOOP)
- KANSAI LINE
- KINTETSU NARA LINE

- NANKAI KOYA LINE

(Legend in map: SHINKANSEN, TOKAIDO LINE, HANKYU KYOTO LINE, HANKYU KOBE LINE)

Osakajo Castle 大阪城

Take the JR Osaka Kanjo (Loop) Line to Morinomiya Station, or the Tanimachi subway line to Temmabashi Station, or the Chuo subway line to Tanimachi-Yonchome Station. Otemon Gate on the western side of the Castle (middle center, map 93) is the main entrance and a 10 – 15 minute walk from any of the above stations.

Osakajo Castle was built in 1585 at the order of Hideyoshi Toyotomi. Even though the modern reconstruction is on a smaller scale than the grand original, the Castle still symbolizes the power Hideyoshi gained by means of his victories over the other feudal lords during the civil wars. After the death of Hideyoshi in 1598, Ieyasu Tokugawa seized political power. With the establishment of the Tokugawa Shogunate in Edo (modern Tokyo), the Toyotomi family realm was reduced to just the immediate Osaka area. Underground movements, however, worked to overthrow the Tokugawas and restore the Toyotomis. To crush these would-be rebels, Ieyasu's troops opened fire on Osakajo Castle in 1614. The Toyotomis and their allies were destroyed in the battle, and the Castle was burned down in 1615.

The present donjon (130 feet or 40 m. tall), reconstructed in 1931, is a replica of the original. The top of the five-roofed eight-story donjon commands an extensive view of the city and its vicinity. Especially fascinating are the Castle's huge rock walls. At the order of the Tokugawa government, the feudal lords of western Japan donated the rocks when the Castle was repaired after the 1615 war. Hokoku Jinja Shrine, which is dedicated to the Toyotomi family, was moved to its present location in 1903 to honor the founder of the Castle. The donjon is open to the public from 9:00 AM to 4:30 PM. Admission is 300 yen.

To the south of Osakajo Castle is the **Namba Imperial Palace Grounds**. Huge stones are reminiscent of the glory of this 7th century capital.

Nissei Baseball Stadium is the home of the professional Kintetsu Buffalos.

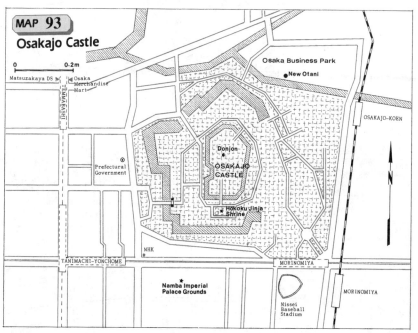

MAP 93
Osakajo Castle

Kita and Nakanoshima 北，中之島

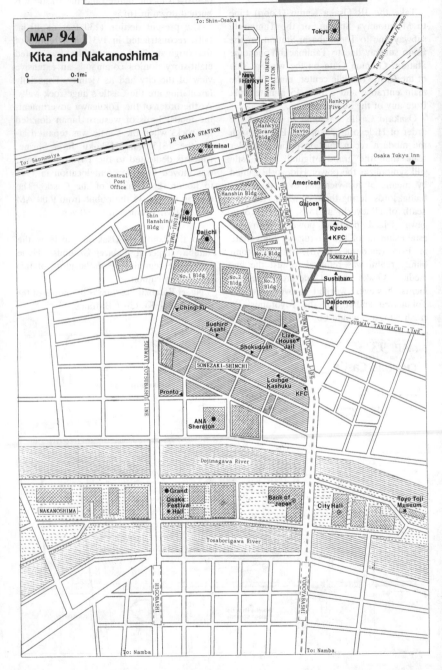

MAP 94
Kita and Nakanoshima

0   0·1mi

To: Shin-Osaka

To: Shin-Osaka/Kyoto

Tokyu

New Hankyu

HANKYU UMEDA STATION

Hankyu Five

Hankyu Grand Bldg

Navio

JR OSAKA STATION

Terminal

UMEDA

Osaka Tokyu Inn

To: Sannomiya

Central Post Office

HIGASHI-UMEDA

American

Hanshin Bldg

Gajoen

Shin Hanshin Bldg

Hilton

Daiichi

Kyoto

KFC

No.4 Bldg

SONEZAKI

NISHI-UMEDA

Sushihan

No.1 Bldg

No.2 Bldg

No.3 Bldg

Daidomon

Ching-Fu

SUBWAY TANIMACHI LINE

Suehiro Asahi

Live House Jail

Shokudoen

SONEZAKI-SHINCHI

SUBWAY MIDOSUJI LINE

SUBWAY YOTSUBASHI LINE

Lounge Kashuku

Pronto

KFC

ANA Sheraton

Dojimagawa River

NAKANOSHIMA

Grand Osaka Festival Hall

Bank of Japan

City Hall

Toyo Toji Museum

Tosaborigawa River

HIGOBASHI

YODOYABASHI

To: Namba

To: Namba

The northern part of the city, called "Kita," has tall concrete buildings rising into the sky, and complicated shopping malls spread underground. The area is centered around JR's Osaka Station, Hankyu Umeda Station, and Umeda subway station. This is the ultra-modern area of the contemporary city.

Hankyu Grand Building 阪急グランドビル (upper center) is a 32-story modern building. There is a free observatory on the 31st floor that commands an extensive, and probably the best, view of the city and Osaka Bay. Many restaurants and shops are located on the 27th through 31st floors: these four floors are called "Hankyu Sanjunibangai" (Hankyu's 32nd Avenue).

Umeda Chika Center 梅田地下センター (Underground Shopping Mall) connects Osaka Station and Umeda subway station with the major buildings around them. The underground paths are lined with stores, restaurants and coffee shops that are very popular with the business people who work in the area. If you want to explore this labyrinth underground mall, you should leave yourself plenty of time because you're sure to get lost.

There are four new office buildings south of Osaka Station. They are numbered No. 1 through No. 4. The 32nd through 34th floors of **No. 3 Building** house restaurants that command a good view of the city.

Toyo Toji Museum 東洋陶磁美術館 (lower right) displays masterpieces of pottery and ceramics that were produced in China and Korea in ancient times and collected by the owner of the now bankrupt Ataka conglomerate (9:30 AM to 5:00 PM. Closed on Mondays).

Osaka Festival Hall 大阪フェスティバルホール (lower center) is the most prestigious concert hall in Osaka. Many concerts by both Japanese and foreign artists are held here year round.

Restaurants in Kita

There are two eating and drinking districts in Kita. **Sonezaki** (middle right) still contains a number of inexpensive eating and drinking establishments as well as many obscure cabarets. An arcade runs through the center of Sonezaki (shaded red on map 94). **Sonezaki-Shinchi** (shaded red in the center of map 94) has many first-class (and generally expensive) bars and restaurants. You will find business people drinking with their colleagues in the Sonezaki district, while business people entertaining guests on expense accounts can be found in the Sonezaki-Shinchi district.

Japanese

Sushihan (middle right) is a reasonable sushi shop. **Kyoto** (upper right) is a Japanese "robatayaki" pub restaurant (reasonable). **Suehiro Asahi** (middle center) serves beef steak, sukiyaki and shabu-shabu (moderate). **Kawakyu,** located on the 33rd floor of No. 3 Building (middle center), is an authentic Japanese restaurant (expensive).

Western and Steaks

L'Omelette, located on the 31st floor of the Hankyu Grand Building (upper center), is an omelette specialist (reasonable). **Din Don** is also on the 31st floor of the Hankyu Grand Building, and serves roast beef and steaks (moderate). **Pronto** (middle center) is an authentic Italian restaurant (moderate). **Lounge Kashuku** (middle center) is a famous Kobe beef steak house (expensive).

Others

Daidomon (middle right) and **Shokudoen** (middle center) are Korean barbecue restaurants (reasonable). **Gajoen** (upper right) is a Chinese restaurant (reasonable). **Ching-Fu** (middle center) serves authentic Chinese cuisine (moderate). **Top of Osaka** is a pub, located on the 33rd floor of No. 3 Building. **Wine House West Coast** is a popular wine house on the 27th floor of the Hankyu Grand Building. **Live House Jail** (middle center) features live rock and roll.

Shinsaibashi and Minami   心斎橋，南

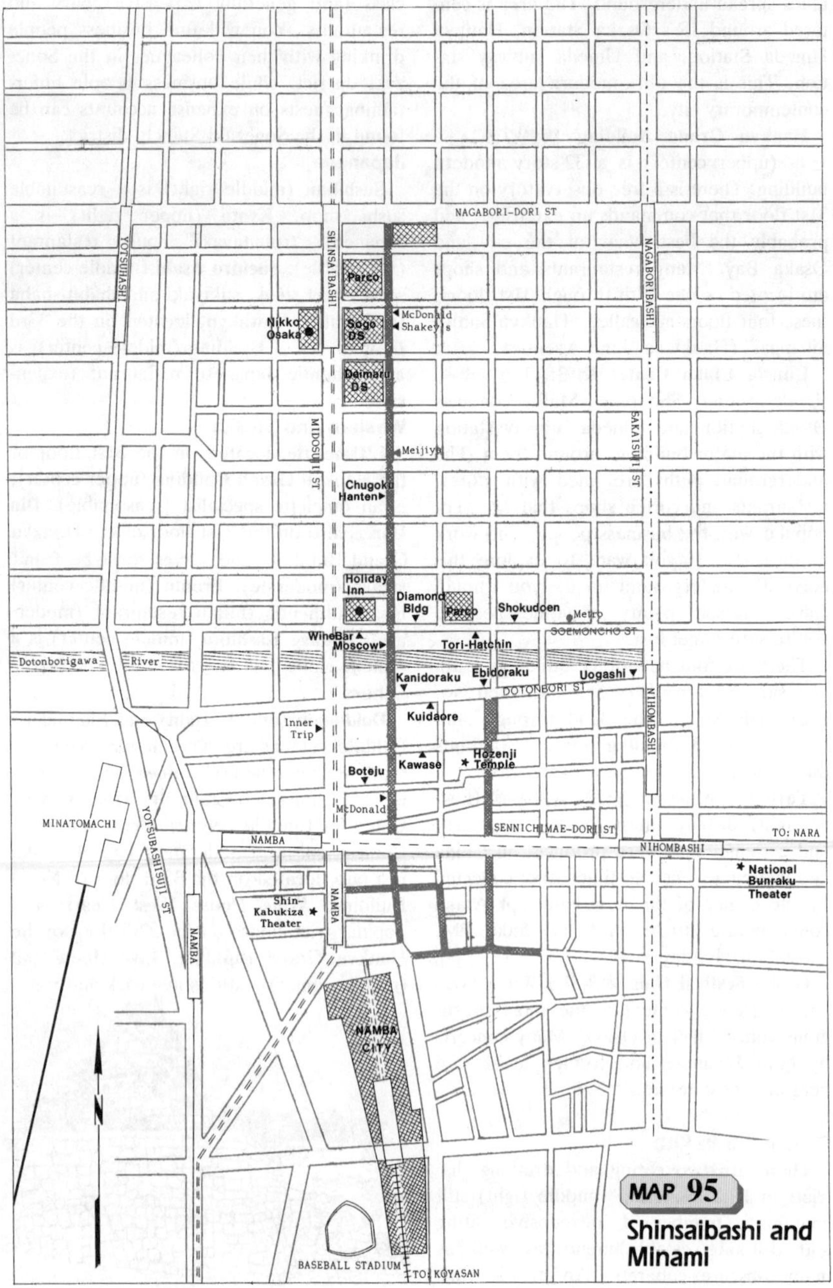

MAP 95

Shinsaibashi and Minami

NAGABORI-DORI ST

NAGABORIBASHI

SHINSAIBASHI

YOTSUBASHI

Parco

Nikko
Osaka

Sogo
DS

McDonald
Shakey's

Daimaru
DS

MIDOSUJI ST

SAKAISUJI ST

Meijiya

Chugoku
Hanten

Holiday
Inn

Diamond
Bldg

Parco

Shokudoen

Metro

SOEMONCHO ST

WineBar
Moscow

Tori-Hatchin

Dotonborigawa   River

Kanidoraku

Ebidoraku

Uogashi

DOTONBORI ST

NIHOMBASHI

Inner
Trip

Kuidaore

Boteju

Kawase

Hozenji
Temple

McDonald

SENNICHIMAE-DORI ST

TO: NARA

NAMBA

NAMBA

NIHOMBASHI

MINATOMACHI

YOTSUBASHI-SUJI ST

* National
Bunraku
Theater

Shin-
Kabukiza
Theater

NAMBA

NAMBA
CITY

N

BASEBALL STADIUM   TO: KOYASAN

There are many shopping arcades in the Shinsaibashi and Minami district (indicated with shaded red on map 95). Three department stores (Daimaru, Sogo, and Parco), and modern shops and boutiques are located near the Midosuji subway line's Shinsaibashi Station and along the arcade that runs parallel to the Midosuji subway line.

National Bunraku Theater 国立文楽劇場 (lower right). Bunraku is a traditional puppet drama developed to new peaks of achievement in the Edo era. Each puppet is manipulated by three puppeteers. The delicate movements of the eyes, mouths, fingers and arms of the puppets are sure to fascinate you even if you cannot follow the story exactly. The plays usually feature tragic stories of the feudal era. You can get information at (06) 212-1122, or at your hotel. There are six runs a year at the National Theater; each lasts for about 20 days.

Shin-Kabukiza Theater 新歌舞伎座 (lower center) stages Kabuki once a year in April (for about a 25 day run).

Hozenji Temple 法善寺 (middle center) has only a small hall and is surrounded by restaurants, bars and cabarets. Decorated with many paper lanterns and filled with the smell of incense, the temple is a symbol of traditional Osaka and the people of the city. Visiting the temple is supposed to be helpful to those in pursuit of true love.

Namba City ナンバシティー (lower center) is a complex of stores and restaurants. Namba Station on the private Nankai Koya Line is located in this building.

Nankai Baseball Stadium near Namba City is the home of the professional Nankai Hawks. This team is not too popular, and tickets should be available even on the day of a game.

Restaurants in Minami

Soemoncho (northern side of the Dotonborigawa River) and **Dotonbori** (southern side of the River) are Minami's two famous eating and drinking streets. The area maintains the traditional atmosphere of Osaka's mercantile past. Inexpensive but good restaurants and pubs line the streets. There are glittering neon signs and unique signboards and displays. Popular wisdom holds that if you are eating and drinking on an expense account you should go to Kita, especially its Sonezaki-Shinchi area. Minami is your destination when you pay from your own pocket. Dotonbori Street is home to many movie and stage theaters.

The following are the three most famous restaurants on Dotonbori:

Kuidaore can't be missed because it has a mechanical clown drummer in front of its entrance. Big plastic samples will help you make your selection (reasonable).

Kanidoraku has a huge mechanical crab over its entrance. A variety of crab dishes are served here (moderate).

Ebidoraku has a huge (but stationary!) shrimp on the wall of its building. The restaurant specializes in shrimp cuisine (moderate).

Other restaurants

Chugoku Hanten (upper center, in the shopping arcade) has 200 different Chinese dishes (reasonable).

Shokudoen (middle center) serves Korean barbecue (reasonable).

Boteju (middle center) serves "okonomiyaki" Japanese-style omelettes (reasonable).

Kawase (middle center) serves tempura, sashimi and other Japanese dishes (moderate).

Tori-Hatchin (middle center) is a typical "yakitori" pub (reasonable).

Uogashi (middle right) is a Japanese pub restaurant, and has a large tank with live fish at its entrance. Fresh seafood, raw and broiled, is priced reasonably.

Moscow (middle center) serves authentic Russian cuisine (moderate).

The Wine Bar (middle center) is a popular wine pub (reasonable).

Shitennoji Temple
四天王寺

MAP 96   Shitennoji Temple

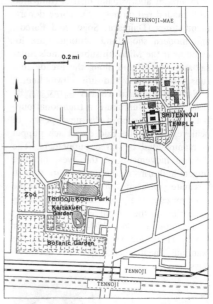

Shitennoji Temple is a five minute walk from Shitennoji-mae Station on the Tanimachi subway line, and a 15 minute walk from the Tennoji Station of either the JR Osaka Kanjo (loop) Line or the Midosuji subway line.

Shitennoji Temple was originally erected in 593 at the order of Prince Shotoku, who later, in 607, had Horyuji Temple in Nara built. Shitennoji is known as the birthplace of Japanese Buddhism. The temple was ravaged many times by fires and the original buildings were lost. The present concrete buildings were constructed in 1965 and have no historical value. They are, however, arranged according to the original design, and all the major buildings are positioned in a straight line. If you are interested in architecture, Shitennoji Temple is a good place to study the development of Japanese Buddhist temple design (9:00 AM to 5:00 PM. Admission 200 yen).

Tennoji-Koen Park 天王寺公園

You can visit Tennoji-Koen Park in conjunction with your visit to Shitennoji Temple. The Park is home to the Botanic Garden (9:30 AM to 5:00 PM), Tennoji Zoo (9:30 AM to 5:00 PM), and Keitakuen Garden (Open to the public on Tuesday, Thursday and Sunday from 9:30 AM to 4:30 PM). Keitakuen Garden was originally built by the owner of the Sumitomo conglomerate and later presented to the city of Osaka. The garden, designed around a pond, is unexpectedly quiet amid the bustle of this great city.

Hotels in Osaka

1. Deluxe Hotels

Royal Hotel ロイヤルホテル
(Middle left, map 91. 1,462 rooms).
Add: 5-3-68, Nakanoshima, Kita-ku,
Osaka.
Tel: (06) 448-1121.

Hotel New Otani Osaka
ホテルニューオータニ大阪
(Middle right, map 91. 610 rooms).
Add: 1-4-1, Shiromi, Higashi-ku, Osaka.
Tel: (06) 941-1111.

Osaka Hilton Hotel 大阪ヒルトンホテル
(Middle center, map 91. 553 rooms).
Add: 1-8-8, Umeda, Kita-ku, Osaka.
Tel: (06) 347-7111.

Plaza Hotel プラザホテル
(Upper left, map 91. 572 rooms).
Add: 2-2-49, Oyodo-Minami, Oyodo-ku,
Osaka.
Tel: (06) 453-1111.

ANA-Sheraton Hotel 大阪全日空ホテル
(Middle center, map 91. 500 rooms).
Add: 1-3-1, Dojimahama, Kita-ku,
Osaka.
Tel: (06) 347-1112.

2. First-class Hotels

Hotel Nikko Osaka ホテル日航大阪
(Middle center, map 91. 651 rooms).
Add: 7, Nishinocho, Daihojimachi,
Minami-ku, Osaka.
Tel: (06) 252-1121.

Miyako Hotel Osaka 都ホテル大阪
(Middle right, map 91. 608 rooms).
Add: 6-1-55, Uehonmachi, Tennoji-ku,
Osaka.
Tel: (06) 773-1111.

Osaka Tokyu Hotel 大阪東急ホテル
(Upper center, map 91. 340 rooms).
Add: 7-20, Chayamachi, Kita-ku, Osaka.
Tel: (06) 373-2411.

Holiday Inn (Nankai) ホリデーイン南海
(Lower center, map 91. 225 rooms).
Add: 28-1, Kyuzaemoncho, Minami-ku,
Osaka.
Tel: (06) 213-8281.

Toyo Hotel 東洋ホテル
(Upper center, map 91. 641 rooms).
Add: 3-16-19, Toyosaki, Oyodo-ku,
Osaka.
Tel: (06) 372-8181.

Osaka Grand Hotel 大阪グランドホテル
(Middle center, map 91. 358 rooms).
Add: 2-3-18, Nakanoshima, Kita-ku,
Osaka.
Tel: (06) 202-1212.

3. Standard Hotels

Osaka Terminal Hotel
大阪ターミナルホテル
(Middle center, map 91. 671 rooms).
Add: 3-1-1, Umeda, Kita-ku, Osaka.
Tel: (06) 344-1235.

Osaka Daiichi Hotel 大阪第一ホテル
(Middle center, map 91. 428 rooms).
Add: 1-9-20, Umeda, Kita-ku, Osaka.
Tel: (06) 341-4411.

Osaka Kokusai Hotel 大阪国際ホテル
(Middle center, map 91. 394 rooms).
Add: 58, Hashizumecho, Uchihonmachi,
Higashi-ku, Osaka.
Tel: (06) 941-2661.

Hotel New Hankyu ホテルニュー阪急
(Upper center, map 91. 1,029 rooms).
Add: 1-1-35, Shibata, Kita-ku, Osaka.
Tel: (06) 372-5101.

Osaka Airport Hotel
大阪エアポートホテル
(In the airport terminal building, 105
rooms).
Add: Osaka Airport Building, Toyonaka,
Osaka Prefecture.
Tel: (06) 855-4621.

4. Business Hotels

Osaka Fujiya Hotel 大阪富士屋ホテル
(Middle center, map 91. 196 rooms).
Add: 2-27-1, Nagahoribashi-suji,
Minami-ku, Osaka.
Tel: (06) 211-5522.

Osaka Tokyu Inn 大阪東急イン
(Middle center, map 91. 402 rooms).
Add: 2-1, Doyamacho, Kita-ku, Osaka.
Tel: (06) 315-0109.

Nakanoshima Inn 中之島イン
(Middle center, map 91. 342 rooms).
Add: 1-13-10, Edobori, Nishi-ku, Osaka.
Tel: (06) 447-1122.

Koyasan 高野山

Koyasan is a 5.6 km. (3.5 mile) long and 2.2 km. (1.4 mile) wide tableland hid amid 900 m. (3,000 foot) high mountains. It is inhabited by 7,000 people, and the area has the usual facilities of a modern town including schools, banks and amusement places, but as a temple town it also has its own character and atmosphere. All accommodations available here are in temples, and they serve only special vegetarian foods, reflecting the traditional diet of the priests. There are about 120 temples scattered throughout the area. They are surrounded by magnificent forests.

To enter Koyasan is to enter a mysterious world of Buddhism. Ever since Kukai (Kobo Daishi), founder of the Shingon sect, opened a temple here in 816, Koyasan has prospered as the capital of Japanese Buddhism. The more than 100,000 monuments commemorating the giants of Japanese history that line the approach to Okunoin Cemetery testify to the respect that Koyasan has been accorded for the past 12 centuries.

Koyasan is an ideal one-night two-days destination from Kyoto or Osaka. Though it is possible to make a one-day excursion here from Osaka, we don't recommend it because your day will be too rushed, and because the overnight stay at a temple accommodation is one of the major reasons for a visit to Koyasan.

Transportation to Koyasan
1. Direct trains from Osaka

The private Nankai Koya Line operates a direct train from Osaka's Namba Station to

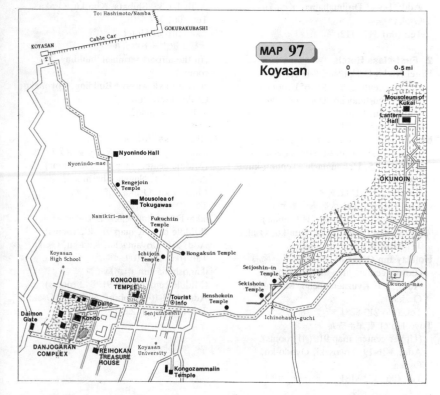

Gokurakubashi via Hashimoto. Nankai's Namba Station is pictured on map 95 (lower center) and can be reached easily by the Midosuji subway line. There are three limited express trains from Namba Station every day. Additional limited express trains operate in spring and fall. The limited express trains use deluxe cars and have only reserved seats. The ride from Namba to Gokurakubashi 極楽橋 takes 1 hour 25 minutes. In addition to the limited expresses, commuter-type express trains operate about once every 30 minutes from early in the morning till late at night. The ride from Namba to Gokurakubashi takes 1 hour and 45 minutes. Because the express trains take only 20 minutes longer than the limited expresses and because the fare is one-half, it might be wise to take an express unless you are intent on a deluxe reserved seat.

2. JR Trains from Kyoto

As explained in the Introduction to Kansai section, you can take four JR trains from Kyoto to Hashimoto: (1) Kyoto to Nara on the JR Nara Line; (2) Nara to Oji on the JR Kansai Line; (3) Oji to Gojo on the JR Wakayama Line; and (4) Gojo to Hashimoto on another JR Wakayama Line. At Hashimoto Station 橋本駅 you transfer to the private Nankai Koya Line for Gokurakubashi. Allow about 4 hours on this route.

Transportation in Koyasan
1. Koyasan Cable Car

A cable car operates every 20 – 30 minutes from Gokurakubashi Station to Koyasan. The ride takes five minutes. The cable car climbs up a steep mountain slope; it is unbelievable that there is such a wide tableland at the top of such a precipitous mountain.

2. Bus Service in Koyasan

Two important bus routes originate at Koyasan cable car station. One operates between Koyasan Station and Okunoin-mae 奥の院前 (lower right, map 97), the other between Koyasan Station and Daimon 大門 (lower left, map 97). Both buses run on the same route till they reach

Senjuinbashi 千手院橋 stop, as indicated with red dotted lines on the map. The buses operate every 20 – 30 minutes, connecting with the arriving cable cars.

*Plenty of taxis are also available in Koyasan.

Places of Interest

Koyasan can be divided into two sections: the western part contains the temple precincts where many grand structures and the Reihokan Treasure House are located; the eastern part is a cemetery where more than 100,000 tombs of historic figures and the mausoleum of Kukai are located. This area is shaded with cedar trees hundreds of years old. Visit one half in the afternoon of the day you arrive and the other half the following day. If your time is limited, skip the places marked optional.

Okunoin 奥の院 (Upper right, map 97)

The stone-paved main approach to Okunoin begins at Ichinohashi, but there is a shortcut to Okunoin from Okunoin-mae bus stop that bypasses some of the approach. You can start your walking tour at either Ichinohashi-guchi or Okunoin-mae. The 2 km. (1.3 mile) long main approach is lined on both sides with a variety of monuments, statues and gravestones. It is very difficult to think of a historical figure for whom there isn't a monument along this path. You'll probably see a number of pilgrims dressed in white and carrying wooden staffs as you walk along the path. At the end of the path is Lantern Hall. There are 11,000 lanterns all through the Hall. There are also two fires in the Hall – one has been burning since 1016 and the other since 1088. The mausoleum of Kukai is behind Lantern Hall. The entire area is densely wooded; the huge trees prevent any sunshine from breaking through. The mysterious atmosphere is enhanced by the pervasive smell of incense. A visit here will help you understand why Koyasan has been so important to Japanese Buddhism.

Kongobuji Temple 金剛峯寺 (Lower left)

Kongobuji Temple was erected in 1592 at the order of Hideyoshi Toyotomi as a fami-

ly temple for his mother, and later became Koyasan's main temple. The chambers of the main building are separated by sliding doors decorated with brilliant pictures by artists of the Kano school (8:00 AM to 5:00 PM. Admission 300 yen).

Danjogaran Complex 檀上伽藍 (Lower left)

The Danjogaran Complex consists of more than 15 halls, and the sight of these magnificent buildings never fails to impress visitors. The complex has suffered repeated fires, but the oldest building dates from 1198. The two most important buildings are Kondo and Daito. Kondo is the main hall of the complex, and Daito is a gigantic pagoda. Though Daito dates only from 1937, it is a very impressive two-story vermilion structure. The entrance to the complex is free of charge. Admission to the interiors of Kondo and Daito is 100 yen each.

Reihokan Treasure House 霊宝館 (Lower left)

Reihokan preserves about 5,000 treasures of Koyasan, 180 of which have been designated National Treasures and Important Cultural Properties. Koyasan's proud artistic achievements are displayed here. The exhibits are changed periodically (9:00 AM to 4:00 PM, till 5:00 PM in summer. Admission 300 yen).

Daimon Gate 大門 (Lower left; optional)

In olden times, the main entrance to Koyasan was through Daimon Gate. This huge structure is located in the western-most part of the tableland and commands a fine view of the surrounding mountains and valleys.

Kongozammaiin Temple 金剛三昧院 (Lower center; optional)

Kongozammaiin Temple dates from 1211 and was erected in commemoration of Yoritomo Minamoto, the founder of the Kamakura Shogunate, Japan's first military government, which was established in 1192. The two-story pagoda, built in 1223, is a National Treasure. Kyakuden Hall (Guest Hall) is famous for the gorgeous pictures on its sliding screens.

Mausolea of the Tokugawas 徳川家霊台 (Upper left; optional)

Mausolea of the first and the second Tokugawa Shoguns are located here. As is the case with many of the shrines, monuments and mausolea related to the Tokugawas, the buildings in Koyasan feature brilliant gold and silver ornamentation (9:00 AM to 5:00 PM).

Accommodations in Koyasan

The only accommodations available in Koyasan are in temples. Fifty-three out of the 120 temples in the area have lodgings. The facilities are basically the same as a regular Japanese-style inn. The greatest differences are that the kitchens prepare the same vegetarian dishes for guests that are served to the priests and that these accommodations are imbued with the solemn atmosphere of the temple precincts. The rates are 8,000 – 12,000 yen per person, including dinner and breakfast.

Sekishoin Temple 赤松院 (lower center)
   Tel: (07365) 6-2734.
Henshokoin Temple 遍照光院 (lower
   center)
   Tel: (07365) 6-2124.
Ichijoin Temple 一乗院 (middle center)
   Tel: (07365) 6-2214.
Hongakuin Temple 本覚院 (middle center)
   Tel: (07365) 6-2711.
Fukuchiin Temple 福智院 (middle center)
   Tel: (07365) 6-2021.
Rengejoin Temple 蓮華王院 (middle left)
   Tel: (07365) 6-2231.

Kobe 神戸

Because the early development of Japan took place in the western part of the archipelago where the calm Inland Sea was the main transportation route, Kobe has been a prosperous port town since the prehistoric period. The early port was called Muko-no-Minato. The area was opened to foreign traders in 1868, at the end of the nation's long period of isolation. Because Kobe has had a large foreign population for more than one hundred years, it has the cosmopolitan atmosphere of an international city. Kobe beef is a famous specialty of the city, and Kobe's sophisticated restaurants feature all sorts of international dishes, making the city a gourmets' paradise. The city's population is 1,416,000.

Outline of the Area

Kobe, sandwiched between the sea on the south and Mt. Rokkosan on the north, is quite long from northeast to southwest.

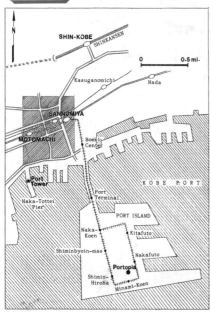

MAP 98 Outline of Kobe

The area around Sannomiya Station is the center of the city. Port Island, a large man-made island, was constructed several years ago to expand port facilities, especially container facilities, and to provide convenient residential and recreational areas for the people of Kobe.

Transportation

Kobe is served by the Shinkansen, and can be reached easily from other major cities. The Shinkansen station is called Shin-Kobe 新神戸駅 and is located about 1.6 km. (1 mile) to the north of Sannomiya Station. Except for those traveling to Kobe from Osaka, the Shinkansen is the most convenient method of transportation even though you need to take a short taxi ride between Shin-Kobe and Sannomiya.

1. From Osaka

JR and private railways operate parallel commuter lines between Sannomiya and Osaka. Refer to the Introduction to Kansai section.

2. From Osaka Airport

A shuttle bus operates between Osaka Airport and Sannomiya Station three times an hour, from 6:00 AM to 8:00 PM. The bus stop is located near the JR and Hankyu Sannomiya Stations (The stop is pictured at the upper right of map 99).

Places of Interest in Kobe

The main areas of Kobe explained in this guidebook can be covered on foot. If you get tired, Kobe has plenty of taxis.

The wide boulevard stretching south from Sannomiya Station is called **"Flower Road"** and is decorated with flowers of the season. On the eastern side of the road are exotic restaurants and pubs. Old western-style buildings reminiscent of the adventurous early foreign traders dot the area. Along the western side of the boulevard there are many sculptures by contemporary artists. City Hall and many businesses, both

Japanese and foreign, are located to the west of Flower Road.

The main shopping district of Kobe stretches along the southern side of the JR and the Hankyu lines. Shopping arcades are indicated with shaded red on map 99. The arcades between Sannomiya and Motomachi Stations contain modern buildings, while the arcade to the south of Motomachi Station features traditional specialty shops.

A small **Chinatown** 南京町 is located to the south of the shopping arcade. Though this Chinatown does not have the scale or brilliance of that of Yokohama, it has a good reputation for excellent food.

There is an extensive **underground shopping mall**, with fashion boutiques, souvenir shops, restaurants and coffee shops located under the northern part of Flower Road, around JR's Sannomiya Station.

Tor Road runs from north to south, crossing under the elevated railroad tracks (upper left, map 99). The street, which slopes gently as it goes north, is lined with horse chestnuts, and is always peaceful and quiet. This favorite promenade of the people of Kobe is dotted with specialty shops and good restaurants.

The northern side of Sannomiya Station is called **Ikuta** 生田. With clusters of eating and drinking facilities, it is Kobe's busiest night life area. In the middle of the glitter-

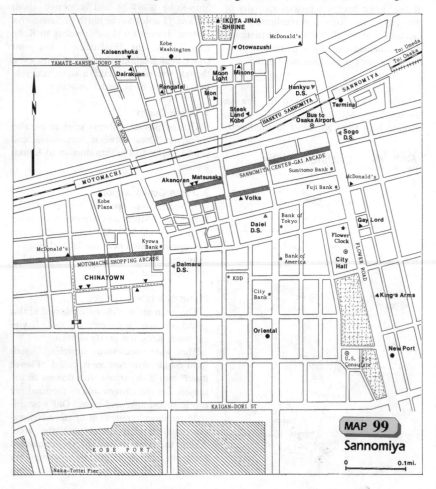

MAP 99
Sannomiya

0   0.1mi.

ing neon signs of the night spots is **Ikuta Jinja Shrine** 生田神宮. The woods behind the vermilion shrine were once quite extensive, and were the subject of a famous poem in olden times.

Port Tower ポートタワー is a good place to get a bird's-eye view of the port and the city. The 108 m. (354 foot) tall tower is located in the middle of Naka-Tottei Pier (lower left, map 99). Elevators take you from the second floor to the observatory on the top (9:00 AM to 9:00 PM. Admission 400 yen). The third and fourth floors of the tower are a museum that displays objects related to the history of Kobe Port and ocean transportation (An observatory ticket includes admission to the museum).

Port Island ポートアイランド

Port Island is connected with Sannomiya Station by automatic monorails called Portliners. The monorail makes a counterclockwise loop and stops at eight stations. The island features large container terminals for international ocean freight, a number of condominiums, an international trade show hall and recreational facilities such as a planetarium and sports fields. If you want to take a stroll in the area, get off the monorail at Shimin-Hiroba Station and walk to Minami-Koen Station. Even if you don't get off and take a walk, it is fun to take the monorail to see the port and the new development. The full loop trip takes 27 minutes. Portliner platforms are located on the second floor at the eastern corner of JR's Sannomiya Station.

Restaurants in Kobe

Japanese: Otowazushi (upper center, map 99) is a sushi bar restaurant. It has a good atmosphere and there is a lot of raw fish neatly displayed in glass cases on the bars (reasonable). **Akanoren** (middle center) serves set menu authentic Japanese meals (reasonable). **Matsusaka** (middle center) serves beef steaks, shabu-shabu and sukiyaki (moderate).

Steak Houses: Volks (middle center) is a reasonable steak house. **Steak Land Kobe** (upper center) is another reasonable restaurant. Both **Misono** (upper center) and **Rengatei** (upper left) are famous Kobe steak houses. You won't have any complaints about the quality, but portions are rather smallish (expensive).

Others: Dairakuen (upper left) serves Korean barbecue (reasonable). **Kaisenshuka** (upper left) is a Chinese restaurant (reasonable). All restaurants in **Chinatown** are priced reasonably. **Gay Lord** (middle right) is an authentic Indian restaurant. **King's Arms** (lower right) is an English-style pub restaurant popular with Kobe's foreign residents.

Hotels in Kobe

Kobe Portpia Hotel 神戸ポートピアホテル
(Deluxe: on Port Island, map 98)
Add: 6-10-1, Minatojima-Nakamachi, Chuo-ku, Kobe.
Tel: (078) 302-1111.

Oriental Hotel オリエンタルホテル
(First-class: lower center, map 99. 190 rooms)
Add: 25, Kyomachi, Naka-ku, Kobe.
Tel: (078) 331-8111.

New Port Hotel ニューポートホテル
(Standard: lower right, map 99. 207 rooms)
Add: 6-3-13, Hamabedori, Naka-ku, Kobe.
Tel: (078) 231-4171.

Sannomiya Terminal Hotel
三の宮ターミナルホテル
(Standard: upper right, map 99. 190 rooms)
Add: 8, Kumaidori, Naka-ku, Kobe.
Tel: (078) 291-0001.

Kobe Washington Hotel
神戸ワシントンホテル
(Business hotel: upper left, map 99. 194 rooms)
Add: 2-11-5, Shimo-Yamatedori, Chuo-ku, Kobe.
Tel: (078) 331-6111.

Kobe Plaza Hotel 神戸プラザホテル
(Business hotel: middle left, map 99. 141 rooms)
Add: 1-13-12, Motomachidori, Chuo-ku, Kobe.
Tel: (078) 332-1141.

Introduction to 瀬戸内海 the Inland Sea Area

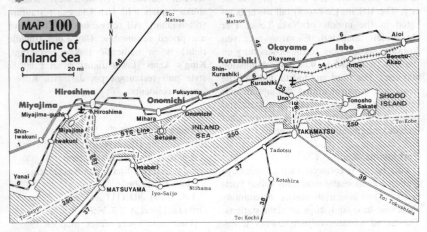

MAP **100**

Outline of Inland Sea

0   20 mi

The Inland Sea lies between the Sanyo area of western Honshu and Shikoku Island. There are a number of historic and scenic destinations on both sides of the Inland Sea.

In this Chapter, we introduce the destinations along the northern side of Inland Sea (i.e., those on Honshu), while those on Shikoku Island are introduced in the Shikoku Chapter below.

The northern Inland Sea area can be divided into two parts – the Eastern Inland Sea and the Western Inland Sea. The Eastern Inland Sea area includes Okayama, Kurashiki and Inbe (for pottery enthusiasts only), while the Western Inland Sea area includes Hiroshima, Miyajima and Onomichi.

We suggest that you plan your itinerary from Kyoto/Osaka to the Inland Sea area as follows:

– If you have only one night: You have two alternatives:

(1) Visit Kurashiki first. You can spend a full afternoon in Kurashiki on the first day. Overnight in Kurashiki. Visit Okayama or Inbe on the second day, and then return to Kyoto/Osaka (You can also return to Tokyo in 4 hours).

(2) Visit Hiroshima first and spend a full afternoon there. You can stay overnight at either a Hiroshima hotel or a Miyajima ryokan. After spending several hours in Miyajima, return to Kyoto/Osaka. We personally prefer the latter itinerary.

– If you have two nights, you can cover both areas as follows:

Day 1.   Kyoto/Kurashiki

Day 2.   Kurashiki/Hiroshima (If you want to stay at a ryokan, proceed to Miyajima.)

Day 3.   Hiroshima/Miyajima/Kyoto.

– If you have three nights, add Onomichi after your visit to Miyajima.

You can also combine an Inland Sea visit with a visit to the San-in area to the north, or Shikoku to the south. Okayama provides good connections to both areas – the JR Hakubi Line (No. 45) to Matsue, and the JR Uno Line (No. 35) and the Uko boat (No. 36) to Takamatsu. JR's direct trains between Okayama and Takamatsu will be inaugurated upon completion of the Seto Ohashi Bridge in 1988.

Himeji is also included in this Chapter, because this castle city is easily incorporated in an Inland Sea itinerary.

Himeji

姫路

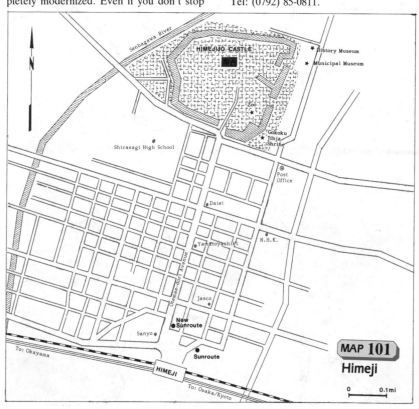

Himeji was a prosperous castle city in the feudal era. Himejijo Castle 姫路城, in an extensive compound of about 80 buildings, was built in 1601 at the order of the feudal lord, Terumasa Ikeda. Though Himeji was devastated during World War II, the Castle survived. Because of its magnificent scale and gracious design, the castle is often called "White Heron Castle" and is considered by many the most beautiful castle in Japan. The donjon and the main buildings are National Treasures (9:00 AM to 4:00 PM. Till 3:30 PM in winter. Admission 200 yen). The Castle is only 0.6 miles (1 km.) north of Himeji Station. Except for the castle, the city has been completely modernized. Even if you don't stop in Himeji, you can catch a glimpse of the castle from the train.

You can even make a day excursion from Kyoto or Osaka to Himeji easily. The ride on the Shinkansen takes only 40 – 50 minutes each way.

Hotels in Himeji

Himeji Castle Hotel 姫路キャッスルホテル
    (Standard: 222 rooms)
    Add: 210, Hojo, Himeji.
    Tel: (0792) 84-3311.
Hotel Sunroute Himeji
    ホテルサンルート姫路
    (Business hotel: lower center. 89 rooms).
Add: 195-9, Ekimaecho, Himeji.
    Tel: (0792) 85-0811.
Hotel Sunroute New Himeji
    ホテルサンルートニュー姫路
    (Business hotel: lower center. 40 rooms).
    Add: 198-1, Ekimaecho, Himeji.
    Tel: (0792) 85-0811.

MAP 101
Himeji

Eastern Inland Sea Area Transportation

Okayama, because it is on the Shinkansen, is the key to transportation in the eastern part of the Inland Sea area. In Kurashiki, the Shinkansen stops at Shin-Kurashiki Station, which is a very inconvenient six miles (10 km.) west of the city center. Okayama should therefore be where you get off the Shinkansen if that's your destination, or if you're headed for Kurashiki. At Okayama, you can transfer to a JR Sanyo Line local for the 17 minute trip to Kurashiki. The trains operate about once every 20 – 30 minutes. The tiny pottery town of Inbe is on the JR Akao Line (local trains only), about 40 minutes from Okayama.

If you plan to continue to Shikoku after a visit to the eastern part of the Inland Sea area, take the JR Uno Line from Okayama to Uno, and transfer there to either a JR hovercraft (23 minutes) or steamship (1 hour) for the trip to Takamatsu. When completed, the Seto Ohashi Bridge will allow for JR's new direct train services between Okayama and Takamatsu.

If you plan to travel on to the San-in

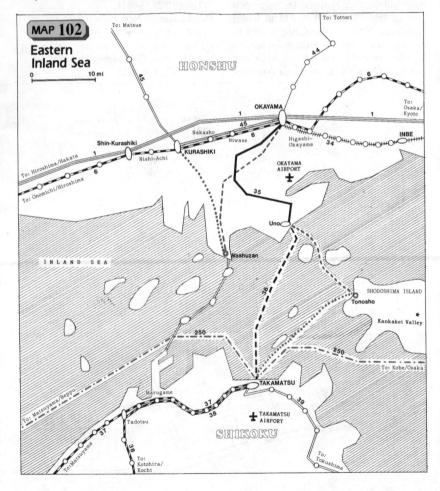

area of Honshu from the eastern part of the Inland Sea area, take the JR Hakubi Line from Okayama or Kurashiki to Matsue (No. 45).

Okayama
岡山

Okayama, a metropolis of 570,000, is a principal city of the Chugoku region, and the capital of Okayama Prefecture. Its train station features a statue of Momotaro, the "Peach Boy" of Japanese mythology.

Korakuen Garden 後楽園 (Upper right, map 103)

Take the bus from Platform 9 in front of the station. Be sure to take a *seiri-ken* fare zone ticket. The ride takes about 12 minutes. The 200 yen admission tickets you need for the park are sold in vending machines.

Korakuen is one of Japan's three most celebrated gardens. It was laid out at the order of Tsunamasa Ikeda, the feudal lord of the area, and was completed in 1700. It features several fields, ponds, waterfalls and tea pavilions, including one that even has a stream flowing through it. The Garden is famous for its vistas: its wide open spaces are a special treat in Japan. Korakuen Garden's reputation is well deserved. Hours: 8:30 AM to 6:00 PM (till 5:00 PM in winter).

Okayamajo Castle 岡山城 (optional) (Middle right, map 103)

Turn left when you leave Korakuen Garden and follow the path to the river. Turn left again and enjoy the short walk to Tsukimibashi Bridge. When you come to the English signboard after you cross the bridge, turn to your right and enter the Castle grounds through Rokamon Gate. The distinctive black castle, nicknamed Crow Castle, was built in 1573 by Lord Ukida, who ruled Bizen Province, as the area was then known. Only the turrets, which are both designated Important Cultural Properties, are originals. The donjon and gates are 1966 reconstructions. Hours:

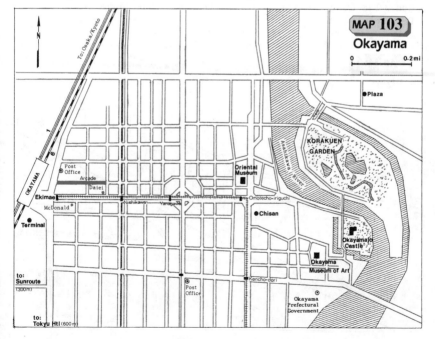

9:00 AM to 5:00 PM. Armor, swords, clothing, screens and lacquer items are on display in the donjon. Admission 200 yen.

Okayama Museum of Art 岡山美術館
(optional) (Middle right, map 103)

This museum displays treasures of the Ikeda family. The building is modeled after a traditional samurai residence and houses a collection of 4,000 items. Hours: 9:00 AM to 5:00 PM. Admission 200 yen.

You can take a streetcar from the Omotecho stop for the five minute trip back to the station, or walk back along Momotaro-dori, the street on which the streetcar runs.

Hotels in Okayama

Okayama Kokusai Hotel 岡山国際ホテル
(First-class: 194 rooms. 15 minutes by taxi from Okayama Station.)
Add: 4-1-16, Kadota-Honcho, Okayama.
Tel: (0862) 73-7311.

Okayama Tokyu Hotel 岡山東急ホテル
(First-class: 240 rooms. 10 minute walk from Okayama Station.)
Add: 3-2-18, Otomo, Okayama.
Tel: (0862) 33-2411.

Okayama Plaza Hotel 岡山プラザホテル
(Standard: upper right, map 103.
85 rooms)
Add: 2-3-12, Hama, Okayama.
Tel: (0862) 72-1201.

Okayama Terminal Hotel
岡山ターミナルホテル
(Business hotel: middle left, map 103.
215 rooms)
Add: 1-5, Ekimotomachi, Okayama.
Tel: (0862) 33-3131.

Hotel Sunroute Okayama
ホテルサンルート岡山
(Business hotel: 125 rooms. 7 minute walk from Okayama Station.)
Add: 1-3-12, Shimo-Ishii, Okayama.
Tel: (0862) 32-2345.

Bizen
備前

Transportation to Inbe

The JR Ako Line (No. 34, local trains only) takes about 40 minutes from Okayama to Inbe 伊部駅.

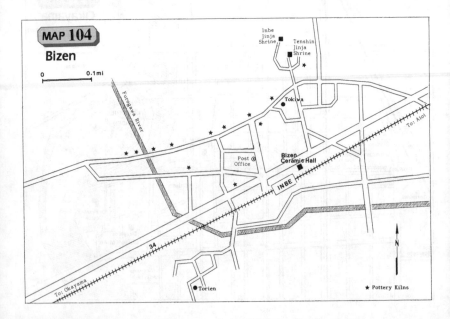

MAP 104
Bizen
0   0.1mi

Furogawa River
Inbe Jinja Shrine
Tenshin Jinja Shrine
Tokiwa
To: Aioi
Post Office
Bizen Ceramic Hall
INBE
34
To: Okayama
N
Torien
★ Pottery Kilns

Places of Interest in Inbe

This tiny town is the traditional home of Bizen pottery, which is distinguished by its warm earthen tones and its lack of a glaze. It only takes a few minutes to explore the whole town, but it is easy to lose yourself for hours in its many pottery shops. If the owners aren't busy, you're likely to be invited into the workrooms and kilns that adjoin most of the shops to see the pottery being made. The town's major kilns are indicated with stars on map 104. Watch the traffic on the busy road that runs parallel to the train tracks and on the curving street on which most of the town's kilns are located.

Bizen Ceramic Hall 備前焼会館 is the large brown building on your right as you emerge from the station. It displays outstanding examples of modern Bizen pottery as well as pieces from the Edo, Momoyama and Muromachi eras. Hours: 9:30 AM to 4:30 PM. Admission 300 yen.

Ryokan in Inbe

Torien 陶里苑
(Standard: lower center. 11 rooms)
Add: 2552, Inbe, Bizen.
Tel: (08696) 4-3363.

Washuzan Hill is located on the southern tip of Kojima Peninsula. There is an observatory (with the inevitable restaurant and souvenir shop) atop the hill, which has long been famous as one of the best places for a grand view of the "Shimmering Inland Sea." A number of small islands dot the peaceful waters, which are highlighted beautifully by the play of the sunshine. The coast line of Shikoku Island is visible in the distance. The view from Washuzan is reproduced over and over again in paintings, scenic photos and travel brochures.

The Seto Ohashi Bridge starts near Washuzan and connects Honshu to Shikoku, linking many small Inland Sea islands along the way. The view from Washuzan now encompasses this example of super modern technology. Some say that the view is now more impressive, while others claim that construction of the bridge has violated both nature and tradition.

Frequent bus service connects Washuzan with both Okayama and Kurashiki Stations (both are private bus companies). The rides take 40 and 70 minutes respectively.

Kurashiki is an arts center and a living museum. During the feudal era it was a rice and cotton shipping and distribution center. The distinctive white walls and black tiles of the granaries that flank the city's picturesque canal are the trademark of modern Kurashiki. It is a compact city, and the best way to appreciate its charms is probably on foot. Most of Kurashiki's attractions are closed on Mondays, and are open other days.

Ohashi House 大橋家 (Middle left, map 105)

Kurashiki's main thoroughfare is pleasantly westernized, and features several shops that specialize in *Bizen-yaki*, the local pottery. Ohashi House is about a 5 minute walk from the station. Turn right off the main street, and it will be the predominantly wooden building on your left, next to a bicycle shop. The house was built in 1796 by a former samurai family that became one of Kurashiki's leading mercantile powers. Make sure you remove your shoes in the tatami rooms, and watch your head.

Ohara Museum 大原美術館 (Lower center, map 105)

Modeled after a Greek temple, the main building of the museum displays Western art, including works of El Greco, Van Gogh, Cezanne, Renoir, etc. Next to the main building are the museum's Pottery Hall and Asian Art Hall, and behind it is the Museum Annex, which features modern Japanese paintings. A 500 yen combination ticket affords admission to all parts of the museum (9:00 AM to 4:30 PM. Closed on Mondays).

Other Attractions Along the Canal (lower right, map 105)

Kurashiki Museum 倉敷美術館 displays Western art (8:30 AM to 5:00 PM. Open year round).

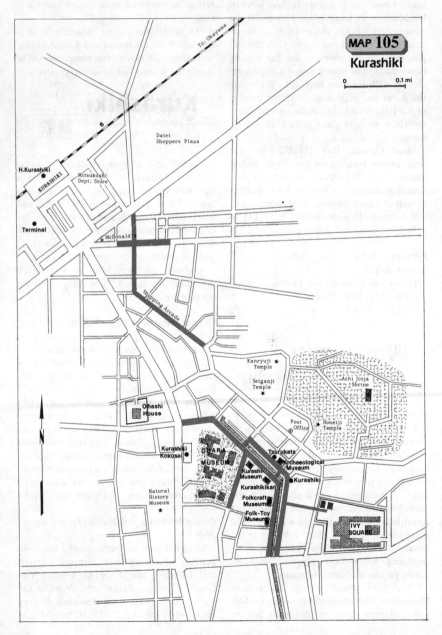

MAP 105
Kurashiki

0   0.1 mi

To Okayama

Daiei
Shoppers Plaza

6

H.Kurashiki

KURASHIKI

Mitsukoshi
Dept. Store

Terminal

McDonald

Shopping Arcade

Kanryuji
Temple

Seiganji
Temple

Achi Jinja
Shrine

Post
Office

Honeiji
Temple

Ohashi
House

Kurashiki
Kokusai

OHARA
MUSEUM

Tsurukata

Archaeological
Museum

Kurashiki
Museum

Kurashiki

Kurashikikan

Natural
History
Museum

Folkcraft
Museum

Folk-Toy
Museum

IVY
SQUARE

Kurashikikan 倉敷館 , a charming example of Japanese Victoriana, houses the city's Tourist Information Office.

Folkcraft Museum 倉敷民芸館 is composed of four rice granaries that house a lovely collection of more than 4,000 Japanese and foreign folkcraft items, including ceramics, woodenware, bamboo ware, textiles, etc. (8:00 AM to 5:00 PM. Closed on Mondays).

Folk Toy Museum 日本郷土玩具館 is six rooms crammed full of toys, including the dolls used for *hinamatsuri*, Girls' Festival, and the flying fish standards used for Boys' Day, as well as animal figures from the Japanese zodiac and the roly-poly *daruma* Buddha dolls that bring good luck (8:00 AM to 5:00 PM. Open year round).

Archaeological Museum 倉敷考古館 displays artifacts unearthed in Japan, including large *haniwa,* along with several finds from China and Latin America (9:00 AM to 4:00 PM. Closed on Mondays).

The canal area also features many souvenir shops, which sell all sorts of traditional Japanese crafts. This is a good place to stock up on presents for those back home.

Ivy Square アイビースクエアー(optional) (Lower right, map 105)

Renovated factory buildings now house fashionable shops, cafes, museums and a hotel. A 400 yen ticket will gain you admission to the three Ivy Square Museums: **Kojima Memorial Museum** 児島虎次郎館 features Middle Eastern and Western art; **Kurabo Memorial Museum** 倉紡記念館 features artifacts of the industrial revolution; and **Ivy Gakken** アイビー学研 , an educational display that explains Western art for Japanese students.

Achi Jinja Shrine 阿知神社 (optional) (Middle right, map 103)

Sitting atop a wooded hill that overlooks the cultural area of the city, Achi Jinja Shrine is a quiet retreat for the weary tourist. The Shrine has festivals on the third weekend of May and October. If you're tired of Kurashiki's official attractions, you can trace the path through the woods. You can detour to Kanryuji Temple and Seigan-ji Temple, and will emerge at a shopping arcade that will give you a taste of local life and which leads you back to Kurashiki Station.

Accommodations in Kurashiki
1. Hotels
Kurashiki Kokusai Hotel 倉敷国際ホテル
   (Standard: lower center, map 105. 70 rooms)
   Add: 1-1-44, Chuo, Kurashiki.
   Tel: (0864) 22-5141.
Hotel Kurashiki ホテル倉敷
   (Business hotel: upper left, map 105. 139 rooms)
   Add: 1-1-1, Achi, Kurashiki.
   Tel: (0864) 26-6111.
Kurashiki Terminal Hotel
   倉敷ターミナルホテル
   (Business hotel: upper left, map 105. 212 rooms)
   Add: 1-7-2, Achi, Kurashiki.
   Tel: (0864) 26-1111.
Kurashiki Ivy Square
   倉敷アイビースクエア
   (Business hotel: lower right, map 105. 157 rooms)
   Add: 7-2, Honcho, Kurashiki.
   Tel: (0864) 22-0011.

2. Ryokans
Ryokan Kurashiki 旅館くらしき
   (Deluxe: lower center, map 105. 20 rooms)
   Add: 4-1, Honcho, Kurashiki.
   Tel: (0864) 22-0730.
Ryokan Tsurukata 旅館鶴形
   (Deluxe: lower center, map 105. 13 rooms)
   Add: 1-3-15, Chuo, Kurashiki.
   Tel: (0864) 24-1635.
Kurashiki Ishiyama Kadan
   くらしき石山花壇
   (First-class: outside of map 105. 80 rooms)
   Add: 1-25-23, Chuo, Kurashiki.
   Tel: (0864) 22-2222.
Misono Ryokan 御園旅館
   (Standard: outside of map 105. 22 rooms)
   Add: 3-4-1, Oimatsucho, Kurashiki.
   Tel: (0864) 22-3618.

Western Inland Sea Area Transportation

The Shinkansen stops at both Mihara and Hiroshima. Both of these cities, as well as Onomichi, are also on the Sanyo (local) Line (No. 6).

The trip from Hiroshima to Miyajima involves a short JR Sanyo (local) Line ride to Miyajima-guchi, and a boat from there to the island.

In addition to being accessible via the JR Sanyo (local) Line, Onomichi can also be reached via a short boat trip from Setoda on Ikuchijima Island, which is connected to Hiroshima and Miyajima by the STS Line hydrofoil. See the Inland Sea Cruise section below.

You can also travel between Onomichi and Kurashiki on the JR Sanyo (local) Line. The ride takes 65 minutes.

Hiroshima is the western gateway to Shikoku Island. Hiroshima (Ujina) Port is connected with JR Hiroshima Station by streetcar (30 minutes). Both steamships and hydrofoils operate between Hiroshima and Matsuyama on Shikoku. The ride takes about 3 hours by steamer and 70 minutes by hydrofoil. See No. 251 for the time-

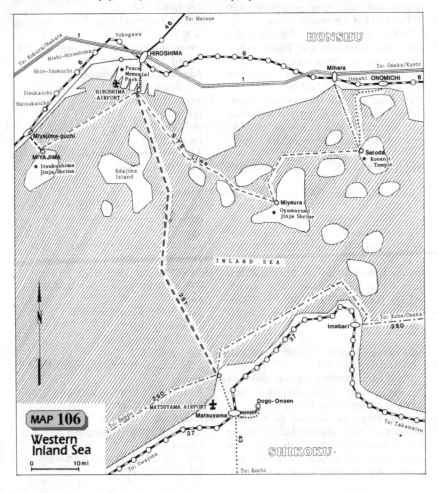

MAP 106
Western Inland Sea
0   10mi

tables of these boats, and see the Matsuyama section below for details on Matsuyama Kankoko Port.

Onomichi
尾道

This inland sea shipping center is a famous tourist attraction for the Japanese because of its lovely temples, three of which are National Treasures. The problem for foreigners is that the walking tour that the most serious Japanese visitors follow is marked only by granite sign posts with the names of the temples carved in characters. It is impossible to reproduce a map or describe in words the complicated twists and turns of the streets and alleys of this ancient town, so we have selected the best of Onomichi's temples and described a half-day walking tour.

Transportation to Onomichi

The JR Sanyo Line (all local trains) serves Onomichi. The ride to Onomichi takes 15 minutes from Mihara, 1 hour 10 minutes from Kurashiki, and 1 hour 30 minutes from Hiroshima. A new Shinkansen Station is planned for Onomichi in the near future.

Transportation in Onomichi

Onomichi has a good bus system, and several routes cater to tourists. Enter at the rear and pay as you leave. Fares vary with

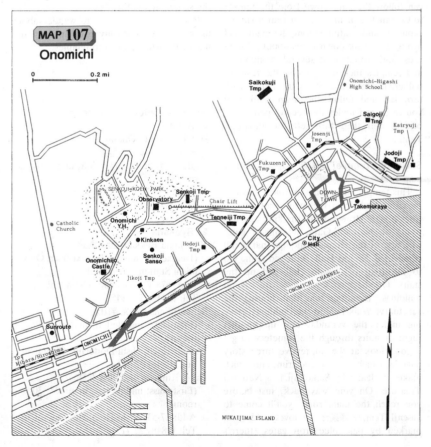

MAP 107
Onomichi

0   0.2 mi

Saikokuji Tmp

Onomichi-Higashi High School

Saigoji Tmp

Kairyuji Tmp

Josenji Tmp

Jodoji Tmp

Fukuzenji Tmp

SENKOJI-KOEN PARK

Observatory

Senkoji Tmp

Chair Lift

DOWN-TOWN

Catholic Church

Onomichi Y.H.

Kinkaen

Tenneiji Tmp

Takemuraya

City Hall

Hodoji Tmp

Onomichijo Castle

Senkoji Sanso

Jikoji Tmp

ONOMICHI CHANNEL

Shopping Arcade

Sunroute

ONOMICHI

To Mihara/Hiroshima

N

MUKAIJIMA ISLAND

the distance traveled: be sure to take a *seiri-ken* fare zone ticket when you enter.

Suggested Itinerary
Senkoji Temple 千光寺 (Upper left, map 107)

Turn right as you leave the station, and walk along Onomichi's main road. It's not pretty, but things will improve! There's an entrance to the Senkoji-Koen Park cable car to your left just as you come to the first pedestrian bridge. When you get off, follow the path to your left to Senkoji Temple. On the way, you'll pass gnarled pines and rocks on which generations of poets have carved their odes to the beauty of the Inland Sea. The temple was founded in 806, and extends out over a platform with another great view of the Inland Sea. You can follow the path down from the temple to Onomichi's main street, or return via the cable car and continue along the main road again. The walk down takes about 20 minutes and you'll pass several monuments and temples tucked in among the residential area. Once you reach the main road, turn left and follow the main road until you've passed under the second pedestrian bridge, and then turn left for Saikokuji Temple.

Saikokuji Temple 西国寺 (Upper center, map 107)

This temple has a long approach and is a bit of a climb from the main road. It features a giant straw sandal (the kind pilgrims wear) on Niomon Gate, its biggest gate. The first of the temple buildings that you'll come to is Kondo Hall, with red trim. Go to the right of Kondo Hall and up the stairs. On the next level there are several buildings, including one that houses the sanctuary. Walk behind the buildings, passing under the veranda, and up another flight of stairs through the cemetery to get a good look at the impressive three story pagoda, which also has red trim, and which makes it clear why Saikokuji is a National Treasure. On your way back, just before you reach the main road, you'll come to **Josenji Temple** 浄泉寺 , a lovely old gem, marked by pale blue iron gates (there's

another entrance on the main road).

Jodoji Temple 浄土寺 (Middle right, map 107)

Continue along the main road again. After you pass another pedestrian bridge, you'll come to a three way intersection. You'll be able to see the harbor on your right. Go up the stone steps under the railroad tracks. Jodoji Temple was founded in 616. It too is a National Treasure and features a pagoda. When you finish at Jodoji Temple, turn left just outside the gate and follow the path to **Kairyuji Temple** 海竜寺 , a small, lovely temple that houses an image of thousand-handed and thousand-eyed Kannon who can see sounds! Go back out to the main street through the entrance to Jodoji Temple, and catch the bus back to the station across the street.

If you have extra time to wander about in this lovely town, any path up from the main road will lead you to temples.

Accommodations in Onomichi
1. Hotel
Hotel Sunroute Onomichi
ホテルサンルート尾道
(Business hotel: lower left, map 107. 68 rooms)
Add: 5-3, Temmancho, Onomichi.
Tel: (0848) 25-3161.

2. Ryokans
Nishiyama Bekkan 西山別館
(Deluxe. 10 minutes by taxi from Onomichi Station. 11 rooms)
Add: 678-1, Sanbacho, Onomichi.
Tel: (0848) 37-3145.
Senkoji Sanso 千光寺山荘
(First-class: middle left, map 107. 49 rooms)
Add: 15-20, Nishi-Dodocho, Onomichi.
Tel: (0848) 22-7168.
Hotel Kinkaen ホテル金花園
(First-class: middle left, map 107. 30 rooms)
Add: 17-53, Nishi-Dodocho, Onomichi.
Tel: (0848) 22-7151.

Hiroshima

広島

This city got its name when the feudal lord Terumoto Mori built a castle here at the end of the 16th century and named it "Hiroshima"-jo (Broad Island Castle). The Mori family was followed by the Fukushima family, and then the Asanos, who, by encouraging industry, laid the foundation for the development of the castle town. On August 6, 1945, at 8:15 AM, Hiroshima was atom-bombed. The city was completely flattened in an instant, and more than 200,000 lives lost. Two years later the citizens of Hiroshima held their first Peace Festival. Its theme was: "No more Hiroshimas." It has since become an annual event to promote world peace. Now the city, with a population of 1,036,000, serves as the administrative, educational and communications center of the Chugoku district.

Outline of the City

There are four major places of interest in Hiroshima – Peace Memorial Park (middle left, map 108); Hiroshimajo Castle (upper center); Shukkeien Garden (upper center to the east of the Castle); and Hijiyama-Koen Park (lower right). The downtown section of the city is on the southern side of the east-west main street (Shopping arcades are indicated with shaded red). Many

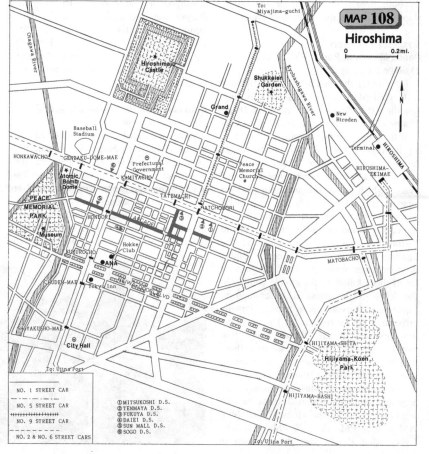

MAP **108**

Hiroshima

0   0.2mi.

NO. 1 STREET CAR
NO. 5 STREET CAR
NO. 9 STREET CAR
NO. 2 & NO. 6 STREET CARS

①MITSUKOSHI D.S.
②TENMAYA D.S.
③FUKUYA D.S.
④DAIEI D.S.
⑤SUN MALL D.S.
⑥SOGO D.S.

drinking spots and obscure cabarets are located around the eastern end of the shopping arcades. Hiroshima Prefectural Government and other governmental offices are located on the northern side of the main street. These places and JR Hiroshima Station are conveniently connected by several streetcars as explained next.

Transportation in Hiroshima

Hiroshima has eight streetcar lines. We have pictured five of them that can be used by tourists conveniently and easily.

* If you are planning to take a half-day cruise from Hiroshima to Setoda, or a sunset cruise in Hiroshima harbor (explained below), you can take either the No. 5 or No. 1 streetcar to Ujina port (the last stop on both lines). The piers for the cruise ships are a one-minute walk from Ujina.

Suggested Itinerary
Peace Memorial Park 平和記念公園
(Middle left, map 108)

Take either the No. 2 or No. 6 streetcar to Genbaku-Domu-mae 原爆ドーム前 stop (middle left, map 108). **Atomic Bomb Dome** (Ruins of Industry Promotion Hall) stands near the stop. The dome, which was part of an impressive building before the blast, serves as a grim reminder of the destructive power of an atomic bomb. **The Flame of Peace**, which is in the northern part of Peace Memorial Park, will be extinguished when all atomic weapons disappear from the earth. **Memorial Cenotaph for A-Bomb Victims** is a large vault shaped like the clay figurines found in ancient Japanese tombs. A stone chest under the vault contains a list of those killed by the atomic bomb. On the front of the chest is an epitaph in Japanese: "Repose ye in peace, for the error shall not be repeated." The cenotaph was designed by Dr. Kenzo Tange, the world renowned architect, so that those standing in front of it can see the Flame of Peace and the Atomic Bomb Dome beyond it. **Peace Memorial Museum** displays objects and photographs that illustrate the devastation caused by the atomic bomb (9:00 AM to 6:00 PM. Till 5:00 PM in winter). Every adult should visit the Museum in order to understand the era in which we live. Even though viewing the displays is an uncomfortable experience, it is one that should not be avoided. On the second floor of the adjacent Peace Memorial Hall, documentary films on the A-bomb are shown from time to time, one in English and another in Japanese.

Hiroshimajo Castle (optional) 広島城
(Upper center, map 108)

The Castle is about 0.5 miles (0.8 km.) from Peace Memorial Park and your two legs are the best means of transportation there. Hiroshimajo Castle was originally constructed in 1589 by Terumoto Mori. The donjon was registered as a National Treasure until 1945, when the bomb explosion destroyed the entire castle. The five-story donjon was reconstructed for the Hiroshima Rehabilitation Exposition in 1958. The interior is a local museum. From the top, there is a panoramic view of the entire city. Entrance to the castle grounds is free of charge.

Shukkeien Garden (optional) 縮景園
(Upper center, map 108)

Shukkeien Garden was designed in 1620 by the feudal lord Nagaakira Asano. It is situated on the Kyobashigawa River, from which water is drawn to make streams and ponds within the garden grounds. The Garden's islets and bridges, colorful carp, fantastically shaped pine trees and surrounding woods combine to give it special beauty (9:00 AM to 6:00 PM. Till 5:00 PM in

winter).

Hijiyama-Koen Park (optional) 比治山公園
(Lower right, map 108)

Unless you are in Hiroshima during cherry blossom season, you should skip this park. It is located on a small hill and there's a good view of the city from the top.

Hiroshima Municipal Baseball Stadium
(middle left, map 108) is the home of the professional Hiroshima Carps.

Hotels in Hiroshima
1. First-class Hotels
ANA Hotel Hiroshima 広島全日空ホテル
　　(Middle left, map 108. 431 rooms).
　　Add: 7-20, Nakamachi, Naka-ku,
　　Hiroshima.
　　Tel: (083) 241-1111.
Hiroshima Grand Hotel
　　広島グランドホテル
　　(Upper center, map 108. 397 rooms).
　　Add: 4-4, Hatchobori, Naka-ku,
　　Hiroshima.
　　Tel: (082) 227-1313.

2. Standard Hotels
Hotel New Hiroden ホテルニューヒロデン
　　(Upper right, map 108. 353 rooms).
　　Add: 14-9, Osugacho, Minami-ku,
　　Hiroshima.
　　Tel: (082) 263-3456.

3. Business Hotels
Hiroshima Tokyu Inn 広島東急イン
　　(Middle left, map 108. 286 rooms).
　　Add: 3-17, Komachi, Naka-ku,
　　Hiroshima.
　　Tel: (082) 244-0109.
Hiroshima Terminal Hotel
　　広島ターミナルホテル
　　(Upper right, map 108. 137 rooms).
　　Add: 2-37, Matsubaracho, Minami-ku,
　　Hiroshima.
　　Tel: (082) 262-3201.
Hokke Club Hiroshima 法華クラブ広島
　　(Middle left, map 108. 372 rooms).
　　Add: 7-7, Nakamachi, Naka-ku,
　　Hiroshima.
　　Tel: (082) 248-3371.

Inland Sea Cruises
瀬戸内海クルーズ

STS Line Half-Day Cruise　ＳＴＳライン
As pictured on map 106, the Setonaikai Steamship Company (private) operates half day cruises, from March 1 through November 30. The boat leaves Miyajima Pier at 8:40 AM and stops at Ujina Port 宇品港 in Hiroshima at 9:10 AM. The boat then makes a stop at Omishima Island so passengers can visit Oyamazumi Jinja Shrine. The boat arrives at Setoda at 1:05 PM (The fare is 6,200 yen). After visiting Kosanji Temple in Setoda 瀬戸田, you can take a connecting ferry to Mihara to catch the Shinkansen (JR's Mihara Station 三原駅 is only a five minute walk from Mihara Port), or another connecting ferry to Onomichi to continue your trip in the area.

The boat back leaves Setoda at 1:45 PM, and arrives at Hiroshima at 5:00 PM, and at Miyajima at 5:20 PM. The boat also stops at Omishima Island to visit Oyamazumi Jinja Shrine.

Oyamazumi Jinja Shrine 大山祇神社. The present buildings are 1427 reconstructions. Because several feudal lords dedicated treasures to the Shrine every time they won a battle in the Inland Sea area, the Treasure House of the Shrine has Japan's best collection of samurai armor and swords.

Kosanji Temple 耕三寺. This Temple was built by a successful businessman born in Setoda. All the buildings are modeled on different famous structures all over Japan, and the Temple itself is a museum of replicas of National Treasures. The replicas include copies of Yomeimon Gate of Toshogu Shrine; Silver Pavilion; and Yumedono Hall of Horyuji Temple.

Sunset Cruises　サンセットクルーズ
Setonaikai Steamship Co. also recently introduced a new sunset harbor cruise. It leaves from Hiroshima's Ujina Port at 6:30 PM every evening and returns at 8:50 PM. The marine scenery is especially beautiful in the sunset glow. The fare is 2,000 yen.

Miyajima

宮島

Miyajima, also called Itsukushima, is an island about 19 miles (30 km.) in circumference. It is famous for its shrine built on supports that extend into the sea. Tame deer wander about the island.

Transportation from Hiroshima

1. Hiroshima to Miyajima-guchi

Commuter trains on the JR Sanyo Line (No. 6) operate about every 15 – 30 minutes, and connect Hiroshima and Miya-jima-guchi 宮島口. There is also streetcar service between Hiroshima Station and Hiroden-Miyajima Station 広電宮島.

2. Miyajima-guchi to Miyajima

The Miyajima-guchi boat piers are a three-minute walk from the train station. JR and a private company operate frequent boat service between Miyajima-guchi and Miyajima. If you have a Japan Rail Pass, make sure you take a JR boat.

Suggested Itinerary in Miyajima

The boat piers on Miyajima Island are located about 0.5 miles (0.8 km.) north of Itsukushima Shrine. The approach to the Shrine is a pleasant promenade along the

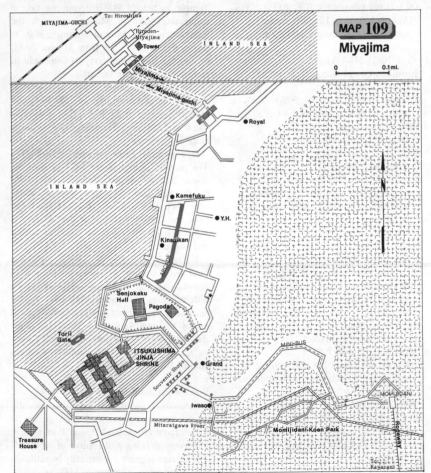

MAP 109
Miyajima

0   0.1 mi.

Inland Sea, the southern half of which is lined with stone lanterns.

Itsukushima Jinja Shrine 厳島神社 is dedicated to the three daughters of *Susano-o-no-Mikoto*, a Shinto god. The buildings, which have been rebuilt several times, consist of a Main Shrine and several minor shrines and halls – all connected by wide corridors or galleries, that are built above the sea on both sides of the Shrine. When the tide comes in, the whole edifice seems to be floating. The major buildings of the Shrine have been designated National Treasures. A vermilion torii gate rises out of the sea about 525 feet (160 m.) from the shore. This 53-foot (16 m.) tall torii gate, the largest in Japan, was erected in 1875, and is a symbol of the island. Itsukushima Jinja Shrine is open to the public from 6:30 AM to 6:00 PM. Admission is 200 yen.

Itsukushima Jinja Shrine Treasure House 厳島神社宝物館 (lower left, map 109) is just across the street from the exit of the Shrine. This modern structure contains nearly 4,000 objects, more than 130 of which have been designated National Treasures or Important Cultural Properties (9:00 AM to 5:00 PM. Admission 250 yen).

Momijidani-Koen Park 紅葉谷公園 **and Mt. Misen** 弥山. Momijidani-Koen Park (Maple Valley Park) is a quiet retreat on a hillside amid groves of maple trees. A free mini-bus operates between the two stops pictured on map 109 (The bus route is indicated with a broken red line) every 20 minutes, but because it's so lovely you should consider walking through the Park to the ropeway station pictured at the lower right of map 109. The ropeways take visitors almost to the top of Mt. Misen. The first ropeway, a small six-passenger car, connects Momijidani Station with Kayatani Station. The cars operate every 30 seconds. A larger gondola, with a capacity of 26, operates every 15 minutes from Kayatani to Shishiiwa. The real summit of Mt. Misen (1,739 feet, or 530 m.) is a 15 – 20 minute walk from Shishiiwa Station. From the gondola, and, of course, from Shishiiwa, visitors have a splendid view of Inland Sea National Park and its innumerable islets. Many wild monkeys live on Mt. Misen.

When they are playing near Shishiiwa, visitors are asked to check their handbags in complimentary lockers in Shishiiwa Station. There is no danger to visitors, but the monkeys are rather naughty. The two ropeways operate from 8:00 AM to 5:00 PM (From 9:00 AM to 4:20 PM in winter).

Senjokaku Hall 千畳閣 (middle center). When you return to the shrine area, visit Senjokaku Hall and the **Five-story Pagoda** 五重塔. These two structures are located on a hill, atop a flight of steep steps. Senjokaku Hall, or the Hall of One Thousand Mats, is an old building that Hideyoshi Toyotomi dedicated to Itsukushima Shrine in 1587. Though the original plans called for Senjokaku Hall to be painted vermilion, it was left unpainted when Hideyoshi died (9:00 AM to 5:00 PM). Nearby, a five-story pagoda soars to a height of 90 feet (27 m.). Thatched with the bark of the Japanese cypress, it is a mixture of Japanese and Chinese architectural styles. A much better view can be obtained from the small hill marked with a black star on map 109.

Ryokans in Miyajima

Iwaso 岩惣
  (Deluxe: lower center, map 109. 45 rooms)
  Add: 345, Miyajimacho, Hiroshima Prefecture.
  Tel: (08294) 4-2233.

Miyajima Grand Hotel 宮島グランドホテル
  (First-class: middle center, map 109. 61 rooms)
  Add: 362, Miyajimacho, Hiroshima Prefecture.
  Tel: (08294) 4-2411.

Kamefuku かめ福
  (First-class: middle center, map 109. 44 rooms)
  Add: 849, Miyajimacho, Hiroshima Prefecture.
  Tel: (08294) 4-2111.

Kinsuikan 錦水館
  (Standard: middle center, map 109. 26 rooms)
  Add: 1133, Miyajimacho, Hiroshima Prefecture.
  Tel: (08294) 4-2133.

Introduction to
San-in

山陰

In our opinion, this is the best of the off-the-beaten-track areas of Japan. This area, which stretches along the Japan Sea in the western part of Honshu, is blessed with a gentle climate, a rich history and lovely coastal and mountain scenery. Due to comparatively inconvenient transportation to this area, it is usually ignored by foreign tourists, who prefer to use the Shinkansen to visit cities along the Inland Sea. We urge that you give serious consideration to the San-in area when you plan your itinerary. It has much to offer.

We introduce four major destinations in this area:

(1) Matsue, a castle town that is also noted for its beautiful lakefront scenery;

(2) Izumo, the site of the famous Izumo Taisha Shrine;

(3) Hagi, an unspoiled historic city famous for its subtly gorgeous pottery; and

(4) Tsuwano, another castle town famous for a variety of handicrafts.

The following is a standard San-in itinerary, starting from Kyoto:

DAY 1. Kyoto/Okayama/Matsue

Shinkansen from Kyoto to Okayama (1 hour 20 minutes), and then a limited express on the JR Hakubi Line (No. 45) from Okayama to Matsue (2 hours 45 minutes). Tour downtown Matsue in the afternoon.

DAY 2. Matsue/Izumo/Hagi

Visit Izumo in the morning, and then catch an early afternoon JR train (No. 25) from Izumoshi to Higashi-Hagi (3 hours).

* If you want to visit the area of Matsue that features 4 – 7th century archeological

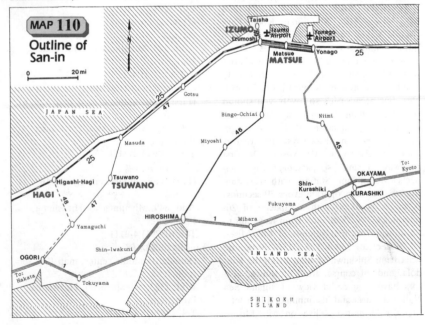

sites, allocate one more night to Matsue.

DAY 3. Hagi

Full day in Hagi. Be forewarned that once you get there you might well want to stay longer.

DAY 4. Hagi/Tsuwano

JR train from Higashi-Hagi to Masuda (No. 25), and then another JR train from Masuda to Tsuwano (No. 47). The combined train ride takes about 2 hours.

* If your time is limited, you should skip Tsuwano and take a JR bus (No. 48) from Higashi-Hagi to Ogori, and return from there to Kyoto by the Shinkansen, or proceed to other destinations.

DAY 5. Tsuwano/Ogori

A JR train to Ogori (No. 47), and then on to your next destination.

You can combine a San-in trip with an Inland Sea trip quite easily, for a thoroughly enjoyable itinerary.

Matsue is very much a water-oriented city. Located near, but not on, the Japan Sea, it is situated at the conjunction of Nakaumi Lagoon and Lake Shinjiko. Matsue is probably most familiar to non-Japanese as the first Japanese home of Lafcadio Hearn (Yakumo Koizumi), the 19th century's foremost interpreter of Japan to the West. This small, graceful city is also a rich repository of archeological treasures.

Transportation to Matsue

See No. 45 for trains to Matsue from Okayama. You can see Mt. Daisen on the right after about 2 hours, as the train approaches Yonago. See No. 22 for trains to Higashi-Hagi, and No. 46 for trains to Hiroshima.

Izumo Airport is served by flights from Tokyo, Osaka and Fukuoka. Buses run between Izumo Airport and Matsue Onsen Station 松江温泉駅 (40 minutes – middle left of map 111).

Transportation in Matsue

The best way to get around Matsue is on the city's excellent bus system. The main bus terminal is located at the train station. Stops 1 and 2 are right in front of the station, and Stops 3, 4 and 5 are on the adjacent traffic island. Enter through the rear door, be sure to take a *seiri-ken* fare zone ticket, and exit from the front.

Places of Interest in Downtown Matsue

Matsuejo Castle 松江城 (Upper left, map 111)

Take any bus from either Stop No. 1 or No. 2 at Matsue Station. The ride to Kenchomae Stop takes about 10 minutes. When you get off the bus, walk to the north, past the modern municipal buildings. The entrance to the Castle compound is on your left.

You'll soon come to Kounkaku, the distinctive, Western-style building that houses the **Matsue Cultural Museum**. Kounkaku was built in 1903 in honor of the Meiji Emperor, and has served as a museum since 1973. It exhibits all sorts of documents and implements of historical interest (8:30 AM to 5:00 PM).

Matsuejo Castle was built in 1611 by Yoshiharu Horio. The donjon (reconstructed in 1642), and a few of the other old structures still stand. The donjon is 98 ft. (30 m.) tall, and the view from its top floor, of Lake Shinjiko and the city, with the mountains in the distance, is fantastic. The lower floors have interesting displays of helmets, armor, swords, screens and scrolls (8:30 AM to 5:00 PM).

Lake Shinjiko

Koizumi Yakumo Memorial Museum
小泉八雲記念館 (Upper left, map 111)

When you leave the donjon, walk to the northern exit of the castle grounds, following the curves of the path. Cross the moat, turn right at the traffic signal, and follow the moat as it curves around. The Koizumi Yakumo Memorial Museum is on your left, across the street from a bus parking lot. It is the first in a long line of traditional buildings – the remnants of the Shiominawate quarter where high-ranking samurai once lived.

Lafcadio Hearn arrived in Matsue in 1890 to teach English, and fell seriously ill early in 1891. Setsu Koizumi, a local woman who nursed him, became his wife when he regained his health. Hearn remained in Matsue for only 15 months, but loved this city and recorded his impressions of it in several of his essays. Hearn had a long and distinguished career in Japan as an editor and a teacher, and his works helped to introduce Japan to the West. He became a Japanese citizen and took the name Yakumo Koizumi. The Memorial Museum provides foreign visitors with English language brochures, which help explain the extensive collection of Hearn memorabilia (8:30 AM to 5:00 PM. Admission 150 yen).

The Koizumi Residence 小泉八雲旧居 (optional) is next to the Memorial Museum (9:00 AM to 4:30 PM. Admission 100 yen. Another 100 yen for an English language pamphlet). Hearn lived in this house for five months in 1891. Visitors can only enter two rooms, but they have a wonderful view of the garden, which is the one Hearn described in "In a Japanese Garden," one of the essays included in his *Glimpses of Unfamiliar Japan*.

Tanabe Art Museum 田部美術館 (optional), next door to the Hearn Residence, displays ceramics and tea ceremony utensils along with calligraphy, paintings and other precious antiques. Local woodblock prints are also occasionally displayed (9:00 AM to 5:00 PM. Closed on Mondays).

Samurai Residence 武家屋敷

Next door to the Tanabe Museum, this typical feudal-era samurai residence was built in 1730 by the Shiomi family, the chief retainers of the Matsudaira daimyo. Today it preserves and displays objects that illustrate everyday life in the warrior class (8:30 AM to 5:00 PM. Admission 150 yen).

Meimeian Tea House 明々庵

Turn left when you leave the Samurai Residence and walk to the next crosswalk and traffic signal. Turn left, walk past the first intersecting street, and then past 3 houses on your left. Go up the stone steps on your left. There are no signs in English. At the top of the steps, if you make a sharp left you'll come to a gravelled area that has a spectacular view of Matsuejo Castle donjon. The original Meimeian was designed by and built for Lord Fumai Matsudaira in 1779. It was rebuilt in 1928 and restored in 1966, to celebrate the 150th anniversary of the Lord's death. Meimeian is a gem. It's quiet, has a beautiful garden and is the perfect place to relax in soothing surroundings (9:00 AM to 5:00 PM. Admission 150 yen).

To get back to downtown Matsue from Meimeian, follow the moat, crossing it at the first bridge you come to, until it ends, and then walk around the corner to a large bus stop called Kenmin Kaikan-mae. Many different bus lines stop here. Use Conversation Card 5 to get help finding a bus headed toward Matsue Station.

Suggestions for Late Afternoon and Evening Strolls in Matsue

Natives and visitors alike agree that Lake Shinjiko at sunset is Matsue's most spectacular natural asset. Among the places you might want to check on an early morning or sunset stroll of the city are the following:

Matsue Ohashi Bridge 松江大橋 is the best place from which to view the beauties of Lake Shinjiko at sunset.

Kyomise Arcade 京店アーケード (pictured in shaded red on map 111) is the center of downtown Matsue.

There is a group of more than 10 temples in the **Teramachi** 寺町 area (lower center, map 111). These modest gems are all small, neat and clean, and have not been exploited or spoiled as "tourist attractions."

Itinerary for An Extra Day in Matsue

If you stay only one night in Matsue, you should ignore this itinerary, which includes a visit to a traditional paper-making village, an excavation site and archeological museum and two of Matsue's most famous shrines. The distances covered are great, and the bus service relatively infrequent.

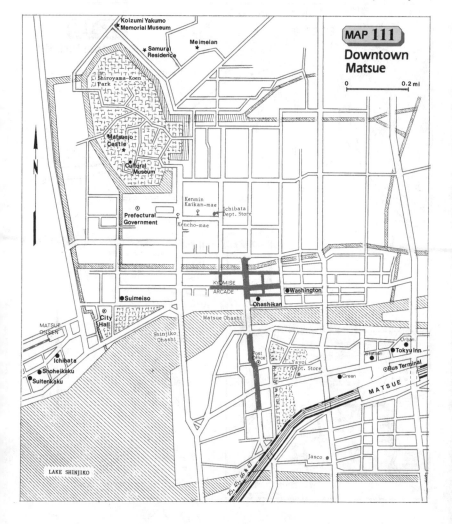

It's important to remember to check return schedules every time you get off a bus. The visits to the shrines also involve a fair amount of walking.

Abe Eishiro Memorial Museum 阿部栄四郎記念館 in Washi-no-Sato Paper Making Village

The bus trip from Matsue Station (Platform No. 3) to Bessho 別所 (the terminus of the bus route) takes 36 minutes. The only buses from Matsue that will get you to Bessho while the Abe Eishiro Memorial

Museum is open leave at 8:15 AM, 9:55 AM, and 12:30 PM.

When you get off the bus, walk straight ahead along the town's main road. Walk past the first cross street, and then past a few more houses and a tiny grocery store on your left. Turn left at the next intersecting road, and walk down the slope to the Memorial Museum, which is the large white building with dark gray tiles.

The Memorial Museum has exhibits on Abe's life, and displays paper making implements as well as samples of the master's

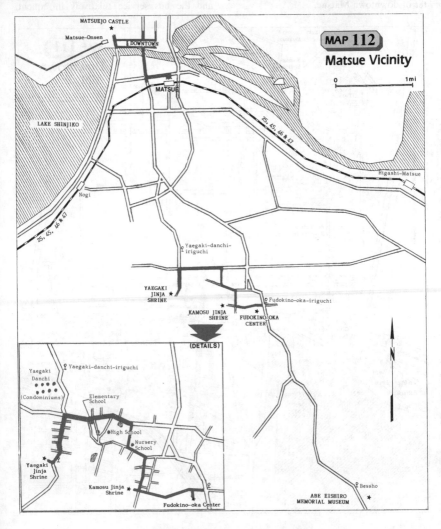

MAP 112
Matsue Vicinity

MATSUEJO CASTLE
Matsue-Onsen
DOWNTOWN
MATSUE
LAKE SHINJIKO
Nogi
25, 45, 46 & 47
Higashi-Matsue
Yaegaki-danchi-iriguchi
YAEGAKI JINJA SHRINE
Fudokino-oka-iriguchi
KAMOSU JINJA SHRINE
FUDOKINO-OKA CENTER
(DETAILS)

Yaegaki Danchi (Condominiums)
Yaegaki-danchi-iriguchi
Elementary School
High School
Nursery School
Yaegaki Jinja Shrine
Kamosu Jinja Shrine
Fudokino-oka Center
Bessho
ABE EISHIRO MEMORIAL MUSEUM

craft. The Memorial Museum also has two videos that tell the story of Eishiro Abe's life. Even though they are only in Japanese, they are not too hard to follow. Eishiro Abe was born in 1902. He used paper making methods first introduced into Japan 1,200 years ago, refining them to a high level of sophistication. Abe, who was named a Living National Treasure in 1968, elevated this craft to an art (9:00 AM to 4:30 PM. Admission 500 yen).

On your way back to the bus stop, you can stop in at the Abe workshop (owned by his son) to see the paper being made. After you pass the grocery on your right, you'll see a traffic mirror on your left. The workshop, a venerable wooden building, is the second building on your left after the traffic mirror. The workers are very gracious about inviting you in to watch the paper making process.

Fudokino-oka Center 風土記の丘センター

The Matsue-bound buses from Bessho stop at Fudokino-oka on the way back to the city. The bus stop is called Fudokino-oka-iriguchi 風土記の丘入口. The trip from Bessho to Fudokino-oka takes about 15 minutes.

An ancient state called Izumo was centered in what are now the southern suburbs of Matsue. Many tumuli of 4th-7th century *kofun* are scattered through the area. The Shimane Prefectural government has established Fudokino-oka Center to preserve and protect the area's precious cultural artifacts. The Fudokino-oka Center building, itself modeled on the ancient tumuli of Izumo, displays various ancient implements and large *haniwa* clay figures that were extracted from tumuli in the area. The observatory on the roof top gives you an excellent opportunity to observe two tumuli in the Center grounds. The grounds also encompass a restored 6th century dwelling and the foundations of a medieval samurai house (9:00 AM to 5:00 PM. Admission to the Museum is 130 yen).

Kamosu Jinja Shrine 神魂神社

When you leave the Fudokino-oka Museum grounds, turn left. When the road deadends, you've arrived at the National Treasure Kamosu Jinja Shrine. Climb up the stone steps. The Shrine is constructed in the *Taisha-zukuri* style, the oldest known architectural style of Japan. The walls and ceilings of the Shrine are ornamented with beautiful paintings.

If you want to return to Matsue from Kamosu Jinja Shrine, go back to Fudokino-oka-iriguchi bus stop. The buses back to Matsue leave about once an hour.

Yaegaki Jinja Shrine 八重垣神社

Thirty minute walk from Kamosu Jinja Shrine. Follow the route on Map 112. This Shrine was the subject of one of Lafcadio Hearn's essays on the Matsue area. The gods enshrined here are believed to have special influence in matters of romance. After you've finished looking at the Shrine, walk to the left and behind it, to the mysterious wood with its miniature shrines and quiet pond. Here you're sure to understand why Lafcadio Hearn found Japan so enchanting.

There's a bus stop just outside Yaegaki Jinja Shrine, but service back to the city is infrequent. If the schedule here doesn't look promising, walk to Yaegaki-danchi-iriguchi bus stop. Buses for Matsue leave from here much more frequently.

Accommodations in Matsue
1. Hotels

Matsue Tokyu Inn 松江東急イン
(Business hotel: lower right, map 111. 181 rooms)
Add: 590, Asahicho, Matsue.
Tel: (0852) 27-0109.

Matsue Washington Hotel
松江ワシントンホテル
(Business hotel: middle center, map 111. 156 rooms)
Add: 2-22, Higashi-Honcho, Matsue.
Tel: (0852) 22-4111.

Green Hotel Matsue
グリーンホテル松江
(Business hotel: lower center, map 111. 160 rooms)
Add: 493-1, Asahicho, Matsue.
Tel: (0852) 27-3000.

2. Ryokans

Hotel Ichibata　ホテル一畑
　　(First-class: lower left, map 111.
　　137 rooms)
　　Add: 30, Chidoricho, Matsue.
　　Tel: (0852) 22-0188.
Suimeiso　水明荘
　　(Standard: middle left,
　　map 111. 50 rooms)
　　Add: 26, Nishichamachi,
　　Matsue. Tel: (0852) 26-3311.
Ohashikan　大橋館
　　(Standard: middle center,
　　map 111. 29 rooms)
　　Add: 40, Suetsugi-Honcho,
　　Matsue.
　　Tel: (0852) 21-5168.
Suitenkaku　水天閣
　　(Standard: lower left, map 111.
　　66 rooms)
　　Add: 39, Chidoricho, Matsue.
　　Tel: (0852) 21-4910.
Shoheikaku　松平閣
　　(Standard: lower left, map 111.
　　14 rooms)
　　Add: 38, Chidoricho, Matsue.
　　Tel: (0852) 23-8000.

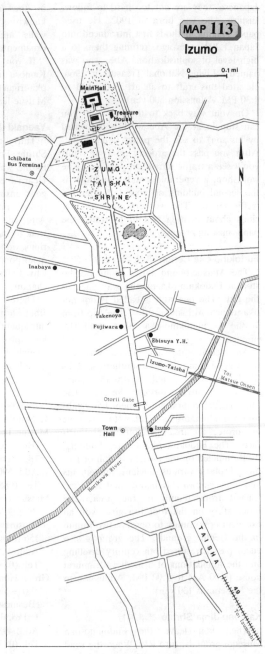

MAP 113

Izumo

0   0.1 mi

Main Hall

Treasure House

Ichibata Bus Terminal

IZUMO TAISHA SHRINE

N

Inabaya

Takenoya

Fujiwara

Ebisuya Y.H.

Izumo-Taisha

To: Matsue Onsen

Otorii Gate

Town Hall

Izumo

Horikawa River

TAISHA

49

To: Izumoshi

Izumo 出雲

Izumo Taisha is the oldest shrine location in Japan. Legend has it that it is the place to which the Shinto god *Okuninushi-no-Mikoto* retired after introducing medicine, agriculture and the art of farming to Japan. Most of the present structures were built in 1874. Nearby Cape Hinomisaki provides scenic views of the Japan Sea. It is recommended only for seascape enthusiasts. If you are planning to take a train between Matsue and Hagi or Tsuwano, you'll see sea coasts just as beautiful from the train windows.

Transportation to Taisha 大社

Take the JR San-in Line (No. 25) between Matsue and Izumoshi, and then the JR Taisha Line (No. 49) between Izumoshi and Taisha. There is also a private rail connection, on the Ichibata Railway, between Matsue Onsen (lower left, map 111) and Izumo-Taisha, via Kawato.

You can visit Izumo from Matsue in a half-day excursion, or you can stop here on your way from Matsue to Hagi.

Izumo Taisha Shrine 出雲大社

When you come out of the JR Station at Taisha (lower right, map 113), you'll see the mountains in the distance. The street is unusually wide and lined with pine trees. It's about a 15 minute walk to the Shrine. A giant torii marks the entrance to the Shrine. Once inside the precincts of the Shrine, the approach to the Main Building is even more impressive. The path has a lovely wooded garden on both sides, with a large number of magnificent pine trees.

The Shrine's Treasure House is open to the public.

There are several noodle shops on the main street. They feature homemade *wari-go-soba*, the specialty buckwheat noodles of the area. Any of them is a good place to stop for a delicious and economical snack.

Cape Hinomisaki 日御碕 (optional)

The stop for the bus to Cape Hinomisaki is at Ichibata Bus Terminal (upper left, map 113). Buses operate about once an hour to the Cape. The trip to Cape Hinomisaki takes about 25 minutes.

Most of the bus ride is along a coast road with beautiful views of the Japan Sea. When the bus turns onto the coast road, you'll be able to see a rocky, pine-clad islet with its own small torii.

When you get off the bus at the Cape Hinomisaki terminus, the entrance to Hinomisaki Jinja Shrine is just to your right. After you explore the Shrine, exit from the gate to the left of its main building and walk down to the water. The pier for glass boat tours is there. From April 29 – September 30, you can take one of these half hour tours. If you plan to continue on foot to the Cape, turn right and follow the path up the hill. The walk to the Cape's famous Lighthouse takes about 10 minutes. The first part is up a wooded hill with lovely views of the Sea. When you reach the commercial street with souvenir and snack shops, bear to your left. Every time there's a choice, bear left. If you feel adventurous or just hungry, try the grilled squid that's for sale in almost every one of the shops along this road.

The **Cape Hinomisaki Lighthouse** is open to visitors from 8:30 AM to 4:00 PM. Eighty yen buys you the privilege of climbing to the top. You have to check your shoes at the entrance, and the attendants there will also kindly hold your bags for you while you make the 127 ft. (38.8 m.) trek to the top. Opened in 1961, this 460,000 candle power lighthouse is Asia's tallest. The view of the Japan Sea is spectacular.

When you descend from the Lighthouse, you can stroll around the walkways laid out along the Cape.

Hagi

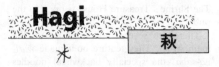

萩

Located on the Japan Sea side of Yamaguchi Prefecture near the southern tip of the main island of Honshu, Hagi is a lovely traditional castle town and port. It is surrounded by hills on the east, west and south. Most of the Hagi's tourist attractions are situated on an island surrounded by the Hashimotogawa River, the Matsumotogawa River and the Japan Sea. The Mori family ruled Hagi for thirteen generations, and eventually generated a revolt against the

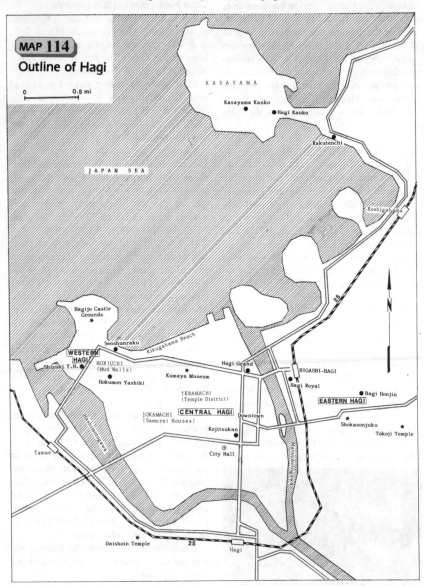

MAP 114
Outline of Hagi

0   0.5 mi

KASAYAMA

Kasayama Kanko

Hagi Kanko

Rakutenchi

JAPAN SEA

Koshigahama

Hagijo Castle Grounds

Senshunraku   Kikugahama Beach

WESTERN HAGI

Shizuki Y.H.   HORIUCHI (Mud Walls)   Hagi Grand   HIGASHI-HAGI

Hokumon Yashiki   Kumaya Museum   Hagi Royal

TERAMACHI (Temple District)   Hagi Honjin

JOKAMACHI (Samurai Houses)   CENTRAL HAGI   Downtown   EASTERN HAGI

Kojitsukan   Shokasonjuku   Tokoji Temple

Tamae

City Hall

Daishoin Temple   25   Hagi

Tokugawas. The late 19th century Meiji Restoration and modernization of Japan were initiated by young Mori samurais, who organized the nation's first farmers' militia, and who worked to break down caste distinctions, activities that were extremely revolutionary even at the end of the feudal era. Hagi is also famous for its 375-year tradition of pottery making. *Hagi-yaki* ware is distinguished by its subtle pastel colors and sophisticated glazes. Tea ceremony masters rank *Hagi-yaki* second only to the austere *Raku-yaki* of Kyoto. There are scores of pottery shops throughout the city.

You can follow the itinerary outlined below in a busy one and a half days or leisurely two days. If you have only one day in Hagi, you should be able to visit the town's Jokamachi (Central Hagi), Horiuchi and Castle areas (Western Hagi), and, if you are lucky, squeeze in visits to Teramachi (Central Hagi) and Tokoji Temple (Eastern Hagi).

Transportation to Hagi

See No. 25 for JR trains from Matsue, and No. 48 for the JR bus to Ogori. When you travel from Matsue (or Izumoshi) to Higashi-Hagi 東萩, be sure to sit on the right hand side of the car. The coast views and light playing on the sea are beautiful.

Transportation in Hagi

The best way to get around this compact city is by bicycle. There are rental shops scattered throughout the city.

Takasugi House

Central Hagi

Jokamachi 城下町

Kumaya Art Museum 熊谷美術館 (upper left, map 115). The museum has no sign in English, but its entrance is marked by a big black metal gate that looks something like an elongated torii. The museum's impressive collection of breathtakingly beautiful scrolls, screens and pottery is housed in traditional Hagi warehouses. You can also walk around and observe the former residence of the Kumayas, who handled all the commercial transactions of the Mori family. The Kumayas were proponents of Western technology and sponsors of the Hagi-based revolutionary movement. Admission 500 yen. Hours 9:00 AM to 5:00 PM.

Kikuya House 菊屋家住宅 (upper left, map 115). Built in 1604, this was the residence of a wealthy merchant family. Walking through this house (with your shoes safely stowed in a plastic bag) will give you a good idea of family life in the Edo period. The garden is beautiful. There is a wonderful museum behind the residence, with old maps of the Hagi area, beautiful scrolls and screens, and gorgeous kimono and *Hagi-yaki* pottery. Admission 350 yen. Hours 9:00 AM to 5:00 PM.

After a visit to the Kikuya Residence, you should stroll or cycle through Jokamachi. The traditional whitewash and lattice architecture adds to the charm of the neighborhood. The camellias and *natsu mikan* (Japanese 'mandarin' oranges) for which Hagi is famous grace many of the gardens in this area, and often, to the delight of passersby, hang over the whitewashed walls that surround the gardens. Other (optional) points of interest in this area include: **Takasugi House** 高杉晋作旧宅 (upper left, map 115). Shinsaku Takasugi learned the philosophy of Shoin Yoshida at his local school. After the teacher's execution, Takasugi inherited his spiritual mantle. He created the *Kiheitai*, a military group, and overthrew the Choshu conservatives, moving the state toward modernization. He died shortly before the Meiji Restoration. No admission charge; **Enseiji Temple** 円政寺 (upper left, map

115). Lovely small garden and temple. A tiny stable with a wooden statue of a horse is the temple's most distinctive feature; **Kido House** 木戸孝允旧宅 (upper left, map 115). Koin Kido worked for modernization of Japan through diplomatic channels, meeting with leaders of other states. His family was of samurai rank, and traditionally served as physicians for the feudal lord. You can look into many of the rooms of the house. Lovely garden, with cacti. No admission charge. Hours: 7:00 AM to 6:00 PM, April – October, 8:00 AM to 5:00 PM, November – March.

If you have an extra hour or two:

We suggest that you explore the many lovely temples in Hagi's **Teramachi** 寺町 section (upper center, map 115). Most Japanese tourists pass these peaceful places by, but they are full of unexpected surprises and delights. An early morning or sunset stroll is the perfect way to enjoy them.

Baizoin Temple 梅蔵院: A charming statue of a relaxed, seated Buddha, and a collection of smaller Buddha statues.

Kyotokuji Temple 亨徳寺 : Much larger. Lovely garden.

Samurai House

Tokoji Temple

Kaichoji Temple 海潮寺 : An impressive two-story gate with a veranda around its second floor.

Chojuji Temple 長寿寺 : A large cemetery surrounded by whitewashed mud walls.

Hofukuji Temple 保福寺 : An old wooden building. Lots of bibbed Jizo statues.

Kounji Temple 広雲寺 : Wooden trimmed temple, jizos, stone memorials.

Jonenji Temple 常念仏 : Note the carvings on the gate. It was transferred here from the Jurakudai Palace of Kyoto, which was built by Hideyoshi and dismantled by Ieyasu.

We've only mentioned a few of the temples in this neighborhood. Have fun exploring on your own!

Ishii Museum 石井茶碗美術館 (upper center, map 115). Located in the midst of Hagi's shopping arcade (shaded red on map 115), this tiny, second-floor museum has no English sign, but is distinguished by its typical Hagi facade of whitewash and lattice. It's sandwiched between a florist and a handbag shop. Push the bell on the first floor as you enter. The collection is a good demonstration of why the restrained beauty of *Hagi-yaki* is so cherished by devotees of the tea ceremony. Admission 300 yen. Hours: 9:00 AM to 5:00 PM. Closed on Wednesdays, December through March.

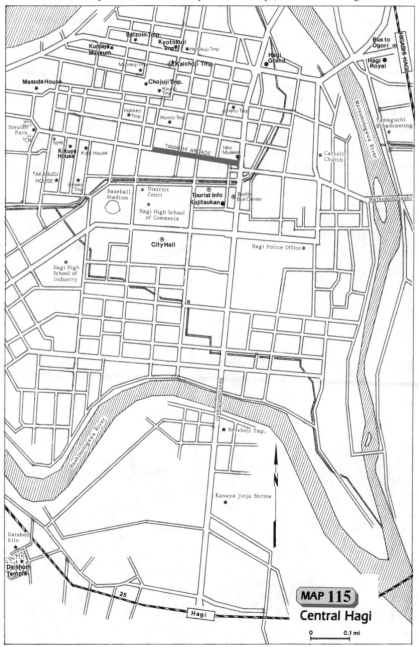

MAP **115**
Central Hagi

0   0.1 mi

Western Hagi

Horiuchi 堀内

Horiuchi was the residential area of high-ranking samurais. Old whitewashed walls, constructed of stone and tiles and held together with mud, still stand in front of most houses in this area.

Masuda House 益田家物見矢倉 (middle right, map 116). Surrounded by a high wall, this was the site of the residence of the Prime Minister of the State Government. **Sufu House** 周布家 (middle right, map 116) is a marvelous old wooden samurai residence. You can enter and look around. The beach is only one block away here, and you may not be able to resist the temptation to wander over there for a few minutes. **Toida Masuda House Walls** 問田益田家旧宅土塀 (middle center, map 116). These are the longest mud walls in Hagi. Typical of the Horiuchi samurai residence area.

Shizuki Kiln 指月窯 (middle right, map 116). If you have time to visit only one *Hagi-yaki* pottery shop, this should be it. For most, this will be just a place to browse: the pieces on display are lovely, but many of them are quite expensive. The kiln is in the adjacent building, and the potters will let you in to observe.

Fukuhara Gate 福原家門 (middle center, map 116) is a beautiful wooden gate. **Tomb of Tenjuin** (middle center, map 116), a memorial to Terumoto Mori, founder of the Choshu Clan and his wife, is a quiet and very romantic place.

Masuda House

Hagijo Castle Area 萩城

Hagijo Castle was built in 1604 by Teru-moto Mori, and destroyed in 1874 as a demonstration of loyalty to the Meiji government. Huge stonewalls and spacious moats are all that remain, but they will give you some idea of the grand scale of the castle. The castle ruins are now part of Shizuki-Koen Park.

Mori House 旧厚狭毛利家萩屋敷長屋 (middle center, map 116). This row house-type structure housed samurai foot soldiers and is 16.5 ft. (5 m.) wide and 170 ft. (51.5 m.) long. Admission 200 yen. Hours: 8:00 AM to 6:30 PM (4:30 PM in winter). The ticket you purchase here will also gain you admission to the Castle ruins.

Christian Cemetery キリシタン殉教者墓地 (middle center, map 116). A forgotten corner of the castle area with lots of atmosphere.

Inside the Castle Grounds (middle center, map 116): **Shizukiyama Jinja Shrine** 指月山神社. Nestled against the mountain, this Shrine was built in 1879. Its fine, mellowed wood makes it seem less austere than many other shrines. **Fukuhara House** 福原家. This was the residence of the Fukuhara family, clan administrative officers. **Hananoe Tea House** 花江茶亭. A beautiful garden and lovely tea house. No admission charge. The attendants will make tea for you in the thatched roof building for 300 yen. A great way to enjoy the tea ceremony in extremely peaceful and informal surroundings. When you leave the Tea House, climb the steps to the top of the Castle walls. At the top, the moat is at your feet, the mountains are both in front of and behind you, and Hagi Bay, with the Japan Sea beyond it, is to your right. There is also a path that goes the more than 2,400 feet to the top of the mountain, for an even better view. It's a hard 20-minute climb.

If you're a pottery enthusiast:

The following are pottery centers that just can't be included in a leisurely sightseeing itinerary, but which will be of interest if you're really interested in *Hagi-yaki* (all middle center, map 116).

Shogetsu Kiln 松月窯. The buildings of this kiln and pottery shop are hidden from the street by shrubbery. You can observe the potters at work, and the prices in the adjacent shop seem relatively reasonable.

Hagijo Kiln 萩城窯. Located in the Castle compound, this is another good place to observe the potters at work. The shop has a large selection.

Hagi Ceramic Center 萩焼陶芸会館. A five minute walk from the castle, this museum is housed in a large, two-story modern building. The first floor has a huge souvenir shop. The museum on the second floor exhibits many pieces of antique *Hagi-yaki,* as well as modern examples of the ceramic art. Admission 300 yen. Pay at the counter on the first floor.

If you have time:

On the other side of the Hashimotogawa River, **Daishoin Temple** 大照院 (lower left, map 115) is about a 10 – 15 minute bicycle trip from the Hagijo Castle area. Cross the river over either the Tokiwabashi Bridge or Hashimotobashi Bridge. Be careful on the busy road. There is no English sign for Daishoin Temple. The Temple foliage is spectacular in the fall, as is the garden in spring. The long approach to the temple is lined with 603 lanterns. Admission 100 yen. Hours: 9:00 AM to 4:30 PM. You can also take the train from Higashi-Hagi to Hagi and walk to Daishoin Temple from there. The local trains between these two stations run at most once an hour.

Eastern Hagi

Tokoji Temple 東光寺 (Lower right, map 117)

Tokoji Temple, the Mori family temple, is about a 10 – 15 minute bicycle ride from downtown Hagi. It was founded in 1691 by Yoshinari, the third Mori lord. Some of the Temple structures date from the 17th century. Hours 8:30 AM to 5:30 PM. You pay the 100 yen admission after you walk through the Temple's first gate. The Temple's impressive, three story main gate, Sanmon, is straight ahead. The Temple's Main Hall houses several gaudy images of Buddha. Behind the Main Building (follow the arrows) are the lanterns for which Tokoji Temple is so famous. Row upon row of lanterns, the smell of the pine trees, the deep, quiet peace of a natural setting: a thoroughly Japanese atmosphere. At the end of the lantern area are ten large stone monuments that commemorate five Mori lords and their ladies.

If you have time:

The additional attractions in the area around Tokoji Temple relate in one way or another to Shoin Yoshida. Yoshida, a pre-Meiji era philosopher, educator and revolutionary, who was born in 1830, was executed by the Tokugawa Shogunate at the age of 29. His influence, however, lived on and shaped the Meiji era. His execution fired the revolutionary movement in the Hagi area, and spurred Takasugi and the rebel faction to take over the conservative officials of the Mori family. **Tamaki House** 玉木文之進旧宅 was home of Shoin's uncle and teacher. The path leading to the **Tomb of Shoin Yoshida** 吉田松陰の墓 is upslope and the climb up is a hard one. You'll pass a grove of *natsu mikan* on your left and a field on your right. At the top of the hill is a statue of Yoshida and his favorite students. To the right is the site of Yoshida's birthplace. The next stop along this route is the **Ito House** 伊藤博文旧宅. Ito, another of Shoin's students, became the first Meiji Prime Minister. There's a statue of Ito, and his thatched house is to the right of the statue. Return to the main street, and follow it until it ends. On your right will be the entrance to the **Shoin Jinja Shrine** 松陰神社. Follow the path through the torii gate, past the stone fence and lanterns, straight back to the Shrine. As you walk away from the Shrine, turn right and follow the stone path. You'll come to **Yoshida House** 吉田家. The next structure on your

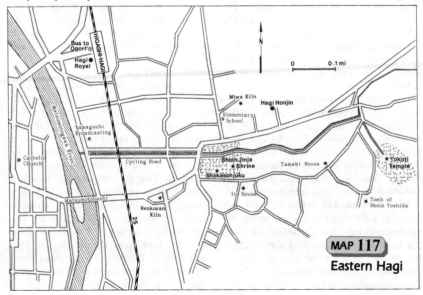

MAP 117
Eastern Hagi

left will be the **Shokasonjuku** 松下村塾, Yoshida's school. On your way out of the Shrine grounds, the **Shoin History Museum** 松陰誕生地 will be on your right. Admission 300 yen. Dioramas tell the story of Yoshida's life. No English explanation.

Ryokans in Hagi

Hagi Grand Hotel 萩グランドホテル
   (First-class: upper center, map 115. 84 rooms)
   Add: 25, Kohagicho, Hagi.
   Tel: (08382) 5-1211.

Hokumon Yashiki 北門屋敷
   (First-class: middle center, map 116. 32 rooms)
   Add: 210, Horiuchi, Hagi.
   Tel: (08382) 2-7521.

Hagi Honjin 萩本陣
   (First-class: middle center, map 117. 99 rooms)
   Add: 385-8, Chinto, Hagi.
   Tel: (08382) 2-5252.

Senshunraku 千春楽
   (First-class: middle center, map 116. 55 rooms)
   Add: Kikugahama, Horiuchi, Hagi.
   Tel: (08382) 2-0326.

Hagi Kanko Hotel 萩観光ホテル
   (First-class: upper center, map 114. 86 rooms)
   Add: 1189, Chinto, Hagi.
   Tel: (08382) 5-0211.

Rakutenchi 楽天地
   (First-class: upper center, map 114. 92 rooms)
   Add: 6509, Chinto, Hagi.
   Tel: (08382) 5-0121.

Hagi Royal Hotel 萩ロイヤルホテル
   (Standard: upper right, map 115. 52 rooms)
   Add: 3000-5, Chinto, Hagi.
   Tel: (08382) 5-9595.

Kojitsukan 好日館
   (Standard: middle center, map 115. 30 rooms)
   Add: 78, Tohicho, Hagi.
   Tel: (08382) 2-0868.

Kasayama Kanko Hotel 笠山観光ホテル
   (Standard: upper center, map 114. 34 rooms)   Add: 1172, Chinto, Hagi.
   Tel: (08382) 5-0311.

Tsuwano

津和野

Perched in the mountains, the 700 year old castle town of Tsuwano is often referred to as the Kyoto of San-in. A great many traditional samurai homes are preserved in Tsuwano. Tsuwano is also famous for the colorful carp that swim in the streams that line the town's streets. Spring and early summer are lovely in this tiny mountain town, and irises bloom all along the streams the carp swim in.

Transportation to Tsuwano

The JR Yamaguchi Line (No. 47) serves Tsuwano. The ride to Tsuwano takes about 1 hour from Ogori, and 3 hours 20 minutes from Matsue. When you travel from Hagi to Tsuwano, you have to change trains (from No. 22 to No. 47) at Masuda Station.

Transportation in Tsuwano

Without a doubt, the best ways to get around in Tsuwano are on foot or by bicycle. Many bike rental shops are scattered throughout the town.

Tsuwano Walking Tour Itinerary

Start your sightseeing at **Tsuwano Catholic Church** 津和野カソリック教会 (middle right, map 118), evidence of what was once a strong Christian influence in Tsuwano. In an effort to completely obliterate Christianity, which had gained many adherents in various parts of Kyushu, the Tokugawa Shogunate dispersed Japan's Christians around the country, isolating and torturing them in unfamiliar and hostile environments to force them to recant. A group of Nagasaki Christians was exiled to Tsuwano. This tatami-matted church, built in 1931, is modeled on Nagasaki's Oura Tenshudo Church.

Once you leave the church, you'll be in the heart of Tsuwano's most famous and most scenic area: the distinctive whitewashed and lattice-patterned buildings are the town's signature.

Bear to your right and go through the

large torii gate. Miei Jinja Shrine, which is located on the lovely Tsuwanogawa River, will be straight in front of you. **Taikodani Inari Jinja Shrine** 太鼓谷稲成神社 (middle center, map 118) is nearby. Enter the approach to the Shrine through the first of the 1,174 closely ranked red torii gates that make a tunnel up the steep mountain slope. Climbing, for the 10 minutes it takes to reach the Shrine, through torii after torii is an amazing experience. The Shrine itself is a relatively large complex, trimmed in the same bright red of the torii gates.

Walk through the Shrine compound, and down the slope on the other side, which will lead you to a chair lift that will take you, in 5 minutes, to the mountain top **Tsuwanojo Castle Grounds** 津和野城跡 483 ft. (127 m.) above the town. When you get off the lift, follow the path through the woods for about 10 minutes, to the Eastern Gate entrance to the Castle ruins. The view from the summit is fantastic: the river and town below and terraced rice paddies and mountains in the distance. From this marvelous vantage point you can easily understand why the *daimyo* would choose this as the site of his castle; you'll also understand how sitting at the top of one's world like this could reinforce an opinion of self-importance and superiority. The view from the lift on the way down is also quite spectacular.

Dento Kogeisha 津和野伝統工芸舎 (middle center, map 118): The workers here, who make paper according to methods more than 1,000 years old, are quite nice about letting visitors observe. The Center has a large shop. Hours 8:00 AM to 5:30 PM (5:00 PM in winter). Closed Fridays December through February. There is no admission charge. The entrance of **Jingasa** 陣笠 is back off the street, past the bakery. Admission 250 yen, which you pay after you go through the door on your right. Hours 8:00 AM to 5:00 PM. This two story museum displays many historical artifacts, such as armor, guns, lacquer ware, household goods and antique coins and paper money. It also displays models wearing the fantastic costumes of Tsuwano's *Sagi-Mai* Heron Dance Festival, an annual event

every July 20th and 27th.

Nishi House 西周旧宅 is on a quiet residential street. It is the only residence on the street with a wall in front, and the house itself has a thatched roof. There is no admission charge. Amane Nishi, 1829 – 1897, was the first Japanese of his era to become interested in and try to promulgate western philosophies, and was an active politician in the exciting Meiji era of Japan.

Cross the bridge over the Tsuwanogawa River. On the other side of the bridge, take a quick right and then a quick left. Go past the house on the corner, and the next building, set back behind a courtyard and garden, is **Mori House** 森家 . Ogai Mori (1862 – 1922), another famous figure of the Meiji era, was an army doctor, a writer and a translator whose life was an unending quest to reconcile western and Japanese traditions.

Continue to **Washi Kaikan** 和紙会館 (Handmade Paper Hall) on the corner. There is no admission charge. The first floor of this building is devoted to demonstrations of the paper maker's craft. The second floor houses a small museum that displays samples of handmade paper from all parts of Japan, and a huge souvenir shop.

If you still have time, you should explore the area behind Tsuwano Station. The hard climb up the hill to Otometoge Pass and **St. Maria Church** 聖マリア教会 (upper right, map 118) takes about 8 minutes. There's a small waterfall to your left as you begin your climb. There is no admission charge. The tiny chapel, which was built in 1951, is a memorial to the Christian exiles who were tortured and martyred at this site. Its stained glass windows depict the sufferings of the martyrs. Otometoge, the Pass of the Virgin, is named for the daughter of a local lord who wandered up this lonely pass and disappeared after being rejected by the prince to whom she was betrothed.

Accommodations in Tsuwano

1. Hotel

Hotel Sunroute Tsuwano
ホテルサンルート津和野
(Standard: upper right, map 118. 50
rooms)
Add: Terada, Tsuwano-machi.
Tel: (08567) 2-3232.

2. Ryokans

Tsuwano Kanko Hotel 津和野観光ホテル
(First-class: upper right, map 118. 30
rooms)
Add: Ushiroda, Tsuwano-machi.
Tel: (08567) 2-0332.

Ryokan Koraku 旅館行楽
(Standard: upper right, map 118. 25
rooms)
Add: Ushiroda, Tsuwano-machi.
Tel: (08567) 2-0501.

Ryokan Yoshinoya 旅館吉野屋
(Standard: upper right, map 118. 27
rooms)
Add: Ushiroda, Tsuwano-machi.
Tel: (08567) 2-0531.

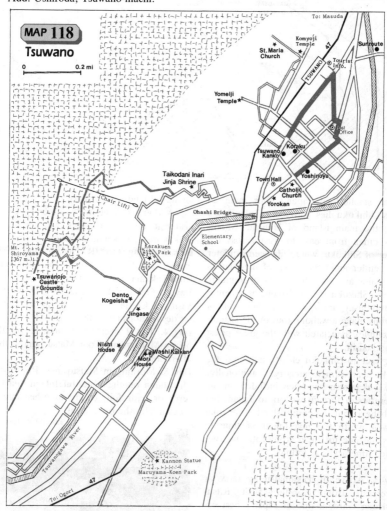

Introduction to
Shikoku

四国

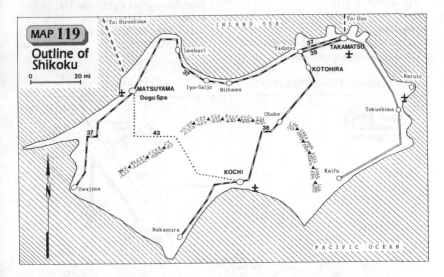

MAP 119

Outline of Shikoku

0   20 mi

To: Hiroshima   INLAND SEA   To: Uno

Imabari   Tadotsu   37   TAKAMATSU
38
KOTOHIRA
Naruto
MATSUYAMA   Iyo-Saijo   Niihama
Dogo Spa   Tokushima
Oboke
37   43   38
KOCHI   Kaifu
Uwajima
Nakamura
PACIFIC OCEAN

The smallest of Japan's four main islands, Shikoku lies across the Inland Sea from the main island of Honshu. Mountains range from east to west across the center of Shikoku, where life seems quieter and gentler amid the green of the island's mountains and the blue of its surrounding waters. Shikoku is also famous as a center of Buddhism, and every year thousands of pilgrims make a walking tour of the island's 88 temples associated with the great priest Kobo Daishi.

A visit to Shikoku clearly falls into the off-the-beaten-track category. Traditionally, only Takamatsu has been included on the itineraries of foreign visitors to Japan, but we believe that the entire island of Shikoku is well worth the investment of time (5 days) needed to travel around it. Our suggested itinerary is as follows:

Day 1. Arrive in Takamatsu by ferry or hovercraft from Honshu. Visit Ritsurin-Koen Garden, one of Japan's best ex-

amples of landscape artistry.

* Add an extra day to the itinerary if you also visit suburban Yashima, which features Shikokumura Open-air Museum.

Day 2. Using the JR Dosan Line, visit magnificent Kotohira Shrine on your way from Takamatsu to Kochi.

Day 3. Full day for sightseeing in Kochi. Visit the Castle and some of the spectacular destinations along the coast.

Day 4. Travel over the mountains by JR bus to Matsuyama. Tour Matsuyama in the afternoon.

Day 5. Morning in Matsuyama. Return to Hiroshima on the beautiful Inland Sea by ferry or hydrofoil, or fly to other major cities in Honshu or Kyushu.

Ritsurin-Koen Garden

Takamatsu

高松

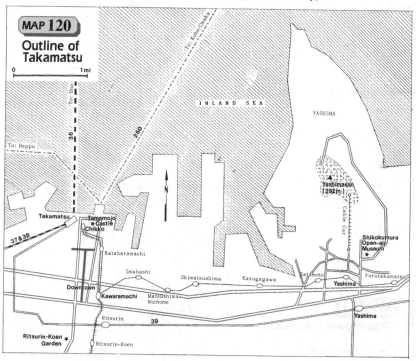

Takamatsu is Shikoku's principal link to the main island of Honshu. Founded as a castle town in 1588, it was the headquarters of the Matsudaira family during the Tokugawa period. The home of Ritsurin-Koen Garden, renowned as one of Japan's most beautiful gardens, Takamatsu today is the capital and cultural center of Kagawa Prefecture. There are two major tourist destinations in Takamatsu: Ritsurin-Koen Garden, and Yashima to the east of the city.

Transportation to Takamatsu

JR ferry and hovercraft service connect Takamatsu to Uno on Honshu. At Uno, local trains to Okayama meet each ferry and provide easy connections to the Shinkansen. The hovercraft trip takes only 23 minutes. The Seto Ohashi Bridge linking Honshu and Shikoku will be completed in early 1988. The long awaited double decker bridge – the upper deck for automobiles and the lower for JR trains – is expected to enhance tourism to Shikoku.

For cruise fans, steamship service from Osaka/Kobe on Kansai Kisen is recommended (No. 250). The trip from Osaka takes 5 hours 30 minutes, and the trip from Kobe 4 hours 30 minutes. The steamship uses Naka-Tottei Pier in Kobe and Bentenfuto Pier in Osaka. Because Naka-Tottei Pier is easily accessible from the train stations, we suggest that you catch the boat (or get off the boat) in Kobe. See the Kobe section for Naka-Tottei Pier.

Shikoku's three major JR lines originate at Takamatsu: the JR Yosan Line to Matsuyama (No. 37), the JR Dosan Line to Kochi (No. 38) and the JR Kotoku Line to Tokushima.

Takamatsu is also connected by air with other major cities such as Tokyo, Osaka and Fukuoka. There is airport bus service between the airport and JR Takamatsu Station (a 25 minute trip).

MAP 120
Outline of Takamatsu

Transportation in Takamatsu

Takamatsu has excellent bus service, and a commuter train line, the Kotoden, that terminates at Chikko Station just across the street from Takamatsu JR Station. Some of Takamatsu's buses still have conductors to collect fares!

Outline of the City

The area sandwiched between the Kotoden Line on the east and Chuo-dori, the city's main street, on the west is Takamatsu's

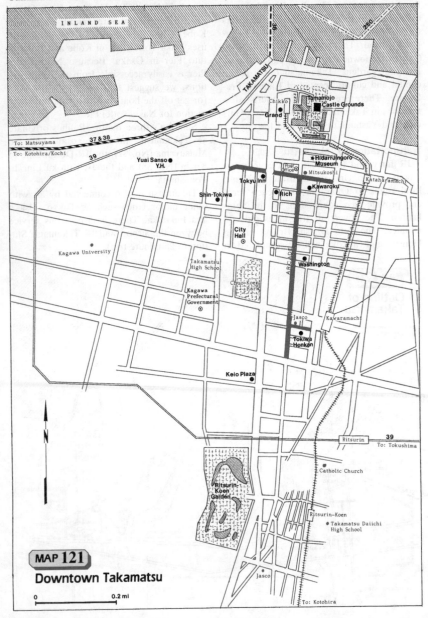

MAP 121
Downtown Takamatsu

INLAND SEA

To: Matsuyama
To: Kotohira/Kochi

Yuai Sanso Y.H.

Shin-Tokiwa

Kagawa University

Takamatsu High School

Kagawa Prefectural Government

Keio Plaza

Chikko

Grand

Tamamojo Castle Grounds

Hidari Jingoro Museum

Post Office

Mitsukoshi

Tokyu Inn

Rich

Kawaroku

Kataharamachi

City Hall

Chuo-Koen Park

Washington

Jasco

Kawaramachi

Tokiwa Honkan

Ritsurin   39
To: Tokushima

Catholic Church

Ritsurin-Koen Garden

Ritsurin-Koen

Takamatsu Daiichi High School

Jasco

To: Kotohira

N

0   0.2 mi

downtown. Two arcades (shaded red) run north to south and east to west. Department stores, souvenir shops, restaurants and coffee shops line the arcades, and bars and cabarets crowd the narrow streets that intersect the arcades.

Places of Interest in the City

Tamamojo Castle Grounds 玉藻城跡 (Upper right, map 121)

The entrance to this park is across the street from Takamatsu Station. Walk back off the street on the path next to the Mister Donut shop. You should be able to see an English language sign. Admission: 20 yen. Hours: 8:30 AM to 6:00 PM. Tamamojo Castle was built in 1588 by Chikamasa Ikoma, and later became the home of the ruling Matsudaira family. Only a few turrets of the castle, and remnants of the moats and the wall remain. The park, however, is lovely, and the perfect place to take a relaxing stroll.

Hidari Jingoro Museum 左甚五郎美術館 (optional) (Upper right, map 121)

If you leave the park through the eastern gate, Hidari Jingoro Museum is a few minutes walk away. The museum is housed in a three-story tan stucco building with two white balconies. This small museum has a fine collection of the works of Hidari Jingoro, who is most famous as the sculptor of the sleeping cat of Nikko's Toshogu Shrine and the designer of the nightingale corridor of Kyoto's Chion-in Temple. Recommended for art history majors only.

Ritsurin-Koen Garden 栗林公園 (Lower center, map 121)

The bus for Ritsurin Koen Garden leaves from Stop No. 2 in front of the Grand Hotel, across the street from Takamatsu Station. The trip to the Garden takes about 10 - 15 minutes. You can also take a Kotoden Line train.

When you get off the bus, keep walking in the same direction the bus was traveling, and use the underpass to cross the street. When you emerge, you'll be at the East Gate of Ritsurin-Koen Garden. The best bargain is the 550 yen combination ticket,

Tamamojo Castle Grounds

which, in addition to the Garden itself, also gains you admission to the **Sanuki Folk Museum** 讃岐民芸館 and the **Kikugetsutei Tea House** 掬月亭.

When you enter the Garden, the second building on your right is the Sanuki Folk Museum, which displays impressive pieces of local pottery, lovely wooden furniture and some antique items such as lacquer ware, etc.

A leisurely stroll around the clearly marked paths of Ritsurin-Koen Garden is a treat in any season. It is dotted with ponds, a variety of lovely bridges and one surprising vista after another. In season, the cherry blossoms, azaleas and irises are magnificent.

The Garden's Kikugetsutei Tea House is the perfect place to experience a taste of the traditional tea ceremony. There's a lovely view of the garden in the room where you're served tea.

Yashima 屋島

This suburb of Takamatsu is famous as a historic battle site, and home of an innovative tradition-conserving museum.

Transportation to Yashima

Take the Kotoden train from either the Ritsurin-Koen Station or the Chikko Station to Yashima. (If you take the train from the Ritsurin-Koen Station you'll have to change at Kawaramachi – where the Yashima-bound trains leave from Platform No. 3. It's a complicated place – use Conversation Card 5!) The Kotoden trains run about once every 15 – 30 minutes. There is also JR service to Yashima, but those trains operate much less frequently - only about once every hour.

Shikokumura Open-Air Museum 四国村
(Middle right, map 120)

As you walk up the hill from the train station, you'll be able to see a shrine in front of you. The entrance to Shikokumura Open-air Museum is next to the shrine. It has a brown signboard with a waterwheel behind it (8:30 AM to 5:00 PM. Till 4:30 PM November through March. Admission 480 yen).

The Open-air Museum features a collection of old farmhouses and other traditional Shikoku structures of the type that have grown rarer and rarer with the years. It is a surprisingly pleasant and educational place. It is attractively laid out, and occasional English signs help you get your bearings. The buildings that have been relocated here include a mill, a paper-making workshop, a stone carving shop, and several traditional farm houses. You should skip the Museum inside the grounds. It only exhibits implements and crafts that you can see displayed in the other buildings for free! A thoroughly enjoyable experience if you have some extra time in the Takamatsu area.

Mt. Yashima 屋島山 (Middle right, map 120)

Mt. Yashima can be reached by cable car in just five minutes. The flat, wide mountain top is covered by pine trees. The observatories on this tableland command a grand view of the Inland Sea. **Yashimaji Temple** 屋島寺 has, in its Treasure House, artifacts gathered from the battleground of the 1185 clash between the Minamoto and Taira clans that lead to the establishment,

by Yoritomo Minamoto, of Japan's first Shogunate in Kamakura.

Accommodations in Takamatsu
1. Hotels
Keio Plaza Hotel Takamatsu
　　京王プラザ高松
　　(First-class: middle center, map 121. 180 rooms).
　　Add: 11-5, Chuo-machi, Takamatsu.
　　Tel: (0878) 34-5511.
Takamatsu Kokusai Hotel 高松国際ホテル
　　(First-class: 10 minutes by taxi from Takamatsu Station. 107 rooms).
　　Add: 2191-1, Kita-machi, Takamatsu.
　　Tel: (0878) 31-1511.
Takamatsu Grand Hotel
　　高松グランドホテル
　　(Standard: upper center, map 121. 136 rooms).
　　Add: 1-5-10, Kotobuki-machi, Takamatsu.
　　Tel: (0878) 51-5757.
Hotel Rich Takamatsu ホテルリッチ高松
　　(Business hotel: upper center, map 121. 126 rooms).
　　Add: 9-1, Furushin-machi, Takamatsu.
　　Tel: (0878) 22-3555.
Takamatsu Tokyu Inn 高松東急ホテル
　　(Business hotel: upper center, map 121. 181 rooms).
　　Add: 9-9, Hyogo-machi, Takamatsu.
　　Tel: (0878) 21-0109.
Takamatsu Washington Hotel
　　高松ワシントンホテル
　　(Business hotel: middle center, map 121. 252 rooms).
　　Add: 1-2-3, Kawara-machi, Takamatsu.
　　Tel: (0878) 22-7111.

2. Ryokans
Hotel Kawaroku ホテル川六
　　(First-class: upper center, map 121. 73 rooms).
　　Add: 1-2, Hyakken-machi, Takamatsu.
　　Tel: (0878) 21-5666.
Tokiwa Honkan 常磐本館
　　(Standard: middle center, map 121. 23 rooms).
　　Add: 1-8-2, Tokiwa-machi, Takamatsu.
　　Tel: (0878) 61-5577.

Kotohira

琴平

An approximately 50 minute express train trip from Takamatsu (the JR Dosan Line; No. 38), the **Kotohiragu Grand Shrine** 金刀比羅宮 , popularly known as **Kompira** or **Kompira-san**, stands halfway up the densely wooded 1,650 ft. (500 m.) Mt. Zozusan. See No. 38 for schedules between Takamatsu and Kotohira. The Shrine is dedicated to *Omono-nushi-no-Mikoto*, who is the patron of seafarers and voyagers and who is regarded as a very accessible god. Presumably, he also looks after tourists, even foreign ones, so you might want to pay your respects. Because it takes about 1 hour to climb the 785 stone steps to the main shrine buildings, we suggest that you get an early morning start, especially in warm weather, so you won't be hiking up Mt. Zozusan in the midday sun.

Turn left when you emerge from JR's Kotohira Station, and walk along until you come to a cross street with an arcade, where you should turn right. Walk through the arcade, cross the bridge, and go straight until you come to the steps. It's about a 15 minute walk to here from the station – this is the beginning of the approach to Kompira-san. Souvenir shops line the ascent up to Daimon, the Main Gate of the Shrine, which is another 10 minute's climb.

Like most Shinto shrines, Kompira-san, which claims its origins in antiquity, has been rebuilt again and again throughout its history. **Daimon Gate** 大門 is an impressive two-story structure, with huge wooden statues standing in its niches. Past Daimon Gate, the path is lined with stone lanterns and memorial tablets. The Shrine's **Treasure House** 宝物館 is the smaller of the two new, white buildings on your right just before the second torii gate after Daimon. Admission 200 yen. Hours: 9:00 AM to 4:00 PM. The Treasure House museum, which most Japanese tourists neglect, displays large vases and other ceramic items, beautiful pieces of sculpture, lovely scrolls and Noh masks, and an impressive collection of swords, helmets and armor.

At the next landing, **Shoin** 書院 , which was built in 1659, is on your right. The carvings on the outside of this "Parlor" building are well worth the detour off the main path. Its interior features sliding

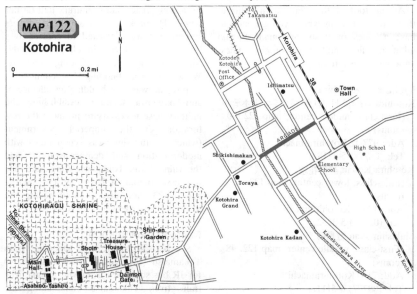

MAP 122
Kotohira

0   0.2 mi

N

To Takamatsu

Kotohira

Kotoden Kotohira
Post Office

Ishimatsu

Town Hall

38

High School

Shikishimakan

Elementary School

Toraya

Kotohira Grand

KOTOHIRAGU SHRINE

To Inner Shrine (90 min.)

Shin-en Garden

Treasure House

Shoin

Kotohira Kadan

Kanekuragawa River

To Kochi

Main Hall

Daimon Gate

Asahino-Yashiro

doors decorated by Okyo Maruyama, the famous 18th century landscape artist.

The climb to the next landing is a rather difficult one, but you're rewarded at the landing with the lovely double-roofed, early 19th century **Asahino Yashiro (Rising Sun Hall)** 旭社 , famous for its beautiful, intricate carvings of animals, flowers, etc.

The main buildings of the Shrine are on the next landing, which also has a fantastic view of Takamatsu and the mountains and water that surround it. The Main Shrine, which is constructed on stilts like Kyoto's Kiyomizudera Temple, was rebuilt about 100 years ago. Walk to the **Votive Picture Hall** 絵馬殿 , the last of the buildings in the main shrine compound, for another grand view, and be sure to take a walk around the Votive Hall's open air display of its surprisingly eclectic collection of pictures.

The ascent up the additional 583 steps to **Okusha Inner Shrine** 奥社 is a climb of another 30 minutes. The Inner Shrine is usually visited by only the most religious of the thousands of pilgrims who come to Kompira-san every year.

The path down from the main shrine compound gives you a good opportunity to observe the carvings tucked under the roof of Asahino Yashiro Rising Sun Hall.

At the foot of the steps to the Shrine, there are two shops where you can stop to have a snack of fresh, handmade Sanuki udon noodles, and a seemingly endless variety of souvenir shops.

Ryokans in Kotohira

Kotohira Grand Hotel 琴平グランドホテル
(First-class: middle center, map 122. 90 rooms)
Add: 977-1, Kotohira-machi.
Tel: (08777) 5-3218.

Kotohira Kadan 琴平花壇
(First-class: lower center, map 122. 42 rooms)
Add: 1241, Kotohiramachi.
Tel: (08777) 5-3232.

Shikishimakan 敷島館
(First-class: middle center, map 122. 48 rooms)
Add: 713, Kotohiramachi.
Tel: (08777) 5-5111.

Toraya Ryokan 虎屋旅館
(Standard: middle center, map 122. 50 rooms)
Add: 814, Kotohiramachi.
Tel: (08777) 5-3131.

Ishimatsu Ryokan 石松旅館
(Standard: upper center, map 122. 34 rooms)
Add: 302, Kotohiramachi.
Tel: (08777) 5-2236.

Kochi 高知

except Sunday

Kochi, with a population of 265,000, is the administrative center of Kochi Prefecture. The city is in a lovely natural setting, surrounded by hills to the north and the east. The Kumagawa and Kagamigawa Rivers flow through the city into Urado Bay, which in turns opens into the much larger Tosa Bay.

The name of Kochi, or Tosa, the name of the feudal era province in this area, is linked in the minds of most Japanese with that of Ryoma Sakamoto, a political genius instrumental in upsetting the Tokugawa feudal system. Sakamoto was born in 1835 to a low class, half-samurai, half-farmer family. He broke away from the rigid class system that was designed to control lives like his, and exiled himself to Nagasaki, where he organized a trading company. While he was building his commercial empire, he was also building an alliance of anti-Tokugawa samurai, establishing the military base necessary to promote the restoration of the imperial government (which, at the time was synonymous with modernization and democratization) and the ruin of the Tokugawa Shogunate. He was assassinated in Kyoto in 1867 at the age of 33, and died without seeing the triumph of his ideas and his alliance.

Transportation to Kochi

See No. 38 for JR train schedules from Takamatsu (the Dosan Line) and No. 43 for JR bus schedules from Matsuyama. The train from Takamatsu runs along the famous Oboke and Koboke ravines. The trip takes 2 hours 30 minutes. Most of the 3 hour and 45 minute JR bus trip between Matsuyama and Kochi is through Shikoku's magnificent mountains.

Air transportation is also available to Kochi from major cities such as Tokyo, Osaka, Nagoya and Fukuoka. Airport buses run between Kochi Airport and the JR Kochi Station – a 60 minute trip.

Outline of the City

Kochi's downtown area is centered at Harimayabashi intersection. The train station and the Castle are located within the urban core, but several of the area's beautiful destinations, such as Godaisan-Koen Park and Katsurahama Beach, are at a bit of a distance, closer to the water.

Transportation in Kochi

Kochi has a streetcar system with two principal lines that cross at Harimayabashi. They run frequently and charge a flat 150 yen fare. Enter at the rear and pay as you exit from the front. These streetcars are not particularly important for tourists. Kochi is also served by several different bus companies, including the Toden Bus Company and the Kochi Ken Kotsu Bus Company. Fares on these buses vary with the distance traveled. You use these buses when you visit Godaisan-Koen Park and Katsurahama Beach.

Places of Interest in Kochi

Kochijo Castle and Park 高知城 (Middle left, map 123)

This was the site of a fortress as early as

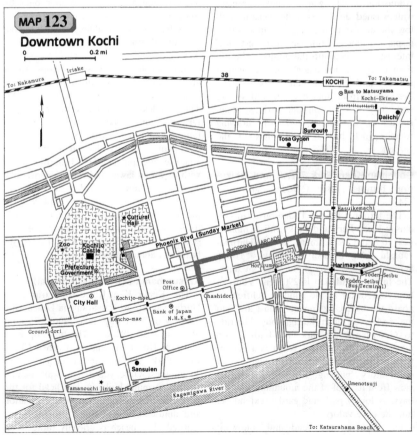

the 14th century. Construction on the present castle began in 1601 at the order of Lord Kazutoyo Yamanouchi, and was completed in 1611. The castle was destroyed by fire in 1727, and reconstruction was completed in 1753. The Castle was again repaired after World War II. The Castle is about a 20 minute walk from Kochi Station or from the Harimayabashi downtown area. If you're in Kochi on Sunday, you'll find the walk particularly interesting because Kochi's famous Phoenix Boulevard Sunday Open Air Market will be in full swing, and you'll be able to sample all sorts of local specialty foods.

As the street to the castle deadends, you'll see Otemon Gate on your right. Enter the Castle grounds there and climb the steps to the Castle (9:00 AM to 5:00 PM. Admission 200 yen). The compact, whitewashed donjon is quite elegant. Follow the arrows to the museum area, which displays armor and other items of historical interest, and then into the donjon. The top floor of the donjon has a fabulous view of the city and the mountains. When you've descended from the donjon, follow the signs to your right, through various tatami rooms, to Kaitokukan, the lord's drawing room, which has a lovely view of the garden.

Godaisan-Koen Park 五台山 and Chikurinji Temple 竹林寺 (Middle right, map 124)

The terminal for the Toden buses to Godaisan-Koen Park and Chikurinji Temple is next to Seibu Department Store at Harimayabashi (An English sign says "Toden Seibu"). Buses leave about once an hour. The fare to Godaisan is 290 yen. You can buy your ticket at the window before you board the bus. Use Conversation Card 5 to make sure you catch the right bus. The ride to Godaisan-Koen Park's Chikurinji stop takes about 20 minutes. When you get off the bus, the path to your right leads to an observatory building. There's a fantastic view from its roof of the mountains and the bays. A lovely park and garden extend below the observatory.

Go back to the road and follow it downhill for about 5 minutes, until you come to a small cluster of souvenir shops. The entrance to Chikurinji Temple is on your left. The approach up the steps is quite impressive. The temple was founded in 724 and has a magnificent five-story red pagoda, matched in its splendor only by some of Kyoto's most famous temples. The areas between the buildings of the temple are dotted with statues of darumas and bibbed Jizos.

Just beyond the souvenir shops are a greenhouse, museum and a park. Admission 200 yen. Hours 9:00 AM to 5:00 PM. The complex is dedicated to the memory of Dr. Tomitaro Makino (1862 – 1957), a famous botanist from the Kochi area. The Greenhouse has a collection of more than 1,000 exotic plants. The beautiful park, with its broad lawns and rolling fields, rock gardens and terraced gardens that descend toward the water, is the perfect place for a picnic. There is also a museum that features science displays appropriate for school children. Buses back to Harimayabashi run about once an hour.

Katsurahama Beach 桂浜 (optional)

The Kochi Ken Kotsu Bus trip from Harimayabashi to Katsurahama Beach, and its view of Tosa Bay, takes about 35 minutes and costs 480 yen. The bus stop is at platform No. 1 in front of Kochi's Chuo-Koen Park. The bus runs about once every 30 minutes. Once you arrive, walk behind the bus terminal building, and head for the park and the beach. There's a recreation and amusement area that's probably best ignored. The beach is gravelly rather than sandy, but is a good place for a cooling dip in hot weather. On clear days, the view out to sea – blue upon blue – is incomparable. You can follow a path up to an observatory that shares the top of a rocky cliff with a red torii gate. There's also a hiking path through the woods. The buses back to Harimayabashi run about once every 30 minutes.

Ryugado Cavern : 竜河洞 (optional)

Located about 25 km. (15 miles) to the east of Kochi, Ryugado is one of the largest caverns in Japan. About a quarter of the total length of the caves – 4 km. or 2.5 miles – is open to the public. Guided tours (in Japanese only) are conducted from time to time, and highlight the secret beauties of this natural treasure.

Toden buses run between Harimayabashi (Toden-Seibu Bus Terminal) and Ryugado about once an hour, and the ride takes one hour. The Cavern is recommended for those who stay in the Kochi area for longer periods.

Accommodations in Kochi
1. Hotels

Kochi Daiichi Hotel 高知第一ホテル
  (Business hotel: upper right, map 123. 118 rooms).
  Add: 2-2-12, Kita-Honmachi, Kochi.
  Tel: (0888) 83-1441.

Hotel Sunroute Kochi
  ホテルサンルート高知
  (Business hotel: upper right, map 123. 110 rooms).
  Add: 1-1-28, Kita-Honmachi, Kochi.
  Tel: (0888) 23-1311.

2. Ryokans

Sansuien Hotel 三翠園ホテル
  (First-class: lower left, map 123. 132 rooms).
  Add: 1-3-35, Takashomachi, Kochi.
  Tel: (0888) 22-0131.

Tosa Gyoen 土佐御苑
  (First-class: upper right, map 123. 26 rooms).
  Add: 1-4-8, Okawasuji, Kochi.
  Tel: (0888) 22-4491.

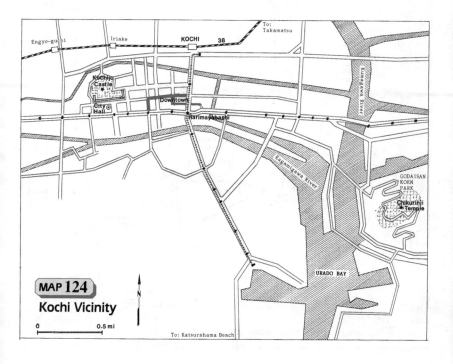

MAP 124
Kochi Vicinity

0   0.5 mi

To: Katsurahama Beach

Matsuyama

松山

Matsuyama, with a population of 428,000, is Shikoku's largest city. It is the capital of Ehime Prefecture, and its educational, cultural and commercial center. Dogo Onsen Spa, located in the eastern part of the city, is one of Japan's oldest hotsprings. In the 14th century this area prospered as a castle town. The present city developed when Matsuyama Castle was built at the order of Yoshiakira Kato in 1602.

Soseki Natsume, a famous Meiji-era novelist, taught English at a high school in Matsuyama when he was young. His novel "Botchan" was based on his experience here.

Transportation to Matsuyama

From Hiroshima: See No. 251 for ferry and hydrofoil schedules. If you have time, we recommend a late afternoon ferry to or from Hiroshima. The 2 hour and 45 minute trip gives you a chance to enjoy the sunset on the beautiful Inland Sea. Matsuyama Kanko-ko Port 松山観光港 is to the northwest of the city. Buses run frequently to the Port from Matsuyama and Matsuyama-shi Stations, as well as from Dogo Onsen Spa.

From Takamatsu: Yosan Line (No. 37)
From Kochi: JR bus (No. 43)

Matsuyama is served by air from Tokyo, Nagoya, Osaka, Fukuoka and Kagoshima. Matsuyama Airport and Matsuyamashi Station (not JR Matsuyama Station) are linked by Airport Bus. The ride takes about 25 minutes.

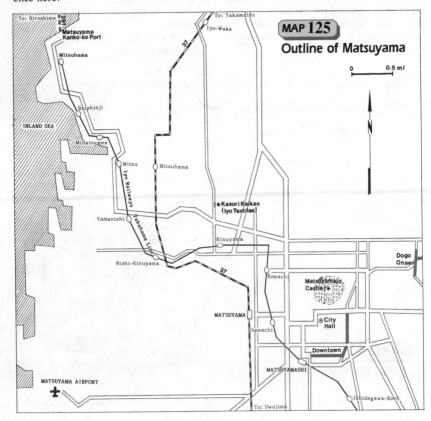

MAP 125

Outline of Matsuyama

Outline of the City

Matsuyama's downtown area is at the foot of the Castle park area (The northern side of Matsuyamashi Station. The JR Matsuyama Station area is less developed). It features several arcades crammed full of department stores, shops and restaurants.

Transportation in Matsuyama

Matsuyama has two main train stations. The first, Matsuyama Station 松山駅, is the JR station and the terminal for long distance and city buses as well as city streetcars. The second, Matsuyamashi Station 松山市駅, on the private Iyo Railway, is a center for local commuter lines and serves as a second major bus terminal.

Places of Interest

Matsuyamajo Castle 松山城 (Middle center, map 126)

Construction of this castle was begun in 1602 at the order of Yoshiakira Kato, and continued until 1627. In 1635, the Castle became the home of the Matsudaira family, which ruled the Matsuyama area during the Tokugawa period. The donjon was reconstructed in the 19th century, after it was struck with lightning, and again in the 20th century, after it was damaged during the war. For the last twenty years, the city has worked hard at restoring this municipal symbol, and has succeeded splendidly. A visit to the Castle, which sits high above' the city, will give you an excellent idea of life in feudal Shikoku. An English language pamphlet will help you to understand what you see (9:00 AM to 5:00 PM. Admission 250 yen).

A 3-minute ropeway (middle center of Map 126) ride to the Castle runs about once every 10 minutes. An English sign for the ropeway arches over the street.

A walk around the many gates and turrets of the Castle will give you a good idea of the scale of many feudal castle compounds. The donjon has a fantastic view of the mountains and the water that frame Matsuyama, and houses a museum that displays a good collection of armor and swords, and lacquer items, scrolls, screens and kimono.

If you have some extra time, we suggest that you walk back down from the Castle rather than taking the ropeway, stopping at **Shinonome Jinja Shrine** 東雲神社 . The path is to the right of the ropeway station as you return to it from the Castle. It's a lovely wooded downslope that parallels and eventually passes under the cable and lift lines. The path will lead you to the back of the Shrine, which features lots of nice dark wood and shining gold trim. From the Shrine, it's another 5-minute walk down the steps back to the street with the ropeway entrance.

Shikido Hall 子規堂 (optional) (Lower left, map 126)

Next to Shojuji Temple, near Matsuyamashi Station, this building is a replica of the residence of Shiki Masaoka (1867 – 1902), a famous Meiji-era *haiku* poet. Touring the house will give you a good idea of middle class Meiji life. The temple cemetery is behind and to the left of the residence, and there's an antique street car in front of the residence that Japanese tourists consider a real delight.

Kasuri Kaikan Iyo Textile Hall 民芸伊予ガスリ会館 (optional) (Middle center, map 125)

A twenty minute Iyo Tetsu Bus ride from Matsuyamashi Station (10 minutes from Matsuyama Station – platform No. 1). Get off the bus at Kumanodai Stop, and walk back the way the bus came about 220 yards (200 m.) to the entrance to Kasuri Kaikan Iyo Textile Hall. The entrance is back off the street, to your left as you walk through the bus parking lot. A clearly marked path leads you through the factory and an explanation of the dyeing and spinning processes. Iyo Kasuri "splashed-pattern" textiles are a specialty of the Matsuyama area, and have been made here for almost 200 years. Many of the beautiful items on sale in the souvenir shop are rather expensive, but after viewing the backbreaking work that goes into their creation, you'll probably have a good idea of why that's so. The buses back to Matsuyama run about once every fifteen minutes.

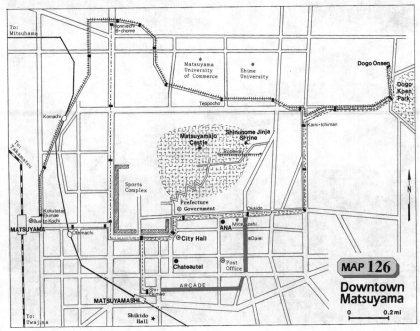

MAP 126
Downtown Matsuyama

Dogo Onsen 道後温泉

Dogo Onsen Spa can be reached by streetcar from either JR Matsuyama Station or the Iyo Railway's Matsuyamashi Station in 15 minutes. Bus service is available to and from Matsuyama Kanko-ko Port. Most Japanese tourists who visit Matsuyama stay here. The modern hotels downtown are used mostly by business people. **Dogo Onsen Honkan** 道後温泉本館 was the original communal hotspring bath house used by all visitors to Dogo in the days before each ryokan had its own baths. The traditional building, now preserved as a monument, is the symbol of Dogo Onsen. **Dogo Koen Park** 道後公園 is located at the site of the 14th century Yuchikujo Castle, and is a lovely place for a stroll.

Accommodations in Matsuyama

1. Hotels in Downtown

ANA Hotel Matsuyama ＡＮＡホテル松山
(First-class: middle center, map 126. 246 rooms).
Add: 3-2-1, Ichibancho, Matsuyama.
Tel: (0899) 33-5511.

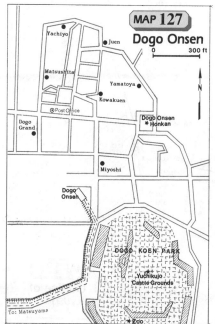

Dogo Onsen

Chateautel Matsuyama シャトーテル松山
(Standard: lower center, map 126. 176 rooms).
Add: 4-9-6, Sanbancho, Matsuyama.
Tel: (0899) 46-2111.

2. Ryokans in Dogo Onsen

Kowakuen 古涌園
(Deluxe: upper center, map 127. 85 rooms).
Add: Dogo, Matsuyama,
Tel: (0899) 45-5911.

Yamatoya 大和屋
(Deluxe: upper center, map 127. 97 rooms).
Add: Dogo, Matsuyama.
Tel: (0899) 41-1137.

Juen 寿苑
(First-class: upper center, map 127. 76 rooms).
Add: Dogo, Matsuyama.
Tel: (0899) 41-0161.

Matsushita Hotel 松下ホテル
(First-class: upper left, map 127. 81 rooms).
Add: Dogo, Matsuyama.
Tel: (0899) 32-1291.

Yachiyo 八千代
(First-class: upper left, map 127. 59 rooms).
Add: Dogo, Matsuyama.
Tel: (0899) 43-7266.

Dogo Grand Hotel 道後グランドホテル
(Standard: middle left, map 127. 67 rooms).
Add: Dogo, Matsuyama.
Tel: (0899) 43-0075.

Introduction to
Kyushu

九州

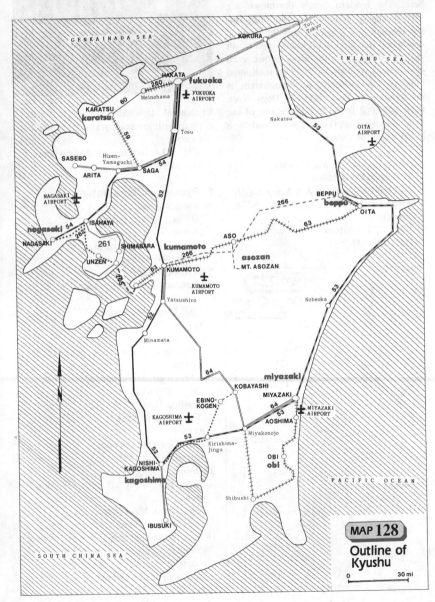

MAP **128**

Outline of
Kyushu

0   30 mi

Kyushu, the third largest of Japan's islands, is at the southwestern end of the archipelago. Kyushu is divided into two zones – North Central Kyushu and Southern Kyushu.

The highlight of **North Central Kyushu** is the trans-island trip from Nagasaki to Beppu via Shimabara, Kumamoto and Mt. Asozan. The standard itinerary for North Central Kyushu takes five days as follows:

Day 1.   Arrive in Nagasaki

You can fly to Nagasaki from Tokyo or Osaka, or you can combine two railways for travel by train: the Shinkansen (No. 1) to Hakata (3 hours 30 minutes from Kyoto), and then the JR Nagasaki Line (No. 54) from Hakata to Nagasaki (2 hours 30 minutes).

* If you have an extra day, we suggest that you make a detour to Karatsu. Then, you can proceed to Nagasaki via the JR Karatsu Line (No. 59) and the JR Nagasaki Line (No. 54).

Day 2.   Nagasaki

Full day in this exotic city.

Day 3.   Nagasaki/Unzen-Shimabara/Kumamoto

There are two ways to travel from Nagasaki to Kumamoto. The easier one is to take a through bus from Nagasaki (No. 262). The bus visits Unzen's "Jigoku" volcanic hells, and then crosses Ariake Bay by ferry to Misumi. After a short detour to Amakusa, the bus proceeds to Kumamoto. The total ride takes 10 hours.

The other route requires you to travel on your own. You take the JR Nagasaki Line to Isahaya, and then the private Shimabara Tetsudo Line to Shimabara (No. 261). After your visit to Shimabarajo Castle, continue by train to Shimabara-gaiko and cross Ariake Bay by boat to Misumi (No. 265). Then take the JR Misumi Line to Kumamoto (No. 63).

Day 4.   Kumamoto/Mt. Asozan/Beppu

Again, there are two ways to travel on this route. A sightseeing bus operates from Kumamoto to Beppu, visiting Mt. Asozan on the way (No. 266). Unless you have a Japan Rail Pass, this 7-hour bus trip is recommended.

If you have a Rail Pass, you can take the JR Hohi Line from Kumamoto to Aso Station (No. 63). Mt. Asozan is 40 minutes away by bus from Aso Station. After your visit to the mountain, you continue on No. 63 train from Aso to Beppu.

Day 5.   Leave Beppu

You can return to Kyoto via the JR Nippo Line (No. 53; from Beppu to Kokura; 1 hour 30 minutes) and the Shinkansen. You can also fly from Oita Airport to Tokyo, Osaka and Nagoya.

If you have more time in Kyushu, take the JR Nippo Line to Miyazaki, and then follow the Southern Kyushu itinerary detailed below.

Due to its long distance from Tokyo and Kyoto, **Southern Kyushu** is seldom visited by foreign tourists. The area, however, has a lot to offer. We suggest the following itinerary:

Day 1.   Arrive in Miyazaki

You can fly to Miyazaki from Tokyo, Nagoya or Osaka. If you are traveling by train, take the Shinkansen (No. 1) to Kokura and then the JR Nippo Line from Kokura to Miyazaki (No. 53; 5 hours).

Day 2.   Miyazaki/Obi/Aoshima/Miyazaki

You make a full day excursion to Obi and Aoshima.

Day 3.   Miyazaki/Ebino-Kogen/Kagoshima

Take the JR Kitto Line (No. 64) to Kobayashi, and then a bus to Ebino-Kogen Plateau. After enjoying the Plateau, take a bus to Kirishima Jingu Shrine, and then to Nishi-Kagoshima.

* If your time is limited, take the JR Nippo Line from Miyazaki directly to Nishi-Kagoshima and enjoy afternoon sightseeing there. Thus you can save one day.

Day 4.   Kagoshima

Full day sightseeing in Kagoshima.

Day 5.   Leave Kagoshima

You can fly from Kagoshima to Tokyo, Osaka, Nagoya or Hiroshima. The JR Kagoshima Line (No. 52) takes 4 hours 30 minutes from Nishi-Kagoshima to Hakata.

* There is another famous hotspring resort, Ibusuki, to the south of Kagoshima. If you have one more extra night in the area, we suggest that you visit this spa and try its famous black sand sauna.

Fukuoka

福岡

Fukuoka, with a population of 1,130,000, is the largest city on Kyushu Island, and the cultural, political, education and transportation center of Southern Japan. Because it is so close to the Asian Continent, advanced continental culture was imported to Japan through the Fukuoka area at the dawn of the nation's history. The Mongolians who conquered China and established the Yuan Dynasty there attacked Japan twice, both times in vain – in 1274 and in 1281 – in this area.

The area got its name in 1600 when Nagamasa Kuroda, a feudal lord, was assigned here and named his new castle "Fukuoka"-jo. From then on the area to the west of the Nakagawa River, where the samurai lived, was called Fukuoka, while the area east of the river, where the merchants and craftsmen resided, was called Hakata. After the Meiji Restoration, when the entire area became a city, the politicians chose Fukuoka as the name for the whole city. But virtually all subsequent development has taken place in the Hakata area (and the nearby Tenjin area), and thus Hakata is now the center of the city. The Japan Railways station is named Hakata instead of Fukuoka. The people of the city seem to be fond of calling it Hakata rather than Fukuoka because that name better represents their economic and cultural achievements. The Fukuoka area now provides the people with recreational facilities, such as Fukuokajo Castle grounds, Ohori-Koen Park and Heiwadai Stadium; these are also the major tourist attractions of the city.

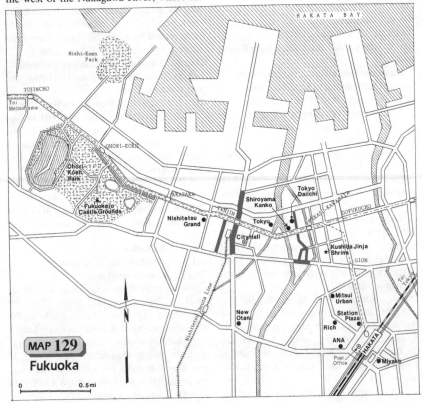

MAP 129
Fukuoka

0   0.5 mi

Transportation to Fukuoka

Hakata Station 博多駅 (lower right, map 129) is the terminus of the 735-mile (1,177 km.) long Tokaido-Sanyo Shinkansen bullet train that originates in Tokyo. Hakata is also the starting point of the major trains operating to many parts of Kyushu, such as Kumamoto and Nagasaki.

Fukuoka Airport is connected by air with all the major airports in Japan, such as Tokyo (both Narita and Haneda Airports), Osaka, Nagoya, Sapporo, and Okinawa. An airport bus runs between Hakata Station and the airport in 30 minutes.

Transportation in Fukuoka

There are two city subways in Fukuoka. No. 1 subway runs between Hakata Station and Meinohama. It connects Hakata Station, the Nakasu-Kawabata night life area, the Tenjin shopping area, and the Ohori-Koen recreational area.

Places of Interest

Fukuokajo Castle Grounds 福岡城跡 (middle left, map 129). Only a few gates and one turret still remain, but the castle is located on a 157-foot (48 m.) high hill and commands a bird's-eye view of the city.

Ohori-Koen Park 大濠公園 (northwest of the castle grounds). The park is laid out around a large pond that is 1.25 miles (2 km.) in circumference. Several bridges provide access to the islet in the center of the pond.

Kushida Jinja Shrine 櫛田神社 (middle right, map 129) is Fukuoka's most important shrine and is dedicated to the Shinto god *Susano-o-no-Mikoto*. The floats used for the Hakata Yamagasa Festival (July 1 – 15) are on display in the museum attached to the shrine. They feature feudal era costumes and objects, and are quite colorful and elaborate but offer no comparison to those on display in Karatsu (The museum is open from 9:00 AM to 5:00 PM. Admission is 200 yen).

Nakasu 中洲 (middle center, map 129). In the center of the city there is an islet surrounded by the Nakagawa and Hakatagawa Rivers called Nakasu (this literally means central sand bar); it is one of Japan's most famous night life centers. The nearby **Tenjin** area is Fukuoka's main shopping area.

Hotels in Fukuoka

1. First-class Hotels

Hotel New Otani Hakata
　　ホテルニューオータニ博多
　　(Lower center, map 129. 436 rooms).
　　Add: 1-1-2, Watanabedori, Chuo-ku,
　　Fukuoka.
　　Tel: (092) 714-1111.

Nishitetsu Grand Hotel
　　西鉄グランドホテル
　　(Middle center, map 129. 308 rooms).
　　Add: 2-6-60, Daimyo, Chuo-ku,
　　Fukuoka.
　　Tel: (092) 771-7171.

ANA Hotel Hakata
　　ＡＮＡホテル博多（博多全日空ホテル）
　　(Lower right, map 129. 363 rooms).
　　Add: 3-3-3, Hakata-ekimae, Hakata-ku,
　　Fukuoka.
　　Tel: (092) 471-7111.

Hakata Miyako Hotel 博多みやこホテル
　　(Lower right, map 129. 269 rooms).
　　Add: 2-1-1, Hakataeki-Higashi,
　　Hakata-ku, Fukuoka.
　　Tel: (092) 441-3111.

Hakata Tokyu Hotel 博多東急ホテル
　　(Middle center, map 129. 266 rooms).
　　Add: 1-16-1, Tenjin, Chuo-ku, Fukuoka.
　　Tel: (092) 781-7111.

2. Business Hotels

Hotel Rich Hakata ホテルリッチ博多
　　(Lower right, map 129. 178 rooms).
　　Add: 3-27-15, Hakata-ekimae,
　　Hakata-ku, Fukuoka.
　　Tel: (092) 451-7811.

Tokyo Daiichi Hotel Fukuoka
　　東京第一ホテル博多
　　(Middle center, map 129. 223 rooms).
　　Add: 5-2-18, Nakasu, Hakata-ku,
　　Fukuoka. Tel: (092) 281-3311.

Karatsu

唐津

If you are a pottery enthusiast, or have extra time in Kyushu before going to Nagasaki, we recommend that you visit Karatsu. There are a number of pottery kilns in Karatsu. Visit the information office in Karatsu Station to check on which kiln is open to the public for the day.

Transportation to Karatsu

The JR Chikuhi Line (No. 60) runs between Karatsu and Meinohama (local trains only). All the trains run beyond Meinohama to JR Hakata Station. The ride takes 1 hour 20 minutes.

The JR Karatsu Line (No. 59) connects Karatsu with Saga. The ride takes 1 hour 20 minutes (local trains only).

Suggested Itinerary

Kinshoji Temple 近松寺 (optional) (Middle left, map 131)

This is the family temple of the Ogasawaras, feudal lords who governed the area during the Edo era. The temple is famous as the burial place of Monzaemon Chika-

matsu. Chikamatsu wrote *joruri* – the chanted dramatic stories from which the modern Bunraku puppet plays evolved. He was extremely prolific and wrote more than 50 plays. He has been called the father of Japanese drama. The temple also has a small museum that displays the family treasures of the Ogasawaras.

Hikiyama Tenjijo Hall 曳山展示場 (Middle center, map 131)

Karatsu Kunchi Festival (November 2 – 4) is famous for its colorful festival floats. Fifteen districts of the city have their own floats, each designed in a distinctive shape, such as a samurai helmet, a dragon, a fish, etc. These impressive floats are displayed in Hikiyama Tenjijo Hall. Magnificently finished with gold and silver foil and lacquer, they testify to the high artistic standards of the area (9:00 AM to 5:00 PM. Admission 200 yen).

Karatsujo Castle 唐津城 (Upper right, map 131)

Karatsujo Castle stands on a small hill facing the Genkainada Sea. Because of its white walls and its ideal location right on the water, the castle is popularly known as Maizurujo or Flying Crane Castle. The pres-

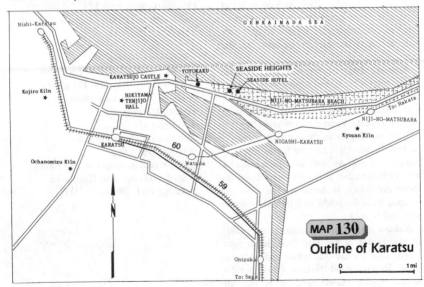

MAP **130**
Outline of Karatsu

ent building is a 1966 reconstruction. The view from the castle grounds of the sea, the city and Rainbow Pine Beach to the east is well worth the effort of climbing the long stone stairway.

Niji-no-Matsubara (Rainbow Pine Beach)
虹ノ松原 (optional; upper center, map 130)

You can walk in 15 minutes from Karatsujo Castle to Niji-no-Matsubara, or take a taxi at the exit of Karatsujo Castle (there are usually many waiting there). This pine forest is 0.6 km. (0.4 miles) wide and 5 km. (3 miles) long. Most of the pine trees are over 350 years old. This is the most beautiful forest of its kind in all Japan.

Pottery Kilns in Karatsu

Karatsu pottery is characterized by its plain dark brown glaze. Simple, and austerely beautiful, it is often used for tea ceremony. If you are unfamiliar with the process of pottery making, you will be impressed with the skillful handiwork of the craftsmen.

Three kilns are pictured on map 130 – **Kyozan Kiln** 鏡山窯 (middle right), **Kojiro Kiln** 小次郎窯 (middle left), and **Ochanomizu Kiln** お茶ノ水窯（妙見屋）(middle left), and one more kiln, **Hanchu Kiln** 帆柱窯, on map 131 (middle left).

There are a number of pottery shops along the city's main street, which runs between Karatsu Station and City Hall.

Accommodations in Karatsu

All the major accommodations in Karatsu are located along the picturesque Niji-no-Matsubara Beach. Fresh seafood from Genkainada Sea is their specialty and their pride.

1. Hotel

Karatsu Seaside Hotel
　唐津シーサイドホテル
　(Standard: upper center, map 130. 52 rooms)
　Add: 4-182, Higashi-Karatsu, Karatsu.
　Tel: (0955) 73-5185.

2. Ryokans

Karatsu Seaside Heights
　唐津シーサイドハイツ
　(Standard: upper center, map 130. 59 rooms)
　Add: 4-182, Higashi-Karatsu, Karatsu.
　Tel: (0955) 73-5185.

Yoyokaku 洋々閣
　(Standard: upper center, map 130. 25 rooms)
　Add: 2-4-40, Higashi-Karatsu, Karatsu.
　Tel: (0955) 72-7181.

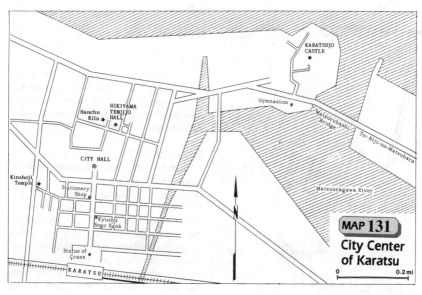

MAP 131
City Center
of Karatsu

Nagasaki

長崎

Nagasaki was a small fishing village until the middle of the 16th century, when the Portuguese started trading there. Christianity, which was introduced by the Jesuits, soon took root in the area, but it was prohibited at the end of the century by Hideyoshi Toyotomi, the military leader who completed the unification of Japan after a long period of civil war. He forced those who had converted to renounce their religion. Twenty-six faithful Christians refused to do so, and were executed in 1597 at what is now Nishizaka-Koen Park. All of these martyrs were named saints by the Pope in 1862.

In 1639, the Tokugawa Shogunate adopted isolationism as a national policy and closed all Japanese ports except Nagasaki to foreign traders. The Tokugawas wanted to shut out the Christian influence of the European traders, and, at the same time, wanted to monopolize foreign trade, keeping all the profits for the Shogunate. Only Dutch and Chinese traders who did not have any connections with Christian missionaries were allowed to continue trading at Nagasaki. Thus, during the nation's long period of isolation, Nagasaki became the eyes through which Japan watched the changes of the world. Until the abandonment of this isolationist policy in the 19th century, all modern ideas, science and technology were introduced into Japan through Nagasaki.

In the modern era, Nagasaki prospered as a port city, and became a shipbuilding center. An atomic bomb was exploded over Nagasaki on August 9, 1945, three days after the explosion at Hiroshima. The city was rebuilt and rehabilitated rapidly, and today, with a population of 450,000, Nagasaki is the center of Western Kyushu.

Transportation to Nagasaki

The JR Nagasaki Line (No. 54) runs between Hakata and Nagasaki. The ride on a limited express takes 2 hours 30 minutes. Though not introduced in this book, the JR Omura Line connects Nagasaki with Sasebo. The ride takes 1 hour 30 minutes by express, and 2 hours 30 minutes by local.

Nagasaki Airport (also called as Omura Airport) is served by flights from Tokyo, Osaka, and Nagoya. An airport bus runs between the airport and Nagasaki Station in 55 minutes.

Transportation in Nagasaki

Most places of interest, night life and shopping centers are conveniently connected by streetcars. The city's four different streetcar lines are pictured on map 133. A one-day pass, which allows unlimited rides on the four lines, can be purchased at major hotels (not on the streetcars).

Outline of the City

Even though there are many shopping, eating and drinking places in its vicinity, JR's Nagasaki Station (middle left, map 133) is rather isolated from downtown (lower center, map 133). The majority of the city's night spots and shopping centers are in the southern part of the city. Local government offices and business properties are located between downtown and Nagasaki Station. Most of the cultural and his-

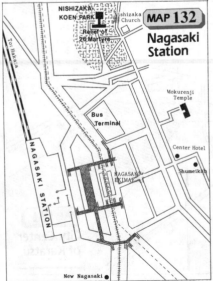

MAP 132
Nagasaki Station

torical relics of Nagasaki are also located in the southern part of the city. The northern part of the city contains A-bomb related sites and monuments. Mt. Inasayama, the best place to view the whole city, is located to the west of Nagasaki Station.

Places of Interest

The suggested Kyushu itinerary provides for only one full day of sightseeing in Nagasaki. However, because two one-day itineraries are ideal for Nagasaki (one full day for the southern historic area, and one more full day for the northern and the cen-

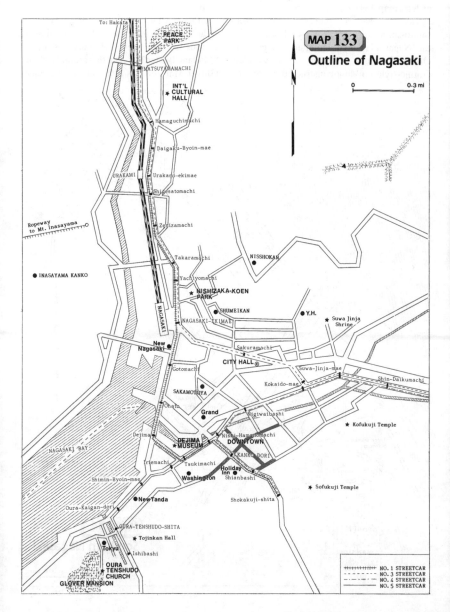

MAP **133**
Outline of Nagasaki

0   0.3 mi

+++++++++ NO. 1 STREETCAR
- - - - - NO. 3 STREETCAR
— - — -   NO. 4 STREETCAR
———————   NO. 5 STREETCAR

tral areas), we have introduced Nagasaki that way, and have, of course, suggested how you can select major sites to construct a one-day itinerary.

Day 1 Itinerary
Oura Tenshudo Church 大浦天主堂 (Lower left, map 134)

Take the No. 5 streetcar to Oura-Tenshudo-shita stop 天主堂下 , and walk past the Nagasaki Tokyu Hotel to the church. Oura Tenshudo Church is a wooden Gothic-style building constructed in 1864 to honor the 26 martyrs of Nagasaki. The Church features impressive stained glass windows, and has been designated a National Treasure (8:00 AM to 6:00 PM. Admission 200 yen).

Glover Mansion グラバー邸 (Lower left, map 134)

Glover Mansion is the oldest Western style building in Japan. The mansion is famous as the scene of Puccini's opera "Madam Butterfly." On the grounds of the Glover Mansion is a living museum consist-

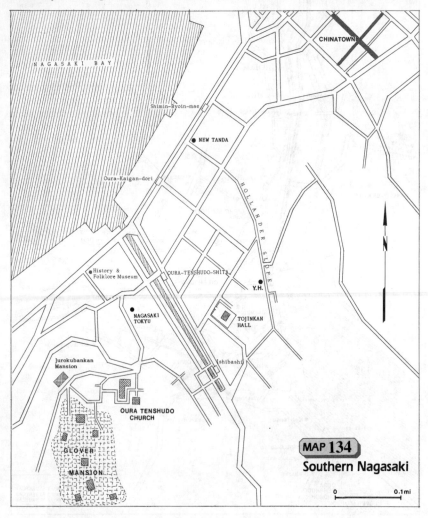

NAGASAKI BAY

CHINATOWN

Shimin-Byoin-mae

● NEW TANDA

Oura-Kaigan-dori

HOLLANDER SLOPE

● History & Folklore Museum

OURA-TENSHUDO-SHITA

Y.H. ●

● NAGASAKI TOKYU

TOJINKAN HALL

Jurokubankan Mansion

Ishibashi

OURA TENSHUDO CHURCH

GLOVER MANSION

N

MAP 134
Southern Nagasaki

0   0.1mi

ing of several Western style buildings which were moved here from their original locations around Nagasaki. They are on a hillside equipped with escalators that ease your trip to the top. Probably the best way to appreciate the museum is to take the escalators to the top, and then walk down, visiting the various houses located on the hillside. You can have a good view of the port of Nagasaki from the grounds (8:30 AM to 5:00 PM. Admission 600 yen).

Jurokubankan Mansion 十六番館 (optional) (Lower left, map 134)

Jurokubankan, another Western style building located right outside the exit of the Glover Mansion grounds, is a museum that contains historical and cultural objects that illustrate the early Western and Christian influence in Japan (8:30 AM to 5:00 PM).

To Ishibashi Streetcar Stop

A narrow street that runs east from Jurokubankan Mansion leads to the square in front of Oura Tenshudo Church. Instead of returning along the same street which you took on your way to the Church, take the narrow path stretching to the southeast. The path travels down a hillside on which are clustered a number of small houses typical of Nagasaki.

* If you are spending only one day in Nagasaki, take the No. 5 streetcar from Ishibashi 石橋 to Tsukimachi 築町 (lower center, map 133), and then transfer to No. 1 streetcar to Matsuyamamachi 松山町 (upper left, map 133) to visit Peace Park.

Tojinkan Hall 唐人屋敷跡 and Hollander Slope オランダ坂 (optional: middle center, map 134)

Tojinkan Hall was built in 1893 by the Chinese residents of Nagasaki and was dedicated to Confucius. The present building was reconstructed after World War II. The Hall contains Chinese arts and crafts, as well as a restaurant and many souvenir shops (8:30 AM to 5:30 PM).

Hollander Slope runs up the hillside. The path was so named because Dutch traders often took walks here. Take the No. 5

streetcar from Shimin-Byoin-mae stop (upper center, map 134) to Tsukimachi (middle left, map 135), or you can continue to walk to Dejima Museum (0.4 miles or 0.6 km.).

Dejima Museum 出島資料館 (Middle left, map 135)

The site of Dejima Museum was the only place foreigners were allowed to live and trade for more than 200 years. The original Dutch traders' residence still stands here. There are also miniature replicas of the secluded trading houses, which were completed in 1957 (9:00 AM to 5:00 PM. Closed on Mondays. Admission free).

Suwa Jinja Shrine 諏訪神社 (optional) (Middle center, map 133)

Returning to the Tsukimachi stop, take the east-bound No. 5 streetcar to Suwa-Jinja-mae 諏訪神社前.

Suwa Jinja Shrine was constructed at the order of the feudal government to promote Shintoism and to help wipe out Christian influence in the area. Slowly, it became very popular with the people of Nagasaki. A 277-step stone stairway leads to the wooded precincts and the magnificent shrine buildings. The shrine is famous as the home of Okunchi Festival, which is held each year from October 7 – 9. The precincts are open year round to worshippers and visitors (No admission charge).

When you finish at Suwa Jinja, it may be around 3 or 4 PM. Take the west-bound No. 4 or No. 5 streetcar to Nigiwaibashi

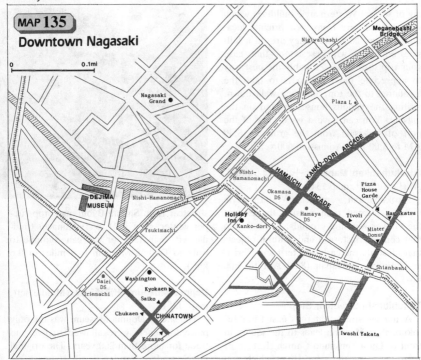

MAP 135
Downtown Nagasaki

stop (or you can walk the distance of about 0.4 miles or 0.6 km.). Then enjoy a stroll across Meganebashi Bridge (Eyeglasses Bridge) and around the downtown area.

Downtown Nagasaki (Map 135)

The street that runs northeast from Kanko-dori streetcar stop is a shopping arcade (indicated with shaded red). Another street, starting at Nishi-Hamanomachi streetcar stop, and also indicated with shaded red, is another shopping arcade. Modern stores and specialty shops crowd

both of these streets. Many restaurants are also located in the area. The southern part of the wide street where the streetcars run is clustered with many drinking places and pachinko pinball parlors (also pictured in shaded red). Chinatown is further to the southwest (lower left, map 135).

Restaurants in Downtown

Pizza House Garde (middle right) serves 11 – 13 inch pizzas (inexpensive).

Restaurant Tivoli (middle right) serves Japanized Italian cuisine (inexpensive).

Hamakatsu (middle right) serves fried pork cutlets (inexpensive).

Chinatown (lower left). Only four Chinese restaurants are indicated on the map. There are many more in the area, and they are reasonably priced.

Iwashi Yakata (lower right) is a Japanese pub specializing in sardines. You can enjoy them here just about every way possible: sliced raw – as sashimi, fried, broiled, minced, as tempura, etc. Try "shochu," a special Kyushu alcoholic drink, to accompany the fresh seafood. Be forewarned: it's strong stuff and rather pungent! Iwashi Yakata is easy to find because a big tank with lots of sardines stands in front of it (reasonable).

Day 2 Itinerary
Peace Park 平和公園 (Map 136)

You should begin your second day with a visit to Peace Park. Take either the No. 1 or No. 3 streetcar to Matsuyamamachi stop 松山町 (refer to map 133 for streetcar connections).

* If you are spending just one day in Nagasaki, you should visit Peace Park after Glover Mansion.

Peace Park was built on a small hill around the spot over which the A-bomb exploded on August 9, 1945. The Park's 32-foot (10 m.) bronze statue is the symbol of the wishes of the people of Nagasaki for

peace. It is the work of Seibo Kitamura. The Park also features many statues and sculptures presented by foreign countries. It is open year round.

Urakami Tenshudo Church 浦上天主堂 (optional) (Upper right, map 136)

* If you are spending just one day in Nagasaki you should skip this church.

If you have visited or are planning to visit Hiroshima's Peace Memorial Museum, you can also skip the International Cultural Hall, and proceed to the next destination – Nishizaka-Koen Park, which is located near Nagasaki Station and which is explained below.

Urakami Tenshudo Church was built by faithful Christians who secretly adhered to their religion throughout the 200 years that it was banned by the Tokugawa Shoguns. When freedom of religion was restored

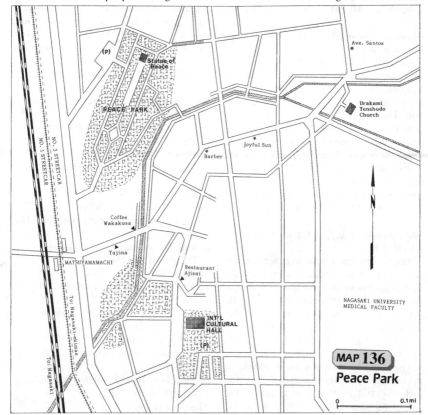

MAP 136
Peace Park

with the Meiji Restoration, these people built the largest Catholic church in the Orient with their own hands. The present building was reconstructed in 1959 to replace the original, which was destroyed by the A-bomb.

International Cultural Hall

(Lower center, map 136) 長崎国際文化会館

International Cultural Hall is located in a quiet park. It displays objects that illustrate the devastation caused by the atomic bomb. Looking at the panel displays and the twisted remains of objects destroyed by the A-bomb is by no means a pleasant experience, but it is an important one and will help you better understand the era we live in (The power of atomic weapons exploded in Hiroshima and Nagasaki is nothing compared to the destructive capacity of today's arsenal). The Hall is open from 9:00 AM to 5:00 PM. Admission is 50 yen.

Nishizaka-Koen Park 西坂公園 (Upper center, map 132)

Take the south-bound No. 1 or No. 3 streetcar from Matsuyamamachi stop to Nagasaki-ekimae 長崎駅前. Nishizaka-Koen is on a small hill northeast of Nagasaki Station. The twenty-six faithful Christians who defied the government mandate to renounce their religion were executed here in 1597. A bronze monument honoring the martyrs was completed in 1962. The Park's museum features objects related to Christianity in Japan (Museum is open from 9:00 AM to 5:00 PM. Admission 200 yen).

Mt. Inasayama 稲佐山 (optional) (Middle left, map 133)

The bus to Inasayama Ropeway Station uses a bus stop located under the huge pedestrian bridge in front of Nagasaki Station. Take the north-bound No. 3 bus. Be sure to take a *seiri-ken* fare zone ticket upon entering the bus. Ropeway-mae stop ロープウェイ前 is your destination. The ride takes about five minutes.

The ropeway station is on a hillside. It operates every 20 minutes from 9:00 AM to 5:00 PM. (till 10:00 PM in summer). The top of Mt. Inasayama (1,089 feet, or 332

Nagasaki was the eyes of Japan during the more than 200-year-long isolation.

m., a five-minute walk from the ropeway station) has a fantastic view of the city of Nagasaki; the summit also commands a beautiful view of Saikai National Park.

For the return trip from Ropeway-mae stop to Nagasaki Station, you have to take a different bus because most buses in Nagasaki operate as one-way loops. You should take the south-bound No. 30 or No. 40 bus to Nagasaki-ekimae.

Nagasaki Harbor Sightseeing Boat

If you are interested in a boat ride in Nagasaki Harbor, take the south-bound No. 1 streetcar to Ohato stop (middle left, map 133) and then walk west for three minutes to the boat pier. A 60-minute sightseeing boat operates three times a day at 10:15 AM, 11:40 AM and 3:15 PM.

Accommodations in Nagasaki

1. Hotels

Nagasaki Tokyu Hotel 長崎東急ホテル
(First-class: lower left, map 133. 225 rooms)
Add: 1-18, Minami-Yamatemachi, Nagasaki.
Tel: (0958) 25-1501.

Nagasaki Grand Hotel 長崎グランドホテル
(First-class: middle center, map 133. 126 rooms)
Add: 5-3, Manzaimachi, Nagasaki.
Tel: (0958) 23-1234.

Hotel New Tanda ホテルニュータンダ
(Standard: lower left, map 133. 161 rooms)
Add: 2-24, Tokiwamachi, Nagasaki.
Tel: (0958) 27-6121.

New Nagasaki Hotel ニュー長崎ホテル
(Standard: middle left, map 133. 60 rooms)
Add: 14-5, Daikokumachi, Nagasaki.
Tel: (0958) 26-6161.

Holiday Inn Nagasaki ホリディ・イン長崎

(Standard: middle center, map 133. 84
rooms)
Add: 6-24, Dozamachi, Nagasaki.
Tel: (0958) 28-1234.

Nagasaki Washington Hotel
長崎ワシントンホテル
(Business hotel: lower left, map 133. 177
rooms).
Add: 9-1, Shinchimachi, Nagasaki.
Tel: (0958) 28-1211.

2. Ryokans

Nisshokan 日昇館
(First-class: middle center, map 133. 166
rooms)
Add: 210-1, Nishizakamachi, Nagasaki.
Tel: (0958) 24-2151.

Shumeikan 秀明館
(First-class: middle center, map 133. 106
rooms)
Add: 3-11, Chikugomachi, Nagasaki.
Tel: (0958) 22-5121.

Sakamotoya 坂本屋旅館
(First-class: middle center, map 133. 20
rooms)
Add: 2-13, Kanayamachi, Nagasaki.
Tel: (0958) 26-8211.

Inasayama Kanko Hotel 稲佐山観光ホテル
(First-class: middle left, map 133. 124
rooms)
Add: 577, Akebonomachi, Nagasaki.
Tel: (0958) 61-4151.

Shimabara and Unzen
島原，雲仙

There are two ways to travel from
Nagasaki to Kumamoto.

The easier route involves taking a
through bus (No. 262) that originates in
Nagasaki at the Bus Terminal in front of
Nagasaki Station (middle center, map 132).
The bus runs along the scenic southern
shore of the peninsula to Obama, and then
climbs up to Unzen. After visiting the volcanic "hells" in Unzen, the bus continues
to Shimabara-gaiko and crosses Ariake Bay
by ferry to Misumi. The bus makes a short
detour to visit the scenic Amakusa-Gokyo
(Five Bridges of Amakusa), and then proceeds to Kumamoto. It stops at JR's
Kumamoto Station, and terminates at Kotsu Center Bus Terminal in downtown
Kumamoto. The trip takes about 10 hours.

The other route requires you to travel on
your own. Take the JR Nagasaki Line (No.
54) from Nagasaki to Isahaya, and then
transfer there to the private Shimabara Tetsudo Line (No. 261) bound for Shimabara.
In Shimabara visit Shimabarajo Castle and
the samurai houses. Then continue on the
Shimabara Tetsudo Line to Shimabara-gaiko. After enjoying a one hour

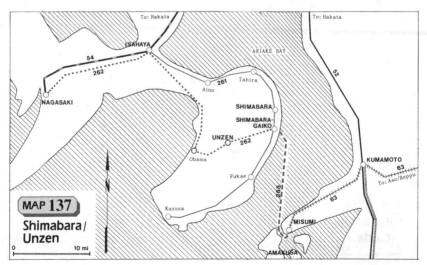

MAP 137
Shimabara/
Unzen
0   10 mi

cruise across Ariake Bay, take the JR Misumi Line (No. 63) from Misumi to Kumamoto. This full day trip is an enjoyable sightseeing event in itself.

Shimabara 島原

Shimabara Station has both a check room and coin lockers. Leave your bags at the station before you start your Shimabara walking tour.

Shimabara, with Ariake Bay to its east and with Mt. Mayuyama (2,687 feet, or 819 m.) rising to the west, is a bright, scenic city. Christian missionaries were very successful in this area. In 1638, the teachings of this new faith, and the severity of the taxes levied by the military government spurred the local farmers to revolt. The Tokugawa Shogunate dispatched a huge force to suppress the rebellion, and, after three months of severe battles, 37,000 rebels were massacred. Amid the peaceful atmosphere of the city today, it is difficult to imagine the bloody tragedy of the Christians and the farmers 350 years ago.

Shimabarajo Castle 島原城

Shimabarajo Castle is located at the end of the main street that begins at the train station. It was originally built in 1625, and the donjon was reconstructed in 1964. The entrance to the castle grounds is on the western side. The grounds are open from 8:00 AM to 6:00 PM (till 5:00 PM in winter), and admission is 10 yen.

There is a great view of Ariake Bay from the top of the donjon. The six-story donjon is also a museum that displays Christian objects on the second floor, samurai weapons and armor on the third, and pottery on the fourth. Especially noteworthy is the collection of Christian objects. They are classified according to the eras when Christianity was introduced in Japan and when it was prohibited by the military government (The 200 yen admission to the donjon includes admission to Seibo Memorial Museum). The eastern turret houses the Seibo Museum, which displays the works of Seibo Kitamura, a famous sculptor born in the area. The Peace Statue in Nagasaki's Peace Park is the work of Seibo. The western turret is used for display of a collection of kokeshi wooden dolls that includes samples

MAP 138
Shimabarajo Castle

0   0.1mi

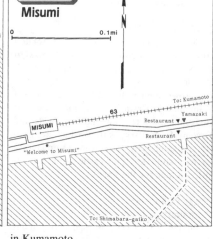

of this popular folkcraft item from all parts of Japan.

Samurai Houses 武家屋敷跡

Samurai houses still stand in Teppocho, northwest of the Castle. A clear creek, which was used for drinking water, still runs between the mud walls which surround the wooden houses. Two houses, which were residences of lower-class samurai, are open to the public. Teppocho preserves the atmosphere of the feudal city and is one of the best of several places like this in various parts of the country.

Kumamoto's prosperity began when Kiyomasa Kato, one of the most influential of Hideyoshi Toyotomi's generals, had a magnificent castle built here in 1601. The city was later granted by the Tokugawa Shogunate to the feudal lord Tadatoshi Hosokawa. Throughout the Edo era, Kumamoto prospered under the rule of successive generations of the Hosokawa family. After the Meiji Restoration, when Japan moved toward modernization and democratization, samurai warriors who resisted the new order fought their last battle in Kumamoto.

Kumamoto is often called the "forested city." The many trees in every neighborhood of this lovely city help create and maintain its fresh and pleasant atmosphere.

Transportation to Kumamoto

Located in the western central part of Kyushu, Kumamoto is conveniently linked with other major cities.

Kumamoto is served by the JR Kagoshima Line (No. 52), which runs between Hakata and Nishi-Kagoshima. Kumamoto is also served by another JR Line (No. 64) and connected with Miyazaki.

From Nagasaki: See the Shimabara and Unzen sections above.

From Beppu: See the Mt. Asozan section below.

Kumamoto Airport is served by flights from Tokyo, Osaka, and Nagoya. An airport bus runs between the airport and Kumamoto Station in 55 minutes.

Transportation in Kumamoto

Streetcars are the most convenient public transportation. As pictured on map 141, there are two streetcar lines – No. 2 and No. 3. The route number is posted on the front of the car. The No. 2 line, which is indicated with a solid line, operates every 5 – 6 minutes. The No. 3 line, which is indicated with a broken line, operates every 15 to 30 minutes. Be sure to take a *seiri-ken* fare zone ticket when you enter.

Outline of the City

JR's Kumamoto Station is rather isolated from the city's downtown, but thanks to the No. 2 streetcar, it is quite easy to reach the downtown area from the station. The downtown area is located to the south of Kumamotojo Castle. The major attractions of Kumamoto are Kumamotojo Castle and Suizenji-Koen Park, both of which are easily accessible by streetcar (Kumamoto-jo-mae stop for the castle and Suizen-ji-Koen-mae for the Park).

Places of Interest
Kumamotojo Castle 熊本城

Kumamotojo Castle is especially famous for its delicately curved stone walls. The curve served a defensive purpose, and prevented attackers from climbing up the walls. The defensive capabilities of the Castle were tested a few years after the Meiji Restoration when samurai who had been deprived of the privileges and social status they enjoyed during the feudal era, holed up in it and battled the imperial forces. The rebels survived for 55 days against the overwhelming force of the imperial army.

The major buildings were burnt down in this battle; the present castle was reconstructed in 1960.

As pictured on map 142, there are two major entrances to the Castle. In order to better see the magnificent stone walls, we recommend that you get off the street car at Kumamotojo-mae stop and use the southwestern entrance. The approach leading to the donjon, which is located on the highest point of the grounds, may help you imagine what it was like for the 17th century samurai who ascended these stone steps on their way to pledge their allegiance to their feudal lord. The interior of the six-story donjon is a museum that houses historical objects related to the feudal lords who governed the Kumamoto area. Take the path headed southeast and leave the grounds near the Shiyakusho-mae streetcar stop. The castle grounds are open from 8:30 AM to 5:30 PM (until only 4:30 PM in winter), and admission is 100 yen. Entrance to the donjon costs an additional 200 yen.

Suizenji-Koen Park 水前寺公園 (optional)

Suizenji-Koen Park is officially open from 7:00 AM to 6:00 PM (Admission 100 yen), but the Park never really closes. Take

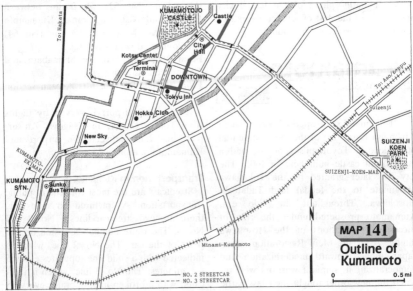

MAP 141
Outline of
Kumamoto

NO. 2 STREETCAR
NO. 3 STREETCAR

0   0.5 mi

either the No. 2 or No. 3 streetcar from Shiyakusho-mae stop after visiting Kumamotojo Castle. Allow 15 – 20 minutes for the trip to Suizenji-Koen-mae stop. Take note that the stops for the west-bound streetcar and the east-bound streetcar are about 0.1 miles away from each other.

Suizenji-Koen Park was established over 300 years ago by Tadatoshi Hosokawa and was improved upon by succeeding lords of the Hosokawa family. The Garden features miniature replicas of the picturesque scenery along the Tokaido Road (the road connecting Tokyo and Kyoto), such as Mt. Fuji and Lake Biwako.

Downtown Kumamoto

The streets indicated with shaded red on map 142 are shopping arcades. Two depart-ment stores – Shiroya and Tsuruya – are located in the arcades, and one more department store – Iwataya-Isetan – is located near Kotsu Center Bus Terminal. Most drinking and eating establishments are located to the northwest of these arcades.

Some Restaurants in Downtown

Daiichi Ginnan Building (middle center, map 142) houses many restaurants and bars. **Kumaichi** (1F) is a Korean-style barbecue restaurant (reasonable), and **Wakaba** (5F) serves a tempura dinner and Japanese-style set menu dinner (reasonable). **Higokko** (lower center, map 142) is an inexpensive "robatayaki" pub. **Chohan** (lower center, map 142) features a variety of Japanese cuisine, including tempura, shabu-shabu, and several set menus (reasonable).

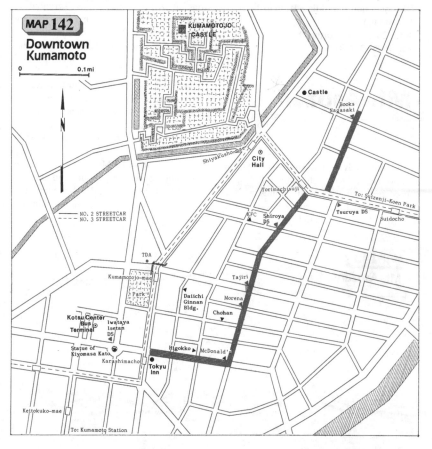

Hotels in Kumamoto

New Sky Hotel ニュースカイホテル
  (First-class: middle left, map 141. 358
  rooms)
  Add: 2, Higashi-Amidajimachi, Kuma-
  moto.
  Tel: (096) 354-2111.

Kumamoto Hotel Castle
  熊本ホテルキャッスル
  (First-class: upper center, map 141. 214
  rooms)
  Add: 4-2, Jotomachi, Kumamoto.
  Tel: (096) 326-3311.

Kumamoto Tokyu Inn 熊本東急イン
  (Business hotel: middle center, map 141.
  140 rooms)
  Add: 7-25, Shin-Shigai, Kumamoto.
  Tel: (096) 322-0109.

Hokke Club Kumamoto 法華クラブ熊本店
  (Business hotel: middle left, map 141.
  139 rooms)
  Add: 20-1, Nishidorimachi, Kumamoto.
  Tel: (096) 322-5001.

Mt. Asozan 阿蘇山

Geologically, Mt. Asozan is a typical
volcano chain. An eighty-mile (128 km.)
ring of outer mountains surrounds a wide
caldera valley. It is in this valley that the
JR Hohi Line runs, and where approximately 100,000 people live. In the center
of the valley rise the main mountains of
Mt. Asozan. There are five main peaks,
which are 4,300 – 5,200 feet (1,300 – 1,600
m.) above the sea level. The crater of Mt.
Nakadake still emits steam and demonstrates the wild and mysterious powers of
nature.

We suggest that you visit Mt. Asozan on
your way to Beppu from Kumamoto. If
you don't take this trans-Kyushu route, you
can still visit the mountain in one day from
Kumamoto (Allow 7 – 8 hours).

There are two ways to travel from
Kumamoto to Beppu via Mt. Asozan.

The easier route involves taking a
through bus (No. 266) from Kumamoto.
The bus originates at Sanko Bus Terminal
in front of JR's Kumamoto Station, and
stops at Kotsu Center Bus Terminal in
downtown Kumamoto. The bus trip includes the visit to Mt. Asozan, and a drive
through the scenic Yamanami (mountain)
highway to Beppu. The ride takes about 7
hours.

The other route requires you to travel independently. This route is especially recommended for those who have Japan Rail
Passes, because the trip involves a ride on
the entire route of the JR Hohi Line (No.
63). You have to make a roundtrip bus trip
from Aso Station to Mt. Asozan. The bus
runs about once every hour, and the trip
takes 40 minutes from JR's Aso Station to
Asozan-nishi ropeway station, and 30
minutes for the return trip.

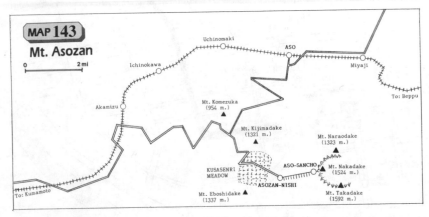

To Asozan-nishi Ropeway Station
阿蘇山西駅

The road leading to Asozan-nishi ropeway station is a well-maintained toll road that zigzags up the mountain slope. The valley between the inner (main) mountains and outer mountains falls away under your eyes. Along the way the bus passes a distinctive mountain shaped like an inverted bowl of rice (called "Komezuka", or rice mound) and a spacious, picturesque meadow (called "Kusasenri" or 2,500-mile meadow). The bus usually makes a short stop at Kusasenri to allow passengers time to get off the bus and enjoy the scenery (and to provide the professional cameramen waiting there the opportunity to take the passengers' photos).

Aso-sancho (Top of Mt. Nakadake)
阿蘇山頂 (中岳火口)

There are many restaurants and souvenir shops in and around the ropeway station. The 0.9 km. (0.6 mile) long ropeway operates every 8 minutes and takes visitors to the top of Mt. Nakadake in only 4 minutes. From the ropeway you can see a pleasant walking path on the lava slope. If the weather permits, and if you are a good walker, it is enjoyable to take the path on your way back to Asozan-nishi bus terminal.

The crater of Mt. Nakadake is 1.1 km. (0.7 miles) wide from north to south, 0.4 km. (0.25 miles) long from east to west and about 100 m. (330 feet) deep. Steam billows forth from the bottom of the crater, and the pedestrian paths along its edge are dotted with shelters.

Beppu
別府

Beppu is Japan's hotspring capital. There are eight hotspring resorts scattered about the Beppu area. More than 200 hotels and ryokans accommodate the hundreds of thousands of tourists from around the world who flock here every year. Beppu is also home to several medical institutions and hospitals that study the role of hotsprings in curing a variety of diseases.

Transportation to Beppu

Beppu is connected with Kumamoto by the JR Hohi Line (No. 61) and the Private "Yamanami Highway" bus (No. 266). You

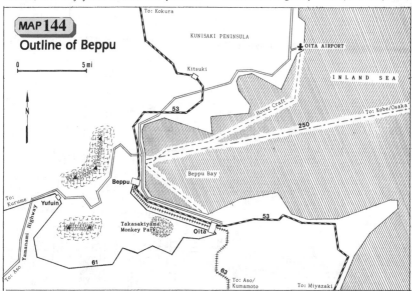

MAP 144
Outline of Beppu

0   5 mi

To: Kokura
KUNISAKI PENINSULA
OITA AIRPORT
Kitsuki
INLAND SEA
Hover Craft
To: Kobe/Osaka
250
Beppu Bay
Beppu
To: Kurume
Yufuin
Takasakiyama Monkey Park
Oita
53
To: Aso/Kumamoto
To: Miyazaki
61
63
N
53
To: Aso Yamanami Highway

will use one of these if you follow our suggested itinerary.

Beppu is also served by the JR Nippo Line (No. 53), and is linked with Kokura to the north and Miyazaki to the south. By combining the Shinkansen (to Kokura) and the Nippo Line (Kokura to Beppu), you can reach Beppu in two and a half hours from Hiroshima, and in four and a half hours from Kyoto.

The airport for Beppu is Oita Airport, which is located to the northeast of Beppu. Several daily flights are available from Tokyo, Osaka, Nagoya and Matsuyama. Airport buses connect the airport and Beppu Station (70 minutes). Hovercrafts also operate between the airport and Beppu Kokusai Kankoko Pier (45 minutes).

You can also travel to Beppu by steamship (No. 260). The Kansai Steamship Company operates three daily trips each way between Osaka and Beppu via Kobe (it is easier to board the boat in Kobe). Unfortunately, all of them are overnight trips, and pass through the beautiful scenery of the Inland Sea in the dark.

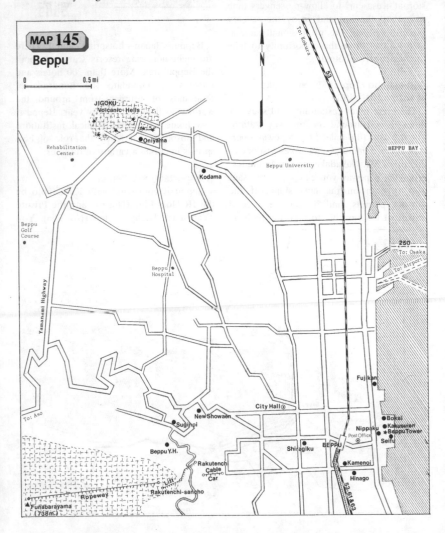

MAP 145
Beppu

Beppu Hotspring by Hotspring

Beppu has eight hotspring resorts – Beppu, Kankaiji, Kannawa, Hamawaki, Myoban, Kamegawa, Shibaseki, and Shin-Beppu. The first three have important tourist facilities and attractions.

The main attractions in Beppu are the large hotspring baths attached to most of the area's accommodations. Like many insular peoples, the Japanese have a great deal of curiosity about foreigners, especially Westerners. In Beppu, your most overwhelming experience is likely to be as an object of curiosity at the large communal baths. If you are with a tour, your group will probably overwhelm the Japanese gawkers, but if you are alone you are likely to be a bit uncomfortable. Most accommodations nowadays have private hotspring baths in each guest room, which should help those who care for privacy.

Beppu Hotspring 別府温泉

Located conveniently close to JR Beppu Station (lower right, map 145), Beppu Hotspring is the town's most developed area: its major streets are lined with souvenir shops, bars, cabarets and other night life/entertainment facilities. It is interesting to see the thousands of tourists strolling in the evening, each wearing a *yukata* robe bearing the name of his or her hotel/ryokan.

Beppu Tower (lower right, map 145), located to the east of Beppu Station, is a 100-meter tall TV tower. Its observatory is 55 meters above sea level.

Cable Rakutenchi (lower center, map 145) is a recreation complex at the western end of Beppu Hotspring. Located in the middle of Mt. Funabarayama, this hillside amusement park contains a zoological garden, a playland, a small museum for hotspring science, and a planetarium.

Kankaiji Hotspring 観海寺温泉

Two of the most deluxe accommodations in Beppu – New Showaen and Suginoi Hotel – are in a quiet, hilly area that overlooks the city. Kankaiji Hotspring is very popular among couples and foreign visitors, as well as deluxe group tours. Suginoi Palace スギノイ・パレス, attached to Suginoi Hotel (but nevertheless open to visitors), is a huge complex of several hotspring baths, including the famous jungle bath; swimming pools; bowling alleys; theater restaurants; etc. Many Japanese tourists spend a full-day at leisure here.

Kannawa Hotspring 鉄輪温泉

Kannawa Hotspring is famous for its "Jigoku" volcanic hells (upper center, map 145). It has more than 10 hells, representing different volcanic activities, and is laid out with an eye to the tourist trade. The easiest way to visit the hells is to join a scheduled sightseeing bus 地獄めぐりバス. Though the tour is designed for Japanese tourists, you should not have much of a problem. The two hour and 20 minute tour starts at Beppu Kitahama Bus Terminal 別府北浜バスターミナル (several minutes walk to the east from Beppu Station) every 30 – 40 minutes from 8:30 AM to 3:40 PM, and visits eight Kannawa "Jigoku".

Takasakiyama Monkey Park
高崎山自然公園

Mt. Takasakiyama (lower center, map 144), a 628 meter tall peak located between Beppu and Oita Stations, is home to approximately 1,600 wild monkeys (15 minutes by taxi from Beppu).

Originally, the monkeys conducted frequent raids on area farms. To keep them away from their crops, the farmers began feeding the monkeys. The Monkey Park, which is now quite a tourist attraction, was the eventual result. The monkeys are divided into three groups: each has its own leader and jealously protects its territory. The Monkey Park has a central feeding area, and during the morning, each of the groups makes a separate visit there. The visits are the highlight for tourists, and offer great photo opportunities.

Accommodations in Beppu
1. Beppu Hotspring
Beppu Fujikan Hotel 別府富士観ホテル
   (Standard ryokan, 91 rooms)
   Add: 122-1, Wakakusa-cho, Beppu.
   Tel: (0977) 23-6111.

Hotel Bokai ホテル望海
  (Standard ryokan, 65 rooms)
  Add: 3-8-7, Kitahama, Beppu.
  Tel: (0977) 22-1241.
Kamenoi Hotel 亀の井ホテル
  (First-class ryokan, 88 rooms. 31 of them
  are Western-style rooms)
  Add: 5-17, Chuo-cho, Beppu.
  Tel:(0977) 22-3301.
Hotel Seifu ホテル清風
  (First-class ryokan, 197 rooms)
  Add: 2-12-21, Kitahama, Beppu.
  Tel: (0977) 24-3939.
Hotel Shiragiku ホテル白菊
  (Deluxe ryokan, 108 rooms)
  Add: 16-36, Uedanoyu-machi, Beppu.
  Tel: (0977) 21-2111.

2. Kankaiji Hotspring

Suginoi Hotel 杉乃井ホテル
  (Deluxe. 89 Western-style rooms and 513
  Japanese-style rooms)
  Add: 2272, Minami-Tateishi, Beppu.
  Tel: (0977) 24-1141.
New Showaen ニュー昭和園
(Deluxe ryokan, 44 rooms)
  Add: 2178, Minami-Tateishi, Beppu.
  Tel: (0977) 22-3211.

Miyazaki
宮崎

The development of Miyazaki started after the Meiji Restoration, when the city
was selected as the capital of Miyazaki Prefecture. Miyazaki now has a population of
279,000. Palm trees line the city's major
streets, and Miyazaki has a pleasant subtropical atmosphere. Miyazaki is a good
base of operations for exploring Aoshima,
Obi and other destinations south of the
city.

Transportation to Miyazaki

Miyazaki is connected by the JR Nippo
Line (No. 53) with Kokura to the north,
and with Kagoshima to the west. JR trains
to Kumamoto (No.64) and to Obi (No. 65)
also originate at Miyazaki. There is fre-

quent air service to Miyazaki from Tokyo
and Osaka. Buses run between the airport
and Miyazaki Station in 25 minutes.
Note:
Miyako City Bus Terminal near JR
Minami-Miyazaki Station is the central
point of the city's bus transportation system. You can take a direct express bus
to Ebino Kogen Plateau from here (Refer to the Kirishima section below).

Downtown Miyazaki

Downtown Miyazaki is to the west of JR
Miyazaki Station (shaded red on map 146).

Miyazaki Jingu Shrine 宮崎神宮

Miyazaki Jingu Shrine is just a 15 minute
walk from JR Miyazaki-Jingu Station. The
shrine was dedicated to Emperor Jimmu, a
rather mythological figure who established
the Yamato imperial court. In the clean,
wide grounds of the shrine is located the
Miyazaki Prefectural Museum. The
museum displays historic and archeological
objects from the area (9:00 AM to 4:30
PM. Closed on Mondays).

Heiwadai-Koen Park 平和台公園

A 15 minute walk from Miyazaki Jingu
Shrine. This spacious garden was constructed in 1940 to celebrate the 2,600th
anniversary of the mythological foundation
of the nation of Japan. The neatly maintained gardens feature ancient clay images
("haniwa").

Hotels in Miyazaki

Sun Hotel Phoenix
  サンホテルフェニックス
  (First-class: upper center, map 147.
  302 rooms)
  Add: 3083, Hamayama, Miyazaki.
  Tel: (0985) 39-3131.
Hotel Plaza Miyazaki ホテルプラザ宮崎
  (First-class: lower right, map 146.
  183 rooms)
  Add: 101, Kawaharacho, Miyazaki.
  Tel: (0985) 27-1111.
Miyazaki Kanko Hotel 宮崎観光ホテル
  (First-class: lower right, map 146.
  103 rooms)
  Add: 1-1-1, Matsuyama, Miyazaki.

Tel: (0985) 27-1212.
Hotel Phoenix　ホテルフェニックス
(Standard: lower right, map 146.

117 rooms)
Add: 2-1-1, Matsuyama, Miyazaki.
Tel: (0985) 23-6111.

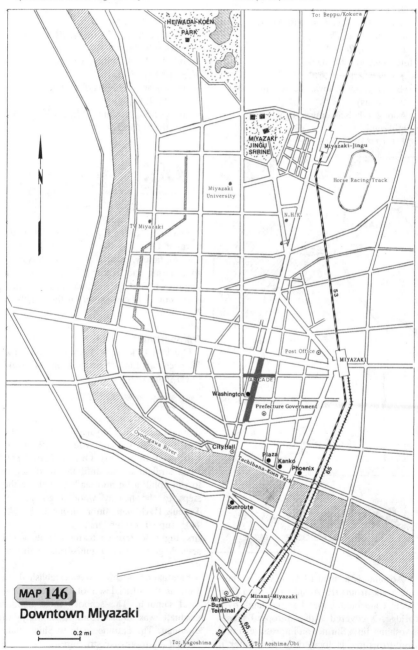

Miyazaki Washington Hotel
宮崎ワシントンホテル
(Business hotel: middle center, map 146.
205 rooms)
Add: 3-1-1, Tachibanadori-Nishi,
Miyazaki.
Tel: (0985) 28-9111.

Hotel Sunroute Miyazaki
ホテルサンルート宮崎
(Business hotel: lower center, map 146.
105 rooms)
Add: 1-1-1, Nakamura-Higashi,
Miyazaki.
Tel: (0985) 53-1313.

the islet. The shallow rocky shore surrounding the islet has eroded into a unique formation called the "Devil's Washboard."

Ryokans in Aoshima

Aoshima Tachibana Hotel 青島橘ホテル
(First-class: 332 rooms)
Add: 2-1-26, Aoshima, Miyazaki.
Tel: (0985) 65-1311.

Aoshima Kanko Hotel 青島観光ホテル
(Standard: 88 rooms)
Add: 3-1-53, Aoshima, Miyazaki
Tel: (0985) 65-1211.

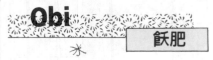

Obi 飫肥

Kyushu's "Little Kyoto," the old castle town of Obi, was the traditional home of the Ito family, which ruled the Miyazaki area during the Tokugawa era. Obi is a small town, and the best way to get around is on foot. You can explore it thoroughly in 2 – 3 hours.

Transportation to Obi

Obi is a little more than 1 hour by the JR Nichinan Line (No. 65) from Miyazaki (local trains only).

Half-Day Itinerary

Turn left when you leave the train station and cross the Shuyagawa River. At the fourth intersection after you cross the river, there will be a Post Office. Turn right. Walk straight ahead until the road begins to run uphill a bit and leads directly to the steps to the heavily wooded grounds of **Tanoue Hachiman Jinja Shrine** 田上八幡神社 (upper center, map 148). After the first flight of steps up to the Shrine, you'll see a huge tree with a mini-shrine built into it.

Shintokudo 振徳堂 was established in 1801 as the official school for the sons of local samurai. The school's most famous graduate was Jutaro Komura, a Meiji-era diplomat. The entrance gate to Shintokudo is itself an impressive structure.

Aoshima 青島

Aoshima is a small islet, only a five minute walk from JR Aoshima Station. The islet, connected with the mainland by a bridge, is covered with subtropical plants. Aoshima Jinja Shrine, an impressive vermilion structure, is located in the center of

Proceed to **Otemon Gate** 大手門 . The size of the huge two-story gate will give you some idea of what the scale of the Castle must have been. Once you've passed through Otemon Gate, turn right and go up the steps behind the wall. At the top of the steps you'll come to the **Historical Museum** 歴史資料館 . Obijo Castle was home to the Ito family for 14 generations, and this well laid-out Museum is a sort of attic for Ito family items. It displays swords, armor, kimono and castle utensils, such as lacquer trays. When you pay the 300 yen admission fee for the Museum you'll get a ticket that will also gain you admission to all other parts of the Castle grounds.

Up the stairway to your left is **Matsunomaru** 松尾ノ丸 , an exact reproduction of the residence of the Ito family. You can walk all through this graceful building, and the bilingual brochure distributed at the Castle grounds explains the function of each of its rooms. Watch your head and enjoy!

When you leave Matsunomaru, walk in the opposite direction from the Historical Museum, and climb the steps to the top of the **Castle Ruins** 飫肥城跡 . The trees there are majestic and the view of the mountains in the distance quite spectacular.

As you leave the Castle grounds through Otemon Gate, you'll come to **Yoshokan** 予章館 on your right. The ticket you got in the Castle grounds will gain you admission here as well. You can walk all around this typical Obi scholarly samurai residence. Before you leave, be sure to explore the garden, which is particularly lush in spring and summer.

Walk along Otemon-dori Street until you get back to the main street. This is the **Honmachi** 本町 section of Obi, traditional home of the merchants of the area. The old neighborhood was destroyed when the road was widened in 1980, but several of the modern merchants had their homes reconstructed in the original style. One of the finest old buildings has become the **Merchants Museum** 商家資料館 . This large, two-story white building has a wooden first floor exterior. It was built by Gohei Yamamoto, a lumber merchant, in 1866. The Museum displays utensils, equipment and furniture of the old Honmachi merchant families.

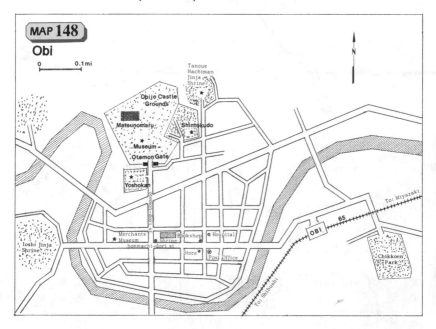

If you have time:

Ioshi Jinja Shrine 五百禩神社 (lower left, map 148) has a lovely garden and a peaceful pond. Behind the Shrine is a cemetery with Ito family graves.

Chikkoen Park 竹香園 (lower right, map 148). The only entrance to this park is from east side of the train station. You can follow the path up the hill. It's an extremely peaceful place – the only sound you can hear is the creaking of the bamboo trees.

Kirishima
霧島

Ebino Kogen Plateau is located on the border between Miyazaki and Kagoshima Prefectures. Surrounded by Mts. Karakuni, Koshiki and Kurino, the plateau is dotted with beautiful lakes and hot springs. The plateau is also famous for its Japanese red

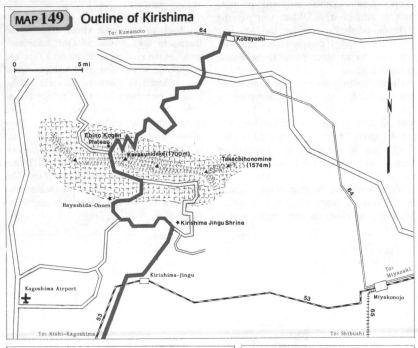

MAP 149 Outline of Kirishima

To: Kumamoto
To: Kobayashi
0   5 mi
Ebino Kogen Plateau
Karakunidake (1700m)
Takachihonomine (1574m)
Hayashida-Onsen
Kirishima Jingu Shrine
Kirishima-Jingu
Kagoshima Airport
Miyakonojo
To: Miyazaki
To: Nishi-Kagoshima
To: Shibushi

Byakushi-ike Pond
Natural Trail
To: Kobayashi
Fudoike Pond
Rokkannon-miike Pond
Ebino Visitor Center
Ebino-Kogen (Bus Terminal)
Ebino Kogen Htl. Annex
Ebino Kogen Htl
MAP 150
Ebino Kogen
To: Kirishima-Jingu

MAP 151
Kirishima Jingu Shrine
To: Ebino-Kogen
Kirishima Jingu Shrine
Kirishima-Jingu-mae
Info.
Kirishima Kogen Y.H.
To: Kirishima-Jingu

pines, azaleas and bird watching opportunities. The autumn foliage is spectacular. You can visit the plateau and nearby Kirishima Jingu Shrine on your way from Miyazaki to Kagoshima. If you have extra time, consider staying overnight either at the plateau or at nearby Hayashida-Onsen.

Transportation to Ebino Kogen Plateau

Take the JR Kitto Line (No. 64) from Miyazaki to Kobayashi 小林. Ebino Kogen Plateau is about one hour from Kobayashi by bus (private). There are also direct buses from Miyazaki (Miyako City Bus Terminal, lower center of map 146) to Ebino Kogen several times a day. If you take the bus from Kobayashi, it's easiest to get the bus at the Miyazaki Kotsu Bus Center. When you leave the train station, walk straight ahead and turn right on the main street. The Bus Center is on the left hand side after the second traffic light – it's the first building on your left after the end of the arcade awnings.

Ebino Kogen Plateau えびの高原 (Map 150)

The trip from Kobayashi to Ebino Kogen Plateau is along the Kirishima Skyline Drive, which features magnificent vistas. There are some lockers at the Ebino Kogen Bus Terminal building. If your bags are too large for the lockers, the woman who runs the souvenir shop next door will check them for you. You're up in the mountains here, so be sure to bring warm clothes.

Across the street from the bus stop is a large parking lot, and beyond it are the Rest House, a souvenir shop and the Visitors' Center. To the left and in front of the Visitors' Center is a big brown signboard. The entrance to the **Ebino Kogen Natural Trail** えびの高原散策路 is just to the left of the signboard. A leisurely hike along this circular path will take less than 2 hours. You'll see three beautiful crater lakes on this walk, and the path is dotted with observatory platforms. When the path goes uphill, there are steps to ease the way. The first of the three ponds is Byakushi-Ike. The second, Rokkannon-miike, the largest of the three, is famous for its magnificent

cobalt blue color. The third pond, a twenty-minute hike from Rokkannon-miike, is Fudoike. On your way back to the Visitors' Center and Bus Center, you'll pass sulphurous hot springs that are a constant reminder of the volcanic origins of the topography of this plateau. You'll also pass the field of *susuki* pampas grass that, in the autumn, takes on an orange-red tint.

In summer months, ambitious hikers can climb to the top of Mt. Karakunidake in about 1 hour.

Accommodations in Ebino Kogen Plateau

Ebino Kogen Hotel えびの高原ホテル
(Standard: lower right, map 150.
20 rooms)
Add: 1495, Nagasue, Ebino.
Tel: (09843) 3-1155.
* Annex has 44 Japanese rooms.

To Kirishima Jingu Shrine

If you travel to Kagoshima on a Hayashida Bus from Ebino Kogen Plateau, you should make a stop on the way at Kirishima Jingu Shrine. The trip between Ebino Kogen Plateau and Kirishima Jingu Shrine takes about 50 minutes, and is quite spectacular. As the bus descends from the Plateau, there are great views of the mountain peaks above and of Sakurajima and Kagoshima Bay below. You can also catch occasional glimpses of plumes of steam escaping from the hot springs that dot the region.

Hayashida-Onsen 林田温泉

Hayashida-Onsen is the largest hotspring resort in Kirishima, and is located between Ebino Kogen Plateau and Kirishima Jingu Shrine. If you are a hotspring enthusiast and have an extra day, you may wish to stay overnight here.

Hotel Hayashida Onsen ホテル林田温泉
(First-class: 458 rooms)
Add: 3958, Takachiho, Kagoshima Pref.
Tel: (09957) 8-2911.

Kirishima Jingu Shrine 霧島神宮 (Map 151)

There are coin lockers at the Kirishima Jingu Shrine bus stop. Recross the red bridge the bus crossed just before the stop, and climb up the steps to the Shrine. Set among Japanese cedars, this lavish shrine is dedicated to *Ninigi-no-Mikoto*, grandson of the Japanese sun goddess *Amaterasu-Omikami*. In addition to the fantastic carvings of flowers and animals on the main building, the Shrine also features a magnificent view of Sakurajima. The maple leaves in the fall are absolutely breathtaking.

Kagoshima 鹿児島

Kyushu's southernmost city, Kagoshima, is situated on a lovely bay. The city is symbolized by Sakurajima, the active volcano located in the bay. Southern Kyushu is an area rich in tourist attractions, and Kagoshima is its administrative, commercial and cultural center. The people of this area are as warm and sunny as the climate.

Outline of the City

Kagoshima's downtown area is centered around the Tenmonkan streetcar stop. Arcades (shaded red) crowded with shops and restaurants cross the street the streetcar runs on and run parallel to it. A pleasant place to take an evening stroll. The backstreets behind Takashimaya Department Store have the seamier sort of establishments.

Transportation to Kagoshima

Kagoshima Airport is served by flights from other major cities, such as Tokyo, Osaka, Nagoya, Hiroshima, Fukuoka, Nagasaki, and Okinawa. Airport buses run between JR's Nishi-Kagoshima Station and the airport (a 60 minute ride).

There are two train stations in Kagoshima: Kagoshima Station 鹿児島駅 and Nishi-Kagoshima Station 西鹿児島駅. The latter is the main station and the terminus of two major long distance trains – the JR Kagoshima Line from Hakata (No. 52) and the JR Nippo Line from Kokura (No. 53).

The JR Ibusuki-Makurazaki Line (local

trains only) runs between Nishi-Kagoshima and Ibusuki, a famous hotspring resort to the south of Kagoshima. Trains run once every 30 to 40 minutes, and the ride takes 1 hour 10 minutes.

Transportation in Kagoshima

Kagoshima is served by the streetcar lines outlined on map 152. In rush hours they run as frequently as once every 4 minutes. At other times, they run about once every 15 minutes. Enter in the rear, exit at the front. You can also get around to many of the city's sightseeing attractions on foot. Several bus companies operate lines in the city and to outlying areas.

Places of Interest in Kagoshima
Iso-Teien Garden 磯庭園 (Upper right, map 152)

About a ten minute ride from the Kagoshima Station stop (25 minutes from Nishi-Kagoshima) on the Hayashida Bus line, Iso-Teien Garden was laid out in 1660 by Mitsuhisa Shimazu, the 19th Lord of Satsuma, whose family ruled this area for 700 years (8:30 AM to 5:30 PM. Admission 500 yen).

Just past the entrance to the Garden is a complex that contains a restaurant, a snack shop and a Rest House. Keep going, and you'll reach the Main Villa, the Shimazu family home, which has a lovely view of Kagoshima Bay. You can walk around the villa but can't enter it. Wander through the rest of the garden: there's a lovely pond, a miniature waterfall, a plum grove, a bamboo grove, a small shrine, and *Kyokusui-no-Niwa*, the site of noble poetry composing parties. Between the Rest House and the Shimazu Villa there's a ropeway that will take you to the top of the mountain behind the Garden in a small cable car in just 3 minutes. The view from **Iso-yama Recreation Ground** 磯山リクリエーショングラウンド (optional) at the summit is unparalleled, with spectacular vistas of Sakurajima and Kagoshima Bay. There's an amusement park-type playland, with go-carts and other rides, but there's also a lovely formal garden and a natural area where you can stroll (after crossing the

Kurenaibashi Suspension Bridge!).

Shoko Shuseikan Historical Museum 尚古集成館 (optional). Your ticket from

Iso-Teien Garden will gain you free admission here, and its hours are the same as those of the Garden. The 28th Lord of Sa-

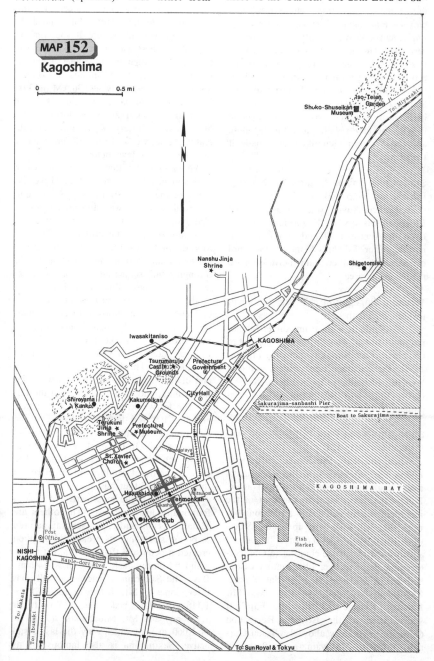

MAP 152
Kagoshima

0   0.5 mi

Iso-Teien Garden

Shoko-Shuseikan Museum

To: Miyazaki

KAGOSHIMA

Nanshu Jinja Shrine

Shigetomiso

Iwasakitaniso

Tsurumarujo Castle Grounds

Prefecture Government

Shiroyama Kanko

Kakumeikan

City Hall

Sakurajima-sanbashi Pier

Boat to Sakurajima

Terukuni Jinja Shrine

Prefectural Museum

St. Xavier Church

KAGOSHIMA BAY

Yamagataya

Hayashida

Tenmonkan

Mitsukoshi

Takashimaya

Hokke Club

Fish Market

Post Office

NISHI-KAGOSHIMA

Naple-dori Blvd.

To: Hakata

To: Ibusuki

To: Sun Royal & Tokyu

tsuma, Nariakira Shimazu, became fascinated with the technology of the West, and built an industrial complex here in the middle of the 19th century, where 1,200 employees manufactured guns, swords, farm implements and Western-style glassware and ceramics. The museum tells the story of this enterprise and displays some of its products, along with items of historical interest related to the history of the Shimazu family. The Museum has no signs in English, but does give visitors a good idea of the fervor with which the Japanese adopted Western technology and made it their own.

St. Francis Xavier Church ザビエル教会 (Middle left, map 152)

St. Francis Xavier was among the first European visitors to Kagoshima. He arrived in August 1549 and stayed for ten months, after Takahisa Shimazu, the Lord of Satsuma, granted him permission to preach in the area.

Terukuni Jinja Shrine 照国神社 (optional) (Middle left, map 152)

A 6 – 8 minute walk from Xavier Memorial and Church. This Shrine is dedicated to the memory of Nariakira Shimazu (1809 – 1858), the Satsuma Lord who introduced Western technology to southern Kyushu before the Meiji Restoration made such pioneering fashionable.

Shiroyama-Koen Park 城山公園 (optional) (Middle left, map 152)

When you leave the Shrine, turn right. Follow the waterway with the white metal fence to the corner, and turn right again. Follow the street back to the foot of the mountain, where you'll find a path on your right that will take you up to the Shiroyama-Koen Park Observatory. It's a relatively hard 15 minute climb. The Observatory is at the site of a 14th century castle, and has a fantastic view of Sakurajima, Kagoshima Bay, and, on clear days, Mt. Kaimon, Kyushu's 'Little Mt. Fuji.' If you've been to the Isoyama Recreation Ground Observatory above Iso-Teien Garden, a trip to Shiroyama-Koen Park will

probably be redundant.

Sakurajima 桜島

If you have extra time, you can take the ferry to Sakurajima, rent a bike and cycle around this volcanic island. If your time is limited, the best way to see Sakurajima is on one of the regularly scheduled Japanese sightseeing buses. The 90 minute "B Course" tour operates twice a day, at 9:30 AM and 3:00 PM, and costs 940 yen. The tour bus makes stops at an observation platform and a *Satsuma-yaki* Pottery Kiln, and the ride features great views of the volcano, the bay and the island's lava fields.

We recommend that you get an early start and take the morning tour. Take the No. 1 or the No. 2 streetcar to Sakurajima Sanbashi stop, and walk toward the water. The block between the street where the streetcars run and the port is a wholesale food distribution center, and, in the morning hours, an open air market. You'll walk through stands selling all sorts of fish, pickles, nuts, beans, flowers and packaged foods. With an early start, you'll have time to linger here and enjoy yourself, perhaps sampling some of the many items on sale.

If you plan to take the 9:30 AM "B Course" tour, you should get on the ferry by 9:00 AM. The ferry entrance is at the end of the street. Go up the stairway with the awning, and walk directly onto the ferry. The ferry ride takes about 15 minutes, and the 100 yen fare is collected at the Sakurajima terminal. At Sakurajima, go down the stairs to the platform for the regularly scheduled sightseeing buses. The clerk at the ticket window will direct you to the "B Course" tour bus.

Sakurajima is the most active of Japan's four major live volcanos. (The others are Mihara, Asama and Aso). Sakurajima used to be an island, but its great 1914 eruption created a peninsula that now links it to the mainland on the eastern side of Kagoshima Bay. The Sakurajima volcano actually has three cones – Mt. Kitadake (3,689 ft or 1,118 m.), Mt. Nakadake (3,663 ft. or 1,110 m.) and Mt. Minamidake (3,498 ft. or 1,060 m.), of which only the last is still active. Sakurajima is also famous for its

MAP 153
Sakurajima
0   2 mi

tiny *natsu mikan* (Japanese 'mandarin' oranges) and its giant white radishes (Ones as large as 5 ft or 1.5 m. in diameter have supposedly been grown here!).

The view from the observation platform where the bus makes its first stop is a great one – on clear days you can see Mt. Kaimon, a graceful cone-shaped extinct volcano, to the south, and Mt. Kirishima to the north. The next stop, at the *Satsuma-yaki* kiln is a rather long one. You'll have a chance to wander through the pottery workshop. The potters are quite gracious about letting you look over their shoulders, and will do their best to explain their craft to those who are interested. *Satsuma-yaki* ceramic ware comes in two varieties: a plain dark brown glaze, and a white glaze decorated with colorful floral patterns. After the stop at the kiln, the bus drives through the vast lava field created by the 1914 explosion of the volcano, which sent three billion tons of debris cascading down from the peaks. The rocks, of all sizes and shapes, create a sort of lunar landscape. The bus returns you to the ferry pier at the end of the tour.

Accommodations in Kagoshima

1. Hotels

Shiroyama Kanko Hotel 城山観光ホテル
  (First-class: middle left, map 152.
  621 rooms)
  Add: 41-1, Shin-Shoincho, Kagoshima.
  Tel: (0992) 24-2211.

Kagoshima Tokyu Hotel
  鹿児島東急ホテル
  (First-class: 10 minutes by taxi from Nishi-Kagoshima Station. 206 rooms)
  Add: 22-1, Kamoike-Shinmachi, Kagoshima.
  Tel: (0992) 57-2411.

Kagoshima Sun Royal Hotel
  鹿児島サンロイヤルホテル
  (First-class: 10 minutes by taxi from Nishi-Kagoshima Station. 306 rooms)
  Add: 1-8-10, Yojiro, Kagoshima.
  Tel: (0992) 53-2020.

Kagoshima Hayashida Hotel
  かごしま林田ホテル
  (Standard: middle center, map 152.
  200 rooms)
  Add: 12-22, Higashi-Sengokucho, Kagoshima.
  Tel: (0992) 24-4111.

Hokke Club Kagoshima
  法華クラブ鹿児島
  (Business hotel: middle center, map 152.
  124 rooms)
  Add: 3-22, Yamanokuchicho, Kagoshima.
  Tel: (0992) 26-0011.

2. Ryokans

Shigetomiso 重富荘
  (First-class: upper left, map 152.
  20 rooms)
  Add: 31-7, Shimizucho, Kagoshima.
  Tel: (0992) 47-3155.

Kakumeikan 鶴鳴館
  (First-class: middle center, map 152.
  53 rooms)
  Add: 5-30, Shiroyamacho, Kagoshima.
  Tel: (0992) 23-2241.

Iwasakitaniso 岩崎谷荘
  (Standard: middle center, map 152.
  62 rooms)
  Add: 14-6, Shiroyamacho, Kagoshima.
  Tel: (0992) 22-2151.

Okinawa

沖縄

Isolated in the South China Sea, away from the Japanese main islands, Okinawa was long an independent kingdom; it was not incorporated officially into Japan until after the Meiji Restoration. When the American occupation after World War II came to an end in the rest of Japan, Okinawa remained under U.S. control, and was used as one of its Far East strategic military bases, especially during the Korean and Vietnam Wars. Returned to Japanese control in 1972, Okinawa embarked on an ambitious development plan. In 1975, it

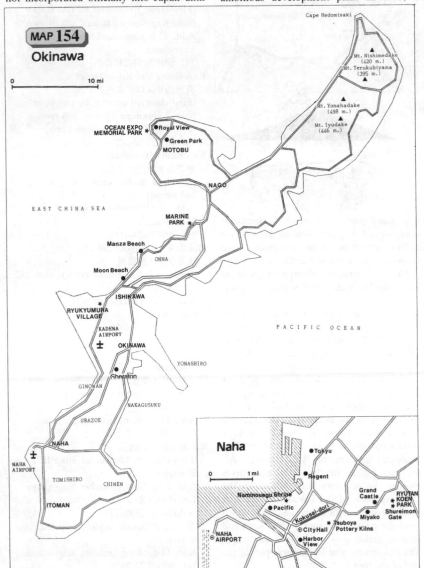

MAP 154
Okinawa

0   10 mi

Cape Hedomisaki

Mt. Nishimedake (420 m.)
Mt. Terukubiyama (395 m.)

Mt. Yonahadake (498 m.)
Mt. Iyudake (446 m.)

OCEAN EXPO MEMORIAL PARK
Royal View
Green Park
MOTOBU

NAGO

EAST CHINA SEA

MARINE PARK

Manza Beach
ONNA

Moon Beach

ISHIKAWA

RYUKYUMURA VILLAGE

KADENA AIRPORT

OKINAWA

YONASHIRO

PACIFIC OCEAN

Sheraton

GINOWAN

NAKAGUSUKU

URAZOE

NAHA

NAHA AIRPORT

TOMISHIRO

CHINEN

ITOMAN

Naha

0   1 mi

Tokyu

Regent

Naminouegu Shrine

Grand Castle
RYUTAN KOEN PARK
Shureimon Gate

Pacific

Miyako

Kokusai-dori

City Hall
Tsuboya Pottery Kilns

NAHA AIRPORT

Harbor View

was host to the World Ocean Exposition. Since then, capitalizing on its subtropical weather, Okinawa has developed many ocean resorts.

Okinawa is popular among Japanese, but is still seldom incorporated in the itineraries of foreign visitors to Japan, except for U.S. military personnel and their families.

Transportation to Okinawa

Several daily flights operate to Naha Airport from Tokyo, Osaka, Nagoya, Fukuoka, Hiroshima, Matsuyama, Miyazaki, Nagasaki and Kagoshima.

Places of Interest

Naha 那覇, with a population of 300,000, is Okinawa's capital and largest city. Kokusai-dori (International) Boulevard is the main street of Naha. Tsuboya pottery, which was developed during the time of the Ryukyu Kingdom, is the area's representative handicraft, and about 10 kilns preserve this tradition.

Shuri 首里 was once the capital of the Ryukyu Kingdom, and is now the cultural center of Okinawa. Surrounding Ryutan-Koen Park are: Shureimon Gate of the former Shurijo Castle, the symbol of Okinawa; and Okinawa Prefectural Museum, which displays historical and cultural objects of the Ryukyu Kingdom.

Okinawa 沖縄, the second largest city, was developed by U.S. military forces, and still has a large population of American and other foreign residents. Very different from other Japanese cities.

Moon Beach ムーンビーチ and **Manza Beach** 万座ビーチ are two typical modern Okinawa ocean resorts. **Ryukyumura Village** 琉球村 is an amusement park, and displays 5,000 *habu* poisonous snakes. **Okinawa Marine Park** 沖縄海洋公園 has ocean sports facilities and a submarine observatory. You can see beautiful tropical fish and corals.

Ocean Expo Memorial Park 海洋博記念公園 was built on the 1975 World Expo site. The park contains an aquarium, a marine museum, an ocean sports complex, a playland, etc.

Hotels in Okinawa

1. Naha

The Regent of Okinawa
リージェント沖縄
(Deluxe, 140 rooms)
Add: 165 Uenoya, Naha.
Tel: (0988) 64-1111.

Okinawa Harbor View Hotel
沖縄ハーバービューホテル
(Deluxe, 346 rooms)
Add: 2-46, Senzaki, Naha.
Tel: (0988) 53-2111.

Okinawa Grand Castle
沖縄グランドキャッスル
(Deluxe, 305 rooms)
Add: Yamakawacho, Shuri, Naha.
Tel: (0988) 86-5454.

Okinawa Miyako Hotel 沖縄都ホテル
(First-class, 318 rooms)
Add: 40, Matsukawa, Naha.
Tel: (0988) 87-1111.

Naha Tokyu Hotel 那覇東急ホテル
(First-class, 280 rooms)
Add: 1002, Ameku, Naha.
Tel: (0988) 68-2151.

Pacific Hotel Okinawa
パシフィックホテル沖縄
(Standard. 378 rooms)
Add: 3-5-1, Nishi, Naha.
Tel: (0988) 68-1118.

2. Other Places

Okinawa Sheraton Hotel
沖縄シェラトンホテル
(Deluxe, 310 rooms)
Add: Kita-Nakagusuku-mura.
Tel: (09893) 5-4321.

Hotel Moon Beach
ホテルムーンビーチ
(Deluxe, 136 rooms)
Add: Maekaneku, Onnason.
Tel: (09896) 5-1020.

Manza Beach Hotel
万座ビーチホテル
(Deluxe, 401 rooms)
Add: Seragaki, Onnason.
Tel: (09896) 6-2301.

Royal View Hotel
ロイヤルビューホテル
(First-class, 92 rooms)
Add: Ishikawa, Motobucho.
Tel: (09804) 8-3631.

Introduction to
Hokkaido 北海道

Hokkaido's cold weather, which made it unsuitable for Japan's early agricultural methods, kept it untouched by the central power of the nation. Traditionally, it has been the province of the Ainu, aborigines with many tribal and cultural characteristics similar to those of American Indians. Their historic destiny has been similar to that of American Indians as well.

When the Matsumae clan established the authority of the central government (the Shogunate) here in the 16th century, its influence extended to only a small southern part of the island. The balance of the vast, undeveloped land was the home of Ainu, who lived as hunters and gatherers in small autonomous family groups.

The development or colonization of Hokkaido got started in earnest under the auspices of the new central government after the 1868 Meiji Restoration. A Hokkaido government was established first in Hakodate in 1869 and then moved to newly developed Sapporo in 1871.

Since then, Hokkaido has been Japan's new frontier. The island comprises 22% of the total Japanese archipelago, but is home to only 5% of the total population. Hokkaido offers magnificent natural wonders, including mysterious caldera lakes, wild forests, volcanic mountains, and hotsprings, as well as a fresh and vigorous frontier

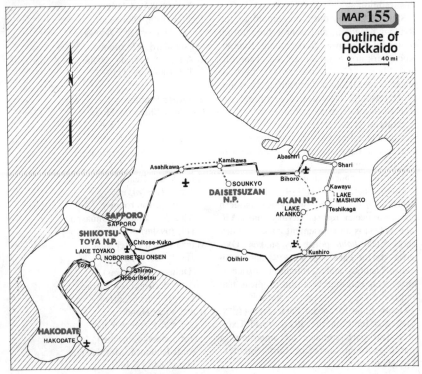

atmosphere.

In this chapter Hokkaido is introduced in two sections – Southwest and Central East.

Southwestern Hokkaido contains such major destinations as Sapporo, Noboribetsu Spa, Lake Toyako and Hakodate. This area illustrates the island's development and displays its natural beauty in Shikotsu-Toya National Park. Thanks to easy access from the mainland and a convenient transportation network between Sapporo and Hakodate, the area attracts the majority of Japanese tourists who visit Hokkaido. We suggest the following 6 day (5 night) itinerary:

Day 1. Arrive in Sapporo by air from Tokyo or Osaka, or, by ferry (Aomori/Hakodate) and train (Hakodate/Sapporo).

*JR ferry service between Aomori and Hakodate will soon be replaced by JR trains, which will use the newly completed Seikan Under-sea Tunnel.

Day 2. Full day in Sapporo.

Day 3. Sapporo/Shiraoi/Noboribetsu Spa.

Day 4. Noboribetsu Spa/Lake Toyako.

Day 5. Lake Toyako/Hakodate.

Day 6. Leave Hakodate for the mainland by either air or ferry.

*If your time is limited, you can continue your trip to Hakodate on Day 4 without staying at Lake Toyako. Or, you can skip Hakodate and catch a flight from Sapporo to Tokyo or Osaka on Day 5.

Central Eastern Hokkaido is less developed. Akan National Park, with many caldera lakes surrounded by wild forests, is one of the most beautiful in Japan. Daisetsuzan National Park is the roof of Hokkaido and is proud of its splendid gorges and mountain scenery. Most accommodations in the area are in hotspring resorts. Starting from Sapporo you need a minimum of 4 days (preferably 7) to visit the area as follows:

Day 1. Sapporo to Kushiro by train, or you can fly from Tokyo directly to Kushiro. Then a bus from Kushiro to Lake Akanko. (If possible, stay 2 nights at Lake Akanko.)

Day 2. Akanko/Lake Mashuko/Lake Kutcharoko/Bihoro by bus. Then a train to

Kamikawa and a bus to Sounkyo. (If you have extra time, visit Abashiri for one or two days, and then proceed to Sounkyo.)

Day 3. Full day in Sounkyo.

Day 4. Sounkyo/Asahikawa/Sapporo. You can stay in Sapporo, or can continue to Sapporo Airport and catch a late afternoon flight to Tokyo or Osaka.

Sapporo 札幌

With a population of 1,528,000, Sapporo, capital of Hokkaido, is the 5th largest city in Japan and the largest north of Tokyo. When Japan was unified by the modern imperial government in 1868, and the development of Hokkaido started under the auspices of the new government, the area of Sapporo was a wild land, with a small Ainu population and a few Japanese families. In just a little over 100 years, Sapporo has developed into a modern city.

Transportation to Sapporo

By Air: Sapporo Airport (locally called Chitose Airport) is about 28 miles to the southeast of Sapporo. Three major Japanese airlines (Japan Air Lines, All Nippon Airways, and Toa Domestic Airlines) maintain daily flights between Sapporo and the following major cities in Japan: Narita and Haneda Airports in Tokyo, Osaka, Fukuoka, Hiroshima, Nagoya, Kanazawa, Niigata, and Sendai. Sapporo Airport is connected with JR Chitose-Kuko Station by a covered bridge, and trains operate to Sapporo Station about once every 10 to 30 minutes (the ride takes about 50 minutes). Buses also operate between the Airport and major downtown hotels (Keio Plaza, Sapporo Prince and ANA Sapporo: a 60 minute ride).

By Train/Ferry: JR's Seikan ferry, connecting Hakodate and Aomori, is still a popular route to Hokkaido from the mainland. (The ferry will soon be replaced by a train which will run directly from the mainland via the Seikan Under-sea Tunnel to Sapporo.) From Hakodate you can reach Sapporo by a limited express train on the JR Hakodate-Muroran-Chitose Line.

Outline of The City

The city of Sapporo spreads to the south of Sapporo Station (upper center, map 156). There are three department stores – Sogo, Tokyu and Sanbankan – near Sapporo Station. Office buildings and hotels cluster between Sapporo Station and Odori Boulevard. Huge shopping malls have been developed around Odori subway station so that the city's bustling life can continue unimpeded even in severe winter weather. To the south of Odori Boulevard there are many department stores and shops, such as Marui Imai, Mitsukoshi, Parco, Daiei, etc. Susukino is a huge restaurant and night life zone. Further to the south of Susukino is Nakajima-Koen Park, a recreation zone for city residents.

Two subways – the Nanboku Line (or South-North Line) and the Tozai Line (or East-West Line) intersect at Odori Station. The Nanboku Line especially provides tourists with handy intra-city transportation. A streetcar that circles around the southern part of the city is another convenient way to get an easy glimpse of the city.

Hokkaido University (upper left, map 156) and the Sapporo Beer Brewery (upper right, map 156), popular tourist destinations, are located to the northwest and northeast of Sapporo Station respectively.

Places of Interest

Sapporo Beer Brewery サッポロビール公園, established in 1876, is the oldest brewery in Japan. The factory is proud of its completely automated modern facilities. A guided tour (in Japanese) of the factory is conducted from time to time every day (except Sunday) from 9:00 AM till 3:30 PM. Applications for the tour are accepted at the reception booth near the entrance gate. The tour visits the automated production facilities and a small gallery exhibiting old machines and beer labels in chronological order. At the end of the tour a complimentary can of beer (or soft drink) is offered to each tour participant.

The old brick factory buildings have been converted to "Sapporo Beer Garden" restaurants. Most people actually visit the factory not to join the tour but to enjoy fresh beer and Mongolian barbecue at the Beer Garden. The Garden is open for dinner as well. The breweries can be reached by taxi for 1,000 yen from the city center.

Odori-Koen Park 大通公園 (middle center, map 157): The median strips of the 100-meter wide Odori Boulevard are designed as parks with flower beds, fountains and statues. The world-famous Snow Festival is held here in early February. At the eastern end of the boulevard stands a 142-meter (469 feet) tall TV Tower, whose observatory commands panoramic views of the city and Ishikari Plain.

Botanic Garden 北大付属植物園 (upper left, map 157), with 5,000 different plants from all over the world, displays flowers of the season from April till November (closed in winter). Batchelor Museum in the Garden, also known as Ainu Museum, displays costumes, arms and everyday objects used by the northern aboriginal races.

Old Hokkaido Government Building 北海道庁旧庁舎 (upper left, map 157), a red-brick western structure, is the symbolic monument of Sapporo. A small museum in the building exhibits paintings related to the developmental history and the life of the people.

Nijo Market 二条市場 (lower right, map 157) is the kitchen of Sapporo. Small stores that sell seafood and other foodstuffs are crowded along narrow alleys. Fresh seafood is sold here at incredibly inexpensive prices. Many Japanese tourists buy bargain souvenirs here.

Nakajima-Koen Park 中島公園 is a huge

recreational area with a sports complex, playland and elaborate gardens. Hoheikan Hall in the Park, a wooden Western build-ing constructed in 1880, is another impor-tant monument of Hokkaido's develop-ment.

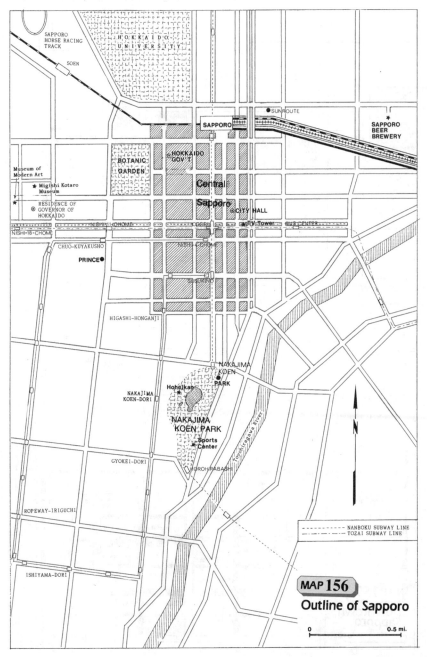

MAP 156
Outline of Sapporo

- - - - - - NANBOKU SUBWAY LINE
- · - · - · TOZAI SUBWAY LINE

0   0.5 mi.

Downtown

Tanuki-Koji Arcade 狸小路 (shaded red on map 157) runs east to west to the south of Odori Boulevard. Along with many clothing stores, it is home to a large number of souvenir shops and restaurants. **Ezo-Goten**

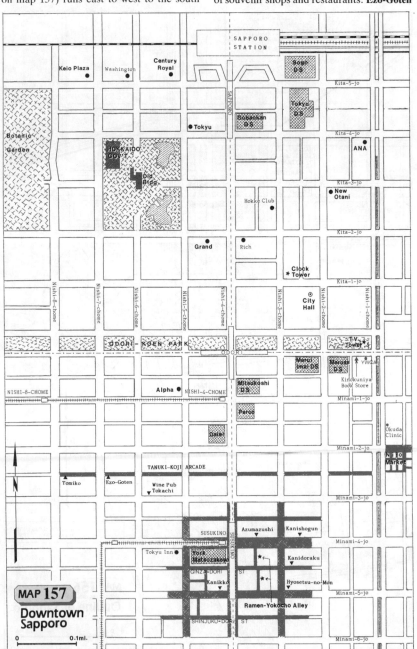

MAP **157**
Downtown
Sapporo

is a famous restaurant that features Hokkaido specialties (reasonable).

Susukino すすきの (lower center of map 157, shaded red) is a huge night life area. **Ramen Yokocho** is a narrow alley lined with *ramen* noodle shops (inexpensive). It is said that there are about 5,000 eating and entertainment facilities in Susukino. They range from the very inexpensive to extremely expensive. **Kanishogun, Kanidoraku, Hyosetsu-no-Mon** and **Kanikko** are crab specialists (reasonable to moderate).

Hotels in Sapporo

Keio Plaza Hotel Sapporo　京王プラザ
　ホテル札幌 (Upper left, map 157. First-class, 525 rooms)
　Add: Nishi-7-chome, Kita-Gojo,
　Chuo-ku, Sapporo.
　Tel: (011) 271-0111.

Hotel Alpha Sapporo ホテルアルファ札幌
　(Middle center, map 157. First-class, 147 rooms)
　Add: Nishi-5-chome, Minami-Ichijo,
　Chuo-ku, Sapporo.
　Tel: (011) 221-2333.

Sapporo Grand Hotel 札幌グランドホテル
　(Middle center, map 157. First-class, 521 rooms)
　Add: Nishi-4-chome, Kita-Ichijo, Kita-ku, Sapporo.
　Tel: (011) 261-3311.

ANA Hotel Sapporo　札幌全日空ホテル
　(Upper right, map 157. First-class. 470 rooms)
　Add: Nishi-1-chome, Kita-Sanjo,
　Chuo-ku, Sapporo.
　Tel: (011) 221-4411.

Hotel New Otani Sapporo ホテルニュー
　オータニ札幌 (Upper right, map 157.
　First-class. 347 rooms)
　Add: Nishi-1-chome, Kita-Nijo.
　Chuo-ku, Sapporo.
　Tel: (011) 222-1111.

Sapporo Prince Hotel 札幌プリンスホテル
　(Middle left, map 156. First-class. 345 rooms)
　Add: Nishi-11-chome, Minami-Nijo,
　Chuo-ku, Sapporo.
　Tel: (011) 241-1111.

Sapporo Tokyu Hotel 札幌東急ホテル
　(Upper center, map 157. First-class 263 rooms)
　Add: Nishi-4-chome, Kita-Shijo,
　Chuo-ku, Sapporo.
　Tel: (011) 231-5611.

Century Royal Hotel　センチュリー
　ローヤルホテル (Upper center, map 157. First-class. 327 rooms)
　Add: Nishi-5-chome, Kita-Gojo,
　Chuo-ku, Sapporo.
　Tel: (011) 211-2121.

Sapporo Park Hotel 札幌パークホテル
　(Middle center, map 156. First-class. 223 rooms)
　Add: Nishi-3-chome, Minami-Jujo,
　Chuo-ku, Sapporo.
　Tel: (011) 511-3131.

Hotel Rich Sapporo ホテルリッチ札幌
　(Middle center, map 157. Business hotel. 165 rooms)
　Add: Nishi-3-chome, Kita-Ichijo,
　Chuo-ku, Sapporo.
　Tel: (011) 231-7891.

Hokke Club Sapporo 法華クラブ札幌
　(Middle center, map 157. Business hotel. 124 rooms)
　Add: Nishi-3-chome, Kita-Nijo,
　Chuo-ku, Sapporo.
　Tel: (011) 221-2141.

Hotel Sunroute Sapporo ホテルサンルート
　札幌 (Upper right, map 156. Business hotel. 128 rooms)
　Add: Nishi-1-chome, Kita-Shichijo,
　Kita-ku, Sapporo.
　Tel: (011) 737-8111.

Shiraoi, Noboribetsu & Lake Toyako

白老，登別，洞爺湖

Transportation

Shiraoi, Noboribetsu and Toya Stations are located on the JR Hakodate-Muroran-Chitose Line (No. 100), which operates a number of limited express trains between Sapporo and Hakodate. Starting from Sapporo, you can reach Shiraoi in 60 – 70 minutes. After your visit to Poroto Cotan (Ainu Folklore Museum), take a short train ride to Noboribetsu. In addition to the limited express trains listed in the attached time table, short-distance local trains also run between Shiraoi and Noboribetsu about once every hour. (If you do not have a Japan Rail Pass, you can cut the fare in half by using a local train.) Noboribetsu Onsen is about 20 minutes by bus (private company) from Noboribetsu Station. The buses operate every 20 to 30 minutes.

A bus (No. 298; private company) runs between Noboribetsu Onsen and Toyako from June through the middle of October, crossing the picturesque Orofure Pass (938 meters or 3,095 feet above sea level). When the mountain road is closed by snow in winter and spring, the bus runs along the coast to Toyako. Alternatively, if you have a Rail Pass, you can take a JR train from Noboribetsu to Toya, and a 15-minute bus ride to Toyako (frequent operation).

To Hakodate you can take a bus from Toyako Bus Terminal to Toya Station, and then a JR limited express train.

The train from Toya to Hakodate runs for the most part along the Pacific Ocean coast, and you should get a left-hand window seat, if possible. Especially beautiful is the view of Mt. Komagatake rising above Onuma Pond.

*If you visit only Sapporo and plan to fly back to Tokyo, you can still visit Shiraoi easily. Leaving Sapporo by limited express train in the morning and spending a few hours in Poroto Cotan, you can still catch an early afternoon flight at Sapporo (Chitose) Airport. The train ride from Shiraoi to Chitose-Kuko takes only 30 – 40 minutes.

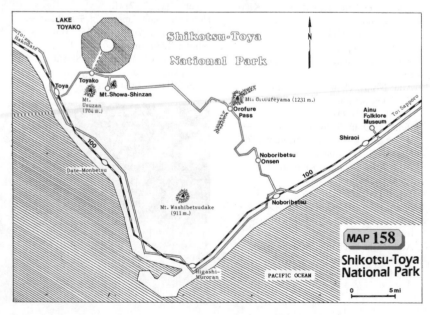

MAP 158
Shikotsu-Toya National Park

Shiraoi 白老

Shiraoi is a tiny local town. It is famous as the site of the Ainu Folklore Museum. Because of its good location – close to the Pacific Ocean with comparatively mild weather, a fairly large number of Ainu settled here long before the development of Hokkaido by Japanese. In 1965, the Ainu village in Shiraoi was moved to the shores of Lake Porotoko (a 10 minute walk from Shiraoi Station), and since then has served as the Ainu Museum. Several original Ainu houses are preserved here to give visitors an idea of their traditional lifestyle. A 18-meter (60 foot) tall statue of "Korobokkuru" (chief of the village) stands at the entrance, and brown bears (believed by Ainu to be messengers of God) are fed in the village. There is a huge building containing a number of souvenir shops. The most popular souvenir item here is a carving of a brown bear holding a salmon in his mouth, a traditional Ainu handicraft. The area is quite touristy, but provides some idea of Ainu culture and history. However, the newly constructed **Ainu Folklore Museum** 民族資料館 , the first one of this kind, not only displays daily life utensils of the Ainu but also gives the visitor a scientific explanation of the history of the Ainu, and other northern minorities. The panel displays are bilingual. Among the many so called "Ainu Museums" in Hokkaido, this is far and away the best.

There are rental row boats on Lake Porotoko. The Lake becomes a natural ice skating rink in winter.

*Shiraoi Station, a very small building, has coin lockers. If your bags won't fit, ask the station staff to keep them while you visit Poroto Cotan.

Noboribetsu Onsen 登別温泉

Noboribetsu Onsen is one of Japan's most famous hotspring spas. Major ryokans are within a few minutes walk of the Bus Terminal (lower center, map 160). To meet the needs of the large number of tourists who visit here throughout the four seasons, most accommodations have built modern concrete buildings with 100 – 400 rooms, which is very large for Japanese ryokans. Fortunately the interiors of the guest rooms remain traditionally Japanese. As is the case with many large hotspring resorts, there are a number of adult entertainment facilities along the main street (shaded red). Daiichi Takimotokan has about 30 large baths and can accommodate 1,000

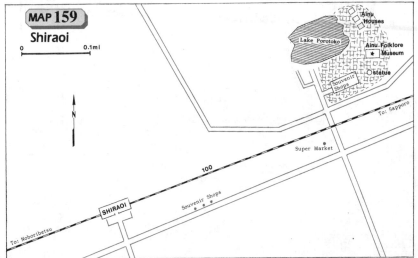

MAP 159
Shiraoi

0   0.1mi

Lake Porotoko

Ainu Houses

Ainu Folklore Museum

Souvenir Shops

Statue

To: Sapporo

N

100

Super Market

SHIRAOI

Souvenir Shops

To: Noboribetsu

bathers at a time. Its baths are open not only to its clients but also to visitors. If you are a hotspring enthusiast, you may want to visit what is described as Japan's largest hotspring facility.

Jigokudani 地獄谷, a volcanic "hell" valley, is at the northern end of the main street and is the source of hotspring waters. Sulphur and steam escape from the valley, demonstrating the wondrous power of nature.

Mt. Shihoreizan 四方嶺山 (549 meters or 1,650 feet high) is another attraction of Noboribetsu. The mountain top can be reached easily by double track ropeways. (A chair lift operates between Noboribetsu Spa and the bottom station of the ropeway (middle center, map 160). You can also easily walk up to the ropeway station in

only five minutes.) There is a brown bear sanctuary on top of the mountain. About 130 bears live here. A reproduction of an Ainu Village, called Yukara-no-Sato, is also located here (quite touristy). The summit commands a panoramic view of the area, including the Pacific Ocean to the south, Lake Kuttarako to the east and Noboribetsu Onsen to the west.

Ryokans in Noboribetsu Onsen

Daiichi Takimotokan 第一滝本館
   (First-class: 356 rooms)
   Add: 55, Noboribetsu-Onsen, Noboribetsu.
   Tel: (01438) 4-2111.
Noboribetsu Park Hotel 登別パークホテル
   (First-class: 185 rooms)
   Add: 100, Noboribetsu-Onsen, Nobori-

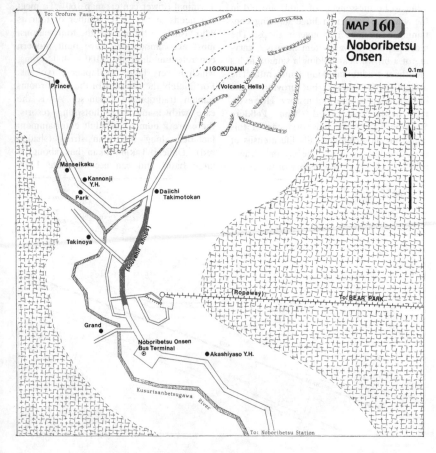

betsu.
Tel: (01438) 4-2335.
Noboribetsu Grand Hotel　登別グランド
ホテル (First-class: 264 rooms)
Add: 154, Noboribetsu-Onsen, Nobori-
betsu.
Tel: (01438) 4-2101.
Noboribetsu Prince Hotel　登別プリンス
ホテル (First-class: 163 rooms).
Add: 203, Noboribetsu-Onsen, Nobori-
betsu.
Tel: (01438) 4-2255.
Takinoya　滝の家 (Standard: 70 rooms)
Add: 162, Noboribetsu-Onsen, Nobori-
betsu.
Tel: (01438) 4-2221.

Lake Toyako   洞爺湖

Lake Toyako is the crown jewel of
Southern Hokkaido. Almost perfectly
round in shape with Oshima Island at its
center, the Lake is especially beautiful
when reflecting the cobalt blue of the clear
sky. Lake Toyako measures about 48 kilometers (30 miles) in circumference and is
19.2 meters deep at its deepest point. Modern accommodations have been developed
along the southern shore of the lake, all of
which feature hotspring baths.

Transportation to Toyako

Buses (private company) operate several
times a day between Noboribetsu Onsen
and Toyako via Orofure Pass (No. 298).
The ride takes one hour and forty minutes.
The bus stops at the top of Orofure Pass
for 10 – 15 minutes to allow passengers to
enjoy a panoramic view. (In winter, when
Orofure Pass is covered with snow, the bus
runs along the Pacific Ocean coast.) Toyako Bus Terminal is also served by buses
from JR Toya Station (frequent service; a

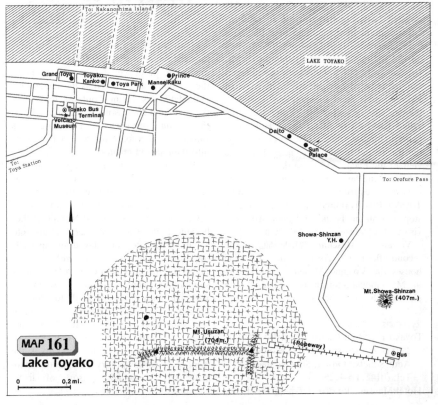

MAP 161
Lake Toyako

0   0.2 mi.

15 minute ride).

Places of Interest

Mt. Showa-Shinzan and Mt. Usuzan. Buses run between Toyako Bus Terminal (upper left, map 161) and Showa-Shinzan (lower right) once every 30 – 60 minutes. **Mt. Showa-Shinzan** 昭和新山 was formed when volcanic Mt. Usuzan erupted in 1943 through 1945, creating a 1,346 ft. (408 m) tall mountain in the middle of a flat farm field. Steam still escapes from the crevices on the mountain side. The summit of **Mt. Usuzan** 有珠山 (725 meters above sea level) can be reached by ropeway. The view of Lake Toyako from the gondola is breath-taking, with graceful Mt. Yoteisan (often called Ezo-Fuji or Mt. Fuji of Hokkaido) rising behind the lake. The observatory on the top of the mountain commands a good view of the Pacific Ocean to the south.

Sightseeing boat: A 90-minute sightseeing boat operates frequently from the pier near Toyako Bus Terminal. The boat makes a stop at Oshima Island and passengers can visit its Prefectural Forest Museum.

Volcano Museum 火山博物館 : The second floor of Toyako Bus Terminal houses the Volcano Museum. The history of Mt. Showa-Shinzan is explained with photographs and models.

Ryokans in Toyako

Toyako Park Sun Palace 洞爺湖パークサンパレス (First-class: 335 rooms)
   Add: Sobetsu-Onsen, Sobetsu-machi.
   Tel: (01427) 5-4126.
Hotel Manseikaku ホテル万世閣 (First-

class: 200 rooms)
   Add: 21, Toyako-Onsen-machi.
   Tel: (01427) 5-2171.
Toya Prince Hotel 洞爺プリンスホテル (First-class: 73 rooms)
   Add: 7, Toyako-Onsen-machi.
   Tel: (01427) 5-2211.
Toya Park Hotel 洞爺パークホテル (First-class: 167 rooms)
   Add: Toyako-Onsen-machi.
   Tel: (01427) 5-2442.
Toyako Kanko Hotel 洞爺湖観光ホテル (First-class: 132 rooms).
   Add: 33, Toyako-Onsen-machi.
   Tel: (01427) 5-2111.
Hotel Daito ホテル大東 (Standard: 132 rooms)
   Add: Sobetsu-Onsen, Sobetsu-machi.
   Tel: (01427) 5-2421.

Hakodate 函館

Hakodate, Hokkaido's third largest city, has a population of 320,000. Hakodate was under the influence of the government of the mainland as long ago as the feudal era. Hakodate was Japan's outpost to protect the mainland from riots by the Ainu. From the Ainu perspective, Hakodate was Japan's advance base for further incursions into their sacred territory.

When Japan abandoned its 250-year-long isolationist policy in 1855, Hakodate was selected as one of the five official international trading ports, together with Nagasaki, Yokohama, Kobe and Niigata. It thus became a gateway of Western culture into Japan. Hakodate Port played an especially important role in trade with Russia. Hakodate has also prospered as Hokkaido's shipbuilding center. In 1869, when the national authorities decided to develop Hokkaido, a local Hokkaido government was established in Hakodate. Two years later, the seat of local government was moved to Sapporo. While Sapporo is the symbol of contemporary Hokkaido, Hakodate has remained a sort of living monument of Hokkaido.

Outline of the City

The city of Hakodate stretches from north to south, with Hakodate Station and Pier located in the middle. Downtown Hakodate is to the east of Hakodate Station/Pier. The southern part of the city is the historic district with several monumental buildings. Mt. Hakodateyama rises at the southern end of the peninsula.

The northern part of the city has been developed into a new downtown. Goryokaku, the first Western-style fort built in Japan, is another historical monument reminiscent of the historic role of Hakodate.

Transportation in the City

Hakodate has an extensive streetcar network that serves the entire city, providing

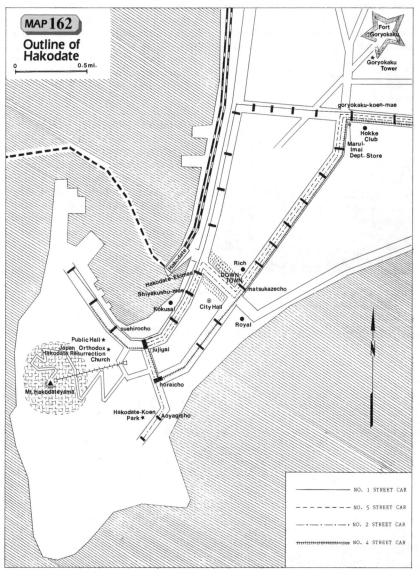

MAP 162

Outline of Hakodate

0   0.5 mi.

Fort Goryokaku

Goryokaku Tower

goryokaku-koen-mae

Hokke Club

Marui-Imai Dept. Store

Hakodate

Rich

DOWN-TOWN

matsukazecho

Hakodate-Ekimae

Shiyakushu-mae

Kokusai

City Hall

Royal

suehirocho

Public Hall ★

Japan Orthodox ★
Hakodate Resurrection Church

jujigai

Mt. Hakodateyama

horaicho

Hakodate-Koen Park ★

Aoyagicho

——————— NO. 1 STREET CAR

– – – – – – – NO. 5 STREET CAR

–·–·–·–·– NO. 2 STREET CAR

++++++++++++ NO. 4 STREET CAR

handy transportation to tourists as well as Hakodate people.

Tourist Attractions

The southern part of the city is the "must-see" area of Hakodate. **Old Public Hall** 旧函館区公会堂 (middle center, map 163), a five minute walk from Suehirocho streetcar stop, is a wooden Western-style building constructed in 1910. It is a symbol of Japanese enthusiasm of that time for Western culture. **Japan Orthodox Hakodate Resurrection Church** ハリストス正教会

(middle center, map 163) was originally built in 1862 and was replaced by the present building in 1916. This impressive wooden Byzantine-style structure enhances the exotic atmosphere of Hakodate (illuminated at night). **Mt. Hakodateyama** 函館山 (lower left, map 163) (335 meters or 1,100 feet high) can be reached by ropeway. There are TV towers and restaurants on the flat mountain top. The summit commands a panoramic view of the city, the Pacific Ocean and the surrounding mountains. The night view of the city from the summit is especially gorgeous. The ropeway operates frequently from 9:00 AM to 10:00 PM in the summer (April 21 through October 20), and 10:00 AM to 6:00 PM the rest of the year.

Goryokaku 五稜郭 (upper right, map 162) is the only tourist attraction in Northern Hakodate. This fort was built in 1857 by the Tokugawa Shogunate to protect against feared Russian aggression against Japan. Instead of being used to defend Japan against the Russians, the fort became the last scene of the battle between the samurais supporting the feudal Tokugawa shogunate and the Imperial Army of the new Meiji government. The fort is now used as a park and is open to the public.

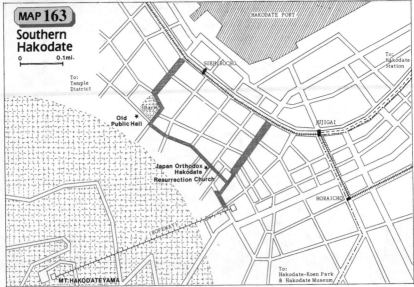

MAP **163**
Southern Hakodate
0   0.1mi.

HAKODATE PORT

To: Hakodate Station

SUEHIROCHO

To: Temple District

Old Public Hall

Park

JUJIGAI

Japan Orthodox Hakodate Resurrection Church

HORAICHO

(ROPEWAY)

MT. HAKODATEYAMA

To: Hakodate-Koen Park & Hakodate Museum

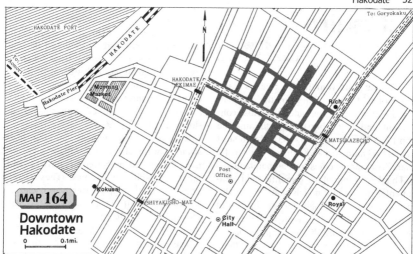

Nearby Goryokaku Tower has an observatory at its top.

Downtown Hakodate

Downtown Hakodate stretches to the east of Hakodate Station (shaded red on map 164). Several department stores are located along the main street where the streetcars run, and many restaurants and night spots cluster on the narrow alleys on both sides of the main street.

Leaving Hakodate

You can leave Hakodate via a JR Seikan ferry to Aomori, or by air to major cities in Honshu. This ferry service will be replaced in 1988 by the new JR railroad that will connect Hakodate and Aomori via the Seikan Under-sea Tunnel. The ferry pier is adjacent to Hakodate train station. Hakodate Airport is to the northeast of the city. Airport buses leave from Hakodate Station and the ride takes about 45 minutes.

Hotels in Hakodate

Hakodate Kokusai Hotel 函館国際ホテル
(Lower left, map 164. First-class. 131 rooms)
Add: 5-10, Otemachi, Hakodate.
Tel: (0138) 23-8751
Hotel Hakodate Royal ホテル函館ロイヤル
(Lower right, map 164. Standard. 117 rooms)
Add: 16-9, Omoricho, Hakodate.
Tel: (0138) 26-8181.
Hotel Rich Hakodate ホテルリッチ函館
(Middle right, map 164. Business hotel. 87 rooms)
Add: 16-18, Matsukazecho, Hakodate.
Tel: (0138) 26-2561
Hokke Club Hakodate 法華クラブ函館
(Upper right, map 162. Business hotel. 123 rooms)
Add: 27-1, Honcho, Hakodate.
Tel: (0138) 52-3121.

Kushiro

釧路

If you start your trip to Central Eastern Hokkaido from Sapporo, the JR Ishikachi-Nemuro Line provides the most convenient and enjoyable transportation. The trip takes four hours (No. 103). If you start your Hokkaido trip at Kushiro, you can fly there from major cities on the mainland.

Thanks to popular, romantic and sentimental poems and novels that feature this city, the name of Kushiro evokes images of the exotic for most Japanese. However, unless you are tracing the footsteps of one of the heroes of these stories or poems, there is nothing special to see here. If you arrive in Kushiro by train in late afternoon, you'll have to stay overnight in Kushiro. The city's main boulevard (shaded red on map 166) stretches to the south from the train station. Nusamai-bashi Bridge, with a harbor view to the west, is especially romantic in cold winter weather. Kushiro's nightlife zone is also marked with shaded red (lower right, map 166).

Kushiro is also famous for the huge swamps north of the city. Japanese cranes, now designated as Special Natural Monuments, inhabit the swamps. They retreat deep into the swamps during warm seasons. In winter, about 200 cranes visit the **Tancho-no-Sato** 丹頂の里 area for feeding. About 20 cranes are kept year round in **Tsuru-Koen Park** 鶴公園 . Because the Park is designed to protect this endangered spe-

MAP 165

Outline of Kushiro/Akanko

cies rather than exhibit the birds to visitors, you may be able to see only a few on the other side of the fence.

If you arrive in Kushiro by train, take a bus to Akanko from the bus terminal adjacent to Kushiro Station. The bus stops at Kushiro Airport on the way. Those who arrive in Kushiro by air can catch it in front of the arrivals building. Away from the modern city, the 2-hour bus ride is a trip into the heart of the natural beauty of Hokkaido.

Hotels in Kushiro

Kushiro Pacific Hotel 釧路パシィックホ
テル (Standard: lower right, map 166. 132 rooms)
Add: 2-6, Sakaecho, Kushiro.
Tel: (0154) 24-8811.

Hotel Sunroute Kushiro ホテルサンルート
釧路 (Business hotel: upper center, map 166. 128 rooms)
Add: 13-26, Kuroganecho, Kushiro.
Tel: (0154) 24-2171.

Kushiro Tokyu Inn 釧路東急イン (Business hotel: upper center, map 166. 150 rooms)
Add: 13-1-14, Kita-Odori, Kushiro.
Tel: (0154) 22-0109.

Kushiro Oriental Hotel 釧路オリエンタル
ホテル (Business hotel: lower center, map 166. 18 Western and 19 Japanese rooms)
Add: 7-1, Saiwaicho, Kushiro.
Tel: (0154) 23-3431

Lake Akanko
阿寒湖

Lake Akanko lies surrounded by wild forests between two graceful mountains – Mt. Oakandake and Mt. Meakandake. About 10 modern ryokans have been built in the hotspring resort along the southern shore of the lake. All the ryokans are within walking distance of the Akanko Bus Terminal (lower right, map 167).

Lake Akanko is especially famous for *marimo*, green weeds shaped like balls. *Marimo* are found only in several lakes in Japan, Switzerland and North America, and the ones in Akanko are considered the most beautiful for their large size and balanced shape. A **Sightseeing Boat** operates frequently on the lake and visits picturesque parts of the lake. The boat also stops at Nakanoshima Island. You can see displays of a number of *marimos* in tanks in a small museum on the island. The **Akanko Visitors Center** 阿寒湖ビジターセンター (middle right, map 167) displays flora and fauna of the area as well as several *marimos*. **Bokke** ボッケ (upper right, map 167) is a hotspring near the lake. Steam from underground constantly creates bubbles on the surface of small muddy ponds, a very unusual natural phenomenon. **Ainu Cotan** アイヌコタン (lower left, map 167) is a cluster of souvenir shops featuring Ainu

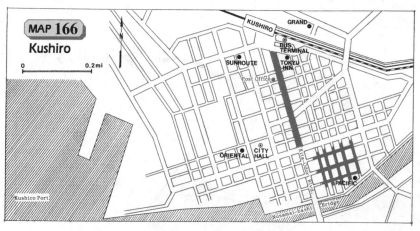

handicrafts. Ainu dances are performed in a small hut at the end of the street from time to time (quite touristy). A number of souvenir shops also line the main street (shaded red). Most tourists, after enjoying hotspring baths in their ryokan, take a walk along the street in *yukata* (a Japanese robe provided by each ryokan).

Ryokans in Akanko

New Akan Hotel ニュー阿寒ホテル (First-class: 215 rooms)
　Add: Akankohan, Akan-machi.
　Tel: (0154) 67-2121.
Akan Grand Hotel 阿寒グランドホテル (First-class: 136 rooms)
　Add: Akankohan, Akan-machi.
　Tel: (0154) 67-2531.

Hotel Akankoso ホテル阿寒湖荘 (First-class: 94 rooms)
　Add: Akankohan, Akan-machi.
　Tel: (0154) 67-2231.
Akan Kanko Hotel 阿寒観光ホテル (Standard. 70 rooms)
　Add: Akankohan, Akan-machi.
　Tel: (0154) 67-2611.
Hotel Yamaura ホテル山浦 (Standard: 60 rooms)
　Add: Akankohan, Akan-machi.
　Tel: (0154) 67-2311.

From Akanko to Bihoro

The bus trip from Akanko to Bihoro covers the highlights of Akan National Park. The scheduled bus stops for 10 – 20 minutes at several scenic points along the route to allow passengers to enjoy the vari-

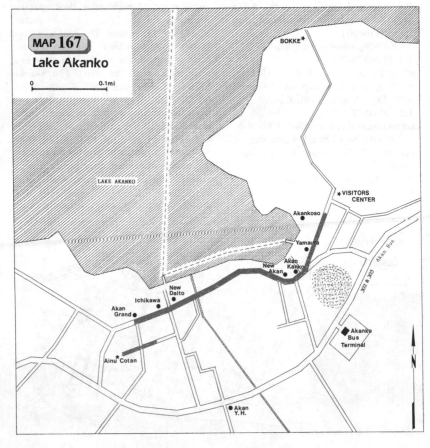

ety of natural beauties and wonders. **Soko-dai** 双湖台 is an observatory overlooking two small lakes – Panketo and Penketo Lakes. The area is still covered by extensive wild forests and is a paradise for wild animals.

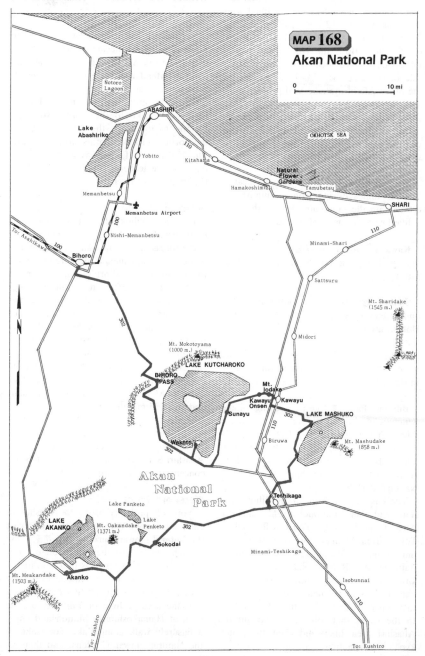

MAP **168**
Akan National Park

0   10 mi

Lake Mashuko 摩周湖 is the gem of Akan National Park. Surrounded by 200-meter (656 feet) high precipitous cliffs, this quiet mysterious caldera lake is filled with dark blue water (212 meters or 696 feet in depth). There is a small island in the center of the lake. Both the No. 1 and No. 3 Observatories are located on the western side of the lake. Mt. Mashudake rises on the other side of the lake as if protecting it. The area is foggy, especially in May through July, and the lake seldom shows its entire shape to visitors. However, some consider the lake much more attractive when it is half hidden by mist.

Mt. Iodake 硫黄岳 is an active volcano. Sulphur fumes escape from a number of crevices on the mountainside and the area is filled with the smell of sulphur.

Kawayu Onsen 川湯温泉 is another famous hotspring resort in the beautiful forest.

Sunayu 砂湯 is a scenic hotspring resort on the eastern shore of Lake Kutcharoko. Hotsprings well up even on the beach.

Wakoto 和琴 is another small hotspring resort. Wind surfing is popular on the lake in this area.

Bihoro Pass 美幌峠 : Leaving Lake Kutcharoko the bus zigzags up to Bihoro Pass. The view from the Pass, especially that of Lake Kutcharoko, is truly breathtaking. Before descending to the north to Bihoro city, you bid farewell to Akan National Park here.

The bus stops in front of JR Bihoro Station, and then continues to Memanbetsu Airport, the last stop. You can fly back to Tokyo from Memanbetsu Airport if your time is limited. We suggest that you take a train on the JR Sekihoku Line to Kamikawa to proceed to Sounkyo. If you have one or two extra nights, we recommend that you visit Abashiri on the Okhotsk Sea. In the pages that follow, we explain the Abashiri area first, and then the Sounkyo/Asahikawa area.

Abashiri

網走

Abashiri has long been called "The Town of Outlaws" because Abashiri Prison used to be reserved for brutal criminals and political offenders serving life sentences (It is no longer true nowadays). Abashiri is located in beautiful natural surroundings – Lake Abashiriko to the south, Notoroko Lagoon to the west, the Okhotsk Sea to the north, and Lake Tofutsuko to the east. The city is also famous as a place where one can see icebergs floating by its shore (February and March).

Access to Abashiri

The JR Sekihoku Line (No. 100) connects Abashiri and Sapporo. Several limited express trains run daily between the two cities. Supplemental local trains run on the same line for short distances to meet local needs. The JR Kunmo Line runs between Abashiri and Kushiro. Because major tourist attractions between them are more conveniently reached by bus, this line is not popular with tourists. Memanbetsu Airport is about 10 miles to the south of the city. Several daily flights are available to and from Tokyo. An airport bus runs between Memanbetsu Airport and Abashiri Station (a 35 minute ride).

Modern ryokans are located in the hotspring area on the eastern shore of Lake Abashiriko (10 minutes by taxi from Abashiri Station), while business hotels are concentrated downtown.

Places of Interest

You will probably arrive in Abashiri in early afternoon. We suggest that you visit the **Natural Flower Gardens** 原生花園 (lower right, map 169) the afternoon of your arrival, checking your bags in a coin locker in Abashiri Station. The Kunmo Line (No. 110) runs along Okhotsk Sea here. If you visit the area in June or July, get off the train at Hamakoshimizu Station and enjoy a leisurely walk along Lake Tofutsuko to the Natural Flower Gardens, and then return to Abashiri by train. (Rental bicycles are available near Hamakoshimizu Station). In other months, we suggest that you enjoy the natural scenery from the train window, especially graceful Mt. Sharidake, and stay on the train until Shari Station.

Shari 斜里 is a small town that functions as a shipping center for the area's logging industry. It is the northeastern-most point in Hokkaido that can be reached by train. If you have a wait for a return train to Abashiri, you should visit the **Shiretoko Museum** 知床博物館 (upper right, map 171), a 15 minute walk from Shari Station. The unexpectedly modern museum displays flora and fauna of the Shiretoko Peninsula as well as daily utensils of northern aboriginal tribes excavated in the area (Closed on Mondays and holidays).

Other Places of Interest

Abashiri Prison Museum 網走監獄博物館 (middle left of map 169): Abashiri Prison has often been featured in *yakuza* (Japanese mafia) movies. The original Abashiri Prison buildings and gates were moved to the current location to be preserved. In

Hokkaido's early frontier period prisoners were important resources of labor in the area. The primitive, simple cells tell the story of the cruel life of the prisoners in this cold northern exile. Thousands of Japanese tourists visit here to satisfy the curiosity created by the films. Several buses run between Abashiri Station and the Museum, but you may end up using a taxi.

Abashiri Municipal Museum 網走・郷土博物館 (lower center of map 170), located in the primitive Ainu fort, has several rooms exhibiting historic objects and daily utensils of the Ainu and other northern aborigines.

Abashiri Museum 網走美術館 (middle center, map 170) displays many paintings

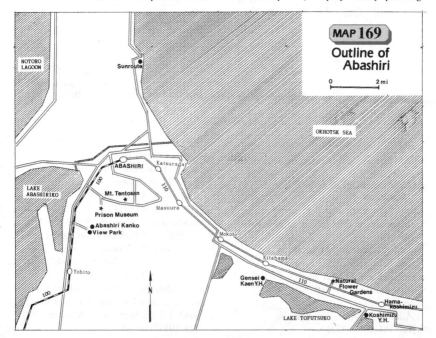

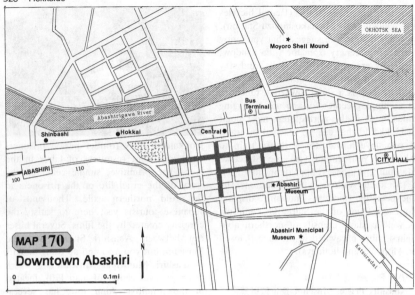

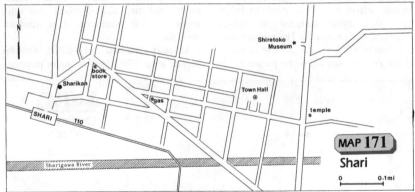

featuring the lifestyles of northern aboriginal peoples.

Accommodations in Abashiri

1. Ryokans

Hotel View Park ホテルビューパーク (Standard: middle left, map 169. 164 rooms)
  Add: 23, Yobito, Abashiri.
  Tel: (0152) 48-2211.

Abashiri Kanko Hotel 網走観光ホテル (Standard: middle left, map 169. 85 rooms)
  Add: 23, Yobito, Abashiri.
  Tel: (0152) 48-2121.

2. Hotels

Abashiri Central Hotel 網走セントラルホテル (Business hotel: middle center, map 170. 80 rooms)
  Add: Nishi 3-7, Minami-Nijo, Abashiri.
  Tel: (0152) 44-5151.

Hotel Sunroute Abashiri ホテルサンルート網走 (Business hotel: upper center, map 169. 87 rooms)
  Add: Futatsuiwa-Kaigan, Abashiri.
  Tel: (0152) 43-4581.

Hotel Shinbashi ホテルしんばし (Business hotel: middle left, map 170. 20 rooms)
  Add: 1-2-12, Shinmachi, Abashiri.
  Tel: (0152) 48-4307.

Sounkyo and Asahikawa

層雲峡, 旭川

Transportation to Sounkyo and Asahikawa

Kamikawa Station 上川 on the JR Sekihoku Line is the gateway to Sounkyo. Buses operate from Kamikawa to Sounkyo about once every hour, meeting all trains. If you follow our suggested itinerary you will catch a bus to Sounkyo here. Some of these buses run to and from Asahikawa beyond Kamikawa. The bus stop in Asahikawa is pictured on map 174 (lower left of map 174, in front of JR Asahigawa Station).

There are several daily flights between Tokyo's Haneda Airport and Asahikawa Airport. Airport buses run between the airport and JR Asahigawa Station in 30 min-

utes. If your time is limited, this air service is a convenient way to finish your Hokkaido trip and return to Tokyo.

Sounkyo 層雲峡

Sounkyo, or Gorges Reaching to the Clouds, is in the heart of Daisetsuzan National Park. The 8-km. (5 mile) long narrow valley between Sounkyo and Obako is flanked by precipitous cliffs that create gorgeous palisades scenery. All the accommodations in Sounkyo have hotspring baths.

Sounkyo Valley

To enjoy the Sounkyo Valley (between Sounkyo Bus Terminal and Obako 大函) you have to either walk or cycle (rental bicycles are available), because the automobile road passes through a tunnel under Kobako Gorge 小函, the most scenic part of the valley. If you walk, we suggest that you take a taxi from your hotel to Obako first, and then walk back on the cycling path to your hotel. The cycling path sometimes runs separately from the automobile road, but for the most part is alongside the road. Watch for buses and cars. A small tunnel near the souvenir shops in Obako marks the beginning of your exploration. A number of small waterfalls tumbling down precipitous cliffs create picturesque scenery. The walk is refreshing and

invigorating.

Sounkyo Ropeway 層雲峡ロープウェー

A 1.6-km (1 mile) long ropeway takes you from Sounkyo terminal to the 5th grade of Mt. Kurodake (a part of the Daisetsuzan mountains). You can then go by chair lift to the 7th grade. The observatory commands a panoramic view of the Daisetsuzan mountains. The balanced shape of Mt. Niseikaushupe rising over Sounkyo valley is especially impressive.

Ryokans in Sounkyo

Hotel Daisetsu ホテル大雪 (First-class: 254 rooms)
  Add: Sounkyo, Kamikawa-machi.
  Tel: (01658) 5-3211.
Sounkyo Grand Hotel 層雲峡グランド ホテル (First-class: 245 rooms)
  Add: Sounkyo, Kamikawa-machi.
  Tel: (01658) 5-3111.
Hotel Soun ホテル層雲 (First-class: 230 rooms)
  Add: Sounkyo, Kamikawa-machi.
  Tel: (01658) 5-3311.
Mount View Hotel マウントビューホテル (First-class: 40 rooms)
  Add: Sounkyo, Kamikawa-machi.
  Tel: (01658) 5-3011.

Sounkyo Kanko Hotel 層雲峡観光ホテル (Standard: 302 rooms)
  Add: Sounkyo, Kamikawa-machi.
  Tel: (01658) 5-3101.

Asahikawa 旭川

Asahikawa, with a population of 365,000, is the second largest city in Hokkaido. The city is modern and clean, but is rather characterless. After your visit to Sounkyo, you can take a train from Kamikawa to Sapporo, skipping Asahikawa. If you have already visited Sapporo and Southern Hokkaido, you can fly back to Tokyo from Asahikawa Airport. An Airport Bus operates between JR Asahigawa Station and the airport. The ride takes about 30 minutes. Incidentally, Asahikawa is the official city name, but JR uses Asahigawa as its train station name.

A Few Places of Interest in Asahikawa

Shopping Park Street: A traffic-free pedestrian mall lined with many department stores, shops and restaurants.

Yukara Textiles 優桂良織工芸館 (middle left, map 174): Yukara Textiles originated

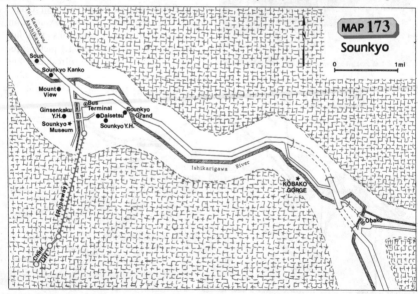

MAP 173
Sounkyo

0   1mi

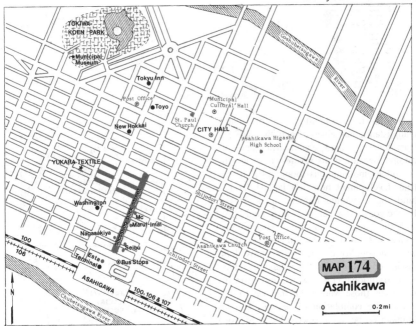

MAP 174
Asahikawa

in Asahikawa. They use the natural beauties of Hokkaido for their design motifs. Stubbornly clinging to manual processes, the textile makers have won a number of awards at major international exhibitions. A small store/exhibition hall in the downtown area (middle left) is just a 10 minute walk from Asahigawa Station. A free shuttle bus operates from here to the Main Workshop/Museum located to the west of the city (about a 15 minute ride).

Tokiwa-Koen Park 常磐公園 (upper left, map 174) contains several public halls and

gardens, as well as statues commemorating the centennial of Hokkaido's development.

Hotels in Asahikawa
New Hokkai Hotel ニュー北海ホテル
(Standard: middle left, map 174. 207 rooms)
Add: 6-chome, Gojo-dori, Asahikawa.
Tel: (0166) 24-3111.
Toyo Hotel トーヨーホテル (Standard: upper center. 108 rooms)
Add: 7-chome, Shichijo-dori, Asahikawa,
Tel: (0166) 22-7575.
Asahikawa Terminal Hotel 旭川ターミナルホテル (Business hotel: lower left. 152 rooms)
Add: 7, Miyashita-dori, Asahikawa.
Tel: (0166) 2-0111.
Asahikawa Tokyu Inn 旭川東急イン (Business hotel: upper center. 110 rooms)
Add: 6-chome, Hachijo-dori, Asahikawa.
Tel: (0166) 26-0109.
Asahikawa Washington Hotel 旭川ワシントンホテル (Business hotel: middle left. 260 rooms)
Add: 6-chome, Ichijo-dori, Asahikawa.
Tel: (0166) 25-3311.

Introduction to **Tohoku**

東北

Tohoku, the northeastern part of Japan's main island, has always been the nation's least developed area, economically and culturally. Because of its severe winter weather and its mountainous topography, industrial development here has lagged far behind the economic miracle areas of the Pacific coast. But nature is unspoiled here, and the area has beautiful coasts. The area's natural beauties and the simple, warm hospitality of the people have long fascinated visitors. The area has also clung to its traditional crafts, which add extra interest for those who make the trip to Tohoku. The completion of the JR Tohoku Shinkansen between Tokyo (Ueno Station) and Morioka has made travel to Tohoku much easier, and many parts of Tohoku nowadays can be visited in a two or three day trip from Tokyo. The following four major destinations in Tohoku are introduced in this book:

Towada Hachimantai National Park

Combination of two local cities – Aomori and Hirosaki – with Lake Towadako (3 days from Tokyo). Aomori/Lake Towadako/ Morioka route is conveniently covered by the JR buses.

Rikuchu-Kaigan National Park

Picturesque marine scenery created by a rugged coast (3 days from Tokyo). Once called the "Tibet of Japan" because of its inconvenient transportation. Thanks to the completion of new railroads it is now easily accessible.

Hiraizumi, Sendai and Matsushima

Combination of the historic city of Hiraizumi, the contemporary city of Sendai, and the poetic natural beauty of Matsushima (3 days from Tokyo).

Bandai-Asahi National Park

Beautiful mountains and lakes of Bandai-Kogen together with historic Aizu-Wakamatsu (2 days from Tokyo).

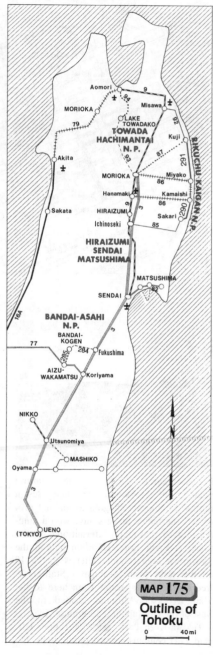

MAP 175
Outline of Tohoku

0   40mi

Aomori, Hirosaki and Lake Towadako 青森, 弘前, 十和田湖

Aomori is the main gateway to Lake Towadako. The bus terminal is adjacent to Aomori Station. You can reach Aomori by JR Seikan ferry from Hakodate. From Tokyo you can use the JR Tohoku Shinkansen (No. 3 from Ueno to Morioka) and then the JR Tohoku Line train (No. 9 from Morioka to Aomori). The combined train rides take about 6 hours. You can also fly from Tokyo (Haneda Airport) to Aomori Airport. An airport bus runs between Aomori Station and the airport in 35 minutes.

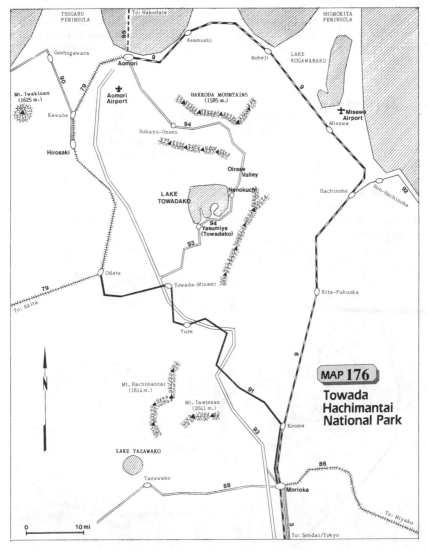

MAP 176

Towada Hachimantai National Park

The following is a typical itinerary in the area:

Day 1. Arrive in Aomori

If you have a full afternoon in Aomori, we suggest that you visit Hirosaki instead of staying in Aomori. (Hirosaki is more interesting from the tourist's view point.)

Day 2. Aomori/Lake Towadako

Morning JR bus to Lake Towadako. Visit Oirase Valley and enjoy a boat ride across the Lake. Overnight on the lake.

Day 3. Lake Towadako/Morioka

Early afternoon JR bus to Morioka, and then return to Tokyo via the Tohoku Shinkansen, or proceed to other destinations in Tohoku.

Aomori 青森

Aomori, with a population of 294,000, is the largest city in the area. The city is especially famous for its Nebuta Festival (August 3 – 7), a colorful event featuring processions of Nebuta floats. **Munakata Shiko Memorial Museum of Art** 棟方式功記念館 (lower left) displays works of Shiko Munakata (1903 – 1975), one of the world's outstanding wood-block print artists. The museum building is shaped like the famous Shosoin Treasure House of Todaiji Temple in Nara. **The Market** near Aomori Station is the kitchen of Aomori. A number of small shops are crowded in the narrow arcades. **Tourism & Products Center** 観光物産館 is a modern building housing souvenir shops and restaurants. **The Main Street** (shaded red) stretches to the east from Aomori Station and is lined with department stores, souvenir shops and restaurants.

Hotels in Aomori

Hotel Aomori ホテル青森 (Standard: middle right, map 177. 100 rooms)
  Add: 1-1-23, Tsutsumicho, Aomori.
  Tel: (0177) 75-4141.

Aomori Grand Hotel 青森グランドホテル (Standard: middle left, map 177. 138 rooms)
  Add: 1-1-23, Shinmachi, Aomori.
  Tel: (0177) 23-1011.

Hotel Sunroute Aomori ホテルサンルート青森 (Business hotel: middle left, map

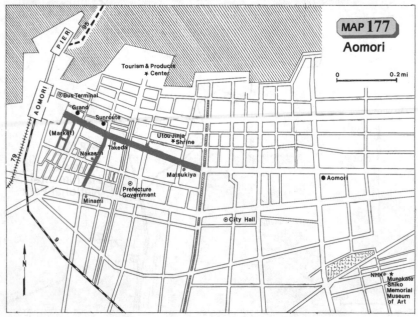

177. 124 rooms)
Add: 1-9-10, Shinmachi, Aomori.
Tel: (0177) 75-2321.

Hirosaki

弘前

Hirosaki prospered as a castle town in the feudal era. Hirosaki is connected with Aomori by the JR Ou Line. The ride takes only 30 minutes by limited express train and 60 minutes by local. Hirosaki is also famous for its Neputa Festival (August 1 – 7), similar to that of Aomori.

Hirosakijo Castle 弘前城 is about a 15 minute walk from JR Hirosaki Station. The castle was built in 1611. The three-story donjon is located in the center of neatly maintained grounds. The castle is especially popular towards the end of April, when 3,000 cherry trees display their beautiful pink flowers.

Neputa-no-Yakata ねぷたの館 is an exhibition hall of festival floats and instruments. With festival music in the background, you can experience the atmosphere of the colorful, gay summer event.

Yokien Garden 揚亀園, attached to Neputa-no-Yakata, is one of Tohoku's most famous landscaped gardens. The garden features pine trees, rocks and ponds. **Samurai Houses** 武家屋敷跡: To the north of the castle is located the old samurai residential district (upper left of map 178, shaded red). Though most of the houses have been replaced with modern ones, the hedges and streets preserve the atmosphere of olden times. **Iwata House** 岩田家 is the most famous one in the area.

Hirosaki's downtown is centered at Hirosaki Chuo Station, which is served by local private commuter trains. The area around JR Hirosaki Station is comparatively less developed, though there are a few department stores and restaurants (both are shaded red on map 178).

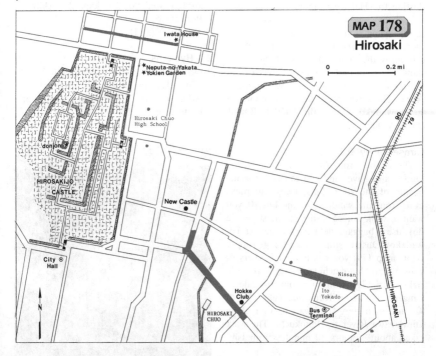

MAP 178
Hirosaki

Hotels in Hirosaki

Hokke Club Hirosaki 法華クラブ弘前
  (Business hotel: lower center, map 178.
  122 rooms)
  Add: 126, Dotemachi, Hirosaki.
  Tel: (0172) 34-3811.
Hotel New Castle ホテルニューキャッスル
  (Business hotel: middle center, map 178.
  62 rooms)
  Add: 24-1, Kamisayashimachi, Hirosaki.
  Tel: (0172) 36-1211.

Lake Towadako
十和田湖

Yasumiya (also called Towadako) is the
last stop of the JR bus from Aomori (lower
center, map 179). You should, however,
buy a ticket to Nenokuchi (middle right,
map 179) so that you can enjoy a boat ride
across the Lake from Nenokuchi to Yasumiya. Leaving the city of Aomori, the bus
runs along a refreshing mountain road,
skirting the Hakkoda mountains. Hakkoda
is a heavy snow zone and a mecca for
spring skiing. On the way, the bus makes
short stops at scenic points so passengers
can enjoy the views. Because of the heavy
snow, the road to Towadako is closed from
the middle of November till the middle of
April. There are two major attractions in
the Towadako area – the lake itself and
Oirase Valley.

Oirase Valley 奥入瀬渓谷

The JR bus from Aomori runs along the
Oirasegawa River and you can enjoy scenic
beauty of the river, falls, trees and rocks
even from the windows of the bus. If you
want to walk Oirase Valley (as most people
do), use a baggage delivery service. At Towadako Onsen stop 十和田温泉 (upper
right, map 179) you can ask for delivery of
your bag to Nenokuchi stop 子の口 (middle
right, map 179). Continue your bus ride to
Ishigedo 石ヶ戸 or Kumoi-no-Taki 雲井の
滝, and then start your walking tour along
Oirasegawa River to Nenokuchi. The walk
takes about 3 hours 30 minutes from Ishi-

gedo, and 2 hours 30 minutes from Kumoi-
no-Taki. You can pick up your bag at the
small hut in front of the Nenokuchi bus
stop.

Lake Towadako 十和田湖

Lake Towadako is a caldera lake 46 km
(29 miles) in circumference and 327 meters
(1,073 feet) deep. You can take a sightseeing boat from Nenokuchi to Yasumiya.
The view from the boat of Ogura Peninsula
and Nakayama Peninsula is especially impressive. Most accommodations are located
in the Yasumiya area (See the upper left
corner of map 179). Enjoy a leisurely walk
along the lake. The "Statue of Girls" is the
final work of Kotaro Takamura, and a symbol of Lake Towadako. Towada Jinja
Shrine is a few minutes walk from the
statue.

Accommodations in Towadako
1. Hotel
Towada Prince Hotel 十和田プリンス
  ホテル (First-class: middle left, map 179.
  66 rooms)
  Add: Towadako, Kosakamachi, Akita
  Prefecture.
  Tel: (017675) 3111.

2. Ryokans
Towada Kanko Hotel 十和田観光ホテル
  (First-class: in Yasumiya. 72 rooms)
  Add: Towada, Towadakomachi, Aomori
  Prefecture.
  Tel: (017675) 2111.

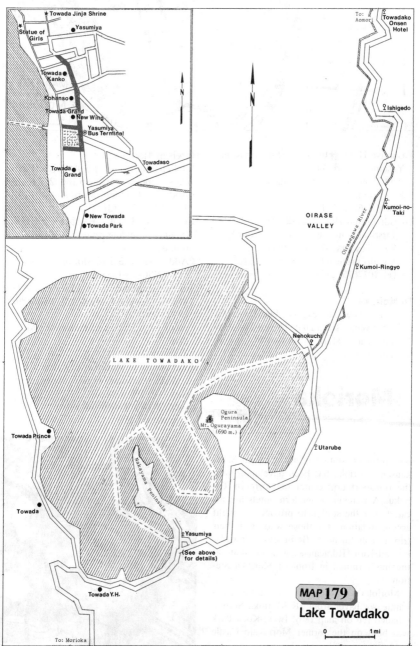

Towadaso 十和田荘 (First-class: in Yasumi-
   ya. 141 rooms)
   Add: Towada, Towadakomachi, Aomori
Prefecture.
Tel: (017675) 2221.

★ Towada Jinja Shrine

Statue of Girls

● Yasumiya

Towada Kanko ●

Kohanso ●

Towada Grand ● New Wing

Yasumiya Bus Terminal

● Towadaso

Towada Grand ●

● New Towada
● Towada Park

To: Aomori

Towadako Onsen Hotel

♨ Ishigedo

OIRASE VALLEY

Oirasegawa River

♨ Kumoi-no-Taki

♨ Kumoi-Ringyo

Nenokuchi ♨

L A K E   T O W A D A K O

Ogura Peninsula

Mt. Ogurayama (690 m.)

♨ Utarube

Nakayama Peninsula

Towada Prince ●

Towada ●

♨ Yasumiya
(See above for details)

Towada Y.H. ●

MAP 179
Lake Towadako

0   1 mi

To: Morioka

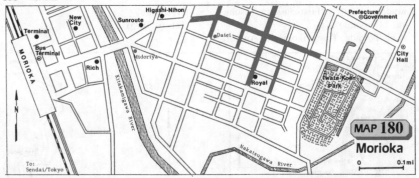

Yasumiya Hotel 休屋ホテル (First-class: in
    Yasumiya. 77 rooms)
    Add: Towada, Towadakomachi, Aomori
    Prefecture.
    Tel: (017675) 2321.
Towada Grand Hotel 十和田グランドホテル
    (First-class: in Yasumiya. 118 rooms)
    Add: Towada, Towadakomachi,
    Aomori prefecture.
    Tel: (017675) 2121

To Morioka

A JR "Towada" express bus (No. 93)
runs between Towadako (Yasumiya Bus
Terminal) and Morioka Station in 2 hours
15 minutes.

Morioka

盛岡

A terminal station of the Tohoku Shinkansen, Morioka has been developing into
the transportation center of Northern Tohoku. A number of modern hotels are located near the station to provide overnight
accommodations for those who start their
trip in Tohoku here. JR buses to Towadako and Kuji (Rikuchu-Kaigan) originate at
the bus terminal in front of Morioka Station.

Morioka's downtown is across the Kita-
kamigawa River from JR Morioka Station
(shaded red on map 180). Iwate-Koen Park
was built on the former Moriokajo Castle
grounds.

Hotels in Morioka

Hotel Higashi-Nihon ホテル東日本 (First-
    class: upper center, map 180. 207 rooms)
    Add: 3-3-18, Odori, Morioka.
    Tel: (0196) 25-2131.
Hotel Royal Morioka ホテルローヤル盛岡
    (Standard: middle center, map 180. 98
    rooms)
    Add: 1-11-11, Saien, Morioka.
    Tel: (0196) 53-1331.
Morioka Terminal Hotel 盛岡ターミナル
    ホテル (Standard: upper left, map 180.
    194 rooms)
    Add: 1-44, Morioka-Ekimaedori, Mori-
    oka.
    Tel: (0196) 25-1211.
Hotel Sunroute Morioka ホテルサンルー
    ト盛岡 (Business hotel: upper center,
    map 180. 188 rooms)
    Add: 3-7-19, Odori, Morioka.
    Tel: (0196) 25-3311.

Rikuchu Kaigan 陸中海岸

Rikuchu Kaigan is famous for the beautiful marine scenery of its rugged rocky coast. Until two new railroads – the private Kita Rias Line (No. 291) and the private Minami Rias Line (No. 290) – were completed several years ago, infrequent bus service was the only transportation available along the narrow coastal roads, and the area was popularly called the "Tibet of Japan." Even though the train service is not as frequent as that of other areas, Rikuchu Kaigan is now an accessible destination. We suggest the following 3-day itinerary from Tokyo:

Day 1. Arrive Kuji

If you start your trip from Morioka (upon arrival from Tokyo by the Tohoku Shinkansen or after a trip to Lake Towadako), take a JR bus from Morioka to Kuji (about a 3 hour ride). The bus passes scenic Hiraniwa Kogen Heights. If you come from the north (upon arrival at Misawa Airport, or on your way back to Tokyo from Hokkaido), take the JR Kuji Line from Hachinohe to Kuji (about a 2 hour ride). Overnight in Kuji.

Day 2. Kuji/Shimanokoshi/Miyako/Morioka

Take a train on the Kita Rias Line from Kuji to Shimanokoshi. Most of the trip is through tunnels, but you can catch occasional views of lovely small fishing villages along the coast. Enjoy a 45 minute boat ride at Shimanokoshi (available about once every 90 minutes).The boat visits the "Alps of the Sea" of Kitayamazaki, a stretch of 200 meter (656 feet) tall precipitous cliffs rising from the sea. After the boat ride, continue by train to Miyako. If you start from Kuji around 8:00 AM you will be in Miyako around noon. Take a bus from Miyako Station to Jodogahama (about a 20 minute ride, frequent service). Jodogahama (Heavenly Beach) is a sunken beach. Its white rocks and green pine trees are a typical Japanese seascape. A 40 minute sightseeing boat trip operates about once

every hour.

* If you plan to go back to Tokyo on Day 3, stay in Miyako. If you plan to visit the Hiraizumi/Sendai area after Rikuchu Kaigan, you should proceed from Miyako to Morioka by late afternoon JR train (No. 86). On Day 3 you can take a JR train (No. 9) from Morioka to Hiraizumi.

Rikuchu Kaigan National Park

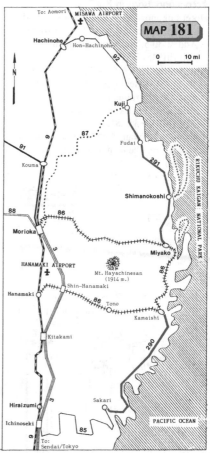

Kuji

久慈

Kuji, which once prospered as a castle town of the Kuji family, is now a small city with a population of 41,000. The JR Kuji Station and Kuji Station on the Kita-Rias Line are located side by side. The city is famous for fresh seafood and for the traditional *Kokuji-yaki* pottery of the area.

Accommodations in Kuji

Hotel Fukunoya ホテル福乃屋 (Standard ryokan: upper left, map 182. 25 rooms)
Add: 1-30-5, Nakanohashi, Kuji.
Tel: (01945) 3-5111.

Kuji Station Hotel 久慈ステーションホ
テル (Business hotel: middle center, map 182. 26 rooms)
Add: 1-37-11, Ekimae, Kuji.
Tel: (01945) 3-5281.

Tatsumiya Ryokan たつみや旅館 (Tourist ryokan: middle center, map 182. 17 rooms)
Add: 5-16-94, Tomoecho, Kuji.
Tel: (01945) 3-3326.

Tashiro Ryokan 田代旅館 (Tourist ryokan: lower center, map 182. 13 rooms)
Add: 5-29, Honcho, Kuji.
Tel: (01945) 3-5151.

Shimanokoshi

島ノ越

Shimanokoshi is a tiny fishing village. The Shimanokoshi Station is a colorful fairy tale building. There is literally nothing in the station area. The pier for the sightseeing boat is about 200 meters (656 feet) from the station (only a 3 minute walk).

A 45-minute sightseeing boat operates about every 60 – 100 minutes. The small boat cruises along the precipitous cliffs of Rikuchu Kaigan National Park. Kitayamazaki, popularly called the "Alps of the Sea," features sunken rocks washed by rough Pacific waves, and is the highlight of the boat trip.

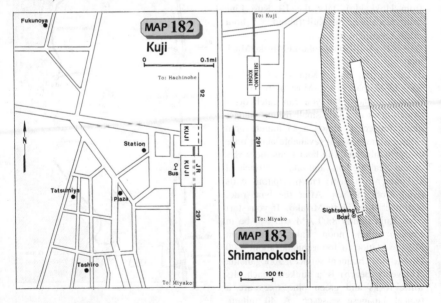

Miyako

宮古

Miyako, with a population of 62,000, is the largest city in the Rikuchu Kaigan area. The small downtown stretching to the north from the station, is typical of local cities. The highlight of Miyako is Jodogahama Beach. Buses operate once every 20 – 30 minutes from the station. The beautiful rock formations there are natural works of art. In the summer the beach is crowded with sea bathers. A sightseeing boat around the rock formations starts from near Jodogahama 浄土ガ浜 bus stop.

Ryokans in Miyako

Jodogahama Park Hotel   浄土ガ浜パークホテル (Standard: upper right, map 184. 46 rooms)
Add: Jodogahama, Miyako.
Tel: (01936) 2-2321.

Sawadaya Shinsenkaku 沢田家新泉閣 (Standard: lower left, map 184. 28 rooms)
Add: 7-2, Kurodacho, Miyako.
Tel: (01936) 2-3753.

Kumayasu Ryokan 熊安旅館 (Standard: lower center, map 184. 25 rooms)
Add: 2-5, Shinmachi, Miyako.
Tel: (01936) 2-3545.

Itoya Ryokan イトウヤ旅館 (Standard: lower center, map 184. 19 rooms)
Add: 1-2-14, Odori, Miyako.
Tel: (01936) 2-1636.

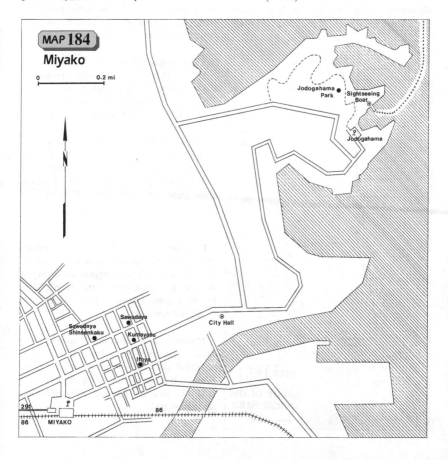

Hiraizumi, Sendai and 平泉、仙台、 Matsushima 松島

Thanks to easy access from Tokyo via the Tohoku Shinkansen (only a 2 hour ride), the Sendai Area is Tohoku's most popular tourist destination. The area includes Tohoku's largest city of Sendai (a population of 683,000), the historic city of Hiraizumi, and scenic Matsushima. We suggest the following three day itinerary from Tokyo.

Day 1. Tokyo/Hiraizumi/Sendai

The Tohoku Shinkansen (No. 3) from Tokyo's Ueno Station to Ichinoseki, and then visit Chusonji and Motsuji Temples in Hiraizumi. Take the Tohoku Shinkansen from Ichinoseki back to Sendai, and stay overnight in Sendai.

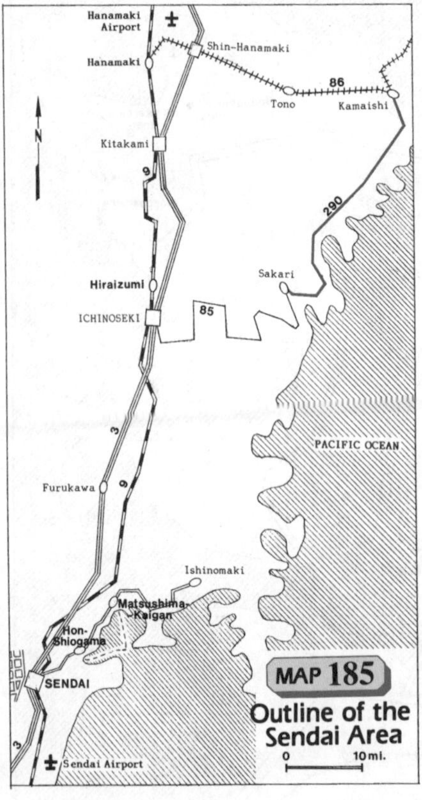

You can also start this itinerary after visiting other Tohoku destinations, i.e., Lake Towadako or Rikuchu Kaigan.

Day 2. Sendai/Shiogama/Matsushima/ Sendai

The JR Senseki Line (local trains only) from Sendai to Hon-Shiogama to visit Shiogama Jinja Shrine. Then, take a sightseeing boat from Hon-Shiogama to Matsushima-Kaigan across the scenic Matsushima Bay. After visiting Zuiganji Temple and other historic places in Matsushima-Kaigan, return to Sendai by the JR Senseki Line.

Instead of returning to Sendai, you can stay overnight in Matsushima.

Day 3. Sendai/Tokyo

After sightseeing in Sendai, return to Tokyo on the Tohoku Shinkansen.

You can visit Bandai Kogen or Nikko on your way back to Tokyo from Sendai.

Sendai is the capital of Miyagi Prefecture, and Tohoku's economic and cultural capital as well. It was established in the 17th century by a *daimyo* named Masamune Date, whose shadow still looms large for the modern inhabitants of this provincial center.

Hiraizumi is the home of one of Japan's most precious National Treasures – Konjikido Hall, which is an impressive legacy of the society established in this remote area by the Fujiwara family, who reigned here in the medieval era.

Matsushima is one of three places in Japan acclaimed as the nation's most beautiful sites. Matsushima (literally, Pine Island) Bay is dotted with hundreds of beautiful islands crowded with pine tree upon pine tree.

MAP 185
Outline of the Sendai Area
0   10 mi.

Hiraizumi

平泉

The Fujiwara family operated a strong local government in Hiraizumi from 1089 to 1189. An efficient economy and political stability enabled three generations of Fujiwaras to nurture a level of culture comparable to that of Kyoto, and unequalled by any other local area. Chusonji Temple and Motsuji Temple are symbols of Tohoku culture in the medieval era. Yoritomo Minamoto, the founder of the first military government in Japan, defeated the fourth leader of the Fujiwaras in 1189, and the 100-year long prosperity of the north disappeared, never to return. The area is also famous for its lacquerware and ironware, such as wind chimes and kettles. Many souvenir shops are located near the Chusonji bus stop and along the approach to the Temple.

Transportation to Chusonji Temple

A visit to Chusonji Temple requires a long walk on a hilly path. You should leave your bag(s) in a coin locker at Ichinoseki Station. The bus going to Chusonji operates every 20 – 30 minutes from early morning till early evening. Take a *seiri-ken* fare zone ticket upon boarding. The ride from Ichinoseki to Chusonji takes 26 minutes.

The JR Tohoku Line operates between Ichinoseki and Hiraizumi almost every hour. However, because Chusonji Temple is away from Hiraizumi Station, you still have to take this same bus, from Hiraizumi to Chusonji. Going this way is much too time consuming. Even if you have a Japan Rail Pass, we recommend that you take the bus from Ichinoseki.

Chusonji Temple 中尊寺

(Upper left, map 186)

Allow at least one and a half hours for this visit. The entrance to the main approach to Chusonji Temple is a stone bridge, which leads to a steep slope. Once you cross the bridge, smoking is prohibited

everywhere in the temple grounds.

Chusonji Temple was erected in the 9th century. It prospered under the reign of the Fujiwara family in the 11th and 12th centuries, and at its peak there were more than 40 buildings in the precincts (which actually cover all of one small mountain). Chusonji Temple lost most of its buildings to fire in 1337. Only Konjikido Hall (Golden Hall) and Kyozo Hall (Sutra Hall) survived the fire. Most of the other buildings were reconstructed in the Edo era. The 0.6 mile (1 km.) long approach to Konjikido Hall is shaded by tall cedar trees; the many small halls along this path add to the solemn atmosphere of the grounds.

The Main Hall of Chusonji Temple 中尊寺本堂 is located about halfway up the approach. Chusonji Temple is still active as a principal temple of the Tendai sect of Buddhism in the Tohoku region (The headquarters is Enryakuji Temple on Mt. Hieizan in Kyoto).

Konjikido Hall 金色堂, **Kyozo Hall** 経蔵 and **Old Protection Hall** 旧金色堂履堂 of Konjikido are located in the enclosed area at the end of the approach. The ticket office is at the entrance to the enclosure (8:30 AM to 5:00 PM). The 500 yen admission also covers admission to Sankozo Treasure House. Konjikido Hall, a small golden hall built in 1124, is coated with black lacquer and covered entirely with gold foil. It is especially famous for the delicate decorative art works of its interior; they testify to the high artistic achievements of the area in the 12th century. Konjikido Hall, which has been designated a National Treasure, is contained within a larger concrete structure completed in 1968. The Old Protection Hall, which used to house Konjikido, has been moved to the north. Kyozo Hall, originally constructed in 1108 as a two-story building, lost its second floor to fire in 1337. The first floor was repaired and preserved.

Noh Hall 能楽堂 is an important historical relic that testifies to the Temple's former preeminence in cultural activities. The Hall has an outdoor stage so that audiences can enjoy open air performances.

Sankozo Treasure House 讃衡蔵 displays the temple's treasures, which include images of Buddha, paintings and other art objects. There is an especially large number of sculpture masterpieces.

Chusonji Temple to Motsuji Temple

Motsuji Temple is 0.4 miles (0.6 km.) from Hiraizumi Station. You can take a bus from Chusonji stop to Hiraizumi Station (The same bus you took from Ichinoseki Station but in the opposite direction). Motsuji Temple is only 10 minutes on foot from Hiraizumi Station. You can, of course, walk from Chusonji Temple to Motsuji Temple in about 30 minutes.

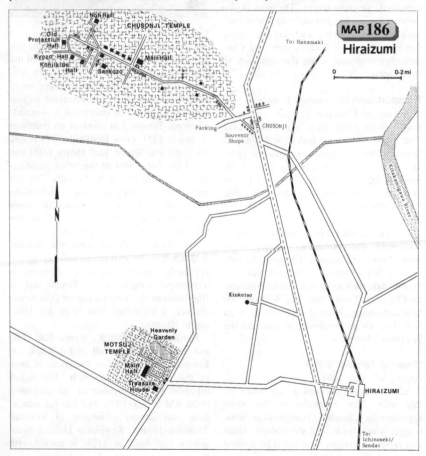

Motsuji Temple 毛越寺
(Lower left, map 186)

Motsuji Temple was originally erected by the priest Ennin (Jikaku Daishi) in 850. In the 12th century, under the protection of the Fujiwara family, the temple precincts contained 40 minor temples and as many as 500 lodgings, and was probably one of the nation's biggest religious establishments. All the structures were lost in repeated fires and only a few were reconstructed later. However, the original garden, which features an imaginary heaven (Jodo) and is considered among the best of those designed in the Heian era, is still intact. This spacious garden is the best place possible to get an idea of what the medieval aristocrats and priests expected their heaven to be like. The grounds are open from 8:30 AM to 5:00 PM. The 500 yen admission also covers the Treasure House in the precincts.

After the visit to Motsuji Temple, walk back to Hiraizumi Station and take a bus (or the JR train) back to Ichinoseki, and then the Tohoku Shinkansen to Sendai.

Ryokan in Hiraizumi
Kinkeiso 金鶏花 (First-class: middle center, map 186. 65 rooms)
Add: 15, Osawa, Hiraizumi.
Tel: (0191) 46-2241.

Hotel in Ichinoseki
Hotel Sunroute Ichinoseki ホテルサンルートー／関 (Business hotel: in front of Ichinoseki Station. 95 rooms).
Add: 53, Kami-Otsukigai, Ichinoseki.
Tel: (0191) 26-4311.

Sendai 仙台

Toward the end of the civil war period (the end of the 16th century), a military genius named Masamune Date unified the smaller feudal lords of the Tohoku district and established a power base in Sendai. Because the capital at Kyoto was so far away, Masamune did not participate in the struggles or the bloody battles then being waged by those seeking central political power. He remained an influential feudal lord under Ieyasu Tokugawa, the first Tokugawa Shogun. The people of Tohoku still say that Masamune would have been the person to complete the unification of Japan if he had been born 20 years earlier and somewhere closer to Kyoto. This belief, regardless of its credibility, reflects the respect the people of the area still have for this one-eyed hero. Throughout the Edo era, Sendai prospered as the largest castle city in Tohoku under the reign of successive generations of the Date family. After World War II, Sendai was redeveloped as a modern city, but its quiet air of a feudal town, surrounded by thick green woods, has been preserved successfully. Even though Sendai lacks buildings of historical interest because of the devastation of the war, it is one of Japan's most livable cities. With its clean shopping arcades and generally pleasant atmosphere, it is also one of the most comfortable cities in Japan for an evening stroll.

Outline of the City
Sendai Station is a four-story building. The Tohoku Shinkansen platforms are located on the fourth floor. Exits are located on the second floor and the ground floor (If you want a taxi, go down to the ground floor). If you are walking to your hotel, use the second floor exit. You will be surprised at the extensive maze of pedestrian bridges outside the station.

Sendai has two shopping arcades, as pictured on map 187 (shaded red). The arcade running east to west is called Chuo-dori Street, and the one running north to south is called Higashi-Ichibancho Street. Both of them are lined with department stores (such as **Daiei, Fujisaki, Jusco** and **Mitsukoshi**), souvenir shops and restaurants. Many drinking spots and obscure cabarets are located on the streets to the west of Higashi-Ichibancho Street. The area is completely safe; don't be afraid to take a look at this colorful night life zone and its jovial people. But if you are a woman alone don't stay in the area after 8:00 PM, unless you want to find out how alcohol can inspire even shy country people to make shockingly indecent proposals. Stick to the shopping arcades after 8:00 PM.

Government offices are located on the northern side of Jozenji-dori Street (upper center, map 187), and business offices are along Hirose-dori, Aoba-dori and Higashi-Nibancho-dori Streets.

Transportation in Sendai

Buses are the only means of public transportation in Sendai. The central part of the city can be reached easily on foot from all the major hotels. A subway, running north to south and passing Sendai Station, is not useful for tourists. Sendai's bus system is perhaps the most complicated one in all of Japan. There are more than 60 bus stops on the western side of the station. Even if

you can read the destination names in Japanese, you really can't use the buses unless you also have a thorough knowledge of the geography of the area. Because you will probably visit only one or two places of interest in Sendai (because there really are no more than one or two), it is better to use taxis.

Places of Interest

Zuihoden Hall 瑞鳳殿 (Lower left, map 187)

Zuihoden Hall is a mausoleum of Masamune Date located on a small hill and surrounded by thick cedar trees. The original hall, a National Treasure, was a splendid structure with elaborate carvings and decorations but it was lost to fire during the war. The present building is an exact replica of the original. **Kansenden Hall** 感仙殿

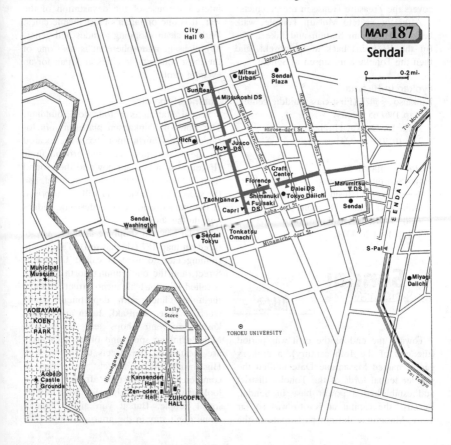

and **Zen-oden Hall** 善応殿, the mausolea of the second and third lords of the Date family, are also located near Zuihoden. Both of them are open from 9:00 AM to 4:00 PM. The 500 yen admission covers all three monuments.

Aobayama-Koen Park 青葉山公園 (Lower left, map 187)

Aobayama-Koen Park was built on the former Aobajo Castle grounds. The grounds are covered with thick woods, and remains of the castle and the statue of Masamune Date are located there. The Sendai Municipal Museum 仙台市立博物館 in the grounds displays historic objects of the area.

Osaki Hachimangu Shrine 大崎八幡宮
(Outside of map 187, about 2 miles to the northwest from Sendai Station)

Osaki Hachimangu Shrine (National Treasure) was built in 1607 at the order of Masamune Date, to offer thanks for the area's prosperity. This magnificent black lacquer building is typical of the designs of the time. The Shrine is located on a small hill, and is surrounded by a thick forest (9:00 AM to 4:00 PM).

Shopping

Craft Center (middle center, map 187, in the Chuo-dori arcade) deals in a variety of handicraft items and antiques. **Shimanuki** (middle center, in the Chuo-dori arcade) has a big inventory of all sorts of *kokeshi* (wooden) dolls produced in the Tohoku district.

Restaurants

Florence and **Capri** (both in the middle center, map 187) serve Japanized Italian food (inexpensive). **Sun Beam** (upper center) is a Korean barbecue restaurant and is recommended if you are starved for beef (reasonable). **Tonkatsu Omachi** (middle center, on Aoba-dori Street) specializes in pork cutlet (reasonable). **Tachibana** is an authentic yet reasonable Japanese restaurant on Chuo-dori Street (middle center). The first floor is a sushi restaurant and the second serves tempura.

Hotels in Sendai
First-class Hotels
Hotel Sendai Plaza ホテル仙台プラザ (Upper center, map 187. 221 rooms)
Add: 2-20-1, Honcho, Sendai.
Tel: (0222) 62-7111.
Sendai Tokyu Hotel 仙台東急ホテル (Middle center, map 187. 302 rooms)
Add: 2-9-25, Ichibancho, Sendai,
Tel: (0222) 62-2411.

Standard Hotel
Sendai Hotel 仙台ホテル (Middle right, map 187. 84 rooms)
Add: 1-10-25, Chuo, Sendai.
Tel: (0222) 25-5171.

Business Hotels
Tokyo Daiichi Hotel Sendai 東京第一ホテル仙台 (Middle center, map 187. 154 rooms)
Add: 2-3-18, Chuo, Sendai.
Tel: (0222) 62-1355.
Miyagi Daiichi Hotel 宮城第一ホテル (Middle right, map 187. 121 rooms)
Add: 122, Higashi-Nanabancho, Sendai.
Tel: (0222) 97-4411.
Hotel Rich Sendai ホテルリッチ仙台 (Middle center, map 187. 242 rooms).
Add: 2-2-2, Kokubucho, Sendai.
Tel: (0222) 62-8811.
Sendai Washington Hotel 仙台ワシントンホテル (Middle left, map 187. 611 rooms)
Add: 2-3-1, Omachi, Sendai.
Tel: (0222) 22-2111.

Matsushima and Shiogama

松島，塩釜

Matsushima Bay, dotted with more than 200 small and uniquely shaped pine-tree-clad islets, is famous for its peaceful and picturesque scenery. Matsushima is also famous for Zuiganji Temple, Tohoku's most important Zen temple. The one-day excursion from Sendai outlined below also incorporates a visit to Shiogama, a leading fishing town and site of the fabulous Shiogama Jinja Shrine, and includes a boat ride in Matsushima Bay as well.

Transportation

As pictured on map 185, the JR Senseki Line (local trains only) runs northeast from Sendai, stopping at Hon-Shiogama (Main Shiogama) and Matsushima-Kaigan (Matsushima Coast) Stations. The commuter trains of this line operate every 30 minutes from early in the morning till late at night. The Senseki Line leaves Sendai from either platform No. 1 or No. 2, located in the northeastern corner of the station. Walk to the north on the ground floor of Sendai Station building until you find the "Senseki Line" signs in English. The signs will lead you to the underground passage that connects with the Senseki Line platforms. The

ride to Hon-Shiogama is about 25 minutes, and the ride to Matsushima Kaigan takes about 35 minutes.

A sightseeing boat runs between Hon-Shiogama and Matsushima-Kaigan across scenic Matsushima Bay, one of the highlights of the itinerary.

Hon-Shiogama 本塩釜

Shiogama is one of Japan's leading fishing ports. The city is filled with the lively spirit of the fishermen as well as a fishy smell! **Shiogama Jinja Shrine** 塩釜神社 is located to the west of Hon-Shiogama Station in a hilly forest (upper left, map 188). The Shrine was erected at the end of the 8th century. Throughout history, it was always well respected by the leading lords of the area. The present buildings were constructed in 1704 at the order of the fourth lord of the Date family. The main approach, up 200 steep stone steps, is on the western side of the shrine. Though the ancient tree-shaded stone steps are very impressive, the approach is a long distance from the train station, and you have to walk on a street with heavy traffic. We therefore recommend a southern approach (indicated with shaded red on map 188). After passing the first large torii gate, the path is a quiet stone-paved traffic-free gentle slope up. There are two shrines, Shiogama Jinja Shrine and Shibahiko Jinja Shrine, on a small hill. The former is the main structure of the precincts. Both of

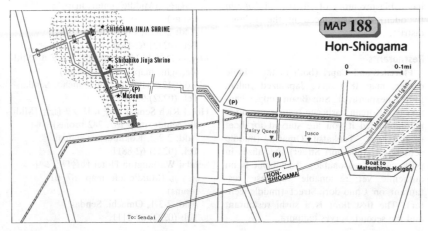

MAP **188**

Hon-Shiogama

SHIOGAMA JINJA SHRINE

Shibahiko Jinja Shrine

★ Museum

(P)

0   0.1mi

Dairy Queen   Jusco

(P)

HON-SHIOGAMA

Boat to Matsushima-Kaigan

To Matsushima-Kaigan

To: Sendai

them are magnificent vermilion buildings. Entrance to the shrine grounds is free of charge. A small museum in a modern two-story building displays miniature festival shrines, swords, hanging scrolls, paintings and armor on its first floor. The second floor features exhibits on whaling and fishery. There is a good view of the city and Matsushima Bay from the museum's roof (8:00 AM to 5:00 PM). The shrine's Harbor Festival, held in early August, is famous for its colorful parade of fishing boats.

To Matsushima-Kaigan by Boat

The pier, where you can catch the boat to Matsushima-Kaigan, is to the east of the train station (middle right, map 188). Sightseeing boats between Shiogama and Matsushima-Kaigan operate every 30 to 60 minutes (less frequently in winter). Two of the boats are very fanciful, one shaped like a dragon and the other like a peacock. If you're lucky you might end up on one of them. There are two classes of seats on the boat — first and second. The ride takes one hour, and the second class cabin is quite comfortable.

The boat cruises Matsushima Bay, skirting numerous small islands, all of which have been formed into grotesque shapes by the waves. Oddly shaped pine trees that look like *bonsai* grow on each island. A newly constructed power station ruins the marine scenery at the beginning of the cruise, but for most of the trip you still see the artistry of nature. This is the scenery that thoroughly fascinated the brilliant *haiku* poet, Basho, more than 300 years ago. You will see a number of bamboo sticks and logs on the surface of the water. The bamboo sticks are frames for cultivating sea weed, and the logs are used by oyster farmers.

Matsushima 松島海岸

All of Matsushima's places of interest are located within walking distance of both Matsushima-Kaigan Pier and the JR train station. You need about three hours to cover the area.

Godaido Hall 五大堂 (middle right, map 189) is located on a tiny island connected to the coast by a small bridge. It was originally built in 807 by Tamuramaro Sakanoue, a military leader who invaded the

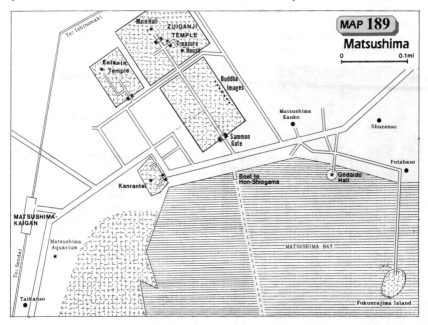

area at the order of the emperor. Masamune Date had the present hall built in 1600. The traditional architecture of the small temple complements the picturesque marine scenery. The inside of the hall is not open to the public.

Fukuurajima Island 福浦島 (lower right, optional) is connected with the coast by a vermilion pedestrian bridge. The island itself is a botanical garden (8:30 AM to 5:00 PM).

Zuiganji Temple 瑞厳寺 (upper center) is the most important Zen temple in northern Japan, and dates originally from 827. The present buildings were constructed in 1609 at the order of Masamune. Sammon Gate is the entrance to the main approach, which leads straight to the main temple precincts. You should turn to the right to see the numerous images of Buddha carved on the cliffs. In the olden days novices at the temple were set the arduous task of carving these images as part of their training. The ticket office is at the entrance to the main precincts (7:30 AM to 5:00 PM. Admission 330 yen). The Main Hall, a gigantic wooden structure, houses masterpieces of carving and painting that reflect the brilliant artistic trends of the early 17th century. The Treasure House displays impressive Buddhist images and historical objects related to the Date family.

Entsuin Temple 円通院 (upper left, optional) is also called Rose Temple because of the large number of rose bushes on its grounds. The mausoleum of Mitsumune Date, a grandson of Masamune, and the landscaped garden are worthy of special attention (8:00 AM to 5:00 PM).

Kanrantei 観瀾亭 (middle center, optional) was used by the lords of each generation of the Date family for moon viewing parties on summer nights. The house was originally a tea house in Fushimijo Castle in Kyoto, and was later presented to Masamune by Hideyoshi Toyotomi. Adjacent to Kanrantei House is Matsushima Museum, which features armor, swords, paintings, etc. of the Date family (8:00 AM to 5:00 PM).

Places for Lunch.

There are a number of restaurants and souvenir shops on the main street along the coast. Eels are a specialty of the area. Many are pleasantly surprised the first time they try eel. You might be too.

Return to Sendai by Train

The JR Senseki Line is the only train that serves Matsushima-Kaigan Station. Take the south-bound train to Sendai, the last stop.

Ryokans in Matsushima-Kaigan

Hotel Taikanso ホテル大観荘 (First-class: lower left, map 189. 212 rooms)
  Add: 10-76, Inuta, Matsushima.
  Tel: (02235) 4-2161.
Hotel Futabaso   ホテル二葉荘
  (First-class: middle right, map 189. 30 rooms)
  Add: 35, Senzui, Matsushima.
  Tel: (02235) 4-5065.
Matsushima Kanko Hotel 松島観光ホテル
  (Standard: middle center, map 189. 28 rooms)
  Add: 115, Chonai, Matsushima.
  Tel: (02235) 4-2121.
Shuzanso 秀山荘 (Standard: middle right, map 189. 24 rooms)
  Add: 35-4, Senzui, Matsushima.
  Tel: (02235) 4-2131.

Bandai-Kogen and Aizu-Wakamatsu 磐梯高原，会津若松

Bandai-Kogen Heights, surrounded by the magnificent Mt. Bandaisan and a number of beautiful lakes and ponds, is the highlight of Bandai-Asahi National Park. Thanks to the completion of the Tohoku Shinkansen and the development of picturesque mountain roads, Bandai-Kogen can be visited easily from Tokyo.

Aizu-Wakamatsu is a historic city. It prospered as the largest Edo era castle town in Southern Tohoku. The loyalty of the Aizu Clan to the Tokugawa Shogunate ultimately led to Aizu resistance against the imperial forces in 1868.

Higashiyama Onsen, located in a narrow valley in the southeastern corner of the city, is a popular hotspring. Most visitors to Aizu-Wakamatsu spend a night there.

We introduce the area in a three-day itinerary from Tokyo. You can also combine this area with other destinations in Tohoku.

Day 1.   Tokyo/Fukushima/Bandai-Kogen

Take the Tohoku Shinkansen from Tokyo's Ueno Station to Fukushima (1 hour 40 minutes), and then take a bus from Fukushima to Bandai-Kogen, via the scenic "Bandai-Asahi Skyline" and "Bandai-Asahi Lakeline" toll roads (an enjoyable 3 hour ride). Overnight in Bandai-Kogen.

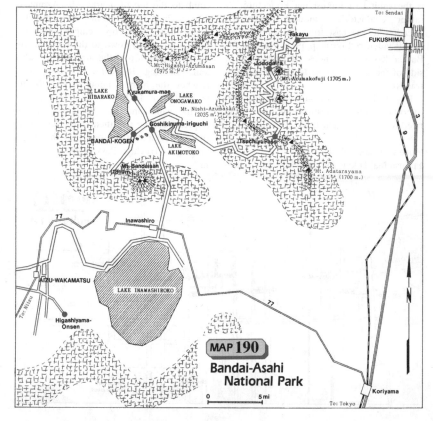

MAP 190
Bandai-Asahi National Park

Day 2. Bandai-Kogen/Aizu-Wakamatsu

Take a bus from Bandai-Kogen to Aizu - Wakamatsu (1 hour 20 minutes). The bus first runs on a pleasant mountain road skirting Mt. Bandaisan, and then along the northern shore of Lake Inawashiroko. Overnight in Higashiyama Onsen.

Day 3. Aizu-Wakamatsu/Tokyo

The JR Bandai-Saisen Line (No. 77) from Aizu-Wakamatsu to Koriyama, and then the Tohoku Shinkansen from Koriyama to Ueno, Tokyo (1 hour 20 minutes).

Fukushima

福島

Fukushima, with a population of 270,000, is the capital of Fukushima Prefecture. A rather characterless modern downtown stretches to the east from Fukushima Station (shaded red on map 191). The bus for Bandai-Kogen originates at the western side of the station (close to the Shinkansen tracks).

If you visit Bandai-Kogen after your trip to other Tohoku destinations, you may need to stay overnight here.

Hotels in Fukushima

Fukushima Tokyu Inn 福島東急イン (Busi-
ness hotel: middle center, map 191. 118 rooms)
Add: 11-25, Sakaecho, Fukushima.
Tel: (0245) 23-0109.
Hotel Sunroute Fukushima ホテル
サンルート福島 (Business hotel: lower center, map 191. 81 rooms)
Add: 2-6, Nakamachi, Fukushima.
Tel: (0245) 21-1811.

Fukushima to Bandai-Kogen

Takayu (upper right, map 190), the starting point of the "Bandai-Azuma Skyline" toll road, is 40 minutes from Fukushima. The bus climbs the mountain on zig-zag curves. At Jododaira, above the tree line, the bus makes a 40-minute rest stop. The rest stop features a restaurant and souvenir shop. Jododaira, located at an altitude of 5,214 ft. (1,580 m.), commands a grand view of the Azuma mountains. You can climb to the top of nearby Mt. Azumako-fuji (5,626 ft., or 1,705 m.) in 10 minutes. The caldera on the top is empty, and if you wish, you can go down to the bottom. The view from the top of the mountain is excellent. Leaving Jododaira, the bus soon reaches the highest point of the Skyline (5,353 ft., or 1,622 m.). The view of Mt. Adatarayama and Mt. Bandaisan is very impressive. The bus then starts descending the zig-zag mountain road into the woods leading to Tsuchiyu Pass (4,059 ft, or 1,230 m.).

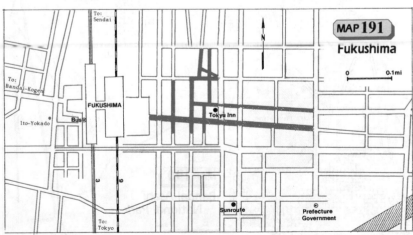

MAP **191**
Fukushima

Turning west at Tsuchiyu Pass, the bus follows the "Bandai-Azuma Lakeline" toll road, through beautiful forests. You can see the lovely trio of Bandai-Kogen: Lake Hibarako, Lake Onogawako and Lake Akimotoko, from time to time through the woods. The blue lakes are a striking contrast to the deep green of the woods. The bus usually proceeds first to Goshikinuma-iriguchi 五色沼入口, then to Kyukamura-mae 休暇村前, and finally to Bandai-Kogen, the last stop.

Bandai-Kogen
磐梯高原

Bandai-Kogen Bus Terminal, near Lake Hibarako, is at the center of the plateau. Many restaurants and souvenir shops are located in this area.

Goshikinuma 五色沼 (Five Colored Ponds) is the name given to many small ponds located between Lake Hibarako and Lake Onogawako. Varied in size and shape, each one of the ponds has water of a different color. **Goshikinuma Natural Trail** 五色沼自然探勝路 is a sylvan promenade that passes most of the Goshikinuma Ponds. Rental row boats are available on Bishamonnuma Pond, the largest one – near Goshikinuma-iriguchi bus stop.

Lake Hibarako 檜原湖 is the largest lake

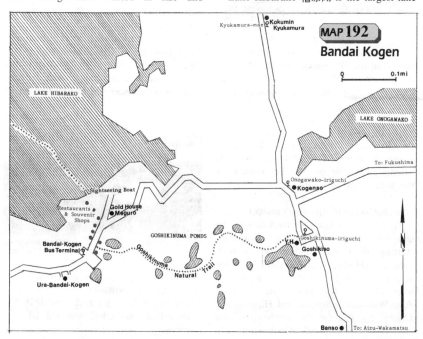

MAP 192
Bandai Kogen

0   0.1mi

LAKE HIBARAKO

LAKE ONOGAWAKO

Kyukamura-mae ● ○ Kokumin
　　　　　　　　　　Kyukamura

To: Fukushima

Onogawako-iriguchi
● Kogenso

Sightseeing Boat

Restaurants
& Souvenir
Shops

Gold House
● Meguro

GOSHIKINUMA PONDS

Goshikinuma
Natural Trail

Goshikinuma-iriguchi
Y.H. ○
● Goshikiso

Bandai-Kogen
Bus Terminal

Ura-Bandai-Kogen

N

Banso ●   To: Aizu-Wakamatsu

in Bandai-Kogen. A 30-minute sightseeing boat operates frequently from the pier near Bandai-Kogen Bus Terminal. Pleasant walking paths run along the eastern shore of the lake.

Accommodations in Bandai-Kogen

Ura-Bandai-Kogen Hotel　裏磐梯高原ホテル　(First-class: lower left, map 192. 47 rooms)
> Add: Hibara, Shiobaramura, Fukushima Prefecture.
> Tel: (0241) 32-2211.

Hotel Kogenso　ホテル高原荘 (Standard: middle center, map 192. 58 rooms).
> Add: Hibara, Shiobaramura, Fukushima Prefecture.
> Tel: (0241) 32-231.

Hotel Goshikiso　ホテル五色荘 (Standard: lower center, map 192. 19 rooms).
> Add: Hibara, Shiobaramura, Fukushima Prefecture.
> Tel: (0241) 32-2011.

Aizu-Wakamatsu 会津若松

The Aizu clan, one of the strongest supporters of the Tokugawa Shogunate, fought the last major battle against the victorious imperial army in 1868. The people in Aizu, young and old, men and women, struggled desperately for as long as one month. Towards the end of the siege, 19 members of the Byakkotai (White Tiger Troop), a group of young soldiers 15 to 17 years old, committed suicide on Mt. Iimoriyama, as the town went up in flames.

Transportation in Aizu-Wakamatsu

There are two loop bus lines around the city (clockwise and counter clockwise), starting from Aizu-Wakamatsu Station. Tsurugajo-Minamiguchi 鶴ガ城南口 , the stop for the castle, is on these loop services. There is also bus service between Aizu-Wakamatsu Station and Higashiyama Onsen 東山温泉 (to the southeast of the city; outside of Map 193). Oyakuen-iriguchi 御薬園入口 and Bukeyashiki are on this line.

Downtown Aizu-Wakamatsu

The city's downtown (shaded red) is to the north of City Hall and is about a 15 minute walk from the station.

Places of Interest

Tsurugajo Castle 鶴ガ城 (Lower left, map 193)

Originally built in 1384, the castle was destroyed in the battle of 1868. A replica of the original donjon was constructed on the site in 1965. The five-story donjon contains museums that display Aizu lacquerware and historic objects of the Aizu clan. Hours: 8:30 AM to 5:00 PM.

Oyakuen 御楽園 (optional) (Lower center, map 193)

Oyakuen is a beautiful landscaped garden laid out around a large pond. At the order of the Aizu lord it was constructed as a herb garden. Hours: 8:00 AM to 5:00 PM.

Bukeyashiki 会津武家屋敷 (optional) (Lower right, map 193)

This museum features the Aizu samurai. Many replicas of Aizu samurai houses are displayed here. The main building is the mansion of Tanomo Saigo, Aizu's Prime Minister. Open 8:30 AM to 5:00 PM.

Accommodations in Aizu-Wakamatsu
1. Hotels in Downtown

Hotel New Palace　ホテルニューパレス (Standard: middle left, map 193. 90 rooms)

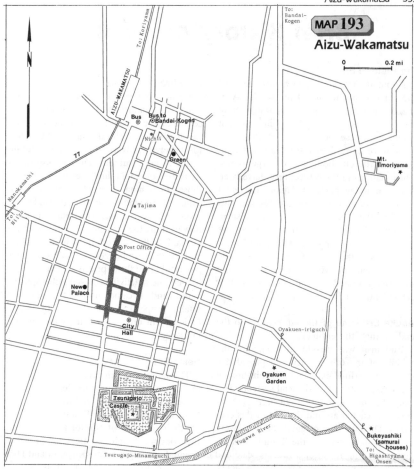

Add: 2-78, Nakamachi,
Aizu-Wakamatsu.
Tel: (0242) 28-2804.
Green Hotel Aizu　グリーンホテル会津
(Business hotel: upper center, map 193.
57 rooms)
Add: Ekimae, Aizu-Wakamatsu.
Tel: (0242) 24-5181.

2. Ryokans in Higashiyama Onsen
Mukotaki　向瀧 (Deluxe: 31 rooms)
Add: Yumoto, Higashiyama-machi,
Aizu-Wakamatsu.
Tel: (0242) 27-7501.
Harataki Shinkan　原瀧新館
(First-class: 36 rooms)
Add: Yumoto, Higashiyama-machi,

Aizu-Wakamatsu.
Tel: (0242) 27-6048.
Matsushimakaku　松島閣
(First-class: 48 rooms)
Add: Yumoto, Higashiyama-machi,
Aizu-Wakamatsu.
Tel: (0242) 27-6022.
Fudotaki Ryokan　不動滝旅館
(First-class: 42 rooms)
Add: Yumoto, Higashiyama-machi,
Aizu-Wakamatsu.
Tel: (0242) 26-5050.
Higashiyama Daiichi Hotel　東山第一ホテル
(Standard: 32 rooms)
Add: Yumoto, Higashiyama-machi,
Aizu-Wakamatsu.
Tel: (0242) 28-1222.

Brief History of Japan

Pre-Historic Era

About 10,000 years ago when the level of the sea rose at the end of the 4th Ice Age, the Japanese archipelago separated from the Asian Continent. According to first century Chinese documents, at that time there were more than 100 small tribal communes scattered about Japan. Large tombs, which date from the 4th century, have been found in many parts of Japan, and giant ones are located in Nara and Osaka. This supports the theory that of the many small "nations" led by powerful families at this time, the most powerful "nation" was located in the Nara-Osaka area. The establishment of what can be considered the first unified nation of Japan was achieved in the 5th century, in Nara.

Asuka Era (End of the 6th century to the end of the 7th century)

Buddhism was introduced to Japan in the middle of the 6th century and provided a common spiritual basis for organization of centralized political and social systems. Horyuji Temple in the Ikaruga area of Nara was constructed around the end of this century. Though the original designs were changed slightly when the Temple was reconstructed in 670 after a fire, its scale and grandeur testify to the power and influence Buddhism had acquired in such a short period of time. The first Japanese Constitution, the "Seventeen Article Constitution," was promulgated by Regent Shotoku.

Fujiwara Era (End of the 7th century to 710)

A large scale capital was constructed in Fujiwara (south of Nara) in 694. An aristocracy was established along with a sophisticated tax collection network that extended to virtually every corner of the country to support it. The East Tower of Yakushiji Temple in Nara is the symbol of the cultural achievements of this era. Its balanced beauty has been described as "frozen music."

Nara Era (710 – 794)

Japan's first permanent capital was constructed in Nara (a little to the west of the center of the modern city) in 710. The imperial court sent cultural missions to China to master the advanced science and culture of the Asian continent. During this era, art treasures of India and Persia as well as those of China were brought back to Japan. Throughout this period, Buddhism, protected by the imperial family and the powerful aristocrats, grew in influence. The Great Buddha at Todaiji Temple in Nara, cast in 752, symbolizes this influence. The powerful Buddhist priests eventually extended their activities beyond the spiritual world and became involved in political affairs. Emperor Kammu moved the capital to Kyoto in order to rid the court of their influence.

Heian Era (794 – 1192)

The new capital in Kyoto was completed in 794, and about this time, leading priests, among them Kukai and Saicho, began a reform movement within Buddhism. As part of their pursuit of spiritual purification, they opened training centers for priests in isolated mountain areas. Koyasan and Hieizan were locations of two of these new monasteries. For hundreds of years Kyoto continued to prosper, and the city's imperial and aristocratic families enjoyed political and economic power. They were also the leaders, along with the priests, of cultural activities.

In the 12th century, economic development in the rural areas resulted in new power for local military leaders. The Taira family, based in western Japan, and the Minamoto family, based in the east, were the two most influential military powers of their time. Under the leadership of Kiyomori, the Taira family won major battles against the Minamotos, and then began its ascent up the political ladders of the imperial court. Kiyomori became the prime minister, and members of the family occupied other important government posts. Kiyomori's daughter, Empress Kenreimon-in, bore Emperor Takakura a son who grew up to be Emperor Antoku. The Taira's prosperity, however, did not last long. After the death of Kiyomori, the reorganized Minamoto force sparked revolts against the Tairas. After three major victories in the Inland Sea area, Yoritomo Minamoto seized power. The rapid rise to power and easy downfall of the Tairas have long symbolized what the Japanese regard as one of history's greatest lessons – that prosperity is like a bubble on the surface of the water, easily formed and just as easily broken, lost and forgotten. While the Taira family prospered in Kyoto, an autonomous government flourished in Hiraizumi, in the northern part of Japan's main island. The Fujiwara family, leaders of this local government, were also patrons of high culture, as symbolized by the Konjikido (Golden Hall) at Chusonji Temple and the Heavenly Garden of Motsuji Temple. After 100 years of prosperity, the Fujiwaras too were destroyed, by Yoritomo Minamoto.

Kamakura Era (1192 – 1333)

Learning his lesson from the rapid deterioration of the Taira military spirit once the family joined the imperial court, Yoritomo established Japan's first independent military government. He made Kamakura, far away from the ruined imperial court in Kyoto, his capital. The simple and straightforward warrior spirit of the Minamoto family became the social norm, and the austere strictures of the Zen School of Buddhism gained countless adherents.

After the assassination of the third Minamoto Shugun, the political power of the Kamakura Shogunate fell into the hands of the Hojos, the family of Yoritomo's wife. In 1274 and again in 1281, the Mongolians, who had established the Yuan Dynasty in China, tried to attack Japan. These unsuccessful assaults were made at Fukuoka, in Kyushu, the southernmost island. Though the Kamakura Shogunate successfully defended the nation, the economic difficulties caused by the wars weakened its leadership. Emperor Godaigo was able to rally the dissatisfied warrior leaders from all parts of the nation and defeated the Shogunate forces in 1333. This new imperial government only survived for three years, however, and another military leader, Takauji Ashikaga, established a new Shogunate in 1336, this time in Kyoto.

Muromachi and Azuchi Momoyama Eras (1336 – 1603)

Though the Ashikagas centered their government in the Kyoto area, their rule over the rural areas did not last long. The financial power of local military leaders allowed them to remain independent from the Ashikaga Shogunate and to set up their own feudal systems. Beginning with the middle of the 15th century, there were frequent civil wars among local feudal lords who sought to expand their territory. The Ikko sect of Buddhism played an influential role in these wars, especially in the central part of the Japan Sea coast area. Members of this sect defeated the feudal lord in Kanazawa and established an autonomous government that endured for as long as 100 years. The famous Gold and Silver Pavilions in Kyoto were constructed by Shoguns of the Ashikaga family and are the representative historic relics of the era. Flower arranging, tea ceremony and the Noh drama also date from this era.

In the second half of the 16th century, Nobunaga Oda, a minor feudal lord and brilliant military strategist from Gifu, near Nagoya, conquered neighboring lords and emerged as one of the nation's greatest military powers. In 1573, Nobunaga attacked Kyoto and defeated the Ashikaga Shogunate. After victories over other influential feudal lords, Nobunaga was on the brink of unifying the nation when he was assassinated in 1582 by his retainer, Mitsuhide Akechi. Another powerful retainer, Hideyoshi Toyotomi, a mere farmer's son who had risen to a position of power, crushed Mitsuhide's rebel force, and then went on to complete the establishment of a centralized government.

In the period of peace that began with the end of the 16th century, all sorts of cultural pursuits flourished; it was a particularly rich and lavish era in the history of Japanese art. The gorgeous paintings of the Kano School are representative of the work of this era. Prototypes of the modern Kabuki and Bunraku puppet dramas also developed at this time.

The reign of the Toyotomi family, however, did not last long. After the death of Hideyoshi, two top retainers of the Toyotomis, Ieyasu Tokugawa and Mitsunari Ishida, vied for power, and their struggle divided the other feudal lords. The two forces had a final decisive battle at Sekigahara, between Kyoto and Nagoya, in 1600, and Ieyasu's victory led to the establishment of a new Shogunate in Edo (modern Tokyo) in 1603.

Toward the end of the period of civil war, Christianity was introduced on Kyushu island. Because the Christian missionaries accompanied the European traders who brought advanced technologies and foreign products into the country, Nobunaga Oda allowed them to act freely, and the new religion spread, especially in Nagasaki and other trading centers of western Kyushu. Some of the feudal lords of that area became Christians and even sent envoys to Rome. It is estimated that Christianity quickly gained 700,000 adherents, but because the new religion was especially popular among those poor farmers who suffered from the heavy taxes and rigid caste system of the Shogunate, it was not acceptable to either Hideyoshi or Ieyasu. Christianity was officially forbidden by the Tokugawa Shogunate in 1613. The bloody battle at Shimabara near Nagasaki between the Christian farmers and the army of the Shogun is symbolic of the tragic destiny of Christians in Japan at this time.

Edo Era (1603 – 1868)

The third Tokugawa Shogun, Iemitsu, closed all the ports of Japan, except Nagasaki, in 1639. His intentions were to shut out Christianity, and, at the same time, to monopolize foreign trade. Only Dutch and Chinese traders with no connections to missionaries were allowed to trade at a secluded area in Nagasaki. This isolationist period, which continued for 225 years, until 1854, was also the longest peaceful era in Japanese history. By the middle of the 18th century, the population of Edo had increased to one million, the largest in the world at that time. Economic progress allowed even the common people to engage in cultural activities, and *ukiyo-e* (woodblock prints) and *haiku* (short stylized poems) achieved great popularity.

By the middle of the 19th century, the rigid feudal system had become an obstacle to development of a modern economy. Despite their low social status, the merchants had great economic power and became underground supporters of a new, freer social system. In 1853, Commodore Perry of the United States brought his fleet to the port of Uraga, near Yokohama, and demanded the opening of Japanese ports for the supply of commodities to foreign fleets, and for international trade in general. The advanced technological level of the West that Perry and his sailors demonstrated helped make the people aware of the need for change. After civil wars between the conservative Shogunate forces, and those who wanted a new order (these included members of the imperial family and the innovative feudal lords of western Japan),the 15th Tokugawa Shogun, Yoshinobu, returned the reins of government to Emperor Meiji. This historic event of 1868 is referred to as the Meiji Restoration.

Modern Era (Meiji, Taisho and the current Showa Eras 1868 –   )

The new imperial government aggressively took the initiative in importing Western culture, technology and social structures. Japan's new government also invested heavily in and promoted industrialization. Despite the many changes that accompanied this modernization, the nation's traditional, unequal social structure survived. Sovereignty rested with the Emperor and, ultimately, he possessed all power. Only aristocrats could be members of the House of Chancellors and only men who paid a certain level of taxes were eligible to vote for members of the House of Representatives (Women gained the right to vote in

1925). After the tragedy of World War II, a genuine democratization took place in Japan. The Emperor was declared to be merely symbolic of the spirit of the nation, and elected officials, wielding all political power, ushered in a period marked by unparalleled efforts and crowned by the achievement of genuine social equality and phenomenal economic growth and success.

Timetables

The timetables listed on the following pages are accurate as of December 1987, and cover all the inter-city transportation – trains, buses and boats – introduced in this guidebook. Throughout this guide, each route has been assigned its own number, e.g., No. 1 for the Shinkansen, No. 30 for the JR Nara Line, No. 280 for the private Tobu Nikko Line, etc. The timetables that follow are listed in numerical order for the various routes so that you can find them easily.

Due to space limitations, we have selected the most convenient train, bus and boat services for each route, thus the time tables do not include all services available. For example, we have listed 37 trains each way for the Shinkansen (No. 1), though there actually are more than 100 daily trains each way on this line. There should, nevertheless, be more than enough choices to enable you to plan a good itinerary.

To distinguish JR from private transportation companies, the numbers 1 through 199 have been assigned to JR routes and the numbers 200 and above are used for private lines. The numbers are not consecutive and many numbers are missing from the tables. Despite their omission, there are actual long distance train, bus and boat services corresponding to these numbers. They are omitted from this book because they are not necessary to visit destinations introduced in this book. However, their numbers are reserved so that we can expand destinations in future editions, if there are requests from readers for off-off-off-the-beaten-track destinations.

The timetables, like official timetables in Japan, use military time. For example, 6:00

AM is expressed as 06:00, while 6:00 PM is 18:00; 11:30 AM is 11:30, while 11:30 PM is 23:30. Numbers larger than 12:00 indicate afternoon. To determine the time for afternoon trains, simply deduct 12:00 from the number listed in the timetable.

Information on fares between major cities is included with each timetable. Because most long distance trains are limited expresses, we have chosen to list fares for reserved seats for limited express trains. Fares for coach class are listed first followed by Green Car (first-class) fares in parentheses. When the timetable shows only local trains, fares listed are for local trains. If both limited express and local trains are listed in the timetable, both fares are detailed.

When planning your itinerary, first find the train, bus or boat you want to use, referring to the district maps (maps 7 to 13) and other destination maps. Determine its number, and then use the number to find its corresponding timetable and fare information.

Once you are accustomed to the system (which is very much like the system Japanese transportation companies use to provide information to Japanese travelers), you'll enjoy planning your itineraries, and you'll begin to gain an appreciation of the extent and the efficiency of Japan's public transportation system.

Important Notice

Timetables and fares are subject to change without notice. Please check the latest ones with your hotel personnel or with local tourist information centers.

1. JR Shinkansen

West-bound from Tokyo to Hakata

TRAIN \ STATION	TOKYO	ODAWARA	ATAMI	MISHIMA	NAGOYA	KYOTO	SHIN-OSAKA	SHIN-KOBE	HIMEJI	OKAYAMA	SHIN-KURASHIKI	FUKUYAMA	MIHARA	HIROSHIMA	OGORI	KOKURA	HAKATA
HIKARI-71	—	—	—	—	06:48	07:38	07:56	08:11	→	08:54	→	→	→	09:41	10:22	10:46	11:08
KODAMA-377	—	—	—	—	—	—	08:14	08:29	08:54	09:25	09:38	09:52	10:07	10:41	11:33	12:02	12:24
HIKARI-21	06:00	→	→	→	07:54	08:40	08:58	→	→	09:51	→	→	→	10:38	11:19	11:43	12:05
HIKARI-221	06:12	06:51	→	→	08:16	09:01	09:19	09:34	09:59	10:31	10:43	10:57	11:10	11:32	—	—	—
HIKARI-1	07:00	→	→	→	08:54	09:40	09:58	→	→	10:50	→	→	→	11:36	→	12:36	12:57
HIKARI-223	07:16	→	→	→	09:16	10:01	10:19	10:34	10:59	11:31	11:43	11:57	12:10	12:32	—	—	—
HIKARI-3	08:00	→	→	→	09:54	10:40	10:58	→	→	11:50	→	→	→	12:36	→	13:36	13:57
HIKARI-225	08:16	→	→	→	10:16	11:01	11:19	11:34	11:59	12:31	12:43	12:57	13:10	13:33	—	—	—
KODAMA-411	08:20	09:01	09:12	09:25	10:57	11:56	12:12	—	—	—	—	—	—	—	—	—	—
HIKARI-23	09:00	→	→	→	10:54	11:40	11:58	→	→	12:51	→	→	→	13:38	14:19	14:43	15:05
HIKARI-227	09:16	→	→	→	11:16	12:01	12:19	12:34	12:59	13:31	13:43	13:57	14:10	14:32	—	—	—
KODAMA-417	09:20	10:01	10:12	10:25	11:57	12:56	13:12	—	—	—	—	—	—	—	—	—	—
HIKARI-163	09:42	→	→	→	11:35	12:22	12:40	12:55	13:15	13:41	—	—	—	—	—	—	—
KODAMA-419	09:51	10:32	10:43	10:55	12:25	13:36	13:52	—	—	—	—	—	—	—	—	—	—
HIKARI-5	10:00	→	→	→	11:54	12:40	12:58	→	→	13:50	→	→	→	14:36	→	15:36	15:57
HIKARI-229	10:16	→	→	→	12:16	13:01	13:19	13:34	13:59	14:31	14:43	14:57	15:10	15:33	—	—	—
KODAMA-421	10:20	11:01	11:12	11:25	12:57	13:56	14:12	—	—	—	—	—	—	—	—	—	—
HIKARI-201	10:47	→	→	→	12:46	13:32	13:50	14:05	14:32	15:04	15:16	15:30	15:47	16:12	17:05	17:34	17:55
HIKARI-7	11:00	→	→	→	12:54	13:40	13:58	→	→	14:51	→	→	→	15:38	→	16:38	16:59
KODAMA-425	11:20	12:01	12:12	12:25	13:57	14:56	15:12	—	—	—	—	—	—	—	—	—	—
HIKARI-141	11:42	→	→	→	13:35	14:22	14:40	14:55	15:15	15:42	→	16:03	→	16:33	—	—	—
HIKARI-25	12:00	→	→	→	13:54	14:40	14:58	→	→	15:51	→	→	→	16:38	17:19	17:43	18:05
HIKARI-203	12:47	→	→	→	14:46	15:32	15:50	16:05	16:32	17:04	17:16	17:30	17:47	18:12	19:05	19:34	19:55
KODAMA-433	12:51	13:32	13:43	13:55	15:25	16:30	16:46	—	—	—	—	—	—	—	—	—	—
HIKARI-9	13:00	→	→	→	14:54	15:40	15:58	→	→	16:51	→	→	→	17:38	→	18:38	18:59
HIKARI-27	14:00	→	→	→	15:54	16:40	16:58	→	→	17:51	→	→	→	18:38	19:19	19:43	20:05
HIKARI-11	15:00	→	→	→	16:54	17:40	17:58	→	→	18:51	→	→	→	19:38	→	20:38	20:59
HIKARI-235	15:12	15:51	→	→	17:16	18:01	18:19	18:34	18:59	19:31	19:43	19:57	20:10	20:33	—	—	—
HIKARI-29	16:00	→	→	→	17:54	18:40	18:58	→	→	19:51	→	→	→	20:38	21:19	21:43	22:05
KODAMA-451	16:20	17:01	17:12	17:25	18:57	19:56	20:12	—	—	—	—	—	—	—	—	—	—
HIKARI-239	16:47	→	→	→	18:46	19:32	19:50	20:05	20:30	21:07	21:19	21:33	21:46	22:09	—	—	—
HIKARI-31	17:12	→	→	→	19:06	19:52	20:10	→	→	21:04	→	→	→	21:50	22:31	22:55	23:17
HIKARI-285	18:00	→	→	→	19:54	20:40	20:56	—	—	—	—	—	—	—	—	—	—
HIKARI-41	18:42	→	→	→	20:35	21:22	21:40	→	→	22:34	→	→	→	23:20	—	—	—
HIKARI-347	19:30	→	→	→	21:31	22:18	22:34	—	—	—	—	—	—	—	—	—	—
HIKARI-293	20:30	→	→	→	22:30	23:20	23:36	—	—	—	—	—	—	—	—	—	—
HIKARI-289	21:00	→	→	→	22:51	23:36	23:52	—	—	—	—	—	—	—	—	—	—

1. JR Shinkansen

Tokyo / Odawara	3,480	(4,780)	Kyoto / Okayama	7,000 (11,200)
Tokyo / Nagoya	10,100	(14,300)	Kyoto / Hiroshima	10,300 (15,700)
Tokyo / Kyoto	12,600	(18,000)	Kyoto / Hakata	14,500 (21,100)
Tokyo / Osaka	13,100	(18,500)	Okayama / Hiroshima	5,600 (8,400)
Tokyo / Okayama	15,600	(22,200)	Okayama / Hakata	11,500 (16,900)
Tokyo / Hiroshima	17,200	(25,000)	Hiroshima / Hakata	8,300 (12,500)
Tokyo / Hakata	20,700	(28,500)		

1. JR Shinkansen

East-bound from Hakata to Tokyo

TRAIN	HAKATA	KOKURA	OGORI	HIROSHIMA	MIHARA	FUKUYAMA	SHIN-KURASHIKI	OKAYAMA	HIMEJI	SHIN-KOBE	SHIN-OSAKA	KYOTO	NAGOYA	MISHIMA	ATAMI	ODAWARA	TOKYO
HIKARI-60	—	—	—	—	—	—	—	06:00	→	06:41	06:58	07:15	08:00	→	→	→	09:59
KODAMA-404	—	—	—	—	—	—	—	—	—	—	07:31	07:48	08:47	10:23	10:33	10:46	11:24
HIKARI-260	—	—	—	—	—	—	—	06:42	07:12	07:37	07:54	08:11	09:01	→	10:17	→	11:04
HIKARI-220	—	—	—	06:12	06:35	06:48	07:02	07:15	07:46	08:10	08:27	08:44	09:30	→	→	→	11:28
KODAMA-412	—	—	—	—	—	—	—	—	—	—	08:54	09:11	10:19	11:52	12:03	12:16	12:55
HIKARI-222	—	—	—	07:12	07:35	07:48	08:02	08:15	08:46	09:10	09:27	09:44	10:30	→	→	→	12:28
HIKARI-224	—	—	—	07:34	07:57	08:11	08:25	08:38	09:14	09:39	09:58	10:15	11:00	→	→	→	12:59
HIKARI-20	06:29	06:50	07:14	07:56	→	→	→	08:44	→	→	09:38	09:55	10:42	→	→	→	12:34
HIKARI-226	—	—	—	08:12	08:35	08:48	09:02	09:15	09:46	10:10	10:27	10:44	11:30	→	→	→	13:28
HIKARI-200	06:51	07:13	07:42	08:34	09:00	09:15	09:29	09:42	10:14	10:41	10:58	11:15	12:00	→	→	→	13:59
HIKARI-22	07:41	08:02	08:26	09:08	→	→	→	09:56	→	→	10:50	11:07	11:52	→	→	→	13:46
HIKARI-228	—	—	—	09:12	09:35	09:48	10:02	10:15	10:46	11:10	11:27	11:44	12:30	→	→	→	14:28
HIKARI-2	08:47	09:08	→	10:08	→	→	→	10:56	→	→	11:50	12:07	12:52	→	→	→	14:46
HIKARI-230	—	—	—	10:12	10:35	10:48	11:02	11:15	11:46	12:10	12:27	12:44	13:30	→	→	→	15:28
KODAMA-432	—	—	—	—	—	—	—	—	—	—	12:31	12:48	13:47	15:23	15:33	15:46	16:24
HIKARI-202	08:51	09:13	09:42	10:34	10:57	11:11	11:28	11:42	12:14	12:41	12:58	13:15	14:00	→	→	→	15:59
HIKARI-4	09:47	10:08	→	11:08	→	→	→	11:56	→	→	12:50	13:07	13:52	→	→	→	15:46
HIKARI-232	—	—	—	11:12	11:35	11:48	12:02	12:15	12:46	13:10	13:27	13:44	14:30	→	→	→	16:28
KODAMA-436	—	—	—	—	—	—	—	—	—	—	13:31	13:48	14:47	16:23	16:33	16:46	17:24
HIKARI-24	10:41	11:02	11:26	12:08	→	→	→	12:56	→	→	13:50	14:07	14:52	→	→	→	16:46
KODAMA-442	—	—	—	—	—	—	—	—	—	—	14:31	14:48	15:47	17:23	17:33	17:46	18:24
HIKARI-6	11:47	12:08	→	13:08	→	→	→	13:56	→	→	14:50	15:07	15:52	→	→	→	17:46
HIKARI-236	—	—	—	13:12	13:35	13:48	14:02	14:15	14:46	15:10	15:27	15:44	16:30	→	→	→	18:28
KODAMA-446	—	—	—	—	—	—	—	—	—	—	15:31	15:48	16:47	18:23	18:33	18:46	19:24
HIKARI-8	12:47	13:08	→	14:08	→	→	→	14:56	→	→	15:50	16:07	16:52	→	→	→	18:46
HIKARI-238	—	—	—	14:12	14:35	14:48	15:02	15:15	15:46	16:10	16:27	16:44	17:30	→	→	→	19:28
HIKARI-26	13:41	14:02	14:26	15:08	→	→	→	15:56	→	→	16:50	17:07	17:52	→	→	→	19:46
HIKARI-240	—	—	—	15:12	15:35	15:48	16:02	16:15	16:46	17:10	17:27	17:44	18:30	→	→	→	20:28
HIKARI-10	14:49	15:09	→	16:09	→	→	→	16:56	→	→	17:50	18:07	18:52	→	→	→	20:46
HIKARI-242	—	—	—	16:12	16:35	16:48	17:02	17:15	17:46	18:10	18:27	18:44	19:37	→	→	→	21:34
HIKARI-204	14:53	15:15	15:44	16:35	17:01	17:15	17:29	17:42	18:14	18:41	18:58	19:15	20:00	→	→	→	21:59
HIKARI-12	15:49	16:09	→	17:09	→	→	→	17:56	→	→	18:50	19:07	19:52	→	→	→	21:46
HIKARI-244	—	—	—	17:12	17:35	17:48	18:02	18:15	18:46	18:10	19:27	19:44	20:30	→	→	21:54	22:32
HIKARI-28	16:41	17:02	17:26	18:08	→	→	→	18:56	→	→	19:50	20:07	20:52	→	→	→	22:46
HIKARI-142	—	—	—	18:42	→	19:12	→	19:34	20:00	20:20	20:37	20:54	21:44	→	→	→	23:46
HIKARI-72	18:07	18:28	18:52	19:34	→	→	→	20:22	→	21:03	21:20	21:37	22:27	—	—	—	—
HIKARI-90	19:13	19:34	19:58	20:45	→	21:16	→	21:41	→	22:23	22:38	—	—	—	—	—	—

2. JR Tohoku Shinkansen

North-bound from Ueno to Morioka

TRAIN \ STATION	UENO	OYAMA	UTSUNOMIYA	KORIYAMA	FUKUSHIMA	SENDAI	ICHINOSEKI	MORIOKA
YAMABIKO-31	06:00	→	06:47	07:21	07:38	08:04	08:36	09:21
YAMABIKO-35	07:00	→	07:47	08:21	08:38	09:04	09:36	10:21
YAMABIKO-41	08:00	→	08:47	09:21	09:38	10:04	10:36	11:21
AOBA-205	08:18	08:57	09:11	10:01	10:19	10:50	—	—
YAMABIKO-1	08:40	→	→	→	10:08	10:34	→	11:25
YAMABIKO-43	09:00	→	09:47	10:21	10:38	11:04	11:36	12:21
AOBA-207	09:18	09:57	10:11	11:02	11:19	11:50	—	—
YAMABIKO-21	09:40	→	10:23	10:57	→	11:35	→	12:26
YAMABIKO-47	10:00	→	10:47	11:21	11:38	12:04	12:36	13:21
AOBA-209	10:18	10:57	11:11	12:01	12:19	12:50	—	—
YAMABIKO-51	11:00	→	11:47	12:21	12:38	13:04	13:36	14:21
YAMABIKO-55	12:00	→	12:47	13:21	13:38	14:04	14:36	15:21
YAMABIKO-61	13:00	→	13:47	14:21	14:38	15:04	15:36	16:21
YAMABIKO-63	14:00	→	14:47	15:21	15:38	16:04	16:36	17:21
YAMABIKO-71	15:00	→	15:47	16:21	16:38	17:04	17:36	18:21
YAMABIKO-73	16:00	→	16:47	17:21	17:38	18:04	18:36	19:21
YAMABIKO-77	17:00	→	17:47	18:21	18:38	19:04	19:36	20:21
YAMABIKO-79	18:00	→	18:47	19:21	19:38	20:04	20:36	21:21
YAMABIKO-81	19:00	→	19:47	20:21	20:38	21:04	21:36	22:21

South-bound from Morioka to Ueno

TRAIN \ STATION	MORIOKA	ICHINOSEKI	SENDAI	FUKUSHIMA	KORIYAMA	UTSUNOMIYA	OYAMA	UENO
YAMABIKO-130	—	—	06:14	06:40	06:57	07:31	07:43	08:22
YAMABIKO-140	—	—	07:00	07:30	07:47	08:26	→	09:10
YAMABIKO-30	06:13	06:58	07:31	07:57	08:14	08:48	→	09:34
YAMABIKO-2	07:29	→	08:21	08:47	→	→	→	10:14
YAMABIKO-34	08:13	08:58	09:31	09:57	10:14	10:48	→	11:34
YAMABIKO-10	09:10	→	10:02	→	10:40	12:13	→	11:55
AOBA-208	—	—	10:50	11:27	11:45	12:30	12:42	13:22
YAMABIKO-20	10:10	→	11:02	→	11:40	→	→	12:57
YAMABIKO-46	11:13	11:58	12:31	12:57	13:14	13:48	→	14:34
AOBA-212	—	—	12:50	13:21	13:38	14:29	14:42	15:22
YAMABIKO-50	12:13	12:58	13:31	13:57	14:14	14:48	→	15:34
AOBA-214	—	—	13:50	14:21	14:38	15:29	15:42	16:22
YAMABIKO-56	13:13	13:58	14:31	14:57	15:14	15:48	→	16:34
AOBA-216	—	—	14:50	15:21	15:38	16:29	16:42	17:22
YAMABIKO-62	14:13	14:58	15:31	15:57	16:14	16:48	→	17:34
YAMABIKO-66	15:13	15:58	16:31	16:57	17:14	17:48	→	18:34
YAMABIKO-68	16:13	16:58	17:31	17:57	18:14	18:48	→	19:34
YAMABIKO-72	17:13	17:58	18:31	18:57	19:14	19:48	→	20:34
YAMABIKO-76	18:13	18:58	19:31	19:57	20:14	20:48	→	21:34

3. JR Joetsu Shinkansen

North-bound from Ueno to Niigata

TRAIN \ STATION	UENO	TAKASAKI	JOMO-KOGEN	ECHIGO-YUZAWA	NAGAOKA	NIIGATA
TOKI-401	06:22	07:16	07:34	07:48	08:17	08:42
ASAHI-333	07:10	07:59	→	08:28	08:52	09:17
ASAHI-381	07:52	08:46	09:04	→	→	09:55
TOKI-403	08:36	09:30	09:48	10:03	10:31	10:56
ASAHI-301	09:10	→	→	→	10:42	11:03
TOKI-405	09:36	10:30	10:48	11:03	11:31	11:56
ASAHI-339	10:10	10:59	→	11:28	11:52	12:17
ASAHI-341	11:10	11:59	→	12:28	12:52	13:17
TOKI-407	11:36	12:30	12:48	13:03	13:31	13:56
ASAHI-361	12:10	12:59	13:17	→	13:52	14:17
ASAHI-343	13:10	13:59	→	14:28	14:52	15:17
ASAHI-391	14:10	14:57	→	15:25	15:54	16:19
ASAHI-349	15:10	15:59	→	16:28	16:52	17:17
ASAHI-303	16:10	→	→	→	17:42	18:03
ASAHI-353	17:10	17:59	→	18:28	18:52	19:17
ASAHI-311	18:10	18:59	→	→	→	20:03
ASAHI-365	19:10	20:00	20:18	→	20:52	21:17
ASAHI-359	20:10	20:59	→	21:28	21:52	22:17
ASAHI-371	21:10	21:59	→	→	22:52	23:17

South-bound from Niigata to Ueno

TRAIN \ STATION	NIIGATA	NAGAOKA	ECHIGO-YUZAWA	JOMO-KOGEN	TAKASAKI	UENO
ASAHI-390	06:25	06:51	07:19	→	07:48	08:34
ASAHI-380	07:13	→	→	08:04	08:22	09:16
TOKI-404	08:06	08:32	09:01	09:15	09:33	10:26
ASAHI-300	08:50	09:12	→	→	→	10:43
ASAHI-310	09:50	→	→	→	10:55	11:43
ASAHI-332	10:36	11:02	11:26	→	11:54	12:43
ASAHI-362	11:36	12:02	→	12:36	12:54	13:43
ASAHI-370	12:36	13:02	→	→	13:54	14:43
TOKI-412	13:06	13:32	14:01	14:15	14:33	15:26
ASAHI-336	13:36	14:02	14:26	→	14:54	15:43
ASAHI-340	14:36	15:02	15:26	→	15:54	16:43
TOKI-414	15:06	15:32	16:01	16:15	16:33	17:26
ASAHI-344	15:36	16:02	16:26	→	16:54	17:43
ASAHI-364	16:19	16:45	→	17:19	17:37	18:26
ASAHI-302	16:50	17:12	→	→	→	18:43
ASAHI-348	17:36	18:02	18:26	→	18:54	19:43
TOKI-418	18:06	18:32	19:01	19:15	19:33	20:26
ASAHI-320	18:50	19:12	→	→	19:59	20:46
ASAHI-352	19:34	20:00	20:24	→	20:52	21:41

4. JR Yokosuka Line

Tokyo to Kurihama							Kurihama to Tokyo						
STATION TRAIN	TOKYO	SHINAGAWA	OFUNA	KITA-KAMAKURA	KAMAKURA	KURIHAMA	STATION TRAIN	KURIHAMA	KAMAKURA	KITA-KAMAKURA	OFUNA	SHINAGAWA	TOKYO
LOCAL TRAIN	08:00	08:09	08:50	08:54	08:57	09:26	LOCAL TRAIN	09:15	09:41	09:44	09:48	10:28	10:37
LOCAL TRAIN	08:34	08:42	09:25	09:28	09:32	10:03	LOCAL TRAIN	10:22	10:54	10:57	11:02	11:43	11:51
LOCAL TRAIN	09:03	09:11	09:53	09:56	09:59	10:34	LOCAL TRAIN	11:21	11:53	11:57	12:02	12:42	12:50
LOCAL TRAIN	09:34	09:42	10:25	10:28	10:33	11:04	LOCAL TRAIN	12:20	12:50	12:53	12:59	13:40	13:48
LOCAL TRAIN	10:05	10:13	10:57	11:00	11:04	—	LOCAL TRAIN	13:21	13:52	13:55	14:01	14:42	14:50
LOCAL TRAIN	10:35	10:43	11:26	11:29	11:32	12:03	LOCAL TRAIN	14:21	14:53	14:57	15:01	15:41	15:50
LOCAL TRAIN	11:35	11:43	12:25	12:29	12:32	13:03	LOCAL TRAIN	15:19	15:50	15:54	15:57	16:39	16:47
LOCAL TRAIN	12:36	12:45	13:27	13:30	13:34	14:02	LOCAL TRAIN	16:17	16:47	16:51	16:56	17:37	17:45
LOCAL TRAIN	13:35	13:43	14:25	14:29	14:33	15:02	LOCAL TRAIN	16:32	17:03	17:06	17:11	17:53	18:01
LOCAL TRAIN	14:35	14:43	15:25	15:28	15:31	16:01	LOCAL TRAIN	16:47	17:16	17:19	17:24	18:05	18:13
LOCAL TRAIN	15:35	15:44	16:27	16:31	16:34	16:59	LOCAL TRAIN	17:18	17:49	17:52	17:57	18:37	18:46
LOCAL TRAIN	16:36	16:45	17:28	17:31	17:35	18:07	LOCAL TRAIN	18:09	18:38	18:41	18:46	19:26	19:35
LOCAL TRAIN	17:34	17:43	18:28	18:31	18:35	19:07	LOCAL TRAIN	19:09	19:39	19:43	19:47	20:27	20:36

2. JR Tohoku Shinkansen

Ueno / Utsunomiya	4,400	(7,200)
Ueno / Fukushima	8,100	(12,300)
Ueno / Sendai	9,900	(14,100)
Ueno / Ichinoseki	11,700	(17,100)
Ueno / Morioka	13,000	(18,400)
Utsunomiya / Sendai	7,800	(12,000)
Fukushima / Sendai	3,420	(4,720)
Sendai / Ichinoseki	3,740	(6,540)
Sendai / Morioka	6,000	(8,800)

3. JR Joetsu Shinkansen

Ueno / Jomo-Kogen	5,300	(8,100)
Ueno / Niigata	9,700	(13,900)
Jomo-Kogen/Niigata	6,000	(8,800)

4. JR Yokosuka Line

Tokyo / Kita-Kamakura	780	(N / A)
Tokyo / Kamakura	900	(N / A)

5. JR Ito Line

Several "Odoriko" trains run between Tokyo Station and Izukyu-Shimoda Station via Ito. Their schedule is listed under No. 202.

6. JR Tokaido/Sanyo Line

Since the completion of the Shinkansen, this old line has been used for short-distance local trains. Trains run every 10 - 30 minutes, and the following two sectors are especially important for tourists:

(1) Between Kyoto and Sannomiya.

Commuter trains connect Kyoto with Shin-Osaka, Osaka, and Sannomiya (Kobe).

(2) Between Okayama and Miyajima-guchi.

Local trains provide frequent service between major Inland Sea destinations such as Okayama, Kurashiki, Shin-Kurashiki, Onomichi, Mihara, Hiroshima, and Miyajima-guchi.

7. JR Shinetsu Line

Ueno to Naoetsu

STATION TRAIN	UENO	TAKASAKI	KARUIZAWA	KOMORO	NAGANO	NAOETSU
ASAMA-3	08:00	09:13	09:59	10:15	10:54	—
HAKUSAN-1	09:30	10:40	11:26	11:42	12:22	13:43
ASAMA-11	11:00	12:12	12:58	13:15	13:54	15:15
ASAMA-17	13:00	14:12	14:58	15:15	15:51	—
ASAMA-19	14:00	15:09	15:55	16:12	16:52	—
HAKUSAN-3	15:30	16:39	17:25	17:40	18:20	19:33
ASAMA-27	17:00	18:09	18:55	19:11	19:50	—
ASAMA-29	18:00	19:14	20:00	20:17	20:57	22:09
ASAMA-33	20:00	21:09	21:57	22:16	22:58	—

Naoetsu to Ueno

STATION TRAIN	NAOETSU	NAGANO	KOMORO	KARUIZAWA	TAKASAKI	UENO
ASAMA-6	—	08:18	08:56	09:18	10:05	11:15
ASAMA-8	08:11	09:24	10:03	10:24	11:12	12:23
ASAMA-12	10:02	11:17	11:54	12:16	13:04	14:15
ASAMA-18	—	13:16	13:56	14:16	15:04	16:15
HAKUSAN-2	13:33	14:49	15:26	15:47	16:35	17:45
ASAMA-24	—	15:44	16:24	16:45	17:35	18:45
ASAMA-28	15:34	16:48	17:25	17:47	18:35	19:46
ASAMA-30	—	17:16	17:56	18:17	19:05	20:15
HAKUSAN-4	17:24	18:43	19:20	19:41	20:28	21:38

8. JR Joetsu Line

Ueno to Nagaoka

STATION TRAIN	UENO	TAKASAKI	MINAKAMI	DOAI	ECHIGO-YUZAWA	NAGAOKA
TANIGAWA-1	07:11	08:33	09:30	—	—	—
LOCAL TRAIN	—	08:22	09:42	09:51	10:17	11:32
TANIGAWA-3	10:11	11:35	12:31	—	—	—
LOCAL TRAIN	—	—	13:21	13:30	14:08	15:25
TANIGAWA-5	12:11	13:33	14:26	—	—	—
LOCAL TRAIN	—	—	16:10	16:19	16:47	18:11
TANIGAWA-7	14:11	15:33	16:30	—	—	—
LOCAL TRAIN	—	—	17:33	17:43	18:14	19:28

Nagaoka to Ueno

STATION TRAIN	NAGAOKA	ECHIGO-YUZAWA	DOAI	MINAKAMI	TAKASAKI	UENO
LOCAL TRAIN	08:36	10:08	10:35	10:47	—	—
TANIGAWA-4	—	—	—	11:12	12:11	13:32
LOCAL TRAIN	10:56	12:15	12:42	12:54	—	—
TANIGAWA-6	—	—	—	15:14	16:12	17:35
LOCAL TRAIN	15:25	16:43	17:09	17:21	—	—
TANIGAWA-10	—	—	—	18:12	19:09	20:30

7. JR Shinetsu Line
Ueno / Nagano   6,400   (9,200)
Ueno / Naoetsu   7,400   (11,600)

8. JR Joetsu Line
Ueno / Minakami   4,900   (7,700)
Minakami / Nagaoka 1,800* (N / A)
    * Local train

9. JR Tohoku Line
Morioka / Aomori   5,700   (9,900)

9. JR Tohoku Line

Morioka to Aomori

STATION TRAIN	MORIOKA	HACHINOHE	AOMORI
HATSUKARI-1	08:23	09:37	10:42
HATSUKARI-3	09:31	10:50	11:57
HATSUKARI-5	10:31	11:44	12:52
HATSUKARI-7	11:37	12:56	14:03
HATSUKARI-9	12:34	13:44	14:47
HATSUKARI-11	13:35	14:51	15:58
HATSUKARI-13	14:31	15:46	16:52
HATSUKARI-15	15:33	16:50	17:56
HATSUKARI-17	16:35	17:54	19:01
HATSUKARI-19	17:31	18:47	19:53
HATSUKARI-21	18:36	19:50	20:58

Aomori to Morioka

STATION TRAIN	AOMORI	HACHINOHE	MORIOKA
HATSUKARI-8	07:30	08:40	10:00
HATSUKARI-10	08:45	09:48	11:03
HATSUKARI-12	09:33	10:43	12:03
HATSUKARI-14	10:48	11:51	13:03
HATSUKARI-16	11:45	12:48	14:03
HATSUKARI-18	12:33	13:41	15:00
HATSUKARI-20	13:50	14:52	16:02
HATSUKARI-22	14:35	15:41	17:00
HATSUKARI-24	15:46	16:49	18:03
HATSUKARI-26	16:40	17:46	19:03
HATSUKARI-28	17:45	18:48	20:03

10. JR Chuo/Oito Line

Shinjuku to Itoigawa

STATION TRAIN	SHINJUKU	OTSUKI	MATSUMOTO	SHINANO-OMACHI	MINAMI-OTARI	ITOIGAWA
AZUSA-1	07:00	08:02	09:58	10:35	11:17	—
LOCAL TRAIN	—	—	—	—	11:19	12:09
AZUSA-5	08:00	→	10:56	—	—	—
LOCAL TRAIN	—	—	11:32	12:29	13:21	—
LOCAL TRAIN	—	—	—	—	14:12	15:06
AZUSA-9	09:00	10:07	11:59	—	—	—
AZUSA-13	10:00	→	12:49	—	—	—
LOCAL TRAIN	—	—	13:27	14:26	15:31	—
LOCAL TRAIN	—	—	—	—	15:33	16:25
AZUSA-17	11:00	12:02	13:56	—	—	—
LOCAL TRAIN	—	—	14:39	15:54	16:53	—
LOCAL TRAIN	—	—	—	—	17:01	17:54
AZUSA-21	13:00	→	15:54	—	—	—
LOCAL TRAIN	—	—	16:47	17:45	18:41	—
LOCAL TRAIN	—	—	—	—	19:04	19:56
AZUSA-27	15:00	→	17:57	—	—	—
AZUSA-31	16:00	→	18:56	—	—	—
AZUSA-37	18:00	19:08	21:08	21:46	22:39	—

Itoigawa to Shinjuku

STATION TRAIN	ITOIGAWA	MINAMI-OTARI	SHINANO-OMACHI	MATSUMOTO	OTSUKI	SHINJUKU
AZUSA-10	—	07:06	07:52	08:38	→	11:25
AZUSA-12	—	—	—	09:31	11:23	12:25
LOCAL TRAIN	08:06	09:11	—	—	—	—
AZUSA-18	—	—	—	11:33	→	14:25
LOCAL TRAIN	—	10:20	11:26	12:29	—	—
AZUSA-24	—	—	—	13:34	15:23	16:24
LOCAL TRAIN	11:03	12:08	—	—	—	—
LOCAL TRAIN	—	12:30	13:55	14:53	—	—
AZUSA-30	—	—	—	15:02	→	17:55
LOCAL TRAIN	14:03	15:01	—	—	—	—
AZUSA-36	—	15:05	15:47	16:35	→	19:25
AZUSA-38	—	—	—	16:55	18:46	19:51
AZUSA-40	—	—	—	17:41	→	20:25
LOCAL TRAIN	15:16	16:21	17:25	—	—	—
LOCAL TRAIN	—	—	17:48	18:46	—	—
LOCAL TRAIN	15:51	16:57	—	—	—	—
LOCAL TRAIN	—	17:28	18:30	19:29	—	—
AZUSA-46	—	—	—	19:34	→	22:25

11. JR Chuo/Shinonoi Line

Nagoya to Nagano

STATION TRAIN	NAGOYA	TAJIMI	NAKATSUGAWA	NAGISO	MATSUMOTO	NAGANO
SHINANO-1	07:00	07:26	07:55	→	09:16	10:09
SHINANO-3	08:00	08:26	08:55	→	10:19	11:09
SHINANO-5	09:00	09:26	09:57	10:10	11:21	—
SHINANO-7	10:00	10:26	10:57	→	12:19	13:12
SHINANO-11	13:00	13:26	13:57	→	15:20	16:13
SHINANO-15	15:00	15:26	15:57	16:10	17:21	18:14
SHINANO-17	17:00	17:26	17:55	18:08	19:20	20:12
SHINANO-19	19:00	19:26	19:57	20:11	21:23	22:16

Nagano to Nagoya

STATION TRAIN	NAGANO	MATSUMOTO	NAGISO	NAKATSUGAWA	TAJIMI	NAGOYA
SHINANO-2	06:04	06:59	→	08:24	08:57	09:24
SHINANO-4	08:03	08:58	10:10	10:24	10:56	11:23
SHINANO-6	09:08	10:04	→	11:27	11:57	12:24
SHINANO-8	11:04	11:57	→	13:22	13:55	14:22
SHINANO-10	13:05	13:58	15:11	15:24	15:54	16:22
SHINANO-12	14:06	14:58	16:10	16:24	16:55	17:22
SHINANO-16	15:20	16:14	17:27	17:43	18:13	18:40
SHINANO-18	17:20	18:14	→	19:38	20:11	20:38

10. JR Chuo / Oito Line

Shinjuku / Matsumoto   6,400 (10,600)
Matsumoto / Shinano-Omachi
                        620* (N / A)
Mtsumoto / Itoigawa   1,800* (N / A)
    * Local train.

11. JR Chuo / Shinonoi Line

Nagoya / Tajimi   1,820 (3,120)
Nagoya / Nagiso   2,940 (4,240)
Ngoya / Matsumoto   5,600 (8,400)
Nagoya / Nagano   6,800 (11,000)

366

15. JR Takayama Line

Nagoya to Toyama

STATION / TRAIN	NAGOYA	GIFU	GERO	TAKAYAMA	HIDA-FURUKAWA	TOYAMA
NORIKURA-1	08:30	09:00	10:49	11:57	12:14	13:34
HIDA-1	09:41	10:08	11:39	12:31	—	—
TAKAYAMA	—	10:31	12:26	13:25	13:40	—
HIDA-3	10:46	11:14	12:53	13:46	—	—
KITA-ALPS	—	—	13:07	14:07	14:21	15:41
HIDA-5	13:01	13:29	15:06	16:07	16:22	—
NORIKURA-3	13:45	14:14	16:03	17:07	17:22	18:47
NORIKURA-5	14:30	15:00	17:02	18:23	—	—
NORIKURA-7	16:37	17:09	19:02	19:59	—	—
HIDA-7	19:01	19:31	21:08	22:06	—	—

Toyama to Nagoya

STATION / TRAIN	TOYAMA	HIDA-FURUKAWA	TAKAYAMA	GERO	GIFU	NAGOYA
HIDA-2	—	—	08:31	09:21	10:59	11:29
NORIKURA-4	—	—	09:50	10:50	12:30	13:02
NORIKURA-6	09:32	10:57	11:20	12:26	14:07	14:35
LOCAL TRAIN	10:23	12:14	12:34	—	—	—
HIDA-4	—	—	13:26	14:27	15:55	16:24
HIDA-6	—	—	14:37	15:35	17:06	17:39
TAKAYAMA	—	14:55	15:14	16:16	17:54	—
NORIKURA-8	13:50	15:28	15:49	16:52	18:31	19:00
HIDA-8	—	16:47	17:04	17:56	19:23	19:51
KITA-ALPS	16:32	18:04	18:23	19:22	—	—

16A. JR Uetsu Line

Niigata to Aomori

STATION / TRAIN	NIIGATA	SAKAMACHI	SAKATA	AKITA	HIROSAKI	AOMORI
INAHO-1	08:52	09:35	11:20	12:50	14:57	15:28
INAHO-5	11:13	11:55	13:35	15:13	—	—
INAHO-7	13:27	14:10	15:48	—	—	—
INAHO-9	15:27	16:09	17:48	19:22	—	—
HAKUCHO	17:27	18:10	19:46	21:11	23:09	23:40
INAHO-11	18:15	19:04	20:43	—	—	—

Aomori to Niigata

STATION / TRAIN	AOMORI	HIROSAKI	AKITA	SAKATA	SAKAMACHI	NIIGATA
HAKUCHO	04:50	05:22	07:23	08:54	10:28	11:10
INAHO-6	—	—	09:37	11:10	12:44	13:26
INAHO-10	10:13	10:45	12:53	14:24	15:59	16:40
INAHO-12	—	—	—	16:23	17:59	18:40
INAHO-14	—	—	17:10	18:42	19:17	20:59

17. JR Nanao Line

Kanazawa to Wajima

STATION / TRAIN	KANAZAWA	WAKURA-ONSEN	ANAMIZU	WAJIMA
NOTOJI-1	08:00	09:17	09:47	10:25
NOTOJI-3	09:56	11:10	11:55	12:35
NOTOJI-7	14:20	15:35	16:10	16:48
NOTOJI-9	15:41	16:59	17:36	18:13
NOTOJI-11	17:38	18:52	19:33	20:10
NOTOJI-13	19:50	21:11	21:59	22:37

Wajima to Kanazawa

STATION / TRAIN	WAJIMA	ANAMIZU	WAKURA-ONSEN	KANAZAWA
NOTOJI-2	07:22	08:08	08:40	09:51
NOTOJI-4	08:16	09:03	09:42	11:03
NOTOJI-8	10:27	11:10	11:40	12:51
LOCAL TRAIN	11:59	12:49	13:29	15:16
NOTOJI-10	—	13:39	14:09	15:22
NOTOJI-14	18:23	19:16	19:46	20:59

15. JR Takayama Line

Nagoya / Gero	4,300	(7,100)
Nagoya / Takayama	5,600	(8,400)
Nagoya / Toyama	6,800	(11,000)
Gero / Takayama	2,100	(3,400)
Takayama / Toyama	3,140	(4,440)

16A. JR Uetsu Line

Niigata / Akita	7,100	(11,300)
Niigata / Aomori	10,000	(15,400)

17. JR Nanao Line

Kanazawa / Wakura-Onsen	1,720	(N / A)
Kanazawa / Wajima	2,700	(N / A)

16. JR Hokuriku Line

Osaka to Niigata

TRAIN \ STATION	OSAKA	SHIN-OSAKA	KYOTO	FUKUI	AWARA-ONSEN	KANAZAWA	TOYAMA	UOZU	ITOIGAWA	NAOETSU	NAGAOKA	NIIGATA
HOKUETSU-3	—	—	—	—	—	07:44	08:36	08:54	09:34	09:59	10:52	11:42
HOKUETSU-5	—	—	—	08:02	08:13	08:55	09:39	09:57	10:33	10:59	11:52	12:42
RAICHO-3	07:50	07:55	08:20	09:55	10:07	10:48	11:37	11:54	12:30	12:56	13:48	14:37
RAICHO-5	08:20	08:25	08:50	10:21	10:33	11:12	—	—	—	—	—	—
RAICHO-7	09:20	09:25	09:50	11:26	11:38	12:19	13:02	—	—	—	—	—
HAKUCHO	10:40	10:45	11:10	12:40	12:52	13:33	14:17	14:33	15:09	15:34	16:30	17:16
HOKUETSU-9	—	—	—	—	—	14:05	14:50	15:07	15:45	16:11	17:02	17:52
RAICHO-13	11:50	11:55	12:20	13:54	14:05	14:47	15:34	15:52	16:28	16:53	17:48	18:44
RAICHO-15	12:20	12:25	12:50	14:24	14:35	15:17	16:02	—	—	—	—	—
RAICHO-17	13:20	13:25	13:50	15:26	15:38	16:19	17:02	—	—	—	—	—
HOKUETSU-11	—	—	—	—	—	16:46	17:33	17:51	18:29	18:56	19:50	20:42
RAICHO-21	14:20	14:25	14:50	16:22	16:34	17:15	17:58	—	—	—	—	—
RAICHO-25	15:20	15:25	15:50	17:24	17:35	18:16	19:06	19:22	19:59	20:25	21:20	22:10
RAICHO-27	16:20	16:25	16:50	18:21	18:33	19:14	19:58	—	—	—	—	—
RAICHO-31	17:20	17:25	17:50	19:23	19:35	20:17	21:01	—	—	—	—	—
RAICHO-33	18:20	18:25	18:50	20:24	20:36	21:17	22:03	—	—	—	—	—
RAICHO-37	19:20	19:25	19:50	21:23	21:35	22:16	23:03	—	—	—	—	—

Niigata to Osaka

TRAIN \ STATION	NIIGATA	NAGAOKA	NAOETSU	ITOIGAWA	UOZU	TOYAMA	KANAZAWA	AWARA-ONSEN	FUKUI	KYOTO	SHIN-OSAKA	OSAKA
RAICHO-4	—	—	—	—	—	06:49	07:40	08:19	08:31	10:10	10:34	10:39
RAICHO-6	—	—	—	—	—	—	08:10	08:51	09:04	10:38	11:02	11:08
RAICHO-8	—	—	—	—	—	08:24	09:10	09:49	10:02	11:37	12:02	12:07
RAICHO-10	—	—	—	—	—	09:25	10:10	10:49	11:02	12:38	13:04	13:09
RAICHO-12	—	—	—	—	—	10:25	11:10	11:49	12:02	13:39	14:03	14:09
RAICHO-14	08:16	09:06	09:59	10:25	10:59	11:19	12:06	12:45	12:58	14:35	14:59	15:05
RAICHO-18	09:04	09:54	10:49	11:15	11:48	12:10	12:58	13:37	13:50	15:26	15:50	15:56
HOKUETSU-2	10:00	10:51	11:45	12:11	12:47	13:05	13:49	—	—	—	—	—
RAICHO-22	—	—	—	—	—	—	14:10	14:49	15:02	16:37	17:02	17:07
RAICHO-24	—	—	—	—	—	13:54	14:40	15:19	15:32	17:09	17:33	17:39
HAKUCHO	11:16	12:03	13:00	13:26	13:59	14:18	15:05	15:44	15:57	17:31	17:55	18:01
RAICHO-26	—	—	—	—	—	14:54	15:39	16:18	16:30	18:08	18:33	18:38
RAICHO-30	13:15	14:05	14:57	15:24	15:58	16:18	17:06	17:45	17:58	19:35	19:59	20:05
RAICHO-34	—	—	—	—	—	17:25	18:10	18:49	19:02	20:39	21:03	21:09
HOKUETSU-4	15:12	16:03	16:57	17:23	17:57	18:17	19:04	—	—	—	—	—
RAICHO-38	—	—	—	—	—	18:32	19:17	19:56	20:09	21:45	22:09	22:15
HOKUETSU-8	17:00	17:51	18:43	19:08	19:41	20:00	20:45	—	—	—	—	—

16. JR Hokuriku Line

Kyoto / Fukui
  4,600 (7,400)
Kyoto / Awara-Onsen
  5,300 (8,100)
Kyoto / Kanazawa
  6,400 (10,600)
Kyoto / Toyama
  7,400 (11,600)
Kyoto / Niigata
  11,000 (16,400)
Awara-Onsen /
  Kanazawa
  2,500 (3,800)
Kanazawa / Toyama
  2,500 (3,800)
Kanazawa / Niigata
  7,900 (12,100)
Toyama / Niigata
  6,800 (11,000)

368

21. JR Narita Line

Narita to Ueno

TRAIN	NARITA	ABIKO	UENO
LOCAL TRAIN	07:24	08:12	08:48
LOCAL TRAIN	08:47	09:33	10:08
LOCAL TRAIN	15:49	16:29	17:04
LOCAL TRAIN	16:39	17:20	17:59
LOCAL TRAIN	18:11	18:56	19:31
LOCAL TRAIN	21:14	22:00	22:35

Ueno to Narita

TRAIN	UENO	ABIKO	NARITA
LOCAL TRAIN	08:55	09:33	10:13
LOCAL TRAIN	15:18	15:52	16:31
LOCAL TRAIN	16:14	16:48	17:27
LOCAL TRAIN	16:36	17:10	17:53
LOCAL TRAIN	17:06	17:41	18:24
LOCAL TRAIN	17:51	18:33	19:15

21. JR Narita Line
Tokyo / Narita
1,060　(N / A)

22. JR Joban Line

Ueno to Taira

TRAIN	UENO	MITO	HITACHI	TAIRA
HITACHI-7	08:00	09:29	09:56	10:50
HITACHI-11	09:00	10:20	10:45	11:33
HITACHI-19	11:00	12:14	12:40	13:29
HITACHI-25	13:00	14:14	14:39	15:29
HITACHI-29	15:00	16:14	16:39	17:30
HITACHI-37	17:00	18:18	18:45	19:38
HITACHI-41	18:00	19:15	19:39	20:28
HITACHI-45	19:00	20:14	20:41	21:35

Taira to Ueno

TRAIN	TAIRA	HITACHI	MITO	UENO
HITACHI-6	06:45	07:34	08:00	09:24
HITACHI-10	07:38	08:31	09:00	10:14
HITACHI-18	09:46	10:34	11:00	12:14
HITACHI-22	11:39	12:31	13:00	14:20
HITACHI-28	—	14:33	15:00	16:15
HITACHI-36	15:37	16:31	17:00	18:17
HITACHI-40	16:42	17:32	18:00	19:14
HITACHI-46	—	19:02	19:30	20:51

24. JR San-in/Miyazu Line

Kyoto to Toyooka

TRAIN	KYOTO	AYABE	MIYAZU	AMANOHASHIDATE	TOYOOKA
ASASHIO-3	09:40	11:02	11:51	11:58	12:59
TANGO-1	10:28	11:54	12:49	12:54	—
TANGO-5	13:40	15:13	16:17	16:24	18:05
TANGO-9	18:08	19:52	20:56	21:06	22:44

Toyooka to Kyoto

TRAIN	TOYOOKA	AMANOHASHIDATE	MIYAZU	AYABE	KYOTO
TANGO-2	05:20	06:49	06:57	08:12	09:49
TANGO-6	09:14	10:31	10:37	11:40	13:10
TANGO-8	—	14:45	14:51	15:53	17:33
ASASHIO-12	16:45	17:46	17:52	18:39	20:07

22. JR Joban Line
Ueno / Mito
3,900　(6,100)
Ueno / Hitachi
4,600　(7,400)

24. JR San-in/Miyazu Line
Kyoto / Amanohashidate
4,300　(7,100)

29. JR Kise Line

Nagoya to Tennoji

TRAIN	NAGOYA	TAKI	SHINGU	KII-KATSUURA	SHIRAHAMA	TENNOJI
KUROSHIO-5	—	—	—	—	09:36	11:41
KUROSHIO-7	—	—	08:41	08:58	10:33	12:41
KUROSHIO-11	—	—	11:00	11:17	12:43	14:41
NANKI-1	08:25	09:57	12:19	12:38	—	—
KUROSHIO-15	—	—	12:58	13:14	14:43	16:42
KUROSHIO-19	—	—	13:55	14:12	15:43	17:46
NANKI-3	10:02	11:33	14:09	14:26	—	—
KUROSHIO-25	—	—	15:58	16:15	17:48	19:49
KUROSHIO-29	—	—	17:26	17:43	19:14	21:18
NANKI-5	14:02	15:32	17:59	18:17	—	—

Tennoji to Nagoya

TRAIN	TENNOJI	SHIRAHAMA	KII-KATSUURA	SHINGU	TAKI	NAGOYA
NANKI-2	—	—	06:11	06:40	09:11	10:45
NANKI-4	—	—	09:14	09:33	12:04	13:34
KUROSHIO-2	08:00	10:09	11:41	11:57	—	—
KUROSHIO-4	09:00	11:05	12:40	12:57	—	—
NANKI-6	—	—	13:19	13:42	16:14	17:43
KUROSHIO-8	10:00	11:58	13:25	13:40	—	—
KUROSHIO-12	11:00	13:04	—	—	—	—
KUROSHIO-16	13:00	14:59	16:39	16:55	—	—
KUROSHIO-20	15:00	17:03	18:36	18:52	—	—
KUROSHIO-22	18:00	18:07	—	—	—	—

29. JR Kise Line
Nagoya / Taki　　　　3,050　(4,350)
Nagoya / Kii-Katsuura　6,430　(10,630)
Kii-Katsuura / Shirahama　2,980　(4,280)
Kii-Katsuura / Tennoji　5,400　(9,600)
Shirahama / Tennoji　4,900　(7,700)

25. JR San-in Line

Kyoto to Shimonoseki

STATION / TRAIN	KYOTO	OSAKA	TOYOOKA	TOTTORI	YONAGO	MATSUE	IZUMOSHI	MASUDA	HIGASHI-HAGI	NAGATOSHI	SHIMONOSEKI
SANBE	—	—	—	05:13	07:40	08:08	08:46	11:01	12:08	12:40	14:09
LOCAL TRAIN	—	—	—	—	08:12	08:47	09:26	—	—	—	—
LOCAL TRAIN	—	—	—	—	—	—	09:28	14:11	15:31	16:50	18:58
LOCAL TRAIN	—	—	—	06:49	09:00	09:47	10:31	—	—	—	—
LOCAL TRAIN	—	—	—	08:21	10:12	10:42	11:22	14:08	—	—	—
LOCAL TRAIN	—	—	—	—	—	—	12:11	15:22	—	—	—
LOCAL TRAIN	—	—	—	—	11:26	12:03	13:16	17:28	—	—	—
ISOKAZE	—	—	—	—	12:03	12:31	13:02	15:13	16:10	16:40	17:59
LOCAL TRAIN	—	—	—	—	—	—	—	15:58	17:20	17:57	—
LOCAL TRAIN	—	—	—	—	—	—	—	17:50	19:42	20:37	22:29
LOCAL TRAIN	—	—	—	—	13:11	13:51	15:08	18:52	—	—	—
ASASHIO-1	09:16	→	11:42	13:05	—	—	—	—	—	—	—
HAMAKAZE-1	—	09:40	12:26	13:56	—	—	—	—	—	—	—
LOCAL TRAIN	—	—	11:26	15:04	17:44	18:27	19:20	—	—	—	—
LOCAL TRAIN	—	—	12:48	14:42	16:33	17:04	18:06	21:02	—	—	—
HAMAKAZE-3	—	12:40	15:30	17:05	18:35	—	—	—	—	—	—
ASASHIO-7	14:40	→	17:23	18:55	20:41	—	—	—	—	—	—

Shimonoseki to Kyoto

STATION / TRAIN	SHIMONOSEKI	NAGATOSHI	HIGASHI-HAGI	MASUDA	IZUMOSHI	MATSUE	YONAGO	TOTTORI	TOYOOKA	OSAKA	KYOTO
ASASHIO-4	—	—	—	—	—	—	07:00	08:22	09:47	→	12:21
ASASHIO-6	—	—	—	—	—	—	07:59	09:57	11:21	→	14:05
HAMAKAZE-4	—	—	—	—	—	—	09:56	11:23	12:53	15:36	—
LOCAL TRAIN	—	—	—	—	09:01	10:01	10:43	—	—	—	—
LOCAL TRAIN	—	—	—	07:47	10:19	10:52	11:22	13:05	14:46	—	—
LOCAL TRAIN	—	07:52	08:20	09:24	12:13	13:08	13:44	—	—	—	—
LOCAL TRAIN	05:45	08:15	09:02	10:18	14:11	—	—	—	—	—	—
LOCAL TRAIN	—	—	—	—	14:12	14:56	16:20	18:41	—	—	—
LOCAL TRAIN	—	09:50	10:29	11:47	—	—	—	—	—	—	—
ISOKAZE	09:29	10:51	11:19	12:13	14:30	15:04	15:35	—	—	—	—
LOCAL TRAIN	—	—	—	—	15:17	16:16	16:50	—	—	—	—
LOCAL TRAIN	—	—	—	—	16:47	17:33	18:04	—	—	—	—
LOCAL TRAIN	—	12:47	13:35	15:01	—	—	—	—	—	—	—
LOCAL TRAIN	—	—	—	—	17:37	18:23	18:57	—	—	—	—
SANBE	12:30	14:02	14:30	15:36	18:04	18:37	19:18	21:15	—	—	—
LOCAL TRAIN	12:42	15:03	15:49	17:08	—	—	—	—	—	—	—
LOCAL TRAIN	—	16:38	17:25	18:42	—	—	—	—	—	—	—

28. JR Sangu Line

Taki to Toba

STATION / TRAIN	TAKI	ISESHI	FUTAMIGAURA	TOBA
LOCAL TRAIN	09:16	09:45	09:57	10:07
LOCAL TRAIN	10:10	10:36	10:46	10:56
LOCAL TRAIN	12:08	12:32	—	—
LOCAL TRAIN	—	12:34	12:44	12:55
LOCAL TRAIN	12:42	13:06	13:15	13:26
LOCAL TRAIN	13:37	14:01	14:10	14:21
LOCAL TRAIN	14:32	14:58	15:08	15:18
LOCAL TRAIN	15:34	15:59	16:09	16:19
LOCAL TRAIN	16:14	16:37	16:47	16:57
LOCAL TRAIN	17:03	17:27	17:36	17:47

Toba to Taki

STATION / TRAIN	TOBA	FUTAMIGAURA	ISESHI	TAKI
LOCAL TRAIN	08:11	08:22	08:32	08:56
LOCAL TRAIN	09:45	09:56	10:05	—
LOCAL TRAIN	—	—	10:08	10:31
LOCAL TRAIN	10:34	10:45	10:56	11:20
LOCAL TRAIN	11:45	11:56	12:07	12:31
LOCAL TRAIN	13:35	13:46	14:00	14:23
LOCAL TRAIN	14:35	14:46	15:00	15:23
LOCAL TRAIN	15:20	15:31	15:42	16:07
LOCAL TRAIN	15:57	16:09	16:20	16:46
LOCAL TRAIN	17:04	17:15	17:26	17:49

25. JR San-in Line

Matsue / Izumoshi
540* (N / A)
Matsue / Higashi-Hagi
6,400 (10,600)
Izumoshi / Higashi-Hagi
5,600 (8,400)
* Local train.

28. JR Sangu Line

Taki / Iseshi 300 (N / A)
Taki / Toba 540 (N / A)
Iseshi / Toba 300 (N / A)

30. JR Nara Line

Kyoto to Nara

STATION / TRAIN	KYOTO	TOFUKUJI	INARI	UJI	NARA
LOCAL TRAIN	06:50	06:53	06:55	07:15	07:55
LOCAL TRAIN	07:47	07:49	07:53	08:11	08:50
LOCAL TRAIN	08:10	08:12	08:15	08:32	09:14
LOCAL TRAIN	08:32	08:34	08:37	08:54	09:31
LOCAL TRAIN	08:52	08:54	08:58	09:14	09:52
LOCAL TRAIN	09:24	09:26	09:30	09:45	10:29
LOCAL TRAIN	09:56	09:59	10:01	10:17	10:57
LOCAL TRAIN	10:28	10:30	10:32	10:50	11:29
LOCAL TRAIN	11:41	11:43	11:47	12:03	12:43
LOCAL TRAIN	12:46	12:48	12:51	13:07	13:46
LOCAL TRAIN	13:49	13:51	13:55	14:11	14:49
LOCAL TRAIN	14:41	14:44	14:48	15:04	15:41
LOCAL TRAIN	15:47	15:50	15:53	16:08	16:49
LOCAL TRAIN	16:41	16:43	16:46	17:03	17:44
LOCAL TRAIN	17:41	17:43	17:48	18:06	18:45
LOCAL TRAIN	18:26	18:29	18:32	18:49	19:33
LOCAL TRAIN	19:36	19:38	19:41	19:57	20:36

Nara to Kyoto

STATION / TRAIN	NARA	UJI	INARI	TOFUKUJI	KYOTO
LOCAL TRAIN	07:38	08:19	08:37	08:40	08:42
LOCAL TRAIN	08:37	09:14	09:29	09:32	09:34
LOCAL TRAIN	09:51	10:27	10:44	10:46	10:49
LOCAL TRAIN	10:51	11:30	11:46	11:49	11:51
LOCAL TRAIN	11:54	12:36	12:52	12:54	12:56
LOCAL TRAIN	12:56	13:39	13:55	13:57	13:59
LOCAL TRAIN	13:52	14:31	14:47	14:49	14:51
LOCAL TRAIN	14:51	15:36	15:53	15:55	15:57
LOCAL TRAIN	15:25	16:09	16:24	16:27	16:29
LOCAL TRAIN	15:51	16:31	16:46	16:49	16:51
LOCAL TRAIN	16:09	16:50	17:10	17:12	17:15
LOCAL TRAIN	16:34	17:12	17:29	17:32	17:34
LOCAL TRAIN	16:50	17:30	17:48	17:51	17:53
LOCAL TRAIN	17:14	17:53	18:09	18:12	18:14
LOCAL TRAIN	17:32	18:14	18:32	18:34	18:37
LOCAL TRAIN	17:54	18:36	18:54	18:56	18:59
LOCAL TRAIN	18:41	19:21	19:41	19:44	19:46

32. JR Wakayama Line

Oji to Wakayama

STATION / TRAIN	OJI	TAKADA	YOSHINOGUCHI	GOJO	HASHIMOTO	WAKAYAMA
LOCAL TRAIN	07:05	07:27	07:45	08:11	08:33	09:38
LOCAL TRAIN	08:10	08:30	08:51	09:11	09:29	10:34
LOCAL TRAIN	09:40	09:57	10:14	10:30	10:47	11:55
LOCAL TRAIN	10:42	10:58	11:17	11:35	11:55	12:57
LOCAL TRAIN	11:34	11:50	12:02	12:29	12:45	13:54
LOCAL TRAIN	12:34	12:50	13:10	13:32	13:48	14:55
LOCAL TRAIN	13:34	13:50	14:10	14:34	14:51	15:55
LOCAL TRAIN	14:34	14:50	15:10	15:35	15:53	16:57
LOCAL TRAIN	15:34	15:50	16:11	16:29	16:46	17:48
LOCAL TRAIN	16:26	16:44	17:04	17:25	17:40	18:47
LOCAL TRAIN	17:14	17:33	17:54	18:22	18:41	19:43

Wakayama to Oji

STATION / TRAIN	WAKAYAMA	HASHIMOTO	GOJO	YOSHINOGUCHI	TAKADA	OJI
LOCAL TRAIN	06:55	08:15	08:32	08:51	09:09	09:25
LOCAL TRAIN	07:41	08:52	09:09	09:28	09:45	10:02
LOCAL TRAIN	08:20	09:28	09:48	10:02	10:22	10:37
LOCAL TRAIN	09:25	10:34	10:53	11:07	11:31	11:47
LOCAL TRAIN	10:35	11:39	11:55	12:10	12:31	12:47
LOCAL TRAIN	11:34	12:34	12:55	13:10	13:31	13:47
LOCAL TRAIN	13:33	14:39	14:55	15:10	15:31	15:47
LOCAL TRAIN	14:34	15:40	15:53	16:11	16:30	16:46
LOCAL TRAIN	15:33	16:33	16:47	17:04	17:21	17:39
LOCAL TRAIN	16:36	17:41	17:56	18:10	18:27	18:43
LOCAL TRAIN	17:34	18:42	19:03	19:23	19:40	19:55

32. JR Wakayama Line

Oji / Hashimoto	900 (N / A)
Oji / Wakayama	1,540 (N/A)

30. JR Nara Line

Kyoto / Nara	700 (N / A)
Kyoto / Uji	220 (N / A)

33. JR Kansai Line

Nara to Osaka

STATION / TRAIN	NARA	HORYUJI	OJI	TENNOJI	OSAKA	MINATOMACHI
LOCAL TRAIN	07:43	07:55	08:00	08:22	—	08:29
LOCAL TRAIN	08:57	09:08	09:12	09:30	09:45	—
LOCAL TRAIN	09:57	10:08	10:12	10:30	10:45	—
LOCAL TRAIN	10:57	11:09	11:13	11:30	11:45	—
LOCAL TRAIN	11:57	12:08	12:12	12:30	12:45	—
LOCAL TRAIN	12:57	13:08	13:12	13:30	13:45	—
LOCAL TRAIN	13:57	14:08	14:12	14:30	14:45	—
LOCAL TRAIN	14:57	15:08	15:12	15:30	15:45	—
LOCAL TRAIN	15:57	16:08	16:12	16:30	16:45	—
LOCAL TRAIN	16:57	17:08	17:12	17:30	—	17:37
LOCAL TRAIN	17:26	17:38	17:42	18:00	—	18:07
LOCAL TRAIN	17:57	18:08	18:12	18:31	—	18:38
LOCAL TRAIN	18:40	18:52	18:56	19:16	—	19:23
LOCAL TRAIN	19:20	19:32	19:37	19:54	—	20:01

Osaka to Nara

STATION / TRAIN	MINATOMACHI	OSAKA	TENNOJI	OJI	HORYUJI	NARA
LOCAL TRAIN	07:53	—	08:00	08:19	08:23	08:35
LOCAL TRAIN	08:31	—	08:38	09:00	09:04	09:16
LOCAL TRAIN	09:04	—	09:10	09:31	09:35	09:46
LOCAL TRAIN	—	09:35	09:50	10:08	10:12	10:24
LOCAL TRAIN	—	10:35	10:50	11:08	11:12	11:23
LOCAL TRAIN	—	11:35	11:50	12:08	12:12	12:23
LOCAL TRAIN	—	12:35	12:50	13:08	13:12	13:23
LOCAL TRAIN	—	13:35	13:50	14:08	14:12	14:23
LOCAL TRAIN	—	14:35	14:50	15:08	15:12	15:24
LOCAL TRAIN	—	15:35	15:50	16:08	16:12	16:23
LOCAL TRAIN	—	16:35	16:50	17:08	17:12	17:23
LOCAL TRAIN	17:03	—	17:10	17:28	17:32	17:44
LOCAL TRAIN	18:03	—	18:10	18:31	18:35	18:47
LOCAL TRAIN	19:03	—	19:10	19:29	19:33	19:44

33. JR Kansai Line

Nara / Horyuji	220	(N / A)
Nara / Oji	300	(N / A)
Nara / Tennoji	620	(N / A)
Nara / Minatomachi	700	(N / A)
Nara / Osaka	780	(N / A)

34. JR Ako Line

Okayama to Aioi

STATION / TRAIN	OKAYAMA	INBE	BANSHU-AKO	AIOI
LOCAL TRAIN	08:31	09:07	09:36	—
LOCAL TRAIN	09:21	10:00	10:37	10:50
LOCAL TRAIN	10:20	11:00	11:37	11:50
LOCAL TRAIN	11:20	12:00	12:37	12:50
LOCAL TRAIN	12:20	13:00	13:37	13:50
LOCAL TRAIN	13:22	14:02	14:37	14:50
LOCAL TRAIN	14:20	15:01	15:37	15:50
LOCAL TRAIN	15:20	16:00	16:37	16:50
LOCAL TRAIN	16:20	16:59	17:37	—
LOCAL TRAIN	17:23	18:02	18:37	—
LOCAL TRAIN	18:06	18:43	19:18	19:32

Aioi to Okayama

STATION / TRAIN	AIOI	BANSHU-AKO	INBE	OKAYAMA
LOCAL TRAIN	—	07:49	08:22	09:12
LOCAL TRAIN	—	09:01	09:39	10:25
LOCAL TRAIN	09:24	09:37	—	—
LOCAL TRAIN	—	10:08	10:39	11:25
LOCAL TRAIN	10:54	11:08	11:40	12:33
LOCAL TRAIN	11:54	12:08	12:38	13:18
LOCAL TRAIN	12:54	13:08	13:40	14:33
LOCAL TRAIN	13:54	14:08	14:40	15:25
LOCAL TRAIN	14:54	15:08	15:39	16:25
LOCAL TRAIN	15:54	16:08	16:39	17:18
LOCAL TRAIN	16:54	17:08	17:42	18:23

34. JR Ako Line

Okayama / Inbe	540	(N / A)
Okayama / Aoi	1,060	(N / A)

35. JR Uno Line

Okayama to Uno

STATION / TRAIN	OKAYAMA	UNO
LOCAL TRAIN	07:56	08:29
LOCAL TRAIN	08:56	09:28
LOCAL TRAIN	09:56	10:28
LOCAL TRAIN	10:56	11:28
LOCAL TRAIN	11:56	12:28
LOCAL TRAIN	12:56	13:28
LOCAL TRAIN	13:57	14:28
LOCAL TRAIN	14:56	15:28
LOCAL TRAIN	15:56	16:28
LOCAL TRAIN	16:56	17:28
LOCAL TRAIN	17:56	18:28

Uno to Okayama

STATION / TRAIN	UNO	OKAYAMA
LOCAL TRAIN	08:08	08:46
LOCAL TRAIN	09:14	09:49
LOCAL TRAIN	10:14	10:49
LOCAL TRAIN	11:14	11:49
LOCAL TRAIN	12:14	12:49
LOCAL TRAIN	13:14	13:50
LOCAL TRAIN	14:14	14:49
LOCAL TRAIN	15:14	15:49
LOCAL TRAIN	16:14	16:49
LOCAL TRAIN	17:14	17:50
LOCAL TRAIN	18:14	18:49

35. JR Uno Line

Okayama / Uno

540 (N / A)

36. JR Uko Boat Line

Uno to Takamatsu

BOAT	PORT UNO	PORT TAKAMATSU
STEAMSHIP	08:36	09:38
STEAMSHIP	09:36	10:38
HOVERCRAFT	09:37	10:00
STEAMSHIP	10:36	11:38
HOVERCRAFT	10:37	11:00
STEAMSHIP	11:36	12:37
HOVERCRAFT	11:37	12:00
STEAMSHIP	12:36	13:38
STEAMSHIP	13:36	14:37
STEAMSHIP	14:36	15:37
HOVERCRAFT	14:37	15:00
STEAMSHIP	15:36	16:38
HOVERCRAFT	15:37	16:00
STEAMSHIP	16:36	17:38
STEAMSHIP	17:40	18:42
STEAMSHIP	18:36	19:38

Takamatsu to Uno

BOAT	PORT TAKAMATSU	PORT UNO
STEAMSHIP	07:00	08:00
HOVERCRAFT	07:38	08:01
STEAMSHIP	08:07	09:07
HOVERCRAFT	08:40	09:03
STEAMSHIP	09:07	10:06
STEAMSHIP	10:07	11:06
STEAMSHIP	11:07	12:07
STEAMSHIP	12:07	13:07
HOVERCRAFT	12:40	13:03
STEAMSHIP	13:07	14:06
HOVERCRAFT	13:40	14:03
STEAMSHIP	14:07	15:07
STEAMSHIP	15:07	16:06
STEAMSHIP	16:07	17:07
HOVERCRAFT	16:07	16:30
STEAMSHIP	17:07	18:07

36. JR Uko Boat
Uno / Takamatsu
(1) Steamship 500 (1,000)
(2) Hovercraft 1,600 (2,100)

37. JR Yosan Line

Takamatsu to Uwajima

TRAIN	TAKAMATSU	TADOTSU	IMABARI	MATSUYAMA	UWAJIMA
SHIOKAZE-1	06:00	06:31	08:11	08:57	—
SHIOKAZE-3	07:00	07:30	09:05	09:46	11:32
SHIOKAZE-5	08:50	09:21	11:06	11:46	—
SHIOKAZE-7	09:50	10:17	11:45	12:24	—
SHIOKAZE-9	10:50	11:17	12:57	13:41	15:25
SHIOKAZE-11	11:50	12:21	13:55	14:39	—
SHIOKAZE-13	12:50	13:17	14:49	15:29	17:13
SHIOKAZE-15	13:50	14:18	15:57	16:43	—
SHIOKAZE-17	14:50	15:21	16:58	17:46	—
SHIOKAZE-19	15:50	16:19	17:59	18:47	20:44
SHIOKAZE-21	16:50	17:18	19:01	19:49	—
SHIOKAZE-23	18:00	18:28	20:04	20:43	22:31
SHIOKAZE-25	19:05	19:33	21:18	22:00	—

Uwajima to Takamatsu

TRAIN	UWAJIMA	MATSUYAMA	IMABARI	TADOTSU	TAKAMATSU
SHIOKAZE-2	—	07:00	07:41	09:22	09:49
SHIOKAZE-4	06:10	08:00	08:42	10:18	10:46
SHIOKAZE-6	07:13	09:00	09:43	11:20	11:47
SHIOKAZE-8	—	10:00	10:42	12:20	12:48
SHIOKAZE-10	09:10	11:00	11:54	13:32	13:59
SHIOKAZE-12	—	12:00	12:45	14:29	14:55
SHIOKAZE-14	—	13:00	13:41	15:20	15:48
SHIOKAZE-16	12:10	14:00	14:40	16:18	16:45
SHIOKAZE-18	—	15:00	15:43	17:28	17:57
SHIOKAZE-20	—	16:30	17:09	18:45	19:12
SHIOKAZE-22	—	17:28	18:11	19:50	20:17
SHIOKAZE-24	17:14	18:55	19:34	21:02	21:29
SHIOKAZE-26	—	20:33	21:18	22:49	23:15

37. JR Yosan Line
Takamatsu / Matsuyama 3,140 (5,940)

38. JR Dosan Line

Takamatsu to Nakamura

TRAIN	TAKAMATSU	TADOTSU	KOTOHIRA	OBOKE	KOCHI	NAKAMURA
NANPU-1	07:16	07:46	07:59	→	09:55	11:56
NANPU-3	08:37	09:12	09:25	10:26	11:26	13:30
ASHIZURI-3	10:03	10:38	10:51	11:56	13:12	15:26
ASHIZURI-5	11:59	12:31	12:45	13:50	14:56	17:19
NANPU-5	13:47	14:15	14:28	→	16:26	—
ASHIZURI-7	15:02	15:39	15:52	17:04	18:11	20:30
TOSA-1	16:53	17:29	17:42	18:42	19:52	—
NANPU-7	19:02	19:29	19:43	→	21:40	23:39

Nakamura to Takamatsu

TRAIN	NAKAMURA	KOCHI	OBOKE	KOTOHIRA	TADOTSU	TAKAMATSU
TOSA-4	—	08:02	09:17	10:16	10:29	10:59
NANPU-2	07:24	09:25	→	11:19	11:31	11:58
TOSA-6	—	10:02	11:11	12:18	12:30	13:00
ASHIZURI-2	08:09	11:04	12:15	13:14	13:26	13:55
ASHIZURI-4	10:43	13:02	14:14	15:17	15:30	16:00
NANPU-4	12:25	14:26	→	16:20	16:32	16:58
NANPU-6	—	16:50	→	18:47	18:59	19:29
NANPU-8	16:00	18:13	19:16	20:10	20:22	20:48

43. JR Bus Matsuyama-Kochi

North-bound

BUS	KOCHI	MATSUYAMA
NANGOKU-2	07:00	10:12
NANGOKU-4	08:00	11:34
NANGOKU-6	09:00	12:09
NANGOKU-8	10:00	13:12
NANGOKU-10	11:00	14:37
NANGOKU-12	12:00	15:37
NANGOKU-14	13:00	16:37
NANGOKU-16	14:00	17:37
NANGOKU-18	15:00	18:37
NANGOKU-20	16:00	19:37
NANGOKU-22	17:00	20:25

South-bound

BUS	MATSUYAMA	KOCHI
NANGOKU-1	07:00	10:12
NANGOKU-3	08:00	11:25
NANGOKU-5	09:00	12:09
NANGOKU-7	10:00	13:12
NANGOKU-9	11:00	14:25
NANGOKU-11	12:00	15:25
NANGOKU-13	13:00	16:25
NANGOKU-15	14:00	17:25
NANGOKU-17	15:00	18:25
NANGOKU-19	16:00	19:25
NANGOKU-21	17:00	20:25

38. JR Dosan Line

Takamatsu / Kotohira	1,900	(3,200)
Takamatsu / Kochi	4,900	(7,700)
Kotohira / Kochi	4,000	(6,800)

45. JR Hakubi Line

Okayama to Izumoshi

TRAIN	OKAYAMA	KURASHIKI	YONAGO	MATSUE	IZUMOSHI
YAKUMO-1	09:09	09:21	11:20	11:43	12:08
YAKUMO-3	10:53	11:05	13:06	13:29	13:59
YAKUMO-5	11:53	12:05	14:08	14:32	15:05
YAKUMO-7	12:53	13:05	15:07	15:35	16:02
YAKUMO-9	14:53	15:05	17:09	17:34	18:03
YAKUMO-11	16:53	17:05	19:12	19:36	20:05
YAKUMO-15	18:53	19:05	21:14	21:39	22:07
YAKUMO-17	20:07	20:20	22:21	22:52	23:28

Izumoshi to Okayama

TRAIN	IZUMOSHI	MATSUE	YONAGO	KURASHIKI	OKAYAMA
YAKUMO-2	06:37	07:06	07:33	09:39	09:50
YAKUMO-4	07:36	08:04	08:31	10:39	10:51
YAKUMO-6	08:18	08:46	09:12	11:24	11:38
YAKUMO-8	10:36	11:09	11:35	13:39	13:51
YAKUMO-10	12:24	12:52	13:17	15:26	15:38
YAKUMO-12	13:32	14:01	14:28	16:39	16:51
YAKUMO-14	14:54	15:19	15:44	17:41	17:52
YAKUMO-18	17:01	17:30	17:55	20:00	20:12

43. JR Matsuyama-Kochi Bus
Kochi / Matsuyama 3,500 (N / A)

45. JR Hakubi Line
Okayama / Matsue 5,600 (8,400)
Okayama / Izumoshi 6,400 (10,600)

46. JR Geibi Line

Yonago to Hiroshima

TRAIN	STATION	YONAGO	MATSUE	BINGO-OCHIAI	HIROSHIMA
CHIDORI		09:55	10:26	13:14	15:50

Hiroshima to Yonago

TRAIN	STATION	HIROSHIMA	BINGO-OCHIAI	MATSUE	YONAGO
CHIDORI		08:28	10:47	13:23	13:58

46. JR Geibi Line
Matsue / Hiroshima   4,900   (9,100)

48. JR Bocho Bus

Higashi-Hagi to Ogori

BUS	STATION	HIGASHI-HAGI	YAMAGUCHI	OGORI
JR-4		07:40	08:50	09:17
JR-12		10:55	12:03	12:30
JR-16		12:30	13:40	14:07
JR-20		14:40	15:48	16:15
JR-24		15:50	16:58	17:25
JR-30		19:00	20:08	20:35

Ogori to Higashi-Hagi

BUS	STATION	OGORI	YAMAGUCHI	HIGASHI-HAGI
JR-1		07:50	08:26	09:36
JR-5		09:50	10:18	11:25
JR-9		11:20	11:48	12:55
JR-15		13:20	13:50	14:57
JR-19		15:30	15:58	17:05
JR-27		19:20	19:48	20:55

48. JR Bocho Bus Line
Higashi-Hagi / Ogori   1,700   (N / A)

49. JR Taisha Line
Izumoshi /Taisha   190   (N / A)

49. JR Taisha Line

North-bound

TRAIN	STATION	IZUMOSHI	TAISHA
LOCAL TRAIN		08:06	08:18
LOCAL TRAIN		09:36	09:48
LOCAL TRAIN		10:53	11:04
LOCAL TRAIN		12:14	12:26
LOCAL TRAIN		13:31	13:43
LOCAL TRAIN		14:01	14:12
LOCAL TRAIN		14:33	14:45
LOCAL TRAIN		16:10	16:22
LOCAL TRAIN		17:18	17:30
LOCAL TRAIN		18:07	18:19

South-bound

TRAIN	STATION	TAISHA	IZUMOSHI
LOCAL TRAIN		08:30	08:42
LOCAL TRAIN		09:56	10:08
LOCAL TRAIN		11:07	11:19
LOCAL TRAIN		12:42	12:54
LOCAL TRAIN		13:45	13:57
LOCAL TRAIN		14:15	14:27
LOCAL TRAIN		14:48	15:00
LOCAL TRAIN		16:25	16:37
LOCAL TRAIN		17:42	17:54
LOCAL TRAIN		18:32	18:45

47. JR Yamaguchi Line

Yonago to Ogori

TRAIN	STATION	YONAGO	MATSUE	IZUMOSHI	MASUDA	TSUWANO	YAMAGUCHI	OGORI
LOCAL TRAIN		—	—	—	07:53	08:40	09:55	10:19
OKI-1		06:15	06:42	07:16	09:25	09:58	10:48	11:03
LOCAL TRAIN		—	—	—	—	10:44	12:11	12:34
LOCAL TRAIN		—	—	—	10:35	11:21	12:39	13:02
OKI-3		09:16	09:43	10:18	12:32	13:06	13:56	14:09
LOCAL TRAIN		—	—	—	13:01	13:49	15:02	15:24
LOCAL TRAIN		—	—	—	14:14	14:55	16:20	16:43
LOCAL TRAIN		—	—	—	16:10	17:03	18:21	18:44
OKI-5		14:36	15:04	15:33	17:46	18:19	19:11	19:25

Ogori to Yonago

TRAIN	STATION	OGORI	YAMAGUCHI	TSUWANO	MASUDA	IZUMOSHI	MATSUE	YONAGO
LOCAL TRAIN		05:47	06:25	08:01	08:40	—	—	—
LOCAL TRAIN		07:34	08:01	09:35	10:14	—	—	—
OKI-2		09:19	09:32	10:25	10:58	13:17	13:46	14:14
LOCAL TRAIN		09:31	09:55	11:18	11:57	—	—	—
LOCAL TRAIN		10:39	11:06	12:42	13:25	—	—	—
OKI-4		11:57	12:12	13:07	13:41	16:04	16:36	17:04
LOCAL TRAIN		12:36	13:02	14:29	15:10	—	—	—
LOCAL TRAIN		13:32	14:03	15:29	16:09	—	—	—
OKI-6		14:48	15:05	16:00	16:33	18:56	19:30	19:56

47. JR Yamaguchi Line

Masuda / Tsuwano	540* (N / A)	Tsuwano / Ogori	2,660 (3,960)
Matsuda / Tsuwano	1,740 (3,040)	Matsue / Tsuwano	5,600 (8,400)
Tsuwano / Ogori	1,060* (N / A)	Izumoshi / Tsuwano	5,300 (8,100)
		* Local train.	

52. JR Kagoshima Line

Hakata to Nishi-Kagoshima

STATION / TRAIN	HAKATA	TOSU	KUMAMOTO	MINAMATA	NISHI-KAGOSHIMA
ARIAKE-3	07:49	08:13	09:24	10:39	12:24
ARIAKE-5	08:50	09:13	10:25	—	—
ARIAKE-7	09:20	09:42	10:53	12:02	13:58
ARIAKE-11	10:22	10:45	11:55	13:06	14:54
ARIAKE-15	11:21	11:43	12:53	14:11	15:59
ARIAKE-19	12:20	12:42	13:48	15:03	16:50
ARIAKE-23	13:20	13:42	14:53	16:11	17:58
ARIAKE-27	14:20	14:43	15:53	17:06	18:52
ARIAKE-31	15:20	15:43	16:53	18:02	19:55
ARIAKE-33	15:50	16:13	17:24	—	—
ARIAKE-35	16:20	16:42	17:48	19:01	20:47
ARIAKE-37	16:50	17:12	18:27	—	—
ARIAKE-39	17:20	17:43	18:54	20:08	21:55
ARIAKE-43	18:20	18:42	19:51	—	—

Nishi-Kagoshima to Hakata

STATION / TRAIN	NISHI-KAGOSHIMA	MINAMATA	KUMAMOTO	TOSU	HAKATA
ARIAKE-4	—	—	07:52	09:03	09:26
ARIAKE-6	—	—	08:52	10:03	10:25
ARIAKE-8	—	—	09:21	10:31	10:51
ARIAKE-12	—	—	10:21	11:33	11:56
ARIAKE-14	08:00	09:41	10:58	12:05	12:25
ARIAKE-18	08:40	10:29	11:53	13:03	13:25
ARIAKE-22	09:45	11:39	12:54	14:03	14:26
ARIAKE-26	10:53	12:41	13:53	15:05	15:26
ARIAKE-30	11:51	13:37	14:54	16:04	16:26
ARIAKE-32	—	—	15:22	16:34	16:56
ARIAKE-34	12:55	14:42	15:58	17:05	17:26
ARIAKE-36	—	—	16:21	17:33	17:56
ARIAKE-40	14:30	16:12	17:25	18:33	18:57
ARIAKE-44	15:58	17:45	18:58	20:04	20:29

52. JR Kagoshima Line

Hakata / Kumamoto 3,600 (6,400)
Hakata/Nishi-Kagoshima 7,500 (11,700)
Kumamoto / Nishi-Kagoshima
5,200 (8,000)

53. JR Nippo Line

Kokura to Nishi-Kagoshima

STATION / TRAIN	KOKURA	BEPPU	OITA	MIYAZAKI	NISHI-KAGOSHIMA
NICHIRIN-3	07:22	08:55	09:08	—	—
NICHIRIN-5	08:11	09:43	09:56	13:16	—
NICHIRIN-9	09:59	11:29	11:43	15:08	17:13
NICHIRIN-11	10:56	12:27	12:39	—	—
NICHIRIN-13	11:54	13:26	13:39	17:00	19:15
NICHIRIN-17	12:54	14:26	14:37	—	—
NICHIRIN-19	13:54	15:30	15:46	19:09	21:16
NICHIRIN-21	14:54	16:25	16:37	—	—
NICHIRIN-23	15:54	17:24	17:41	21:14	—
NICHIRIN-25	16:54	18:28	18:41	—	—
NICHIRIN-29	17:55	19:22	19:36	22:56	—

Nishi-Kagoshima to Kokura

STATION / TRAIN	NISHI-KAGOSHIMA	MIYAZAKI	OITA	BEPPU	KOKURA
NICHIRIN-4	—	—	08:10	08:20	09:52
NICHIRIN-6	—	—	09:10	09:20	10:52
NICHIRIN-10	—	06:41	10:10	10:20	11:52
NICHIRIN-12	—	—	11:10	11:20	12:52
NICHIRIN-14	—	08:39	12:10	12:20	13:52
NICHIRIN-16	07:39	09:43	13:10	13:20	14:52
NICHIRIN-18	—	—	14:10	14:20	15:52
NICHIRIN-22	09:31	11:36	15:10	15:20	16:52
NICHIRIN-24	—	—	16:10	16:20	17:52
NICHIRIN-26	—	—	17:35	17:45	19:20
NICHIRIN-28	12:35	14:42	18:10	18:20	19:52

53. JR Nippo Lines

Kokura / Beppu 3,900 (6,700)
Kokura / Miyazaki 7,700 (11,900)
Kokura / Nishi-Kagoshima 9,800 (15,200)
Beppu / Miyazaki 5,700 (9,900)
Beppu / Nishi-Kagoshima 8,000 (12,200)
Miyazaki / Nishi-Kagoshima
3,900 (6,700)

54. JR Nagasaki Line

Hakata to Nagasaki

TRAIN	HAKATA	SAGA	ISAHAYA	NAGASAKI
KAMOME-1	07:05	07:45	09:01	09:20
KAMOME-3	09:15	09:55	11:04	11:29
KAMOME-5	10:18	10:57	12:14	12:40
KAMOME-7	11:18	11:56	13:07	13:29
KAMOME-9	12:15	12:55	14:08	14:27
KAMOME-11	13:15	13:55	15:07	15:27
LOCAL TRAIN	—	—	15:39	16:09
KAMOME-13	14:15	14:54	16:08	16:27
LOCAL TRAIN	—	—	16:28	17:07
LOCAL TRAIN	—	—	17:47	18:16
KAMOME-15	15:15	15:53	17:08	17:33
KAMOME-17	16:15	16:55	18:13	18:39
KAMOME-19	17:15	17:55	19:15	19:35
KAMOME-21	18:15	18:54	20:04	20:22
KAMOME-23	19:15	19:54	21:07	21:25

Nagasaki to Hakata

TRAIN	NAGASAKI	ISAHAYA	SAGA	HAKATA
KAMOME-2	07:19	07:38	08:54	09:33
LOCAL TRAIN	07:37	08:50	—	—
KAMOME-4	08:18	08:42	09:51	10:31
LOCAL TRAIN	08:35	09:08	—	—
KAMOME-6	09:14	09:35	10:51	11:31
LOCAL TRAIN	09:26	10:19	—	—
KAMOME-8	10:12	10:37	11:53	12:32
KAMOME-10	11:10	11:30	12:52	13:34
KAMOME-12	12:21	12:40	13:52	14:32
KAMOME-14	13:24	13:43	14:51	15:31
KAMOME-16	14:21	14:42	15:51	16:31
KAMOME-18	15:21	15:42	16:51	17:29
KAMOME-20	16:21	16:42	17:52	18:32
KAMOME-22	17:35	17:54	19:07	19:47
KAMOME-24	18:20	18:38	19:52	20:32

59. JR Karatsu Line

Nishi-Karatsu to Saga

TRAIN	NISHI-KARATSU	KARATSU	SAGA
LOCAL TRAIN	08:44	08:55	10:05
LOCAL TRAIN	10:06	10:24	11:48
LOCAL TRAIN	11:14	11:25	12:39
LOCAL TRAIN	12:45	12:49	14:03
LOCAL TRAIN	14:30	14:46	15:58
LOCAL TRAIN	16:07	16:24	17:39
LOCAL TRAIN	17:26	17:45	19:03

Saga to Nishi-Karatsu

TRAIN	SAGA	KARATSU	NISHI-KARATSU
LOCAL TRAIN	08:59	10:12	10:16
LOCAL TRAIN	10:00	11:18	11:22
LOCAL TRAIN	11:00	12:11	12:15
LOCAL TRAIN	12:58		14:12
LOCAL TRAIN	14:37	15:50	15:54
LOCAL TRAIN	16:16	17:30	17:34
LOCAL TRAIN	17:46	19:15	19:19

60. JR Chikuhi Line

Hakata to Nishi-Karatsu

TRAIN	HAKATA	MEINOHAMA	KARATSU	NISHI-KARATSU
LOCAL TRAIN	08:03	08:24	09:20	09:24
LOCAL TRAIN	09:03	09:24	10:23	10:26
LOCAL TRAIN	09:30	09:51	10:45	10:48
LOCAL TRAIN	10:30	10:51	11:45	11:48
LOCAL TRAIN	11:30	11:51	12:49	12:53
LOCAL TRAIN	12:30	12:51	13:45	13:49
LOCAL TRAIN	13:30	13:51	14:46	14:49
LOCAL TRAIN	14:30	14:51	15:46	—
LOCAL TRAIN	15:30	15:51	16:45	16:48
LOCAL TRAIN	16:30	16:51	17:45	17:49
LOCAL TRAIN	17:43	18:04	19:05	19:09

Nishi-Karatsu to Hakata

TRAIN	NISHI-KARATSU	KARATSU	MEINOHAMA	HAKATA
LOCAL TRAIN	08:31	08:34	09:39	09:58
LOCAL TRAIN	—	09:09	10:06	10:26
LOCAL TRAIN	—	10:12	11:07	11:27
LOCAL TRAIN	11:05	11:13	12:07	12:27
LOCAL TRAIN	12:07	12:13	13:07	13:27
LOCAL TRAIN	13:09	13:13	14:07	14:26
LOCAL TRAIN	14:02	14:13	15:07	15:27
LOCAL TRAIN	15:00	15:04	16:07	16:26
LOCAL TRAIN	15:30	15:36	16:37	16:57
LOCAL TRAIN	16:37	16:49	17:42	18:02
LOCAL TRAIN	—	17:34	18:30	18:50

59. JR Karatsu Line
Karatsu / Saga   780 (N / A)

60. JR Chikuhi Line
Meinohama / Karatsu   700 (N / A)
Hakata / Meinohama   200* (N / A)
* City subway.

54. JR Nagasaki Line
Hakata / Saga   2,300 (3,600)
Hakata / Nagasaki   4,500 (7,300)
Saga / Nagasaki   3,600 (6,400)
Isahaya / Nagasaki   540* (N / A)
                        1,740 (3,040)
     * Local train.

63. JR Misumi/Hohi Line

Misumi to Beppu

STATION TRAIN	MISUMI	KUMAMOTO	ASO	OITA	BEPPU
LOCAL TRAIN	—	07:33	09:02	—	—
HINOYAMA-1	—	08:35	09:43	11:41	11:57
LOCAL TRAIN	09:18	10:06	—	—	—
LOCAL TRAIN	—	10:37	12:02	—	—
LOCAL TRAIN	10:56	11:45	—	—	—
HINOYAMA-3	—	12:34	13:43	15:34	15:48
LOCAL TRAIN	11:57	12:47	—	—	—
LOCAL TRAIN	12:57	13:47	—	—	—
LOCAL TRAIN	13:57	14:47	—	—	—
LOCAL TRAIN	15:01	15:51	—	—	—
HINOYAMA-5	—	16:38	17:47	19:44	20:02
LOCAL TRAIN	16:02	16:53	—	—	—
LOCAL TRAIN	17:04	17:58	—	—	—

Beppu to Misumi

STATION TRAIN	BEPPU	OITA	ASO	KUMAMOTO	MISUMI
LOCAL TRAIN	—	—	—	07:28	08:18
LOCAL TRAIN	—	—	—	08:20	09:13
LOCAL TRAIN	—	—	—	09:37	10:28
LOCAL TRAIN	—	—	—	10:37	11:26
HINOYAMA-2	08:09	08:27	10:25	11:26	—
LOCAL TRAIN	—	—	—	12:02	12:49
LOCAL TRAIN	—	—	12:19	13:41	—
LOCAL TRAIN	—	—	—	15:02	15:52
HINOYAMA-4	12:30	12:45	14:48	15:50	—
LOCAL TRAIN	—	—	—	16:06	16:56
LOCAL TRAIN	—	—	16:33	18:03	—
HINOYAMA-6	16:11	16:27	18:28	19:34	—

63. JR Misumi / Hohi Lines

Misumi / Kumamoto 620* (N / A)
Kumamoto / Aso 900* (N / A)
1,600 (N / A)
Kumamoto / Beppu 3,800 (N / A)
Aso / Beppu 2,700 (N / A)
* Local train.

64. JR Kitto / Hisatsu Line

Miyazaki / Kobayashi 2,080 (N / A)
Miyazaki / Kumamoto
`, 5,300 (N / A)
Kobayashi / Kumamoto
3,800 (N / A)

64. JR Kitto/Hisatsu Line

Miyazaki to Kumamoto

STATION TRAIN	MIYAZAKI	MIYAKONOJO	KOBAYASHI	KUMAMOTO
EBINO-2	08:22	09:26	10:04	12:58
EBINO-4	13:35	14:39	15:16	18:15
EBINO-6	16:21	17:31	18:08	21:02

Kumamoto to Miyazaki

STATION TRAIN	KUMAMOTO	KOBAYASHI	MIYAKONOJO	MIYAZAKI
EBINO-1	08:32	11:42	12:18	13:12
EBINO-3	10:56	13:59	14:35	15:30
EBINO-5	15:42	18:48	19:27	20:29

65. JR Nichinan Line

Miyazaki to Shibushi

STATION TRAIN	MIYAZAKI	AOSHIMA	OBI	SHIBUSHI
LOCAL TRAIN	09:02	09:30	10:12	11:38
LOCAL TRAIN	09:51	10:22	11:05	12:35
LOCAL TRAIN	12:00	12:25	13:06	14:27
LOCAL TRAIN	12:54	13:26	14:08	15:35
LOCAL TRAIN	14:50	15:19	16:06	17:32
LOCAL TRAIN	16:38	17:16	18:02	19:41
LOCAL TRAIN	18:11	18:40	19:21	20:54

Shibushi to Miyazaki

STATION TRAIN	SHIBUSHI	OBI	AOSHIMA	MIYAZAKI
LOCAL TRAIN	07:25	08:50	09:32	09:59
LOCAL TRAIN	08:46	10:13	10:58	11:25
LOCAL TRAIN	10:54	12:18	13:01	13:30
LOCAL TRAIN	13:48	15:20	16:00	16:29
LOCAL TRAIN	–	–	17:18	17:45
LOCAL TRAIN	15:53	17:16	17:52	18:22
LOCAL TRAIN	16:54	18:25	19:17	19:43

72. JR Sobu Line

Tokyo to Narita

STATION TRAIN	NARITA	SAKURA	CHIBA	TOKYO
LOCAL TRAIN	10:04	10:18	10:38	11:20
LOCAL TRAIN	11:05	11:19	11:36	12:19
LOCAL TRAIN	12:05	12:19	12:37	13:19
LOCAL TRAIN	13:04	13:19	13:38	14:20
LOCAL TRAIN	14:04	14:18	14:37	15:19
LOCAL TRAIN	15:04	15:18	15:38	16:21
LOCAL TRAIN	16:05	16:20	16:38	17:20
LOCAL TRAIN	17:08	17:22	17:38	18:22
LOCAL TRAIN	18:05	18:19	18:37	19:21
LOCAL TRAIN	19:05	19:19	19:38	20:22
LOCAL TRAIN	20:05	20:19	20:36	21:19
LOCAL TRAIN	21:07	21:22	21:40	22:23

Narita to Tokyo

STATION TRAIN	TOKYO	CHIBA	SAKURA	NARITA
LOCAL TRAIN	07:18	08:04	08:21	08:34
LOCAL TRAIN	08:15	09:00	09:16	09:30
LOCAL TRAIN	09:09	09:56	10:14	10:27
LOCAL TRAIN	10:12	10:58	11:14	11:27
LOCAL TRAIN	11:08	11:57	12:13	12:26
LOCAL TRAIN	12:11	12:59	13:16	13:29
LOCAL TRAIN	12:53	13:41	13:58	14:11
LOCAL TRAIN	14:08	14:54	15:10	15:23
LOCAL TRAIN	15:07	15:52	16:08	16:21
LOCAL TRAIN	16:08	16:54	17:10	17:23
LOCAL TRAIN	17:06	17:54	18:11	18:24
LOCAL TRAIN	18:09	18:58	19:16	19:29

65. JR Nichinan Line

Miyazaki / Aoshima
300 (N / A)
Miyazaki / Obi 780 (N / A)
Aoshima / Obi 540 (N / A)

72. JR Boso Line

Tokyo / Narita 1,060 (N / A)

74. JR Mito Line

Oyama to Mito

TRAIN	OYAMA	SHIMODATE	MITO
LOCAL TRAIN	08:11	08:33	09:36
LOCAL TRAIN	09:14	09:36	10:35
LOCAL TRAIN	10:04	10:24	11:24
LOCAL TRAIN	11:12	11:34	—
LOCAL TRAIN	12:09	12:29	—
LOCAL TRAIN	13:28	13:44	14:48
LOCAL TRAIN	14:50	15:06	16:04
LOCAL TRAIN	15:51	16:11	17:10
LOCAL TRAIN	16:52	17:15	18:10

Mito to Oyama

TRAIN	MITO	SHIMODATE	OYAMA
LOCAL TRAIN	08:38	09:35	09:51
LOCAL TRAIN	09:42	10:40	11:02
LOCAL TRAIN	10:41	11:47	12:04
LOCAL TRAIN	11:51	12:57	13:18
LOCAL TRAIN	—	14:13	14:33
LOCAL TRAIN	14:19	15:18	15:37
LOCAL TRAIN	15:10	16:11	16:28
LOCAL TRAIN	16:14	17:16	17:33
LOCAL TRAIN	17:07	18:05	18:26

74. JR Mito Line
Oyama / Shimodate 300 (N / A)
Oyama / Mito 1,060 (N / A)
Shimodate / Mito 900 (N / A)

75. JR Moka Line

Oyama to Motegi

TRAIN	OYAMA	SHIMODATE	MASHIKO	MOTEGI
LOCAL TRAIN	09:35	10:16	11:01	11:25
LOCAL TRAIN	14:04	14:24	—	—
LOCAL TRAIN	—	14:26	15:01	15:25
LOCAL TRAIN	15:20	15:42	—	—
LOCAL TRAIN	—	15:47	16:24	16:48
LOCAL TRAIN	16:52	17:11	—	—
LOCAL TRAIN	—	17:17	18:00	18:24

Motegi to Oyama

TRAIN	MOTEGI	MASHIKO	SHIMODATE	OYAMA
LOCAL TRAIN	08:35	08:58	09:32	—
LOCAL TRAIN	12:15	12:39	13:17	—
LOCAL TRAIN	—	—	13:23	13:43
LOCAL TRAIN	14:08	14:32	15:13	—
LOCAL TRAIN	—	—	15:18	15:37
LOCAL TRAIN	15:30	15:53	16:42	17:08
LOCAL TRAIN	17:05	17:29	18:16	18:41

75. JR Moka Line
Oyama / Mashiko 700 (N / A)
Shimodate / Mashiko 460 (N / A)

76. JR Nikko Line
Utsunomiya / Nikko 700 (N / A)

77. JR Banetsu-Saisen Line
Aizu-Wakamatsu / Koriyama
1,060* (N / A)
1,760 (N / A) * Local train.

76. JR Nikko Line

North-bound

TRAIN	UTSUNOMIYA	NIKKO
LOCAL TRAIN	08:59	09:35
LOCAL TRAIN	09:54	10:42
LOCAL TRAIN	11:00	11:44
LOCAL TRAIN	11:57	12:42
LOCAL TRAIN	12:57	13:42
LOCAL TRAIN	13:57	14:42
LOCAL TRAIN	14:57	15:42
LOCAL TRAIN	15:30	16:18
LOCAL TRAIN	16:24	17:14
LOCAL TRAIN	17:41	18:29

South-bound

TRAIN	NIKKO	UTSUNOMIYA
LOCAL TRAIN	08:11	08:52
LOCAL TRAIN	10:05	10:41
LOCAL TRAIN	12:01	12:42
LOCAL TRAIN	13:01	13:41
LOCAL TRAIN	14:01	14:41
LOCAL TRAIN	15:01	15:41
LOCAL TRAIN	16:34	17:14
LOCAL TRAIN	17:00	17:37
LOCAL TRAIN	17:25	18:10
LOCAL TRAIN	18:00	18:45

77. JR Banetsu-Saisen Line

West-bound TRAIN	KORIYAMA	AIZU-WAKAMATSU	NIIGATA	East-bound TRAIN	NIIGATA	AIZU-WAKAMATSU	KORIYAMA
LOCAL TRAIN	09:16	10:46	13:18	LOCAL TRAIN	—	08:27	09:34
LOCAL TRAIN	10:15	11:51	—	AIZU	—	09:36	10:33
LOCAL TRAIN	11:34	12:33	—	LOCAL TRAIN	08:23	10:48	12:03
LOCAL TRAIN	13:28	14:34	—	LOCAL TRAIN	—	12:40	14:13
LOCAL TRAIN	14:14	15:39	—	LOCAL TRAIN	—	13:48	14:58
LOCAL TRAIN	15:03	16:24	—	LOCAL TRAIN	—	14:42	16:03
LOCAL TRAIN	16:10	17:40	—	LOCAL TRAIN	—	15:28	16:35
AIZU	17:15	18:13	—	LOCAL TRAIN	13:35	17:01	18:37

79. JR Ou Line
Aomori / Hirosaki 620* (N / A)
* Local train.

82. JR Senseki Line
Sendai / Hon-Shiogama 300 (N / A)
Sendai / Matsushima-Kaigan
380 (N / A)

85. JR Ofunato Line
Ichinoseki / Sakari 1,800 (N / A)

86. JR Kamaishi / Yamada Line
Morioka / Miyako 1,800 (N / A)
Miyako / Kamaishi 900 (N / A)

87. JR Hiraniwa-Kogen Bus
Morioka / Kuji 2,200 (N / A)

79. JR Ou Line

Aomori to Fukushima

STATION / TRAIN	AOMORI	HIROSAKI	ODATE	AKITA	FUKUSHIMA
TSUBASA-10	—	—	—	08:39	13:11
LOCAL TRAIN	08:41	09:43	—	—	—
INAHO-10	10:13	10:45	11:21	12:51	—
LOCAL TRAIN	11:21	12:14	—	—	—
LOCAL TRAIN	12:41	13:26	—	—	—
LOCAL TRAIN	—	—	—	14:10	22:28
LOCAL TRAIN	13:21	14:16	—	—	—
TAZAWA-16	14:27	14:59	15:36	17:07	—
LOCAL TRAIN	16:03	16:50	18:09	20:35	—

Fukushima to Aomori

STATION / TRAIN	FUKUSHIMA	AKITA	ODATE	HIROSAKI	AOMORI
LOCAL TRAIN	—	05:18	08:12	09:51	10:41
TSUGARU	02:55	09:03	10:55	11:38	12:17
LOCAL TRAIN	—	—	—	12:50	13:43
LOCAL TRAIN	—	—	—	13:37	14:19
LOCAL TRAIN	—	—	—	14:15	15:08
LOCAL TRAIN	—	—	—	15:13	16:23
LOCAL TRAIN	—	—	—	16:23	17:17
LOCAL TRAIN	—	—	—	17:13	18:05
LOCAL TRAIN	—	—	—	18:05	19:00
TSUBASA-13	15:23	16:45	—	—	—

82. JR Senseki Line

Sendai to Ishinomaki

STATION / TRAIN	SENDAI	HON-SHIOGAMA	MATSUSHIMA-KAIGAN	ISHINOMAKI
LOCAL TRAIN	07:34	08:01	08:14	08:54
LOCAL TRAIN	08:16	08:43	08:53	09:37
LOCAL TRAIN	09:20	09:35	09:42	10:08
LOCAL TRAIN	10:16	10:35	10:46	11:18
LOCAL TRAIN	11:06	11:33	11:43	12:24
LOCAL TRAIN	12:24	12:51	13:03	13:48
LOCAL TRAIN	13:28	13:55	14:05	14:51
LOCAL TRAIN	14:24	14:51	15:00	15:47
LOCAL TRAIN	15:31	15:58	16:08	16:50
LOCAL TRAIN	16:20	16:39	16:48	17:21
LOCAL TRAIN	17:44	18:11	18:21	19:01

Ishinomaki to Sendai

STATION / TRAIN	ISHINOMAKI	MATSUSHIMA-KAIGAN	HON-SHIOGAMA	SENDAI
LOCAL TRAIN	09:13	09:43	09:51	10:06
LOCAL TRAIN	10:15	10:46	10:55	11:15
LOCAL TRAIN	10:44	11:25	11:35	12:02
LOCAL TRAIN	11:41	12:15	12:24	12:44
LOCAL TRAIN	13:15	13:42	13:49	14:04
LOCAL TRAIN	13:53	14:39	14:49	15:16
LOCAL TRAIN	15:10	15:40	15:49	16:09
LOCAL TRAIN	15:30	16:19	16:29	16:56
LOCAL TRAIN	16:26	16:57	17:06	17:26
LOCAL TRAIN	17:14	17:52	18:01	18:21
LOCAL TRAIN	17:42	18:28	18:38	19:04

85. JR Ofunato Line

West-bound

STATION / TRAIN	SAKARI	KESENNUMA	ICHINOSEKI
LOCAL TRAIN	09:33	10:31	11:51
LOCAL TRAIN	10:57	12:09	13:49
LOCAL TRAIN	14:40	15:52	17:24
LOCAL TRAIN	16:04	17:02	18:17
LOCAL TRAIN	18:24	19:47	21:30

East-bound

STATION / TRAIN	ICHINOSEKI	KESENNUMA	SAKARI
LOCAL TRAIN	09:46	11:03	12:03
LOCAL TRAIN	12:45	14:20	15:27
LOCAL TRAIN	14:10	16:09	17:31
LOCAL TRAIN	16:14	18:03	19:11
LOCAL TRAIN	19:20	20:58	22:06

87. JR Bus

Morioka to Kuji

STATION / BUS	MORIOKA	KUJI
SHIRAKABAGO	07:10	10:00
SHIRAKABAGO	09:40	12:30
SHIRAKABAGO	11:40	14:30
SHIRAKABAGO	13:40	16:30
SHIRAKABAGO	14:40	17:30
SHIRAKABAGO	16:40	19:30
SHIRAKABAGO	18:00	20:50

Kuji to Morioka

STATION / BUS	KUJI	MORIOKA
SHIRAKABAGO	07:00	09:50
SHIRAKABAGO	08:05	10:55
SHIRAKABAGO	09:40	12:30
SHIRAKABAGO	10:40	13:30
SHIRAKABAGO	12:50	15:40
SHIRAKABAGO	14:50	17:40
SHIRAKABAGO	16:50	19:40

86. JR Kamaishi/Yamada Line

Morioka to Hanamaki

STATION / TRAIN	MORIOKA	MIYAKO	KAMAISHI	SHIN-HANAMAKI	HANAMAKI
RIKUCHU-4	—	09:04	10:19	12:06	12:14
LOCAL TRAIN	—	09:44	11:09	—	—
LOCAL TRAIN	—	—	11:41	14:14	14:23
LOCAL TRAIN	08:26	11:05	—	—	—
LOCAL TRAIN	—	11:24	13:04	15:16	15:25
LOCAL TRAIN	11:38	13:48	—	—	—
LOCAL TRAIN	—	13:51	15:34	—	—
LOCAL TRAIN	—	—	15:37	18:08	18:18
LOCAL TRAIN	15:05	17:55	19:15	—	—

Hanamaki to Morioka

STATION / TRAIN	HANAMAKI	SHIN-HANAMAKI	KAMAISHI	MIYAKO	MORIOKA
RIKUCHU-1	08:15	08:23	10:04	11:53	—
LOCAL TRAIN	—	—	—	11:56	14:19
LOCAL TRAIN	09:07	09:20	11:46	13:06	—
RIKUCHU-3	11:09	11:17	13:07	14:18	—
LOCAL TRAIN	—	—	—	13:52	15:14
LOCAL TRAIN	—	—	—	15:32	17:57
LOCAL TRAIN	13:08	13:17	15:17	—	—
LOCAL TRAIN	—	—	—	15:25	17:03
LOCAL TRAIN	—	—	16:30	18:20	21:01

92. JR Hachinohe Line

Hachinohe to Kuji

STATION / TRAIN	HACHINOHE	KUJI
LOCAL TRAIN	07:14	09:10
LOCAL TRAIN	10:55	12:51
LOCAL TRAIN	12:57	14:50
LOCAL TRAIN	14:09	15:38
LOCAL TRAIN	15:48	17:39
LOCAL TRAIN	16:51	19:00
LOCAL TRAIN	18:08	19:59

Kuji to Hachinohe

STATION / TRAIN	KUJI	HACHINOHE
LOCAL TRAIN	07:30	09:35
LOCAL TRAIN	09:13	10:41
LOCAL TRAIN	10:47	12:44
LOCAL TRAIN	13:33	15:38
LOCAL TRAIN	16:23	18:29
LOCAL TRAIN	17:47	19:48
LOCAL TRAIN	20:15	22:10

93. JR Bus

South-bound

STATION / BUS	TOWADAKO (YASUMIYA)	MORIOKA
TOWADA-74	10:20	12:35
TOWADA-78	12:20	14:35
TOWADA-80	13:20	15:35

North-bound

STATION / BUS	MORIOKA	TOWADAKO (YASUMIYA)
TOWADA-71	08:50	11:05
TOWADA-81	13:50	16:05
TOWADA-85	15:50	18:05

94. JR Bus

South-bound

STATION / BUS	AOMORI	NENOKUCHI	TOWADAKO
MIZUUMI-4	07:30	10:19	10:43
MIZUUMI-6	08:30	11:20	11:44
MIZUUMI-8	09:30	12:16	12:40
MIZUUMI-10	10:30	13:16	13:40
MIZUUMI-12	11:30	14:19	14:43
MIZUUMI-14	12:30	15:16	15:40
MIZUUMI-16	13:30	16:17	16:41
MIZUUMI-18	14:30	17:20	17:44
MIZUUMI-20	16:20	19:10	19:34

North-bound

STATION / BUS	TOWADAKO	NENOKUCHI	AOMORI
MIZUUMI-3	08:00	08:29	11:00
MIZUUMI-5	09:00	09:29	12:00
MIZUUMI-7	10:00	10:29	13:00
MIZUUMI-9	12:00	12:29	14:58
MIZUUMI-11	13:00	13:29	15:58
MIZUUMI-13	14:00	14:29	16:58
MIZUUMI-15	15:00	15:29	17:58
MIZUUMI-17	16:00	16:29	19:01
MIZUUMI-19	17:00	17:29	19:58

95. JR Seikan Boat

North-bound

PORT / BOAT	AOMORI	HAKODATE
No. 23	07:30	11:20
No. 25	10:10	14:05
No. 3	12:10	16:05
No. 5	15:00	18:50
No. 7	17:05	20:55
No. 9	19:50	23:45

South-bound

PORT / BOAT	HAKODATE	AOMORI
No. 4	07:20	11:15
No. 6	10:10	14:05
No. 8	12:15	16:10
No. 20	15:00	18:55
No. 22	17:00	20:55
No. 24	19:45	23:35

92. JR Hachinohe Line
Hachinohe / Kuji
1,220 (N / A)

93. JR Towada-Minami Bus
Towadako / Morioka
2,300 (N / A)

94. JR Towada-Kita Bus
Aomori / Nenokuchi
2,100 (N / A)
Aomori / Towadako
2,400 (N / A)

95. JR Seikan Boat
Aomori / Hakodate
2,000 (3,600)

100. JR Hakodate / Muroran / Sekihoku Line

Hakodate / Toya	4,900	(7,700)
Hakodate / Noboribetsu	4,100	(10,300)
Hakodate / Chitose-kuko	7,100	(11,300)
Hakodate / Sapporo	7,400	(11,600)
Hakodate / Asahikawa	9,700	(15,100)
Sapporo / Chitose-kuko	700*	(N / A)
	1,900	(3,200)
Sapporo / Shiraoi	3,140	(4,440)
Sapporo / Noboribetsu	4,000	(5,300)
Sapporo / Toya	5,300	(8,100)
Sapporo / Asahigawa	4,300	(7,100)
Sapporo / Kamikawa	5,600	(8,400)
Sapporo / Bihoro	8,700	(12,900)
Chitose-kuko / Shiraoi	1,980	(3,280)
Chitose-kuko / Noboribetsu	2,660	(3,960)
Chitose-kuko / Toya	4,300	(7,100)
Shiraoi / Noboribetsu	300*	(N / A)
	1,500	(2,800)
Noboribetsu / Toya	2,500	(3,800)
Asahigawa / Kamikawa	2,100	(3,400)
Asahigawa / Bihoro	6,200	(10,400)
Asahigawa / Abashiri	7,100	(11,300)
Kamikawa / Bihoro	5,300	(8,100)
Kamikawa / Abashiri	6,100	(10,300)
Bihoro / Abashiri	540*	(N / A)
	1,740	(3,040)

100. JR Hakodate/Muroran/Sekihoku Line

Hakodate to Abashiri

STATION / TRAIN	HAKODATE	TOYA	NOBORIBETSU	SHIRAOI	CHITOSE-KUKO	SAPPORO	ASAHIGAWA	KAMIKAWA	BIHORO	ABASHIRI
OKHOTSK-1	—	—	—	—	—	07:02	08:41	09:24	12:02	12:27
OKHOTSK-3	—	—	—	—	—	09:28	11:06	11:51	14:38	15:04
LILAC-9	—	—	10:38	10:51	11:24	12:00	13:36	—	—	—
HOKUTO-5	08:11	10:08	10:52	→	11:40	12:10	—	—	—	—
HOKUTO-7	09:31	11:23	12:07	→	12:55	13:25	—	—	—	—
LILAC-13	—	—	12:38	12:51	13:25	14:00	15:36	—	—	—
OTORI	11:35	13:27	14:11	→	14:58	15:34	17:15	17:58	20:32	20:57
HOKUTO-9	13:02	14:58	15:42	→	16:29	16:59	—	—	—	—
OKHOTSK-5	—	—	—	—	—	17:10	18:49	19:32	22:06	22:33
LILAC-21	—	—	16:36	16:50	17:25	18:00	19:36	—	—	—
HOKUTO-11	14:30	16:27	17:13	→	17:58	18:28	—	—	—	—
HOKUTO-13	17:12	19:09	19:53	→	20:42	21:11	—	—	—	—
HOKUTO-15	19:00	20:57	21:42	→	22:28	22:58	—	—	—	—

Abashiri to Hakodate

STATION / TRAIN	ABASHIRI	BIHORO	KAMIKAWA	ASAHIGAWA	SAPPORO	CHITOSE-KUKO	SHIRAOI	NOBORIBETSU	TOYA	HAKODATE
HOKUTO-2	—	—	—	—	07:50	08:21	→	09:07	09:51	11:53
HOKUTO-4	—	—	—	—	08:54	09:24	→	10:17	11:02	13:01
HOKUTO-6	—	—	—	—	09:35	10:05	→	10:53	11:37	13:41
LILAC-4	—	—	—	08:30	09:42	10:13	10:47	11:00	—	—
LILAC-8	—	—	—	10:00	11:42	12:15	12:49	13:02	—	—
OKHOTSK-2	06:42	07:09	09:50	10:35	12:17	—	—	—	—	—
HOKUTO-8	—	—	—	—	12:42	13:12	→	13:59	14:43	16:41
LILAC-12	—	—	—	12:00	13:40	14:12	14:46	14:59	—	—
HOKUTO-10	—	—	—	—	14:27	14:56	→	15:42	16:27	18:39
OTORI	10:00	10:25	12:57	13:40	15:22	15:52	→	16:39	17:23	19:21
LILAC-16	—	—	—	14:00	15:40	16:12	16:46	16:59	—	—
HOKUTO-12	—	—	—	—	17:20	17:51	→	18:37	19:22	21:25
OKHOTSK-4	13:46	14:13	16:48	17:38	19:18	—	—	—	—	—

103. JR Nemuro Line

Sapporo to Kushiro

STATION / TRAIN	SAPPORO	CHITOSE-KUKO	OBIHIRO	KUSHIRO
OZORA-1	08:04	08:35	10:52	12:45
OZORA-3	09:26	09:56	12:25	14:25
OZORA-5	11:30	12:00	14:26	16:29
OZORA-7	14:33	15:03	17:29	19:28
OZORA-9	16:28	16:58	19:07	20:57
MARIMO	22:25	23:07	03:31	06:10

Kushiro to Sapporo

STATION / TRAIN	KUSHIRO	OBIHIRO	CHITOSE-KUKO	SAPPORO
OZORA-6	09:03	10:52	12:58	13:28
OZORA-8	11:20	13:19	15:32	16:04
OZORA-10	14:07	16:04	18:34	19:06
OZORA-12	15:50	17:43	20:09	20:41
OZORA-14	17:17	19:20	21:34	22:05
MARIMO	22:25	01:20	06:01	06:52

103. JR Nemuro Line
Sapporo / Kushiro   8,400   (12,600)
Chitose-kuko / Kushiro
                    7,900   (12,100)

110. JR Kunmo Line
Abashiri / Hamakoshimizu
                    380   (N / A)
Abashiri / Shari   700   (N / A)
Abashiri / Kushiro   3,100   (N / A)

110. JR Kunmo Line

Abashiri to Kushiro

STATION / TRAIN	ABASHIRI	HAMA-KOSHIMIZU	SHARI	KAWAYU	TESHIKAGA	KUSHIRO
LOCAL TRAIN	06:44	07:15	07:41	09:00	09:19	10:59
LOCAL TRAIN	10:02	10:31	10:54	11:51	12:10	13:53
LOCAL TRAIN	11:05	11:34	12:03	—	—	—
LOCAL TRAIN	13:09	13:45	14:09	—	—	—
LOCAL TRAIN	15:41	16:16	16:35	—	—	—
LOCAL TRAIN	17:15	17:45	18:07	19:05	19:25	21:11

Kushiro to Abashiri

STATION / TRAIN	KUSHIRO	TESHIKAGA	KAWAYU	SHARI	HAMA-KOSHIMIZU	ABASHIRI
LOCAL TRAIN	06:23	07:55	08:16	09:09	09:27	09:57
LOCAL TRAIN	—	—	—	11:08	11:35	12:04
LOCAL TRAIN	08:54	10:24	11:01	12:05	12:28	12:57
LOCAL TRAIN	—	—	—	13:25	13:44	14:13
LOCAL TRAIN	—	—	—	14:40	14:59	15:28
LOCAL TRAIN	—	—	—	15:56	16:15	16:44

200. Odakyu Railways Hakone Romance Car

West-bound

STATION / TRAIN	SHINJUKU	ODAWARA	HAKONE-YUMOTO
SAGAMI-3	07:30	08:45	09:00
HAKONE-9	09:30	10:40	10:55
HAKONE-11	10:00	11:10	11:25
HAKONE-13	10:30	11:39	11:55
HAKONE-15	11:00	12:08	12:25
HAKONE-17	11:30	12:39	12:55
HAKONE-19	12:00	13:09	13:25
HAKONE-21	12:30	13:38	13:55
HAKONE-23	13:00	14:09	14:25
HAKONE-25	13:30	14:39	14:55
HAKONE-27	14:00	15:08	15:25
ASHIGARA-37	16:30	17:39	17:55
ASHIGARA-1	17:00	18:10	18:25

East-bound

STATION / TRAIN	HAKONE-YUMOTO	ODAWARA	SHINJUKU
ASHIGARA-4	09:13	09:32	10:40
HAKONE-6	10:13	10:32	11:39
HAKONE-10	11:13	11:32	12:40
HAKONE-14	12:13	12:32	13:40
HAKONE-18	13:13	13:32	14:40
HAKONE-22	14:13	14:32	15:40
ASHIGARA-26	15:13	15:32	16:43
ASHIGARA-30	16:13	16:32	17:47
ASHIGARA-34	17:13	17:32	18:46
ASHIGARA-38	18:13	18:32	19:47
ASHIGARA-40	18:43	19:02	20:15
SAGAMI-42	19:13	19:32	20:48
ASHIGARA-44	19:43	20:02	21:09

201. Izu-Hakone Railways

Tokyo to Shuzenji

STATION / TRAIN	TOKYO	MISHIMA	IZU-NAGAOKA	SHUZENJI
ODORIKO-3	09:00	10:48	11:03	11:14
ODORIKO-5	10:00	11:47	12:01	12:12
ODORIKO-15	13:30	15:15	15:29	15:39

Shuzenji to Tokyo

STATION / TRAIN	SHUZENJI	IZU-NAGAOKA	MISHIMA	TOKYO
ODORIKO-4	09:34	09:44	09:58	11:48
ODORIKO-10	12:42	12:53	13:07	14:56
ODORIKO-18	15:47	15:57	16:11	17:58

202. Izukyu Railways

Tokyo to Izukyu-Shimoda

STATION / TRAIN	TOKYO	ODAWARA	ATAMI	ITO	IZU-ATAGAWA	IZUKYU-SHIMODA
ODORIKO-5	10:00	11:08	11:31	11:55	12:29	12:57
ODORIKO-11	12:00	13:08	13:28	13:54	14:24	14:49
ODORIKO-15	13:30	14:38	14:58	15:22	15:51	16:15
ODORIKO-17	14:30	15:38	15:59	16:28	16:55	17:19
ODORIKO-19	15:30	16:38	17:01	17:27	—	—

Izukyu-Shimoda to Tokyo

STATION / TRAIN	IZUKYU-SHIMODA	IZU-ATAGAWA	ITO	ATAMI	ODAWARA	TOKYO
ODORIKO-2	08:00	08:24	08:52	09:15	09:34	10:43
ODORIKO-10	12:11	12:36	13:04	13:30	13:48	14:56
ODORIKO-14	13:12	13:37	14:04	14:27	14:45	15:53
ODORIKO-18	15:09	15:33	16:06	16:33	16:52	17:58
ODORIKO-22	17:25	17:51	18:21	18:46	19:04	20:10

203. Fuji-Kyuko Railways

Shinjuku to Kawaguchiko

STATION / TRAIN	SHINJUKU	OTSUKI	FUJIKYU-HIGHLAND	KAWAGUCHIKO
LOCAL TRAIN	07:05	08:42		
LOCAL TRAIN		08:58	09:48	09:50
LOCAL TRAIN	08:22	09:38		
LOCAL TRAIN		10:08	10:58	11:00
LOCAL TRAIN	08:49	10:32		
LOCAL TRAIN		10:45	11:35	11:37
LOCAL TRAIN	11:25	12:59		
LOCAL TRAIN		13:07	13:57	13:59
LOCAL TRAIN	13:02	14:28		
LOCAL TRAIN		14:40	15:30	15:32
LOCAL TRAIN	14:39	16:17		
LOCAL TRAIN		16:38	17:28	17:30

Kawaguchiko to Shinjuku

STATION / TRAIN	KAWAGUCHIKO	FUJIKYU-HIGHLAND	OTSUKI	SHINJUKU
LOCAL TRAIN	07:49	07:51	08:41	
LOCAL TRAIN			09:14	10:57
LOCAL TRAIN	09:36	09:38	10:28	
LOCAL TRAIN			10:38	12:03
LOCAL TRAIN	13:43	13:45	14:35	
LOCAL TRAIN			15:01	16:42
LOCAL TRAIN	16:21	16:23	17:13	
LOCAL TRAIN			17:38	19:06
LOCAL TRAIN	17:34	17:36	18:26	
LOCAL TRAIN			18:57	20:19
LOCAL TRAIN	18:26	18:28	19:18	
LOCAL TRAIN			19:57	21:18

200. Odakyu Railways Hakone Romance Car

Shinjuku / Odawara	1,050	(N / A)
Shinjuku / Hakone-Yumoto	1,280	(N / A)

201. Izu-Hakone Railways

Tokyo / Izu-Nagaoka	4,590	(7,390)
Tokyo / Shuzenji	4,750	(7,550)
Mishima / Izu-Nagaoka	290	(N / A)
Mishima / Shuzenji	450	(N / A)

202. Izukyu Railways

Tokyo / Atami	4,000	(6,800)
Tokyo / Ito	4,300	(7,100)
Tokyo / Izu-Atagawa	4,980	(8,080)
Tokyo / Izukyu-Shimoda	5,540	(8,790)
Atami / Ito	1,500	(2,800)
Atami / Izukyu-Shimoda	2,740	(4,490)
Ito / Izukyu-Shimoda	1,240	(1,690)

203. Fuji-Kyuko Railways

Shinjuku / Otsuki	1,380*	(N / A)	* Japan
Otsuki / Kawaguchiko	980	(N / A)	Railways.

205. Sado Steamship Company

Niigata to Ryotsu

BOAT	PORT NIIGATA	PORT RYOTSU
JETFOIL	07:00	08:00
JETFOIL	08:00	09:00
STEAMSHIP	09:25	11:45
JETFOIL	10:00	11:00
JETFOIL	11:00	12:00
STEAMSHIP	12:10	14:30
JETFOIL	13:00	14:00
JETFOIL	14:00	15:00
STEAMSHIP	15:25	17:45
JETFOIL	16:00	17:00
STEAMSHIP	18:10	20:30

Ryotsu to Niigata

BOAT	PORT RYOTSU	PORT NIIGATA
JETFOIL	08:30	09:30
STEAMSHIP	09:10	11:30
JETFOIL	09:30	10:30
JETFOIL	11:30	12:30
STEAMSHIP	12:25	14:45
JETFOIL	12:30	13:30
JETFOIL	14:30	15:30
STEAMSHIP	15:10	17:30
JETFOIL	15:30	16:30
JETFOIL	17:30	18:30
STEAMSHIP	18:25	20:45

228. Kintetsu Railways
Nagoya to Kashikojima

TRAIN	NAGOYA	ISESHI	UJI-YAMADA	TOBA	KASHIKOJIMA
LTD EXPRESS	08:50	10:13	10:16	10:33	11:10
LTD EXPRESS	09:50	11:13	11:16	11:34	12:10
LTD EXPRESS	10:50	12:13	12:16	12:33	13:10
LTD EXPRESS	11:25	—	12:44	12:56	13:29
LTD EXPRESS	11:50	13:13	13:16	13:33	14:10
LTD EXPRESS	12:50	14:13	14:16	14:35	15:09
LTD EXPRESS	13:25	—	14:44	14:55	15:30
LTD EXPRESS	14:50	16:13	16:16	16:35	17:09
LTD EXPRESS	15:25	—	16:44	16:56	17:30
LTD EXPRESS	15:50	17:13	17:16	17:32	18:10
LTD EXPRESS	16:50	18:13	18:16	18:32	19:10

Kashikojima to Nagoya

TRAIN	KASHIKOJIMA	TOBA	UJI-YAMADA	ISESHI	NAGOYA
LTD EXPRESS	08:20	09:00	09:12	09:14	10:40
LTD EXPRESS	09:20	10:00	10:12	10:14	11:39
LTD EXPRESS	10:00	10:40	10:52	10:54	12:20
LTD EXPRESS	11:20	12:00	12:12	12:14	13:39
LTD EXPRESS	12:40	13:13	13:25	—	14:43
LTD EXPRESS	13:20	14:00	14:12	14:14	15:39
LTD EXPRESS	14:00	14:40	14:52	14:54	16:20
LTD EXPRESS	14:40	15:13	15:25	—	16:43
LTD EXPRESS	15:20	16:00	16:12	16:14	17:39
LTD EXPRESS	15:40	16:13	16:25	—	17:45
LTD EXPRESS	16:00	16:40	16:52	16:54	18:20

232. Kintetsu Railways
Kyoto to Kashikojima

TRAIN	KYOTO	YAMATO-SAIDAIJI	ISESHI	TOBA	KASHIKOJIMA
LTD EXPRESS	07:15	07:46	09:16	09:59	10:11
LTD EXPRESS	08:15	08:45	10:16	10:33	11:10
LTD EXPRESS	09:15	09:45	11:16	11:33	12:10
LTD EXPRESS	10:15	10:45	12:16	12:33	13:10
LTD EXPRESS	12:15	12:45	14:16	14:33	15:10
LTD EXPRESS	13:15	13:45	15:16	15:33	16:10
LTD EXPRESS	14:15	14:45	16:16	16:35	17:09
LTD EXPRESS	15:15	15:45	17:16	17:32	18:10
LTD EXPRESS	16:15	16:45	18:16	18:32	19:10

Kashikojima to Kyoto

TRAIN	KASHIKOJIMA	TOBA	ISESHI	YAMATO-SAIDAIJI	KYOTO
LTD EXPRESS	08:20	08:57	09:12	10:50	11:20
LTD EXPRESS	09:20	09:57	10:12	11:50	12:20
LTD EXPRESS	10:20	10:57	11:12	12:50	13:20
LTD EXPRESS	11:20	11:57	12:12	13:50	14:20
LTD EXPRESS	13:20	13:57	14:12	15:50	16:20
LTD EXPRESS	14:20	14:57	15:12	16:50	17:20
LTD EXPRESS	15:20	15:57	16:12	17:50	18:20
LTD EXPRESS	16:20	16:57	17:12	18:50	19:20
LTD EXPRESS	17:20	17:57	18:12	19:50	20:20

205. Sado Steamship Company
Niigata / Ryotsu
(1) Steamship	1,730	(3,460)
(2) Jetfoil	5,300	(N / A)

228. Kintetsu Railways
Nagoya / Ise-Shima Line
Nagoya / Iseshi	2,050	(N / A)
Nagoya / Toba	2,260	(N / A)
Nagoya / Kashikojima	2,720	(N / A)

232. Kintetsu Railways
Kyoto / Ise-Shima Line
Kyoto / Iseshi	2,750	(N / A)
Kyoto / Toba	2,960	(N / A)
Kyoto / Kashikojima	3,370	(N / A)

233. Kintetsu Railways

Namba to Kashikojima

TRAIN	KINTETSU-NAMBA	UJI-YAMADA	TOBA	KASHIKOJIMA
LTD EXPRESS	07:20	09:03	09:17	09:50
LTD EXPRESS	08:20	10:04	10:18	10:52
LTD EXPRESS	09:20	11:03	11:17	11:52
LTD EXPRESS	10:20	12:03	12:18	12:49
LTD EXPRESS	11:20	13:03	13:14	—
LTD EXPRESS	12:20	14:03	14:16	14:49
LTD EXPRESS	13:20	15:03	15:16	15:52
LTD EXPRESS	14:20	16:03	16:16	16:49
LTD EXPRESS	15:20	17:03	17:17	17:52

Kashikojima to Namba

TRAIN	KASHIKOJIMA	TOBA	UJI-YAMADA	KINTETSU-NAMBA
LTD EXPRESS	10:00	10:34	10:45	12:30
LTD EXPRESS	11:00	11:34	11:45	13:30
LTD EXPRESS	12:00	12:34	12:45	14:30
LTD EXPRESS	14:00	14:34	14:45	16:30
LTD EXPRESS	15:00	15:34	15:45	17:30
LTD EXPRESS	16:00	16:34	16:45	18:30
LTD EXPRESS	17:00	17:34	17:45	19:30
LTD EXPRESS	17:40	18:15	18:28	20:22
LTD EXPRESS	18:00	18:34	18:45	20:30

234. Kintetsu Railways

Kyoto to Nara

TRAIN	KYOTO	KINTETSU-NARA
LTD EXPRESS	08:30	09:06
LTD EXPRESS	09:00	09:34
LTD EXPRESS	10:00	10:34
LTD EXPRESS	11:00	11:34
LTD EXPRESS	12:00	12:34
LTD EXPRESS	13:00	13:34
LTD EXPRESS	14:30	15:03
LTD EXPRESS	15:30	16:03
LTD EXPRESS	16:30	17:03
LTD EXPRESS	17:30	18:03
LTD EXPRESS	18:00	18:33
LTD EXPRESS	18:30	19:03

Nara to Kyoto

TRAIN	KINTETSU-NARA	KYOTO
LTD EXPRESS	08:30	09:05
LTD EXPRESS	09:30	10:05
LTD EXPRESS	11:00	11:35
LTD EXPRESS	12:00	12:35
LTD EXPRESS	13:00	13:35
LTD EXPRESS	14:00	14:35
LTD EXPRESS	15:00	15:35
LTD EXPRESS	16:00	16:35
LTD EXPRESS	16:30	17:05
LTD EXPRESS	17:00	17:35
LTD EXPRESS	18:00	18:35
LTD EXPRESS	18:30	19:05

235. Kintetsu Railways

Namba to Nara

TRAIN	KINTETSU-NAMBA	KINTETSU-NARA
LTD EXPRESS	09:35	10:07
LTD EXPRESS	11:35	12:07
LTD EXPRESS	12:35	13:07
LTD EXPRESS	13:35	14:07
LTD EXPRESS	15:35	16:07
LTD EXPRESS	16:35	17:07
LTD EXPRESS	19:35	20:07

Nara to Namba

TRAIN	KINTETSU-NARA	KINTETSU-NAMBA
LTD EXPRESS	08:45	09:02
LTD EXPRESS	10:15	10:47
LTD EXPRESS	12:15	12:47
LTD EXPRESS	13:15	13:47
LTD EXPRESS	14:15	14:47
LTD EXPRESS	15:15	15:47
LTD EXPRESS	16:15	16:48

236. Nankai Railways

South-bound

TRAIN	NAMBA	HASHIMOTO	GOKURAKU-BASHI
KOYA-1	09:20	10:04	10:50
KOYA-5	13:20	14:03	14:45

North-bound

TRAIN	GOKURAKU-BASHI	HASHIMOTO	NAMBA
KOYA-2	11:25	12:12	12:54
KOYA-8	16:05	16:54	17:38

233. Kintetsu Railways
Osaka / Ise-Shima Line

Namba / Iseshi	2,340	(N / A)
Namba / Toba	2,800	(N / A)
Namba / Kashikojima	3,010	(N / A)

234. Kintetsu Railways
Kyoto / Nara Line

Kyoto / Kintetsu-Nara	880	(N / A)

235. Kintetsu Railways
Osaka / Nara Line

Namba / Kintetsu-Nara	850	(N / A)

236. Nankai Railways Koya Line

Namba / Gokurakubashi	1,760	(N / A)

250. Kansai Steamship Company

Osaka to Beppu

SHIP	OSAKA	KOBE	TAKAMATSU	BEPPU
STEAMSHIP	08:30	09:50	14:00	—
STEAMSHIP	14:20	15:40	20:10	07:00
STEAMSHIP	19:00	20:30	—	08:00
STEAMSHIP	21:00	22:30	—	11:55

Beppu to Osaka

SHIP	BEPPU	TAKAMATSU	KOBE	OSAKA
STEAMSHIP	—	14:30	18:40	20:00
STEAMSHIP	16:30	—	06:00	07:30
STEAMSHIP	19:20	—	06:50	08:20
STEAMSHIP	21:00	07:30	11:50	13:10

251. Setonaikai Steamship Company

South-bound

SHIP	HIROSHIMA	MATSUYAMA
HYDROFOIL	08:00	09:10
STEAMSHIP	08:40	11:25
HYDROFOIL	09:20	10:30
STEAMSHIP	10:10	12:55
HYDROFOIL	11:20	12:30
STEAMSHIP	11:20	13:50
STEAMSHIP	12:40	15:25
HYDROFOIL	13:40	14:50
STEAMSHIP	15:20	18:05
HYDROFOIL	15:40	16:50
STEAMSHIP	17:00	19:45

North-bound

SHIP	MATSUYAMA	HIROSHIMA
HYDROFOIL	08:00	09:10
STEAMSHIP	08:20	10:50
STEAMSHIP	09:20	12:05
HYDROFOIL	10:00	11:10
STEAMSHIP	10:35	13:20
HYDROFOIL	12:00	13:00
HYDROFOIL	13:40	14:50
HYDROFOIL	15:00	16:00
STEAMSHIP	15:15	17:45
STEAMSHIP	16:15	19:00
HYDROFOIL	16:20	17:20

261. Shimabara Railways

Isahaya to Kazusa

TRAIN	ISAHAYA	SHIMABARA	SHIMABARA-GAIKO	KAZUSA
LOCAL TRAIN	08:38	09:40	09:49	10:52
LOCAL TRAIN	09:32	10:34	10:44	11:48
LOCAL TRAIN	10:41	11:44	11:54	12:56
LOCAL TRAIN	11:37	12:40	12:48	13:51
EXPRESS TRAIN	12:45	13:34	13:44	14:42
LOCAL TRAIN	13:27	14:31	14:39	15:40
LOCAL TRAIN	14:31	15:36	15:44	16:49
LOCAL TRAIN	15:23	16:37	16:45	17:48
LOCAL TRAIN	16:20	17:30	17:40	18:43

Kazusa to Isahaya

TRAIN	KAZUSA	SHIMABARA-GAIKO	SHIMABARA	ISAHAYA
LOCAL TRAIN	07:47	08:53	09:02	10:09
LOCAL TRAIN	08:42	09:49	09:57	11:02
EXPRESS TRAIN	09:46	10:44	10:55	11:43
LOCAL TRAIN	11:11	12:15	12:29	13:35
LOCAL TRAIN	12:18	13:22	13:33	14:38
LOCAL TRAIN	13:14	14:19	14:31	15:31
LOCAL TRAIN	14:05	15:12	15:24	16:26
LOCAL TRAIN	15:02	16:04	16:13	17:26
LOCAL TRAIN	15:59	17:07	17:18	18:18

262. Kyushu Shosen

East-bound

BOAT	SHIMABARA-GAIKO	MISUMI
FERRY	10:05	11:05
FERRY	11:00	12:00
FERRY	12:00	13:00
FERRY	12:55	13:55
FERRY	13:50	14:50
FERRY	14:40	15:40
FERRY	15:35	16:35
FERRY	17:15	18:15
FERRY	18:15	19:15

West-bound

BOAT	MISUMI	SHIMABARA-GAIKO
FERRY	07:05	08:05
FERRY	08:50	09:50
FERRY	09:40	10:40
FERRY	10:30	11:30
FERRY	11:30	12:30
FERRY	12:35	13:35
FERRY	13:20	14:20
FERRY	14:20	15:20
FERRY	15:10	16:10

250. Kansai Steamship Company
Osaka-Kobe / Takamatsu 2,300 — 9,100
Osaka-Kobe / Beppu 5,700 — 18,700

251. Setonaikai Steamship Company
Hiroshima / Matsuyama
(1) Steamship 1,800 (3,600)
(2) Hydrofoil 4,800 (N / A)

261. Shimabara Railways
Isahaya / Shimabara 990 (N / A)
Isahaya / Shimabara-gaiko 1,040 (N / A)
Shimabara / Shimabara-gaiko 100 (N / A)

262. Kushu Shosen Boat
Shimabara-gaiko / Misumi 810 (1,620)

265. Kyushu Kokusai Kanko Bus

Nagasaki to Kumamoto

STATION / BUS	NAGASAKI	UNZEN	SHIMABARA	KUMAMOTO STATION	KUMAMOTO KOTSU CENTER
NAGASAKI-12	07:50	10:16	10:47	14:35	14:44
NAGASAKI-14	08:40	11:11	11:42	15:25	15:34
NAGASAKI-2	11:15	13:51	14:22	18:05	18:14

Kumamoto to Nagasaki

STATION / BUS	KUMAMOTO KOTSU CENTER	KUMAMOTO STATION	SHIMABARA	UNZEN	NAGASAKI
NAGASAKI-1	08:40	08:49	12:30	13:01	16:02
NAGASAKI-11	09:40	09:49	13:35	14:06	16:37
NAGASAKI-13	11:25	11:34	15:20	15:51	18:22

266. Kyushu Kokusai Kanko Bus

Kumamoto to Beppu

STATION / BUS	KUMAMOTO STATION	KUMAMOTO KOTSU CENTER	AR. ASOZAN-NISHI	LV. ASOZAN-NISHI	BEPPU
ASO-1	08:20	08:30	10:21	11:21	14:53
ASO-3	08:50	09:00	11:13	12:13	15:45
UNZEN-11	11:10	11:20	14:02	15:02	18:14

Beppu to Kumamoto

STATION / BUS	BEPPU	AR. ASOZAN-NISHI	LV. ASOZAN-NISHI	KUMAMOTO KOTSU CENTER	KUMAMOTO STATION
UNZEN-12	08:00	11:08	12:08	14:35	14:44
ASO-2	08:30	11:48	13:18	15:03	15:12
ASO-6	09:30	14:02	15:02	17:20	17:29

270. Miyazaki Kotsu Bus

West-bound

BUS STOP / BUS	MIYAZAKI (MIYAKO CITY)	KOBAYASHI	EBINO-KOGEN	HAYASHIDA-ONSEN
EXPRESS BUS	08:20	09:41	10:35	10:55
EXPRESS BUS	09:05	10:26	11:20	11:40
EXPRESS BUS	12:10	13:31	14:25	—
LOCAL BUS	—	14:10	15:07	15:27
EXPRESS BUS	14:20	15:41	16:35	16:55

East-bound

BUS STOP / BUS	HAYASHIDA-ONSEN	EBINO-KOGEN	KOBAYASHI	MIYAZAKI (MIYAKO CITY)
EXPRESS BUS	08:46	09:04	09:54	11:21
EXPRESS BUS	09:50	10:08	10:58	12:25
EXPRESS BUS	12:30	12:48	13:38	15:05
LOCAL BUS	13:30	13:48	14:45	—
EXPRESS BUS	—	15:00	15:48	17:15

271. Hayashida Sangyo Kotsu Bus

South-bound

BUS STOP / BUS	EBINO-KOGEN	HAYASHIDA-ONSEN	KIRISHIMA JINGU SHRINE	NISHI-KAGOSHIMA
BUS	—	08:10	08:33	10:09
BUS	09:06	09:30	09:53	11:30
BUS	—	11:25	11:48	13:42
BUS	—	13:25	13:48	
BUS	—	14:20	14:43	16:23
BUS	16:06	16:30	16:53	18:29
BUS	—	17:25	17:48	19:40

North-bound

BUS STOP / BUS	NISHI-KAGOSHIMA	KIRISHIMA JINGU SHRINE	HAYASHIDA-ONSEN	EBINO-KOGEN
BUS	08:05	09:45	10:13	10:28
BUS	09:25	11:05	11:33	11:48
BUS	11:25	13:15	13:38	—
BUS	12:25	14:14		—
BUS	—	—	14:42	15:01
BUS	14:25	16:01	16:37	—
BUS	15:25	17:01	17:37	—

265. Kyushu Kokusai Kanko Bus
Nagasaki / Kumamoto   7,290 (N / A)

266. Kyushu Kokusai Kanko Bus
Kimamoto / Beppu   7,500 (N / A)

270. Miyazaki Kotsu Bus
Miyako City / Ebino-Kogen 2,100 (N / A)
Kobayashi / Ebino-Kogen 1,000 (N / A)
Ebino-Kogen / Hayashida-Onsen
                           290 (N / A)

271. Hayashida Sangyo Kotsu Bus
Ebino-Kogen / Hayashida-Onsen   290 (N / A)
Ebino-Kogen / Kirishima-Jingu-mae 350 (N / A)
Ebino-Kogen / Nishi-Kagoshima   1,150 (N / A)
Kirishima-Jingu-mae / Nishi-Kagoshima
                                1,050 (N / A)

280. Tobu Railways

Asakusa to Nikko

TRAIN	ASAKUSA	TOBU-NIKKO
KEGON-1	07:20	09:08
KEGON-3	08:00	09:43
KEGON-9	09:00	10:41
KEGON-13	10:00	11:43
LOCAL TRAIN	11:20	13:22
LOCAL TRAIN	12:20	14:24
LOCAL TRAIN	13:20	15:15
LOCAL TRAIN	14:20	16:24

Nikko to Asakusa

TRAIN	TOBU-NIKKO	ASAKUSA
LOCAL TRAIN	09:47	11:56
LOCAL TRAIN	12:42	14:56
LOCAL TRAIN	13:42	15:56
LOCAL TRAIN	14:42	16:56
KEGON-26	16:40	18:25
KEGON-28	17:00	18:45
KEGON-32	17:40	19:25
LOCAL TRAIN	18:52	20:54

284. Fukushima Kotsu Bus

West-bound

BUS	FUKUSHIMA	GOSHIKINUMA-IRIGUCHI	KYUKAMURA	BANDAI-KOGEN
BUS	08:00	10:55	11:01	11:10
BUS	10:40	13:35	13:41	13:50

East-bound

BUS	BANDAI-KOGEN	KYUKAMURA	GOSHIKINUMA-IRIGUCHI	FUKUSHIMA
BUS	13:00	13:10	13:17	16:10
BUS	14:30	14:40	14:47	17:40

* Nos. 284 and 285 buses run from the end of April through the beginning of November.

285. Aizu Noriai Jidosha Bus

South-bound

BUS	KYUKAMURA	BANDAI-KOGEN	GOSHIKINUMA-IRIGUCHI	AIZU-WAKAMATSU
BUS	09:20	09:35	09:40	11:10
BUS	12:55	13:10	13:15	14:30
BUS	14:55	15:10	15:15	16:30
BUS	16:00	16:15	16:20	17:35

North-bound

BUS	AIZU-WAKAMATSU	GOSHIKINUMA-IRIGUCHI	BANDAI-KOGEN	KYUKAMURA
BUS	08:52	10:10	10:15	10:30
BUS	10:12	11:30	11:35	11:50
BUS	13:42	15:00	15:05	15:20
BUS	15:32	16:50	16:55	17:10

290. Sanriku Railways Minami-Riasu Line

South-bound

TRAIN	KAMAISHI	SAKARI
LOCAL TRAIN	08:30	09:16
LOCAL TRAIN	09:26	10:15
LOCAL TRAIN	10:21	11:06
LOCAL TRAIN	11:09	11:56
LOCAL TRAIN	13:23	14:12
LOCAL TRAIN	14:24	15:13
LOCAL TRAIN	15:30	16:19

North-bound

TRAIN	SAKARI	KAMAISHI
LOCAL TRAIN	09:28	10:16
LOCAL TRAIN	10:32	11:20
LOCAL TRAIN	12:08	12:58
LOCAL TRAIN	13:00	13:48
LOCAL TRAIN	14:26	15:14
LOCAL TRAIN	15:32	16:20
LOCAL TRAIN	16:32	17:20

291. Sanriku Railways Kita-Riasu Line

Kuji to Miyako

TRAIN	KUJI	SHIMANOKOSHI	MIYAKO
LOCAL TRAIN	08:08	09:01	09:42
LOCAL TRAIN	09:30	10:20	11:03
LOCAL TRAIN	10:52	11:48	12:33
LOCAL TRAIN	12:15	13:08	13:49
LOCAL TRAIN	12:57	14:01	14:41
LOCAL TRAIN	14:03	14:56	15:38
LOCAL TRAIN	14:55	15:47	16:31
LOCAL TRAIN	16:19	17:09	17:50

Miyako to Kuji

TRAIN	MIYAKO	SHIMANOKOSHI	KUJI
LOCAL TRAIN	07:42	08:29	09:22
LOCAL TRAIN	09:03	09:48	10:41
LOCAL TRAIN	10:26	11:11	12:03
LOCAL TRAIN	11:57	12:38	13:28
LOCAL TRAIN	13:10	13:53	14:44
LOCAL TRAIN	14:22	15:14	16:08
LOCAL TRAIN	15:18	16:05	16:58
LOCAL TRAIN	15:54	16:37	17:30

280. Tobu Railways
Asakusa / Tobu-Nikko
1,100* (N / A)
2,100 (N / A)
* Local train.

284. Fukushima Kotsu Bus
Fukushima / Bandai-Kogen
2,500 (N / A)

285. Aizu Noriai Jidosha Bus
Bandai-Kogen / Aizu-Wakamatsu
1,400 (N / A)

290. Sanriku Railways Minami-Riasu Line
Kamaishi / Sakari 800 (N / A)

291. Sanriku Railways Kita-Riasu Line
Kuji / Shimanokoshi
800 (N / A)
Kuji / Miyako 1,460 (N / A)

298. Donan Bus

West-bound

BUS STOP / BUS	NOBORIBETSU ONSEN	OROFURE-TOGE PASS	TOYAKO ONSEN
DONAN BUS	09:30	10:10	11:10
DONAN BUS	11:30	12:10	13:10
DONAN BUS	12:20	13:00	14:00
DONAN BUS	14:20	15:00	16:00
DONAN BUS	15:30	16:10	17:10

East-bound

BUS STOP / BUS	TOYAKO ONSEN	OROFURE-TOGE PASS	NOBORIBETSU ONSEN
DONAN BUS	08:20	09:20	10:10
DONAN BUS	09:20	10:20	11:00
DONAN BUS	11:20	12:20	13:00
DONAN BUS	13:00	14:00	14:50
DONAN BUS	15:10	16:10	17:00

300. Dohoku Bus

South-bound

BUS STOP / BUS	ASAHIGAWA STATION	KAMIKAWA STATION	SOUNKYO
DOHOKU BUS	08:10	09:30	10:05
DOHOKU BUS	09:10	10:30	11:05
DOHOKU BUS	10:50	12:10	12:45
DOHOKU BUS	11:50	13:10	13:45
DOHOKU BUS	12:45	14:05	14:40
DOHOKU BUS	14:00	15:20	15:55
DOHOKU BUS	15:00	16:20	16:55
DOHOKU BUS	15:40	17:00	17:35

North-bound

BUS STOP / BUS	SOUNKYO	KAMIKAWA STATION	ASAHIGAWA STATION
DOHOKU BUS	07:45	08:25	09:40
DOHOKU BUS	08:45	09:25	10:40
DOHOKU BUS	11:10	11:50	13:05
DOHOKU BUS	11:50	12:30	13:45
DOHOKU BUS	12:30	13:10	14:25
DOHOKU BUS	13:40	14:20	15:35
DOHOKU BUS	14:55	15:30	—
DOHOKU BUS	15:30	16:10	17:25

303. Akan Bus

Kushiro to Akankohan

BUS STOP / BUS	KUSHIRO STATION	KUSHIRO AIRPORT	TANCHO-NO-SATO	AKANKOHAN
AKAN BUS	07:25	→	08:30	09:25
AKAN BUS	09:55	10:40	11:15	12:05
AKAN BUS	11:25	12:10	12:45	13:40
AKAN BUS	14:40	15:25	16:00	17:00
AKAN BUS	17:25	18:10	18:35	19:25

Akankohan to Kushiro

BUS STOP / BUS	AKANKOHAN	TANCHO-NO-SATO	KUSHIRO AIRPORT	KUSHIRO STATION
AKAN BUS	07:30	08:12	08:40	09:30
AKAN BUS	09:45	10:27	11:05	11:55
AKAN BUS	11:30	12:12	12:50	13:40
AKAN BUS	14:40	15:22	16:00	16:50
AKAN BUS	17:20	18:02	→	19:15

302. Akan Bus

Akankohan to Memanbetsu

BUS STOP / BUS	AKANKOHAN	TESHIKAGA	MASHU NO. 1	KAWAYU ONSEN	BIHORO PASS	BIHORO STATION	MEMANBETSU AIRPORT
AKAN BUS	07:20	08:20	08:55	09:50	11:20	12:00	12:15
AKAN BUS	09:00	10:00	10:35	12:05	13:30	14:10	14:25
AKAN BUS	11:30	12:35	13:10	14:05	15:35	16:15	16:30

Memanbetsu to Akankohan

BUS STOP / BUS	MEMANBETSU AIRPORT	-BIHORO STATION	BIHORO PASS	KAWAYU ONSEN	MASHU NO. 1	TESHIKAGA	AKANKOHAN
AKAN BUS	—	09:30	10:20	12:15	13:30	13:50	14:55
AKAN BUS	10:35	10:55	11:45	13:30	14:45	15:05	16:10
AKAN BUS	12:25	12:45	13:35	14:50	16:05	16:25	17:30

298. Donan Bus
Noboribetsu / Toyako   1,300 (N / A)

300. Dohoku Bus
Asahikawa / Sounkyo   1,700 (N / A)
Kamikawa / Sounkyo   710 (N / A)

302. Akan Bus
Akankohan / Bihoro   5,200 (N / A)
Akankohan / Memanbetsu Airport

5,500 (N / A)

303. Akan Bus
Kushiro / Akankohan   2,300 (N / A)
Kushiro-kuko (Airport) / Akankohan
1,850 (N / A)

* No. 302 bus may be cancelled in winter due to snow.

INDEX

下の電車または地下鉄の駅を教えてください

STATION

Where is the following train/subway station?
(Circle either train or subway and fill in the name of the station and the name of the line.)

Circle either one		路線名 Line Name	駅名 Destination
Train 電車	Subway 地下鉄		
1 電車	地下鉄		
2 電車	地下鉄		
3 電車	地下鉄		
4 電車	地下鉄		
5 電車	地下鉄		

下の駅までの運賃を教えてください

TICKET

How much is the fare to the following station?
(Fill in the name of your destination and the name of the line you want to take.)

路線名 Line Name	目的駅 Destination
1	
2	
3	
4	
5	

下の電車の発車ホーム番号を教えてください

PLATFORM

What is the platform number for the following train to the destination listed below?
(If the train is a local and does not have a name, write "Donko" in the train name column.)

路線名 Line Name	電車名 Train Name	目的駅 Destination
1		
2		
3		
4		
5		

1 下の電車または地下鉄の駅を教えてください

STATION Where is the following train/subway station?
(Circle either train or subway and fill in the name of the station and the name of the line.)

Circle either one		路線名 Line Name	駅名 Destination
	Train 電車	Subway 地下鉄		
1	電車	地下鉄		
2	電車	地下鉄		
3	電車	地下鉄		
4	電車	地下鉄		
5	電車	地下鉄		

2 下の駅までの運賃を教えてください

TICKET How much is the fare to the following station?
(Fill in the name of your destination and the name of the line you want to take.)

	路線名 Line Name	目的駅 Destination
1		
2		
3		
4		
5		

3 下の電車の発車ホーム番号を教えてください

PLATFORM What is the platform number for the following train to the destination listed below?
(If the train is a local and does not have a name, write "Donko" in the train name column.)

	路線名 Line Name	電車名 Train Name	目的駅 Destination
1			
2			
3			
4			
5			

座席指定申込書
Application for reserved seats

If you have a Rail Pass, you can request reservations for JR trains free of charge. Show the Pass with this form.
Your Rail Pass cannot be used for private railways.

乗車日 Date of Trip	月 (month)	日 (date)	人数 No. of Psns	大人 ___ 枚 Adults	子供 ___ 枚 Children

出発駅 Departure _____ Station	目的駅 Destination _____ Station

座席の種類 (Check either one) Class of Seat	□グリーン車 First Class	□普通車 Coach Class	□禁煙席 Nonsmoking section, if available

第一希望 First Choice	電車名 Train Name	出発時間 Dep. Time	時 (hour)	分 (minute)
第二希望 Second Choice	電車名 Train Name	出発時間 Dep. Time	時 (hour)	分 (minute)
第三希望 Third Choice	電車名 Train Name	出発時間 Dep. Time	時 (hour)	分 (minute)

座席指定申込書
Application for reserved seats

If you have a Rail Pass, you can request reservations for JR trains free of charge. Show the Pass with this form.
Your Rail Pass cannot be used for private railways.

乗車日 Date of Trip	月 (month)	日 (date)	人数 No. of Psns	大人 ___ 枚 Adults	子供 ___ 枚 Children

出発駅 Departure _____ Station	目的駅 Destination _____ Station

座席の種類 (Check either one) Class of Seat	□グリーン車 First Class	□普通車 Coach Class	□禁煙席 Nonsmoking section, if available

第一希望 First Choice	電車名 Train Name	出発時間 Dep. Time	時 (hour)	分 (minute)
第二希望 Second Choice	電車名 Train Name	出発時間 Dep. Time	時 (hour)	分 (minute)
第三希望 Third Choice	電車名 Train Name	出発時間 Dep. Time	時 (hour)	分 (minute)

座席指定申込書
Application for reserved seats

If you have a Rail Pass, you can request reservations for JR trains free of charge. Show the Pass with this form.
Your Rail Pass cannot be used for private railways.

乗車日 Date of Trip	月 (month)	日 (date)	人数 No. of Psns	大人 ___ 枚 Adults	子供 ___ 枚 Children

出発駅 Departure _____ Station	目的駅 Destination _____ Station

座席の種類 (Check either one) Class of Seat	□グリーン車 First Class	□普通車 Coach Class	□禁煙席 Nonsmoking section, if available

第一希望 First Choice	電車名 Train Name	出発時間 Dep. Time	時 (hour)	分 (minute)
第二希望 Second Choice	電車名 Train Name	出発時間 Dep. Time	時 (hour)	分 (minute)
第三希望 Third Choice	電車名 Train Name	出発時間 Dep. Time	時 (hour)	分 (minute)

4 RESERVATION

座席指定申込書
Application for reserved seats

If you have a Rail Pass, you can request reservations for JR trains free of charge. Show the Pass with this form.
Your Rail Pass cannot be used for private railways.

乗車日 Date of Trip	月 (month)	日 (date)	人数 No. of Psns	大人____枚 Adults	子供____枚 Children

出発駅 Departure _____ Station	目的駅 Destination _____ Station

座席の種類 (Check either one) Class of Seat	□グリーン車 First Class	□普通車 Coach Class	□禁煙席 Nonsmoking section, if available

第一希望 First Choice	電車名 Train Name		出発時間 Dep. Time	時 (hour)	分 (minute)
第二希望 Second Choice	電車名 Train Name		出発時間 Dep. Time	時 (hour)	分 (minute)
第三希望 Third Choice	電車名 Train Name		出発時間 Dep. Time	時 (hour)	分 (minute)

4 RESERVATION

座席指定申込書
Application for reserved seats

If you have a Rail Pass, you can request reservations for JR trains free of charge. Show the Pass with this form.
Your Rail Pass cannot be used for private railways.

乗車日 Date of Trip	月 (month)	日 (date)	人数 No. of Psns	大人____枚 Adults	子供____枚 Children

出発駅 Departure _____ Station	目的駅 Destination _____ Station

座席の種類 (Check either one) Class of Seat	□グリーン車 First Class	□普通車 Coach Class	□禁煙席 Nonsmoking section, if available

第一希望 First Choice	電車名 Train Name		出発時間 Dep. Time	時 (hour)	分 (minute)
第二希望 Second Choice	電車名 Train Name		出発時間 Dep. Time	時 (hour)	分 (minute)
第三希望 Third Choice	電車名 Train Name		出発時間 Dep. Time	時 (hour)	分 (minute)

4 RESERVATION

座席指定申込書
Application for reserved seats

If you have a Rail Pass, you can request reservations for JR trains free of charge. Show the Pass with this form.
Your Rail Pass cannot be used for private railways.

乗車日 Date of Trip	月 (month)	日 (date)	人数 No. of Psns	大人____枚 Adults	子供____枚 Children

出発駅 Departure _____ Station	目的駅 Destination _____ Station

座席の種類 (Check either one) Class of Seat	□グリーン車 First Class	□普通車 Coach Class	□禁煙席 Nonsmoking section, if available

第一希望 First Choice	電車名 Train Name		出発時間 Dep. Time	時 (hour)	分 (minute)
第二希望 Second Choice	電車名 Train Name		出発時間 Dep. Time	時 (hour)	分 (minute)
第三希望 Third Choice	電車名 Train Name		出発時間 Dep. Time	時 (hour)	分 (minute)

5 下の行先の市電またはバス乗場を教えてください

BUS STREETCAR

Where is the stop for the streetcar (or bus) going to the following destination?
(Circle either streetcar or bus and fill in the name of your destination.)

Circle either one		目的駅 Destination
1	Streetcar 市電　Bus バス	
2	市電　バス	
3	市電　バス	
4	市電　バス	
5	市電　バス	

6 私は下の目的地まで行きます 目的地が近づいたら教えてください

DESTINATION

I am going to the following place. Please let me know when we near the destination.
(On the train, streetcar or bus)
(Fill in the name of your destination and show the card to a fellow passenger.)

1		6	
2		7	
3		8	
4		9	
5		10	

7 下の目的地まで行ってください

TAXI

Please take me to the following place.
(For a taxi driver) (Fill in the name of your destination.)

1		7	
2		8	
3		9	
4		10	
5		11	
6		12	

5 下の行先の市電またはバス乗場を教えてください

BUS STREETCAR

Where is the stop for the streetcar (or bus) going to the following destination?
(Circle either streetcar or bus and fill in the name of your destination.)

Circle either one		目的駅 Destination
1	Streetcar 市電 / Bus バス	
2	市電 / バス	
3	市電 / バス	
4	市電 / バス	
5	市電 / バス	

6 私は下の目的地まで行きます 目的地が近づいたら教えてください

DESTINATION

I am going to the following place. Please let me know when we near the destination.
(On the train, streetcar or bus)
(Fill in the name of your destination and show the card to a fellow passenger.)

1		6	
2		7	
3		8	
4		9	
5		10	

7 下の目的地まで行ってください

TAXI

Please take me to the following place.
(For a taxi driver) (Fill in the name of your destination.)

1		7	
2		8	
3		9	
4		10	
5		11	
6		12	

8 BAGGAGE

手荷物一時預り所
または
コインロッカーを
教えてください

Where are the coin lockers or
a short-term baggage check room?

9 REST ROOM

お手洗の場所を
教えてください

Where is a rest room?

---

4 RESERVATION

座席指定申込書
Application for reserved seats

If you have a Rail Pass, you can request reservations
for JR trains free of charge. Show the Pass with this
form.
Your Rail Pass cannot be used for private railways.

乗車日 Date of Trip	月 (month)	日 (date)	人数 No. of Psns	大人 _____ 枚 Adults	子供 _____ 枚 Children
出発駅 Departure _____ Station			目的駅 Destination _____ Station		
座席の種類 (Check either one) Class of Seat	□グリーン車 First Class	□普通車 Coach Class		□禁煙席 Nonsmoking section, if available	
第一希望 First Choice	電車名 Train Name		出発時間 Dep. Time	時 (hour)	分 (minute)
第二希望 Second Choice	電車名 Train Name		出発時間 Dep. Time	時 (hour)	分 (minute)
第三希望 Third Choice	電車名 Train Name		出発時間 Dep. Time	時 (hour)	分 (minute)

---

4 RESERVATION

座席指定申込書
Application for reserved seats

If you have a Rail Pass, you can request reservations
for JR trains free of charge. Show the Pass with this
form.
Your Rail Pass cannot be used for private railways.

乗車日 Date of Trip	月 (month)	日 (date)	人数 No. of Psns	大人 _____ 枚 Adults	子供 _____ 枚 Children
出発駅 Departure _____ Station			目的駅 Destination _____ Station		
座席の種類 (Check either one) Class of Seat	□グリーン車 First Class	□普通車 Coach Class		□禁煙席 Nonsmoking section, if available	
第一希望 First Choice	電車名 Train Name		出発時間 Dep. Time	時 (hour)	分 (minute)
第二希望 Second Choice	電車名 Train Name		出発時間 Dep. Time	時 (hour)	分 (minute)
第三希望 Third Choice	電車名 Train Name		出発時間 Dep. Time	時 (hour)	分 (minute)

④ RESERVATION

座席指定申込書
Application for reserved seats

If you have a Rail Pass, you can request reservations for JR trains free of charge. Show the Pass with this form.
Your Rail Pass cannot be used for private railways.

乗車日 Date of Trip	月 (month)	日 (date)	人数 No. of Psns	大人 ____ 枚 Adults		子供 ____ 枚 Children	

出発日 Departure _____ Station	目的駅 Destination _____ Station

座席の種類 Class of Seat	(Check either one)	□グリーン車 First Class	□普通車 Coach Class	□禁煙席 Nonsmoking section, if available

第一希望 First Choice	電車名 Train Name	出発時間 Dep. Time	時 (hour)	分 (minute)
第二希望 Second Choice	電車名 Train Name	出発時間 Dep. Time	時 (hour)	分 (minute)
第三希望 Third Choice	電車名 Train Name	出発時間 Dep. Time	時 (hour)	分 (minute)

④ RESERVATION

座席指定申込書
Application for reserved seats

If you have a Rail Pass, you can request reservations for JR trains free of charge. Show the Pass with this form.
Your Rail Pass cannot be used for private railways.

乗車日 Date of Trip	月 (month)	日 (date)	人数 No. of Psns	大人 ____ 枚 Adults		子供 ____ 枚 Children	

出発駅 Departure _____ Station	目的駅 Destination _____ Station

座席の種類 Class of Seat	(Check either one)	□グリーン車 First Class	□普通車 Coach Class	□禁煙席 Nonsmoking section, if available

第一希望 First Choice	電車名 Train Name	出発時間 Dep. Time	時 (hour)	分 (minute)
第二希望 Second Choice	電車名 Train Name	出発時間 Dep. Time	時 (hour)	分 (minute)
第三希望 Third Choice	電車名 Train Name	出発時間 Dep. Time	時 (hour)	分 (minute)